Reimagining Capitalism

Applying Negative Dialectics for a Better Future

David M. Atkinson
York St John University

Series in Economics

VERNON PRESS

www.vernonpress.com

In the Americas:
Vernon Press
1000 N West Street, Suite 1200
Wilmington, Delaware, 19801
United States

In the rest of the world:
Vernon Press
C/Sancti Espiritu 17,
Malaga, 29006
Spain

Series in Economics

Library of Congress Control Number: 2022950692

ISBN: 978-1-64889-595-1

Cover design by Gareth D. Atkinson.

For my wife, Yvonne

Table of contents

List of Figures

List of Tables

Foreword

This important book is written with Love, Care, Knowledge, Craft, Compassion, Thoughtfulness, and Positive Negativity! With such an endorsement, it cannot but fail. Hopefully, this cynical prediction will be disproved by the success that this book deserves, for David Atkinson deals with important and difficult, indeed "wicked" problems. This book deals with a vital, indeed perhaps *the* most vital, issue confronting the human race at this juncture, that of understanding the nature of the crisis that confronts us all. In developing this objective, he turns to Adorno's conceptualisation of "negative dialectics". To paraphrase a well-known legal meme, this reviewer avers that in Skirpenbeck, M'Lud they talk of little else.

At the time of writing this foreword, many of the world leaders are meeting at COP 27 to discuss in Egypt at the Red Sea resort city, Sharm El Sheikh. The conference is being live-streamed around the world and the preparation documents are widely available; the very title of the conference clearly demonstrates the many previous meetings that have failed to deal with these issues and there are countless implicit evidences and subtle reminders of the inevitability of consequential failure. But an apparently bland and almost unstated paragraph in one of the background papers circulated widely already notes the continuing lack of agreement about the definitions, multiple, competing and sometimes contradictory definitions in the official discourse of the very phenomena that are being discussed. It needs no latter-day Wittgenstein, even one who celebrated the possibility of writing a philosophical text consisting entirely of jokes, to remind us that if language is central to decision and must be understood in usage and practice, that this omission cannot be accidental but represents a symptom of a deeper and far more deadly malaise. For this is no joke. Doubtless the Wittgenstein who held that language must be logical had never heard Ken Dodd, Ivor Cutler or Stanley Unwin, although these sages and others could argue that its very illogicality and capability of multiple exceptions to its so-called grammar may help better than post-colonialism to understand why English has become the dominant language of the global markets. Reality trumps theory again as does the awful reality of Trump. (See what we did there?). The representative of Barbados at the COP talks has presciently recommended that the globe requires "a changed financial architecture" and Atkinson advises that if we want to agree to do that, we may have to go further back into the mind-sets that have generated the current versions of those structures.

Atkinson interrogates the nature of depicting some of the potential future worlds that may prove to have developed ways of supervening the category mistakes that frame the political and social errors even 100 economists are capable of making, as they develop critiques of the current crisis. He invites the reader to "re-imagine" a post-capitalist society. To some like Fukuyama, who has risibly protested the "total exhaustion of viable alternatives to Western liberal capitalism", culminating in the "ineluctable spread of consumerist Western culture", possibly such outcomes may be literally unimaginable, inconceivable and incapable therefore of being dealt with by the available instruments of collective agency. To Marx, what is occurring was always inevitable (despite the distress these assertions were to cause the cautious Isaiah Berlin, who inveighed against the absurdity of Historical Inevitability) but had merely been somewhat delayed and as a balancing implication was not-surprisingly to cause not merely a new system and structures of economic organization, but the end of the hegemony of the human animal species on this planet.

Atkinson explores the nature of the contemplation of futures, following Robert Burns in noting that the "best-laid plans of mice and men gang aft agley" and implicating the logical inconsistency in believing both that the future is unknowable but that it may be controllable, thus depicting the impotence of the rational, economistic, individualistic model of the social order implicit in Fukuyama's celebration of a corpse that is already rotting.

His starting point is Theodor Adorno, relatively unknown in our current enfeebled Business school curricula, but known even outwith this barren territory, if at all, as a founder of the Frankfurt School, and familiar of the wild notions that to understand Marx, it was necessary to understand Hegel and also to deal with Freud and aesthetics, of musicology and modern music, and to embody these wider knowledge-spaces in concert-level performance and practice. Atkinson does not deal with the apparently broad scope of Adorno's formation but focusses on his treatment of the Hegelian dialectic in a discussion of the Theory of Mind (ToM) that supports it. Atkinson wishes to emphasize the importance of foundational and primitive concepts in situating simple mental assumptions about cognitive processes, such as the assumption that individuals necessarily think in the same way. Instead, he understands that they do not and assumptively cannot, thus "the axiomatic variability of an individual's mental states, ensures there can be no level of universal access to reality."

So Atkinson notes that a "dominant deconstructive interpretation" in Western philosophical construction has privileged a desire for immediate access to meaning" and "built its own metaphysics around the privileging of presence over absence". Thus in moving from "presencing" as a simple feature, Atkinson adds " a 'sixth sense' of social presence, comprises both 1) a rational mode of being with others in relation to a specified medium: a rationally bounded finite whole, that has both form and content, in essence a presence in a temporal, finite reality, and 2) an individual's sense of being with others, an irrational mode of being, influenced by the individual's personal psychology—a degree of mental presence" as an " irrational mode of 'sensory' being which is characterised, not by some ToM, but by its 'absence' ('ab-sense', or 'away/from-sense')". In returning to the classical formulation of thesis/antithesis/synthesis, Atkinson develops Adorno's concept of a "negative dialectic" and his critique of dialectics does not go along with the perhaps facile dismissal by Habermas in favour of the post-event acceptance of positive science or with Rose's argument that negative dialectics does not incorporate the phenomenological complexity of social relations. The Not-thing cannot be nothing even if it is a denial of the thing.

Along the way, Atkinson deals creatively with topics like Entrepreneurship, that current go-to Imaginary of the MBA classes, and with the doctoral naif's inescapable worrying about the status of auto-ethnographic reportage as the denial of self through the Othering of Self-involved in writing what one knows because one saw it, knows it or lives with its diurnal obligations; and he uses his own experience as an entrepreneur, scholar and administrative virtuoso to associate helpfully Montaigne and Morris Holbrook in a single sentence of assured and relevant scholarship. He draws out unfamiliar gems from textbook icons such as Maynard Keynes' treatment of the "Animal Spirits of Capitalism" and succinctly the more recent insights of the enormously important Damasio to explain *en passant* what Keynes probably did not mean by that curious phrase.

In this book, Atkinson deals with some complex imaginaries and the going does not always facilitate the swift skim-read or the injudicious and premature "I get it".

This is a really important book by a really thoughtful scholar that demands serious attention and *vaut bien le detour*. Read it, please and then read it again. There will be really hard questions much sooner than our current imaginaries permit us to sketch out. If we cannot re-imagine capitalism, it will not be the suspense that kills us first.

Skirpenbeck, November 2022 David T. H. Weir

Preface

In August 2020, as I sat writing the first draft of the final chapter of this book, the European Commission (EC) issued a press release: *Commission Unveils Its First Strategic Foresight Report: Charting the Course towards a More Resilient Europe*. In the release, the EC quoted Vice-President Maroš Šefčovič, the person in charge of inter-institutional relations and foresight, as saying:

> 'The [Covid] pandemic has not only thrown a sharp light on our vulnerabilities, but has presented opportunities that the EU cannot afford to miss. It has also reaffirmed the need to make our policies evidence-based, future-proof and centred on resilience. We cannot expect the future to become less disruptive—new trends and shocks will continue to affect our lives. The first-ever Strategic Foresight Report therefore sets the scene for how we can make Europe more resilient—by boosting our open strategic autonomy and building a fairer, climate-neutral and digitally sovereign future.' [1]

In this single quote, I find the rationale for this book. Two words. One—*resilience*—an objective I believe is a distraction. The other—*open*—a thing I believe our autonomous societies are not. And the evidence? Well, this book is an antidote to the idea of 'evidence-based' policies. The idea that we might be able to future proof some 'thing', let alone a policy, and centre any such 'thing' on the concept of resilience, is questionable. Yes, the Covid-19 pandemic cast a spotlight onto our volatile, uncertain, ambiguous and complex world, as did Putin's invasion of Ukraine in February 2022—and those spotlights might well have reaffirmed a need for change in the future—but to many observers that need has existed for some time. As I will relate in this book, for at least 300 years.

The preface of a book is a place—an opportunity—for the author to convey something of the 'why' of the book's content. Many would gloss over this 'why'. Indeed, I have, on many occasions, done just that: glossing over the prefaces of other authors. But I believe it is important to at least set out my 'why'. This book follows a journey. That journey might be considered, variously: a journey of some 60 plus years of living in social systems; or of 40 plus years of working within socio-economic systems; or of 50 plus years

---

[1] European Commission, "Commission Unveils Its First Strategic Foresight Report: Charting the Course towards a More Resilient Europe."

being an active component of educational systems—both being taught and sharing my academic knowledge; or of 50 plus years being an active subject of capitalism; or knowingly being party to legal systems—both subject to and seeking to apply justice. It might even be considered as a 60-plus year journey of being a minority—an autistic journey of learning 'systems' capabilities, not to change them, but to realise my strongly individual performance within them. However, these journeys represent the potential of other books to come. Largely, this present book follows a 20-year journey of critical study. I offer this book as a second-order, critical observation on the economy, work and enterprise. However, as I shall suggest in the chapters to come—drawing on the work of sociologist Niklas Luhmann—one cannot understand the true nature of a second-order observation if one does not understand the perspective of the observer.

As a minority—an autistic in a neurotypical world—I have drawn on an inherent adaptability as a human to adjust to my environment. To me, that is not resilience but adaptability. Resilience is a capacity to withstand or recover quickly from difficult conditions. Withstanding some difficulty is OK, if that difficulty is not so great that it fails to deviate you from your route or other goal-seeking activity. Recovery is OK if the difficulty is time or quantum limited and, once encountered, fades to an acceptable limit and you can return to that route or goal-seeking. One can be resilient in following a certain path. In the path of life, we might be resilient in health, continuing to work through a cold or minor irritation. Or we might show resilience in recovering from a more substantial ailment, like Covid-19, making a full or sufficient recovery to again function in the economic environment. We might even be resilient in becoming an amputee or suffer blindness or a life-changing stroke. But here, we must adapt before we are able to resume our meaningful purpose. Resilience assumes a status quo to be returned to, either desired, or necessarily so. We assume a resilient economy should 'bounce back' to that which subsisted before it encountered difficult conditions. We assume similar with a resilient society.

Economies and societies that persist in seeking resilience over adaptability are closed to ideas that change is required on the path ahead. This book is an argument—a provocation—that our socio-economic systems, our 'autonomous' societies, are not open but closed. One either fits within or does not. It really is that simple. It is our choice. If we choose not to fit, or are unable to fit for whatever reason, then we must adapt. If the environment outside us changes so drastically that difficulty is the new norm, then we had better improve our adaptability—and in short order, too. We must learn when to be resilient and, importantly, when not to be. In a volatile, uncertain, complex and ambiguous world, we must learn adaptability over resilience. If not, we are collectively headed only one way—our demise. It may be as simple as that.

This book's origin lay in a polemic, grounded in a critical perspective. It was inspired by a novel method of considering the future that I developed under the watchful eye of Jeff Gold. As a colleague and an established Professor of Organizational Learning, Jeff is a strong advocate of futures learning and actionable knowledge. He founded York St John University's Futures Research Group. I was an eager, early member. It is instrumental to my adoption of futures thinking that I found there to be a lack of any substantial underlying critical philosophy within it. In the chapters that emerged as my first draft of this book, I provided a conceptual-level text of critical, diverse thought about core, future uncertainties in economics, a post Covid-19 world of work, and enterprise in general. It introduced what amounted to me to be an (autistic) inquiry and provocation into the dance of capitalism, work and aesthetic enterprise. My aim at that point was simply to allow my ideas—as tentative (neuro)diverse and embryonic ideas—to inform future theory and practice; to allow them the space to enrich the ideas of others—part of a cycle of reflective, reflexive learning. I had thoughts that, in part, the book would champion the autistic, neurodivergent voice as a valuable contribution to problem-solving—a demonstration of cognitive diversity in the manner of Matthew Syed's *Rebel Ideas*.

I had offered my first draft of this manuscript for peer review. Kindly, Dr Marcel Lamoureux, a US political scientist, historian, and philosopher, affiliated with the UK's Staffordshire University—concerned with areas of interest to my work that I had only just begun to engage with—took up the challenge. In an early response, Marcel noted an implicit 'dialectical' theme. He made the instrumental recommendation that I consider a more explicit and analytic approach, further recommending that I look at Theodor W. Adorno's conception of *Negative Dialectics*. Here was the underlying critical (social) philosophy I had sought to support my mode of critical thought. Consequently, the book now aims to both deliver its provocation into capitalism and enterprise, and also—by setting it at the intersection with the idea of an imaginary plane—use its inquiry as an exemplar of a philosophically grounded approach to futures-focussed thinking. I have come to call this approach *Applied Negative Dialectics*.

In the manner of my previous work, *Thinking the Art of Management*, I hope I offer what is an interesting yet challenging and provocative read. In establishing and employing my conception of Applied Negative Dialectics to frame my inquiry, I ask you, what if we have got our ideas about change wrong? One of the most oft (and over) used idioms about our life in general, is that the only constant is change. This is with reference to the Greek philosopher Heraclitus, who was known for his doctrine on change and the idea that one may never step into the same river twice. We cannot change our conditions so that we can take up a given position within a given river, at a given time. We might only control the conditions that lead us to it. Importantly, this leads me to value the purpose of science in understanding our environment, not so that we can learn to exploit it to the maximisation of capital, but so that we can learn to manage our own poietic change toward our immortality within it—toward our own position in the river that constantly flows.

Unlike my previous work, I do not offer an *apolitical* perspective. As I explicate, siding with Foucault, all challenge to an incumbent source of power is political. However, although not siding with any specific political agenda (in the UK at least), I find my politics more drawn to the present UK Labour party. This is not that I see myself as in any way a socialist (of any flavour). Certainly, in my reading of Adorno's (and others') work on negative dialectics, I have purposefully avoided its typical application to Marxist thought. Yet, at the time of writing, I feel that in the UK, Labour is only the party in opposition that has the ability (as an insider to the political system) to enact some of the change I might seek. But it will require education and leadership. I am not so naïve as to believe my work will be accepted as an agenda for change. But if it can move one person to an alternative perspective. I shall feel a modicum of success.

Pickhill, 2022 D M A

Acknowledgments

After a twenty-year (part-time) foray into academic study, one meets many people who are more than worthy of an acknowledgement for their contribution to one's thoughts and words. On the journey of exploration that preceded this work, I have had the great fortune to have been richly influenced by a great number of such people in both the real and virtual (online) worlds. Here I would like to acknowledge a few, particularly representative of the many. Most fundamentally, as a past student of Lancaster University's MPhil/PhD programme in Critical Management, I shall forever remain indebted to its co-founders Professor Julia Davies and Professor Jonathan Gosling. It was Julia's passion for critical thought that encouraged me to challenge conventional wisdom, and to embrace the alternative thinking of which I have been capable. All others involved with that course of study, remain in my affections.

I am indebted to the thinking and wisdom of, and conversations with, Professor David Weir. I have never lost my desire to learn from him, from being a student over 20 years ago at Lancaster, to being a colleague at York St John University. With stimulating conversations over a glass or two of claret in one of our local York restaurants, David has provided thought-provoking comments on various drafts of my ideas—influencing some turns in my narrative. He has also been kind enough to provide the Foreword, introducing this work. Also, in similar regard, I am indebted to Professor Jeff Gold for his guidance and mentorship in my use and adaptation of futures and foresight thinking. As colleagues in the York St John University Futures Research Group, I delighted in learning from Jeff; much of the work in Part II of this book has benefitted from his sage advice, comments and encouragement.

As I highlighted in the Preface, I am indeed indebted to Dr Marcel Lamoureux. Without Marcel's generous support in peer-reviewing my earlier manuscript, and his helpful suggestions and critique on my revisions as I incorporated Adorno's negative dialectics, this book's critical foundations would be much less firm. Marcel's support has been unwavering and if there was only room for one name in this acknowledgment, it would be his.

I also remain grateful to my colleague (then PhD student), Enas Dahadha. We met at York St John University in 2018, on an introduction by David Weir. Chapter 9, "Emergence and the non-hero", is a much-adapted version of a paper we co-authored under the title *Entrepreneurship as the Art of Enterprise: Re-conceptualising the Small Business Universe in Search of New Insights.* Enas and I persevered in seeking an academic journal of standing, favourable to our ideas. We were unable to achieve that goal. Consequently, while Chapter 9 no-longer reflects Enas' contribution around small businesses and entrepreneurial orientation, its existence cannot hide from her effort and support through the many discussions we held as we worked on its predecessor together. While it was a disappointment to us both that journal publication eluded us, it is a joy to reflect on her recent successful PhD defence. Beyond Chapter 9, several of the other chapters benefitted from peer-review feedback during the review process of earlier journal-format submissions; it would be remiss of me not to acknowledge the importance of such feedback. I therefore wish to also express my gratitude to the various editors and un-named peer reviewers for their contributions; I take my academic responsibilities seriously and have taken note of many of their comments in refining the manuscript before you.

As a practicing entrepreneur and manager, and therefore only a part-time academic, I have been privileged with membership of many eclectic groups of people in business over the years. There are many who come and go; some who pass by, never seen again—yet I learn from all of them. In the virtual space on LinkedIn, I learn from my many connections as they post from time to time. To single-out any name or group would be inordinately difficult and underplay the value I gain from the others. As reflected later in this work, I make no distinction, lest I set up some 'Others' as, in anyway, less important than other 'Others'. Safe to say, I value all my digital connections, regardless of the activity that may or may not occur between us.

If I am also not to 'other' Others from the academic world, I am grateful to Dr Bob Gammie, Dean of the York Business School, and my academic and non-academic colleagues at York St John University. While Bob's support has given me the opportunity to re-enter academic work, my colleagues have made me welcome. Finally, from the non-academic world, I owe a debt of thanks also to my friends and business partners, past and present, and to those who have lost or gained from my entrepreneurship. To my friend and neighbour, Ian Cross, a professional journalist and teacher of its practice, I offer many thanks for his companionship and his ability to craft a headline—several of which I have used in Chapters 4 and 5. To my friend and ex-Royal Air Force colleague, Anthony Robinson, I owe much for his support as a crucially valuable sounding-board, coach, mentor, investor and friend. I also thank my deceased parents for my autism—I have no doubt this work would not exist without it. Lastly, I thank my wife, Yvonne—to whom this book is ultimately dedicated—for her long-suffering forbearance of my generally nocturnal and weekend writing habits, and for her unwavering love and support.

Chapter 1

An inspector calls

'T' enjoy the World's Conveniences, Be famed in War, yet live in Ease,
Without great Vices, is a vain Eutopia seated in the brain...

...So Vice is beneficial found, When it's by Justice lopt, and bound...'[1]

THE ECONOMIC CRASH OF 2008, the Covid-19 pandemic of 2019/20 and Vladimir Putin's weaponisation of energy assets following his February 2022 invasion of Ukraine, all reinforce a widely held perception that capitalism, despite the progress and gains it has delivered, is in crisis.[2] In terminology first utilised by the US Army in the 1980s, such crises and the futures they foreshadow (our futures) are held as volatile, uncertain, complex and ambiguous (VUCA). This is the concept of a VUCA world.[3] Here, increasingly,

---

[1] Mandeville, The Fable of the Bees, 76. Spelling as per cited version.

[2] The nature of present crises bears resemblance to past crises, being expressed as having 'multiple dimensions—not only economic and financial but also ecological and social'. See: Fraser, "A Triple Movement? Parsing the Politics of Crisis after Polanyi," 29.

[3] It is accepted that the VUCA concept originated with the US Army War College, with the 'U' occasionally referring to Unstructured, in Johansen and Euchner, "Navigating the VUCA World, An Interview with Bob Johansen." It appears to date from the end of the cold war, when the United States 'looked out over the emergence of a diverse, rather than monolithic, global landscape.' in Millar, Groth, and Mahon, "Management Innovation in a VUCA World: Challenges and Recommendations," 6. Although by no means definitive, the US Army Heritage and Education Centre dates the term to 1987, with its use in the curriculum of the Army War College at that time. In USAHEC, "Q. Who

our thinking about the future, and our ability to manage and organize ourselves and others, our economy, and our work within it, is a challenge for which we are seemingly ill-equipped. We have, in our Western capitalist economies at least, seemingly emerged into an epoch of social precarity.[4] In this respect, I adopt a simple definition of capitalism as a system of political and economic organization in which a country's (or society's) commercial enterprise is controlled by private owners for profit, rather than by the state. In the West then, amid a growing sense of despair, we might well ask, what can we learn from 100 economists, a hive of bees and a police inspector?

In August 2020, the UK's Guardian Newspaper published, as an opinion piece, an open letter from 100 economists.[5] It outlined the economists' collective belief that the existing carbon-based economy amplifies racial, social and economic inequality—systemic injustices seen to contribute to a profoundly unstable socio-economic system. However, from the despair of 'dire and deeply interconnected emergencies', to the hope that Covid-19, might have been 'the' crisis opportunity to 'end the carbon economy', the 100 economists merely expressed an opinion as to a single causal factor. Notwithstanding the prevailing economic crisis of 2022, their collective opinion elicits a question. In a journey from such 'despair' to whatever 'hope', what other contributing factors are there to social and economic instability? Given the 'progress' of capitalistic economic enterprise, what else lies at the heart of the contradictory, systemic injustices we face? And—knowing 'what'—might we hope to better influence our future?

First Originated the Term VUCA (Volatility, Uncertainty, Complexity and Ambiguity)?" As an acronym,I consider VUCA a useful shorthand for its constituent dimensions. In this sense, I attibute no additional meaning to my use of the term in this text.

[4] In introducing the word precarity, I acknowledge the work of Albena Azmanova in Capitalism on Edge. However, while Azmanova writes of the mutation of (neoliberal) capitalism into a 'malignant form' she calls 'precarity capitalism', I will argue that precarity is simply an emergent property—the natural progression of the capitalist removal of discretionary political interference. The distinction is subtle, but informative. While we may undoubtedly be emerging in an epoch of social precarity it is not because we have changed the form of capitalism. Rather, I shall argue that it is because of the unbridled success of the champions of the neoliberal form of capitalist economic organization, in their dismantling of the institutions that might control for such precarity. Precarity is, in this sense, an emergent phenomenon of an autopoietic neoliberal capitalism, it is not a form of economic organization.

[5] Jeffrey Sachs and others, 'Letter from Economists: To Rebuild Our World, We Must End the Carbon Economy', The Guardian, 2020 [accessed 13 August 2020].

Over the centuries that Western capitalism has emerged, a great deal has been said and written by economists and social and political philosophers alike. Alongside the Scottish economist and philosopher Adam Smith (1723-1790), French economist and businessman Jean-Baptiste Say (1767-1832) and British philosopher, political economist and politician John Stuart Mill (1806-1873) were key figures in shaping capitalist thought and its eighteenth and nineteenth-century tradition of liberal, free-trade. Key to this text, Say was an early pioneer in situating the entrepreneur. He argued that the entrepreneurial agent was a necessary part of any economic production process, situated between the owners of capital and labour. Here, alongside commercial enterprise controlled by private owners for profit, the democratic ideal of liberty as freedom of the individual and business from constraint took root in opposition to the state and social control. These classical economists and others produced a theory of free-market economics as largely self-regulating systems, governed by 'natural' laws of production and exchange: the basis of the flourishing of nineteenth and twentieth-century capitalism.

Other contemporaries of these early figures of economics also stand out. The British Economist and Politician David Ricardo (1772-1823) challenged the then-prevailing idea that the purpose of international trade was merely to accumulate gold or silver. With his theory of 'comparative advantage',[6] Ricardo argued for industry specialisation and free international trade. From a more social perspective, the British economist, cleric and scholar Thomas Robert Malthus (1766-1834) considered the economic dimension of demography. Here, in what has become known as the 'Malthusian Trap', Malthus challenged another prevailing view of his time—one that held society as improving and as perfectible in principle. He argued that because food production generally lagged population growth, such growth was necessarily temporary, since a population could only sustain growth if its lower classes were free of hardship, famine and disease. This would not be the case if there was insufficient food to feed them. Here, another relatable social dimension was introduced by the British philosopher, jurist and social reformer Jeremy Bentham (1748-1832), associated with the concept of (modern) utilitarianism. This provides a system of ethics that suggests the measure of right and wrong can be logically based on outcomes that provide for the greatest happiness of the greatest number within a population.

The history and development of 'liberal' capitalism—and its contemporary variety in 'neoliberal' capitalism—is well covered by many authors better qualified than me to comment on these perspectives. In highlighting the

---

[6] A 'comparative advantage' over others exists if an economic agent can produce their good(s) at a lower relative opportunity cost to those others.

above luminaries, I merely acknowledge a certain historical perspective. My intent in this manuscript is not to offer a contribution of new economic knowledge that simply follows a series of changes of state (or varieties) in what might be classed as forms of ontic capitalism. Rather, my socio-philosophical argument centres on capitalism's emergence as a pre-ontic[7] state of always becoming. I simply suggest that these classical economists and political theorists provide a present-day ideological theme of capitalism that is vulnerable to re-imagination. Juxtaposed against this theme, is the narrative of failure concerning its present-day neoliberal flavour. And with vulnerability so exposed, my staring point can only be an immanent critique of its increasingly entrepreneurial nature.

History aside, climate change, exacerbated by carbon-based economic utility, is a present danger. Its negative impacts on our environmental sustainability are accepted.[8] They should be neither misunderstood, nor neglected. However, lest we be accused of fiddling while Rome burns, we should ask: is there anything else, more pressing, more deserving of our collective, immediate attention? In their letter, the 100 economists appear to acknowledge a 'fundamental instability' in the existing economy. If this is the case, while ending carbon utilisation may mitigate some symptoms of socio-economic failure, might it be the wrong approach to the overriding question of systemic injustice? As systems thinker Russell Ackoff would have questioned, are the 100 economists seeking to do the wrong thing righter?[9] Paradoxically, a list of recommendations to government and industrial policy makers—concerning actions to de-carbonize the economy—will rely on the existing, unjust socio-economic system for their implementation. This paradox invites counter-intuitive, if not contradictory thinking. Thus, my challenge to VUCA crises, the absurdity of our reality, systemic economic

---

[7] In the sense that the ontic relates to the concrete properties and characteristics of, for example, a certain form of capitalism, the pre-ontic suggests the coming into being of that form. In the sense that the properties and characteristic of capitalism have varied and continue to vary over time, I argue that any identified form of ontic capitalism is historic in nature.

[8] I draw on the concept of sustainability as may be implied from the notion of sustainable development introduced in by the World Commission on Environment and Development, that is sustainability is an outcome of human and social development (or action) that 'meets the needs of the present without compromising the ability of future generations to meet their own needs.' Importantly, these 'needs' are constrained as 'the essential needs of the world's poor'. The notion of 'development' also implies the idea of limits to action imposed by 'the state of technology and social organization on the environment's ability to meet present and future needs. See: World Commission on Environment and Development, "Our Common Future."

[9] Ackoff, "A Lifetime Of Systems Thinking," 2.

injustices, and our (in)ability to organize ourselves and others, is to turn to the counterfactual[10] question: 'what if, before taking all such action, we consider changing the socio-economic system first?' In Ackoff's terms: 'what is the right thing to do, even if we make mistakes along the way, trying?'

The edge of the abyss?

In *Capitalism on Edge*,[11] central to Azmanova's critical thesis is a radical idea. Capitalism itself is not in crisis. Rather, capitalism is in good health. As 'an engine of prosperity', it is doing well.[12] To trace Azmanova's line of argument, the health of capitalism appears to be down to a presumed failure to meet three typical assumptions of capitalism's demise.[13] Firstly, that capitalism is delivering poor economic performance and the exhaustion of natural resources; secondly, that the institutions of liberal democracy have, or are about to capitulate; and thirdly, that capitalism has lost its legitimacy in public support. There is some merit in this analysis. Yet, while eschewing a crisis in capitalism, Azmanova nevertheless proposes a focus toward discerning 'opportunities for *overcoming* it, rather than stabilizing or overthrowing it'.[14]

To Azmanova, her immanent critique is one of conceptualising a democratic capitalism—an amalgam of a democratic system of political organization and a capitalist system of social organization.[15] This is problematic; capitalism, as I have defined it above, is simply a system of political and economic organization. Furthermore, since both political and economic organization are inherently social acts, I argue we may talk confidently of the socio-political. Yet if the system of socio-political organization is capitalism itself—when capitalism pervades the socio-political sphere—and, as Azmanova

---

[10] Counterfactual relates to or expresses that which has not happened or is not the case (Oxford English Dictionary, 12th Edition). Counter factual conditional statements in arguments provide the basis for examining 'what if'. I explore the concept more thoroughly in Chapter 4, as the basis for looking toward the future.
[11] Azmanova, Capitalism on Edge: How Fighting Precarity Can Achieve Radical Change Without Crisis or Utopia.
[12] Azmanova, Capitalism on Edge: How Fighting Precarity Can Achieve Radical Change Without Crisis or Utopia, 2.
[13] Azmanova, Capitalism on Edge: How Fighting Precarity Can Achieve Radical Change Without Crisis or Utopia, 13.
[14] Azmanova, Capitalism on Edge: How Fighting Precarity Can Achieve Radical Change Without Crisis or Utopia, 3–4.
[15] Azmanova, Capitalism on Edge: How Fighting Precarity Can Achieve Radical Change Without Crisis or Utopia, 5.

contends, capitalism (in isolation) is in 'unfailing good health',[16] then the problem must lie solely in the system of political organization. If this is the case, then why a focus of attention on overcoming capitalism through its subversion?

The contradiction under critique is that a healthy capitalism must be overcome to reconcile a failed system of political organization. However, to continue this line of reasoning, how might capitalism be overcome? Here, the political and ideological Left meet their contradictions in the political and ideological Right and vice versa, in which there is a perceived failure in achieving a dialectic synthesis of democratic capitalism. Thus, there is a sense of a desired, ideological synthesis in a political movement that eschews the dialectic of a Left of social protections and a contradictory Right of free markets. Yet, arguably, what has emerged in praxis is a pronounced 'shift' of the Left. In the USA, a large proportion of the Left seem to have aligned, politically, with the economic freedoms and 'politically correct' ideology espoused by a significant Right.[17] Here, especially, Left-leaning members of the billionaire class[18] and the monopolistic activities of international businesses, turn away from the working class and ideas of individuality, political freedoms, free speech, and social protections.[19]

While the shift of the Left has become most visible since the turn to the twenty-first century, it has reached an undeniable level of cultural and political impact in the decade since the 2007-8 financial crisis. Seemingly the American 'Left', having largely abandoned the classically liberal pursuit of societal equality, now emphasizes ethnic and racial divisions and promotes racial discrimination in the pursuit of equitable social and economic *outcomes.*[20] Consequently, a recent concern (reported in the US) is the political Left's promotion of critical race theory (CRT), argued as slowly undermining the tenets of the 60s and 70s Civil Rights Movement.[21] While CRT has been seen as a radical progression of social theory, emerging in the

---

[16] Azmanova, Capitalism on Edge: How Fighting Precarity Can Achieve Radical Change Without Crisis or Utopia, 7.
[17] Lamoureux and Atkinson, "Email Correspondence: Insertions on Precarity (Capitalism)."
[18] See, for example: Schouten, "These Democratic Billionaires Could Help Shape the 2020 Election."
[19] See, for example: MacLean, Democracy in Chains: The Deep History of the Radical Right's Stealth Plan for America.
[20] Lamoureux and Atkinson, "Email Correspondence: Insertions on Precarity (Capitalism)."
[21] See, for example: Murawski, "Critical Race Theory Is About to Face Its Day (s) in Court."

USA since the 1980s,[22] in England it has been an academic concern since the early 2000s.[23]

Here in the UK, the 'politically-Right' government has declared itself 'unequivocally against' CRT.[24] Yet my purpose here is not to enter the debate over CRT *per se*, nor do I wish to draw CRT into what is already an extensive field of inquiry. Rather, casting an eye over the abyss, I illuminate CRT's presence as an empiric example of a dialectic contradiction that fails to offer promise in synthesis. The contradictions inherent and perfectly alive in both CRT and Nancy Maclean's explication of a 'blue-print' for a radical Right, are real. And, on the edge of the abyss, they are being played out in their respective long-games since the late 1950s.[25] These games cross a global field, at least between the USA and the UK, where the voice of a political Left—favouring social equality—struggles against the turn to economic freedoms, as US-funded radical think tanks are charged with reshaping the UK's political Right.[26]

A turn in immanent critique?

Although Azmanova charts a landscape of varieties of democratic capitalism, arising from the spread from a capitalist organization of the economy to a capitalist organization of society, she neither acknowledges the narratives of the radical-Right influencers of economic freedoms nor the followers of CRT. Rather, the shift of the Left to the Right arises as she changes the axes of her ideological analysis from the twentieth to the twenty-first century.[27] While the net results are similar, and thus our immanent critiques are comparative, the change of axes is problematic; it obscures why these shifts have occurred. We did not just shift from a liberal-conservative versus regulated-free market view, to a cosmopolitan-national versus closed-open view of socio-economic organization in the year 2000. I suggest that is an absurdity, in and of itself.

---

[22] Cabrera, "Where Is the Racial Theory in Critical Race Theory?: A Constructive Criticism of the Crits."

[23] Warmington, "Critical Race Theory in England: Impact and Opposition."

[24] Trilling, "Why Is the UK Government Suddenly Targeting 'Critical Race Theory'?"

[25] MacLean, Democracy in Chains: The Deep History of the Radical Right's Stealth Plan for America.

[26] Lawrence et al., "How the Right's Radical Thinktanks Reshaped the Conservative Party."

[27] Azmanova, Capitalism on Edge: How Fighting Precarity Can Achieve Radical Change Without Crisis or Utopia, 71–78.

The longevity of issues with a capitalist colonisation of the political system inherit almost two centuries of ideology,[28] from the likes of John C Calhoun, and James McGill Buchanan, whose primary concern appeared to the 'failure of democracy to preserve liberty'.[29] The precarious scene of conflict on the edge of the abyss is thus the disparity between, on the one hand, the failure of economic liberty for the minority to fully overcome the chains of political democracy, and on the other hand, the failure of those very political chains of democracy to safeguard the interests of the majority from the abuses of libertarianism.

Despite the longevity of the issues at the core of our respective critiques, to Azmanova 'The past offers no solutions.'[30] Rather, turning to the future, she invokes ideas of 'no [social] protection without emancipation'.[31] This suggests a utopian (or at least idealistic) movement—a dialectic charge toward a synthesis, led by the 'partisans of emancipation':[32] an irregular army of 'insider' insurgents, seeking freedom from the relational, structural and systemic injustices of the competitive production of profit. This utopian ideal rejects both the pragmatism of 'common sense' and its unwitting institutionalisation of the causes of crises,[33] and its contradiction in 'the morally ambitious', who seek a prosperity for all that will serve only to 'destroy the planet'.[34] Thus, Azmanova advocates a turn to the space in between—to the 'political hopeful',[35] where the progressive partisans will need to step beyond the ideologies of both the political Left and the political Right.

---

[28] MacLean, Democracy in Chains: The Deep History of the Radical Right's Stealth Plan for America, Prologue.
[29] MacLean, Democracy in Chains: The Deep History of the Radical Right's Stealth Plan for America, 1.
[30] Azmanova, Capitalism on Edge: How Fighting Precarity Can Achieve Radical Change Without Crisis or Utopia, 169.
[31] Fraser, "A Triple Movement? Parsing the Politics of Crisis after Polanyi," 40.
[32] Fraser, "A Triple Movement? Parsing the Politics of Crisis after Polanyi," 38.
[33] Azmanova, Capitalism on Edge: How Fighting Precarity Can Achieve Radical Change Without Crisis or Utopia, 170.
[34] Azmanova, Capitalism on Edge: How Fighting Precarity Can Achieve Radical Change Without Crisis or Utopia, 171.
[35] Azmanova, Capitalism on Edge: How Fighting Precarity Can Achieve Radical Change Without Crisis or Utopia, ibid.

In acknowledging the value of Azmanova's insights, I argue the contradictions at the heart of our respective immanent critiques are different.[36] While the distinctions may be problematic, the outcomes of our critiques bear similarity: we both turn our attention from a focus on 'social relations of class' to an 'overarching logic of the social system'; the point of difference being Azmanova's concept of 'system'. While in no way does she argue for an objective system, Azmanova posits one of 'structured social relations', in which the system is 'stabilised' by rules that regulate those relations.[37] To Azmanova, a system of social organization is one in which its purpose is characterised by a certain ruleset. In the complex adaptive systems approach I shall initially adopt, I will argue that purpose only emerges from a system's praxis.

The rules of the game?

To Azmanova, the potential in her analysis lies in the opportunities to overcome capitalism by replacement (through radical, subversive change) of a defined ruleset, offering the promise of policies to address three trajectories of relational, structural, and systemic injustices. Firstly, she advocates for action against relational domination, that is, tackling the injustices of the unequal distribution of power. Here, the enacting of redistribution policies for poverty alleviation, would aim to enhance political agency amongst the poor. As Azmanova suggests, 'Tax the rich is a good place to start'.[38] Secondly, there is a requirement for action against structural domination. Thus, tackling injustices of 'institutionalised' competitive profit production is seen to require policies toward controlling ownership and money as a source of power and political influence.[39] And thirdly, there is a requirement in the new policy 'ruleset' to act against systemic domination. This will require policies that tackle injustices caused by the actual 'practices' of competitive profit production. As Azmanova suggests, this is 'the proper object of radical, revolutionary practice'; it is 'the unprecedented potential... for overcoming

---

[36] I apply the term critical theory as set out by Buchanan "Critical Theory." in which the critical theorist practices against the traditional conception of theory "which holds that it is a system of abstract (i.e. ahistorical, asubjective, and asocial) propositions which can be verified empirically". In this sense, the theoretical approach set out in this paper acknowledges its subjectivity and its historic potential as a foundation for an emerging society.

[37] Azmanova, Capitalism on Edge: How Fighting Precarity Can Achieve Radical Change Without Crisis or Utopia, 5.

[38] Azmanova, Capitalism on Edge: How Fighting Precarity Can Achieve Radical Change Without Crisis or Utopia, 173.

[39] Azmanova, Capitalism on Edge: How Fighting Precarity Can Achieve Radical Change Without Crisis or Utopia, 174.

capitalism'. It will leverage both the losers of relational domination (the poor) and those who may be the moderate winners in the game of structural domination, but who, nevertheless, are harmed by the incessant competitive practice of systemic domination.[40]

Despite the advocating of a new policy ruleset for a purposive, capitalist system of social organization, the vexed question of politic agency (the victim of relational domination) is problematic. As Azmanova acknowledges, in 'conditions of uncertainty, the creative energies of social discontent are trapped by conservative instincts—it is fear that currently directs social unrest into the reactionary path of xenophobia and autocratic calls for law and order.' Such calls and (re)actions serve to support the existing system.[41] They simply resolve—as a good place to start—to 'tax the rich'? Yet is this the right 'system' thing to do? Would the Guardian's 100 economists welcome such a path? Or is there another way? Is there a more 'pragmatic', conceptual and practical approach to identifying problems, then focusing on a more equitable remediation that *avoids utopian tropes*?

In this book, I set out an alternative immanent critique. I argue that rather than a series of changes of state in an ontic capitalism, capitalism exits in pre-ontic state of always becoming. As I substitute my own axes of individual-social identity versus Left-Right power distribution, I venture that the shifts in capitalism are less prone to classification, but no less insidious than the idea of a Capitalism of Precarity. On the edge of this abyss, technology is a mediating factor that has accelerated liberal individualism. And, as we may observe, we have an arms race in the pursuit of individualistic *competitive, anti-meritocratic*, non-inclusive divergent *equity*. Individual freedoms are naturally exclusive; technology has given marginalised voices new capabilities to be heard and others new capabilities to suppress them. Here, I believe, the Left need a new language of meritocratic inclusivity, built on responsibility, not individual rights—this is the *raison d'être* of this present work.

The fable of the bees

The Fable of the Bees—originally published as *The Grumbling Hive: OR, Knaves Turn'd Honest*—is an infamous satire by Bernard Mandeville (1670-1733). It follows the story of a successful hive inhabited by a society of selfish, hypocritical, yet content and prosperous bees. 'A spacious Hive well stock'd

---

[40] Azmanova, Capitalism on Edge: How Fighting Precarity Can Achieve Radical Change Without Crisis or Utopia, 175.
[41] Azmanova, Capitalism on Edge: How Fighting Precarity Can Achieve Radical Change Without Crisis or Utopia, 176–77.

with Bees, That lived in Luxury and Ease.'[42] However, the bees are gradually influenced by the moralising bee-priests of Jove, to the extent the decision is taken for the bee-society to live more virtuously, dispelling fraud and other vices. The contradictory, paradoxical result is precarity—a society in crisis. The virtuous triumph but, absurdly perhaps, at the cost of many bees who die or leave the hive, as the essence of their society—their being—is denied. Undermined, they are reduced to a small colony where, in the final words, avoiding even the extravagance of living in a large, but now largely empty hive, the bees '...flew into a hollow Tree, Blest with Content and Honesty.'[43]

To Mandeville, what underpins the norms of acceptable and unacceptable societal behaviour, are the animal passions. In the human, these passions differ from the animal only by a matter of degree.[44] In Mandeville's human society, as in that of the bees, the animal passions interact in animating the individual, society and its body politic. Avoiding the controversy of Mandeville's work, I simply introduce it as relevant to my aim in this book. This is to investigate the (oftentimes) absurd dance of capitalism, work and enterprise, in speculatively addressing the question: in respect of social injustice, what if we change the socio-economic system, first? As Elisabeth Wallmann observed, 'Mandeville wrote at a time when the classical debate about the effects of luxury on morality where revived and commentators worried about the decline of civic virtue and honour in the face [of] increasing wealth.'[45] Paradoxically, despite our progress, such concerns remain prevalent. It seems little has changed.

We see, in the subtext of the letter of the 100 economists of August 2020, a persistent and general concern over injustice and a decline in civic virtues and honour, all in the face of an absurd increase in the wealth of a minority of the global population: members of the global 'billionaire class'. The politics of Right and Left aside, as the pre-covid-19 Western economies seek their post-Covid future, the trend of increasing wealth based on 'mobile capital' and enhanced by advances in technology is set to continue. This is despite (as I add the final edits to this manuscript) the threat of a global recession, brought on by, inter alia, inflationary pressures and the disruption to energy supplies caused by the latest Russian incursion into Ukraine. This is crises pushing crises, where the cost-of-living is driving a reported 71 million more people

---

[42] Mandeville, The Fable of the Bees, 63.

[43] Mandeville, The Fable of the Bees, 75.

[44] Wallmann, "The Human-Animal Debate and the Enlightenment Body Politic: Emilie Du Châtelet's Reading of Mandeville's Fable of the Bees."

[45] Wallmann, "The Human-Animal Debate and the Enlightenment Body Politic: Emilie Du Châtelet's Reading of Mandeville's Fable of the Bees.".

into extreme poverty.[46] Mandeville's poem warrants reflection. As he suggested in his Preface to *The Fable of the Bees*: 'Laws and Government are to the Political Bodies of Civil Societies, what the Vital Spirits and Life itself are to the Natural Bodies of Animated Creatures…'.[47] As Wallmann argues, 'once humans enter society, just like bees in human-kept hives, they do not lose their animal nature.[48] Here we see the potential in Mandeville's 'good governors' who channel those animal passions, creating a new system, or 'oeconomy'.[49] The excesses of 'Vice', are controlled through 'Justice lopt, and bound.'

The inconvenience of vice

To Robin Douglass, 'Mandeville's account [of the development of human sociability and government,] challenges anyone… who seeks to defend the moral character of commercial society'.[50] Thus, I suggest that what we might take from Mandeville's *Fable of the Bees* is a certain knowledge of the inconvenience of the idea of 'vice': the wilful, individual practice of animal passions, unchanneled in the (useful) service of a social system, or economy. As Mandeville suggests, in *An enquiry into the origin of moral virtue*, 'All untaught Animals… naturally follow the bent of their own Inclination, without considering the good or harm that from their being pleased will accrue to others.'[51] Thus, in many respects, animal passions channelled for the good, albeit indirect good of society, are a virtue, whereas practised with bad societal outcomes, even indirectly, such passions are a vice to be controlled. In a society, vice is an inconvenience—a certain contradiction. Vice is a natural proclivity of the human animal that has not been controlled in the service of (a) society.

In the commercialised—now precariously situated—Western economies that have emerged through the epochs following Mandeville's social commentary, entrepreneurial (neoliberal) capitalism has seemingly made a virtue of all vices. Even Adam Smith's (1723-1790) *The Wealth of Nations*[52] and his *Theory*

---

46 Georgieva, "Facing a Darkening Economic Outlook : How the G20 Can Respond."
47 Mandeville, The Fable of the Bees, 53.
48 Wallmann, "The Human-Animal Debate and the Enlightenment Body Politic: Emilie Du Châtelet's Reading of Mandeville's Fable of the Bees."
49 Oeconomy, derived from the Aristotelian model of oikos, is a term referring to the practice of managing the economic and moral resources of a household for the maintenance of good order. See, for example: Harvey, "Oeconomy and the Eighteenth-Century House"; Wallmann, "The Human-Animal Debate and the Enlightenment Body Politic: Emilie Du Châtelet's Reading of Mandeville's Fable of the Bees."
50 Douglass, "Morality and Sociability in Commercial Society: Smith, Rousseau-And Mandeville," 599.
51 Mandeville, The Fable of the Bees, 81.
52 Smith, The Wealth of Nations: Books I-III; Smith, The Wealth of Nations: Books IV-V.

of Moral Sentiments,[53] underpinning much contemporary capitalist thinking, can be argued to have drawn, in part, on *The Fable of the Bees*. Here, perhaps absurdly, the inconvenience of vice is waived aside by 'an invisible hand'. The (animal) self-interest of the individual is drawn-on for the greater good of society, suppressing the notion of vanity in Mandeville's line: 'T' enjoy the World's Conveniences… Without great Vices, is a vain Eutopia seated in the brain'—scant regard is taken of the need for Justice to *lop and bind*.

A provocation of capitalism, work and enterprise

We see, in *The Fable of the Bees*, the powerful idea of systems thinking. Over the course of the poem, Mandeville expounds on the complexity of causal relationships in his allegoric description of a society of bees. I argue this is a fine provocation in the dance of capitalism, work and enterprise. It demonstrates the role an extensive array of both virtuous and non-virtuous non-mechanical components can play in the achievement of common purpose. The allegoric poem clearly depicts the impacts that such components can have, when working for or against a given purposeful enterprise. By arguing against Mandeville's treatment of vice and virtue as, in effect, the same thing[54]—animal passion—Smith maintained a distinction between vices that seemed to adopt, as a virtue, the great Vice of self-interest, guided only by a virtuous 'invisible hand'. Thus, the present Western capitalist system of neoliberal economics[55] pays scant regard to the need to channel certain freedoms. Here, from Smith's economic systems perspective, people's behaviour is assumed to manifest (through invisible guidance) in the virtue of self-interested prudence, far more than the vice of self-interested greed.[56]

In reflecting on VUCA crises, in an immanent critique of both systemic injustices and our ability to organize our 'selves' and 'others', I eschew Azmanova's rule-based systemic approach to a utopian emancipation from capitalism's hegemonies. I also challenge her idea that 'The past offers no solutions'. Rather, in asking the (counterfactual) question: 'what if we change the socio-economic system first?' I see value in the continuity of the past as it

---

53 Smith, The Theory of Moral Sentiments.

54 Smith, The Theory of Moral Sentiments, 362.

55 The neoliberal turn in the general direction of capitalism may be seen in the rise of the neoliberal politics of the 1970s, in which Thatcherism (in the UK), and Reagonomics (in the US), applied neoliberal theory, for example that of Milton Friedman, in a politico-economic practice 'aimed at the commodification of everything'. See, for example: Fuchs, Commun. Capital. A Crit. Theory, 1.

56 Douglass, "Morality and Sociability in Commercial Society: Smith, Rousseau-And Mandeville," 619.

shapes a systemic becoming. I choose to do so, initially inspired by an 'adaptive systems' thinking perspective. Here, contrary to a purposive ruleset, I take Ackoff's position that the promise of systems thinking is that 'it attempts to derive understanding of parts from the behaviour and properties of wholes, rather than derive the behaviour and properties of wholes from those of their parts.'[57] However, against both Azmanova and Ackoff, I also adopt Friedrich W. Nietzsche's critical distrust of systematisers, for 'The will to a system is a lack of integrity.'[58]

Much naïve systems thinking sees systems as the sum of some set of parts, or components, put together by design, to achieve some purpose. Such naïve systems are designed on the basis that the designer understands certain properties of certain components, relying on those properties to achieve certain interactions with other components. Even in hard, technical systems, this does not necessarily work. As a young radar technician in the UK's Royal Air Force, I worked in repairing complex electronic equipment, where the 'system' diagrams showed the value of a particular component as: 'S.O.T'—Select on Test. Due to the tolerances on hundreds of different interconnected components, I had to experiment with the final piece of the jigsaw to realise the desired system functionality to operational specifications.

In general terms, if we cannot expect a given hard system component, such as a resistor or a capacitor manufactured to a given tolerance, to restore a certain electronic system to operational capability, how can we expect the constant movement of people across, through and in-between our social systems, to allow their consistent, stable function? Here, again absurdly, even the weather or a 'bad hair' day can upset the balance of an individual's animal passions, resulting in what, to some, might seem an irrational (component) performance in their socio-economic role.[59] It is not surprising that, beyond their moralising controversy, Manderville's 'Bees' have received little attention in the histories of economic thought—histories that have set the foundations for modern neoliberal capitalism, such as the work of Joseph Schumpeter and others. The 'Bees' offer 'little "formal" economic theory'.[60] Here, the 100 economists' concerned acceptance of a pre-existing 'fundamental instability' in the economy, 'rooted' in systemic injustice, or Azmanova's epoch of precarity, are emergent properties of a socio-economic system. However, such instability

---

[57] Ackoff, "A Lifetime Of Systems Thinking," 2.
[58] Cited in: Adorno, Lectures on Negative Dialectics, 220 (Lecture 3, Note 18).
[59] The recent publication of Noise, highlights the role that 'small and seemingly random factors, can [play in producing] major differences in [expected] outcomes. Kahneman, Sibony, and Sunstein, Noise: A Flaw in Human Judgement, 16.
[60] Chalk, "Mandeville's Fable of the Bees: A Reappraisal."

and precarity are not by virtue of some flawed set of components, or a ruleset that can be understood and corrected for, but, paradoxically, by the very fact that the components themselves are inherently unstable and precarious.

The complexity and management of a complicated 'system' of social and economic organization, developed from a set of complex and inherently instable components, goes beyond the norms of general systems thinking. It defies (or rather, contradicts) theories of equilibrium and attempts to generate stable, effective and efficient systems based on rational theorising. And while such theoretical advances as game theory, and Nash's equilibria, have had an undeniable impact on our social and economic existence, the assumptions made, essential to such rationality, require that the system's human components, as individual agents, act rationally.[61] The introduction of a contradictory (human) irrationality is the scourge of naïve systems designers, striving to achieve perfect, efficient, effective and thus homeostatic systems.

Thinking about human irrationality as a given in systems design, requires a form of thinking discrete from the individualist or collectivist views of society. We cannot simply consider people as biological organisms with predefined identities and characteristics. They are not self-reliant and independent of the social system in which they live and function. Such a system merely reflects a sum of its parts. Neither can we simply consider individuals as component sponges, soaking up the economic systems' environmental collective purpose, each component capable of, and trusted in, faithfully replicating that purpose, as and when the system requires. Rather, our mode of systems thinking should regard critical thought about its components that is relational. Here, what we might call *relational critical systems thinking*, implies a mode of thought—beyond the dialectic—in which the identities and characteristics of its components are not 'bestowed upon them in advance of their involvement with others[,] but are the condensations of histories of growth and maturation within fields of… relationships.'[62] Every system component is a 'locus of development', capable of adaptive variation, capable of transformation under both its own actions, and its interaction with others and its environment.

---

[61] Stacey, Griffin, and Shaw, Complexity and Management: Fad or Radical Challenge to Systems Thinking?, 53:45.

[62] Ingold, The Perception of the Environment: Essays in Livelihood, Dwelling, and Skill, 43:3–4.

An inspector calls

In the words of J. B. Priestley's Inspector Goole:

> 'We don't live alone. We are members of one body. We are responsible for each other. And I tell you that the time will soon come when, if [we] will not learn that lesson, then [we] will be taught it in fire and blood and anguish.'[63]

Set in 1912, two years before the outbreak of the first Great War, and first performed the year after the end of the second, *An Inspector Calls* provides an allegorical commentary on what appear to be the trappings and consequences of capitalist excess: a comfortable existence in the large suburban home of a prosperous manufacturer. As an Inspector calls, the inhabitants of this microcosm of capitalism are celebrating a special occasion. They are dressed in their finery and served by their parlour maid; they are, as Priestley notes at the opening of Act One, 'pleased with themselves'.[64] Yet, by the time of the Inspector's 'blood and anguish' line, the audience has been taken, systematically, through the causal relationship that each of the capitalist diners held with the unfortunate suicidal demise of the play's absent protagonist: an ex-employee of the capitalist employer. Through a series of five avenues of inquiry, the Inspector reveals a systemic suppression by way of the capitalist 'code'—a Levinasian dereliction of an ethical responsibility to face their Other—of the dignity of a young woman and her expectations of a meaningful, purposeful and/or purposive[65] role in society.

The Inspector arrives. He informs the collected family gathering of a young woman who has committed suicide by drinking disinfectant. He has some questions for the diners. He commences his inquiry. The owner of the house, it is revealed, had sacked the young woman from his business, for going on

---

[63] Priestley, "An Inspector Calls," 207.

[64] Priestley, "An Inspector Calls," 161.

[65] I refer to the definitions of purpose, purposeful and purposive as provided by Peter Checkland. Purpose being an end pursued but never achieved; purposeful being a 'willed' activity or 'action'; and purposive as that activity seen by an observer as serving a purpose. See: Checkland, Systems Thinking, Systems Practice, 316–17. In this sense, as a wilful action, purposeful is associated with the 'self', an individual desire or need to achieve a purpose. On the contrary, a purposive action may simply be the action of the 'self' driven to meet some externally imposed purpose, such as in an obligation to serve the purpose of an other's desire or need. A purposive action may be beneficial to the self, as in serving the purpose of a greater social good, or a job of employment in return for a fair wage; or it may be objectional to the self, as in a Conscientious Objector forced to take military action, or the action of an individual enslaved to the will of an other.

strike. He refuses to accept any responsibility for her death. The owner's daughter is then revealed to have caused the young woman's sacking from another position, after making a complaint to her new employer. The daughter is ashamed. But her fiancé is subsequently revealed to have had an affair with the young woman, who was then without means and vulnerable. The owner's wife, in a position to provide charitable support after the young woman becomes pregnant, is revealed to have refused the provision of help. And finally, the Inspector reveals that it was the owner's son who got the young woman pregnant. The son is also accused of stealing money from his father's business to help her. Are these characters victims of animal passions?

Following the Inspector's warning of 'fire and blood and anguish', he leaves. The owner telephones the infirmary, but there is no record of a girl dying from drinking disinfectant. At this point, the family take a little time considering their situation; they convince themselves there is nothing for them to answer for, despite the truths revealed among them. Then, the phone rings. The owner answers it. It is the police. He learns a young woman has just died from drinking disinfectant and an inspector is on his way to question them about it. At this point, the play ends. In a later film adaptation of the play (2017), the audience may be left speculating that, had the family quickly reached an alternative conclusion on learning the truth from the infirmary—taking the initiative to quickly search for the girl—they may have interceded in her suicide, perhaps making some reconciliation against the violence to her dignity and affording her the care and attention they had the responsibility and capacity (if not the motivation) to provide. An inspector with the capability of inquiring into the future is an interesting and provocative fictional device. It provides a useful (imaginative) perspective, and one which—along with a letter from 100 economists and a poem about a bee colony—forms a general *motif* for this book's approach—examples of a certain 'empiric of the imagination'.[66]

---

[66] Given the term empiric is generally associated with what is traditionally concerned with, or verifiable by, observation or experience of our reality, an empiric of the imagination allows me to consider the imagination on similar terms. In this sense, I deploy the idea of an empiric of the imagination as associated with what is experienced within the imagination. While in context, the subject of a letter, or a poem, or a play does not (in reality) exist, their socially acknowledged existence is evidence of a certain collective (meaningful) interpretation of an imaginative possibility. The empiric value of the imagination lies in the extent to which the experience of the imaginaition can be shared or held in common meaning. In this sense, to praphrase Vega Balbás, "The Performative Nature of Dramatic Imagination," 12., such interpretations (as in acting) permit 'an empirical approach to the imagination'. This somewhat overcomes the limits of a purely philosophical approach.

'So who is to blame?' the Inspector demands, as Peter Marks observed, in a review of the stage play performed in the US in 2018;[67] 'a line that pretty much sums up the Inspector's whole line of inquiry.' However, the Inspector is not so much seeking a culprit to whom he can pin a charge of 'guilty', but more an inquiry into causality. While this perspective on the play was lost on some critics,[68] in following the form of the Inspector's inquiry into a future event, in this book, I set out to interrogate selected incumbents on our present state of capitalism.

1912 and all that

The significance of setting in *An Inspector Calls,* was not lost on its audience. Set in 1912 (late-Edwardian) England, it expressed the idealism and anxiety of its historical moment.[69] The foretold second coming of the Inspector in the play's closing moment, was prescient of the looming 1914-1918 great war. Written in the winter of 1944-1945, Priestley imbued the play with a sense of *déjà vu.* Over the course of time, from well before 1912, the idealism and anxiety of critical historical moments might have held considerable promise of less *fire and blood and anguish,* had foresight been available (and if available, considered with due attention). Had an inspector called prior to the financial 2008 crash, or the global pandemic with its origin in China in late-2019, or any other lessor or equally significant moments in time and asked this book's central question: 'what if we change the socio-economic system first?', what then?

It is not sufficient to simply employ the *motif* of an inspector calling. The Inspector must transcend the scope of Mandeville's 'Bees' and offer a 'formal' framework of critique. Thus, in this Inquiry, I adopt the lens of Theodor W. Adorno's negative dialectics. In doing so, I aim to document a conceptual inquiry over systemic injustices faced in the 'progress' of capitalistic economic enterprise. These are the contradictions. I further aim to posit reparative socio-economic interventions. These are the reconciliations. In setting out these aims, I also offer a heterodox starting point for the conceptual advancement of the negative dialectic, given contemporary and emergent societal conditions. My thesis is that the complex geometry of social reconciliations resists objectification by virtue of their existence at the intersection of a rational plane of material reality, and an irrational, imaginary plane of aesthetic sensibility. While traditional empiricism may address the

---

[67] Marks, "The Rich Haven't a Clue in 'Inspector.'"
[68] Seligman and de Llosa, "God's Economics."
[69] See, for example: Baxendale, "'Now We Must Live up to Ourselves': New Jerusalem and Beyond."

(historic) material reality, it is with an (ahistoric) 'empiric of the imagination' that we must address the imaginary plane.

Inquiry structure...

My proper concern is the intersection of social philosophy with the fields of socio-economic work and neoliberal capitalistic enterprising praxis. It is not, *per se*, with the fields of academic literature that presently represent this juxtaposition. Thus, let me assume an Inspector calls, alerted by a context of impending crises, social and economic injustices, and our seeming inability to organize our 'selves' and 'others' within them. To get to the counterfactual question: 'what if we change the socio-economic system first?', my Inspector must perform an inquiry. I remember, imbued with a sense of déjà vu, that this is a special form of inquiry: it is an inquiry into a future crisis. But, following Russell Ackoff, I can have no interest in attempting to forecast the future[70]—I do not attempt to forecast, for example, the death of capitalism, or the next great technological advance, or the outbreak of a social revolution in work—velvet or otherwise. My interest in the future is in creating it, by acting appropriately, cognisant of its VUCA antagonisms: its volatility, uncertainty, complexity and ambiguity. I want to know how our thinking about the future, can help us rise to the challenge of better equipping our 'selves' to manage and organize our 'selves' and 'others', and our 'economy' and our 'work', within it. Thus, also challenging a Nietzschean distrust of systematising my inquiry, I adopt a search for a (provisional) truth through a methodology of negative dialectics.

With my Inspector's hat firmly atop my head, I present a discursive inquiry into capitalism, work and enterprise in three parts. This is the classic detective's approach of addressing motive, means and opportunity. I set aside despair. In Part I, by way of a discussion of methodology, I offer two inquiries *on motivation*. This covers both Adorno's conception of speculation as mimetic motivation—a need to reveal the absurd, the 'absent other' rooted in the negative dialectics of a common purpose, such as in the idea of a purposive system—and the motivation evidenced in the (sometimes) perceived irrationality of purposeful, individual action. This later inquiry focuses on the individual 'entrepreneurial' action I reason lies at the core of an emergent entrepreneurial capitalism. In Part II, I address the *means*: the negative dialectics and method. Here, I offer inquiries into future contradictions of four perspectives: entrepreneurship, work, international business, and capitalism itself. It is here that the empirics of the imagination move a provisional

---

[70] Ackoff, "A Lifetime Of Systems Thinking," 1.

conclusion from the fact that change is required, to address the emergent potential of that change. Finally, in Part III, in a discursive reconciliation of my empiric findings of the imagination, I hint at *opportunities* for change, from the inside out. These draw on provocations of reconciliatory hope: conceptualisations of a Design Capitalism, Meaningful Work and an Aesthetic Enterprise. I outline these Parts and their Chapters in the following sections.

On motivation

In Part I, I address a need to understand the *motivation* of creative thought and action. In Chapter 2, "In Defence of the Absurd", I extend my previous writing on the concept of dance as a metaphor for collective movement, now set in the context of the VUCA challenges of organizational leadership, management and human relations. I draw on key concepts of social presence, rhythm and finding common purpose to explicate the idea of the absurd as the motivation for this inquiry. Pivoting on the 'absurd', I then explicate a methodology of negative dialectics. This draws heavily on a close reading of Theodor W. Adorno's lectures on the subject. This methodology allows me to set my inquiry as a 'means' to the intellectual experience of understanding difference rather than sameness. I offer a certain autistic[71] primacy of thought in action—a thinking that negative dialectic thought starts from the point of view of the individual, gazing upon 'other' individuals in the richness of their differences. Here, Adorno's dialectic of non-identity makes the other unlike the self.[72] It presents a Levinasian ethical and responsible 'facing of the Other' without violating their oftentimes contrary otherness.[73] However, to overcome a problematic with negative conditions, I introduce reconciliatory pathways through the responsible introduction of the imaginary plane of human possibility. Thus, a responsibility to speculate on the infinite differences of the absurd in the face of the Other, provides the motivation for a methodology of negative dialectics.

In Chapter 3, "The contrary entrepreneur",[74] I continue the theme of motivation, seeking to reveal something of the nomothetic social promise that

---

[71] I use the term autistic in relation to its etymology in the Greek word autos meaning 'self'. I am conscious that this use might perturb some readers. However, as an autistic person, (in the contemporary sense of the word), I find no issue in the use of the term in the context of self-interest. Indeed, it is, perhaps, a function of my own autism and thinking style, that I can take up the position of negative dialectic thinking I develop in this text.

[72] Adorno, Lectures on Negative Dialectics, 1.

[73] Lévinas, "Ethics and Infinity."

[74] An earlier version of Chapter 3 was presented at the University of Suffolk Storytelling Conference 2018, benefiting from some feedback from its audience.

emerges from within entrepreneurial idiographies—the private stories of enterprising Others. This, again, is an ethical and responsible gaze upon the face of Others in the richness of their difference. Here, I use story to extend the methodology of negative dialectics, enabling an exploration of the essence of the social character: The Entrepreneur. This allows me to resurface Maslow's seminal Needs Theory. It is here that I suggest that Mandeville's *Fable of the Bees* sees its most overt relevance to my inquiry, as animal passions become a focus of attention in terms of the contrariness of individual motivation and action. Therefore, through speculating on the conscious and unconscious needs that motivate an entrepreneur's entry into J-B Say's entrepreneurial agency—at times a seemingly irrational or even absurd action—I argue that the inquiry into the entrepreneurial call to capitalist enterprise, contributes a notion that the individual's motivation to action depends upon a balance of needs.

On means

In Part II, set within a methodology of negative dialectics, I turn to address a need for creative methods—or *means*—of thinking and speculating about the future. These methods, illustrated over the course of four separate inquiries, centre on the idea of counterfactuals as the non-conceptual identities of empiric[75] aspects of an emergent, antagonistic (VUCA) reality (the 'imaginations'). In Chapter 4, "Entrepreneurship and unicorns"—in the first of these 'means' inquiries—I build on the intellectual use of fictional story. I take inspiration from a critical, counterfactual application of science fiction. Although both science fiction and counterfactuals in futures studies are not uncommon, I set out a distinct negative dialectic rationale for their use in the speculative analysis of futures narratives. To do so, I first theorise on both the critical counterfactual and the emergent and its ontological character. In doing so, I make a distinction between two modes of emergence: the phenomenal and the epiphenomenal. I then apply the *critical counterfactuals* (CCF) method to inquire into an emergent, indeterminate (rather than determinate) non-concept of entrepreneurship.

In the method of choice, fictional news headlines from the future—'science fictions'—provide me with an empiric set of 'imaginations'. These are counterfactual vignettes: small scenes from the future that are concerned with the experience of another's imagined reality. These empiric imaginations are then used to explore the epiphenomenal emergence of the (non)concept of entrepreneurship. The method employs a truth table to assign relative truth values to the fictional news stories. It enables an exploration of their

[75] I refer the reader to the earlier note 66.

coherence with a range of projected future moments of an antagonistic reality, based on three critical uncertainties: the productivity paradox; the future of work; and a need for sustainable economic growth. I posit that this approach to investigating the future, overcomes several limitations in the use of fiction within counterfactual analysis, including the indeterminacy intuition—the accepted wisdom that impossible or wholly implausible (absurd) scenarios are unfeasible. In the futures mould, I follow, for example, Andrew Atherton,[76] and Antonio García-Olivares and Jordi Solé,[77] in challenging the contemporary study of entrepreneurship. I argue there is a value in considering its future sustainability through the provocation of an emergent, indeterminate non-concept of entrepreneurship. In this context, my provisional conclusion is, simply, that change is required.

In Chapter 5, "Work: experts and storytellers", I look at the functional interchangeability of technology and institutions in the development of a post Covid-19 future of work. Building on the negative dialectic inquiry into entrepreneurship in previous chapters, I undertake this separate yet related 'means' inquiry into the 'other' (negative) side of enterprising work—the individual as an employee, or worker. In Chapter 5, I thus offer a negative dialectic response to increasing interest in the impacts of new technology on work. Here, facing a post Covid-19 future, I ask: do we use foresight to develop better social systems of work, or do we turn our backs on the challenge and opportunity it presents? Following Martin Heidegger, I argue a concern with the equipmentality of technology in the interchange of technology and institutions.

In Chapter 5, I develop the theme of work on a localised basis. Here, the inquiry is facilitated by an opportunity to reflect on an 'expert' led view of work, technology and institutions, arising from a Futures and Foresight Workshop held at York St John University, UK, in March 2020. The workshop, funded by the University's Institute for Social Justice, was held to develop regional-level social justice scenarios for the year 2030. While the detail of the workshop is beyond the scope of this book, it offered a form of validation of the critical counterfactuals method, allowing me to triangulate on expert scenarios and fictional news stories—providing an amalgam of the empiric of the real with the empiric of the imagination. In this case, I set the coherence of imaginative news from the future of work against the three critical uncertainties—the negative dialectics of: varying power bases; the changing

---

[76] Atherton, "A Future for Small Business? Prospective Scenarios for the Development of the Economy Based on Current Policy Thinking and Counterfactual Reasoning."
[77] García-Olivares and Solé, "End of Growth and the Structural Instability of Capitalism-From Capitalism to a Symbiotic Economy."

nature of a population's social values; and social concerns over environmental and other issues.

Centred on work and employment, my investigation in Chapter 5 highlights the close relationship of the contemporary nature of work to the non-concept of entrepreneurship. This resolves to a politically influenced problematic of non-identity. I argue that a dialectic entrepreneurship simply represents its own industry, giving only an illusion of an entrepreneurial actor's self-control, in which entrepreneurship merely produces insecure short-term (self-) employment opportunity for many. This suggests a provisional direction for change: to consider Jim Dator's archetypal, yet ideological, 'conserver/ disciplined' future society.[78]

In Chapter 6, "Horsemen in the land of Oz", I offer a variation on the use of the critical counterfactuals method of futures analysis. In this third 'means' inquiry, I critically consider the long-term horizon of international business. This is a nod to David Ricardo's idea of 'comparative advantage' and its role in the evolution of capitalism. This inquiry builds on the problematic of the non-concept of identity (or non-identity) surfaced in Chapter 5, by taking a more global perspective. Thus, I take up the three critical and antagonistic uncertainties of power, technology, and identity, and I ask the question: what future: the neoliberal colonisation by, or of, post-pandemic international business? Given the accelerating sense of global insecurity and the absurd level of hyper-turbulence arising from the seismic impact of Covid-19, will neoliberalism continue to drive global dimensions in shaping a post-pandemic world of international business? If so, what does this say about power, technology and identity?

In Chapter 6, I posit an initial complex adaptive system view of international business.[79] And I again project three antagonistic uncertainties as the basis of future possibility. However, rather than the empiric 'imaginations' of fictional news stories, in a variation of futures vignette development, I 'imagine' a related story at the pole of each antagonism. The truth table then balances

---

[78] Bezold, "Jim Dator's Alternative Futures and the Path to IAF's Aspirational Futures."

[79] In May 2020, a 'full text' keyword search on the term 'complex adaptive system" in the leading Journal of International Business Studies (JIBS) returned just four articles. Widening the comb of enquiry to other journals, a search of article 'abstracts' with '"complex adaptive system" + "international business"' revealed just three additional articles. The selected JIBS articles ranged from one in 1992, to three in the period 2013-2014; the remaining two articles came from Studies in Business and Economics and the British Journal of Management. The search was by no means exhaustive. However, I reason it is illustrative of the limited extent to which such 'complex adaptive systems' thinking might have featured in the study of international business to-date.

coherence across the related dimensions. In following the counterfactual futures approach, I draw on elements of design thinking. I replace the triangulation of 'experts' with a Wizard-of-Oz view of a range of antagonistic 'moments in time', in the future reality of international business praxis. This involves an allegoric visit of the Four Horsemen of the Apocalypse to the Land of Oz, as I assign them the collective status of antagonist.[80] While extending a critical, negative dialectic understanding of the ways in which institutions (including businesses and governments) might influence their own global futures, in this further inquiry, I reveal a shift in the provisional conclusion for a change to a 'conserver/disciplined' future society. This calls on a requirement for an immanent critique of capitalism itself.

In setting out to critique capitalism, I introduce, in Chapter 7, some "Ghosts of democracy". I offer a conceptual, critical futures-based inquiry into the long-term antagonistic horizon of neoliberal capitalist economies. In invoking the ghosts of Karl Marx, Joseph Schumpeter and Martin Luther King Jr, I develop non-conceptual perspectives on post-Covid socio-economic systems. Here, characteristic of the economic future, lies the accelerating sense of the absurd: the volatility, uncertainty, complexity and ambiguity in the VUCA world. Again, these conditions are particularly exacerbated by the seismic impact of Covid-19. International business aside, in Chapter 7, I, therefore, extend the previous concerns by posing the question: does neoliberal (entrepreneurial) capitalism have a future in the context of organizing our post-Covid-19 national economies? If so, I ask what might be its scope for development?

In Chapter 7—in this fourth of the 'means' inquiries—I again work from the negative dialectic perspective of the economy as an epiphenomenally emergent non-concept of a complex adaptive subsystem. Here, its foundation is based on a complex inter-relationship of the underlying critical, antagonistic uncertainties of: the role and regulation of identity; the nature of the power-politic; and the emancipatory paradox of technological liberation in the development and transfer of economic value. However, from this (non-conceptual) systems perspective, I argue that a neoliberal capitalist ideology—romanced by what has clearly been achieved for its incumbents and those enfranchised to its (positivistic) dialectic identity—has failed to understand the true nature of a self-organizing system. Again, following the critical counterfactuals method, I project the highlighted uncertainties as a complex function of economic possibility. In setting out six exemplar antagonistic futures outcomes, I reflect on the empiric value of three vignettes of economic thought from Marx, Schumpeter and King. The ensemble of ghosts, of futures yet to come, are recruited as antagonists. They reveal what some might

---

[80] Foucault, Aesthetics, Method, and Epistemology, 234.

consider a capitalist sleight-of-hand. This sets the ground for an exploration of possible 'reconciliations': designs on what Paul Mason has described as a transition to postcapitalism.[81]

On opportunity

In Part III, I turn to the question of *opportunity*. In effect, I direct my inquiries toward ruminations on 'reconciliations'—toward 'designs' for the future: a potential negative dialectic, or non-conceptual, epiphenomenal emergence of postcapitalism. In effect, I build on the empiric value (of the imagination) that I believe is realisable from the foregoing 'means' inquiries. I argue that this approach acknowledges a need to both address the opportunity for change, and to examine how best to unlock its potential, *from the inside out*. In Chapter 8, "The invisible hand, emergent", I entertain a discursive exploration that builds on the provocations of the preceding inquiries, using them as metaphors of a certain empirical value. Amid the now less-than-absurd images of autonomous taxis and autonomous additive manufacturing units, operating on de-centralised blockchain-facilitated self-enforcing contracts, the signifiers (the imaginations) apply their associated implications (provocations) to the set of antecedent conditions (the signified) from which a new conceptual form of a post-economic system might emerge. Thus, I explore the reconciliatory idea of Design Capitalism, its problematic and its potential. This expands on the idea of a design capitalism with roots in mid-twentieth-century discourse. It reveals its contemporary problematic as making invisible (negating) its own potential. I argue that a non-concept of Design Capitalism has a role in a post-Covid-19 society, as perhaps the only pragmatic reconciliation of an idealistic notion of capitalism.

Chapter 8 highlights a need to negate a perceived trend for fine-tuning an educational curriculum that strives to produce the ideal yet synthetic neoliberal capitalist. It implies that to better prepare humanistic responses to a VUCA environment, society and its people will require different skills. Perhaps a new language and a typology of meaningful, enterprising work may be necessary to encourage poietic responses that pitch creativity, experimentation, problem-solving capabilities and ingenuity against an antagonistic reality that promises less repetitiveness, less predictability, and less regularity. With roots in the concept of design, Chapter 8 starts to light the shadows of the needs of society. It thus lays the groundwork for a subsequent re-introduction of the aesthetic theory from *Thinking the Art of Management*, setting a scene for highlighting the real potential for change in society.

---

[81] Mason, Postcapitalism: A Guide to Our Future, 145.

In Chapter 9, "Emergence and the non-hero", I return specifically to (re)question the (non)concept of entrepreneurship, in which the entirety of this inquiry is inextricably bound. If Chapter 8's implicit conclusion is that a new typology of enterprising work is required, then what might it look like? This question strikes at the heart of the birth of capitalism and Jean-Baptiste Say's situating of the entrepreneurial agent as a necessary part of the economic production process, between the owners of capital and labour. Here, I argue against the overly simplistic idea that, in enterprising work, there are simply entrepreneurs and non-entrepreneurs (labourers) who combine with sources of capital. This naïve dialectic fails to respect the adaptive variability (or contrariness) of the humans that constitute society, which a (sub)system of economic organization must function to serve. To speculate on new ideas about enterprise, I seek to understand the 'myths' and 'othering' that are socially constructed through the dialectic concepts of the entrepreneur, entrepreneuring and entrepreneurship. This invokes a (non-conceptual) theory of art-related management practice, in which the craft of management is subsumed into a generic set of craft skills, all associated with the socially inclusive variety of enterprising work. Here, enterprising artforms emerge epiphenomenally through praxis.

The inquiry in Chapter 9 thus turns on the critical perspective that dialectic entrepreneurship theory stands accused of reifying the Western 'hero' entrepreneur. Avoiding this reification, I explore the non-concept of entrepreneurial identity in the context of the more socially inclusive practice of enterprising work. As a reconciliation, this offers an immanent critique of entrepreneurship, coherent with entrepreneurial identity and the practice of entrepreneuring. Here, I draw on ideas of entrepreneurial emplacement, highlighting both an aesthetic cause-effect, and the structure of enterprising space. This leads to the development of a typology of personas of practice. While artists, designers, innovators and dreamers are not uncommon in the field of entrepreneurship, I position them as MacIntyrean 'social characters', in which an interpretation of their actions-of-practice in the context of a complex and adaptive system of enterprising work, hints at how the structure of an education system for an antagonistic future of work might be envisaged. Such a structure would, by design, and for a post Covid-19 society, be better prepared for an absurd level of volatility, uncertainty, complexity and ambiguity.

In Chapter 10, "On experts and wizards", I revert to the critical counterfactuals method of 'means'. My purpose is to question the future state of learning with regard to the argument for a change in our approach to education—that is, in relation to the education of a population toward a more inclusive concept of enterprising work. My focus is the university business school. Although an oft-discussed topic, unsurprisingly, the absurdly disruptive event of the Covid-19 pandemic is, again, a catalyst for considering the antagonistic futures of business schools. I highlight the context of their position in universities, as bastions of higher education (HE). Here, I relate to three further critical antagonisms: the role and value of the university in society; the core function of higher education; and the regulatory (or controlling) framework within which HE is delivered. I pose the core questions: will business schools maintain an HE role in our future society? And if so, what might that role look like?

In Chapter 10, I speculate on what way or ways, the institution of education might prepare for a shift in focus: toward inculcating the knowledge and skills required to leverage society's creativity, experimentation, problem-solving capabilities and ingenuity. I begin by taking a historical perspective, highlighting the changing nature of our social reality. I then speculate on possible antagonistic realities, using the counterfactual futures method. From an expert perspective, the coherence between future antagonistic moments, and the range of critical uncertainties, suggests the potential for a student movement seeking the decolonisation of a perceived neoliberal capitalist curriculum. Yet there is hope in the potential of business schools to drive a new academic agenda, in differentiation of the commercialisation of its space. In seeking further empiric value from the imagination, I recast the Wizard of Oz's original antagonistic visitors: the Tin Woodman; the Scarecrow; and the Cowardly Lion. This allows me to discuss a need for both a heart and courage in reassessing the knowledge to be delivered to students, as they enter the world of enterprising work. In this respect, however, I also argue there is significant inertia and elasticity to be overcome in the educational system.

On bringing it all together

Inertia and elasticity are symptomatic of *autopoiesis*, the dialectic order of *homeostasis* and the contrast of a desired *poiesis*. These are (non)concepts I introduce in the Chapters ahead. It is here I turn to question the need for *resilience*. I posit that resilience is the wrong word. Do we really need a more resilient economy and society?[82] This is not the resilience of individuals. Here, the word resilience[83] is 'a measure of the persistence of systems and of their

---

[82] European Commission, 2020 Strategic Foresight Report: Charting the Course Towards a More Resilient Europe.

[83] Resilience, according to the Oxford English Dictionary (12th Edition), is the ability of an object, such as a system, to recoil or spring back into shape after bending, stretching or being compressed. Or it is the ability of a person or animal to withstand or recover quickly from difficult conditions. Therefore, there is a sense in which system resilience may be characterised by a certain property of elasticity (in the first interpretation) or

ability to absorb change and disturbance and still maintain the same relationships between populations or state variables.'[84] If, as we—author and reader— collectively proceed though these inquiries, we conclude that the antagonistic issues we face are within the systems themselves, do we really want to absorb the disturbance of crises and return to a status quo? Do we honestly wish to retain the same relationships among our populations, reflecting high levels of social injustice? Do we wish to return to, or maintain, the same conditions as Bernard Mandeville commented upon in *The Fable of the Bees,* as early as 1705, or as J. B. Priestley reflected upon in *An Inspector Calls,* in 1947? Such conditions, we have been told by 100 leading economists, are symptomatic of an already broken, socially unjust, economic system.

In Chapter 11, "Dancing the VUCA: Emergence", I reject the autopoiesis of dialectic complex adaptive systems. Drawing on a reading of Niklas Luhmann's lecture on Observing,[85] and the contemporary aesthetics of Giorgio Agamben,[86] I call for an enhancement of first-order poietic action through inculcating an aesthetic sensibility. This sees the convergence of my inquiries into entrepreneurship, work and enterprise. In rising to the antagonistic challenges of VUCA crises, rising economic injustice, and a limited ability to organize our 'selves' and 'others', socially or economically, I turn to answer the question: 'what if we change the socio-economic system first?' Here, I argue that change is an activity we must attempt—a reconciliation of a dialectic neoliberal capitalism that has reached the end of its useful life. In doing so, I deny an ontological certainty and divert attention from the conceptually ontological to a pre-ontic state of constantly becoming—the emergent, non-conceptually real. Thus, in a reprise to Chapter 2's invocation of dance as a metaphor for collective movement, my question resolves to how do we make society and the economy dance?

In Ackoff's terms, if making society and the economy dance is the right thing to do, this book, this inquiry, must also be a source of ideas—of recommendations. In Chapter 11, I argue for a praxis of Design Capitalism, built on this book's reconciliations, and serving a society that provides for a greater, more flexible, and aesthetically educated people. Yet design is a mode of operation on praxis; it requires a target: a reality of field problems. Thus, to illustrate—to imagine—the application of Design Capitalism, I set the

---

inertia in being unaffected by, or able to quickly recover a previous path or track from, a perturbation or deviation in movement (in the second interpretation).

[84] Holling, "Resilience and Stability of Ecological Systems."

[85] Luhmann, Introduction to Systems Theory, 101–20.

[86] Agamben, The Man Without Content.

example of extruding the doughnut of Kate Raworth's *Doughnut Economics.*[87] I posit that Doughnut Economics exists on the imaginary plane, across the antagonistic horizon. In reconciling its potential, Design Capitalism suggests that working toward its possibility—of a regenerative and distributive economy—will require experimentation. In designs to shape society's logos of identity, technology and power—now at the core of society's foundation—we should permit mistakes to be made along the way. Solving such mistakes would be solving toward emergent success, not failure. Thus, in seeking the capacity to change, the act of integrating 'systems thinking' and 'design thinking' with a futures approach, suggests a basis for arguing a de-othered, aesthetic, non-concept of enterprise—a praxis of the 'work' of society and its social and economic organization. Here, the de-othered entrepreneur co-emerges with other forms of enterprising work, in shaping a safe and just space for humanity and society.

In the final Chapter, 12, "An emergent conclusion", I reiterate the value in negative dialectics inherent in its surfacing of ideas—imaginations of empiric value—for application to the design of policy and practice in economic enterprise, including the need for the reform of both educational and justice subsystems. While change must come from the inside out, I argue that it can only do so if the state regains its capacity to exercise the justice necessary to lop and bind antagonistic, socially unproductive vices. There can be no invisible hand. Despite my having posited a re-reading of Platonic love (Chapter 8), without a degree of social control, the productive vice of self-interest stops being socially relevant. Too much control, and sclerosis sets in. It will be a fine balance. Recalling another fable, that of *The Boiling Frog,* I argue there is no time like the present to institute change. But last words must go to the *Fable of the Bees,* and to J. B. Priestley, who maintained the possibility of achieving a community in which every citizen felt himself to be something of an artist and every artist knew himself to be a citizen.

A note on readership

Critiques of capitalism, or of neoliberalistic enterprise culture, or of entrepreneurship in general, are not new. One can also find multiple engagements with negative dialectics, critical thinking, futures thinking, systems thinking, design thinking, and the like. They are spread across the gamut of academic and non-academic literature. Here, as an aid to my readers, I have reflected the intersection of related academic disciplines in Figure 1.1, circumscribed by the discipline of Social Philosophy. Indeed,

---

[87] Raworth, Doughnut Economics: Seven Ways to Think Like a 21st-Century Economist.

Adorno has been categorised as a social philosopher,[88] and I believe that the strong negative dialectic theme makes this work a contribution to social philosophy. In particular, this work sits at the intersection of social philosophy and its application to capitalism and its emergence from (social) enterprise and (social) innovation.

Scholars in individual disciplines may be frustrated with what, on the face of it, suggests either one more variation on a well-wrung theme, or the potential of an incoherent and straggling or sprawling attempt at their reconciliation. This, I argue, would be a somewhat short-sighted view. In grounding my ambitious inquiry in negative dialectics, I must resist the tendency to resolve contradictions by simply resorting to their dialectic. As I hope to show, even Adorno acknowledged a contradiction in negative dialectics that risks inviting such a dialectic treatment. I believe one must seek to persevere the negative, to find not what is an elusive positive, but what is of meaning in either the negative or the positive.

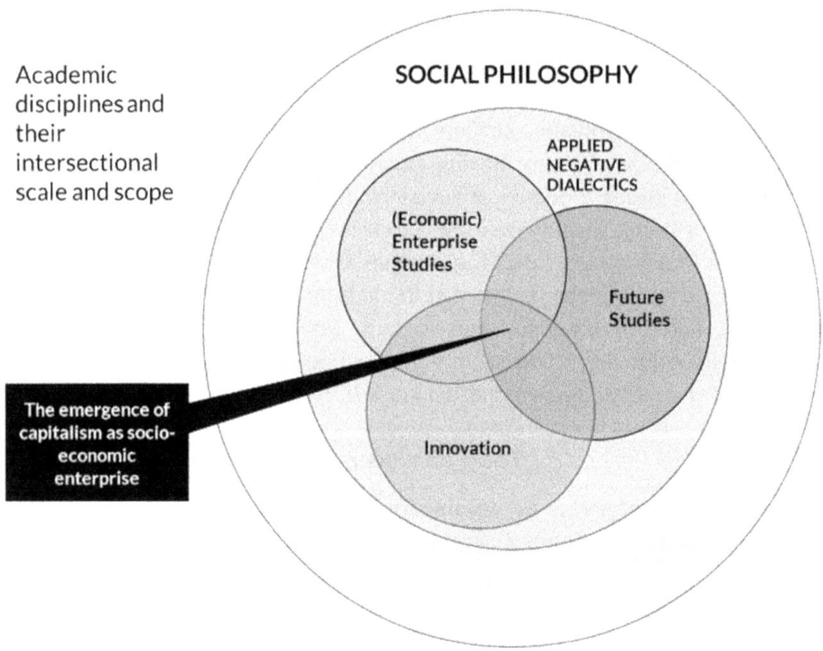

Figure 1.1. Academic scope of inquiry

[88] Zuidervaart, "Theodor W. Adorno."

There will be readers who may be disappointed by the book's paucity of empirical analysis of present events, and such readers may well challenge my association of the imagination with empirical value. However, fundamentally, the manuscript is not about an analysis of the present; it is about an approach to the future. It concerns a re-interpretation of the past in highlighting its role in emergence. In this sense, I do not deny traditional empiricism. Rather, as I set out in this introduction, I offer an 'empirics-of-the-imagination'. In doing so, I must acknowledge the critique of Jonathan Egeland, who suggests the imagination cannot justify empirical belief because of its doxastic foundation.[89] Yet I counter this critique with the simple proposition that an imagination shared through story, or any other means, can transcend its doxastic nature and attain a truth value—however provisional—in the apotheosis of a collective imagination.

Ultimately, this book is an academic provocation. It offers, if you like, a theory of provocation. Thus, I envisage that my core readership will lie within three groups. Firstly, I include those interested in the application of post-disciplinary critical thought and/or negative dialectics to the fields of the economy, work and enterprise. Secondly, I include scholars of futures and foresight thinking and its application to the economy. Here, I argue that invoking negative dialectics offers an alternative basis for critical futures scholarship. Finally, I seek to provoke those interested in critical systems thinking and complexity theory.

In an academic context, I believe I have followed the traditions of my scholarly training in critical management studies. I am not an empiricist. I do not offer evidence for a future yet to come. What I offer is a structured, if somewhat idiosyncratic inquiry, in which I draw together many (non)concepts and ideas, grounded in many fields of academic study. I consider these through a lens of negative dialectics. I consider this a post-disciplinary work—a non-concept of a discipline. As such, my readership may also include scholars from various disciplines who, not seeking an in-depth, gap-in-existing-knowledge-filling monograph, may appreciate the potential in the ideas that such an approach engenders, including an introduction to the integration of future thinking in a research context. Ultimately, through its exploration of the potential empiric value of its imaginations (and with further reference to Figure 1.1), I believe this work will offer its readers:

---

[89] Egeland, "Imagination Cannot Justify Empirical Belief."

- A contribution to social philosophy through an application of negative dialectics.
- A contribution to enterprise studies through a scholarly treatment of practical, socio-economic concerns about our emergence in an antagonistic VUCA world.
- A contribution to future studies in the form of a new critical counterfactual method for contemplating futures in context, coherent with a methodology of negative dialectics.
- Innovative perspectives in the critical review of the future of entrepreneurship, work, international business, capitalism and higher education.
- And, in an accumulative sense, perspectives on a post-capitalism as future-focussed socio-economic enterprise, including:
    - insights into the (non-)concept of a Design Capitalism;
    - a new, inclusive typology of enterprising work; and
    - ideas on the negative dialectics and design of interventions into education, and (social) justice.

I also hope that this book may be of interest to policy makers and postgraduate practitioners in the world of work, the economy, and enterprise. All may share a common concern over the precarity and 'idealism and anxiety' of the moment. All may also share a common concern over the perceived inadequacy of much current thinking and theorising to aid societal practise toward a volatile, uncertain, complex, and ambiguous future. Though it may be a challenge to some readers less familiar with its philosophical and academic style, such readers may nevertheless benefit from this more scholarly approach to introduce new thinking—as insight into the potential for imaginative solutions to some of the world's trickiest, most 'wicked' problems. In this regard, policy makers and practitioners who are able to accept a transcendence of traditional empirical analysis of present events as the basis for imagined policy interventions, may benefit from a firm grasp of Chapter 2, in which the philosophy of the negative dialectic is introduced.

Readers are also likely to include people who would welcome a call for an enlightened form of economic enterprise. Such a readership may have always struggled with uncertainty and the limits of ideas. In this respect, while the extent of academic literature covered is significant, I have not sought to render any single author's perspective as some 'rabbit hole' to a magical, yet frustrating promised land. My touch on the work of others is intentionally light, inspired by (non)concepts and their potential negation, rather than a need for any empirical follow-up.

In the Chapters that follow, I do not shy away from approaching complex problems through complex perspectives. While my objective is not to offer advice, the inquiry approach I take challenges a tendency of others to offer noncomplex advice for complex problems.[90] Words like autopoiesis may not trip off everybody's tongue with the ease of water, but the complex idea it offers—that of referring to a system that has the capability and capacity to maintain and reproduce itself—is helpful in coming to understand how and why society, and its subsystems—for example, the economy—might function. Ultimately, this book is simply a provocation—an inquiry, through the imagination, as a source of ideas.

---

[90] See, for example: Valentinov, "From Equilibrium to Autopoiesis: A Luhmannian Reading of Veblenian Evolutionary Economics."

Part I.
On motivation

Chapter 2

In defence of the absurd[1,2]

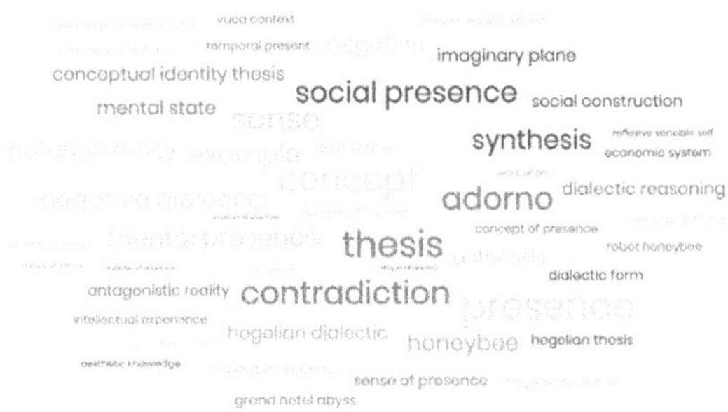

UNPRECEDENTED, ABSURD TIMES? Uncertain global stability? Financial crises? Global pandemics? Conflict scenarios, special military operations and war? Amid these negative signs of an absurd, seemingly irrational world of volatility, uncertainty, complexity and ambiguity—our VUCA world—I choose to speculate about 'changing the socio-economic system' of organization and enterprise. As I do so, I check into a room in the Lukácsian *Grand Hotel Abyss*: an elegant, comfortable accommodation on the edge of absurdity. There, I am in good metaphorical company with members of the Frankfurt School of critical social philosophers.[3] However, there is a caveat: before making any, even tentative, recommendations for speculative action, I shall need to

---

[1] This Chapter is based on an article previously published as Atkinson, "Dancing 'the Management': On Social Presence, Rhythm and Finding Common Purpose." It reproduces some of that article's arguments, particularly in respect of the definition of social presence. It has been shaped under the watchful eye and critique of Dr Marcel Lamoureux, whose contributions through our email correspondence bely their instrumental nature in reforming my ideas around the writings of Adorno and Lévinas.

[2] I use the word Absurd in its common English Language usage, referring to that which may be described as highly unreasonable, illogical, or inappropriate. See Oxford English Dictionary (12th Edn.) There is also the sense in which the absurd is an extension of the mathematical concept surd, meaning an irrational number, from the Latin, surdus, and Greek, algos, meaning irrational, speechless. In this sense, the irrational number is one that is speechless about its magnitude?? For example, an irrational infinity. The absurd: ab as prefix (away, from); thus away from the irrational—further away from that which remains speechless about its nature.

[3] Jeffries, Grand Hotel Abyss: The Lives of the Frankfurt School.

carefully diagnose any situation of practice, any reality—for example: the economy and enterprise—for what it is, lest the finite resources available to me and others are misappropriated to address what might simply be a phantom threat.[4]

Against this context, it is a basic premiss that the proper concern of an organized system of leadership and management, whether social, public or private, profit or non-profit enterprise, is the means of movement of the organization and its people from one place in time to another place in-time—a movement from a *present moment* to a *future moment*—in the achievement of some common 'end' of its socio-economic purpose. In this Chapter, as I start to examine the motivation for my inquiry, and surface its core methodology, our future time is obscured by the antagonistic VUCA context. Here, such a premiss adopts 'wicked', even 'absurd' dimensions, admirably illustrated by the insurrection event on Capitol Hill, Washington DC, 6th January 2021, as pro-Trump rioters stormed the U.S. Capitol on the day then-President-elect Joe Biden was certified as the 46th President of the United States.[5]

Leaving aside, for a moment, my fellow guests in the *Grand Hotel*, I note that in a 2019 interview, Vikki Heywood CBE, Chair of the UK's Royal Society of Arts, advocated the benefits of considering the VUCA context 'through the lens of culture and creativity'.[6] Heywood related particularly to the idea of leading through both art and culture. I posit that such a consideration of the artistic process and the social construction of culture is highly relevant to our emergence in a future place in time. Relatedly, I have previously written on the concept of *dance* as a metaphor for linking future leadership, management and the challenges of human-relations. In a 2008 article, I posited the finding of a common purpose through the concepts of social presence and rhythm.[7] However, in the VUCA context and our means-ends premiss, I now wish to elicit the meaning of the absurd[8] that is embedded in such challenges.

Human relationships, as functions of a *moment-to-moment* movement in the time and space of organizational praxis, invoke the idea of synchronizing such movement in concert with a concept of organizational *rhythm*, such as

---

[4] Bennett and Lemoine, "What a Difference a Word Makes: Understanding Threats to Performance in a VUCA World," 317.

[5] Thomas and Parti, "Biden Calls Attack on Capitol an 'Insurrection.'"

[6] Edwards and O'Regan, "Leading Through Art: An Interview With Vicki Heywood CBE, Chair, Royal Society of Arts," 72.

[7] Atkinson, "Dancing 'the Management': On Social Presence, Rhythm and Finding Common Purpose."

[8] The Oxford English Dictionary (12th Edn.) notes the etymology of the word absurd as deriving from the Latin absurdus, meaning 'out of tune', hence 'irrational'.

might be characteristic of forms of dance. As with many forms of dance rhythm, I argue that an *organizational rhythm* may be identifiable within the culturally socialised, and historic embeddedness of an *a posteriori* system (or pattern) of rules (or conventions) arising within its relationships. Patterns of convention—as metaphoric 'dances'—give rise to the many diverse ways in which organizations might be seen to respond, rhythmically, to their challenges. Metaphorically, I suggest an 'organizational dance' can help position the human body in relation to the organization, providing a place for the individual—a social sense of *presence* (or being) within the organization, its environment and its culture.

Given the concept of an *organizational dance*, there is a coherence in relating it to the idea of the *absurd*—a dance performed out of tune—and its effect on *presence*. This is not so much the idea of embracing a form of Absurdism—where we might perform and live-out our organizational dances within a purposeless, chaotic universe—but that our lives and dances (our 'means') lead us to absurd places (or 'ends'), despite a desire for purpose and order. Here, I use the metaphor of dance to usefully describe the dynamics of emergent change, as organizations respond to the turbulent, increasingly dissonant rhythms of their VUCA environments.[9] In the coming sections, I will explore the notion of absurdity, building a case for its consideration as a prime motivator of this inquiry. Re-joining my fellow guests in the *Grand Hotel Abyss*, I will then defend the absurd within a negative dialectic dialogue, between a material and an imagined, antagonistic reality. First, however, I will reproduce,[10] and further develop, some of the argument for the concept of social presence and its aesthetic root.

The presence of mind

The concept of *presence* generally relates to the subjective feeling of an existence within some reality.[11] For example, it is increasingly seen in the study of virtual reality (VR) environments. Here, Mel Slater notes that '[presence] is considered as a perceptual mechanism for selection between alternative hypotheses: "I am in this place" or "I am in that place".'[12] In this respect, presence has a place in considering our emergence in alternate future realities or scenarios: a sense of *being* within an organized future. Presence

---

[9] Maimone and Sinclair, "Dancing in the Dark: Creativity, Knowledge Creation and (Emergent) Organizational Change."

[10] Atkinson, "Dancing 'the Management': On Social Presence, Rhythm and Finding Common Purpose."

[11] Zahorik and Jenison, "'Presence as Being-in-the-World', Presence."

[12] Slater, "Presence and the Sixth Sense," 435.

has also been ascribed a biological function, as a 'feeling' of being in an externally existing world.[13] More generically, Georg Franck noted that presence may be thought of in terms of a *mental presence,* a 'feeling' of being a conscious mind. In this context, *mental presence* is a byword for concreteness.[14] Yet, as Franck also suggested, *mental presence* is alien to us—we cannot experience it with our senses, nor can we access it through abstract thought. Mental presence, we might say, is born of the imagination. If so, is there not a counterfactual case for positing *presence* as a sense in its own right?

What if a 'sense of presence' lay at the root of our faculty for accumulating a tacit knowledge concerning our place in a future *order of things*? Is it knowledge that constitutes our sense of reality and our place in the world? Here, I posit that a state of presence is *embodied* knowledge: I imagine, therefore I am. In this respect, a knowledge arising from a sense of presence is in the same category, and inextricably linked to the aesthetic knowledge that arises from our other sense faculties.[15] Thus, I argue that we are frequently called upon to act, based only on such knowledge. This places aesthetic knowledge as a way of knowing, as part of action.[16] Aesthetic knowledge sits alongside *phronēsis*—a wisdom associated with practical action—as a reflection of a deeper engagement with life, or *praxis.* This is thoughtful, practical doing; it engages both cognition and emotion in construing meaning.[17] Thus, in an organizational context, if presence is a *sixth sense,* then we might conclude it has a bearing on our ability to hypothesize and judge between alternate (future) organizational scenarios. We might call on a sixth sense of presence to better aid our judgement in determining some future course—or scenario—of organizational action, particularly under VUCA conditions.

To distinguish between the 'subjective' feeling of being a conscious mind (*mental presence*) and the 'objectivity' of being present within a sensed environment (a reality of things and events perceived), Franck notes the concept of the *temporal present*—what Peter Senge et al.[18] would refer to as

---

[13] Waterworth and Waterworth, "'The Meaning of Presence', Presence-Connect."
[14] Franck, "Mental Presence and the Temporal Present," 48.
[15] See, for example: Ewenstein and Whyte, "Beyond Words: Aesthetic Knowledge and Knowing in Organizations," 689.
[16] Cook and Brown, "Bridging Epistemologies: The Generative Dance between Organizational Knowledge and Organizational Knowing."
[17] Antonacopoulou, "Organisational Learning for and with VUCA: Learning Leadership Revisited."
[18] Senge et al., Presence: Exploring Profound Change in People, Organizations, and Society.

being fully conscious and aware in the present moment.[19] Within the individual, first-person context, *mental presence* and the *temporal present* are one—the 'oneness' of a Heideggerian *being-in-the-world.* However, in the social, or third-person context, there is a logical yet paradoxical disconnect between the mental and temporal domains. While the perspectives of all persons are seemingly bound to the universal objectivity of the *temporal present*—the here and now of a material reality—what might be perceived phenomenologically is dependent on an individual's state of *mental presence,* for which, I argue, there can be no corresponding mode of universal subjectivity.

Franck notes, '[the] only way we have access to the reality deemed to exist independently of being experienced is conscious thought'.[20] Here, a Theory of Mind (ToM) invokes 'a folk psychology—the [first-order] ability to ascribe beliefs and desires to others in order to predict their behavior.'[21] It suggests that, through conscious thought, we may predict the behaviour of others—within the reality we access—based on mental states that we ascribe to them. It is the case that such ascriptions can be 'richly predictive of a surprisingly wide variety of behavioural effects'[22] However, reflexively, we subjectively access a reality only through observations of the behaviours of others, based on beliefs and ideas we ascribe to them. On a complex level, these ascribed beliefs and ideas may be *about* beliefs and ideas (a second-order ascription).[23] Here, through subjectification, ToM assumes a rationality of action that may be irrationally violated by an 'Other'. We are shaken when an absurd action is taken by an 'Other' that appears to us as irrational, or wrong, or immoral, or illegal; we question mental states we have ascribed to that 'Other', and whether they are an 'other' at all.[24] Thus, I argue that the axiomatic variability of an individual's mental state ensures there can be no level of universal access to reality.

---

[19] Senge et al. suggest a move from understanding presence as a temporality to understanding it as a process of "deep listening". Senge et al., 13. This present work rejects this notion on the basis that, philosophically, an understanding of the temporal nature of a reality must be maintained. I do not, however, argue that Senge et al's work is flawed in any way—it merely adopts an alternative viewpoint. Metaphorically, I acknowledge that while there is a need to dance into the future, there is also a need to dance the present.

[20] Franck, "Mental Presence and the Temporal Present," 49.

[21] Jarrold et al., "Linking Theory of Mind and Central Coherence Bias in Autism and in the General Population.," 126.

[22] Dennett, "Beliefs about Beliefs."

[23] Dennett, "Conditions of Personhood."

[24] Dennett, "Conditions of Personhood," 194.

The paradox of phenomenology is that, nomothetically, there is no true, social construction of 'oneness' to be found in the concept of *presence.* Paraphrasing Sartre, 'Although I live in and experience this world as others do, I cannot... experience the reality of this world as others do, and neither can others see and experience the reality... I do.' [25] To explore this paradox and elicit grounds for a common purpose, I shall (initially) adopt a dialectic form of reasoning.

The dialectic form and its incompleteness

The dialectic form of reasoning is well-rehearsed in the literature. With its origins in Platonic and Aristotelian logic, and further developed, for example, by Georg Wilhelm Friedrich Hegel, dialectics follows the triadic development of thesis, anti-thesis, and synthesis.[26] While the dialectic form has its appropriations—for example, in the work of Marx, Engels, and Lenin—it also has its critics, notably Karl Popper and Mario Bunge. However, it will suffice for my purposes to consider dialectic's Hegelian and Greek roots, but with my acknowledgement that there must, perhaps, be some ring of truth within Bunge's opinion that "...'dialectics' denotes a thick fog without precise boundaries, quite unlike, say, the propositional calculus or classical mechanics... incompatible with science [and] materialism."[27]

With reference to Figure 2.1, I identify the thesis ('B') as a statement or theory about some aspect of a domain of material interest ('A'); it is advanced as a premise to be maintained or proven about the nature of 'A'. In Hegelian logic, 'B' is a proposition that forms the first stage dialectical reasoning about 'A'. However, here I note that within the etymology of thesis, from its relationship to Greek and Latin verse, there is a sense that a thesis is only a part of some 'thing'—an unstressed syllable, or part of a metrical foot[28]—thus a thesis is, by definition, also something that is, in and of itself, incomplete.

---

[25] Sartre, Being and Nothingness: An Essay on Phenomenological Ontology.
[26] Popper, "What Is Dialectic?"
[27] Bunge, "Comment on Apostol' s Paper," 137–38.
[28] Stevenson and Waite, Concise Oxford English Dictionary.

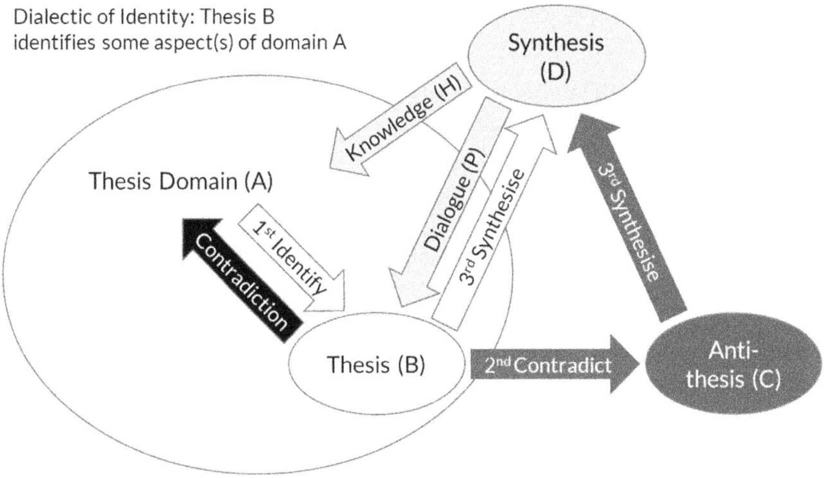

Figure 2.1. The dialectic form

An anti-thesis is a thing that is in direct opposition (or contradiction) to another thing: the expression of the opposing or contradictory idea (or *concept*). Thus, as the second stage of Hegelian dialectic reasoning, the thing being contradicted is the thesis 'B'. This is problematic if I stop to consider the anti-thesis ('C') as being directly opposed to something that is, by its nature, incomplete.[29] In 'C's' contradiction of 'B', we lose something of the sense of the domain of interest: 'A'. This problem is compounded when I turn to the 3rd stage of Hegelian dialectic reasoning, in which the notion of synthesis seeks to combine the components (or aspects) of the incomplete thing (thesis) and its contradiction (anti-thesis) to form a new thing, or synthesis, in this case, 'D'. Thus, a traditional process of dialectical reasoning, in which the new synthesised idea (concept or theory) resolves the conflict (or contradiction) between (an incomplete) thesis and its anti-thesis, as synthesis 'D', can itself only ever be incomplete. For example, an antithesis to a ToM suggests that when one is shaken by an absurd action-in-praxis of another, the other is no other at all, and is, therefore, deficient in some respect. A synthesis arises in that a deficiency of the human ToM is attributable to, for example, autism.[30] Such a synthesis may be considered incomplete—it does not attribute to the

---

29 The Hegelian anti-thesis plays on the use of indeterminateness to suggest some 'thing' that has not been determined. However, that the thing may be undetermined does not suggest that there is a lack of determinates. In this sense, the thing is incomplete in its self.

30 See, for example: Baron-Cohen, "Theory of Mind and Autism: A Review."

classification 'autistic person' any positive contribution to an autistic ability to access their own reality.[31]

In Aristotelian and Platonic logic, the dialectic process is dialogic. To Plato, the synthesis enters a new dialogue ('P') with its thesis, in what Gadamer termed the 'art of carrying on a conversation' [about the thesis], in 'an endless process of establishing meaning' [about the thesis in relation to the domain].[32] Thus, in a cyclic fashion, the traditional or Platonic process of dialectic reasoning is to 'give an [ideological] account' of something.[33] But, by its nature, that account can only ever be provisional, can only ever be contingent, and can only ever be incomplete. There is no sense in which the dialectic process leads to a congruence of account and thing. An issue arises in the later Hegelian logic, in its systematising of the dialectic process. Here, a synthesis, as a concretised resolution of the contradiction between thesis and antithesis is offered as absolute knowledge ('H'), in some way transcending experience (the observations identifying the thesis)—an attempt to (re)integrate it into the present.[34] Thus, a synthesis that accords some people a classification of autistic, inserts a deficiency in a reality of praxis that is purely negative, devaluing the autistic experience.

On the one hand, while a traditional or Platonic dialectic forms an idealist philosophy, it promises the revision of contingent knowledge through dialogue. Yet the nature of this dialogue is that it remains ideologically detached from any material practice. On the other hand, while Hegelian dialectics offers a form of objective idealism, the concretizing of a provisional (partial or incomplete) knowledge as an absolute, raises the possibility of misplaced concreteness—the mistaken existence of a provisional knowledge in some material form, as the basis for a material practice. Certainly, a practice in any material domain, based on a false ideological precept of a complete knowledge of its concepts, can only ever be a false practice.[35]

---

[31] A recent review of the literature on Theory of Mind and Autism is critical of the received wisdom that Autistic people lack a Theory of Mind. Gernsbacher and Yergeau, "Empirical Failures of the Claim That Autistic People Lack a Theory of Mind." The implication, here, is that there is the potential for an alternative Theory of Mind, in which both autistic and non-autistic minds may find a valid place.
[32] Moran, Introduction to Phenomenology, 268.
[33] Moran, Introduction to Phenomenology, 269.
[34] Moran, Introduction to Phenomenology, 276.
[35] Making real that which is not real.

The duality of Hegelian and Platonic contradiction

Returning to the concept of *presence*, I suggest that we may identify it by its thesis, relating it to our domain of interest. From an idealist perspective, *presence* provides a subjective feeling of existence within a material environment; it is identified from both the determinate temporally present and the indeterminate mentally present. But, despite a ToM, we have no objective basis for a unity of thought about being mentally present; *presence* sets up its own (internal) conflict (contradiction) with the domain of interest. Here, for the concept of presence to be of rational use in determining an existence in, say, a non-random future practice, I argue that we must move beyond what might be an interesting, but ultimately non-practical Platonic dialogue over the (external) contradiction of its *thesis* and anti-thesis. We must also avoid the fallacy of adopting an incongruent Hegelian false conception of presence of limited value in praxis (save, perhaps, in the idea of VR). Thus, the question arises, how can we reconcile the internal contradiction between a concept (thesis) of presence and its domain of practice? To Theodor W. Adorno, a principal guest in the *Grand Hotel Abyss*, the dual (internal and external) nature of a dialectic contradiction is neither irrational nor random.[36]

Re-expressing the above problematic, the concept (Thesis 'B') enters a contradiction with the thing it represents (Domain 'A'). When a 'B' is defined as an 'A', it is always less than 'A'. Thus, since the ideology of (a ToM in) *presence* requires a unity of thought about being *mentally present*, the privileging of any one subjective idea of being *mentally present* suppresses or resits 'other' subjective ideas of mental presence. However, the concept is 'always also *different from and more than*' the 'A'.[37] Here, the ideological thesis of *presence* pretends to be a generalisation—a representation of the group or class of experiences we might classify as *presence*: 'B' is always more than and less than 'A'—a contradiction (or paradox). Whatever resists coercion (the identification) of the thesis 'B'='A' is a (material) contradiction. But this is not the same contradiction that is established in the antithesis. While our interest might properly be concerned with the former (material) contradiction, our minds are diverted (certainly in complex concepts) to the consideration of the latter (ideological) contradiction.

Conceptually, in a naïve dialectic process, the synthesis operates on only what does not resist coercion, on what is not (materially) denied (in contradiction) in the identification of the thesis. And, as Adorno suggested, once the anti-thesis is postulated, the synthesis tends to occur only through

---

[36] Adorno, Lectures on Negative Dialectics, 7.

[37] Adorno, Lectures on Negative Dialectics, 7.

the thesis re-asserting itself within the ideological, in its anti-thesis, rather than its domain.[38] A dialectic of ideological *presence* fails to illuminate a future, material practice. The naïve error is to conflate the duality of the contradiction as an ideological unity and co-opt the ideological concept within the material, assuming an ideological perspective on the material. A surfeit of naïve concepts exists in an 'official world-view that dominates a very large portion of the globe'[39]: simulacrum—waypoints on Jean Baudrillard's map of hyperreality.[40]

The social construction of presence

'Social presence', also called 'co-presence', is another term finding use in VR studies. However, as a concept, the roots of *social presence* reach into the fields of psychology and interpersonal communications theory. Social presence has been defined as the '...degree of salience of the other person in a mediated communication and the consequent salience of their interpersonal interactions'.[41] In this sense, *social presence* is defined in relation to a medium of communication, where the medium functions to '...collapse space and time to provide the limited illusion of being there in other places and being together with other people'.[42] This 'limited illusion' is analogous to the idea of a local *telos*,[43] as the emergence of, or identification of, a (limited or localised) shared vision or sense of purpose. This lifts a veil on any material volatility, ambiguity, complexity or uncertainty—an avoidance of what might be a tendency to dance in the dark.[44] With its predisposition to multiple perspectives, the suggestion is that a *social presence* resists the contradiction of the unity perspective on *mental presence* that is implicit in a naïve dialectic of *presence*. In this respect, *social presence* can be seen to constitute a mediated bridge to understanding the paradox of multiple perspectives of a sensed reality.

I define 'social presence' as the degree to which an individual can sense the perspective of an 'other', and thus be able to take a perspective on a material reality that includes the self and others as participating objects. Importantly, I suggest this is in no way subjective. Rather, social presence evokes an inter-

---

[38] Adorno, Lectures on Negative Dialectics, 29–30.
[39] Adorno, Lectures on Negative Dialectics, 10.
[40] Baudrillard, Simulacra and Simulation, 1.
[41] Short, Williams, and Christie, "The Social Psychology of Telecommunications," 65.
[42] Biocca et al., "Criteria and Scope Conditions for a Theory and Measure of Social Presence."
[43] An ultimate object or purpose; an 'end'.
[44] See, for example: Allard-Poesi, "Dancing in the Dark: Making Sense of Managerial Roles during Strategic Conversations."

subjective (respons-)ability[45] of the 'sensible' self to perceive, objectively, a socially constructed reality in which they are able, in the first moment, to separate out the autistic[46] oneness of their own mental presence from what might be temporally present. In this respect, social presence allows the existence of the reflexive, sensible self. In the second responsible moment, this autistic dialectic of mental presence is combined, in a mediated construction with a multiplicity of the sensed mental presences of others, without prescribing antecedent mental states. In this second responsible moment, the reflexive sensible self, integrates its objective perceptions of others' mental presences. This implies a form of arithmetic summation of objective perspectives, in which the self's perception of mental presence is subject to the complication of others. A sense of social presence does not suggest a subjectification of the perspective of others—as might be envisaged under a ToM. Rather it represents a retention of objectivity—a form of negative ToM (or precognition) built from the reactions of others.[47]

In introducing a complication, I must be mindful to determine what I mean by this. The words complicated (adjective) and complicate (verb) are derivations of the Latin *complicat;* they take the form of a folding together, or the making of some 'thing' more complex. Some 'thing' that is complicated comprises many interconnecting parts.[48] In the sense of a socially constructed mental presence—a constituent element of a concept or theory of *social presence,* applied to some future domain of practice—there are many interconnecting, potentially contradictory perspectives. However, some 'thing' that *is* complex (as opposed to being made more complex) goes beyond the complicated. Here, I suggest that the arithmetic sum of several

---

45 Such an ability of the self to respond to the Other implies a responsibility (response-ability), of the self in respect of or to the Other. There is a sense, to be explored further in this work, that this response-ability (responsibility) is intrinsic to the intersubjectivity of the self with the Other. In this sense, social presence holds, as intrinsic to itself, an ethical responsibility for the Other. In engaging with the Other, the self is responsible for the Other, 'without even having taken on responsibilities in [this] regard' (Lévinas, "Ethics and Infinity", 194.).

46 Autism: from the Greek autos: self; plus -ism: Greek ismos, isma: as in action, principle, or pathology. For example, self-isolation, self-interest, self as preoccupation or focus. See Oxford English Dictionary (12th Edn.).

47 In his lectures on negative dialectics, Adorno notes that a reduction (elimination) of 'the subjective qualities [of an object] always implies a reduction of the object.' A theory of mind which subjectifies the mental experiences of others in contemplation of an object—for example a subjectification of an external reality—constitutes a dismissal of the individual reactions of others as subjective, and 'the loss of the qualitative determinants of object.' Adorno, Lectures on Negative Dialectics, 141.

48 Stevenson and Waite, Concise Oxford English Dictionary.

views, such as in determining a small group or small organization's sense of *social presence*, while complicated, is a different order of magnitude (and challenge) to determining the sense of social presence of a large body of people or, greater still, of a society or religion. When I consider the variation of human perspectives of any 'one' thing, I invoke the notion of the infinite. While, conceivably, a Hegelian thesis of social presence, postulated on the basis of a 'meagre, finite number'[49] of perspectives, suggests the potential for a less than naïve dialectic process of theorising about a future (social) practice, I argue that this can only hold valid where the finite number bears comparison with a comprehendible (rational) infinity.

The irrationality of social presence

At the heart of the traditional practice of both qualitative and quantitative social science research lies the idea that a complicated thesis, identified by a sample of rational, determinate perspectives, set against a certain domain or population universe, bounded by a rational infinity,[50] is, in some respects, and under certain rational conditions or assumptions, representative of that domain or population. Given that the population comprises the sum of both determined and undetermined determinates, the *assumption of representation* suppresses differences (contradictions) between sampled and unsampled. The assumption of representation is present in a ToM. It subjectifies the positive mental states of some—a majority—yet assigns negative otherness to the remainder—a minority. In the limit that the determinates/samples approach the size of the domain, there remains little that is undetermined in identifying a thesis. Conversely, in the limit that the (unsampled) indeterminates approach to the size of the domain, then there remains little that is determined. Therefore, a rational infinity suggests the limits of usability of even a process of complicated dialectic theorising.

---

[49] Adorno, Lectures on Negative Dialectics, 78.

[50] A rational infinity is one that is not speechless about its magnitude. In Greek thought, the infinite was that magnitude beyond the limit that could be comprehended in thought. In set theory, in the context employed in the Chapter, taking the domain as a finite set, the infinite is that which is not equivalent to that finite set. (See, for example: Sia, "Describing the Concept of Infinite among Art, Literature, Philosophy and Science: A Pedagogical-Didactic Overview.") A rational infinity is thus comprehensible in the sense that it may be rendered (in thought) as if it had an imaginable magnitude, such as in comparing a single human against the magnitude (a finite set) of humanity. It is rational in the sense that a number may be rational. See also endnote: 2. By contrast, an irrational infinity is one that is speechless about its magnitude. It is incomprehensible in the sense that it cannot be rendered (in thought) as if it had an imaginable magnitude.

The issue with the traditional practice of social science/research is the rational assumption of representation, in that the selected determinates are both necessary and sufficient to identify the thesis. However, as I posit above, this assumption suppresses contradictory difference; it denies other differentiating factors (including partial factors) that, while indeterminate, are necessary to adequately identify a materialistic thesis, one with direct application in its material domain. Left suppressed, indeterminates take the nature of contradictions. To assume that an idealised, even if complicated, thesis of social presence is usefully representative of a given future practice is of limited value. To confront the suppression of an unknown number of indeterminates is to challenge (critically) the ideological theory of social presence, with its reliance on a rational idea of infinity, and to open it to the idea of the irrational, including an irrational infinity, and the transformation of the complicated into the complex. Here, I include—in the concept of an irrational infinity—the idea of the infinite sum of fractions (infinitesimal parts of a whole) needed to represent the idea of an irrational quantity. This is an idea rejected by Aristotle.[51] However, it is useful to think of it in these terms, particularly regarding any whole domain as a finite set.

Given the concepts of the infinite, both rational and irrational, I argue that any contemplation (such as a dialectic theorising) of a domain of enquiry (a finite set) 'creates an infinity of everything we know and don't... perspectives, acts, desires, thoughts of thoughts within acts, molecular routines...'.[52] This is both a space for science and a space for art, where the rational sits alongside the irrational, where the real subsists alongside the imagined—as a speculation about the possibility of the real. This is a space where a material reality of social presence can be considered complex. Certainly, in mathematics, a complex expression includes both real (rational) and imaginary (irrational) parts. For example, the complex expression allows for the negation of a negation to be a negative value, as in the square root of minus one: an imaginary number '*i*'. And, in psychoanalysis, the complex invokes the repression, or part repression, of emotionally significant ideas, characterised by abnormal mental states or behaviours.[53] Both forms of expression of the irrational, infinite nature of complexity, may be applied to a dialectic of social presence.

In a concept of social presence, some 'thing'—the single human in the whole of humanity—may be complex without being complicated, comprising an irrationally infinite set of mental states of behaviours. A small group of

[51] See, for example: Pesic, "Hearing the Irrational: Music and the Development of the Modern Concept of Number."
[52] Field, "Irrationality, Situations, and Novels of Inquiry," 1 (pagination as downloaded).
[53] Stevenson and Waite, Concise Oxford English Dictionary.

humans becomes both more complicated and is complex at the outset. This is a complexity born of the contradiction between thesis and domain; it is reflected through the thesis, as an *absence* of the *irrational*, now present in the (incomplete) contradiction between its thesis and its antithesis. A ToM suppresses the difference in its subjectivity.

Following Popper's critique of dialectics, a naïve, or even complicated form of dialectic reasoning is a valid form of social science, only if we are not willing 'to accept, and to put up with, the [external] contradiction between the thesis and the antithesis.' However, given the incompleteness of the contradiction in, say, social presence, it cannot simply be the case that 'it is… our decision… not to agree to [such external] contradictions, which induces us to look out for a new [synthesis] enabling us to avoid them'. The acceptance of incomplete contradictions, implied by virtue of an intentional, or naïve ignorance of the absurd, amounts to an 'end of criticism, and thus the collapse of science.'[54] Thus it cannot be the case that, if we allow for the contradictory presence of the absurd, as an absence of the irrational, that we 'have to give up on any kind of scientific activity'.[55] *Ex ante*, we can neither ignore nor put up with the absence of the irrational in social science. And while, in the *Grand Hotel Abyss*, Adorno advocated that the challenge of philosophy was to retain a grasp of this (pessimistic) absolute truth about the social world, his perspective was not without criticism from its other guests. The younger Jürgen Habermas, one-time student of Adorno, eschewed such negativity in favour of a non-absolute truth in which philosophy is restricted to the critique of science, *ex-post*.[56]

From absence to social presence

Leaving aside the critique of negativity for the moment, in confronting the absent irrational in an idealised dialectic reasoning—what has been expressed elsewhere as 'secondary thinking in social theorising'[57]—there are echoes of the reflexive, *sensible self*. This *sensible self* can be seen in the work of the great Romantics. For example, in the opening of a lecture given on 8 March 1819, Samuel Taylor Coleridge said:

> '[We] find [man] gifted… with a threefold mind; the one belonging to him… arising… necessarily, out of the peculiar mechanism of his nature and by which he beholds all things perspectively from his relative position as man; the second, in which these views are… modified—too

---

[54] Popper, Conjectures and Refutations, 322.
[55] Popper, "What Is Dialectic?"
[56] Zuidervaart, Social Philosophy after Adorno.
[57] Cooper, "Primary and Secondary Thinking in Social Theory: The Case of Mass Society."

> often distributed and falsified—by his particular constitution and position, as [a] particular individual; and the third, which exits in all men potentially… though it requires both effort from within and auspicious circumstances from without to evolve into effect—by this… higher power he places himself [at one with] Nature and contemplates all objects, himself included, in their permanent and universal being and relations.'[58]

By virtue of this third and higher power, the promise of humanity is the human capacity to contemplate all objects in their permanent and universal being and relations. This is a recognition of a primary (first-order) mode of thought that recognises the unconscious, the indeterminate, the negative, and the irrational that, while absent in a naïve or merely complicated dialectic, is nevertheless 'an immanent and ever-present source of all social and cultural action'.[59] It is a human capacity to comprehend both the rational and irrationally infinite nature of being and being present. This is a capacity not to be shaken when an (absurd) action is taken by others that appears irrational, or wrong, or immoral, or illegal. It is to forego the ascription of subjective mental states and to embrace the inclusivity of all others, without question. But, of what relevance to organizational practice (in its broadest sense) is the working up to some primary theory of social presence, in which sensible individuals place themselves within a state of consciousness where they can begin to consider (or speculate on) the relationships between themselves, others and their environment from an equal perspective?

Intuitively, the reflexive *sensible self* lies at the heart of what Otto Scharmer called *presencing*, a leadership discipline for emerging business environments, including VUCA ones. Presencing employs the highest form of *self* as a vehicle for 'sensing, embodying, and enacting emerging futures.'[60] However, I argue *presencing* is one-dimensional. It shifts the focus from the temporal present. Here, in their 2004 article in the journal of Cyber Psychology & Behavior, Rosa Baños and her colleagues suggested that *social presence* consists of both a media dimension, with characteristics of form and content, and a user dimension, referring to individual characteristics of, for example: age, gender and cultural variables.[61] Thus, rather than *presencing*, I suggest a 'sixth sense' of *social presence*, which comprises both 1) a rational mode of being with

---

[58] K. Coburn, Samuel Taylor Coleridge—The Philosophical Lectures, Lecture XI (London: The Pilot Press, 1949).

[59] Cooper, "Primary and Secondary Thinking in Social Theory: The Case of Mass Society," 151.

[60] Scharmer, "Presencing: Learning From the Future As It Emerges," 4.

[61] Baños et al., "Immersion and Emotion: Their Impact on the Sense of Presence," 734.

others in relation to a specified medium: a rationally bounded finite whole, that has both form and content, in essence, a presence in a temporal, finite reality, and 2) an individual's sense of being with others, an irrational mode of being, influenced by the individual's personal psychology—a degree of mental presence. It is this irrational mode of 'sensory' being which is characterised, not by some ToM, but by its 'absence' ('ab-sense', or 'away/from-sense').[62]

The above conceptualisation of *social presence* might be described as a metaphysics of presence. However, a dominant deconstructive interpretation holds that the entire history of Western philosophy and its language and traditions has emphasised the desire for immediate access to meaning. Deconstruction has built its own metaphysics around the privileging of presence over absence. If this is the case, in adapting the colloquial notion of a 'sixth sense'[63]—an individual's faculty for the realization of social presence—are we not appealing to a more constructive paradigm that embraces equally both presence (concept) and absence (non-concept)? Here, the social domain of mass society takes on the dimension of the 'social mass', revealed in the 'ever-present absence'[64] of its irrational complexity. Thus, I argue, what is required in a theory of *social presence* as a 'sixth sense', is a cognizance of its two modes—a cognizance grounded in social construction. However, before returning to the (speculative) social construction of social presence, I will reflect further on Adorno's critique of dialectics.

Adorno's dialectic of non-identity

With reference to Figure 2.2, positing an anti-thesis as an *externalised* contradiction (negation) of a thesis, itself the *internalised* contradiction (negation) of either a naïve or complicated dialectic within the thesis domain, leads Adorno to suggest that the synthesis is no more than a negation of dialectic negation. If the thesis emerges in contradiction to the field of somethings, that is, a field of determinates and indeterminates (non-conceptual things) that constitute the whole domain, then the synthesis resolves toward the field of nothings.

---

[62] I will return to explore the irrationality in personal psychology more fully in Chapter 3.

[63] One that is frequently used to refer to some power of discernment of what might, for most of us, be considered absent—frequently in terms of the discernment of some psychic presence. An exemplar often quoted is the 1999 film "The Sixth Sense", written and directed by M. Night Shyamalan.

[64] Cooper, "Primary and Secondary Thinking in Social Theory: The Case of Mass Society."

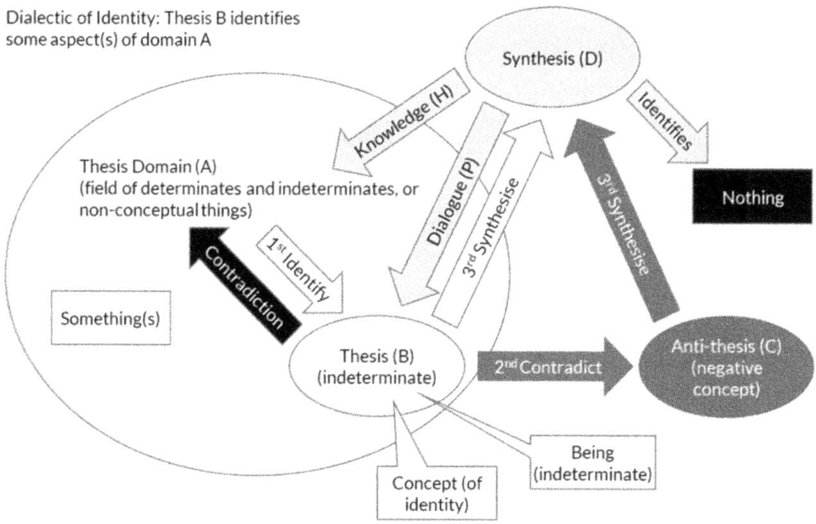

Figure 2.2. Being, nothing, concept

In the above sense, with complexity supressed, Adorno posited that the value of synthesis is much reduced and is to be resisted. For example, a synthetic ToM—which ultimately underpins a dialectic of presence—may be held to critique the disenfranchisement of certain others; a synthetic ToM is inherently discriminatory. Rather, Adorno's concern was with how the concept moves towards its opposite—the non-concept, the field itself—and not toward its (externalised) contradiction and synthesis.[65] In supressing the contradictions of the field, the thesis leaves behind what Adorno described as 'the dregs of the concept', the 'field of somethings' in which the thesis arises, and which are not, themselves, part of that concept.[66] They represent what remains absent.

Following the notion of the 'dregs of the concept',[67] it might be said that just as the thesis of a thing contains both the *being* of the thing and its *concept*, so the determinate something of a thesis contains both an element of the nonconceptual (a sense of the absurd or irrational) and a relevance (an essential importance *for the concept*).[68] In considering the concept of *social presence*, the realm of the unconscious mental presence lies within the non-

---

65 Adorno, Lectures on Negative Dialectics, 6.

66 Adorno, Lectures on Negative Dialectic, 63.

67 This refers to Adorno's reflection on Freudian psychology, in particular Freud's attention to the 'dreg's of the phenomenal world'.

68 Adorno, Lectures on Negative Dialectics, 69.

conceptual. We can thus see how the overtly absurd and irrational (in character), such as the variety of unconscious and conscious mental states of a population's individuals that do not accord with a thesis, are the non-conceptual somethings denied their conceptual relevance. As Adorno suggests, the *denied* 'may well contain the very thing that cries out for [consideration].[69]

A Hegelian anti-thesis, in naïve or complicated form, makes absent the element of *being* that is its complexity: its absurdity, its irrationality. This leads to an uncritical and false concretization of *being*. For example, being *there* in social presence falsely identifies its 'self' in contradiction to nothing, rather than in contradiction to its determinate(s). The Hegelian dialectic, in denying the essence of *being* (the thing), allows the concept (of the thing), in its purest form, to be equated with nothing. Thus, the *identification* of the anti-thesis with its thesis results in a synthesis of conceptual knowledge that is, in and of itself, in contradiction to both its thesis (the thing) and its determinates. For example, a Hegelian synthesis of non-autistic and autistic, by virtue of it being purely conceptual, can be no 'thing' (nothing)—it is a 'thesis of non-identity'. Thus, I return to the notion of a praxis rooted in the naivety of a dialectic theorising that is nothing if not a false practice. The conclusion I must draw at this juncture is that a praxis rooted in the naivety of Hegelian dialectic thinking is nothing if not problematic.

Toward a dialectic of praxis

As Adorno argued in the 5th of a published 1953 series of lectures:

> '...[in these times] thinking itself has become paralysed and impotent, chance practice has become a substitute for the things that do not happen. [The] more people sense that this is not actually true practice, the more doggedly and passionately their minds become fixated on it... The only thought that can be made practical is the thought that is not restricted in advance by the practice to which it is directly applied.'[70]

Let me set the context of a practice of *social presencing*. For example, taking a perspective on organizing a future material reality that includes our 'selves' and 'others' as participating objects. I might call this a systematised practice of futures thinking or thinking about the future—limited by a dialectics of non-identity. Here, are we surprised when what we might plan for does not happen? We are subject to happenchance. I argue that the irony in absenting the absurd and irrational in our identities is that, particularly in the VUCA

---

[69] Adorno, Lectures on Negative Dialectic, 70.
[70] Adorno, Lectures on Negative Dialectic, 53–54.

context, we emerge in a future that is more '*nothing* that we practised for', than '*something* we hypothesised'. A future where we are shaken by the absurd actions of others that appear irrational, or wrong, or immoral, or illegal—when socio-economic systems fail and we emerge in chaos and disorder.

Returning to the social construction of presence, in terms of both a temporal reality and a faculty for mental presence, I have argued that the sensible human must be presented with a medium for the (speculative) exploration of relationships.[71] This suggests space within which we allow form, content and their relations to allude to that which might be absent from either naïve or complicated dialectic perspectives—a concern with how the complex concept emerges from the non-concept. I now suggest we can associate this concern with Adorno's observation that the reason change does not occur (as we might envision it) is that 'too little is interpreted', that is to say: there is an insufficient critique of (or an uncritical acceptance of) the absent in the systematisation of a dominant dialectic thought. As Adorno argued, 'the reality of history has shaken [dialectic] thinking to its innermost core.'[72] We are left with the feeling that the history of happenchance has replaced the predications and aspirations of our dialectic reasoning; our emergent[73] futures appear poor substitutes for the things that were supposed to happen.

As Adorno observed, we are left to reflect on why the (predicted) transformation (or change) 'from theory to practice' did not occur.[74] Ultimately, as we continue to face increasing global instability, financial crises and the real threat of global pandemics, we are left with the feeling that we are increasingly unprepared for praxis in a VUCA world. We ask: are we simply to be left to a world of (indeterminate) happenchance? Why consider changing the socio-economic system if its practice may only lead to happenchance? I posit that to entertain such (new) thinking, we must revert to theory—to the concept antecedent to the dialectic itself, and to its limitations—the suppression of identity, the absurd and the irrational.

The absurdity of dance

I posit one social space that addresses the dichotomy of absence and presence may be found through the medium of art. In a sense of being with others, the roles of artist and audience are correspondent: art interrupts an individualistic

---

[71] Atkinson, "Dancing 'the Management': On Social Presence, Rhythm and Finding Common Purpose."

[72] Adorno, Lectures on Negative Dialectics, 55–56.

[73] I shall go on to provide a more explicit notion of emergence within Chapter 4, identifying two distinct modes of emergence.

[74] Adorno, Lectures on Negative Dialectics, 56.

sense of place. Through a socially constructed, yet individual engagement in the artist-audience relationship, the individual 'viewer' is guided to sense the perspective of an 'other' (the artist) and may take a perspective on a reality that includes the viewer's self as a participating object. Art, in this 'sixth' sense allows the 'sensible individual' the self-awareness necessary to contemplate what might be absent, by '...being aware without being aware *of* something, an attitude for which there are no words.'[75]

In a transitive, interactive form of disinterested mediation, Art allows new possibilities of knowledge to emerge.[76] Art invokes, within the sense of presence, the requirement for an experiential notion of *aesthetic reflexivity*.[77] Art enables a social audience to gain a mental presence of being in another temporal place through a reflex-like interaction with a changing material context. This allows me to extend the artistry of dance to the organizational space. But what if our dance is out of tune? What if we become overwhelmed, perhaps, by the apparently absurdly irrational arising from the innately infinite nature of a future materiality? What happens when the aspirational foundation of our future social presence is undermined by the unanticipated determinates within a dialectic of non-identity? What then?

In reverting to theory, an artistic practice promises a concept antecedent to any dialectic limitation and the suppression of identity. A theory of art promises the potential of the absurd and the irrational. It offers a step beyond a Hegelian thesis of social presence, postulated on a finite but meagre number of perspectives. As Adorno observed, in a sense, works of art are both finite and infinite. They are finite in their objective existence 'circumscribed [by] givens in time or space, while... [possessing] an infinite quantum of implications that do not reveal themselves spontaneously'.[78] The (prototypical) interpretation of a work of art, such as a dance, or a painting, is a process of integrity, progressively (gradually) yielding the truth content (or knowledge)

---

[75] Franck, "Mental Presence and the Temporal Present," 48.

[76] Atkinson, Thinking the Art of Management: Stepping into "Heidegger's Shoes," 202; Here, disinterestedness signifies that Art is not to be contemplated merely as an end-in-itself. As Dewey, Art as Experience, 258. remarked, disinterestedness does not mean un-interestedness. Along with "detachment" and "physical distance", disinterestedness expresses the notion of ideas that apply to '...raw primitive desire and impulse...' but are irrelevant to the '...matter of experience artistically organized.' This Kantian notion of "disinterest" is one in which the subject is contemplative; it is indifferent as regards the Art (object or performance) itself; it focuses on the represented not the representation per se.

[77] Ewenstein and Whyte, "Beyond Words: Aesthetic Knowledge and Knowing in Organizations."

[78] Adorno, Lectures on Negative Dialectics, 84.

of its object: the dance in performance; the painting in disinterested contemplation. In comparison with the non-intellectual experience of empirical observation, the interpretation of a work of art is a subjective, intellectual experience—an openness to the object itself.

In contrast to the intellectual experience of artistic interpretation, Adorno equates the non-intellectual experience with 'everything that can be described as the so-called controlled advance of abstraction or as the mere subsumption under concepts' within the *meta*-concept of 'technology in the broadest sense'.[79] In this sense, technical knowledge, 'that fails to go beyond the already known is in danger of… being declared false, untrue and obsolete. …[Here,] truth content contains an element of time [rather than] subsisting in time and appearing… eternal and indifferent to it.'[80] In the absurdity of the contemplation of the art object—a performance of dance, for example—technology, in its broadest sense, mediates and/or moderates truth. Technology, based on dialectic abstraction, denies objective truth, or fixes it relative to nothingness. It both confines (a requisite) variation with its ideological advancement of the abstract—a model of some aspect of a material reality, denying the truth of its absent indeterminates—and fixes its limited truth value in time, systemically projecting the historicity of its ideology into the systematised faux-practice of a future present.

On systems of dance

In this inquiry into capitalism, work and enterprise, the dance metaphor may be questioned; yet the concept of dance is evident in various domains of academic interest.[81] In some cases, there is a distinct sense of the absurd. For example, Landgraf and others reported on a biomimetic honeybee robot that mimics a real honeybee returning from a 'valuable' location, performing a 'waggle dance' on its hive's honeycomb surface. While the reported robot could be 'configured comfortably using a graphical interface', with parameters to control its dance action, the authors did not observe a real bee following the robot bee for more than one dance cycle.[82]

---

[79] Adorno, Lectures on Negative Dialectics, 85.

[80] Becker, "Arts and Crafts."

[81] An EBSCO Connect search of full-text, peer-reviewed scholarly articles on 23 December 2020, using the search string 'system + dance', revealed the following: 343 articles with both words appearing at least once in the title; 3523 articles with both words appearing at least once in the article abstract; and 288,378 articles with both words appearing at least once in the full text.

[82] Landgraf et al., "A Biomimetic Honeybee Robot for the Analysis of the Honeybee Dance Communication System."

Other overt examples of systematising dance include the development of a computer-based system for ballet dance training in VR environments. Here, acknowledging 'aesthetic ideals' of classical ballet, systematising dance concerns the recognition and assessment of 'the precise alignment of the postures of trainees.'[83] The development of (dance) gesture recognition systems[84] also promises the possibility of changing the tune to which dancers dance—altering even the concept of artistic improvisation and interpretation itself. Others seek to resolve the 'colliding reciprocal dance problem', where two improvising, 'dancing' agents seem unable to pass each other, despite an expanse of space available in which to move. While the reciprocal dance is frequently enacted on the streets by passers-by, attention to systematising the dynamics of 'free agents' in time and space is relevant to driverless vehicles.[85] Systematised dance is also used to explore a means to make robots appear more humanoid and familiar by introducing 'systems' to make a robot dance 'automatically' to music.[86]

The sense of the absurd, if not explicit, hovers in a space somewhat adjacent to reality, like a robot honeybee checking out a flower. Here, the honeybee dance is posited as a means of communicating, in which the honeybee employs four key sense modes of smell, sight, taste and touch. Furthermore, there is 'evidence that honeybees have a form of hearing and an undefined ability to sense the Earth's magnetic field.'[87] That the communication (of a mode of presence) from one honeybee to another might be theorised and replicated on the complicated dialectic of (dance) movement alone, demonstrates little more than a naivety of praxis: a denial of the absurd of the real that courts its own sense of the absurd, by virtue of its abstraction in technology. In such a light, this 'will' to systematise in the realm of the scientific, can be argued to lack a degree of integrity[88] of truth content.

A lack of truth was noted by Nietzsche, who mistrusted and avoided all systematisers as lacking integrity.[89] Reaching after something that is already

---

83 Sun et al., "An Advanced Computational Intelligence System for Training of Ballet Dance in a Cave Virtual Reality Environment," 159.

84 Qian et al., "A Gesture-Driven Multimodal Interactive Dance System."

85 Johnson, "The Colliding Reciprocal Dance Problem: A Mitigation Strategy with Application to Automotive Active Safety Systems*."

86 Seo et al., "Autonomous Humanoid Robot Dance Generation System Based on Real-Time Music Input."

87 Beynon-Davies, "Dances with Bees: Exploring the Relevance of the Study of Animal Communication to Informatics."

88 Integrity: as in the state of being whole or the condition of being unified or soundly constructed, internally consistent. See Oxford English Dictionary (12th Edn.).

89 Nietzsche, Twilight of the Idols, 8.

known—for example, a Hegelian synthesis of conceptual knowledge—as cause of some experienced element of material praxis, is no more than following the maxim of 'any explanation is better than none'. Such an explanation—a knowledge merely held true—might provide relief from the anxiety of the unknown, but it denies '[the] new, the unexperienced, the alien'. The absurd is 'ruled out as a cause.' Here, following Nietzsche, an idealised conceptual knowledge forms 'a *select* and *privileged...* explanation.'[90] Systematised, select and privileged explanations—such as a ToM—become dominant, dispelling notions of the absurd; other causes: the alien, the new and unexperienced—to Nietzsche the most usual explanations—are simply ruled out.

We tend to experience the material consequences of our systems of praxis as caused, not by the absurd, but by failures of theory to predict them. Bee stings found on the body of a dancing robot bee are attributed to the silicon body having a repellent smell,[91] rather than to the absurdity of replicating a dance of nature through the mediating technology of a 'robot' bee. Certainly, a robot bee, as a systematisation of natural communication between real honeybees—a scheme of presentation in technology—somewhat hides the truth. Yet, our need to create 'systems' is perceived to be far greater than the idea of discrediting them.[92]

The negativity of dialectic systems

As I explore here, the (pre)dominance of Hegelian dialectics drives the thinking about systems that provide form to, and an explanation of, the world as a whole. This includes systems of art. As a dialectic process, such systematising has become a uniform mode of presentation, yielding systems of undifferentiated objects and subjects, all 'ontic' classifications from the realm of the existent and the conscious. Although Adorno's notion of system is embedded in thinking about the system of philosophy, in this respect philosophy is taken to be the last critique of praxis. His distinction between system and systematisation posits the former as a process of the dynamic development of fact from principles, while systematisation concerns the non-philosophical process of construing 'systems' through classification. This latter form provides a mere 'pale imitation' of, and 'substitute' for, a whole.[93]

---

[90] Nietzsche, Twilight of the Idols, 30.

[91] Landgraf et al., "A Biomimetic Honeybee Robot for the Analysis of the Honeybee Dance Communication System," 3101.

[92] Adorno, Lectures on Negative Dialectics, 36.

[93] Adorno, Lectures on Negative Dialectics, 36.

The divergence between a desired system of material praxis and a naïve systematisation, is due to the system's tendency to work only on what can be ontically classified. While systematisation aspires to an objective whole, it can only do so in the abstract, renouncing *that which remains ontologically unclassified*—that which lies in the realm of the unconscious. In praxis, facing the divergent outcomes of systems construed through systematisations that fail to yield what was materially expected of them—because of causal factors (indeterminates) we are unconscious of—our dominant mode of reconciliation is to redefine the field of praxis: the system does what it does. Our locus of understanding shifts from the system's domain of interest to its governance and control. Our concern is no longer why we might communicate with honeybees, but how we make a robot bee dance a perfect waggle. An understanding of the absurd remains in the unconscious.

The above systems view, derived from Adorno's critique of Hegelian dialectics, is mirrored in the field of cybernetics[94]—the interdisciplinary study of the regulation of systems.[95] Here, an analysis of the *faux practice* of a dancing robot honeybee tends to a study of the system's 'regulatory phenomena',[96] for example: controlling the robot honeybee's temperature to regulate the evaporation of odours that are assumed to have caused real bees to sting it.[97] In the further example of the 'system of horror'—inaugurated on the September 11th, 2001, attack on the Twin Towers, New York, USA—Stafford Beer cited the cybernetic dictum that the purpose of a system is what it does (POSIWID).[98] This aligns with Adorno's critique of the idea that abstract systematisations should be treated as that which 'the system' aspired to be.[99] Working backwards from praxis to concept is to construct something from nothing. It negates the domain through a substitution of the positive by a negative of the negative. Thus a world of robot honeybees that look like bees, smell like bees and dance like bees cannot do what a honeybee does—produce honey.

---

[94] The word cybernetics is a derivation of cybernetes, from the Greek word kubernetes meaning steersman on an ancient Greek long ship. In this sense, cybernetics concerns the communication and control (governance) of the vessel (system of animal and machine) at sea (in a complex environment). It was first used in defining the field during the early 1940s by the distinguished mathematician Nobert Wiener. See for example: Beer, "What Is Cybernetics?"

[95] Beer, "What Is Cybernetics?"

[96] Beer, "What Is Cybernetics?" 217.

[97] Landgraf et al., "A Biomimetic Honeybee Robot for the Analysis of the Honeybee Dance Communication System," 3102.

[98] Beer, "What Is Cybernetics?," 217–18.

[99] Adorno, Lectures on Negative Dialectics, 37.

Following Beer's critique of the 9/11 'system of horror' and its predictable outcome—the retaliation against Afghanistan—the question arises, was not the resultant conflict something constructed from nothing? While I do not offer a direct response to that question, I wish to reflect on the more esoteric and ask: is this what Adorno refers to, when he posited his concept of negative dialectics as 'the consciousness, the critical and self-critical consciousness of... a change in the idea [that it is possible to bring the totality of all that exists within a unified concept]?[100] In the two examples cited, is it possible to understand 'an infinite number of inexplicit threats'[101] as some sort of whole (system of horror), and develop solutions for their governance and control (war)? Is it possible, also, to understand the infinitesimal array of 'various stimuli and behaviours' associated with the honeybee as some sort of whole (dance) and communicate with real honeybees through robots enacting that dance?

Guided by the dominant shape of positivism, we may accept Adorno's critique and call for negative dialectics—the speculative transformation of the ontological unconscious—as a means of understanding. Following Adorno, I posit that the unity of a systematised idea or thesis arises from the coercion that the material (ontic) reality exercises over the idea/thesis. This is in contrast to the speculative 'free action' of the idea/thesis itself.[102] I believe that what is required, therefore, is a renunciation of the idealist, systemic comprehension of a material reality—one which resists an absurdist descent into randomness or arbitrariness. What is required is an acceptance of the need for systems to be considered, but which simultaneously guards against the pale imitations of positivist systems. It is as if, to paraphrase Adorno, 'we should cease to speak as if we [can] explain a substantive [(ontic) concept] from within itself... given that [the concept's] substantiveness [is beyond the reach of the conscious].[103]

Instead of a positivist system, we might envisage an 'a-systematic' coercion of ontological determinates, in which we experience the dynamic ('epistemic') development of facts from principles—a drawing in of every antecedent thing, including absurdities, into its ('ontological') 'self'.[104] This is the speculative motivation for my inquiry. It is a guarding against the belief that it is possible to understand the whole of the existing (carbon-based) economy as the amplifier of racial, social and economic inequality, contributing to a profoundly

---

[100] Adorno, Lectures on Negative Dialectics, 38.
[101] Beer, "What Is Cybernetics?," 218.
[102] Adorno, Lectures on Negative Dialectics, 39.
[103] Adorno, Lectures on Negative Dialectics, 41.
[104] Adorno, Lectures on Negative Dialectics, 36.

unstable socio-economic system. It is a guarding against the belief that replacing that economy will, in some way, provide a necessary and sufficient solution for the governance and control of economic outcomes. It is a guarding against a ToM-driven, privileged access to a material reality. To ignore this motivation—to borrow a phrase from Beer—in the call for a new economic order, we are simply expected to '[dance] into battle against an abstract noun [neoliberalism], and to assault any [business] unwilling to mobilize in such folly.'[105]

Adorno's negative dialectic of non-identity

What is the absurdity denied by the 100 economists? To paraphrase Adorno, 'the more everything is sacrificed to pre-existing objects of conscious [neoliberalism], and the less is left over for ideology to feed off, the more abstract all ideologies necessarily become.'[106] In the theatre of society and the systemic dances of economic life, what does it mean to be identified as a capitalist? What is an anti-capitalist? What absurdities are denied a role? Underlying the conscious objects of neoliberalism, Adorno critiqued the conviction that such objects were positive, in and of themselves. Thus, within the praxis of capitalist enterprise, I see the assumption that the entrepreneur (as object) is in some way intrinsically positive for society. Yet this positivity contains within it a social ambivalence. Questions arise. What (exactly) is it about the entrepreneur that contributes positivity? Is it a fallacy that the entrepreneur, possessed of that which makes them good ('the approvable attributes'), actually exists? On what ToM may we reliably invoke a folk psychology of entrepreneurship to ascribe beliefs and desires to others to predict their entrepreneurial behaviour? Such questions face a positivist conviction. On the one hand, 'positive' refers to the positivism of what is given or is there, or is postulated (a thesis), and on the other hand, it refers to what is good, approvable or, in a sense, ideal.[107]

Despite their being founded on dialectic identities, a Hegelian synthesis of capitalism and its antithesis of non-capitalism, or work and its antithesis of non-work, or entrepreneurship and its antithesis of non-entrepreneurship, resolve to theses of non-identity. Denied their internal contradictions with the field of praxis, any such syntheses are of limited value and incongruent with reality and its praxis. Here, Adorno's conceptualisation of a negative dialectics resists the idea of such synthesis in its concern with how the concept itself (rather than its synthetic self), moves towards its (material) opposite. With

[105] Beer, "What Is Cybernetics?," 218–19.
[106] Adorno, Lectures on Negative Dialectics, 17.
[107] Adorno, Lectures on Negative Dialectics, 18.

reference to Figure 2.3, a negative dialectics thus reduces the value of the concept of synthesis.

The principle behind Adorno's negative dialectic is the formation of a complex *thesis of the non-concept of identity* ('E'). This amounts to a critique of an idealised identity dialectics. While thesis 'B' identifies some aspect(s) of domain A, identifying an ideal concept or thing, the dialectic negation of that concept simply produces its antithesis ('C'), a concept of non-identity. However, if rather than negating the concept of an identity, we introduce its non-concept, defining that identity by virtue of all the possible (contradictory) determinates and indeterminates or non-conceptual things that do not identify it, conceptually, then we find that a complex, *non-conceptual identity thesis* ('E') subsumes both thesis and anti-thesis. Thus, for example, rather than a ToM, and its antithesis of a deficiency in ToM, we are presented with a complex non-conceptual ToM derived from its field of contradictions.

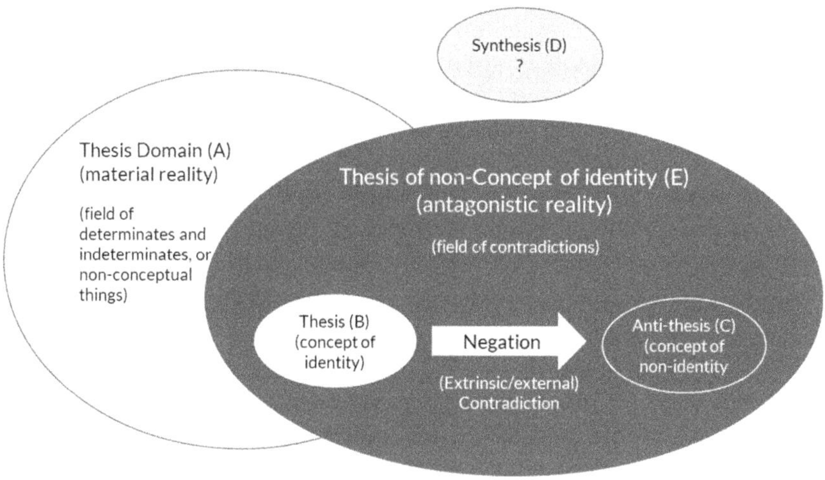

Figure 2.3. Adorno's (critical) negative dialectic

Although an initial concept or idea will form its basis, a non-conceptual identity thesis does not presuppose a fully determinate identity. Unlike a Hegelian thesis, which is a presupposition, central to idealist thinking, 'B' need only approximate itself. In retaining within it both internal and external contradictions, 'B' acknowledges 'the divergence of concept and thing, subject and object, and their unreconciled state.'[108]

---

[108] Adorno, Lectures on Negative Dialectics, 6.

Rather than negate the thesis 'B' as anti-thesis 'C', we negate the concept 'B' to yield the complex thesis of the non-concept 'E'; 'E' thus comprises the field of all possible contradictions identifying 'B'. We identify 'B' by reference to all the contradictory determinates, indeterminates and non-conceptual things that 'B' is not. Yet, by subsuming the external contradictions of an identity's antithesis, we recognise that, just as the idealist 'B' cannot truly represent (an aspect of) 'A', neither can the complex non-conceptual identity thesis ('E') in itself, represent 'A'. However, the divergence of a non-conceptual identity thesis from its material reality, differs from the divergence of an idealised, synthetic thesis from that reality by virtue of its contradictions. Here, Adorno offers the example of the concept of profit.[109]

A Hegelian thesis of capitalist motivation might be that economic profit, generated through enterprising work, identifies society's capacity to 'reproduce its own existence'; the antithesis being that profit 'divides society and potentially tears it apart.' Here, a naïve, idealised, dialectic is evident in Adam Smith's conceptualisation of 'an invisible hand'. Smith's synthetic theorising in *The Wealth of Nations*[110] builds on the identity theory of moral sentiment, in which an invisible hand is given synthetic (positive dialectic) form—an incongruent theory about no 'thing'. Conversely, a non-conceptual identity thesis of profit, while not resolving to a material reality, nevertheless exists because of the contradictions congruent with, and represented by, a society that, in praxis, simultaneously reproduces itself while creating internal divisions and conflict. Negating an idealised, incongruent model reality, a *non-conceptual identity thesis* models a congruent, if *antagonistic reality.*

To take a further example, a Hegelian thesis of a virtuous economic society might be that purposeful businesses that perform to a scheme of social values, rather than simply the delivery of profit, identity a form of sustainable, value capitalism. The naïve antithesis would be that businesses that practise for profit are neither sustainable, nor provide value. Here, such a naïve, idealised, dialectic must ignore many of the motivations for establishing businesses, including the absurdity of those who find no gainful employment open to them, other than what they can generate in the creation of their own enterprise (even if unlawful). A Hegelian synthesis is offered through, perhaps, the (complicated) conceptualisation of a values framework that addresses a range of 'approved' values, from profit to dignity. But here, contradictions envisaged in defining a common set of values are certainly non-trivial. What would a non-conceptual identity thesis of a virtuous economic society look like? This, in a nutshell, is the concern of the present

---

[109] Adorno, Lectures on Negative Dialectics, 8–9.
[110] Smith, The Wealth of Nations: Books I-III; Smith, The Wealth of Nations: Books IV-V.

inquiry: working toward a *non-conceptual identity thesis* that models a congruent if *antagonistic reality* of the economy, work and enterprise.

Reconciling divergence

What if a 'sense of presence' lies at the root of our faculty for accumulating a tacit knowledge concerning our place in a (future) *order of things*—of the economy, work and enterprise? To Adorno, the distinction between a (non)conceptual model and its material reality is the extent to which the model sublimated its antagonisms.[111] Given that an antagonism is a (hostile) form of opposition or contradiction, we can say that in the general case, the non-concept (or thesis of non-identity) of, for example, an antagonistic society, is one that exists by virtue of its contradictions, not with or despite them.[112] In the limit that all contradictions are sublimated, negated or neglected, the idealised concept of an (non)antagonistic society (a utopia) would bear no relevance to its material reality. In the limit that all contradictions are identifiable, the (negative) non-conceptual thesis of such a society would be mimetically representative of its reality. At this limit, society, a human collective, is inherently contrary.[113] This offers a theory of the *contrariness of society*, one which subsumes an antithetical humanity.

Taking Adorno's example of profit, we may say that profit applies to all humanity and is thus inclusive of the contrariness of all humans. In terms of a ToM and the pursuit of profit, this contrariness is manifest in the tendency for some humans to do the opposite of what is (ideologically) expected or desired of them. While mimetically reflective of a material reality, we cannot say—as a 'negative' form of reality—that the product of such negative theorising about an antagonistic society will have a positive mimetic reflection on a material reality. The question is raised, are conceptual reconciliations without some form of synthesis (of the human as an identified object in society) even possible? Here, it has been observed that Adorno detested the idea of

---

[111] Adorno, Lectures on Negative Dialectics, 168.

[112] Stacey, Griffin, and Shaw, Complexity and Management: Fad or Radical Challenge to Systems Thinking?

[113] While the term contradictory represents mutually opposed or inconsistent propositions, ideas or things, in logic it is the case that one or more, or none may be true or right. The contrariness of the human is the perverse inclination or tendency of the human to do the opposite of what is expected or desired. See: Oxford English Dictionary (12th Edn.). For a society consisting of multiple humans, all capable of acting in contradictory ways, the term contrary best describes the collective potential for the contradictions and antagonisms arising from human agency and action within a given society or social grouping.

reconciliations with negative conditions.[114] Having highlighted that it is not the case that the negation of a negation is always positive, we might accept contradictions will continue to exist, and that these will need to be mitigated (or controlled), rather than reconciled.

It is outside the scope of this present work to offer a detailed critique of Adorno's negative dialectics. However, it is worth reflecting on how some others have applied or critiqued negative dialectics to differentiate the present work and its methodology. Associated, as it is, with the Frankfurt School, the idea of adopting/extending Adorno's negative dialectics first butts up against a Lukácsian critique. György Lukács' conceived of society as a process, not a thing.[115] Concerned, as this present work is, with a science of society, the idea of society as a process does hold within it an essential relationship between theory and praxis, in which the objects of study (processes) are, innately, representations of ongoing praxis. To Lukács, the dialectic reification of aspects of society as things (concepts and theories) tended to a rationalisation in which all objects take the form of the abstracted models and theories investigated.[116] While the shortcomings of positive idealised objects of a Hegelian dialectic are readily discernible, as argued herein, to Lukács, the pessimism inherent in Adorno's negative dialectic fairs no better, seemingly offering little real challenge to the miseries of the world.[117] Yet, here, faced with the task of illuminating a future world in which the persistence of dialectic reasoning continues to characterise future praxis, a Lukácsian critique rooted in present praxis does not offer the freedom to speculate with future objects.

Beyond a Lukácsian critique, Gillian Rose presented a case for a speculative reading of Hegelian philosophy, in which she purported to attend to the 'broken middle' between the conceptual and the real (or actual). In her analysis of Rose's Speculative Dialectics, Kate Schick suggested that while Adorno's own (negative) dialectic is Hegelian in method, in its emphasis on the complex variability of the individual—overemphasising the particular at the expense of the universal—it fails to provide an adequate, practical and historical account of society itself.[118] We see something of this criticism in the challenge of reconciling (or mediating) the 'particular' of Adorno's non-concept of, for example, an antagonistic society of individuals, with a 'general'

---

[114] Bonefeld, "Negative Dialectics in Miserable Times: Notes on Adorno and Social Praxis."

[115] Feenberg, "Why Students of the Frankfurt School Will Have to Read Lukács."

[116] Joll, "Adorno's Negative Dialectic: Theme, Point, and Methodological Status."

[117] Gunderson, "A Defense of the 'Grand Hotel Abyss': The Frankfurt School's Nonideal Theory."

[118] Schick, "Speculative Dialectics."

understanding of a praxis of societal contradictions. In short, to Rose, Adorno's negative dialectics fails to offer an account of social relations—yielding only a praxis of thought, not action. This theme, of there being, in Adorno's negative dialectics, a lack of the positive—of there being no guide for practise—is a common one levied in the critique of the Frankfurt School, as residents of the Grand Hotel Abyss.[119] To his critics, Adorno's philosophy was 'substantially disconnected from the historical reality of socio-political praxis.'[120] Indeed, to Adorno himself, negative dialectics was a form of interpretation only.[121] This criticism leads to Habermas' rejection of negativity, in favour of a non-absolute truth in which philosophy is restricted to the critique of science, *ex-post*. However, lest such critique be a diversion, I argue the importance of the matter at hand is to address, in the words of Alain Badiou, the question 'how is the Real of the present [to be] deployed for the future?'[122]

While Rose's critique of Adorno turns her to a speculative reading of Hegel—acknowledging Hegel also advocated a form of speculative 'positive' reasoning, in which 'it is impossible to comprehend concepts in isolation'[123]—the positive, ideal nature of a Hegelian dialectic remains problematic. Ultimately, I argue that both a Hegelian (positive) dialectics and an Adornian negative dialectics leave us with an unreconciled theory-praxis divergence. We may conclude that dialectic reasoning has its place, yet I suggest we are in danger of producing little more than a rich olio of social theories, which can only ever be applied in praxis with extreme caution. Consequentially, I argue that (social) science has lost its way; it is now a world of abstract theories: robot bees rather than real bees; and virtual rather than material realities. Here, the academic press might be seen, in provocation, as little more than a graveyard of spent dialectic dialogue, feeding limited *zombie markets* of niche interests, beyond sight and reach of their esteemed alters of practice. However, if, in contrast to an idealised model of reality, we accept a *non-conceptual identity thesis* model of an *antagonistic reality*, I posit that we can, at least, return to the (speculative) social construction of presence.

Critique aside, moving the dialectic on to address Badiou's deployment of the present Real, I speculate (imagine) about the possibilities of the future. Here, a non-conceptual identification of *presence* becomes a complex social construction of the Real and Imaginary contradictions that support it. Rather

---

119 Buchholz, "'Grand Hotel Abyss?' On the Actuality of Theodor W. Adorno's Critical Theory [Transl.]."
120 Giannakakis, "Adorno, Badiou and the Politics of Breaking Out," 18.
121 Joll, "Adorno's Negative Dialectic: Theme, Point, and Methodological Status."
122 Badiou and Woodward, "Interview."
123 Schick, "Speculative Dialectics," 26.

than seek immediate relief from the anxiety of identifying our presence in the unknown, we may speculate about the new, the unexperienced, and the alien as a complex extension of the Real. Thus, rather than rule out the presently *Real absurd* as having a causal relationship with a future presence, I posit that we may defend its potential. Rather than satisfy ourselves with systematised, privileged accounts of the ideal objective-subjective—a focus on a belief in the possible, plausible, preferable, and a negation of the undesirable—we may speculate on the Nietzschean idea of the most usual. This is the alien, the new and the unexperienced. Here, I argue that our focus of study shifts to also embrace the complexity of the seemingly impossible, the improbable, and/or implausible. However, to achieve this, we must suspend our disbelief in the causal possibilities of the Real absurd.

The imaginary plane

Suspending our disbelief in the relevance of indeterminates calls for suspending a belief in the primacy of the ontic, of the plausible, preferable, and the negation of undesirable determinates. In doing so, we may actively speculate on the transformation of the indeterminate to its determinate. We may ask: what if this? Or: what if that? Thus, I return to a 'sixth sense' of *social presence*, and its two modes. Firstly, there is the rational mode of the self being faced with Others, in relation to a specified medium. This is a rationally bounded finite whole, that has both form and content—in essence, a presence in a temporal, finite material reality: the here and now. Secondly, there is the irrational mode of Being, influenced by the complex collective of individual human (or personal) psychology. Here there is a degree of inter-subjective mental presence in an infinite, antagonistic reality. Following Emanuel Lévinas,[124] the irrational mode is reached through our facing the Other with a responsible speculation of the (often unconscious) possibilities of the absurd in human behaviour. This responsibility to the Other also calls for a new, non-conceptual ToM, in which the autistic dialectic of mental presence is combined, in a mediated construction with a multiplicity of the sensed mental presences of others, without prescribing antecedent mental states. In this second responsible moment, the reflexive *sensible self*, integrates its objective perceptions of others' mental presences.

I posit that we may legitimately ask: what if humanity was like this? What if it was like that? Therefore, I argue that what a negative dialectics offers us is a form of dialogue. But this is not a Platonic dialogue that practises the (re)insertion of some idealistic synthesis within its thesis, but a *dialogue of*

---

[124] Lévinas, "Ethics and Infinity."

reconciliation between a material reality and its antagonisms and contradictions with the aim of better identifying the relationship between that reality, aspects of it, and its antagonisms. It is also an ethical dialogue of inclusion.

Speculating about the possibilities of the absurd and the irrational in a material reality is the equivalent of the introduction of counterfactual components in a dialogue about being in some place, in some time. Such counterfacts are, by definition, non-factual. They are imaginary. It is the equivalent, I suggest, of introducing the concept of the imaginary number '*i*' in mathematics. Conceptually, an imaginary fact (an 'imagination') allows the product of a negation and a negation to result in a negative (contradictory) material outcome.[125] Thus, in assuming an imaginary counterfactual determinate exists, we introduce an imaginary (contradictory) plane at an intersection with, and with the same locus as, a hypothetical plane representative of our material reality (Figure 2.4). In doing so, I argue that a complex negative dialectics provides an ethically grounded, philosophical methodology, in which counter-facts may be perceived as factual, to allow for a (responsible/scholarly) dialogue on a material reality, without having to strive for an objective reconciliation of the contrariness of humanity.

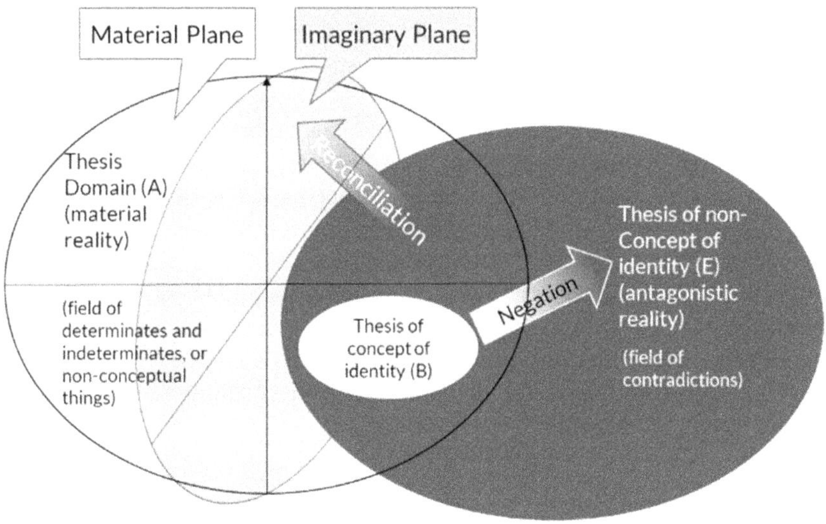

Figure 2.4. An imaginary plane

[125] Adorno, Lectures on Negative Dialectics, 17.

A complex negative dialectics 'does not pacify the contradiction, be it by means of reconciliation, integration, incorporation, or simply formalistic indifference to social contents.'[126] Thus, considering our presence in some future (material) praxis of economic organization, work and enterprise, I argue that there must be a motivation to include, in my inquiry, a dialogue of complex negative dialectics, between what we know of our present reality, and what we might conceive of as the antagonisms and contradictions that will shape its progress. Speculation is *the* motivation to think further than the facts that we perceive.[127]

To overcome Adorno's detestation of reconciliation with negative conditions—the idea that the negation of a negation is positive and makes no sense—I advance the possibility of introducing reconciliatory pathways through the responsible introduction of the imaginary plane of human possibility. I posit that only through the intersection of an imaginary plane—a complex insertion into a material reality—can we avoid any presupposition of positivity, and fully contemplate the potential reconciliation of an antagonistic reality with its potential materialism. Just as with the case of '*i*', the imaginary square root of minus one, I argue that the imaginary plane allows us to overcome the '[irreconcilability] of negative dialectics with negative conditions... [that appear to] render impotent its practical dimension.'[128]

An imaginary plane 'outside' the domain of the real and the material is untethered to pure perception; it is not holistically objective. Yet its ability to respond (its responsibility) to the 'face' of the Other offers an act of 'signifyingness' of an intentional ethical relationship between the self and the Other, through the imaginary plane. Here, following Lévinas,[129] "the rawness of what can be identified with negative dialectics is the open 'face' of the Other and the proximity of responsibility in subjectivity—the immanence of responsibility, face to face".[130] To deny the responsibility of a dialogue with the Other through the imaginary plane, is to deny the Other its possibility of Being, an act of violence against the Other[131] in its contrariness. Thus construed, I argue that negative dialectics presents a Levinasian ethical and responsible method of 'facing the Other' without violating their oftentimes

---

126 Bonefeld, "Negative Dialectics in Miserable Times: Notes on Adorno and Social Praxis," 130.

127 Adorno, Lectures on Negative Dialectics, 88.

128 Bonefeld, "Negative Dialectics in Miserable Times: Notes on Adorno and Social Praxis," 131.

129 Lévinas, "Ethics and Infinity."

130 Lamoureux and Atkinson, "Email Corrspondence: Chapter 2 and Some Thoughts."

131 Lévinas, Entre Nous.

contrary otherness. In Chapter 3, I will explore the contrary nature of the Other, through an exemplar explication of the dialectic concept of the entrepreneur, seeking a responsible reconciliation of the entrepreneurial character through a point of access on the imaginary plane that does not violate its Being.

Chapter 3

The contrary entrepreneur

"LEEDS, AUGUST 2008. I am an entrepreneur, on the brink of listing my company. ...We share our new offices on the outskirts of Leeds, a short pebble-skim from the M1 [motorway], with the company we are to merge with ...prior to floating on London's Plus Markets – a junior stock exchange. ...I will be moving roles from Chief Executive... to joint Managing Director of the combined company. I can handle that. It is the price of progress. [I am followed into my office] by my business partner, Stuart.

'David,' Stuart shakes his head. '...sorry, but it's been a terrible few days.' ...His expression gives me no comfort.

'Yes. Well...' he pauses, briefly. Then rushes onward. 'Yes. Well, the board want you out.'

'Out?' I say."[1]

Who is 'The Entrepreneur'?

Despite: the study of entrepreneurship's eclectic tradition[2]; its growth, from isolated groups of small business researchers to a global community of

[1] Excerpt from: Atkinson, Unpublished Manuscript.
[2] Landström and Harirchi, "The Social Structure of Entrepreneurship as a Scientific Field."

departments, institutes, and foundations[3]; its delineation[4]; and its conceptual models,[5] a question remains largely unanswered. Who is the entrepreneur? Within an entrepreneurial capitalist economy, who embraces the risks and contradictions of entrepreneurship when its oftentimes absurd outcomes include boardroom coups, and the loss of position, income and status?[6]

In Chapter 2, I introduced a methodology of negative dialectics. There, in the limit that all (un-)conscious contradictions might be identifiable, I observed the inherent contrary nature of human action. My suggestion, albeit provisional, is that we cannot naively assume a dialectic ToM. In Chapter 2, I concluded with positing an ethical responsibility to face the contrariness of the Other. As a further motivation for this inquiry into capitalism, work and enterprise, I cannot, therefore, from a critical perspective, assume the subjective being of an entrepreneur—an adjudged agent and mainstay of capitalist economic work and enterprise. I cannot assume that, by some extant thesis of entrepreneurial practice, we might ontically classify a set of other beings to which we can ascribe certain beliefs and desires about entrepreneurship, to predict their entrepreneurial behaviour in a future praxis. Inclusively, human nature is too contrary for such a ToM. In this Chapter, I shall explore this contrary nature further through an autistic, non-conceptual lens of entrepreneurship. In doing so, I seek a responsible reconciliation of the entrepreneurial character through a point of access on the imaginary plane that does not violate its Being. This expands my inquiry into motivation by revisiting Maslow's Needs Theory. In doing so, I elicit something of the nomothetic promise of non-conceptual entrepreneurial idiographies—the private stories of enterprising Others.

From a traditional, dialectic perspective, perhaps spurred by William Gartner's assertion that 'Who is an entrepreneur?' is the wrong question,[7] entrepreneurship researchers turned to consider the process and functional theory. Gartner's argument was based on the premise that, with the entrepreneur as the unit of analysis, the (positive) trait-based approaches of study (the ideals

---

[3] Aldrich, "The Emergence of Entrepreneurship as an Academic Field: A Personal Essay on Institutional Entrepreneurship."

[4] Venkataraman, "The Distinctive Domain of Entrepreneurship Research."

[5] See, for example: Shane and Venkataraman, "The Promise of Entrepreneurship as a Field of Research."

[6] The opening excerpt retells the scene that preceded my exit from a company I had founded, my loss of income and status as CEO, and a lengthy period of unemployment. At the time, I held the largest single shareholding in the company, but did not have overall control. My business partners were able to secure the votes necessary to dispense with my services.

[7] Gartner, "'Who Is an Entrepreneur?' Is the Wrong Question."

of who, why, what and how) were largely unfruitful. However, the resulting shift to the organization as a unit of analysis has also been challenged. It, too, appears to have failed to change the nature of much entrepreneurship understanding, resolving to the analysis of a series of survey questionnaires.[8] In challenging the Gartner-influenced organizational turn to entrepreneurship study, Brian McKenzie and his colleagues gave renewed credence to the idea that entrepreneurship is, *inter alia*, influenced by the intentions and capacity of certain individuals (or groups of individuals)—the entrepreneurs.

In this Chapter, I wish to face the motivation behind an individual's *social presence* in a (negative) dialectic of entrepreneurship. With reference to Figure 3.1, I extend the negative dialectic methodology and its insertion of the imaginary (nonconceptual) plane with a provocation of 'story', to (provisionally) reconcile a nomothetic essence—a moment or state of being a (non)character: *The Entrepreneur.* This is an essence imagined, in the first instance, to emerge from within the oftentimes contrary idiographies of entrepreneurial activity. While providing something of a contribution to the idea of entrepreneurial intent (EI)—an antecedent of entrepreneurial action—the main aim of this Chapter is an appeal to the idea of aesthetic knowledge introduced in Chapter 2.

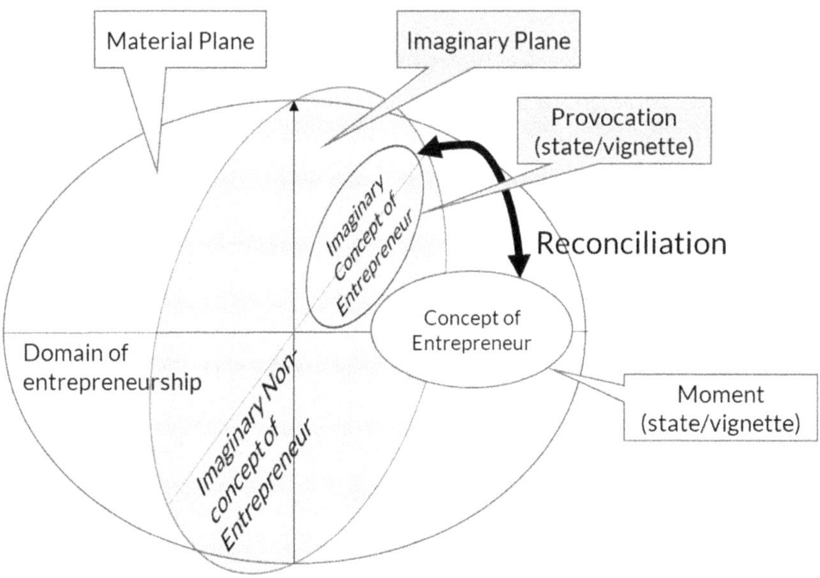

Figure 3.1. Imaginary plane of entrepreneurship

[8] McKenzie, Ugbah, and Smothers, "'Who Is an Entrepreneur?' Is It Still the Wrong Question?"

Firstly, I explore story as both methodology and method. While story provides a framework for multiple points of interpretation, my focus is on the story's call-to-action. Secondly, I use both autoethnographic creative non-fiction and fictional narrative to illustrate the personal psychology of the call. This re-surfaces Maslow's work on individual needs. Here, I draw on an application of Maslow's Needs Theory (NT),[9] offering a needs-consciousness model to inform a provisional (aesthetic) knowledge concerning the contrariness of entrepreneurial motivation. Antecedent to the investigations that follow, this motivation reflects a point of departure in applying negative dialectics in practice, revealing its capacity to make explicit something of the irrational, unconscious nature of an entrepreneurial praxis.

Story: methodology and method

Story is a methodology in which the creation and sharing of new understandings may disrupt dominant narratives, opening up new possibilities of meaning.[10] It avoids the challenge that what may appear to be generic qualitative research, obscures the author's position.[11] Rather, story as methodology represents an evolution of its form.[12] Holistically, story unlocks understanding of our many states of (un-)consciousness, linking dreams to waking[13] and helps unlock understanding of unconscious thinking.[14] Importantly, from Chapter 2, given the ethical responsibility to face the Other, story invokes antagonisms without violating the Other. In context, story places its methods within the constructivist paradigm to present a new (provocative) approach to face the Other and to answer the question: 'Who is the entrepreneur?'

Here, I invoke an autoethnographic[15] method of entrepreneurial story research. This is a juxtaposition of intervention, invention and introspection (the '3i' approach), told through story. It is guided by the principles of

---

[9] D'Souza and Gurin, "The Universal Significance of Maslow's Concept of Self-Actualization."
[10] Rice and Mündel, "Story-Making as Methodology: Disrupting Dominant Stories through Multimedia Storytelling."
[11] Caelli, Ray, and Mill, "'Clear as Mud': Toward Greater Clarity in Generic Qualitative Research."
[12] Putney et al., "Evolution of Qualitative Research Methodology: Looking Beyond Defense to Possibilities."
[13] Goldin, "Storylines."
[14] Martin, "Uncovering Unconscious Memories and Myths for Understanding International Tourism Behavior."
[15] Holbrook, "Customer Value and Autoethnography: Subjective Personal Introspection and the Meanings of a Photograph Collection"; Ellis and Adams, "The Purposes, Practices, and Principles of Autoethnographic Research."

autoethnographic research postulated by Carolyn Ellis and Tony Adams,[16] including: familiarity with existing research; using personal experience to describe and critique cultural experience; taking advantage of, and valuing, insider knowledge; and breaking silence. It aims to reclaim the entrepreneurial voice—an appeal to a narrative research method[17] in the interpretivist tradition, in which (a provisional) knowledge emerges from the intellectual experience of both the materially real (exogenous) and imaginative (endogenous) sources.

Autoethnography is an autobiographical genre of qualitative research.[18] Within the '3i' approach, firstly, intervention equips the entrepreneurship inquirer with a form of enactive research in which movements, initiated by the inquirer themself, culminate in an event,[19] where the researcher both creates and investigates the situation being studied.[20] Secondly, to aid introspection, the approach employs conceptual and fictitious 'invention', rooted in the aesthetic and the political.[21] Thirdly, 'introspection' relies on gathering and analyzing an olio[22] of illustrative story material where, given the axiomatic social complexity of the field of entrepreneurship, the concept of intègraphy[23] draws together the variety of perspectives presented. As a researcher, I am thus at the heart of this inquiry, drawing upon my olio's diverse data from both autoethnography and my creation and use of fiction as exemplars.

Autoethnography as enactive research

By enactive research, I invoke an objective of knowledge emancipation through my role as initiator of an event that creates an opportunity for critical reflexivity. Here, reflexivity goes beyond reflection. It involves self-

---

[16] Ellis and Adams, "The Purposes, Practices, and Principles of Autoethnographic Research."

[17] Soin and Scheytt, "Making the Case for Narrative Methods in Cross-Cultural Organizational Research."

[18] Boje and Tyler, "Story and Narrative Noticing: Workaholism Autoethnographies."

[19] Johannisson, "Between Arm's Length Research and Policy Practices: Interactive Approaches in Entrepreneurship Studies"; Steyaert, "Entrepreneurship as in(Ter)Vention: Reconsidering the Conceptual Politics of Method in Entrepreneurship Studies."

[20] Steyaert, "Entrepreneurship as in(Ter)Vention: Reconsidering the Conceptual Politics of Method in Entrepreneurship Studies."

[21] Steyaert, "Entrepreneurship as in(Ter)Vention: Reconsidering the Conceptual Politics of Method in Entrepreneurship Studies."

[22] Levy, "Olio and Intègraphy as Method and the Consumption of Death."

[23] Levy and Kellstadt, "Intègraphy: A Multi-Method Approach to Situational Analysis."

consciousness and intentional self-introspection.[24] Thus, I argue my enactive research may open up new (autistic) forms of inquiry that do not centre on subjective ToM assumptions. However, autoethnography can be risky.[25] In the following sections, I address some of these risks.

The entrepreneur as the Other

As researchers, people we study are assigned to an outgroup, 'them', different from 'us'. As we do not belong to 'them', we cannot avoid representing 'them' as the Other,[26] a negation of our own identity. Thus, entrepreneurial research and its outgroups tend to have any number of conceptual characterizations. For example: 'bureaucratic entrepreneurs' exist in Public Administration[27]; 'social entrepreneurs' in Organization Science[28]; 'environmental entrepreneurs' in Business Venturing[29]; and 'agripreneurs' in Community Mobilization and Sustainable Development.[30] We identify these outgroups as apart from non-entrepreneurs and the 'us' that are researchers.

'Othering' has its critics.[31] 'Others' may be sealed in a social science narrative '...long on texts that inscribe some Others, preserve other Others from scrutiny, and seek to hide the researcher/writer under a veil of neutrality or objectivity...'.[32] Here, traditional social science constructs, legitimizes and distances Others, banishing them to cultural margins. Othering is an act of suppression and violence. With the phrase: '*I am an entrepreneur*', I may claim 'Otherness' but, with a given entrepreneurial identity, I may violate my identity as a researcher, worker, and the essence of my enterprise. Alongside such contradictions, I even witness social science writing 'for' a class of 'drop-out' entrepreneur, identifying them as an 'Other' to aspire to,[33]

---

24 Brannick and Coghlan, "In Defense of Being 'Native': The Case for Insider Academic Research."
25 Cunliffe, "Alterity: The Passion, Politics, and Ethics of Self and Scholarship."
26 Fitzsimmons, "Us, Them, and Others in Management Research."
27 Teske and Schneider, "The Bureaucratic Entrepreneur: The Case of City Managers."
28 Dacin, Dacin, and Tracey, "Social Entrepreneurship: A Critique and Future Directions."
29 O'Neil and Ucbasaran, "Balancing 'What Matters to Me' with 'What Matters to Them': Exploring the Legitimation Process of Environmental Entrepreneurs."
30 Ahmed, Hasan, and Haneef, "Entrepreneurial Characteristics of the Agripreneurs under the Scheme of Agriclinics & Agri - Buisness Centres."
31 Fitzsimmons, "Us, Them, and Others in Management Research."
32 Fine, "Working the Hyphens: Reinventing Self and Other in Qualitative Research," 73–74.
33 Peverelli and Song, "Chinese Entrepreneurship: A Social Capital Approach."

with the absurdity of an 'academic drop-out' hailed (positively as) a 'hero' by academia.[34]

The researcher as the Other

While autoethnography implicitly avoids 'Othering' the objects of study—that is to say, avoids committing the entrepreneur 'subject' to the class Other—the danger is that, with the suppression of identity, the researcher becomes the Other: no longer a member of 'us', the class of academe. The researcher becomes either a self-absorbed narcissist, failing their scholarly duty to hypothesize, analyse, contextualize, and theorize; or is simply a 'literary poseur', caring little for nuanced literary imagination.[35]

Carolyn Ellis argues that the autoethnographer's challenge is to resist a defensive or attacking posture against the critics of autoethnography and their 'Othering'. Rather, autoethnographers must first establish the efficacy of their approach, particularly given the difficulty of intellectually referencing supporting techniques and procedures for controlling subjectivity.[36] Here, autoethnography (or self-ethnography, or insider research), with its introspective focus, is problematic. Insider researchers are perceived to be 'too close'. They are held to lack the intellectual distance and objectivity required for valid research.[37] Furthermore, their focus on their own experiences to the exclusion of other 'Others', unnecessarily narrows a rich field of inquiry.[38]

Resolving the 'us' in Others

As a point of resolution, I take Stephen Gould's suggestion that the uniqueness of a behaviour, and its recognition by introspection, is such an evident and prominent part of lived experience that we should not ignore it.[39] Paraphrasing Michel de Montaigne, the sixteenth-century philosopher, Morris Holbrook commented: 'I believe that—because I am human—when I write about myself, I inevitably describe some aspect of the human condition'.[40]

---

[34] Watt, "The Rise of the 'Dropout Entrepreneur': Dropping out, 'Self-Reliance' and the American Myth of Entrepreneurial Success."

[35] Ellis, "Fighting Back or Moving on an Autoethnographic Response to Critics."

[36] Alvesson, "Methodology for Close up Studies - Struggling with Closeness and Closure."

[37] Brannick and Coghlan, "In Defense of Being 'Native': The Case for Insider Academic Research."

[38] Wallendorf and Brucks, "Introspection in Consumer Research: Implementation and Implications."

[39] Gould, "The Emergence of Consumer Introspection Theory (CIT): Introduction to a JBR Special Issue."

[40] Holbrook, "Customer Value and Autoethnography: Subjective Personal Introspection and the Meanings of a Photograph Collection," 45.

Holbrook's autoethnographic goal was to illuminate some aspect of humanity. In context, when the entrepreneur as researcher writes about their 'self', s/he inevitably describes some aspect of the human condition that is enterprise.[41] Here, the value of autoethnography lies in exploring multiple layers of (un-)consciousness, multiple selves, and the interplay of narrative and story.[42]

Stories are a specific type of narrative which reflect the voice, thinking, and perceptions of people; their interpretations provide a valuable basis for sensemaking. They provide a means for transposing a *social presence* that respects both its rational mode of being in specified temporal, finite reality, and an irrational mode of being influenced by individual psychology. Stories are separated from narrative by the concept of plot, a link between the rationality of setting and events, and the feelings and emotions of its actors.[43] In the critical perspective of a negative dialectic, stories are evocative; they can loosen readers' ties, creating spaces of ambiguity; and allow contradictory paradigms to co-exist.[44] They can also be antagonistic and absurd. Therefore, resolving the 'us' in 'Others' requires that other researchers discover my research experience, interpreting my analysis through their own experiences.[45] In this respect, my challenge is to present both narrative and story in a form that, together, or separately, the 'we' that is 'us', may constitute a meaningful understanding of the 'Others'. Viewing my autobiographical story through an olio of (non)conceptual, fictional perspectives, allows for a critical introspection with me firmly at the heart of my inquiry.

Writing the 'self' as the Other

The final piece of the methodic jigsaw is the form of the autoethnographic writing itself. Here, Creative Non-fiction (CNF) provides a genre in which: situation, story, character, scenes, summaries and exposition find a place in ethnographic writing[46]; it provides reflections on cross-cultural study[47]; it helps explicate the lived and living fieldwork process in organizational and management research[48]; and it links narrative accounts in consumer

---

[41] Venkataraman, "The Distinctive Domain of Entrepreneurship Research."
[42] Boje and Tyler, "Story and Narrative Noticing: Workaholism Autoethnographies."
[43] Soin and Scheytt, "Making the Case for Narrative Methods in Cross-Cultural Organizational Research."
[44] Islam, "Finding a Space for Story: Sensemaking, Stories and Epistemic Impasse."
[45] Ricci, "Autoethnographic Verse: Nicky's Boy: A Life in Two Worlds."
[46] Narayan, "Tools to Shape Texts : What Creative Nonfiction Can."
[47] Waldern, "Impressing Heaven: Creative Non-Fiction as Reflective Practice in Foreign Language Teaching and Cross Cultural Study."
[48] Cole, "Stories from the Lived and Living Fieldwork Process."

research.[49] Yet it has its critics, with much CNF-labelled output neither good writing nor useful social commentary.[50] However, while not specifically citing CNF, Stephen Brown[51] offers a useful rebuttal:

> '...well-written introspective accounts succeed in capturing the world in a grain of sand.... [They] do not represent the truth in any absolute, neo-positivistic sense... but they are not necessarily unreliable, invalid or untrue either... If they were, creative writers—not to mention autobiographical literary critics—would be in very serious trouble... introspection is an integral part of literary insight and expression'.

I argue, therefore, that the aim of using CNF in writing the Other must, first and foremost, be a well-written account, calling on the appropriate CNF tools to shape the introspective text.[52] It must use scenes, dialogue, description, and first-person points of view, yet consistently remaining truthful and factual.[53] Here, I argue that truth speaks to our responsibility as human beings to answer to Others, for—and to—our lives. This responsibility carries with it the acceptance that the only truth the 'self' can hope to approach, will be the truth of the 'self'[54]—a truth that speaks to Montaigne's entire human estate.[55]

I am an entrepreneur. I seek, in writing my 'truthful self' as the Other, to close the gap between my 'self' and the Other, reconciling my 'self' as entrepreneur and the Other as entrepreneur. My aim is not that I conceptualise a reified, objective hero(ine) in the Other, nor my 'self'. Rather—in story terms—it is that I believe we should come to understand, as an intellectual experience, the entrepreneur as the non-conceptual character 'hero(ine)' as s/he emerges from an antagonistic reality, on an entrepreneurial journey, in which Joseph Campbell's classic image is: '...the man or woman who has been able to battle past his [sic] personal and local historical

---

49 Hackley, "Auto-Ethnographic Consumer Research and Creative Non-Fiction: Exploring Connections and Contrasts from a Literary Perspective."

50 Hackley.

51 Brown, "The Wind in the Wallows: Literary Theory, Autobiographical Criticism and Subjective Personal Introspection," 27.

52 Narayan, "Tools to Shape Texts : What Creative Nonfiction Can."

53 Gutkind, "Roundtable: What Is Creative Nonfiction? Two Views - Why I Chose the Creative Nonfiction Way of Life."

54 Lott, "Roundtable: What Is Creative Nonfiction? Two Views - Toward a Definition of Creative Nonfiction."

55 The word estate, in this sense, is relatively obsolete. It is taken in this study to relate to concepts such as race, breed, caste, and class. Jünger, The Worker: Dominion and Form.

limitations to the generally valid, normally human forms'.[56] Understanding the non-conceptual identity of the entrepreneur as hero(ine) is understanding the entrepreneur as a MacIntyrean 'social character'[57]: 'a stock figure which provides an interpretation of the actions of those individuals who act in character… a moral representative of their socio-cultural origin'.[58] This objectively positions the 'entrepreneur', along with the 'manager', 'scientist', and 'artist', among the essential stock characters of society.

Non-conceptually, the social character plays a similar role to Max Weber's (Weberian) concept *idealtypus.* However, in the context of entrepreneurship, the social character of 'The Entrepreneur' is the negation of the *conceptually pure* ideal *entrepreneur.* Following Thomas Segady,[59] the social character forms a heuristic against which we may seek to better understand the social behaviour of entrepreneurs and the culture of entrepreneurship. Like the *idealtypus,* the social character of 'The Entrepreneur' is a construct, neither historical reality nor true reality. It is a synthesis of a great many diffuse, discrete, more-or-less present and occasionally absent, concrete individual entrepreneurs which are arranged according to those idiographic viewpoints into a unified whole.[60] Yet, unlike the *idealtypus,* the social character respects the nature of the absurd. Here, I am not so much concerned with the 'self' as entrepreneur, as with the journey of the 'self' to the Other—how the 'self' emerges within the oftentimes absurd, antagonistic reality. Thus, I posit that coming to know the social character of 'The Entrepreneur' requires an intimate, truthful knowledge of the journey. Writing the 'self' as Other is writing the journey of the 'self' to the Other—a quest for 'Otherness'. Critically, this eschews the elevation of the self to hero(ine)—avoiding the fantasy of the heroic entrepreneur[61] as the Žižekian *Sublime Object.*[62] Thus, facing the Other, and in writing my 'self' as the Other, I seek neither to reify nor violate 'The Entrepreneur' as Other.[63]

The story: setting the plot…

Heroic images of entrepreneurs, such as Mark Zuckerberg, Steve Jobs, Bill Gates and Richard Branson, dominate the general perception of entrepreneurship.[64] Here, the dominant (written) narratives comprise

---

[56] Campbell, The Hero with a Thousand Faces, 14.
[57] MacIntyre, After Virtue.
[58] Atkinson, Thinking the Art of Management: Stepping into "Heidegger's Shoes," 4.
[59] Segady, "The Utility of Weber's Ideal Type: Verstehen and the Theory of Critical Mass."
[60] Segady, "The Utility of Weber's Ideal Type: Verstehen and the Theory of Critical Mass."
[61] Johnsen and Sørensen, "Traversing the Fantasy of the Heroic Entrepreneur."
[62] Žižek, The Sublime Object of Ideology.
[63] Segady, "The Utility of Weber's Ideal Type: Verstehen and the Theory of Critical Mass."
[64] Johnsen and Sørensen, "Traversing the Fantasy of the Heroic Entrepreneur."

biography and autobiography. The biographic form may provide a non-theoretical, heuristic role in offering insight into individual cases and broad subjects, such as entrepreneurship.[65] However, in reviewing exemplars in the biographies of both Steve Jobs and Van Gogh, Joep Cornelissen argued that narrative study suggests there may be important oversights and oversimplifications in extant entrepreneurship scholarship. This argument is qualified with the observation that, if anything, the unrivalled access of the biographers (in both exemplars) results in narratives that favour the single person—the single entrepreneur—and their success, or lack of it. Others with a relationship to the entrepreneur appear side-lined. And an extant dialectic ToM posits that we then subjectify their experience of entrepreneurship.

Christian Johnsen and Bent Sørensen take the autobiographic form as their mode of investigation of Richard Branson, commenting that Branson's narrative of the 'self' generates the paradoxical desire for transgression and authenticity. The autobiographical 'self', circulating in social media and popular culture, is seen to be 'ridden with paradoxes, impossibilities and contradictions'.[66] But, while such contradictions promise a rich narrative, 'the cultural reception of the story is not focused on the storytelling but on the entrepreneur telling the story... admired and attributed with sometimes mythical capabilities'.[67] Thus, both the idiographic biographic and the autobiographic 'self' appear to offer little insight into the essential stock social character of the entrepreneur. This lack of insight is a herald's call to a journey—the Quest—not for the hero(ine), but the making of the hero(ine).

> "It is nearly Christmas. Next year, 2012, I must steel myself for the inevitable journey. A quest to regain meaning and purpose. Over the years, I have come to define my purpose in life is to travel, almost regardless of direction, always across the boundary of my knowledge—a relentless pursuit of entrepreneurship.
>
> I ask myself, 'do I feel lucky?' [68]

Here plot privileges action in the name of character. But it is not a device to facilitate the theoretical reduction of the autoethnographic narrative into the

---

[65] Cornelissen, "Portrait of an Entrepreneur : Vincent van Gogh , Steve Jobs , and the Entrepreneurial Imagination."

[66] Johnsen and Sørensen, "Traversing the Fantasy of the Heroic Entrepreneur."

[67] Steyaert, "Of Course That Is Not the Whole (Toy) Story: Entrepreneurship and the Cat's Cradle," 734.

[68] Excerpt from: Atkinson, Unpublished Manuscript.

generic plot of the Quest.[69] Andrew Popp and Robin Holt [70] are critical of narratives emplotted through structures with a dominant beginning, middle and end—they argue they foreclose on the very 'undecidedness' by which entrepreneurship is made possible. However, their argument obscures the point of story as a vehicle for understanding. Rather, I argue the construction of the narrative of the 'self', through plot structure, simply ensures a 'good story'; something worth telling, that the world wants to hear,[71] and that resonates with its readership—'us'—by permitting a wide, diverse engagement with the Other. We have only to follow, as Joseph Campbell commented:

> '...a multitude of heroic figures through the classic stages of the universal adventure ...to see again what has always been revealed. This will help us to understand not only the meaning of those images of contemporary life, but also the singleness of the human spirit in its aspirations, powers, vicissitudes, and wisdom.' [72]

As Christopher Booker reminds us, no story plot is more recognisable than the Quest (Table 3.1).[73] Aligning the entrepreneurial narrative within a recognisable structure leverages the innate understanding of a story that is culturally embedded in the human psyche. We—the 'us'—are not left with an indeterminate Other; we are able to call on our stock, MacIntyrean, social characters, within a recognisable plot structure. We are thus guided to approach something of the meaning of 'the Other' through a familiarity of context, if not detail. As Booker relates:

'Stories take shape in the human imagination round certain archetypal patterns and images which are the common property of mankind... [At] the deepest level, the essence of the message they [relay] is always the same'.[74]

Table 3.1. The quest: an overview

Journey Aspect	**Plot point in brief...**
The Call	The Hero(ine) is given visionary direction as to the distant, life-renewing goal for which s/he must aim.

---

[69] See, for example: Booker, The Seven Basic Plots: Why We Tell Stories.
[70] Popp and Holt, "Entrepreneurship and Being: The Case of the Shaws."
[71] McKee, Story: Style, Structure, Substance, and the Principles of Screenwriting.
[72] Campbell, The Hero with a Thousand Faces, 28.
[73] Booker, The Seven Basic Plots: Why We Tell Stories.
[74] Booker, The Seven Basic Plots: Why We Tell Stories, 543.

The Hero(ine)'s Companions	The distinctive mark of the Quest is that The Hero(ine) is not alone on the adventure.
The Journey (its antagonisms):	A succession of terrible, often near-fatal ordeals (things) mixed with periods of respite (other things):
Monsters	To be overcome
Temptations	To be resisted
The deadly opposites	To travel between, on an exact and perilous path
The journey to the underworld	To consider or consult with the lives of those who have lived before – the spirits of the dead
The Helpers	Provide positive assistance—from shelter and rest to advice and guidance, including the benevolent and wise, and the young and beautiful.
Arrival & Frustration	In sight of the goal, but far from reaching it.
The Final Ordeals	A last series of tests to prove worthiness, including the last great battle for the goal.
The Goal	Attainment of the life-transforming goal (the Object of Desire), with the promise of renewed life.

(Source: author, adapted from Booker[75])

While Booker's classic work maps seven basic plots, of which *The Quest* is one, Robert McKee argues all stories take the form of a quest:

> 'For better or worse, an event throws a character's life out of balance, arousing ...the conscious and/or unconscious desire for that which ...will restore balance, launching ...a Quest for the Object of Desire against forces of antagonism (inner, personal, extra-personal). [The character] may or may not achieve it. This is story in a nutshell.'[76]

In March 2014, I launched a new restaurant and craft beer bar. Within weeks, the business was nominated for, and won, 'Best Newcomer' in the local hospitality and tourism awards. In its first year, we garnered three awards from nine shortlists. In our second year, we launched a franchise and raised significant funds through crowdfunding. We launched a range of fresh food products into UK supermarkets in late 2016 and were rewarded with a national food magazine's 'Best New Product' award in August 2017. But, by the

---

[75] Booker, The Seven Basic Plots: Why We Tell Stories, 69-86.
[76] McKee, Story: Style, Structure, Substance, and the Principles of Screenwriting, 196.

end of September 2017, the company was in administration. Despite our achievements and its potential, it failed.

Given my desire to draw on this experience, I decided to frame an autoethnographic narrative within the plot structure of the Quest. *How to Start a Business and Fail*[77] is the working title of an unpublished manuscript. It tells a true story—a narrative introspective on the business of food and entrepreneurship. The story of the company is set to the archetypal plot of the Quest. It is also a design in five parts: an *Inciting Incident* (or Call to Action), which puts into motion the other four parts of *Progressive Complications, Crisis, Climax* and *Resolution.*[78] The story *How to Start a Business and Fail* presents material concerning the business in a way that is analogous to learning about the culture of entrepreneurship in the field.[79]

The poetics of the story

Suspending the distinction between fiction (the imaginary plane) and non-fiction (a material reality) within story, Aristotelian 'Poetics'[80] gives us plot as comprising the characteristics of completeness, magnitude, unity, determinate structure, universality, and its objects of character, in which everyone is differentiated in character by (negative) defect or (positive) excellence. In applying story to entrepreneurship, I follow Aristotle. The plot is the source and soul of the entrepreneurship story: it is the imitation of an action in praxis (of entrepreneurship) that is: admirable; complete; has magnitude; is performed by actors—agents of a certain (social) character; and effects emotional catharsis.

While plot is the source, characters are second. On the one hand, a character is a story's agent: it aspires to its goal and is the object of action, while other characters may help or hinder access to the goal. On the other hand, actions within the plot are held as expressions of its characters. They reveal the characters for who they are, objectively. Thus, story analysis reveals not only what characters do, but also who they are. Characters, as autonomous figures, allow us to assess them as we assess real people.[81] This is counter to the prevailing idiographic focus on character as symptomatic of the dominant

---

[77] Atkinson, Unpublished Manuscript.
[78] McKee, Story: Style, Structure, Substance, and the Principles of Screenwriting.
[79] Maggio, "The Anthropology of Storytelling and the Storytelling of Anthropology."
[80] Aristotle, Poetics.
[81] Nanda and Kropf, "Financing Entrepreneurial Experimentation"; Rhoads, Dewey, and Michie, Mark as Story: An Introduction to the Narrative of a Gospel.

(subjective) myth of the 'self-determining individual'[82]—an ideological impetus calling for critical reflection. As Aristotle argued, there could not be an imitation of an action without action, but there can be without character.[83] Plot holds an implicit recognition that the quest cannot be achieved, let alone attempted, without a cast of others—characters as substantive entities offering better access to the 'truth' of a story; plot remains primary.

The unpublished story of my business is complete in the Aristotelian sense. It has a beginning which does not necessarily follow from anything else, yet it gives rise to things which naturally occur after it. It has an end, which naturally follows the things which precede it, but which does not have anything naturally to follow it. And it has a middle, which comes after something else; some other thing occurs after it. My story neither begins nor ends at arbitrary points in the history of my venture. It has a magnitude (as a manuscript) that is significant (the size of an average novel), and it does not stray from convention. The story possesses unity—yet it does not aim to relay all things that happened between its beginning and its end. Neither is the plot unified by one single character; it is unified through the 'entrepreneurial' action in praxis, from the beginning of the venture to its end. Finally, it is structured such that the removal of any one section of the story would dislocate and change the whole.

Having suspended the distinction between fiction and non-fiction, between the imaginary and the real, it is necessary to acknowledge that, at its heart, the story of my business is a true story, based on historical record (effectively a journal). Its function is two-fold. On the one hand, it tells of what things have happened. However, the call to creative non-fiction and the determinate structure of Booker's archetypal plot—'The Quest'—suggests the story's potential for universality. Thus, on the other hand, the story tells of the things that would (or could) happen in an entrepreneurial action. The aim of the story is to reveal its nomothetic promise in praxis. Whereas a fictional story's narrative must be designed around its premise,[84] the nomothetic promise of the non-fiction story is that its premise is revealed through narrative, *post hoc*.

A call to action

I begin with the reason why. For my Hero(ine) I adopt the fictitious persona, 'Hermaphroditus', avoiding gender stereotyping and the association with the

---

[82] Rhisiart and Jones-Evans, "The Impact of Foresight on Entrepreneurship: The Wales 2010 Case Study"; Elliott, "'Witless in Your Own Cause': Divine Plots and Fractured Characters in the Life of Aesop and the Gospel of Mark."

[83] Aristotle, Poetics.

[84] Egri, The Art of Dramatic Writing: Its Basis in the Creative Interpretation of Human Motives.

typically reified masculine hero concept. Thus, for Hermaphroditus to remain quietly in place, in some form of *status quo,* is impossible (or at least untenable). 'Some fearful threat has arisen. The "times are out of joint". Something has gone seriously and terrifyingly wrong'.[85] While such stimuli to entrepreneurship may, on the face of it, seem a little too creative, even the threat of (the consequence of) inaction in the face of overwhelming opportunity might constitute an untenable position in which to remain. Certainly, the absurdly volatile markets of recent years can be argued to represent *times out of joint* and, given the turbulence caused by the impact of the Covid-19 pandemic, the loss of secure employment represents a feasible stimulus to action.

> 'Yes. It's not working. ...There's just no money about. ...We want your resignation. We're going to put the head-hunting subsidiary into liquidation. When you've signed that off, that's it, I'm afraid.' He pauses, briefly. 'That's it,' he says.
>
> 'That's it?' I should shout. ...I am silent. From somewhere within my fog of confusion, I hear Stuart tell me he has arranged an appointment with a Company Administrator. I turn and stare out of the window. ...I do not know what to say. I say nothing. Stuart leaves my office.[86]

Identifying the entrepreneur by a 'calling' is a non-functional definition, referring to a value system based on some divine or otherwise non-empirical source.[87] It is a non-conceptual definition, in which the entrepreneur emerges as consequential to some other aspect(s) of reality. It is allied to the study of entrepreneurial motivations and intent, where Scott Shane and his colleagues argue the importance of understanding the role of motivation in the entrepreneurial process.[88] Even sociologists who have argued against trait-based entrepreneurship research, implicitly acknowledge that motivation must matter. Entrepreneurship involves human agency; it occurs because people act to pursue opportunity. But the question remains: why? What is it about certain people—entrepreneurs—that drives them to take on the (oftentimes absurd) risk, the uncertainty and the independent structure of entrepreneurship?[89] Why answer the entrepreneurial Call to Action?

---

[85] Booker, The Seven Basic Plots: Why We Tell Stories, 70.
[86] Excerpt from: Atkinson, Unpublished Manuscript.
[87] Hartmann, "Managers and Entrepreneurs: A Useful Distinction?"
[88] Shane, Locke, and Collins, "Entrepreneurial Motivation Objectives."
[89] Segal, Borgia, and Schoenfeld, "The Motivation to Become an Entrepreneur."

The pull and push of desire

The Call to Action is fundamental to the plot. Here, Gerry Segal, Dan Borgia, and Jerry Schoenfeld[90] argued that, as humans can think about possible future outcomes, decide which outcomes are most desirable, and whether it is feasible to pursue attaining these outcomes, it is contradictory to expect people to pursue outcomes that they perceive to be either undesirable or unfeasible. This argument implies a dialectic ToM; it is framed by Victor Vroom's Expectancy Theory (ET).[91] The entrepreneur questions: 1) is entrepreneurship desirable to me? and 2) is entrepreneurship feasible for me?[92] But a Call to Action that invokes (potentially absurd) risk and uncertainty is counter-intuitive—it is also counter-theoretical from the ET perspective. However, it would be reasonable to expect that people might pursue outcomes that they perceive to be either somewhat undesirable or somewhat unfeasible, if other possible outcomes (including the *status quo*) were more undesirable or more unfeasible. Here, there is a sense in which undesirability and unfeasibility evoke individualistic notions of distress, including fear and pity—distinctive features of Aristotle's notion of plot. Certainly, drawing on Neil Anderson, Carsten De Dreu, and Bernard Nijstad's work,[93] the notion of a distress-related Call to Action appeals to the sense in which negatively connotative phenomena, such as: global pandemics, threats to job security, job dissatisfaction, conflict, budget deficiencies and shrinking markets, may all generate creative, entrepreneurial responses to alleviate distress.

In my ethical and responsible facing of the Other, I am left with a non-conceptual,[94] Pull-Push hypothesis for The Call to Entrepreneurial Action,[95] either: a Pull—a consequence of the positive attraction of independence, self-fulfilment, wealth, and other desirable outcomes; or a Push—a consequence of negative external forces, such as job dissatisfaction, low income, or inflexible work arrangements—a desire for something better (more positive). There is an empirical foundation to this hypothesis. For example, Benjamin

---

[90] Segal, Borgia, and Schoenfeld, "The Motivation to Become an Entrepreneur."
[91] Vroom, Work and Motivation.
[92] Segal, Borgia, and Schoenfeld, "The Motivation to Become an Entrepreneur."
[93] Anderson, De Dreu, and Nijstad, "The Routinization of Innovation Research: A Constructively Critical Review of the State-of-the-Science."
[94] The pull-push hypothesis is non-conceptual in the sense that one might experience a pull or a push to what might only later be identified as entrepreneurial action, without acknowledging or presuming any such prior concept as entrepreneur, entrepreneurship, or entrepreneuring. (See, for example: Heck, "Nonconceptual Content and the 'Space of Reasons.'")
[95] See, for example: Amit and Muller, "'Push' and 'Pull' Entrepreneurship."

Gilad and Philip Levine[96] concluded that some individuals are pulled into the entrepreneurial game by the opportunity prospect associated with expected economic expansion, while others are pushed into entrepreneurship by lingering unemployment. As a further example, anecdotally at least, there are multiple stories of parents who have helped start an autistic child's business, simply so that they may overcome the difficulty of finding employment.[97] Granted, the ontic classification entrepreneur by a media extolling positivity may be attractive, yet it hides a discourse of violence against the autistic Other's true self. Thus, the Pull-Push hypothesis fits the plot's requirement for a Call to Action. The Pull or Push must suggest that the plot's outcome(s) will be such that not to embark on the entrepreneurial journey will lead to outcomes that are significantly less desirable than the risk of failure. Thus, after McKee,[98] the story begins:

> 'Hermaphroditus [lives] a life that's more-or-less in balance. There are successes and failures, ups and downs. Who doesn't have those? But life is in relative control. Then, decisively, something occurs that radically upsets its balance, swinging the value-charge of Hermaphroditus' antagonistic reality either to the negative (push) or to the positive (pull).

Understanding the motivation of Hermaphroditus is key to understanding The Quest. What does Hermaphroditus want, to restore balance to his/her life?

McKee suggests that, for the most admirable Hero(in)es, the Call to Action arouses both conscious and unconscious desires (or interests). The significance I draw is that entrepreneurial motivation is complex. It exists on both conscious and subconscious levels, where the notion of subconscious entrepreneurial motivation appeals to Keynes' account of the 'Animal Spirits' of Capitalism,[99] and is rooted in Sigmund Freud's writings on the content of the unconscious.[100]

---

[96] Gilad and Levine, "A Behavioral Model of Entrepreneurial Supply."

[97] See for example Stolman, "Entrepreneurship Is How Families Are Creating Meaningful Jobs for Their Children With Autism Spectrum Disorder." Also, I reflect, my own entrepreneurial journey started around 2000, after I (at the time an undiagnosed autistic adult) found it difficult to obtain meaningful employment.

[98] McKee, Story: Style, Structure, Substance, and the Principles of Screenwriting, 190.

[99] Winslow, "Keynes and Freud: Psychoanalysis and Keynes's Account of the 'Animal Spirits' of Capitalism"; Barnett, "Keynes, Animal Spirits, and Instinct: Reason plus Intuition Is Better than Rational."

[100] Freud, The Essentials of Psycho-Analysis.

The psychology of the call

Given the mind-self connection in this inquiry, linking autoethnography and psychology appears to be a good methodological fit.[101] To Freud, the conscious and un- or sub-conscious interests are related. Conscious interests are transformations of primary ones.[102] Here, Freud argued that through childhood, many (natural) primary interests are repressed—becoming unconscious—replaced by conscious interests that preserve a symbolism with the primary ones, but which do not provoke hostility and opposition to the same extent. Primary interests are the natural drives and instincts that guide our human nature and *supra-instinctual* propensity for survival.[103] Yet, as children, we are conditioned to repress the excesses of these primary instincts, to subsist within an agreed ethical[104] and socially moral framework—to be good citizens.

Intellectually, the (dialectically informed) conscious interests of our conditioning become the focus of our attention on their own account; our attention is directed to them because of their (ideologically) real properties and not merely because of their symbolic connection with our unconscious interests. 'This is why human hunger, desire, and explosive anger do not proceed unchecked toward feeding frenzy, sexual assault, and murder'.[105] We become progressively more (ideologically) rational about our conscious interests.[106] Conversely, we are seen to be irrational about our suppressed primary interests. Here, Freud further argued that rationalism may regress to irrationalism if the transformative process (from subconscious primary interest to conscious interest) is interrupted or faces obstacles at an earlier stage. This can lead to a mix of rational and irrational motivations, which will vary, dependent on (*inter alia*): an individual's environmental and constitutional situation.

---

101 Ellis and Adams, "The Purposes, Practices, and Principles of Autoethnographic Research."

102 Winslow, "Keynes and Freud: Psychoanalysis and Keynes's Account of the 'Animal Spirits' of Capitalism."

103 Damasio, Descartes' Error.

104 Following Lévinas (see Chapter 2), an agreed ethics in this context is counter to the more fundamental (natural) ethic of responsibility in facing the Other. In a sense, there is no provision that may prevent an agreed ethic denying the ethic of responsibility to face the Other, and may therefore, under certain conditions of 'agreement' constitute (or at least risk) an ethic of violence toward certain Others. The case of labeling autistic self-employed individuals as entrepreneurs may constitute a legitimated violence against those autistic individuals excluded from the workplace.

105 Damasio, Descartes' Error, 123.

106 Winslow, "Keynes and Freud: Psychoanalysis and Keynes's Account of the 'Animal Spirits' of Capitalism."

Keynes refers to the subconscious (irrational) interests of Money-loving, Money-making, and a Sadistic-love-of-power.[107] His call on the primitive instinct (or irrational, subconscious primary interest), and the more deliberate reason (or rational conscious interest), as existing as natural animal spirits or evolved functions of the human mind (respectively)—and their relation to each other—is significant for understanding how economic and other policies might be framed by policymaking bodies.[108] In context, a call to Entrepreneurial Action raises the question: What is the balance of 'rational' and 'irrational' needs in entrepreneurial motivation?

John Maynard Keynes' call on instinct is evident in his 'Animal Spirits' and the notion of a 'spontaneous urge to action'.[109] However, despite the notion of spontaneity, as in any sense relevant to entrepreneurial action,[110] there can be no suggestion of a general spontaneous urge to entrepreneurship without premeditation or external stimuli (our Call to Action). This gives some efficacy to the notion that human actions are weighed on the conscious and/or subconscious levels. Following Antonio Damasio,[111] we are generally not given to spontaneous *feeding frenzies, sexual assaults, and murders.* We would not expect spontaneous action toward hoarding money. Such action first requires a conscious or subconscious desire to assuage a Keynesian Money-loving interest. Venturing is thus an action that might assuage a Money-making urge. Here we can usefully substitute the term 'irrational' for 'spontaneous'. To paraphrase Keynes, we might say that:

> '...there is the instability due to ...human nature that a large proportion of our positive activities depend on **irrational** optimism. Most, probably, of our decisions to do something [seemingly] positive, [are due to our] animal spirits – [to] an **irrational** urge to action.' [112]

---

[107] Winslow, "Keynes and Freud: Psychoanalysis and Keynes's Account of the 'Animal Spirits' of Capitalism."

[108] Barnett, "Keynes, Animal Spirits, and Instinct: Reason plus Intuition Is Better than Rational."

[109] Keynes, "The General Theory of Employment, Interest and Money."

[110] Chiles, Bluedorn, and Gupta, "Beyond Creative Destruction and Entrepreneurial Discovery: A Radical Austrian Approach to Entrepreneurship"; Hmieleski and Corbett, "The Contrasting Interaction Effects of Improvisational Behavior with Entrepreneurial Self-Efficacy on New Venture Performance and Entrepreneur Work Satisfaction"; Lachmann, The Legacy of Max Weber.

[111] Damasio, Descartes' Error.

[112] Cited in: Barnett, "Keynes, Animal Spirits, and Instinct: Reason plus Intuition Is Better than Rational," 383.

This substitution supports Keith Hmieleski and Andrew Corbett's conclusion that effective entrepreneurship tends to a blend of both planned (rational) and unplanned (irrational) action.[113]

Turning Maslow on his head

I follow McKee's suggestion that, for the most admirable Hero(in)es, the Call to Action arouses both conscious and unconscious desires. What does Hermaphroditus want (or need), to restore balance to his/her life? What conscious and subconscious interests motivate what kinds of entrepreneurial action, to restore balance to the entrepreneur's life—to reach a new *status quo*? Here, I turn to one of the most influential motivation theories in management and organizational behaviour. Abraham Maslow's NT posits that individuals prioritize physiological needs, moving through a hierarchy, from the satisfaction of basic, essential safety and social needs (belonging and self-esteem), through to the higher needs associated with self-actualization.[114]

Over time, Maslow's NT has garnered major critiques. One of these is NT's relevance to social interaction and culture, which is subverted by its reductionist, individualistic approach to the human being. Social needs, which include love, esteem, prestige and status, are relegated to stages three and four, and hardly feature at all at the fifth level of self-actualization.[115] Such individualism results in a needs-based ethics that understands goodness, virtue, and rights in instinctual, subjectivist, and relativist terms; its moral imperative is 'be yourself'.[116] But, despite its critics, NT holds contemporary relevance as an existential-humanistic-positive theory of motivation, in which individuals construe the ideal life as one which holds no threat to the gratification of one's most dominant need.[117]

---

[113] Hmieleski and Corbett, "The Contrasting Interaction Effects of Improvisational Behavior with Entrepreneurial Self-Efficacy on New Venture Performance and Entrepreneur Work Satisfaction."

[114] Winston, Maher, and Easvaradoss, "Needs and Values: An Exploration"; D'Souza and Gurin, "The Universal Significance of Maslow's Concept of Self-Actualization"; Winston, "An Existential-Humanistic-Positive Theory of Human Motivation"; Acevedo, "A Personalistic Appraisal of Maslow's Needs Theory of Motivation: From 'Humanistic' Psychology to Integral Humanism"; Trigg, "Deriving the Engel Curve: Pierre Bourdieu and the Social Critique of Maslow's Hierarchy of Needs."

[115] Trigg, "Deriving the Engel Curve: Pierre Bourdieu and the Social Critique of Maslow's Hierarchy of Needs."

[116] Acevedo, "A Personalistic Appraisal of Maslow's Needs Theory of Motivation: From 'Humanistic' Psychology to Integral Humanism."

[117] Winston, "An Existential-Humanistic-Positive Theory of Human Motivation."

Maslow's NT employs two key notions relevant to my inquiry. Firstly, individuals move up the hierarchy of needs in relation to changes in their income.[118] However, I extend this notion by proposing that individuals move up the hierarchy by whatever means, or resource, may be on-hand or reasonably accessible at the time. This may include income but, importantly, it may also include debt. This proposal permits the consideration of evil in its humanistic psychology, a factor critically absent in Maslow's rendering.[119] For example, a required resource might be unreasonably, or unlawfully accessible, yet (perhaps absurdly, or irrationally) an individual may still be motivated to acquire it. Secondly, Maslow proposed that gratification of lower-order needs results in the emergence of higher-order needs, culminating in the need for self-actualization.[120] The suggestion is that all individuals progress sequentially through the levels, until the highest is reached. Here, I modify this notion, merely proposing that all individuals progress through the levels until they achieve a state of balance—until their current need is satiated. This may result in a simple or substantial interruption, or a cessation of progression.

The first four needs of Maslow's NT are referred to as deficit or deficiency needs (D-needs), while the need for self-actualization is referred to as a growth or being need (B-need). Here, Christine Winston notes that 'Deficit needs are qualitatively different from the higher-order needs, in that an individual is "driven" to satisfy the former but "drawn" to meet the latter'.[121] This correlates with the Pull-Push hypothesis of my Call to Action, in which the entrepreneurial individual might be drawn (Pulled) towards the satisfaction of B-needs or be driven (Pushed) towards satisfaction of D-needs. Thus, after McKee:

> '...Hermaphroditus is living a life that's more-or-less in balance. There are successes, failures, ups and downs. Who doesn't have those? But life is in relative control. Then, decisively, something occurs that radically upsets its balance. One or more D-needs arise which must be assuaged (a loss of employment and income reduces the food available for the family table; a dispute with a manager leads to toxic work conditions; an existing enterprise fails), swinging the value-charge of Hermaphroditus' antagonistic reality negative, pushing Hermaphroditus into (a new) entrepreneurial action. Or, a B-need arises. With all D-needs in

118 Trigg, "Deriving the Engel Curve: Pierre Bourdieu and the Social Critique of Maslow's Hierarchy of Needs."

119 Acevedo, "A Personalistic Appraisal of Maslow's Needs Theory of Motivation: From 'Humanistic' Psychology to Integral Humanism."

120 Winston, "An Existential-Humanistic-Positive Theory of Human Motivation."

121 Winston, "An Existential-Humanistic-Positive Theory of Human Motivation," 142.

> balance, the B-need is a focus for action (a vision or a market opportunity intrigues; boredom leads to the recall of an unstated past desire; a friend approaches with a great business plan), swinging the value-charge of Hermaphroditus' antagonistic reality positive, pulling Hermaphroditus into entrepreneurial action, putting residual D-needs into perspective.'

Given Hermaphroditus' situation, with the balance of life interrupted, why would s/he choose an entrepreneurial action over a non-entrepreneurial action? At least two possible cases arise. Firstly, if I assume a negative disturbance, such as a loss of food through loss of employment (a D-need)—both entrepreneurial and non-entrepreneurial actions might lead to a recovery of income and therefore food on the table. New employment might suggest certainty in restoring Hermaphroditus' life balance. But why take a relatively absurd high-risk action—such as the start-up of a new venture—particularly if exposed to statistics on business failure? What predisposition might there be to determine that balance might be restored, entrepreneurially?

Maslow provides little insight in relation to the above predisposition. He merely suggests that all that is on a hungry person's mind is food: 'he or she dreams food, remembers food, thinks about food, emotes only about food, perceives only food, and wants only food'.[122] The subject 'self', observing the object 'Other', might conclude a rational Other would secure food through the least-risk option. Should the Other choose a high-risk option, then it might be concluded that the Other is acting irrationally.

Secondly, if I assume a positive disturbance—such as Hermaphroditus spotting a gap in the market for a new product—the choice of action may be to embark on an indeterminate, high-risk entrepreneurial adventure, or seek some other means of assuaging the desire for positive change (a B-need). This might simply be to talk to a friend, who might assuage the positive charge by arguing their view of the irrationality of entrepreneurial action. For example, the friend might suggest the substitution of a low risk, non-entrepreneurial action. Both actions might recover balance. However, in this case, entrepreneurial action puts the balance of existing D-needs at risk. Again, why might Hermaphroditus decide to take the high-risk action? What predisposition determines that balance might be restored, entrepreneurially?

In both the above cases, the suggestion is that the entrepreneurial individual is pre-disposed to one or more (as-yet-to-be-identified) B-needs. In Maslow's NT, this is a pre-disposition to self-actualization. However, one of the most

---

[122] Winston, Maher, and Easvaradoss, "Needs and Values: An Exploration," 296.

widely contested aspects of Maslow's NT is the premise that the gratification of D-needs is a necessary precondition for self-actualization.[123] The initial conclusion must be that Maslow's NT does not fully support my analysis.

The concept of self-actualization has been found to correlate strongly with prominent theories of morality, spirituality, and utilitarianism.[124] Here, beyond further contemporary validation of Maslow's work, Jeevan D'Souza and Michael Gurin offered a need-based activity chart which describes, for differing age-groups, the measure of time that an individual might devote to their different needs to approach self-actualization. Their work acknowledged Maslow's sub-division of self-actualization, providing an eight-level hierarchy.[125] However, given the above discussion, the notion of a hierarchical structure, with each level being a pre-condition of the previous, remains unhelpful.

In Table 3.2, I follow D'Souza and Gurin by positing a Needs-consciousness model. Here, for example, I consider that it is axiomatic that children inhabit the aesthetic realm; children learn through play—creativity, touch, taste and smell are their *modus operandi.* Rather than suggesting (as D'Souza and Gurin do) the measure of time a child spends satisfying aesthetic-based needs is 'low', I have substituted the measure of *time* with *consciousness.*[126] For example, we might relate to time spent acknowledging the nature of the need, rather than fulfilling the need. In Table 3.2, in positing a Needs-consciousness model, the only change I offer to the values proposed by D'Souza and Gurin, is that childhood consciousness may be inferred as 'Low' for both love/belonging and esteem. This is not to say these needs are not present in a child, merely that the level of consciousness of the need is low.

Table 3.2. Needs-consciousness model

Need Type	Need	Consciousness			
		Childhood	**Young Adult**	**Middle Adult**	**Late Adult**
D-needs	Physiological	Low	High	Medium	Low
	Safety	Low	High	Medium	Low

---

123 Winston, Maher, and Easvaradoss, "Needs and Values: An Exploration."

124 D'Souza and Gurin, "The Universal Significance of Maslow's Concept of Self-Actualization."

125 Maslow, Motivation and Personality.

126 D'Souza and Gurin, "The Universal Significance of Maslow's Concept of Self-Actualization," 213.

	Love/Belonging	Low	High	Medium	Low
	Esteem	Low	High	Medium	Low
B-needs	Cognitive	Low	Medium	Medium	High
	Aesthetic	Low	Low	Medium	High
	Self-actualization	Low	Low	Medium	High
	Self-transcendence	Low	Low	Low	High

Note. D-needs—deficient needs; B-needs—being needs
(Source: author, based on D'Souza and Gurin)

As children, we are conditioned toward knowledge of D-needs as we learn values associated with the physiological, safety, love and belonging, and esteem. These are needs and values, conscious knowledge of which is required, more or less (dependent on our environment and/or society), to subsist within an agreed (or culturally emergent) ethical and moral framework. As young adults, we may hold a high level of consciousness about our D-needs. Intellectually, the conscious interests of our conditioning become the focus of our attention on their own account; it is directed to them, because of their real properties and not merely because of their symbolic connection with our unconscious interests. Our B-needs are negated. They are suppressed—unreachable or unattainable or unwanted and unnecessary. As we move through adulthood, we lose consciousness of our D-needs; we take them for granted. As we age, we internalize our D-needs into the realm of the unconscious. We are free to explore the boundaries of our knowledge, going beyond the limit of the current conscious, to (re)explore our B-needs.

This Needs-consciousness model supports Winslow's thesis, that we become progressively more rational about our conscious interests.[127] We become irrational about our suppressed interests. As we age, facing the observing Other, we may appear irrational about our D-needs, since we become progressively more unconscious of them. This is supported by Freud's argument that our rationalism may regress to irrationalism, where the interruption (perhaps through ill-health) of a transformative process from subconscious interest to conscious interest—such as through education—can affect our level of consciousness of any given need. Table 3.2 illustrates that the transformative process may lead to a mix of rational (high-consciousness)

[127] Winslow, "Keynes and Freud: Psychoanalysis and Keynes's Account of the 'Animal Spirits' of Capitalism."

and irrational (low-consciousness) needs. Intuitively, while this argument supports Maslow's NT at the conscious needs level, the introduction of unconscious needs—which exist in every individual—suggests the motivation necessary for people to act sub-consciously and seemingly irrationally in absurd, contrary ways.

Reflecting on Adorno's example of profit motivation (Chapter 2), transposing its reductive dialectic concept by the (negative) possibilities of the unconscious mind, the negative dialectic is simultaneously more expansive. Here, I posit that we may envisage the profit motive under the influence of Keynes' subconscious (irrational) interests of Money-loving and Money-making. Dependant on an individual's subjective interest, profit can be, for example: aesthetic (money is beautiful, more money is sublime); or self-actualisational (an instinctive call on the love of money and money making); or self-transcendental (a love of money's capacity to enable higher purpose). It may be any of these things or more.

Keynes' call on the primitive instincts (or irrational, subconscious primary interests) is resolved to B-needs. (In the newborn child all interests are subconscious, natural animal spirits.) The more deliberate instincts—or rational conscious interests, as evolved functions of the human mind—are resolved to D-needs. By allowing (or imagining) the introduction of subconscious motivations, I address the rigidity of Maslow's NT without subverting it. Thus, I return to the question in *The psychology of the call:* What is the balance of 'rational' and 'irrational' needs in entrepreneurial motivation? That is to say, does an entrepreneur have a particular balance (or mix, or ratio, or logos) of rational and irrational needs in their motivation? In response, I posit that at the start of their entrepreneurial journey, each entrepreneur has a unique balance of rational (conscious) D-needs and irrational (often suppressed, unconscious) B-needs. These needs are assumed to be more or less in balance. A disturbance in the balance of one or more needs sets up a motivation for action, which may take one of four modes, as follows.

Conscious to unconscious motivation. This is a high-risk, irrational motivation; it is either a Pull from D to B (a belief in an opportunity), or a Push from D to B (a belief in a better way). The individual is conscious of their D-needs and the associated risks of unfulfillment, but they do not fully understand their sub-conscious desire for a known opportunity (Pull), or a belief that one is worth looking for—a better way (Push), but they understand the implications of a failure in their action. However, because they are unaware of why the opportunity means so much, they remain unable to make a fully rational and objective assessment of it. The individual exposes themselves to greater risk and their action may be deemed, by degree, as being from irrational to the absurd.

Unconscious to conscious motivation. This is a high-risk, irrational motivation; it is either a Pull from D to B (knowledge of an opportunity), or a Push from D to B (knowledge of a better way). The individual is unconscious of their D-needs (and the risks associated with their unfulfillment). They fully understand what it is about the higher-level, B-needs, that interests (motivates) them about a known opportunity (Pull), or the knowledge that a better way is possible (Push). However, because they are unaware of the consequences of a failure in their action upon their D-needs, they are unable to make a fully rational, objective assessment of it. The individual is exposed to greater risk and their action may be deemed, again by degree, from the irrational to the absurd.

Conscious to conscious motivation. This is a low-risk, rational motivation; it is either a Pull from D to B (knowledge of an opportunity), or a Push from D to B (knowledge of a better way). The individual is conscious of their D-needs, and the risks associated with their unfulfillment. They fully understand what it is about the higher-level, B-needs, that interests (motivates) them about a known opportunity (Pull), or about the knowledge that a better way is possible (Push). Because they are aware of the consequences of a failure in their action upon their D-needs, and understand their motivation for it, they can make a rational and objective assessment. The individual is exposed to no greater risk—their action may be deemed rational.

Unconscious to unconscious motivation. This is a high-risk, irrational motivation, either a Pull from D to B (a belief in an opportunity), or a Push from D to B (a belief in a better way). The individual is unconscious of their D-needs, and the risks associated with their unfulfillment. Neither do they understand what it is about their higher-level B-needs, that interests (motivates) them about some opportunity (Pull), or some belief that there is a better way (Push). Because they are unaware of the consequences of a failure in their action upon their D-needs, they are unable to make a rational, objective assessment of it. In action, the individual is exposed to greater risk and their action may be deemed, by degree, from the irrational to the absurd.

Coda: March 2012

From August 2008, having suffered a failure in a venture first launched in 1999, I had reached mid-adulthood. While employment was elusive, I had restored some measure of balance. I had completed a PhD at the end of 2006, and my hard-won experience had resulted in me not taking my lot for granted. I was fully conscious of the D-needs essential in my life. Being well-educated and well-read, I was also aware of the economic and political conditions of the time. Though, in a sense, a natural risk-taker, I am also conservative and introspective. My PhD in Critical Management Studies had resulted in a great deal of time reflecting on matters. As such, I considered myself to have a high level of understanding of what life meant to me, and those close to me. My successes and failures, my ups and downs, were numerous. But there are those who have been through far worse in their lives. I was philosophical about my downs and had thought about what would happen if… But my life was in relative control. I had secured a settlement with my ex-business-partners, and I had a little capital to invest…

> 'Christ, why …don't we have one of those?'
>
> …I am relaxing, taking a break… watching American food shows on Freeview. …[I've] just seen …a fantastic idea. A five-minute piece on [a restaurant] in New York City. It's a small chain of three casual dining restaurants. …I am impressed. Filmed in the late or early hours, [it is] full of people eating …and drinking [craft] beer. It looks fun… I can't shake the idea from my head. It is a herald's call.' [128]

Given the centrality of Maslow's NT to the idea of an 'entrepreneurial' Needs-consciousness model, it is necessary for me to address one of its remaining critiques. That is, as individual needs are native, NT's relevance to social interaction and culture is subverted by its reductionist, individualistic approach to the human being.[129] Motivation is, by its nature, an individualistic phenomenon. It is antecedent to action. But motivation is directly related to actions in a praxis that generally occurs in a social milieu. I do not find a validity in the criticism levied. Indeed, it is implicit in embedding NT in the (non)concept of the enterprising Entrepreneurial Quest, that others (entrepreneurial and non-entrepreneurial) are indispensable in entrepreneurial action. As Booker argues: 'we can say "the hero and his [sic] companions" because a distinctive mark of the Quest is the extent to which, more than in any other kind of story, the hero is not alone in his adventures'.[130] Hermaphroditus does not (and cannot) venture alone.

I had no prior experience or knowledge of running a restaurant—the motivation for considering the idea of a specialist restaurant and craft beer bar was of the irrational ***Conscious to unconscious mode.*** To reduce the risk, I spent considerable time in developing the belief of the idea into knowledge,

---

[128] Excerpt from: Atkinson, Unpublished Manuscript.
[129] Trigg, "Deriving the Engel Curve: Pierre Bourdieu and the Social Critique of Maslow's Hierarchy of Needs"; Acevedo, "A Personalistic Appraisal of Maslow's Needs Theory of Motivation: From 'Humanistic' Psychology to Integral Humanism."
[130] Booker, The Seven Basic Plots: Why We Tell Stories, 71.

through a process of research, planning and forming an entrepreneurial team. At the launch of my restaurant business, in 2014, the motivation mode had become ***Conscious to conscious.*** While risks remained, they were mitigated.

The call to action

> 'The whole exercise looks academic. Is [the business] such a good idea? I haven't spent much money on developing the idea yet—only my time. It's like planning a major expedition. I've merely been gathering details, checking equipment, checking the feasibility of the journey. Would I be happier using all the money from the sale of my shares to pay down all my debts? ...We would have to sell the house, of course. ...I would never again get back onto the property ladder. Is that what I want?[131]

In this Chapter, I have taken—as a point of departure in positing a negative dialectics—a finding that the question: 'Who is The Entrepreneur?' is open to interpretation. This is not least since it is founded upon a dialectic ToM which cannot, legitimately, presume a unity of entrepreneurial action. While others have argued that a drift to an interpretive study of extant entrepreneurship practice risks losing sight of the very rationale for its being,[132] (non)conceptually, I have employed a method of story to identify something of the MacIntyrean social character of the contrary entrepreneur and their motivation. Here, axiomatically, 'story' has a far longer tradition of being used to make sense of our world than any number of extant interpretive methods.

The world of enterprise is full of stories. In the field of entrepreneurship studies, researchers have been exposed to their elements since the dawn of interest. I have grounded my argument in a theorising about negative dialectics (Chapter 2), and about story and autoethnographic narrative (in this Chapter). I have played with established concepts and the fictitious character Hermaphroditus. This has allowed me to develop an embryonic Needs-consciousness model, founded on Maslow's NT. This resurfacing of NT suggests that there are four modes of a non-concept of motivated, entrepreneurial action, each presenting a pull-push hypothesis by which an individual may be seen to determine the entrepreneurial call to enterprising action based not so much on a hierarchy but on a balance of individual needs.

Although I acknowledge the embryonic nature of this model, I argue that it has the potential to offer significant insight into the socio-economic world of enterprising work, and in understanding the place of entrepreneurial

---

131 Excerpt from: Atkinson, Unpublished Manuscript.

132 Jones and Spicer, Unmasking the Entrepreneur.

motivation. The model provides one point of access to the imaginary plane on which the contrariness of human action within an antagonistic reality can be rationalised against the positivity of an extant level of dialectic theorising. The single call for action I now offer, is an invitation to engage in storying the future of economic enterprise and entrepreneurship. In the quest ahead—an inquiry and provocation into the oftentimes absurd dance of capitalism, work and enterprise, I shall focus attention on the conscious interests of societal conditioning. But I shall do so ethically, with responsibility, with the door open to the (unconscious) contrariness of the enterprising actors I face.

Part II.
On means

Chapter 4

Entrepreneurship and unicorns?

WHAT VALUE, SCIENCE FICTIONING? While in Part I, I focussed on motivation, in this Part II, I turn to the means, to reveal something of the empiric value of the imagination. In doing so, I will develop narratives of presence in a future antagonistic reality, with four perspectives: entrepreneurship, work, international business, and capitalism itself. Here, extant futures thinking occurs in the present; it turns to reflect on the past, then forward to consider options: possible, plausible, preferable, undesirable or even surprising futures.[1] This thinking is typified in the Houston Framework Foresight (HFF) method, used to develop a 'start-to-finish' view of a domain of interest.[2] Such thinking invokes learning about 'new facts, ideas, trends, forecasts, scenarios and images of the future'.[3] While this learning occurs in the present reality, we may turn to its material past to identify trends, drivers and weak signals: patterns in historical and near-present information, indicators of possible, plausible, preferable and undesirable change; or to hint at the potential for wild cards, shocks or discontinuities—plausible uncertainties and conceivable surprises.[4] Thus, while some consider

---

[1] Mićić, The Five Futures Glasses.

[2] Hines and Bishop, "Framework Foresight: Exploring Futures the Houston Way."

[3] Rogers and Tough, "Facing the Future Is Not for Wimps," 492.

[4] Saritas and Smith, "The Big Picture - Trends, Drivers, Wild Cards, Discontinuities and Weak Signals."

futures a division of historical sociology,[5] others turn to narrative, seeking weak signals of the future in the cultural products of society.[6]

To build on the intellectual use of (fictional) story, in this Chapter, I have three objectives. Firstly, as part of my overall inquiry into capitalism, work and aesthetic enterprise, I wish to move beyond the historical and narrative themes and consider the value of a negative dialectic approach—in the first instance, within the broad, yet extant dialectic understanding of entrepreneurship praxis.[7] This is the present mainstay of capitalist enterprise. Then, in extending the application of science fiction (SF) in Futures Studies,[8] I highlight what I believe is a gap in the ontological and epistemological understanding of the use of *counterfactuals.* My second objective is therefore to close this gap by arguing for the adoption of the negative dialectic approach. Thirdly, in closing the gap, my objective is to provoke and challenge the received wisdom that futures thinking is resistant to scientific theory.[9] Given these objectives, I propose and develop the critical counterfactuals (CCF) method of a negative dialectic futures study. I then validate it by exploring the fictional future of a (non)concept of entrepreneurship.

The CCF method offers a framework well suited to studies invoking the negative dialectics of an emergence into an unknown VUCA future. In a critical scholarship vein, I seek to open a future praxis to a more reflexive critical inquiry, rather than offer a reductive, dialectic closing-down on any preferred, idealised future form. In this respect, I position CCF as a negative compliment to the HFF model. In presenting CCF, I take inspiration from asking the question: can CCF, employing SF, be useful in future thinking the

---

[5] Sardar, "The Namesake: Futures; Futures Studies; Futurology; Futuristic; Foresight-What's in a Name?"

[6] Schwarz, "The 'Narrative Turn' in Developing Foresight: Assessing How Cultural Products Can Assist Organisations in Detecting Trends."

[7] See, for example: Atherton, "A Future for Small Business? Prospective Scenarios for the Development of the Economy Based on Current Policy Thinking and Counterfactual Reasoning"; García-Olivares and Solé, "End of Growth and the Structural Instability of Capitalism-From Capitalism to a Symbiotic Economy."

[8] See, for example: Bell et al., "Science Fiction Prototypes: Visionary Technology Narratives between Futures"; Keane, Graham, and Burnes, "Literary Praxiphorical Analysis: Using Science Fiction and Fantasy to Shape Organizational Futures"; Schwarz and Liebl, "Cultural Products and Their Implications for Business Models: Why Science Fiction Needs Socio-Cultural Fiction"; Schwarz, Kroehl, and von der Gracht, "Novels and Novelty in Trend Research - Using Novels to Perceive Weak Signals and Transfer Frames of Reference."

[9] Fergnani and Chermack, "The Resistance to Scientific Theory in Futures and Foresight, and What to Do about It."

narrative of a (non)concept of entrepreneurship, as it emerges from a constellation of speculations?

I proceed as follows. Briefly, I set out the background to this inquiry into entrepreneurship—the first of my 'means' inquiries. I then explicate the negative dialectic methodology's theoretical context for a critical counter-factual method. This emerges from a distinct ontological and epistemological positioning of the emergent and its ontological character, in which I make a distinction between two modes of emergence: the phenomenal and the epiphenomenal. I then apply the negative dialectic method of CCF to explicate the emergent (non)concept of entrepreneurship, drawing on Rafael Popper[10] and others to set out its essential steps. The method starts with a process of domain mapping and future casting, identifying three core *critical uncertainties*. When combined as a complex function, using a *truth table*—a variation of a logic chart[11]—these *critical uncertainties* produce a set of *contradictory themes*, logical historical progressions. Each theme suggests a future moment—a small vignette of dialectic possibility. The set of *future moments* represent *the contradictions*.

Counterfactually, I introduce SF as a set of antagonistic vignettes of negative dialectic possibility, called *imaginations*. On an *imaginary plane*, these *imaginations* are brief SF stories—in this instance, in the form of news headlines of antagonistic events occurring in the future. My objective with this set of *imaginations*, is to overcome a narrative drive in SF, yet draw on its 'considerable illustrative force'.[12] To overcome limitations in the use of fiction as a basis for serious strategizing and policymaking, I explore relationships of coherence across the *antagonistic horizon*, between the *contradictions* grounded on the plane of a *material reality*—and the *'imaginations'* on the *imaginary plane*. Coherent relationships reveal *imaginations* of interest—'*provocations*'—which provide a focus for a rational dialogue connecting historically grounded scenarios and vignettes that are coherent, *counterfactually*, with images represented from SF (creative, imaginative thought). I end the Chapter by drawing out initial implications—*speculations* and *reconciliations*—relevant to a future, emergent (non)concept of sustainable entrepreneurship.

---

[10] Popper, "Foresight Methodolgy."
[11] Popper, "Foresight Methodolgy," 59.
[12] Popper, "Foresight Methodolgy," 60.

Background to the inquiry into entrepreneurship

In setting my ambition with this book's inquiry into the dance of capitalism, work and (aesthetic) enterprise, I am drawn to the (positive) *assumption of representation* that entrepreneurial innovation is necessary for society's growth and prosperity.[13] Certainly, historically, Jean-Baptiste Say's entrepreneurial agent was a necessary part of economic production. Yet, in considering the future around 1947, aged 19yrs, SF author Philip K. Dick (1928-1982) penned one of his first short stories: *Stability*. Dick tells of a dystopian future in which society's further progress was impossible, recalling the point in time at which it was declared that only two major inventions had been filed in the preceding years: 'The great well of human ingenuity had run dry…'.[14] Stability was declared. Draconian measures were enacted to maintain it, lest any future innovation threatened the new status quo. Thus, if value is to be perceived in examining this dystopian 'imagination'—a fictional vignette of an antagonistic future—might it raise valid questions for future entrepreneurship policy and practice?

Schumpeter's link between entrepreneurship's essential innovation and growth, set out in a *Theory of Economic Development*, is widely accepted.[15] Yet, paradoxically, might too much innovation simply tend to the marginal improvement of what has gone before, no more than variation or imitation? As William J. Baumol suggested, 'one must recall that the ease of entry for imitators calls for expectable economic profits to be driven to zero'.[16] Thus, despite entrepreneurship's global promotion, its practical success is equivocal.[17] At the end of 2019, global growth had regressed to 2016 levels, with Gross Domestic Product (GDP) estimates at circa 3% in 2019-2021. Pre-Covid-19 economies were forecast GDP growth of only 1.5% for 2022-2026, while emerging and developing economies were forecast 4.5% for the same period.[18] But, if poor growth is a global problem, what might be driving it? Given the potential for new insights, what might proponents of a dialectic

---

[13] Mckeever, Anderson, and Jack, "Entrepreneurship and Mutuality: Social Capital in Processes and Practices"; Forsman, "Innovation Capacity and Innovation Development in Small Enterprises. A Comparison between the Manufacturing and Service Sectors."
[14] Dick, "Stability," 2.
[15] Baumol, "Joseph Schumpeter: The Long Run, and the Short."
[16] Baumol, "Joseph Schumpeter: The Long Run, and the Short," 42.
[17] Wiklund and Shepherd, "Entrepreneurial Orientation and Small Business Performance: A Configurational Approach"; Lerner, "The Boulevard of Broken Dreams: Innovation Policy and Entrepreneurship"; Lucas et al., "Visions of Entrepreneurship Policy."
[18] Euromonitor International, "Global Economic Forecasts Q4 2019."

entrepreneurship do to contradict a poor growth record and enhance a long-term sustainability, in an antagonistic VUCA world?

This inquiry appeals, in part, to Atilla Öner and Özlem Kunday's call for more research into the dynamics and exploitation of technology innovation.[19] Here, reflecting in part on Chapter 3—"The contrary entrepreneur"—the reified Western 'hero' entrepreneur offers little more than a reductionist and inferior 'othering' of the 'rest'.[20] And, amid the pains of slowing economic growth, we see the paradoxical rise of the unicorn venture[21]—a mythical animal of fiction.

Theory: the critical counterfactual method

Invoking ideas from fiction, including SF, sets an ontological position.[22] Here, at least some of the objects we investigate are potentially wholly imaginary. Invoking SF in a futures thinking context is not novel,[23] yet much of its contemporary application tends to SF prototyping (SFP) or experimenting with the future as creative extrapolations of the present, along some existing technological dimension.[24] In a similar vein, I acknowledge the idea of Creative Fiction Prototyping (CFP) as inclusive of both a hard, science-based SFP and a 'softer' conceptual prototyping of social and economic issues.[25] I also highlight the idealist view of some authors that a 'prototype' expresses 'hope'—a 'consolidation of inspiration'.[26]

---

[19] Öner and Kunday, "Linking Technology Foresight and Entrepreneurship."
[20] Muñoz and Kimmitt, "Entrepreneurship and the Rest: The Missing Debate."
[21] Henrekson and Sanandaji, "Schumpeterian Entrepreneurship in Europe Compared to Other Industrialized Regions."
[22] Mason, Qualitative Researching.
[23] de Cock, "Jumpstarting the Future with Fredric Jameson: Reflections on Capitalism, Science Fiction and Utopia"; Skeates, "The Infinite City"; Livingston, "Science Fiction Models of Future World Order Systems"; Miles, "Stranger than Fiction. How Important Is Science Fiction for Futures Studies?"; Suvin, "On the Poetics of the Science Fiction Genre."
[24] Stahl et al., "The Empathic Care Robot: A Prototype of Responsible Research and Innovation"; Graham and Mehmood, "The Strategic Prototype 'Crime-Sourcing' and the Science/Science Fiction behind It"; Roberts and Middleton, "Evolving Products: From Human Design to Self-Organisation via Science Fiction Prototyping"; Nelder, "Auditory Crescendo"; Graham, Greenhill, and Callaghan, "Technological Forecasting and Social Change Special Section: Creative Prototyping"; Graham, Greenhill, and Callaghan, "Exploring Business Visions Using Creative Fictional Prototypes."
[25] Nelder, "Auditory Crescendo"; Graham, "Exploring Imaginative Futures Writing through the Fictional Prototype 'Crime-Sourcing'"; McCullagh, "Superhighway Patrolman."
[26] Bell et al., "Science Fiction Prototypes: Visionary Technology Narratives between Futures."

Some authors use the form of the SF-novel as a basis for the narrative prototyping[27] or critique[28] of specific contexts. Such applications run alongside the more traditional application of SF novels as cultural artifacts—a basis for detecting the weak signs or signals of a potential future.[29] Here, Dennis Livingston commented that '[in] the absence of data directly connected with the subject at hand it seems logical to turn to the literature of [SF] as a source of possible insight into the future'.[30] But using SF to explore the future is at least somewhat problematic.

Leaving aside the issue that to create new SF requires an ability to write a good story,[31] a skill not necessarily associated with the intellectual or academic search for meaning,[32] there are issues of a more prosaic nature. For example, Paul Raven[33] discusses the popular expectations that the SF genre carries, as having little bearing on the task in hand. It may even act against it. We see, perhaps, images of pulp fiction.[34] As Jen Southern and others suggest, much SF is optimistic and, as such, deserving of a critically reflexive approach, lest too much positivistic and idealistic optimism mislead some, and distance others.[35] As the creative process relies to a great extent on tacit knowledge, there is also the issue of any one person's creative vision of the future introducing unexamined biases—whether grounded in: hard existing science; something 'extra-terrestrial'; or the 'social', yet to be realised.[36] While such biases can be countered by a team approach to futures thinking, this is not always possible, acting to exclude some potential, more individualistic contributions.

---

27 Lee, "Schrödinger's Notebook: Shifting Real."

28 Keane, Graham, and Burnes, "Literary Praxiphorical Analysis: Using Science Fiction and Fantasy to Shape Organizational Futures."

29 Schwarz, Kroehl, and von der Gracht, "Novels and Novelty in Trend Research - Using Novels to Perceive Weak Signals and Transfer Frames of Reference"; Livingston, "Science Fiction Models of Future World Order Systems"; Bell et al., "Science Fiction Prototypes: Visionary Technology Narratives between Futures."

30 Livingston, "Science Fiction Models of Future World Order Systems," 255.

31 Graham, Greenhill, and Callaghan, "Exploring Business Visions Using Creative Fictional Prototypes."

32 Graham, Greenhill, and Callaghan, "Technological Forecasting and Social Change Special Section: Creative Prototyping."

33 Raven, "The Future's Four Quarters: Proposing a Quadrant Methodology for Strategic Prototyping in Infrastructural Contexts."

34 Miles, "Stranger than Fiction. How Important Is Science Fiction for Futures Studies?"

35 Southern et al., "Imaginative Labour and Relationships of Care: Co-Designing Prototypes with Vulnerable Communities."

36 Graham, Greenhill, and Callaghan, "Technological Forecasting and Social Change Special Section: Creative Prototyping."

In offering a critical approach, my aim is to avoid the positive, idealist 'hope' intrinsic in SFP. I also distinguish between SF and fantasy—rather than enjoin them as SF fantasy (SSF), as described by John Keane and his colleagues.[37] Here, I draw on literary criticism,[38] defining SF as the narrative genre that could not arise in the world we know (the present, material reality) but which is hypothesised on some (non)dialectic aspect of science or technology, whether human or extra-terrestrial in origin. In contrast, fantasy is primarily a heroic narrative, including swords and sorcery. It is set in invented worlds of unicorns and other mythical beasts, where magic really works. Thus, while there are cases where fantasy might be used allegorically, I do not include it in the theoretical perspective of a material (negative) dialectics. Therefore, I circumscribe a critical counter-factual method of futures thinking, as it emerges from a distinct ontological and epistemological position within a methodology of negative dialectics.

The emergent and its ontological character

In the context of scenarios, mini-scenarios and vignettes, a narrative representation may be said to be both a social construction and a mechanism for social construction. I avoid the term prototype as simply an application, rather than class of narrative. This avoidance averts, for example, the idea that I might need to (prematurely) introduce further 'types' or ontic classifications, such as socio-cultural fiction.[39] Thus, conceptually, a whole scenario (or a reduced mini-scenario) might form a prototype for exploring a new world order; while a vignette—as just one piece, scene or cameo of that scenario—might hint at one or more dimensions, aspects or states of that order, but in a denser form.[40] Here, conceptually, even fictional narrative images of a future may pose as dialectically legitimised, social constructions of a plausible truth.[41] Yet this is a systematised truth that lacks integrity.

---

[37] Keane, Graham, and Burnes, "Literary Praxiphorical Analysis: Using Science Fiction and Fantasy to Shape Organizational Futures."

[38] See, for example: Mandala, "Science Fiction and Fantasy: Language, Style, and the Critics."

[39] Schwarz and Liebl, "Cultural Products and Their Implications for Business Models: Why Science Fiction Needs Socio-Cultural Fiction."

[40] Rhisiart, "Exploring the Future for Arts and Culture Organisations through Scenarios and Vignettes."

[41] Fuller and Loogma, "Constructing Futures: A Social Constructionist Perspective on Foresight Methodology."

While some have explored the ad-hoc, even improvised nature of a 'social poetics'[42] by which emergent images of the future are created,[43] I imagine the future through SF narrative as a form of emergent '[ontological] abstraction characterised by a dialogic language of negotiated practice', much like the origin of an artwork.[44] However, before taking this idea further, I require an explication of the notion of emergence as having two distinct modes.

I acknowledge that the concept of emergence has a long tradition, spanning multiple literatures.[45] As Serhat Burmaoglu and colleagues have recently observed, the study of emergence has illuminated its inherent dynamics, with both unpredictability and predictability as competing aspects.[46] From a philosophical standpoint, the phenomenon of the emergent can be seen as a cumulative form of change, in which a theory of emergence includes the proposition that it is impossible to deduce that which marks the emergent from that which marks the conditions of its emergence.[47] This points to a contradiction inherent in the concept of emergence itself: either the emergent outcome (change) is not cumulative—that is it does not build upon that from which it emerges, or it is an epiphenomenon: a secondary occurrence emerging alongside or in parallel to that with which its emergence is associated. Here, Pepper argued that the unpredictability of an emergent situation is a possible characteristic of emergence, only if it is an epiphenomenal one.[48] Certainly, in the sense of a future emergence, or an emergent (social) future, there must exist the possibility of its unpredictability; therefore, we may assume the ontologically emergent may either be a phenomenon or an epiphenomenon.

In his treatise on emergence, John H Holland expounds on a simple concept of emergence, in which its 'hallmark' is the sense of 'much coming from little',[49] as in a tree might grow from a nut (its fruit). The DNA of the concept of a tree exists within the nut (and only the nut); given appropriate conditions,

---

42 Shotter and Katz, "Articulating Practices: Methods and Experiences: Articulating a Practice from within the Practice Itself: Establishing Formative Dialogues by the Use of a 'Social Poetics'"; Cunliffe, "Social Poetics as Management Inquiry: A Dialogical Approach."
43 Ramsey, "Reflective Practice or Poetic Mindfulness: A Role for Social Poetics in Constructing and Performing Futures."
44 Atkinson, Thinking the Art of Management: Stepping into "Heidegger's Shoes," 149.
45 See, for example: Burmaoglu, Sartenaer, and Porter, "Conceptual Definition of Technology Emergence: A Long Journey from Philosophy of Science to Science Policy"; Holland, Emergence: From Chaos to Order; Pepper, Stephen, "Emergence."
46 Burmaoglu, Sartenaer, and Porter, "Conceptual Definition of Technology Emergence: A Long Journey from Philosophy of Science to Science Policy," 5.
47 Pepper, "Emergence," 241.
48 Pepper, "Emergence," 245.
49 Holland, Emergence: From Chaos to Order, 1.

the future tree emerges into the real. We can look at the nut, and imagine the future tree, and it will emerge—its complex form (its size and shape) will be revealed within limits dictated by its ecology. But this is not the same as a social emergence, in which some other little thing (for example, a fiction or artwork) may emerge, in praxis, from many other things. For further example, to focus on a concern of this present work, the DNA of capitalism is not in the seed of any one thing (or one type of thing). We do not look at a market within an extant idea of capitalism and imagine a predictable postcapitalism. However, we may imagine an epiphenomenal, fictional postcapitalism. While the future tree is realised as the emergence of a phenomenon, the emergence of a postcapitalism is an epiphenomenon. I argue capitalism only exists because, in the moment of its contemplation, we see the confluence of many related, adjacent things, and use the concept of capitalism to classify that confluence. Without a clear distinction in these two modes of emergence, there is a danger of mistaking the epiphenomenal for the phenomenal, to the neglect of the real underlying phenomenal structure, for example, in a mistaken belief that a certain form of capitalism might be an attainable phenomenon.

The ontology of (socially) emergent futures

As I discuss above, the form of 'fictional' social construction of an emergent ontological abstraction acknowledges the epiphenomenal mode of an emergent future. However, this is at odds with the traditionally sought, monologic language of a deterministic, concrete future—a dialectic practice of reaching out for an ideal, yet unattainable, absolute truth.[50] Here I posit that a preoccupation with an ontology inclusive of epiphenomena—for example, through inclusion of the fiction of an economic man, *homo economicus*, as in any sense real—in the belief that such an ontology comprises only emergent phenomenon, is at least problematic.[51] But, to paraphrase an earlier observation:

> '...it [would be] difficult to rationalise the existence of [a future] until at least an "abstract idea" of it had, itself, been [socially] accepted as a legitimate (a priori) object in its own right—a fiction [or imagination], no longer a mere representation of an idea.'[52]

---

[50] The notion of truth used herein follows the commonly held definition of truth as the quality or state of being true, that is in accordance with fact, or reality, or real or actual, or accurate or exact, or correctly positioned or aligned, or faithful, as opposed to being untrue or false. See, for example: Stevenson and Waite, Concise Oxford English Dictionary.

[51] Stanfield, "Phenomena and Epiphenomena in Economics."

[52] Atkinson, Thinking the Art of Management: Stepping into "Heidegger's Shoes," 149–50.

Therefore, the critical importance of the two modes of emergence is the need to distinguish between the real and the imagined.

While the time machine in *Stability* [53] might be implausible—with no discernible quality of being true—it is a device, an '*imagination*', for exploring the impact of unanticipated innovation: an 'absolutely new' device or *novum*, in a world unprepared for such innovation. It sets up a cognitive estrangement.[54] This compels us to conceive of the future differently—a '*counterfactual*' plough for the fertile field of an emergent future. Therefore, whereas Sergio Urueña favours "[the] deliberative process around 'the plausible' ...as a resource to foster awareness of the contingent, intentional, and malleable",[55] I do not restrict the idea of *counterfactuals* to plausible phenomenon. Nor should I distinguish them from scenarios, mini-scenarios or vignettes. I argue that, in our '*imaginations*', we may conceive of *counterfactuals* as forms of narrative that embrace what is also seemingly impossible, improbable, or implausible. This confronts the accepted wisdom that impossible or wholly implausible ideas are unfeasible[56] and of limited or little value. Rather, I suggest that we accept Philip K. Dick's observation that SF writers 'worry about trends, worry about possible dystopias growing out of the present... a cardinal value of the field [of SF writing]'.[57]

Science fiction counterfactuals: an epistemology

I follow others in considering counterfactuals in the study of futures.[58] However, having introduced SF counterfactuals, their ontological status challenges our epistemology: what can we know about our fictional futures?[59] I must ask: what might constitute knowledge or evidence of the SF counterfactuals as legitimate objects of investigation? Here, an ontology-driven epistemology has received little consideration,[60] with the question of

---

[53] Dick, "Stability."

[54] Suvin, "On the Poetics of the Science Fiction Genre."

[55] Urueña, "Understanding 'Plausibility': A Relational Approach to the Anticipatory Heuristics of Future Scenarios," 23.

[56] Booth et al., "Scenarios and Counterfactuals as Modal Narratives."

[57] Dick, The Shifting Realities of Philip K. Dick: Selected Literary and Philosophical Writings, 97.

[58] Booth et al., "Scenarios and Counterfactuals as Modal Narratives"; Todorova, "Counterfactual Construction of the Future"; Gordon and Todorova, Future Studies and Counterfactual Analysis: Seeds of the Future.

[59] Mason, Qualitative Researching.

[60] Bergman, Karlsson, and Axelsson, "Truth Claims and Explanatory Claims-An Ontological Typology of Futures Studies."

scientificness often left unattended.[61] From a critical perspective, this lack of consideration represents a gap in our understanding. Here, Mariana Todorova somewhat avoids the issue by restricting counterfactuals to three forms: dormant facts, reinterpreted facts, and rumours.[62]

While counterfacts are, by definition, non-factual, I suggest that we must perceive them to be factual if they are to be of scholarly use. While I might uncritically adopt dormant or reinterpreted facts, as holding some inherent truth value, the notion of my accepting a rumour (or hypothesis) as a basis for critical study is open to academic challenge. Though of considerable potential value, rumours and hypotheses—to which I suggest we now include counterfactual fictions—require some form of testing.

In his 1962 novel, *The Man in the High Castle,* Philip K. Dick explored the counterfactual in thinking of an alternate outcome to WWII. Antagonistic *imaginations* of a USA divided between German and Japanese control, followed. As Ian Miles observed, the power of such exploration is that it offers parables to our present reality.[63] However, from a critical perspective, I argue that while extending counterfactual thinking through some element of 'fictioning' suggests the basis of a methodology for exploring futures,[64] it can only do so with an epistemology that accepts the possibility of *an imaginary plane.* Here, Charles Booth and colleagues' proposal of a realist or actualist ontology of possible worlds is vague.[65] They suggest either a realist epistemology, where facts (truth values) about possible (fictional) worlds exist independently of ourselves, or an actualist/modal epistemology, with truth values existing for all propositions. Either way, the truth exists to be found; how, is left to the imagination.

Making sense of emergent futures: an empiric of the imagination

Locating truth values in previously published SF novels is one thing.[66] As is finding grains of truth in rumours circulating in the present. Counterfactual

---

[61] Lauster and Hansen-Casteel, "On Some Fundamental Methodological Aspects in Foresight Processes."

[62] Todorova, "Counterfactual Construction of the Future."

[63] Miles, "Stranger than Fiction. How Important Is Science Fiction for Futures Studies?"

[64] Todorova, "Counterfactual Construction of the Future."

[65] Booth et al., "Scenarios and Counterfactuals as Modal Narratives."

[66] Fergnani and Song published an interesting article setting out a range of archetypal scenarios based on a review of 140 science fiction films. To an extent, the architypes might be argued as providing a provisional truth value through their grounded theory approach. Fergnani and Song, "The Six Scenario Archetypes Framework: A Systematic Investigation of Science Fiction Films Set in the Future."

reasoning, based on modal logic and 'possible worlds' scenarios, has some credence, particularly in exploring future outcomes of decisions in the present or very near future.[67] However, with uncertainty inevitable[68], the further into the future we explore, the more imagined our SF, the harder it is to identify sufficient truth value to adopt our counterfactuals, and make sense of emergent possibilities. Here, I invoke a philosophy of Socially Negotiated Alternativism (SNA).[69] While a detailed review of SNA is beyond the scope of this book, it does provide for an infinitely malleable ontology—'a view of the social world that is open to various legitimate interpretations'—in which an anti-foundationalist epistemology accepts that '[all] concepts can be considered as legitimate candidates to a (negotiated) knowledge of the world', including a researcher's own ideas about it.[70] Thus, I argue that we need only be critically reflexive about a contingent or provisional truth about the value of a counterfactual (an imagination, for example), for it to be of use in a social negotiation of a future reality.

It is in the above sense that I argue there is at least an embryonic (empiric) value in the experience of the imaginations of the self and others, in which the empiric value of an emergent truth is negotiated. Making such sense, of course, engages the scholar or student of the future with others. And, having thus explicated the theoretical position of CCF within a methodology of negative dialectics, I now turn to set out the method by which I will implement it.

Critical Counterfactual Futures (CCF) Method...

The negative dialectic CCF method follows a six-step framework, drawing on several established tools of futures studies, particularly those of Rafael Popper[71] and Andy Hines and Peter Bishop:[72]

1. Domain mapping—identifying *critical uncertainties*
2. Baseline projections—casting *future moments*
3. Uncertain futures—back-casting scenarios
4. Counterfactual futures—positing *the imaginations*

---

[67] Sylvan and Majeski, "A Methodology for the Study of Historical Counterfactuals."
[68] Johnson, "Engineering Uncertainty: The Role of Uncertainty in the Design of Complex Technological and Business Systems."
[69] Atkinson, Thinking the Art of Management: Stepping into "Heidegger's Shoes."
[70] Atkinson, Thinking the Art of Management: Stepping into "Heidegger's Shoes," 155.
[71] Popper, "Foresight Methodolgy."
[72] Hines and Bishop, "Framework Foresight: Exploring Futures the Houston Way."

5. Coherent futures—illuminating *the provocations*
6. Implications analysis—speculations and reconciliations

The six steps of the CCF method are set out in the following paragraphs, with examples given in the inquiry that follows.

Domain mapping: identifying critical uncertainties

As with the HFF method,[73] I start the CCF process by investigating and mapping the domain of interest—the *plane of our material reality.* Given my focus on (non)conceptual studies, the domain is centred on a major field or area of interest, rather than the concept itself. In this Chapter's inquiry, I outline a broad field of entrepreneurship as it relates, fundamentally, to economic growth. Here, the process involves a review of literature on the field, including both academic and non-academic sources, in which I seek to identify both key- and sub-categories of interest. This activity is closely related to the horizon scanning process detailed by Rafael Popper,[74] however, the CCF review tends to be more open, and less concerned with following specific themes or theories at this stage. The purpose of the review is to develop a map of the domain as a guide to its principle causal relationships, and to identify three fundamental dimensions of *critical uncertainty*—the essential parameters defining a set of *contradictions.*

Hines and Bishop provide a useful template for domain mapping,[75] with my own application also drawing on ideas from systems thinking and rich pictures.[76] The domain map is an information visualization, providing the potential for subconsciously internalizing a domain structure.[77] The three identified *critical uncertainties* are expressed as *possibility statements (**'P'**),* concerning the state of uncertainty about a single, but critical, dimension **'P'** of the mapped field. Each **'P'** statement usually takes the form of *<one possible outcome>* rather than *<another possible outcome>*; it characterises the variable nature of the *field of (non)concepts.* The process of developing **'P'** statements is like backcasting,[78] in the sense that one works back from the *present moment* in time to identify possible themes, technologies, policies or strategies, the uncertainties of which contribute to the *present moment.*

---

[73] Hines and Bishop, "Framework Foresight: Exploring Futures the Houston Way."
[74] Popper, "Foresight Methodolgy."
[75] Hines and Bishop, "Framework Foresight: Exploring Futures the Houston Way."
[76] Checkland, "Soft Systems Methodology: A Thirty Year Retrospective."
[77] Hook, "Domain Maps: Purposes, History, Parallels with Cartography, and Applications."
[78] Popper, "Foresight Methodolgy."

Baseline projections: casting future moments

I posit that the *present time—moment zero* **(m_0)**—arises, in large part, due to the historical nature of the changing dimensions of the identified *critical uncertainties.* The *present moment* zero **(m_0)** is a *historical progression* **(h_0)** from a *prior moment* in time **(m_{-1})**, where the *prior history* **(h_0)** is a function of the three emergent *critical uncertainties,* **'P'**, expressed as:

$$\mathbf{m_0} = \mathbf{m_{-1}} + \mathbf{h_0}, \text{ where } \mathbf{h_0} = f_n(\mathbf{P_1}, \mathbf{P_2}, \mathbf{P_3})$$

$$\text{therefore } \mathbf{m_0} = \mathbf{m_{-1}} + f_n(\mathbf{P_1}, \mathbf{P_2}, \mathbf{P_3})$$

Consequently, in making projections about the future, I further posit that any *future moment* **(m_n)** is a *historical progression* **(h_n)** from the *present moment* **(m_0)** and may be expressed in the following form:

$$\mathbf{m_n} = \mathbf{m_0} + \mathbf{h_n} \text{ where } \mathbf{h_n} = f_n(\mathbf{P_1}, \mathbf{P_2}, \mathbf{P_3})$$

$$\text{therefore } \mathbf{m_n} = \mathbf{m_0} + f_n(\mathbf{P_1}, \mathbf{P_2}, \mathbf{P_3})$$

Here, a material future emerges on an *antagonistic horizon,* as a confluence of three infinitely expanding cones of uncertainty from any present point in time, characterised by the *critical uncertainties* **P_1, P_2, P_3**. Such a range of uncertain future materiality is, however, clearly unmanageable. Yet, expressing the future in this manner allows me to employ a form of logic chart.[79] Here, I draw on the work of John Macfarlane and employ the logic of truth tables to develop a manageable range of contingent *future moments.*[80] These emergent phenomena provide a set of *contradictions*—small vignettes, each a 'thin' description of an emergent state, contingent on the uncertainty inherent in our present. Their main application is in assigning relative truth values to *counterfactual imaginations* on the *imaginary plane.*

Uncertain histories: back-casting scenarios

This step is optional. I believe it is useful in developing analyses to call on what we might describe as 'thick' descriptions of each uncertainty, written as mini scenarios. Accepting that the future is a complex function of the three identified *critical uncertainties,* a thick description provides a richer narrative on which I suggest we can draw on, in backcasting from any other *future moment.* In backcasting a mini scenario, I employ a systems-like approach

---

[79] Popper, "Foresight Methodolgy."
[80] Macfarlane, "Future Contingents and Relative Truth."

drawing from the domain map. For each **'P'** statement, I work back from a future point in time, in two equal periods. Thus, for a 10-year projected uncertainty, its uncertain (future) history is expressed in terms of: a) what I believe to be a most likely outcome in year +10; b) what I believe would have happened in year +5 to lead to year +10; and c) what I believe is happening now to suggest the action foreseen in year +5.[81] Although I backcast from the future, my preference is to set the narrative of *historical progression* from the current time. As I mentioned, this step is optional; it best applies where an analysis centres on the content of the domain-mapped literature, rather than drawing on the external perspectives of counterfactual futures from SF/fictional sources. I simply include it here for completeness in describing the CCF method.

Counterfactual futures: positing the imaginations

In this fourth and defining step of the CCF method, I *counterfactually* introduce science fictioning—*the 'imaginations'*—acknowledging Rafael Popper's observation that the method is not typically considered 'serious'.[82] Nevertheless, I argue that we may introduce *imaginations* as fictional short stories (headlines/news) of provocative events inspired by creative thought. Although, generally, we use the term SF and speak of such luminaries of the genre as Philip K. Dick, in practice, all I need do in this fourth step is to 'imagine' a set of future news events: news stories with their headlines ('**HL**'). Here I suggest a set of six is ideal **($HL_{1\text{-}6}$)**, though it could be more. These stories are, themselves, also vignettes; they need not be lengthy narratives. They also need no inherent connection to the present though, in practice, if written by the futures practitioner, they will be influenced by the review of the domain. As a method, I draw on Kenneth Hansen's review of future-oriented journalism, where 'time is manipulated to make the future event seem more imminent' a process of anticipation, fading the boundary between the present and the (antagonistic) future.[83]

Coherent futures: illuminating the provocations

While we might witness the 'image of news [arising] as a distorted and biased interpretation of reality and the reporter as an unreliable messenger',[84] we should be reminded that the journalist's obligation is to the truth. It is this

---

[81] See, for example: Gold, "The Future of HRD: Scenarios of Possibility."

[82] Popper, "Foresight Methodolgy."

[83] Hansen, "News from the Future: A Corpus Linguistic Analysis of Future-Oriented, Unreal and Counterfactual News Discourse," 116.

[84] Broersma, "The Unbearable Limitations of Journalism: On Press Critique and Journalism's Claim to Truth," 22.

notion of truth, at least in a contingent sense, that the CCF method seeks to uphold in reflecting on such fictional headlines. To make science fictioning a 'serious' futures method, and worthy of consideration in the 'serious realm' of political, governmental or business policymaking, it is not sufficient for me to cite a rumour. Nor is it sufficient to simply declare a realist or actualist ontology. I argue that it is not sufficient, from either basis, to make a statement that a fiction is true-enough for it then to form the basis of an analysis considered serious-enough for government work. What I seek, here, is a method of establishing coherence between the projected material reality of possible future moments, and their intersection with antagonistic provocations—imaginations of the imaginary plane.

To retain a critical perspective, I argue for the adoption of a *counterfactual* definition of causation.[85] Here, event **'E'** (such as news story $\mathbf{HL_n}$), would not have occurred if it were not for cause **'C'** (such as history, $\mathbf{h_n}$). This places $\mathbf{h_n}$ (and its antecedents) as a necessary cause of $\mathbf{HL_n}$. However, Judea Pearl pointed to two areas of difficulty in this *counterfactual* approach: confounding and sensitivity to the generative process. On the one hand, cause and effect may both be influenced by a third factor (confounding) and on the other hand, cause and effect relationships may themselves be affected by (sensitive to) the counterfactual antecedent. Here, I avoid a rigorous semantic framework in favour of a simple narrative use of the terms, sufficient for the purpose of my inquiry and its aim in provocation. However, two other terms I consider relevant to a counterfactual analysis are the probability of necessity ($\mathbf{P_N}$) and probability of sufficiency ($\mathbf{P_S}$). These terms play a key role in understanding causation, its events and antecedent conditions. Here, a cause may be considered necessary-or-sufficient or necessary-and-sufficient. It is the role that such considerations play in counterfactual analysis that points to its critical value. In the CCF method of applying negative dialectics, I identify a plausible, coherent truth by making informed, subjective judgments about the coherence between *the contradictions*—the set of *future moments* grounded in present *critical uncertainties*—and *the imaginations*—the *counterfactual* fictional news Headlines.

Implications analysis: on speculations and reconciliations

Having established plausible levels of coherence between *the contradictions* and *the imaginations* from the future, the final step is to select, or prioritise, those potential SF headlines as future antagonistic perspectives (*the provocations*). Here, I *speculate* on what might, or might not, be the consequences of

[85] Pearl, "Probabilities of Causation : Three Counterfactual 1 Introduction."

provocative action or inaction along the lines of the *contradictory themes*. This final stage of *reconciliation* is between the *contradictions* on the *plane of reality* and the *speculations* about the impact of *provocations* from the *imaginary plane*. Reconciliation occurs along the line of the *antagonistic horizon*. In this respect, a *speculation* is a *provocation* transformed onto the *real plane* for the purpose of comparison in the moment. In practice, this process of *reconciliation* invokes a dialogue about, for example, the implications and/or avoidance of problematic policies, drawing (non)conceptual conclusions concerning the domain of enquiry and its (non)concepts. As this is a method designed for (non)conceptual work, it is not intended to develop a detailed set of outcomes and recommendations—steps to be taken to achieve or avoid any given future—but it may form part of a further process that leads to them. The development of a set of *speculations*—realisations in a *future moment* of coherent *provocations*—constitutes a *constellation of speculations*, from which one can discern one or more *reconciliations* as (non)conceptual ideas.

An inquiry into future entrepreneurship

Having explicated my methodology, theoretical position, and method, I now apply it to this inquiry. I ask, can negative dialectics and a CCF futures application of SF be useful in future thinking the narrative of an emergent, indeterminate concept of entrepreneurship? I follow the steps set out above, omitting the optional Step 3. My inquiry commences with domain mapping, in which the following text gives a flavour of the inquiry, with keywords underlined.

Domain mapping entrepreneurship

While various approaches to entrepreneurship study are subject to prolific debate,[86] a reification of the entrepreneur as some mythical hero (Western or not) plays to a study locus favouring Schumpeter's dynamic capitalism, and an entrepreneurship that creatively destroys existing markets.[87] Schumpeter's work continues to guide policy in the long-run[88] where, faced with an omnipresent uncertainty, economic growth (as in GDP) matters.[89] It

---

86 Aldrich and Martinez, "Many Are Called, but Few Are Chosen: An Evolutionary Perspective for the Study of Entrepreneurship."

87 Kirchhoff, Entrepreneurship and Dynamic Capitalism: The Economics of Business; Greene and Brown, "Resource Needs and the Dynamic Capitalism Typology"; Kirchhoff, Linton, and Walsh, "Neo-Marshellian Equilibrium versus Schumpeterian Creative Destruction: Its Impact on Business Research and Economic Policy."

88 Baumol, "Joseph Schumpeter: The Long Run, and the Short."

89 Although, for an analysis of GDP's structural limitations as a continuing measure of growth, see Watanabe, Tou, and Neittaanmäki, "A New Paradox of the Digital Economy - Structural Sources of the Limitation of GDP Statistics."

represents the 'value added' produced within and by a given nation, within a given time frame—a measure of progress with factors that include innovation, technology, financial and human capital, investment and entrepreneurship.[90]

Generally, entrepreneurs take advantage of opportunity, creating and/or exploiting change for profit 'by innovating, accepting risk and moving resources to areas of higher return'.[91] They not only innovate, they are also important agents for economic growth, 'breaking the "circular flow" of macroeconomic equilibrium'.[92] Entrepreneurs disrupt stability. Yet there is a noted disagreement on key issues regarding what entrepreneurship constitutes,[93] while the rewards for its practice are at best mixed.[94] It is not surprising that the future trajectories of entrepreneurship education—including 'why' teach it and 'what' and 'how' it is to be taught[95]—are open to interpretation; the question of 'why entrepreneurship?' is implicit.

High growth—the acme of unicorn wranglers, Schumpeterians, policymakers and politicians alike—offers 'great potential in terms of an increase in opportunities, improvement in living conditions, and decreasing poverty levels'.[96] Here, we assume that many such stakeholders are subject to the continually shifting local, regional, and national economic powerbases that lie behind much geopolitical uncertainty. This assumption is upheld by others. In his essay *Economic Shocks and International Politics*,[97] Jeffrey Frankel supports the argument that, given historical patterns, the risk of new crises in the future (certainly in emerging markets), cannot be overlooked. Certainly, Covid-19, first identified at the end of 2019, has impacted global economics, with movement and trade significantly disrupted.

Shifting economic power is—alongside technology, population change, environmental shifts and pressures, and changing societal values—one of the

---

[90] Chiappero-Martinetti, von Jacobi, and Signorelli, "Human Development and Economic Growth."

[91] Burns, Entrepreneurship and Small Business : Start-up, Growth and Maturity, 10 (emphasis added).

[92] Hornaday, "Dropping the E-Words from Small Business Research: An Alternative Typology," 22.

[93] Rauch et al., "Entrepreneurial Orientation and Business Performance: An Assessment of Past Research and Suggestions for the Future."

[94] Hamilton, "Does Entrepreneurship Pay? An Empirical Analysis of the Returns to Self-Employment"; Luzzi and Sasson, "Entrepreneurial Skills or Reward for Success? Does Entrepreneurship Pay in Future Paid Employment?"

[95] Kuratko and Morris, "Examining the Future Trajectory of Entrepreneurship."

[96] Chiappero-Martinetti, von Jacobi, and Signorelli, "Human Development and Economic Growth," 224 (emphasis added).

[97] Frankel, "Economic Shocks and International Politics."

key drivers shaping the market attitudes and behaviours from which growth emerges.[98] While technology raises questions over the uncertainty of the productivity paradox and the future of work, issues of population change, environmental shifts and pressures, and changing social values, can be brought under the uncertainty of sustainable growth. These questions are symptomatic of a world 'turned upside down'.[99] As important issues, they have the potential to affect 'many people, deeply, for long periods of time'.[100] There is, therefore, an imperative to think about future growth, and to plan for and facilitate decision-making concerning it.[101]

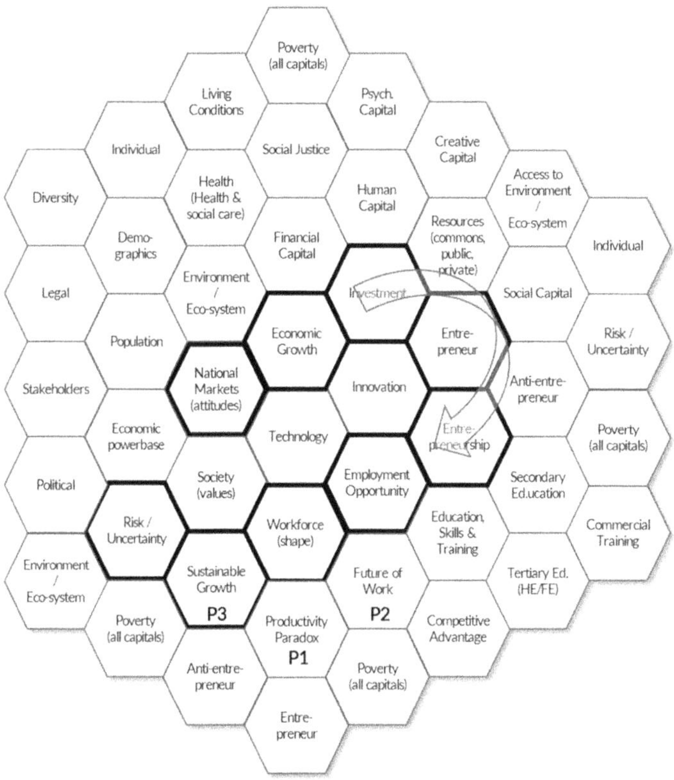

Figure 4.1. Domain mapping entrepreneurship

---

98 Euromonitor Passport, "Understanding the Five Drivers Shaping Megatrends."
99 Cooke, "World Turned Upside down: Entrepreneurial Decline, Its Reluctant Myths and Troubling Realities."
100 Gordon and Todorova, Future Studies and Counterfactual Analysis: Seeds of the Future, 3.
101 Bengston, "Principles for Thinking about the Future and Foresight Education."

The underlined text above provides keywords used to produce a domain map. The text itself is a 'thick' description of the domain—a resource in forming subsequent narratives. Figure 4.1 depicts the domain map used throughout this inquiry. It forms a variation of domain maps produced under other methods; it draws visual inspiration from the honeycomb of a Hive of Bees. In terms of a negative dialectic, this form of domain mapping graphically supports the emergence of, for example, a concept of the entrepreneur from its non-concept—the constellation of other concepts and ideas that are not the entrepreneur (Figure 4.2), but from which the entrepreneur, in praxis, emerges. In practice, it has been possible to draw on this map for the other inquiries that follow, expanding it and refining it as necessary.

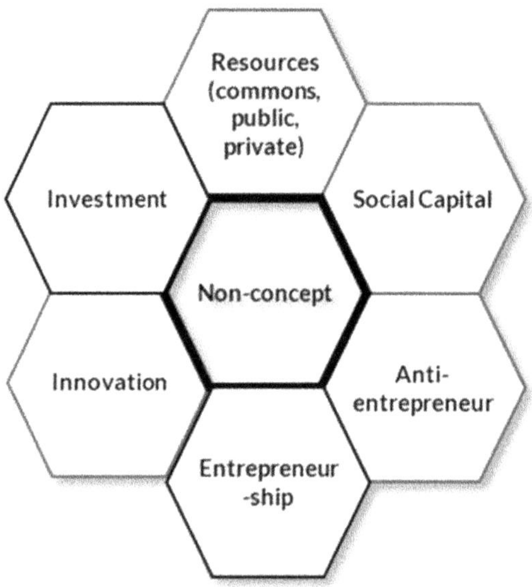

Figure 4.2. Non-concept of the entrepreneur

Drawing on the domain map (Figure 4.1), I can explicate three *critical uncertainties* in line with the United Nations' 17 sustainable development goals (SDGs).[102] In the domain, economic development and environmental protection are not mutually exclusive.[103] Choosing socially responsible, 'green'

---

[102] See, for example: Schaltegger, Beckmann, and Hockerts, "Collaborative Entrepreneurship for Sustainability. Creating Solutions in Light of the UN Sustainable Development Goals."
[103] Hawkins, Kwon, and Bae, "Balance Between Local Economic Development and Environmental Sustainability: A Multi-Level Governance Perspective."

growth under the banner[104] of sustainability seems a necessity, but the path to take is not clear. Entrepreneurship's promise is its potential to boost innovation, stimulate economic growth, and provide the means to reduce poverty and enhance social and environmental sustainability. Entrepreneurship can be a catalyst for sustainability.[105] Thus, it seems the more entrepreneurship develops innovative responses to the environment, the better our chances of survival, growth and well-being are.[106] Yet, the following sections identify *three critical uncertainties* as potentially emergent phenomena.

The productivity paradox

Technology, particularly the internet, shapes what we do and how we do it.[107] It also shapes the workforce.[108] However, investment in information and communication technology (ICT)—assumed to generate a competitive advantage[109] and productivity growth[110]—lacks a solid theoretical explanation and has evidenced only unconvincing empirical success.[111] The observation that technology's impact can be seen everywhere, but in the productivity statistics is widely recognised as Solow's *productivity paradox*.[112] For example, there is little evidence of differential productivity growth in ICT-intensive manufacturing since the late 1990s[113]; with the paradox also reflected in the digital economy.[114] Thus, I make the following statement about the *critical uncertainty* of future productivity:

---

104 See, for example: Sandberg, Klockars, and Wilén, "Green Growth or Degrowth? Assessing the Normative Justifications for Environmental Sustainability and Economic Growth through Critical Social Theory."

105 İyigün, "What Could Entrepreneurship Do for Sustainable Development? A Corporate Social Responsibility-Based Approach."

106 Shapero, "Why Entrepreneurship? A Worldwide Perspective."

107 Watanabe, Tou, and Neittaanmäki, "A New Paradox of the Digital Economy - Structural Sources of the Limitation of GDP Statistics."

108 Card and Nelson, "How Automation and Digital Disruption Are Shaping the Workforce of the Future."

109 Porter and Millar, "How Information Gives You Competitive Advantage."

110 Baily and Solow, "International Productivity Comparisons Built from the Firm Level."

111 Kijek and Kijek, "Is Innovation the Key to Solving the Productivity Paradox?"

112 Solow, "We'd Better Watch out, Review of SS Cohen and J. Zysman. Manufacturing Matters: The Myth of the Post-Industrial Economy."

113 Acemoglu et al., "Return of the Solow Paradox? It, Productivity, and Employment in US Manufacturing."

114 Watanabe, Tou, and Neittaanmäki, "A New Paradox of the Digital Economy - Structural Sources of the Limitation of GDP Statistics."

P1: The economy is more or less characterised by <persistent low productivity from an increasing number of the self-employed>, rather than by <full, high-productivity employment>.

The future of work

In *Race Against the Machine*, Erik Brynjolfsson and Andrew McAfee observe that ICT is 'rapidly encroaching into areas that used to be the domain of people only, like complex communication and advanced pattern recognition',[115] making markets and businesses more efficient to benefit society's consumers. Daron Acemoglu and colleagues suggest that while ICT continues to promise efficiency and flexibility, its encroachment deepens the productivity paradox.[116] Here, as a subset of ICT, continuing advances in Artificial Intelligence (AI) and robotics illuminate the further question of ICT's replacement of traditional workers, reducing the role of labour in the future workplace. Other relevant trends include: the consideration of society and the individual, including demographics and diversity; changing economic perspectives; law and politics; and concern over the environment and scarce resources.[117] I, therefore, make the second statement of *critical uncertainty*:

P2: The future is characterised by <more or less 'soft' skills; technology favours greater workforce feminisation & neurodiversity>, rather than by <greater dexterity and precision>.

Sustainable growth

The cited 2022-2026 growth differential between advanced economies (1.5%) and emerging and developing economies (4.5%) is reflected in the observation that these two groups have different patterns of natural resource use.[118] At the more developed end, GDP growth has an increasing impact on the environment. Whereas less developed economies rely more on their

---

[115] Brynjolfsson and McAfee, "Race against the Machine: How the Digital Revolution Is Accelerating Innovation, Driving Productivity and Irreversibly Transforming Employment and the Economy," 8.
[116] Acemoglu et al., "Return of the Solow Paradox? It, Productivity, and Employment in US Manufacturing."
[117] Rhisiart, Störmer, and Daheim, "From Foresight to Impact? The 2030 Future of Work Scenarios."
[118] This does not take into consideration the 2022 Russian incursion in Ukraine and its impact on global economies and the cost of living crises affecting many countries. Due mainly to increaes in world gas supply prices, this later 2022 crisis is a further reflection of a certain pattern of natural resource use.

environmental eco-systems for income.[119] Assuming a global convergence on a developed (high-income) economic model—the profile adjudged responsible for most of the world's environmental pollution[120]—the trend will continue toward exhausted resources, depleted eco-systems, and underemployed populations. Within this, I can imagine something of the potential of Philip K. Dick's dystopian *Stability*. Thus, I state that the third *critical uncertainty* is:

> $\mathbf{P_3}$: The future is characterised by <more or less unsustainable, global growth>, rather than by <innovative growth with less exploitation of natural resources and degraded eco-systems>.

The baseline: a promise of (sustainable) entrepreneurship

Both the domain map and 'P' statements provide the basis to project a baseline of *future moments*. Here, I am confronted by the possibility of both confounding and sensitivity to the generative process. Firstly, considering any one projected *critical uncertainty* (for example, $\mathbf{P_1}$), its causes and effects may be confounded by a third factor ($\mathbf{P_2}$ and/or $\mathbf{P_3}$). Secondly, the cause-and-effect relationships within any single *historical progression* will be sensitive to its counterfactual antecedents—that is to say, the extent to which an effect may vary, depending on a variation of its cause. Furthermore, I should consider the probability of necessity ($\mathbf{P_N}$) and the probability of sufficiency ($\mathbf{P_S}$). These require me to consider to what extent a future state might require a certain history ($\mathbf{P_N}$) and to what extent may other *historical progressions* be excluded ($\mathbf{P_S}$). To acknowledge these issues, I adopt the technique of a truth table. This allows me to consider the branching of *alternate histories*, to deduce a range of possible *future moments*, based on assigning **T** (true) of **F** (false) values to the range of P.

In Table 4.1, I set out eight vignettes, *future moments* $\mathbf{m_{1\text{-}8}}$, based on the branching of the *critical uncertainties* ($\mathbf{P_1}$, $\mathbf{P_2}$, $\mathbf{P_3}$). Diagrammatically, in Figure 4.3, I then depict the branching of *alternate histories* ($\mathbf{h_{1\text{-}8}}$), anticipating the emergence of each in some *future moment* ($\mathbf{m_{1\text{-}8}}$) characterised by extant dimensions of history, or *prior history* ($\mathbf{h_0}$). The set of *future moments* ($\mathbf{m_{1\text{-}8}}$) represent *the contradictions.*

[119] Cumming and von Cramon-Taubadel, "Linking Economic Growth Pathways and Environmental Sustainability by Understanding Development as Alternate Social-Ecological Regimes."

[120] Omri, "Entrepreneurship, Sectoral Outputs and Environmental Improvement: International Evidence."

Table 4.1. Truth table: contradictions in entrepreneurship

Branch	**P_1**	**P_2**	**P_3**	**Future moment/vignette**
$m_1 = m_0 + h_1$, where $h_1 = h_0$	F	F	F	Historical discontinuity. Changes in perception that low productivity and low growth are bad and a reduction in widespread adoption of AI & robotics
$m_2 = m_0 + h_2$, where $h_2 = f_n(P_3)$	F	F	T	No change in perception of poor growth is bad
$m_3 = m_0 + h_3$, where $h_3 = f_n(P_2)$	F	T	F	No reduction of widespread adoption of AI and robotics (because we can)
$m_4 = m_0 + h_4$, where $h_4 = f_n(P_2, P_3)$	F	T	T	No reduction of widespread adoption of AI & robotics, and no change in perception of poor growth is bad
$m_5 = m_0 + h_5$, where $h_5 = f_n(P_1)$	T	F	F	No change in perception that low productivity is bad
$m_6 = m_0 + h_6$, where $h_6 = f_n(P_1, P_3)$	T	F	T	No change in perception that low productivity and low growth are bad
$m_7 = m_0 + h_7$, where $h_7 = f_n(P_1, P_2)$	T	T	F	No change in perception that low productivity is bad and no reduction in widespread adoption of AI/robotics
$m_8 = m_0 + h_8$ where $h_8 = f_n(P_1, P_2, P_3)$	T	T	T	Status quo: No change in perception that low productivity and low growth are bad and no reduction of widespread adoption of AI & robotics

(T=True, F=False)

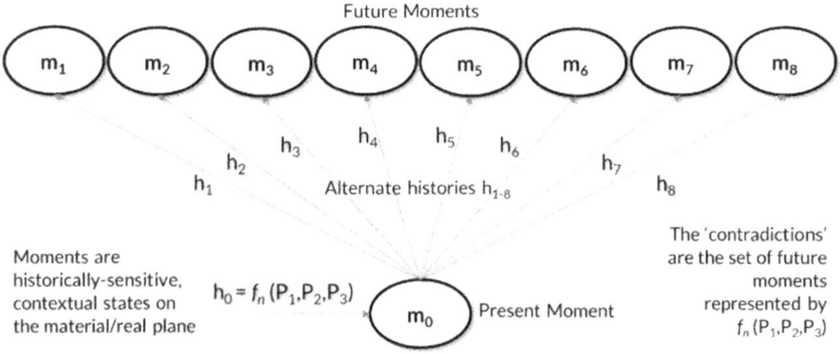

Figure 4.3. Alternate histories, contradictions in entrepreneurship

The counterfactuals: news from the future

Across the antagonistic horizon, I now 'imagine' six contingent, future news headlines **($HL_{1\text{-}6}$)**. I have set out these 'imaginations' as further vignettes in Table 4.2. Although far from being immediate comparisons with a SF novel or short story, as might have been penned by Philip K. Dick, the vignettes are nevertheless fictional. Thus, these fictions are objects of the imagination (*imaginations*). They are consistent with the genre of narrative that cannot arise in the present, but which are hypothesised, based on a belief in the possible consequences of technological progress. In the present moment **(m_0)** there is nothing to suggest that any fictional headline may be true or not. Given this *indeterminacy intuition,*[121] to determine the efficacy of any *indeterminate* headline statement **($HL_{1\text{-}6}$)** I need to attach a 'truth' value to it. While MacFarlane provides a rigorous framework for examining this value, here I simply seek to identify a provisional coherence—between the headlines and their respective histories—a 'necessary' property in respect of sensemaking.[122]

Coherent futures: the provocations of history...

In considering the complex proposition that the future is some function of the projected *critical uncertainties*, $f_n(\mathbf{P_1, P_2, P_3})$, I ask: to what extent might any future news headline **($HL_{1\text{-}6}$)**, be coherent with a *future moment* **($m_{1\text{-}8}$)**. In Figure 4.4, I plot the (intuitive) coherence I find between the imagined headlines and the *future moments* of an emergent entrepreneurship.

Table 4.2. Six headlines from our entrepreneurial future ($HL_{1\text{-}6}$)

News from the Future: Headlines
Headline HL_1: It's official...World stops turning
The United Nations announces 'Global Stability' forecast for 2035. USA productivity flat-lined with 0% growth in GDP; world economies rapidly converging on the USA's situation. Rate of innovation (measured by filed patents) reduced to negligible levels, globally. Increasing population, stagnant productivity and no innovation leads to one-day work week. ***(coherent with moments: m_6, m_8)***
Headline HL_2: Life of leisure beckons as robots take the strain

[121] Macfarlane, "Future Contingents and Relative Truth."

[122] Karl. E. Weick, Sensemaking in Organizations (Vol. 3) (Sage, 1995); Karl E. Weick, Kathleen M. Sutcliffe, and David Obstfeld, 'Organizing and the Process of Sensemaking', Organization Science, 16.4 (2005), 409–21.

Amazon announces the acquisition of Scotland as a 'dark' factory. New innovations (advances in AI tech/ICT) lead to autonomously thinking robots replacing humans in most work/production settings, with personal 'Amabots' now used as family income generators, allowing most humans to pursue non-work-related leisure/self-actualisation activities. ***(coherent with m_1, m_2, m_5, m_6)***
Headline HL_3: Taxing times ahead as Boris turns red
Tax, Tax, Tax: King's speech declares Conservative intent. Following Prime Minister B Johnson's reveal of a new social-engineered capitalist ideology, and election to an historic 3rd term on the back of dropping the "party-of-low-taxation" mantra, economists debate a future in which capitalism now serves society. (coherent with m_2, $m_{4\text{-}8}$)
Headline HL_4: PM takes the wheel of UK Plc
The King moves to Balmoral on permanent basis as Labour sweeps to power. Following the Conservative 'Brexit' project's complete failure, the break-up of the United Kingdom, and on the back of a historic electoral victory, 'New Labour 3.0' promises to nationalise all manufacturing and production, transport and infrastructure services. ***(coherent with m_2, $m_{4\text{-}8}$)***
Headline HL_5: Governments unite to free talent from global stranglehold
New United Nations launches global entrepreneurship model. As global GDP growth continues to converge to under 0.5%, and SMEs fail or are acquired by the few remaining global businesses, national heads of government agree to push for new unicorns in a bid to break the corporate monopolies. ***(coherent with m_1, m_3, m_5, m_7)***
Headline HL_6: Class act to breathe new life into dying economy
Painting by numbers: Art ruled out of UK national curriculum. As GDPs flatline, businesses fail and unemployment increases, entrepreneurship stagnates. The government seizes on a US think-tank paper to make entrepreneurship studies compulsory at all stages on the curriculum. HE Start-up Bursaries are offered to kick-start the struggling, post-Brexit economy. ***(coherent with m_1, m_3, m_5, m_7)***

In simple terms, identifying coherence is a process of considering each headline (*imagination*) in turn, from the position of each *moment*, asking the question: could this *moment* be antecedent to the headline being considered. This allows me to attach contingent and relative 'truth' values, where appropriate, to the headline statements. I argue that this process overcomes, to an extent, the *indeterminacy intuition* about any news from the future and supports my *counterfactual* stance. It allows me to approach a determination of any headline statement $\mathbf{HL_{1\text{-}6}}$, through an assessment of its antecedent *alternate histories* ($\mathbf{h_1}$ **to** $\mathbf{h_8}$).

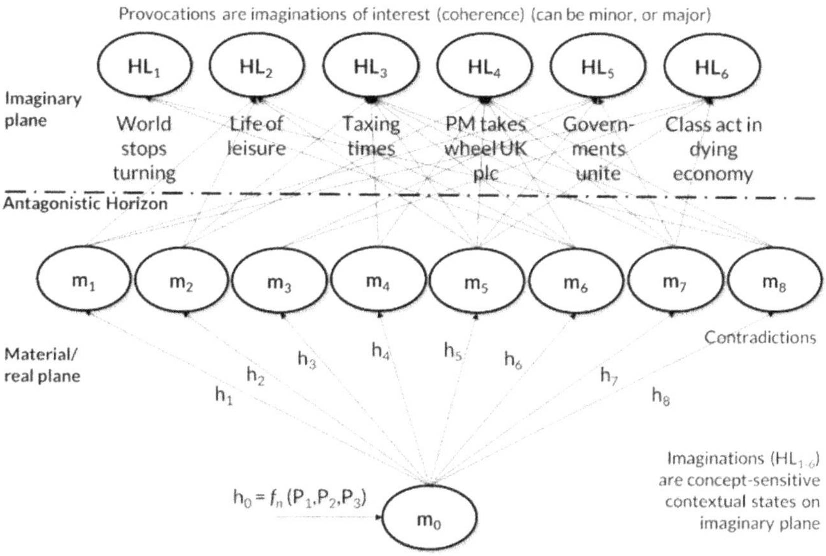

Figure 4.4. Finding truth in the future of entrepreneurship news

Following Figure 4.4, I argue that the coherence visible between the range of uncertainty and headlines **HL3** and **HL4**, suggests a greater contingent truth. That is to say, the probability of necessity (**P_N**) is relatively high. I posit that, on the one hand, a high **P_N** is indicative of an *imagination* of interest, or *major provocation*; on the other hand, a low **P_N** represents an imagination of *minor provocation.* A probability of sufficiency (**P_S**) is more difficult to identify. Here, I suggest that other factors not considered, may also be relevant. However, I believe this approach does at least represent a step in the right *counterfactual* direction.

Speculations from the future of entrepreneurship

The principle of *counterfactual* headlines is that, in the context of thinking about the future, they should represent some aspect of it, however impossible, improbable, or implausible they seem. From my analysis, I determine that there is a greater 'truth' value to consideration of Headlines **HL3** and **HL4** in respect of the projections **P_1, P_2, P_3**. Taken together, I posit that these headlines—as symptomatic, narrative vignettes—represent two possible outcomes and *major provocations.* They are *major provocations* of a future, beyond the antagonistic horizon, predicated as a function of three projected uncertainties. Their UK focus does not necessarily suggest that the antecedent histories do not have a global application.

In the UK of 2030, the idea that a Conservative government should end its 'party-of-low-taxation' mantra is symptomatic of an economy that has singularly failed to generate the returns from capitalism required to support its people. (*Headline **HL3**: Taxing times ahead as Boris turns red.*)[123] I *speculate* that the theme of entrepreneurship central to the antecedent histories of such a future, suggests that either the concept of entrepreneurship upon which much economic policy is predicated is flawed, or that its application is at least problematic, or (more likely) both. That 2030 sees economists debating whether capitalism serves society is intuitively necessary (if not too late). A declaration of Tax, Tax, Tax in a future King's Speech on the opening of a new Conservative parliament is a *major provocation.* If an empiric truth in this argument is allowed, then my *speculation* suggests a *reconciliation* in considering, in detail, how the projected histories of an extant entrepreneurship might be re-engineered. While a new social-engineered capitalist ideology might sound far-fetched, the potential for smaller changes (*reconciliations*) in the trajectories of current trends may be enough to avoid such a headline.

In the UK of 2030, the idea that The King moves to Balmoral on a permanent basis, as Labour sweeps to power is, in effect, a restatement of the same problematic (*Headline **HL4**: PM takes the wheel of UK Plc*). Here, rather than a right-of-centre government reaching its conclusion for change, a new left-of-centre government forces a similar change. However, as an alternate *major provocation*, the risk is that a New Labour '3.0', and a promise to nationalise all manufacturing and production, transport and infrastructure services, runs a risk of throwing away the proverbial 'baby with the bath water'—throwing away that which might be good about enterprise, entrepreneurship and capitalism. Having engineered a culture of entrepreneurship, emergence into a future which promises a severe reduction in entrepreneurial opportunity, in favour of increased state employment, risks an environment of increased tension and anxiety. Again, a projected failure (for example) of the Conservative 'Brexit' project and a consequential break-up of the United Kingdom is a *major provocation*; however, it reinforces the potential that *reconciliatory* changes in the trajectories of extant trends may avoid such a headline.

Reconciling a sustainable entrepreneurship?

Concluding this initial 'means' inquiry: an inquiry into a sustainable future for entrepreneurship, I follow Frances Bell and colleagues who suggested that the most impact is achieved with seedling images of a future that germinate and

---

[123] At the time of the final edits to this manuscript (September 2022), Liz Truss had taken on the mantle of Prime Minister from Boris Johnson. However, there was little to suggest that before 2030, 'Boris' might not make a return in a future Conservative Government.

give fruit in a more distant time.[124] In terms of a contribution to the understanding of a future of Entrepreneurship (study), my aim has been to identify seeds with the most promise. The question I asked at the outset requires an answer. Can a negative dialectic CCF method, employing SF, be useful in future thinking the narrative of a (non)concept of entrepreneurship, as it emerges from a constellation of speculations? I argue that it can. Yet this first phase of my inquiry offers only a provisional conclusion. At this stage, I have not sought to detail changes to better shape a future entrepreneurship praxis or its policies, including those that may impact the delivery of its education and support. My provisional conclusion is limited to merely *speculating* that *reconciliatory* change in this area is most likely to be required.

---

[124] Bell et al., "Science Fiction Prototypes: Visionary Technology Narratives between Futures."

Chapter 5

Work: experts and storytellers

THE NATURE OF WORK and the functional interchangeability of technology and institutions is a concern in a post-Covid-19 VUCA future. With perceived high levels of uncertainty, do we seek to design better social systems of work? Or do we avoid the challenge and opportunity presented, reverting to 'traditional' values and institutions? Jim Dator's essay *De-Colonizing the Future,*[1] first published in 1975, remains prescient. Exhortations for 'development', 'progress' and 'modernisation' persist in the face of accelerating technological change, including the ever-present promise of AI and robotics.[2] In a contemporary twist, social movements, for example, *Extinction Rebellion, Black Lives Matter,* and *Me Too,* all reflect in some way, Dator's floods of nostalgia and the calls for neglected and ignored institutions and values.[3] But what do we, really, exhort for? Do we exhort new, technology-enhanced, real and productive societies or, in a Baudrillardian sense, might we be confronting the maps that precede their founding?[4] In this Chapter, for the second of my 'means' inquiries, I shift the focus to the 'other' (negative) side of enterprising work—to the individual as an employee, or worker. In doing so, I examine the potential of CCF in developing a post Covid-19 future of work, where the hope of many rests on the influence of too few.

---

[1] Dator, "De-Colonizing The Future."

[2] See, for example: BEIS, Industrial Strategy: Building a Britain Fit for the Future.

[3] Dator, "De-Colonizing The Future," 98.

[4] Baudrillard, Simulacra and Simulation.

Dator drew on Marshall McLuhan's (1911-1980) dictum that 'in operational and practical fact, the medium is the message'.[5] Thus, I argue that our concern may reasonably be over what changes persistent advances in technology (for example, AI and robotics) cause to our contemporary societies; it need not be over what our contemporary societies choose to do with such innovation. Here, the medium of technology both 'shapes and controls the scale and form of human association and action'.[6] This respects both the observation that new technologies have already had profound consequences for society,[7] and that technology has, in some sense or another, always lain at the root of impacts on society's work and labour.[8] In this sense, it is AI itself that matters; it is the concept of AI that will shape and control society, not AI's specific applications. And it is the concept of robotics that will also shape and control our societies, not the idea that some home-robot will cook our favourite meal. Thus, I argue, my proper concern is the equipmentality of a technology, not its applications. In the sense that the object 'hammer' exists only 'in order to' accomplish the act of hammering,[9] I may question what is the 'thing' technology is, in order to 'be'? In this manner, I can embrace the totality of its societal assignment, speaking to the Heideggerian *pre-phenomenon*[10] or Adornian (non)concept of the thing 'technology', rather than technology as any phenomenal or ontological object, *per se.*

I follow McLuhan's observation that, generally, electric light escapes consideration as a medium of proper concern because it is assumed light possesses no content; but light *is* the message. Society may be concerned with the phenomenal, or ontic applications of electric light, yet it was its conceptualisation that provided for the radical control and shaping of society in its time. Thus, contemporaneously, the internet and social media escape proper consideration because the (non)concept of the medium does not possess content (or at least so its controllers might argue). I posit that a proper concern is therefore not over what applications the internet and social media are put to, but over the idea that the (non)concept of the internet and social media might not be the message of relevance to societies and the world of work and labour.

---

[5] McLuhan, "The Medium Is the Message," 107.
[6] McLuhan, "The Medium Is the Message," 108.
[7] Baldry, "Editorial: Chronicling the Information Revolution."
[8] See, for example: Albo, Panitch, and Zuege, Capitalism, Technology, Labor: A Socialist Register Reader, Vol 2.
[9] Heidegger, Being and Time.
[10] Heidegger, Being and Time, 67-69.

Arguably, the democratisation of content advanced by many as a basic principle (or freedom) of the digital medium is ineffectual in controlling and shaping the society it serves. Rather, it is the medium itself that controls and shapes; those that control the medium thus control the society. Here, in our media-controlled societies, a surfeit of democratised content devours itself, it devours communication, and it devours meaning.[11] On such grounds, how do we interpret the interchangeability of technology and institutions, their effect on shaping and controlling the scale and form of human associations and actions, and transition from devouring to facilitating? How do we empower better social systems of work for the future? In this Chapter, I contribute to the rising interest in the effects of technology on work where, facing a post Covid-19 future, I shall address these questions by reflecting on the Adornian (non)conceptual meaning attached to the Heideggerian pre-phenomena of employment and work, as projected into that future. I will highlight the close relationship of the contemporary nature of work to the non-concept of entrepreneurship and work to resolve a politically influenced problematic of non-identity.

Social justice

The opportunity to reflect on technology and institutions in a post-Covid-19 future of work, arose through a Futures and Foresight Workshop (FFW) held at York St John University in March 2020. This was a response to an internal call for research from the university's Institute for Social Justice (ISJ). Members of the University's Futures Research Group (FRG) held the FFW to develop regional-level social justice scenarios for 2030. It brought together expert participants from academe and professional life to collaborate in developing future social justice scenarios, to develop insights to be considered by the ISJ as part of its agenda and for use by the participants within their organizations. At the outset, the FRG had no indication of the unfolding Covid-19 crisis that characterised the FFW and much of its write-up.[12]

> The FRG adopted the United Nations (UN) interpretation of social justice as:
>
> 'the fair and compassionate distribution of the fruits of economic growth that is sustainable, that respects the integrity of the natural environment, that rationalises the use of non-renewable resources,

---

[11] Baudrillard, Simulacra and Simulation, 80.

[12] Waehning et al., "Social Justice in York, 2030 (Extended Summary)."

and that enables future generations to enjoy a beautiful and hospitable earth'. [13]

The FFW considered the key inhibitors of social justice with respect to the manifestation of inequality and inequity in the city of York, UK and its regional area, covering the phenomena of: Poverty; Housing and Rough Sleeping; Health and Social Care; and Employment and Skills. In this Chapter, I draw only on the focus on Employment and Skills.

Mixing it up: experts and storytellers

While the CCF method outlined in Chapter 4 has developed throughout this book's inquiries, the opportunity to compare and contrast its 'imaginations' with more traditionally produced (expert) scenarios, was insightful, and an opportunity not to be missed. While researching the future may be paradoxical,[14] to conceptually explore the pre-phenomena of employment in the future of work, by employing both CCF's 'imaginations', and traditional expert-derived (mini)scenarios, enabled a process of triangulation on alternative methods.[15] Here, beyond simply a synthesis of the qualitative and quantitative,[16] there is a tradition of using two dissimilar techniques to forecast a given phenomenon. For example: the objective encounters the subjective in hindsighting the Czechoslovakian invasion of 1968;[17] the constructivist is synthesised with the realist in researching risk in industrial societies;[18] and the quantitative and qualitative combine to foresee industrial change.[19]

Within futures research, the purpose of scenarios is 'to discover or invent, examine and evaluate, and propose possible, probable and preferable futures'.[20] Where scenarios are employed as part of mixed methods research, it is frequently the case that it is the scenario 'analysis' that is subject to mixed

---

[13] For example, as cited in: UN ESCWA, "Social Justice Matters: A View from the Economic and Social Commission for Western Asia," 3.
[14] Blass, "Researching the Future: Method or Madness?"
[15] Marshall and Rossman, Designing Qualitative Research; Mason, Qualitative Researching.
[16] See, for example: Molina-Azorin et al., "Mixed Methods in the Organizational Sciences: Taking Stock and Moving Forward."
[17] Andriole, "Comparative Forecasting: Hindsighting the Czechoslovakian Invasion."
[18] Metzner-Szigeth, "Contradictory Approaches? On Realism and Constructivism in the Social Sciences Research on Risk, Technology and the Environment."
[19] Huan-Niemi et al., "Combining Quantitative and Qualitative Research Methods to Foresee the Changes in the Finnish Agri-Food Sector."
[20] Bell, Foundations of Futures Studies—Vol. 1: History, Purposes and Knowledge, 73 Cited in; Blass, "Researching the Future: Method or Madness?"

methods, rather than its generation;[21] or else, the scenario is compared with outcomes from other methods.[22]

Scenarios are a traditional method of eliciting 'stories of possibility'. However, the social construction of scenarios, for example, through a workshop of experts, reflects the biases and prejudices of those experts; as Jeff Gold remarks, scenarios are generally positive and optimistic.[23] This is not surprising; scenarios are often used to consider 'preferred' futures. Therefore, a method of triangulating the production of scenarios that develops a greater range of 'stories of possibility' may embrace the 'nonpreferred' futures and compensate for expert and social desirability bias. This is not to compare the efficacies of alternative methods of scenario production, rather the aim is to supplement existing methods, adding richness to possibility, embracing the subjectivity of social reality'.[24]

Triangulation in developing scenarios is not new. Alternative futures, developed from the projections of experts, those of futurists themselves, and those developed from the images that people in differing contexts hold, have been a recurring feature, for example, in the work of Jim Dator. As Clement Bezold observed:

> 'Dator's focus on alternative futures evolves, reflecting movement in what people see as the future and what futurists/experts see[;]... the future will likely be a mixture of several of these images'.[25]

Both Dator and Bezold point to a movement for alternative 'aspirational futures', in which a set of scenarios would ideally include: 1) a 'best estimate' of the likely, 2) an exploration of the downside of 'continued growth' and 3) one or two 'official' visionary scenarios exploring what could be.[26] However, while including the downside, the bias of analysis tends to the idea of one or more 'preferred' futures futures.

---

[21] See, for example: Lipiec et al., "Mapping out Climate Change: Assessing How Coastal Communities Adapt Using Alternative Future Scenarios"; Venturini, Hansen, and Andersen, "Linking Narratives and Energy System Modelling in Transport Scenarios: A Participatory Perspective from Denmark."

[22] See, for example: Harris-Lovett, Lienert, and Sedlak, "A Mixed-Methods Approach to Strategic Planning for Multi-Benefit Regional Water Infrastructure."

[23] Gold, "The Future of HRD: Scenarios of Possibility," 80.

[24] Mason, Qualitative Researching, 190.

[25] Bezold, "Jim Dator's Alternative Futures and the Path to IAF's Aspirational Futures," 131.

[26] Bezold, "Jim Dator's Alternative Futures and the Path to IAF's Aspirational Futures," 132.

From a critical perspective, there appears to be little triangulated analysis of alternative scenario production methods and their subsequent synthesis in a single futures research case. As discussed, the general tradition of scenarios is to propose *possible, probable* and *preferable* futures, reflecting what Toni Ahlqvist and Martin Rhisiart have argued is a trend toward utilitarian research.[27] Such scenarios are generally built on causal, intuitive logics (IL). Indeed, others have critiqued an inherent determinism within these traditional IL scenarios, since 'surprise' futures with no salient causality[28] are seemingly precluded.[29] Thus, scenarios are simply recognised as a key method in futures research rather than, perhaps, supporting the 'deeper understanding of the political moorings of anticipatory societal systems'.[30] Such a 'deeper understanding' is implicit in my aim that, in this inquiry, I interpret, (non)conceptually, the interchangeability of technology and institutions in the future VUCA world of work.

Although James Derbyshire and George Wright have proposed an augmented IL approach to scenario development, which broadens the range of causality,[31] a more explicit exception to the *possible, probable* and *preferable* triad was previously outlined by George Cairns, Martyna Śliwa, and George Wright in 2010.[32] This latter group of authors proposed a critical scenario method rooted in Aristotle's *phronēsis*, as a wisdom associated with practical action (introduced in Chapter 2). Here, analysis reaches beyond what might be good and advantageous (that is: *possible, probable* and *preferable*) to also consider, pragmatically, things that might be bad for society (the *nonpreferable*). The idea of practical action allows us to question the development of undesirable trends, their negative impacts (on who) and the need for (and extent of) any required mitigation, such as reflected in Dator's downside of 'continued growth'. Thus, our point of methodic departure in this Chapter's inquiry is to triangulate on aspirational (*preferred*) and alternative non-aspirational (*nonpreferred*) emergent futures.

---

27 Ahlqvist and Rhisiart, "Emerging Pathways for Critical Futures Research: Changing Contexts and Impacts of Social Theory."

28 'No salient causality' includes no explicit exaptation nor evidently evolutionary relationship.

29 Derbyshire and Wright, "Augmenting the Intuitive Logics Scenario Planning Method for a More Comprehensive Analysis of Causation."

30 Ahlqvist and Rhisiart, "Emerging Pathways for Critical Futures Research: Changing Contexts and Impacts of Social Theory," 92.

31 Derbyshire and Wright, "Augmenting the Intuitive Logics Scenario Planning Method for a More Comprehensive Analysis of Causation."

32 Cairns, Śliwa, and Wright, "Problematizing International Business Futures through a 'Critical Scenario Method.'"

Ahead of the FFW, members of the FRG met to decide on the social justice themes. As the facilitator of the employment and skills theme, I provided a background paper for the 'expert' participants that considered relevant key factors. That paper was distributed to participants a week prior to the FFW. Within the theme, participation on the day included a member of The City of York Council and regional members of The UK Ministry of Justice, The Institute of Directors, The Local Enterprise Partnership, and an independent expert. The group collaborated on developing a mini-scenario, testing its assumptions, and setting out actions required for consideration within the remaining months of 2020. The outcome of the workshop is recorded in the report: *Social Justice in York, 2030.*[33] As a parallel activity, this Chapter reflects the application of the negative dialectic CCF method, and its use of SF news headlines on the imaginary plane (Chapter 4). This speculative activity is developed in the following sections, before I offer a (non)conceptual dialogue on a range of identified provocations.

An inquiry into future growth and employment

Having expended a little of this Chapter on developing the theoretical position for adopting a more mixed-methods approach, I now turn to the body of the inquiry itself. I ask, what interpretations can be placed on the interchangeability of technology and institutions, and their effects on facilitating and empowering better social systems of work for the future? I follow the steps of the CCF method, omitting the optional Step 3.

Domain mapping employment opportunity

The domain mapping exercise explores existing trends and patterns to determine a set of three key critical uncertainties **(P_1, P_2, P_3)** characterising the present moment (**m_0**) in the context of economic growth and employment opportunity. Here, I adopt the UN approach to equality of (employment) rights, equality of access to (employment) resources, and eroding barriers restricting such access to disadvantaged groups. Here, notwithstanding the regional pursuit of a just and 'good-growth' economy,[34] I am drawn inexorably into what Klaus Schwab of the Word Economic Forum has labelled the Fourth Industrial Revolution. Schwab cautions us that:

---

[33] Waehning et al., "Social Justice in York, 2030 (Extended Summary)."

[34] Good Growth was a term employed in the Local Enterprise Partnership's draft local industrial strategy YNYER LEP, "YNYER Local Industrial Strategy (Draft January 2020)."

> '...the profound uncertainty surrounding the development and adoption of emerging technologies means that we do not yet know how the transformations driven by this industrial revolution will unfold'.[35]

Here, knowledge of emerging trends at global, national, regional and local levels, has a fundamental role in shaping employment opportunity in the Yorkshire region and beyond.

Growth represents the 'total value added' within a given economy, within a given timeframe. It is a measure of progress, with factors that include innovation, technology, financial and human capital, investment and entrepreneurship.[36] High growth offers 'great potential in terms of increase of opportunities, improvement in living conditions, and decrease of poverty levels'.[37] Yet there is an uneasy relationship between growth and the creation of employment opportunity. On the one hand, Pre Covid-19, we witnessed low levels of unemployment,[38] on the other hand, technology and innovation-led growth may have created (short-term) unemployment through competitive pressure, automation or through a lack of new skills required in the workforce,[39] forcing a long-term displacement of some employment.

Employment displacement can be seen, for example, in the proportion of UK businesses that employ others; this had fallen from one-third of all businesses in 2000, to one-quarter in 2019.[40] The relative decline in employers appeared offset by a disproportionate increase in self-employment. In 2000, there were approximately 2.1 times more non-employing than employing businesses, whereas in 2019, there were 3.2 times as many, at 4.5m (2.1m more than in 2000, and 76% of a total of 5.9m).[41] More recently, the growth in self-employment had turned problematic. At the outset of the 2019/2020 Covid-19 pandemic, the UK government appeared slow to provide an adequate income safety net for many

---

35 Schwab, The Fourth Industrial Revolution, 2.
36 Chiappero-Martinetti, von Jacobi, and Signorelli, "Human Development and Economic Growth."
37 Chiappero-Martinetti, von Jacobi, and Signorelli, 224.
38 For three months ending Nov 2019, the ONS provides headline unemployment rate for the Enterprise Partnership region. https://www.ons.gov.uk/employmentandlabourmarket/peopleinwork/employmentandemployeetypes/bulletins/uklabourmarket/january2020.
39 Eriksson, "Is There a Trade-off between Employment and Growth?"; Schubert and Turnovsky, "Growth and Unemployment: Short-Run and Long-Run Tradeoffs."
40 Rhodes, "Business Statistics."
41 See also https://assets.publishing.service.gov.uk/government/uploads/ system/uploads/attachment_data/file/852919/Business_Population_Estimates_for_the_UK_and_regions_-_2019_Statistical_Release.pdf.

of those self-employed and affected by the economic shutdown, many whose contracts and income had ceased, almost overnight.

In the long term, reallocation of labour may occur through the attainment of new skills and the creation of new opportunity. But how much of the growth in self-employment—through divesting responsibilities to employees, reducing costs, and maximising margins—is facilitated by new technology-based business such as Uber? And, in this mode, is the past in any sense a reliable reflection of the future? Might we be able to rely on new opportunities and skills as a means of allocation of financial capital, when, notwithstanding the impact of Covid-19 on the employment market in 2020, some observers had already pointed to labour's falling share of national income,[42] while workforces are, in general, ageing?[43]

Growth, itself, emerges from an economic market's attitudes and behaviours, which are shaped by the five key drivers of shifting economic powerbases, technology, population change, changing (social) values and concerns, and environmental shifts and pressures.[44] Thus, I posit that future opportunity will tend to a function of these drivers; it may operate at the city, district, region, national and/or global levels. At the local level, and internal to both national and international/global levels, consideration must be given to the concepts of endogenous (internally driven) and exogenous (externally driven) growth. Therefore, I suggest that some of the drivers may remain outside the means of control or influence at the level of their impact. A local strategy cannot, therefore, be disassociated from other challenges, for example, the impact of AI and robotics (technology), an ageing population, environmental sustainability (clean growth) and regional transport infrastructure (the future of mobility). Drawing on a domain map (Figure 5.1), I now explicate three critical uncertainties in detail.

Changing powerbases

Power can usefully be considered as the capacity to exercise control or influence over the drivers of change. Reasonably, local power might be assumed to rest in the politics of councils and their officers and agents, whereas regional power might be bestowed on development agencies, or through devolution arrangements, and national power through governments. Given present levels of global geo-political uncertainty, alongside the shifting

---

[42] Acemoglu et al., "Return of the Solow Paradox? It, Productivity, and Employment in US Manufacturing."

[43] Leopold, Ratcheva, and Zahidi, "The Future of Jobs: Employment, Skills and Workforce Strategy for the Fourth Industrial Revolution."

[44] Euromonitor Passport, "Understanding the Five Drivers Shaping Megatrends."

sovereign power of nations, I ask what trends lie in power shifts among the capitalists and managerialists[45]—the owners and propagators of technological innovation, resources and the means of production—or through the discursive power of technological rhetoric in the hands of a society-at-large?[46]

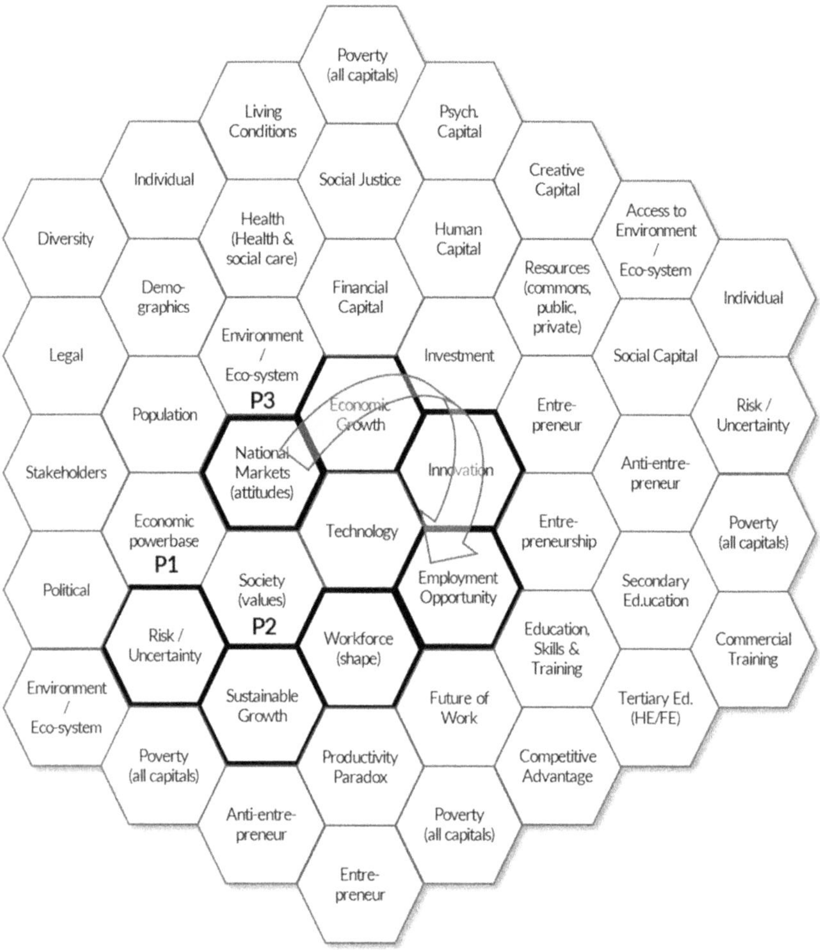

Figure 5.1. Domain mapping employment opportunity

---

[45] See, for example: Baldry, "Editorial: Chronicling the Information Revolution."

[46] See, for example: Boyd and Holton, "Technology, Innovation, Employment and Power: Does Robotics and Artificial Intelligence Really Mean Social Transformation?"

Shifting power relations, allied to events such as the 2008 global financial crisis, have seen varying levels of global austerity and a preoccupation with policies to re-ignite stagnating economies. In 2018, the European Commission set out a policy for rebalancing 'labour power' for an innovation-fuelled, sustainable inclusive growth.[47] Linking Schumpeterian economics of creative destruction and Keynesian demand with a 2020 horizon, they explored the relationship between labour market organization, technological change, and income distribution. They critiqued the deteriorating link between productivity and wage growth, noting the trend toward employment income being held hostage to the threat of unemployment—a consequence of uncertain markets, where income is set through individual bargaining processes that do not respect the principle of equal pay for work of equal value. Here, the capital providers have the last say, presiding over a decline in collective representation.[48]

Over the last decades, a shifting powerbase is visible in a trend for local public sector employment to transition to central government control. With levels of overall public sector employment in 2019 compared to 1999, UK local government employment had fallen by over 0.75m to 2m in that time, while central government employment has risen almost 1m, to 3.25m.[49] A shifting powerbase is also visible in the employment displacement previously noted. While the trend toward increasing self-employment may give an illusion of self-control, as a band-of-one there is little an individual can do to control the uncertainty and risk engendered by the agency of others. I, therefore, arrive at my first critical uncertainty of work's future nature:

> **P_1**: Work is more or less characterised by increasing self-employment, with employers reducing employment costs through technology use rather than by increasing their employee numbers.

From the social justice perspective, self-employment goes hand in hand with fewer, rather than greater (employment) rights, with risk transferred from employer to the self-employed.

Population values

Trends in population values that impact on employment opportunity include work-life balance—adjustments to work patterns that allow one to combine

[47] Dosi, Virgillito, and Roventini, "Rebalancing Labour Power for an Innovation-Fuelled Sustainable Inclusive Growth."
[48] Baldry, "Editorial: Chronicling the Information Revolution."
[49] For an analysis of public sector employment see https://www.ons.gov.uk/employmentandlabourmarket/peopleinwork/publicsectorpersonnel/bulletins/publicsectoremployment/september2019

work with other responsibilities (such as parenting) or aspirations (such as the pursuit of leisure activities). John MacInnes highlighted two relevant features of the concept of work-life balance.[50] Firstly, aside from individual-level motivations, such as reducing work hours and levels of work-related stress, neoliberal family-friendly policies encourage parenting and counter the trend for falling young demographics in emerging markets. Such policies aim to secure long-term labour supply yet, paradoxically, they may prevent the older generations from retiring, restricting opportunity for younger generations. Secondly, changing demographics highlight the importance of the inter-generational transfers of resources. Following MacInnes, consideration of work-life balance in the face of indeterminate future opportunities, shaped by complex, complicated and inter-dependant trends and patterns of influence, speaks little to the importance of 'work' toward people's income and their capability to enjoy such balance. Anecdotally, futures are replete with talk of universal basic incomes[51] and reduced working weeks.

MacInnes' article points to trends that advance the work-life balance perspective. These include 1) the decline of the male breadwinner system, 2) work intensity, long hours and globalisation, and 3) issues of life in general, including both new life (child-care) and old life (care of the elderly and infirm). In the UK, exacerbated by Covid-19,[52] I also point to anecdotal evidence of the increasing inability of the state or its regions to offer adequate levels of support, including social care, to an increasingly ageing population (let alone the disabled and otherwise disadvantaged in society). Here, 'those with the least [are set to] suffer uncertain futures the most'.[53] In practice, older members of society who have the most, are best able to transfer resources to younger generations (within family units) to facilitate the attainment of some form of balance.[54] But, in the face of increasing inequalities in the distribution of assets, any failure to support those unable to afford their own support, is of growing dystopic concern. This leads me to form my second critical uncertainty of the future nature of work:

---

[50] MacInnes, "Work-Life Balance in Europe: A Response to the Baby Bust or Reward for the Baby Boomers?"

[51] For a useful review of the Universal Income policy debate see Martinelli (2017).

[52] Dunn et al., "Briefing: Adult Social Care and COVID-19 - Assessing the Policy Response in England so Far"; Hodgson et al., "Briefing : Adult Social Care and COVID-19 - Assessing the Impact on Social Care Users and Staff in England so Far."

[53] Atkinson, "Class Habitus and Perception of the Future: Recession, Employment Insecurity and Temporality."

[54] MacInnes, "Work-Life Balance in Europe: A Response to the Baby Bust or Reward for the Baby Boomers?"

P2: Work is characterised by a more or less deterministic need for income (ends) rather than by an indeterminacy in the nature of work (means) available to meet that income.

From the social justice perspective, **P2** suggests that while a deterministic, growing need for income implies a greater need for access to (employment) resources, the deterministic yet limited nature of those resources provides no guarantee of equality of access to them.

Environmental and social concerns

Growth often drives unexpected or undesired consequences. Increasingly, the spotlight has fallen on the impact of a 'recent past' of economic development, in which growth has been driven by a technological determinism and toxic debt that neglects unintended outcomes,[55] and rapid development and high profit-related goals.[56] Venkatesh Mani and his colleagues cite two examples from the last decade, of an Indian coffee-bean company having negative social impact on its plantations, and a global clothing brand unethically using health-damaging chemicals in its manufacturing processes.[57] These are just two images of concern raised by growth models that neglect environmental sustainability and social issues in favour of profit. But, will the adoption of more sustainable practices have a positive or negative impact on economies, and therefore opportunity, equity and equality? Here, alongside an inevitable requirement to consume at least some of the remaining environmental resource, there are pressures and obstacles to sustainability. Notwithstanding the clear needs of under-developed economies, even the basic needs of many in developed regions (for food, clothing, shelter, care and jobs) are not adequately met;[58] this includes the North Yorkshire enterprise region.[59]

I have already set the context of the future VUCA environment. Here, there is a growing evidence base that the continuing high levels of environmental abuse and social inequality will require accelerated attention to sustainable practice(s) to avert dystopic catastrophes. But, as Joachim Spangenberg and

---

[55] See, for example: Howcroft and Taylor, "'Plus ca Change, plus La Meme Chose?'-Researching and Theorising the 'new' New Technologies."
[56] See, for example: Mani, Agrawal, and Sharma, "Impediments to Social Sustainability Adoption in the Supply Chain: An ISM and MICMAC Analysis in Indian Manufacturing Industries."
[57] Mani, Agrawal, and Sharma, "Impediments to Social Sustainability Adoption in the Supply Chain: An ISM and MICMAC Analysis in Indian Manufacturing Industries."
[58] Mani, Agrawal, and Sharma, "Impediments to Social Sustainability Adoption in the Supply Chain: An ISM and MICMAC Analysis in Indian Manufacturing Industries."
[59] YNYER LEP, "YNYER Local Industrial Strategy (Draft January 2020)."

his colleagues have observed from the literature, there is a debate between the 'long-term limits to economic growth [due to] the [constant] coupling factor between economic growth and environmental pollution' and the rhetoric of 'no limits to the potential substitution of resources as a result of emerging or as yet unknown technologies'.[60] These two 'images' of the future suggest a need to critique trends which might be inevitable and beneficial or dangerous and dystopic. I therefore advance my third critical uncertainty concerning the future shape of work:

> **P_3**: Work is characterised by an indeterministic need for more or less economic growth, rather than the deterministic need to reduce the misuse of natural resources/eco-systems.

From the social justice perspective, the increasing conflict between the indeterminacy of increasing needs and the determinacy of limited resources, suggests the erection rather than erosion of barriers between equitable solutions and disadvantaged groups.

The baseline: future moments in evolution of work

Following the CCF Method, I question to what extent—under constant technological and innovative change—does demand for economic growth impact on employment opportunity, and how might this be moderated in the interests of social justice? This allows me to explore what David Spencer has argued is technology's impact on the quality of work, as opposed to its loss.[61] I therefore proceed by future casting toward the antagonistic horizon, projecting a set of future moments **($m_{1\text{-}8}$)**. These represent contradictions in the evolution of work as a function of the baseline critical uncertainties **$f_n(P_1,P_2,P_3)$**. I repeat the technique of using a truth table to consider the branching of alternate histories, to deduce a range of possible futures. Here a future history **($h_{1\text{-}8}$)** has the dimensions of: an individual burden of employment risk *(changing powerbases)*, the indeterminacy of income *(population values)*, and the determinacy of limited resources *(environmental and social concerns)*. These dimensions leverage socially responsible opportunity. Table 5.1 sets out the projected contradictions **($m_{1\text{-}8}$)**.

---

[60] Spangenberg, Omann, and Hinterberger, "Sustainable Growth Criteria Minimum Benchmarks and Scenarios for Employment and the Environment."
[61] Spencer, "Fear and Hope in an Age of Mass Automation: Debating the Future of Work."

Table 5.1. Truth table: contradictions in future employment & skills

m	P_1	P_2	P_3	Future moment/vignette
m_1	F	F	F	Historical discontinuity. Changes in the perception that the individual accepts all the burden of employment risk, for an indeterminately (low) income, and has determinately limited resources to leverage socially responsible opportunity.
m_2	F	F	T	No change in perception that the individual accepts determinately limited resources to leverage socially responsible opportunity.
m_3	F	T	F	No change in perception that the individual must accept an indeterminately (low) income.
m_4	F	T	T	No change in perception that the individual must accept and indeterminately (low) income, and determinately limited resources to leverage socially responsible opportunity.
m_5	T	F	F	No change in perception that the individual accepts all the burden of employment risk.
m_6	T	F	T	No change in perception that the individual accepts all the burden of employment risk, and determinately limited resources to leverage socially responsible opportunity.
m_7	T	T	F	No change in perception that the individual accepts all the burden of employment risk, for an indeterminately (low) of income.
m_8	T	T	T	Status quo: No change in perception that the individual accepts all the burden of employment risk, for an indeterminately (low) income, and determinately limited resources to leverage socially responsible opportunity.

(T=True, F=False)

The counterfactuals: news from the future

Following the CCF method, beyond the antagonistic horizon, I now 'imagine' a set of six fictionalised, contingent news headlines (**$HL_{1\text{-}6}$**), as 'tall stories' that characterise nonpreferred images of the future of 2030. These headlines, detailed in Table 5.2, may be influenced by the horizon scanning process and the highlighted uncertainties, but they do not require to be empirically supported by them in any way.

Coherent futures: the provocations of history...

From Table 5.1 and Table 5.2, I intuit the potential coherence between the set of future moments (**$m_{1\text{-}8}$**) and the imaginations, the set of future 'news headlines' (**$HL_{1\text{-}6}$**). Figure 5.2 plots this intuitive coherence between the imagined headlines, and the antecedent moments, ranging from a historical discontinuity where none of the three projected histories bears any relation to the future (**m_1**), to a continuation of the status quo (**m_8**) where all three combine. These outcomes represent truth values assignable to the (fictional) forecasts of the news headlines—non-preferable symptoms of the future of my domain of interest.

Table 5.2. Six headlines from the future of enterprise ($HL_{1\text{-}6}$)

News from the Future: Headlines
Headline HL_1: Welcome to the United Socialism of America
Second US Civil War averted as Republicans agree to gun control reforms, and implementation of universal free health care provision. The reforms follow escalating and high-levels of civil unrest and violence, and evidence of the coalescence of individual groups around a new form of social democracy, and with violence aimed at the wealthy. Republicans in both houses agree on reforms. The new politics of socialism is traced back to the emergence of a new, populist, non-Ivy-league democratic leader, after the disastrous attempt to seize power from the Republicans in 2025. ***(coherent with: m3, m4, m5, m6, m7, m8)***
Headline HL_2: Publish and be sued
UK government bows to social pressure and enacts new law classifying all on-line social media entities as publishers. The US government refuses to extradite AmaPharm's CEO to face a class-action lawsuit in the UK, over the failure of its AI to properly interpret its dataset, leading to the deaths of over 2000 UK individuals wrongly prescribed and delivered medication by the NHS' contracted-out RoboCare in-home service. Consequently, new laws place the burden of responsibility of data accuracy, on those that publish it. ***(coherent with m1, m2, m3, m4)***
Headline HL_3: Capitalism isn't working
Third UK VC firm in three months to be hit by assassination of its CEO, amid public cries for an end to capitalism. Populist concern has set on the deterioration of the link between productivity and growth and people's income. Activist groups have seized on recent reports of increased government investment of public funds in a series of high-profile tech start-up failures, as austerity measures and falling employment opportunities fail to halt the surge in both in-work and out-of-work poverty. Police increase presence by providing 24-hour guarding of foodbanks. ***(coherent with m3, m4, m7, m8)***
Headline HL_4: What price good health?
UK health minister resigns as fears of new novel coronavirus mount following two unexplained deaths in city hospital. In the latest example of the negative impacts of the perceived return to excessive capitalism, public sentiment, fuelled by the popular media, has called into question the decision to sell Barts of London to the US healthcare provider, AmaCare, a Caymen Island registered subsidiary of Amazon. While the sale provided much-needed revenue to the exchequer, rising public concern continues to threaten the government's strong majority in both houses. ***(coherent with m2, m4, m5, m6, m7, m8)***

Headline HL_5: Public lose again as another longshot gamble fails
UK's flagship on-line marketplace fails as false accounting reveals £ 30 billion public investment fraud. Entrepreneurship is receiving bad press. Public concern continues to rise over yet another in a series of high-profile examples of capitalist-excess, as unscrupulous venture capitalists are seen to highjack the goodwill of entrepreneurial agents in pursuing ever-more-dubious propositions, destined to fail, but not before earning high levels of transaction fees. Increasingly, the self-employed are turning away from the epithet 'entrepreneur'. ***(coherent with m2, m4, m5, m6, m7, m8)***
Headline HL_6: Violent night at the opera highlights public revolt
King calls for peace, after Glyndebourne bombed by protest group championing fair income for all. Timed to coincide with the release of the latest Joseph Rowntree Foundation report on Poverty in the UK, the recent bombing of the Glyndebourne opera, leaving 20 hospitalised, is widely condemned. However, the bombing sheds light on the growing public concern of the falling availability of jobs per 100 of working age, the net increase of the economically inactive, and the inability of the conservative government to provide a social safety net. ***(coherent with m3, m4, m7, m8)***

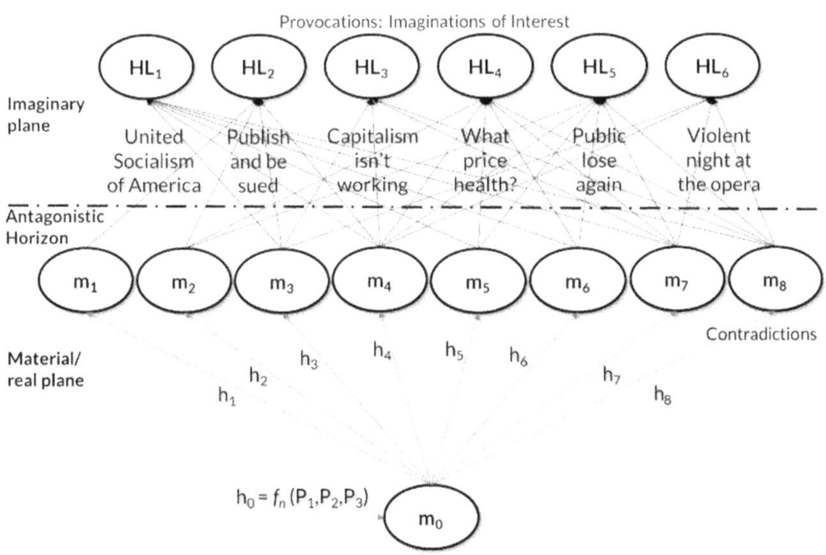

Figure 5.2. Finding truth in the future of work

Intuitively, given the range of possible outcomes of $f_n(\mathbf{P_1}, \mathbf{P_2}, \mathbf{P_3})$, I argue that: 1) the counter-factual headlines $\mathbf{HL_1}$, $\mathbf{HL_4}$ and $\mathbf{HL_5}$ represent those with a greater possibility of truth; and 2) moment ($\mathbf{m_0}$) bears least coherence with any nonpreferred future. This does not suggest that other factors not considered may not be relevant, nor that the truth is absolute.

Speculations from the future of work

As with my inquiry in the future of entrepreneurship in Chapter 4, the idea of considering fictionalised, counterfactual future news headlines—the imaginations—is to focus the context of thinking about the future, or a representation of some aspect of it. In this case the future of employment and work. This is irrespective of however 'impossible, improbable, or implausible' that representation might seem. Headlines **HL_1**, **HL_4** and **HL_5** are thus symptomatic provocations, narrative imaginations of interest from a future predicated as a function of the projected critical uncertainties **(P_1, P_2, P_3)**. While both UK and US perspectives are included, for the present analysis, I shall concentrate solely on the UK and therefore on **HL_4** and **HL_5**.[62]

Given the Headline **HL_4**, '***What price good health?***', the provocation that a UK health minister might resign is hardly of major conceptual concern. As is the idea that a subsequent novel virus pandemic might occur. Throughout the course of time, ministers have come and gone for many reasons, and pandemics are a recurrent feature of history.[63] Another novel coronavirus at some future point can be expected. However, Covid-19, along with (for example) the financial crash of 2008, have tested nations' abilities to respond to extreme, if not strictly unprecedented levels of global, socio-economic impact. In the UK, for example, on the one hand, the 2008 financial crash led to a decade of deterministic austerity measures, enforced by a government moved to cover the costs of the national interventions to mitigate that crisis. Here, consequential cuts to health and social care, and other public services, weakened the resilience of essential social institutions. On the other hand, the UK government exhorted the need for 'development', 'progress' and 'modernisation' through accelerating technological change—they sought private capital-funded solutions to indeterministic economic growth, on the promise of new technologies such as AI and robotics. It is therefore reasonable to envisage a potential long-term response to the Covid-19 crisis as invoking further cost-cutting and even greater 'cries' for technological innovation.

---

[62] Despite the focus on the UK headlines, it is interesting to note that Headline HL1: Welcome to the United Socialism of America (first drafted in an earlier version of this Chapter in December 2019) is somewhat prescient of the growing levels of unrest, and growth in evidence of armed militias present on US streets in the run up to the 2020 US Presidential elections.

[63] See, for example, *https://www.weforum.org/agenda/2020/03/a-visual-history-of-pandemics/*.

Certainly, exacerbated by the growing 2022 cost-of-living crisis, candidates for the UK's summer'22 Conservative Party leadership competition for a new prime minister, received calls for greater investment in innovation.[64]

Can a private-capital-managed, technology-led creative-destructive growth strategy offer a solution to the socio-economic impact of the current crises? Faced with a new imperative to reduce national debt, it is conceivable that the UK government might feel compelled to privatise remaining public institutions (or parts of them). A decision to sell London's Barts Health NHS Trust to the US healthcare provider, AmaCare, a fictional subsidiary of Amazon, is not entirely implausible. Such a sale would provide much-needed revenue to the exchequer and need not represent the widespread dismantling of the NHS. Thus, intuitively, we envisage rising public concern fuelling the growth of social movements that actively lament neglected institutions and values. I suggest that we might anticipate concern growing to very high if not unprecedented levels of activism, which might well threaten even a strong government majority. Unexplained deaths even mistakenly attributed to capitalist excess, could trigger social unrest and violence.

From the Headline **HL_5**, '***Public lose again as another longshot gamble fails***', I argue that we can further critique the continuation of technology-led creative destruction. In a renewed attempt to grow the UK economy out of its post-Covid-19 economic crisis, I suggest that we might envisage that public funds—channelled through the British Business Bank's patient capital initiative—are invested against the promise of returns that are, in their own right, fictions. These fictions constitute wholly indeterminate outcomes. It is conceivable that, in the desire to achieve, for example, a new flagship online market to rival Amazon, one or more unscrupulous parties might conceive of an accounting scheme to rival Enron's.[65]

A dialectic conceptualisation of entrepreneurship is the epithet of technological innovation and creative destruction. Yet, by and large, it is little more than J-B Say's agent of privately managed capital. For the individual, there is an illusion of (self) control in the concept of entrepreneurship. But falling levels of innovation, amid a growth in self-employment and the increase in (employment) risk transferred to the individual, raises many questions. Although there are exceptions, entrepreneurship represents its own industry—the industry of entrepreneurship. It simply produces insecure short-term (self-) employment opportunity for many. A growing reality is that

---

[64] Rathbone, "The UK's next PM Should Build on R&D Spending Commitments."

[65] McLean and Elkind, The Smartest Guys in the Room: The Amazing Rise and Scandalous Fall of Enron.

self-employment is a different matter when the probability and impacts of risk are experienced. Post Covid-19, it is conceivable that many may rethink the illusion of control offered by entrepreneurship and seek new opportunities for employment, turning away from the epithet 'entrepreneur', yet having nowhere to go (in the short term). The concern of a post-Covid-19 future of work, one where the hope of many rests on the influence of too few is that those 'too few' continue to exhort 'development', 'progress' and 'modernisation', while at the same time further undermining institutions as bastions of employment opportunity. Provocatively, I posit that this will be increasingly ill-received.

On experts and storytellers

A post-Covid-19 future does not preclude either social justice or inclusive access to employment opportunities. Here, I draw a comparison with the expert-led questions and issues developed within the FFW report, outlined at the head of this Chapter.[66] Firstly, the FFW determined that, in order that employment opportunities in 2030 may be better quality (in terms of pay, conditions, work-life balance etc.), the local region of the City of York and its wider environs may need to accept that it remains an economy predominantly based on hospitality, tourism and agriculture. Here, it can be argued that this is an institutional view—where, for example, the concept of the institution of hospitality provides form to its industry, market and resources, imposing social coherence on the practices and habits of human thought and action within that institution.[67] An institutional view of hospitality, tourism and agriculture does not preclude the idea of better-quality employment for the region, nor indeed globally, and it is coherent with the FFW's positive scenario of better quality employment opportunities in 2030.

The traditional view suggests employment opportunity is negatively affected by institutional limitations—such as regulated employment practices. However, in considering institutional determinants of unemployment in OECD countries, Lucio Baccaro and Diego Rei found no systematic support for a deregulatory view.[68] Conceptually, de-institutionalisation—whether deregulatory, or creatively destroyed through the interchange of some functional (human) practices with technology—appears to have little ground for positive impact on employment opportunity. In a post-Covid-19 future, a resurgence of

[66] Waehning et al., "Social Justice in York, 2030 (Extended Summary)."

[67] See for example: Qian and Burritt, "The Development of Environmental Management Accounting: An Institutional View."

[68] Baccaro and Rei, "Institutional Determinants of Unemployment in OECD Countries: Does the Deregulatory View Hold Water?"

austerity and a doubling-down on the functional interchangeability of technology and institutional practices, suggests little promise for better-quality opportunity. This is particularly so considering the apparent failure of such interchangeability to overcome a perceived severe productivity crisis since at least 2005.[69]

Secondly, the FFW determined that technology developments will only lead to better quality of life outcomes—creating enhanced employment opportunities—if it is accepted that technology can, and must, be applied to those issues that can be deterministically envisioned. While the FFW called for a shift from the indeterministic development of technology for technology's sake, the news from the post-Covid-19 future suggests that any decision to re-enter austerity is likely to see a doubling down on, rather than a reduction of, such behaviour.

Conceptually, the application of technology to strengthen institutions, rather than creatively de-institutionalise them (in search of new unicorns) may hold greater promise for socially-just employment. However, following Alfred Kleinknecht, the flexibility of a dominantly 'entrepreneurially-focussed' self-employed labour force may have a negative impact on any desire to better develop institutional-level economic activity.[70] Here, innovation at the institutional level suggests a requirement for high levels of tacit knowledge concerning any institution's functional practices and habits. Yet, a flexible, transient labour force may well find itself re-deployed in low-technology manufacturing and less-knowledge-driven services.

Thirdly, the FFW's aspirational scenario of better-quality work, suggests employers must be enabled to make more effective use of their own resources, to develop the potential of their workforces. Taking the institutional view, the long-run suggestion is that recruitment, development, and retention is best seen through the need to establish the high levels of tacit knowledge commensurate with innovation in institutional functional practices. While this idea invokes support for the employer (and the employee) to take responsibility for a life-long learning that acknowledges an indeterminate future, it does so in conflict with the deregulation of workforces of recent decades. A return to austerity and continued investment in (functional) technological substitution will further weaken institutions, forcing transitions of flexible, often highly educated workers to low-technology manufacturing and low-knowledge-led services.

---

[69] Kleinknecht, "The (Negative) Impact of Supply-Side Labour Market Reforms on Productivity: An Overview of the Evidence."

[70] Kleinknecht, "The (Negative) Impact of Supply-Side Labour Market Reforms on Productivity: An Overview of the Evidence."

Finally, the FFW scenario suggested the necessity for employers, particularly SMEs, to be supported to better identify, recruit, retain and develop their employees to meet their requirements. Again, a post-Covid-19 austerity pitches the institutionally desirable against the institutionally disruptive potential of hyper-active, often short-cycled and indeterminate technological innovation. Thus, while we might desire greater institutionalisation, offering enhanced opportunities for the identification, recruitment and retention of employees, such a move would be seen as counterintuitive when faced with increased national debt and a perceived need to enhance productivity and growth.

Reconciling a future of employment and skills

Concluding this second of my future-based 'means' inquiries, to what extent are our institutions interchangeable with technology? What interpretation can be placed on the interchangeability of technology and institutions, and their effect on facilitating and empowering better social systems of work for the future? What is the potential to *shape and control the scale and form of human associations and actions* and move to design better social systems of employment and work? Should we, as Jim Dator suggested, look to *de-colonize the future*? Or conceptually, might we be better moved to guard against the future as some form of failed or failing Schumpeterian creative-destructive project?[71] Should we, instead, look to *re-colonize the present*? Is there an opportunity to control technology in the service of institutional reform, conservation and renewal, letting the future take care of itself? One might well argue that, in a utopian future, unicorns can happily take care of themselves.

Acknowledging a perceived need for greater visibility of the employment and skills challenges faced by the City of York and its environs, the FFW determined there was an immediate requirement for the establishment of some form of (regional) agency for the co-ordination of action. However, as I have unfolded in the above analysis, the Covid-19 crisis and its projected histories provocatively hint at a national and global need for a unity of purpose which will, inevitably, provide the visibility of purpose sought both locally and regionally. While events have overtaken the immediate needs elicited from the workshop, the FFW scenario holds ground in a national and global context. Usefully, it has proven to be a valid foil to the counter-factual histories presented in this Chapter. It is not good enough to simply desire a future and aim toward it, neither is it good enough to simply alter a course of action if no thought has been given to what alternatives might be presented or

---

[71] A failed Schumpeterian project implies a failure in the generally perceived requirement to create new opportunity through the process of destroying old orders.

possible. The former represents a naïve neglect of restrictive forces, the latter a naïve neglect of opportunity.

I have argued a dialectic entrepreneurship's own industry as an illusion of entrepreneurial self-control, in which the entrepreneur is a worker in 'creative destruction', but under insecure short-term (self-)employment. Here, there is some sense in considering Dator's four archetypes of the future: 1) continued growth, 2) collapse/decline, 3) a conserver/ disciplined society, and 4) high-tech transformation.[72] These represent potential strategies. However, consideration of the FFW scenario in isolation does not easily guide selection of an archetypal (let alone hybrid) development strategy. Yet, in considering the counterfactual provocations, I suggest that high-growth and high-tech transformation (while superficially attractive) may be ill-advised in the face of recovery from their impact on the underlying institutions of society. While no one wishes economic or societal collapse or decline, there is sense in conceptually looking toward a more conserver/disciplined society. Perhaps such a society would lay a better foundation for 'technology as a social product... [better reflecting] the priorities of the holders of social and economic power',[73] in which a better future is predicated on broader changes in ownership.[74] The inquiry continues.

---

[72] Bezold, "Jim Dator's Alternative Futures and the Path to IAF's Aspirational Futures."
[73] Baldry, "Editorial: Chronicling the Information Revolution," 180.
[74] Spencer, "Fear and Hope in an Age of Mass Automation: Debating the Future of Work."

Chapter 6

Horsemen in the land of Oz

IN THIS FUTURE-FOCUSSED INQUIRY into the dance of capitalism, work and enterprise, I have so far taken a (science) fictional perspective for the imaginations on the imaginary plane, both on the future of an indeterminate entrepreneurship (Chapter 4), and on the functional interchangeability of technology and institutions in the context of the future of work (Chapter 5). In the latter case, I balanced the fictional perspective against the views of experts. While, in Chapter 4, my initial 'means' inquiry appealed—in part—to a call for more understanding of the dynamics and exploitation of technology innovation,[1] that part remains inconclusive; I did not seek to detail changes to better shape a future technology-driven entrepreneurship. Rather, I simply concluded that such changes were most likely required.

Technology aside, a common theme is the agential act of entrepreneurship itself. While this was explicitly the case in Chapter 4, in Chapter 5's second, 'means' inquiry into work in general, I nevertheless found the disenfranchisement of a class of workers, transitioning from employment to self-employment—a liminal form of entrepreneurship. This, I argue, is a neoliberal colonisation of the institutional practice of employment. It is a significant question of the 'identity' of the individual, between 'employee' and a member of the class of 'self-employed'. Here, in this liminal space, and potentially motivated by a range of factors discussed in Chapter 3, while I may

[1] Öner and Kunday, "Linking Technology Foresight and Entrepreneurship."

call my 'self' an entrepreneur, alongside the disenfranchised others of an 'unmasked' entrepreneurship, I risk losing sight of my rationale for being.[2]

While in Chapter 5, I indirectly surfaced the 'identity' issue in a local/ regional context, I acknowledged the more global implications of change and its driving forces. In particular, I noted that we should consider the concepts of endogenous (internally driven) and exogenous (externally driven) influences. Such influences are, in effect, sources of power. Maintaining my ambitious line of inquiry, the future of enterprising work—inclusive of both employment and self-employment—therefore appears closely associated with the individual concepts of power, technology and identity. In this Chapter—the third of my 'means' inquiries—I choose to single out these concepts and apply them to a more global analysis of enterprise. I therefore continue with an inquiry into neoliberal colonisation, as it relates to the long-term, post-pandemic horizon of international business. In a sense, this critiques David Ricardo's idea of 'comparative advantage' and its role in the evolution of capitalism.

An inquiry into the future of international business

Any conceptual-level inquiry into a field of interest is a provocation. My objective in this one is thus a critical provocation toward a broad view of IB, insofar as it delineates the activities, strategies, structures, and decision-making processes of the multi-national corporations (MNCs) and businesses that operate within the international milieu of varying cultural, economic, legal and political dimensions.[3] While this definition covers two of the six possible sub-domains of interest in IB proposed by Lorraine Eden and her colleagues, it shall suffice for the purpose of my inquiry. I do not, for example, focus on cross-border activities, nor cross-country comparatives. My scope is simply the general impact of the international environment on IB. However, following Jean Boddewyn's definition of the IB field's conceptual boundaries and levels[4], I also set my analysis of IB at the network and global levels, where IB is held as a response to issues of globalisation.[5] This sets my focus on the big issues with potential for global impact: how IB can have impact globally, and how global issues can impact on IB. In this sense, my use of the terms

---

[2] Jones and Spicer, Unmasking the Entrepreneur.
[3] Eden, "Letter from the Editor-in-Chief"; Eden, Dai, and Li, "International Business, International Management, and International Strategy: What's in a Name?"
[4] Boddewyn, "The Conceptual Domain of International Business: Territory, Boundaries, and Levels."
[5] Ricart et al., "New Frontiers in International Strategy."

global, globalised and globalisation are simply taken to mean a 'world-wide' extent in general, and not exclusively in terms of a global capitalist market.[6]

While adopting a non-specific use of the term global, I nevertheless position a critical concern over the idea of a neoliberal capitalist colonisation of societies, as it might be conceived of in a global context. Here, I simply accept neoliberalism as a form of capitalism. It is characterised by a certain 'freedom from the state (deregulation), freedom of the market (privatisation) and freedom of the consumer (possessive individualism)'.[7] This approach is consistent with the non-conceptual idea of studying a subject without looking at it as an object.

Having separated neoliberalism from globalisation, I move from Martin Bosman's four approaches to a neoliberal capitalism, to just two.[8] Firstly, neoliberal capitalism is an emergent (epi)phenomenon, one that is ever-expanding, emerging from world affairs according to the choices made at a local level, as domestic and foreign affairs converge. I accept that, to some, choice might well be influenced by a utopian ideology, but it is a choice. Here, the spread of a mainstream neoliberal capitalism is simply symptomatic of evolutionary, cultural change—potentially on a global scale. Secondly, the global spread of neoliberal capitalism is a dream-vision, a utopian ideal, a project directed by one or more influential forces of power. This amounts to a colonisation of global space. In this second approach, where the forces of power are rivalist nations (whether individual or, in some way, aligned) or, indeed, the collective holders of capital ('the capitalists'), then I am presented with neoliberal capitalism as a form of imperialist colonisation project, or neo-imperialism. Thus, having explicated some basic terminology, in looking toward the future I now pose the questions of the inquiry:

> Will neoliberalism continue to drive global dimensions in shaping a post-pandemic world of international business? If so, what does this say about power, technology and identity?

I proceed with my inquiry in the CCF method, as follows. Firstly, in mapping the domain, I adopt a critical, complex adaptive systems perspective. This allows me to trace individual lines of inquiry into IB under the three core themes of power, technology and identity. However, rather than use fictional

---

[6] See, for example: Levitt, "The Globalization of Markets."
[7] Bosman, "The Political Rhetoric of Corporate Globalisation and the Possibilities for Counter-Hegemonic Projects," 126.
[8] Bosman, "The Political Rhetoric of Corporate Globalisation and the Possibilities for Counter-Hegemonic Projects."

headlines from the future, I simply imagine the potential impact of Covid-19 upon each theme. This sets up six exemplar future outcomes—the imaginations. I then apply the truth table to reflect on the relative coherence of these outcomes to the range of future moments—the contradictions—projected as a function of their thematic history. Finally, in a departure from the triangulation of the experts, I introduce a novel use of allegory. This draws from design thinking to provide a Wizard-of-Oz view on the imagined futures of interest—the provocations. This technique presents the appearance of a future reality that is merely a manipulation by the inquirer.[9] It allows me to critically reflect on a mediated future, through an allegorical discussion that invokes the (fictional) myth of the Four Horsemen of the Apocalypse in a journey to the Wizard of Oz, to seek answers to the questions posed.

IB as a complex, adaptive system

Given the unprecedented global situation presented by the Covid-19 pandemic, my aim in this inquiry is to provoke new, critical thinking. I align this to the challenge of making sense of, for example, the effect of the insecurity and hyper-turbulence of the external VUCA environment on a neoliberal colonisation by, or of, post-pandemic IB. In achieving my aim, I seek to extend a critical understanding of the ways in which the institutions of IB might better influence their own futures. In considering both my aim and the interconnectedness and interrelatedness of IB with the global communities it serves, my first antagonism is that IB, as an entity—a global organization of MNCs and businesses in its own right—is a complex adaptive system.[10] Its components interact with each other and with their local and global environments. Here, Walter Buckley noted that the interchanges among a complex adaptive system's components may result in '*significant changes in the nature of the components themselves,* with important consequences for the system as a whole'.[11] This suggests that critical thinking aimed at sense-making about IB, can only be maintained if my understanding of IB acknowledges, *inter alia,* both the fluidity of its conceptualisation and the malleability of its actors—the MNCs and other businesses, providing a variety pool for adaptive variability.

---

[9] Dahlbäck, Jönsson, and Ahrenberg, "Wizard of Oz Studies - Why and How"; Kinsley, "Futures in the Making: Practices to Anticipate 'Ubiquitous Computing'"; Strömberg et al., "Designing for Social Experiences with and within Autonomous Vehicles-Exploring Methodological Directions."

[10] Kilduff, "Performance and Interaction Routines in Multinational Corporation"; Buckley, Schwandt, and Goldstein, "Classic Paper Section: Society as a Complex Adaptive System (1968)."

[11] Buckley, "Society as a Complex Adaptive System," 490 Reprinted in; Buckley, Schwandt, and Goldstein, "Classic Paper Section: Society as a Complex Adaptive System (1968)."

Following Walter Buckley, IB—as both complex adaptive system and continuing entity—is not to be confused with the structure of IB and its businesses (as might be represented by that system from time to time). The IB system exists, itself, as one component (a sub-system) in another complex adaptive system—the economy.[12] Reflexively, as an inquirer stepping outside of IB and looking in, I may seek to understand the effect that the global (VUCA) environment can have on IB. Reflexively, inside IB looking out, I may seek to understand the effect that IB can have on that same global environment; while I may also seek to make sense of the effect that IB can have on itself. Here, many of the interchanges I observe between the components of such complex adaptive systems are social interactions. They form the social practice of IB. My critical inquiry is thus framed by a need to understand the integral complexity of reflexivity set within the integral complexity of adaptive systems that are, themselves, characterised by high levels of the embedded social practice of (economic) work.[13]

Three themes of a complex adaptive system of IB...

Framing my inquiry, I usefully note the idea of critical futures studies (CFS) advocated by Richard Slaughter.[14] This evokes a search for a 'deeper and broader' understanding of future realities—a process of social construction and legitimation, in which the aim is to isolate and draw attention to, aspects of a present reality which require urgent, critical attention. In this sense, therefore, my application of CFS to IB directly appeals to the deeper and higher meaning of the subject, sought by Christoph Dörrenbächer and Snejina Michailova.[15] It is an exploration of such meaning, around the effects of IB activities,[16] including the subjugation of many of its actors in their post-modern global societies, to a precarious position at the margins of IB.[17]

I draw on the Ricoeurian-influenced notion of 'distentive capability', to offer a creative, narrative construction of a future of IB. This allegorically stretches consciousness through the '*simultaneous attention to memory and*

---

[12] Witt, "Capitalism as a Complex Adaptive System and Its Growth."
[13] Billett, "Work as Social Practice: Activities and Interdependencies."
[14] Slaughter, "From Forecasting and Scenarios to Social Construction: Changing Methodological Paradigms in Futures Studies"; Slaughter, "Farewell Alternative Futures?"
[15] Dörrenbächer and Michailova, "Editorial."
[16] Dörrenbächer and Gammelgaard, "Critical and Mainstream International Business Research: Making Critical IB an Integral Part of a Societally Engaged International Business Discipline."
[17] Prasad and Durepos, "From Margin to Center: Listening to Silenced Subjectivities in International Business."

expectation'.[18] In doing so, I identify three underlying, critical uncertainties. Drawing from the work of Joan Enric Ricart and colleagues,[19] I take an initial position that there are several forces which have combined—under the rubric of globalisation—as either having an external affect on IB or are—to one extent or another—generated by IB and affective globally. Table 6.1 provides a precis of these forces, grouping them as either dominantly externally affective, or dominantly internally affective, that is to say: productive of outcomes that are globally affective on, or by, IB. I also categorise these forces as (dominantly, and in the broadest context) issues of either the exercise of power, the impact of technology, or a question of identity. That power itself is closely related to identity is indicative of the interconnectedness and interrelatedness of these forces and issues.

Power

I follow Elizabeth Armstrong and Mary Bernstein in identifying that my use of the concept of power in relation to the social milieu of a global, complex adaptive system of IB, holds a distinct and narrow definition of the related concept of politics.[20] The exercise of power, of any form, is a challenge to a constituted institutional or non-institutional authority. Thus, in context, all forms of challenge via the exercise of power are, by definition, political. Following Michel Foucault,[21] the power-politic dynamic cannot be exercised successfully—that is, nothing can or will be changed—if the mechanisms of power outside, below and alongside the requirement for change, do not also change.

Table 6.1. Drivers of global change

Affectiveness	**Driver**	**Type**
External affective on IB	Extent of barriers/restrictions to trade and investment	Power
	Extent of globalisation of financial markets	Power
	Extent of globalisation of access to/use of technology	Technology
	Extent of globalisation of knowledge via ICT	Technology

---

[18] Sarpong, Eyres, and Batsakis, "Narrating the Future: A Distentive Capability Approach to Strategic Foresight."
[19] Ricart et al., "New Frontiers in International Strategy."
[20] Armstrong and Bernstein, "Culture, Power, and Institutions: A Multi-Institutional Politics Approach to Social Movements."
[21] Foucault, Power/Knowledge: Selected Interviews and Other Writings 1972–1977.

	Extent of influence/power of supranational organizations	Power
Affecting global IB environ	Extent of active expansion of multinational firms	Power
	Extent of the blurring of nationality of multinationals	Identity
	The emergence of border transcending regional identities	Identity
	The decentralisation of activity within and between firms	Power
	Extent of ICT-facilitated digital communities/markets	Technology

(Based on: Ricart and others[22])

Following this power-politic dynamic then: the extent to which global barriers and/or other restrictions exist to prevent trade and investment; the extent to which financial markets are globalised; the extent to which the power and/or influence of supranational organizations, such as the European Union (EU) and the UN; the extent to which MNCs and business actively participate in international expansion; and the extent to which decentralised activity occurs within and between firms, resolves to an issue of power, moderated by a multi-level perspective of politics. In this respect, at least since the global financial crash of 2008, I also consider populism, as a form of (supra)national organization, and the co-option of a popular voice as movements with the power to politic—for example, Brexit, Trumpism, or populism in general.[23]

Power and politics are typically viewed from within IB, where the institutions of power politics shape and constrain strategies and create costs. Yet, where such institutions are distant or weak, IB must 'institute' its own power-politic to control and shape its environment.[24] Thus, a power politic, at whatever level, can have a systemic affect on IB. It can hide, dilute, or restrict valuable sense-making, and turn preferred (sensible) action into 'sense-censored' inaction.[25] Power thus impacts the interconnectedness of IB's system components, restricting the effectiveness of the variety pool for adaptive variability. Power, individually exercised by nation states, can reasonably be held to shape regional IB. Here, despite the rhetoric of former-UK Prime Minister Boris Johnson's declaration of projecting British power

[22] Ricart et al., "New Frontiers in International Strategy."

[23] Robinson and Bristow, "Riding Populist Storms: Brexit, Trumpism and beyond, Special Paper Series Editorial."

[24] Jackson and Deeg, "Comparing Capitalisms: Understanding Institutional Diversity and Its Implications for International Business."

[25] Whittle et al., "Sensemaking, Sense-Censoring and Strategic Inaction: The Discursive Enactment of Power and Politics in a Multinational Corporation."

worldwide,[26] it is doubtful that such politicking could ever amount to a new form of imperialism—a reflection of the UK's Imperial past. The existence of non-aligned external power structures would resist such global change. Rather, as Mehdi Boussebaa suggests, the important point is understanding how the 'Global Britain' rhetoric might shape and constrain strategies and create costs by 'being incorporated into, and being promoted by, various sectors of the [UK] economy'.[27]

Despite the political rhetoric of moderate powerbases—both institutional and non-institutional—there are those, for example, the USA and China, that do hold considerable power. There are also MNCs with significant economic power. Reflexively, stepping outside IB and looking in, I seek to understand the effect the global environment can have on IB. Reflexively, inside IB looking out, I see the effect of, for example, the IB powerbase of international banking at the centre of the 2008 crises—I understand the potential for negative, global impact. And reflexively, turning inside, I try to make sense of the effect IB has on itself. This includes the subjugation of multiple voices of challenge from complex, adaptive components 'outside, below and alongside'—where the language and politics of power is increasingly used to push dissent to the periphery of IB discourse.[28] Societies, communities, and individuals with no power of influence on the operation of such a complex, adaptive system can be 'subject to death and/or displacement', while those with power 'may expropriate vast resources'.[29] In the face of such power, Ricardo's theory of comparative advantage in industry specialisation and free international trade can do little to guarantee mutually beneficial trade.[30]

The international banking system is an exemplar. Devoid of critical, socio-political reflexivity, enhanced by the neoliberal dismantling of its barriers and the lifting of restrictions to the expansion of its financial markets, international banking's potential was lost in homeostasis.[31] Its ability to remain stable—

---

[26] Boussebaa, "In the Shadow of Empire: Global Britain and the UK Business School."

[27] Boussebaa, "In the Shadow of Empire: Global Britain and the UK Business School."

[28] Prasad and Durepos, "From Margin to Center: Listening to Silenced Subjectivities in International Business."

[29] Jessica Srikantia, 'The Structural Violence of Globalization', Critical Perspectives on International Business, 12.3 (2016), 222–58 (p. 223).

[30] Siddiqui, "David Ricardo's Comparative Advantage and Developing Countries: Myth and Reality."

[31] Homeostasis refers to the ability (of a system) to maintain a stable equilibrium (of operation). See Oxford English Dictionary (12th Edition). Homeostasis is a principle of equilibrium applied to a system's environment. Systems can be said to tend to either a steady state of dynamic homeostasis, in which the system works to preserve its character, importing energy from its environment to fuel its growth—as in an open

despite changes in its environment—saw its power-base push the study and refinement of a reified social 'banking' practice of profiteering: the 'routines' of international banking. As the international banking powerbase steadied its internal system conditions in search of optimal functioning, homeostasis played out to the service of *pleonexia*, ignoring the growing signals of fracture in its environment. Thus, as I might envisage a post-Covid-19 future for IB, I postulate the first critical uncertainty:

> **P_1:** IB is characterised by more or less directed neoliberal capitalist colonisation of global economies, rather than by co-operative, regional and evolutionary capitalism.

Critical uncertainty **P_1** covers a range of concerns, from the idea that 'states' can cause or alleviate deviation from 'efficient' international markets[32] (perceived as necessary in economic development or recovery), to questions of whether IB can be a force for good,[33] and the extent to which *market*

---

system; or a system may tend toward adaptation, in which its preservation involves an adaptation of the character of the system—such systems may be referred to as complex adaptive systems. See, for example: Marguerite Schneider and Mark Somers, 'Organizations as Complex Adaptive Systems: Implications of Complexity Theory for Leadership Research', Leadership Quarterly, 17.4 (2006), 351–65. Seen as a 'living system', social systems, such as systems of social or economic organization, may be held to inherit characteristics studied within the field of physiology. Thus, homeostasis has also been assumed by some as a necessary and desirable feature of complex adaptive systems. (See, for example: Carol Sanford, 'A Theory and Practice System of "Systems Thinking": With an Executive's Story of the Power of "Developmental" and "Evolutionary" Systems Thinking. Why a New Typology of Systems Thinking?', in International Conference on Systems Thinking in Management-ICSTM-ICSTM, 2004.) Such beliefs may arise from assertions that complex organisms require homeostasis to maintain their internal environment 'fairly constant in the face of challenges from the external world' (Harold Modell and others, 'A Physiologist's View of Homeostasis', Advances in Physiology Education, 39.1 (2015), 259–66). Here, homeostasis is related to the control of internally regulated system variables. Intuitively, a complex system's internal values may be set to regulate the system's outputs into an uncontrollable external environment. Thus, we might argue that it is the external environment that (purposively) dictates its internal value(s). And, therefore, in a living, social system, the only way of regulating internal human values is control (for example, power-politics, identity and /or technology). But such control cannot be reliably maintained because of the human condition of contrariness. Therefore, while homeostatic regulation may seem desirable, it reduces the adaptable nature of a complex, human-based adaptive system, and is best not desired.

32 Lenway and Murtha, "The State as Strategist in International Business Research."

33 Ellis, "Can Global Business Be a Force for Good?"

reforms are embraced or sought to drive profitability.[34] These are questions of the directed pursuance of neoliberal capitalism, versus de-colonisation—a turn to a more cooperative, regional form. For example, recovery of the unprecedented costs on all national governments arising from the Covid-19 crisis, allows me to project a future with dominant nationalistic agendas, where governments are driven, in part, by direction toward 'the desire of the super-rich to enjoy pristine safe city spaces with clean streets and immaculate parks';[35] where the BRICS (Brazil, Russia, India, China and South Africa) focus on the exploitation of their globally valuable resources.[36] Thus, I imagine (**P1$_1$**) a future of 'structural violence'.[37]

Alternatively, I guard against 'too strong' a critical bias toward the negativity of 'power, domination and social imperfections'.[38] I balance the potential for an increasingly directive neoliberal capitalism by imagining (**P1$_2$**) a post-Covid19 turn to a more compassionate capitalism.[39] This is a potential, I argue, that exists in the idea of a complex adaptive economic system. It promises a more regionally influenced, cooperative, incremental and evolutionary capitalism that allows the sense-making of its adaptive, human components to reflect a more authentic, power- and context-sensitive voice.[40]

---

34 Dau, "Learning across Geographic Space: Pro-Market Reforms, Multinationalization Strategy, and Profitability."

35 Roberts, "Luxury International Business: A Critical Review and Agenda for Research," 230.

36 Shahrokhi et al., "The Evolution and Future of the BRICS: Unbundling Politics from Economics"; Wallace, "Brazil ' s New Leader Promised to Exploit the Amazon — but Can He ?"

37 Srikantia, "The Structural Violence of Globalization."

38 Venkateswaran and Ojha, "Strategic Management Research on Emerging Economies: Cultural Imperialism in Universalizing Research Paradigms," 222.

39 Edward Boyd, 'Compassionate Capitalism Can Underpin Our Coronavirus Recovery', City AM, 2020 <https://www.cityam.com/compassionate-capitalism-can-underpin-ou rcoronavirus -recovery/>; Mariana Mazzucato, 'The Covid?19 Crisis Is a Chance to Do Capitalism Differently', The Guardian, 2020<https://www.theguardian.com/ commentis free/2020/mar/18/the-covid-19-crisis-is-a-chance-to-do-capitalism-differently> [acces sed 22 May2020]; Kevin Stankiewicz, 'Mark Cuban Says Coronavirus Will End up Improving Capitalism with Companies Putting Employees First', CNBC, 2020 <https:// www.cnbc.com/2020/04/08/mark-cuban-says-coronavirus-will-end-up-improving-cap italism-with-companies-putting employees-first.html> [accessed 22 May 2020]; R. Balasubramaniam, 'Compassionate Capitalism in Covid Era', The New Indian Express, 2020, pp. 1–2 <https://www.newindian express.com/opinions/2020/may/21/compas sionate-capitalism-in-covid-era-2146048.html> [accessed 22 May 2020].

40 Boussebaa and Morgan, "Pushing the Frontiers of Critical International Business Studies: The Multinational as a Neo-Imperial Space."

This allows for an effective challenge to power structures that threaten to uphold or even direct a new form of (neo) liberal colonisation.

Technology

A powerful force drives the world. That force is technology. It has 'proletarianized communication, transport, and travel'.[41] Almost 40 years since Theodore Levitt's words, technological advancement, particularly ICT, has continued apace. It has proletarianized, variously: the international hotel industry (Airbnb); publishing (Amazon: Kindle Direct Publishing, Smashwords); the music industry (Spotify); the film industry (Netflix, YouTube, Amazon: Prime Video); and the global news and communications media industry (YouTube, Twitter, Facebook, WhatsApp, Instagram and TikTok). Now, with costs falling, technologies such as additive manufacturing (AM) are positioned to proletarianize the global factories of IB.[42] It is, however, beyond the scope of my inquiry to comment on the range of technology and its potential. I simply call on ICT and AM as exemplars.

Previously, I noted technology shapes and controls the scale and form of human association and action.[43] In this sense, it shapes and controls the components of the complex adaptive systems of both IB and the economy, as they interact with each other and with their local and global environments. Here, the interchanges among the complex adaptive system components may result in 'significant changes in the nature of the components themselves'.[44] Thus, the paradoxical issue I must consider is the extent to which technology is both a catalyst and accelerator for, and a moderator of, change. For example, technology allows greater levels of 'proletarianization', yet at the same time, it acts to emulsify social practice. Technology, I argue, achieves the stabilisation of the substance of practice into new, technology-enhanced 'routines' of IB, devoid of the reflexivity necessary to maintain the fluidity and malleability of the systems they are designed to enhance.

Paradoxically, technology is a double-edged sword. On the one hand, it can cut through space and time,[45] shrinking distances,[46] eliminating intermediaries

---

[41] Levitt, "The Globalization of Markets," 92.

[42] Hannibal and Knight, "Additive Manufacturing and the Global Factory: Disruptive Technologies and the Location of International Business."

[43] McLuhan, "The Medium Is the Message."

[44] Buckley, "Society as a Complex Adaptive System," 490.

[45] Hydle, "Temporal and Spatial Dimensions of Strategizing."

[46] Ogrean and Herciu, "The Complex, Yet Small World of Global Multinationals – Insights on Some Apparent Paradoxes."

and effecting closer integration of economies.[47] On the other hand, it can cut the bonds of flexibility between a system's actors, revealed in the dichotomy of choice between 'online' scale and 'offline' sensitivity.[48] The technological refinement of a reified social practice of international trade, as a technological 'routine' of IB, emulsifies the internal, physical, and environmental conditions in search of optimal functioning. It sets the conditions for homeostasis.

Following Heidegger,[49] I again question the 'thing' technology 'is', in order to 'be', embracing the totality of its societal assignment. I speak to the equipmentality of the concept: the non-concept of technology, rather than technology as an object *per se*. My concerns are the forces of technology that serve to: 1) extend globalisation through the provision of access to it, or of its use; 2) extend the globalisation of knowledge (via ICT in particular); and 3) extend communities and markets (again via ICT). Here, critically, the application of technology is a matter of human choice, directed or influenced by power from outside, below or alongside that choice. It might also be evolutionary and incremental—a creative and innovative activity. Here, the source of power is more aesthetic. Thus, following my line of argument—and drawing from the world of entrepreneurship—technological change is exercised if the mechanisms of power, outside, below and alongside it, give voice to an 'affective' IB. Here, affections are 'actions and passions, where the former is a power to act and the latter a power to be acted upon'.[50] But even evolutionary change embodies risk and failure. Passions for technological solutions may over-rule senses, and actions may not realise anticipated results. They can hide, dilute, or restrict valuable sense-making, turning preferred (sensible) action into 'sense-censored' inaction. Thus, in a post Covid-19 future of IB, I postulate my second critical uncertainty:

> **P2**: IB is characterised by more or less directed technological application and homeostasis, rather than its emergent, reflexive, creative and innovative adaptation.

P2 delivers the prospect of greater systemic homeostasis in search of the internal, physical, and environmental conditions required for optimal growth

---

[47] de la Torre and Moxon, "Introduction to the Symposium E-Commerce and Global Business: The Impact of the Information and Communication Technology Revolution on the Conduct of International Business."

[48] Kotabe and Mandviwalla, "Information Technology and International Business: Theory and Strategic Development."

[49] Heidegger, Being and Time.

[50] Hjorth, "Absolutely Fabulous! Fabulation and Organisation-Creation in Processes of Becoming-Entrepreneur," 215.

and profits. Such conditions call on new levels of (de-)institutionalisation through, for example, greater levels of directed ICT diffusion. In post Covid-19 territory, I posit that we may imagine a state **(P2$_1$)** where, through increased homeostasis, socially- and even state-contested corporate activity continues undisturbed. This is even after conflicts associated with challenges to, and by, their exercise of power, are escalated to the courts.[51] Here, beyond even state capitalism, the corporate colonisation of regions by (elements of) IB, is as much a damaging prospect to global social interests as the action of, say, Brazil's intended exploitation of the Amazonian rainforest (under Bolsonaro).

Under **P$_2$**, I also address such uncertainty as the impact of ICT on IB itself, where, for example, José de la Torre and Richard Moxon highlighted the idea of the 'end of geography', including the nature of infinitely responsive and elastic supply chains.[52] But the fallibility of this phenomenon was exposed by the Covid-19-enforced shut-down of swaths of global trade, freezing supply chains and raising national concerns over a lack of productive capacity. Thus, I imagine **(P2$_2$)** the positive potential of commercial AM capabilities (3D-printing) being pivoted to re-localise manufacturing and supply—for example, producing necessary personal protective equipment (PPE) in meeting demands disrupted by broken international logistics chains. Here, from the USA[53] to Australia,[54] IB should be aware of the proletarianization of their global factories, as the accessibility to such technology also rests in the hands of smaller, local businesses, crafters and individual members of the public. All of these are increasingly connected, separately by ICT-enabled networks of influence, on a global scale. An idea from an individual in the USA can be manufactured in Australia in minutes, circumventing any requirement for an institutionalised IB. While the dichotomy between 'online' scale and 'offline' sensitivity remains, the risks under the double-edged sword of technology are clear.

Identity

I position my exploration of identity through the precept of identity theory (IT). One might reasonably say that IB, as a social, group or organizational phenomenon, is socially constructed and therefore a candidate for analysis

---

[51] Villo, Halme, and Ritvala, "Theorizing MNE-NGO Conflicts in State-Capitalist Contexts: Insights from the Greenpeace, Gazprom and the Russian State Dispute in the Arctic."
[52] de la Torre and Moxon, "Introduction to the Symposium E-Commerce and Global Business: The Impact of the Information and Communication Technology Revolution on the Conduct of International Business."
[53] Banker, "COVID-19 And 3D Printing."
[54] Knaus, "Manufacturing Face Shields within Days: How Australian Industry Is Pivoting to Fight Coronavirus."

via social identity theory (SIT).[55] However, I argue that as SIT mainly addresses group processes and inter-group relations; IT—which addresses individuals' role-related behaviours[56]—is more relevant to my critical position. Here, in the context of IB as a complex adaptive system and its function in the global economy, my interest is in how identity impacts the individual's role as an aesthetically operating, adaptive component—one able to contribute to the system's variety pool for adaptive variability.

My concern turns to how identity is constructed within a society that is complex and differentiated yet organized.[57] This accepts a view of society as represented, *inter alia*, by the co-existing complex adaptive systems of IB and the economy, at global, national and regional levels. Reflexively, I envisage the potential variability in an individual's identity (that is, identity dispersion[58]), as they negotiate multiple roles through their aesthetically informed, social practice of work and day-to-day living. Here, in contrary fashion, individuals are all, independently, subject to the uncertainties, tensions and conflicts arising under the influence of power structures existing outside, below and alongside them. This complex differentiated view of the construction of identity is further complicated by the advent of ICT, and by the rise of complex, informal organized networks of social identity through, for example, social media platforms such as LinkedIn, Facebook and others.

My broad assumption is that self-identity—as individual power or influence—represents a source of positive flexibility or subversive resistance. It amounts to a contrary inconsistency, in terms of a functioning systemic role in IB. Thus, following Peter Burke,[59] I suggest the cognitive dissonance arising from identity dispersion moderates flexibility and enhances resistance. Identity inconsistency therefore raises questions. For example, how might an individual's identity affect the extent of the blurring of nationality within MNCs and multinational businesses? Or how might emergent border-transcending regional or virtual networked identities impact role effectiveness? While I may observe that, under national conditions of cognitively challenging uncertainty, positive role behaviours can be fostered by organizational

---

[55] Ambos et al., "Imbalance and Isolation: How Team Configurations Affect Global Knowledge Sharing"; Munjal, Budhwar, and Pereira, "A Perspective on Multinational Enterprise's National Identity Dilemma."
[56] Hogg, Terry, and White, "A Tale of Two Theories: A Critical Comparison of Identity Theory with Social Identity Theory."
[57] Hogg, Terry, and White, "A Tale of Two Theories: A Critical Comparison of Identity Theory with Social Identity Theory."
[58] Burke, "Identity Dispersion: Flexibility, Uncertainty, or Inconsistency?"
[59] Burke, "Identity Dispersion: Flexibility, Uncertainty, or Inconsistency?"

formalization,[60] I challenge the idea that a general uncertainty-identity theory[61] is helpful in the context of my inquiry.

As the IB individual navigates their social practice of work and day-to-day living, the influence of power structures outside, below and alongside their role, act to construct and mediate their identity. This mediation is consistent with the idea of 'identity regulation', where the systemic, socio-political construction of identity within IB is affected by a multiplicity of individual narratives and national discourse. These include historical (neo)colonial power relations, managerial elitism and past divisions of labour.[62] Here, I intuit that the greater the distance an individual actor is from identity-regulating power structures—for example, an imperialistic MNC's home-centric hierarchy—the greater the influence of (local) power structures below and alongside the individual actor become. Thus, as IB expands globally, it is more difficult to control its peripheral activity. Power-wielding resources are thus distributed to the regions to improve control, de-centralising imperialistic activity in a form of corporate-colonialism.[63] Corporate identities and their power structures, once external, are now exposed to those previously below them (now alongside)—and with new structures appearing below.

Questions of identity—national, regional and local—matter. As the influence of external power reduces over distance, the systemic social practice of work and day-to-day living becomes more context and power sensitive. Individuals able to transcend the dominant surrounding power structures can tend to either: a strong, individualistic self-identity; or a cosmopolitan identity of non-national openness.[64] Thus, layers of uncertainty surround self-identity. The varying influence of power structures under conditions of national and global external uncertainties, may therefore challenge positive organizational behaviour. In a post Covid-19 future, I postulate my third critical uncertainty:

> **P3:** IB is characterised by more or less individualisation or cosmopolitanisation and the dispersion of corporate identity, rather than assent to corporate/neo-imperialism.

---

[60] Fischer et al., "Does Organizational Formalization Facilitate Voice and Helping Organizational Citizenship Behaviors? It Depends on (National) Uncertainty Norms."

[61] Hogg and Adelman, "Uncertainty-Identity Theory: Extreme Groups, Radical Behavior, and Authoritarian Leadership."

[62] Boussebaa, "Identity Regulation and Globalization."

[63] Boussebaa and Morgan, "Pushing the Frontiers of Critical International Business Studies: The Multinational as a Neo-Imperial Space."

[64] Skovgaard-Smith and Poulfelt, "Imagining 'Non-Nationality': Cosmopolitanism as a Source of Identity and Belonging."

Here I accept technology as a double-edged sword, where—through increasing social networking on a global scale—there is greater uncertainty over the outcomes of identity construction and/or dispersion. In an era witnessing increasing levels of both nationalism and populism (for example: Brexit and Trumpism)—yet characterised by global connectedness—I can imagine **(P3$_1$)** a future state of increasing national power distances, where weaker cross-border corporate/neo-imperialistic structures suggest that greater national, cosmopolitan or individual identities flourish within IB. This effectively facilitates growing levels of (semi-)autonomous activity—a source of potential resistance to corporate/MNC-level goals, with the potential for counter-hegemonic projects to surface.[65]

Alternatively, I can imagine **(P3$_2$)** the potential failure of either national politics or cosmopolitanised non-national populism to derail existing corporate hegemony and forms of neoliberal capitalist colonisation, such as neo-imperialism. Thus, increasingly, IB imposes from the outside in, greater influence on the identity of the individual. This influence may or may not encourage positive performance in role. In turn, this suggests a greater requirement on IB to exercise forms of identity regulation. Where IB operates in local and regional climates—where the power structures, external to, alongside and below its operations, are weak—the self-identity of its operating individuals is subjugated to the periphery of silence. Here, the grounds are set for homeostasis. Where such power structures are strong, the ground is set for conflict.

The baseline: power, technology and identity—IB's future

At the time of writing, an EBSCO Discovery literature search on the compound term <"power + technology + identity">, returned just 13 relevant articles, with a context review revealing just two of interest. Firstly, Michael Brocklehurst's analysis of a group of professional workers moving from conventional 'office working' to 'home working' is apposite, considering the Covid19 necessity of such social practice.[66] In considering the triad of power, technology and identity in the context of a social practice of work, Brocklehurst suggested that while technology-induced change is not inherently corrosive of identity, it restricts space for aesthetic reflexivity. In context, I suggest such an aesthetic restriction amounts to an emulsification of certain internal, physical, and environmental conditions in search of optimal functioning. In a contemporary observation, water-cooler meetings give way to constrained 2-D exchanges of compressed

---

[65] Bosman, "The Political Rhetoric of Corporate Globalisation and the Possibilities for Counter-Hegemonic Projects."

[66] Brocklehurst, "Power, Identity and New Technology Homework: Implications for 'new Forms' of Organizing."

screen images and the emergence of 'Zoom Fatigue'.[67] Secondly, Andrew Wood and Deanna Fassett combined the three perspectives in discussing classroom communications, where an autoethnographic analysis suggested that experiences of technology use, reveal a complex understanding of how identities interact under conditions of power that are distributed, embodied and malleable.[68] For my own analysis of the triad of power, technology and identity uncertainties facing IB, I project a baseline of future moments in time in the CCF form of future possibility—the contradictions. Table 6.2 depicts the associated truth table.

The counterfactuals: transposing the future

The Covid-19 crisis brought the uncertainty and unpredictability that underpins society to the fore. Here, I draw from Slavoj Žižek's *Living in the End Times*[69] and his premise that the global capitalist system is approaching an 'apocalyptic zero-point', marked by the system's *four riders of the apocalypse*: the ecological crisis; the biogenetic revolution and its consequences; systemic imbalances; and the social inequality and exclusion we now see exemplified, for example, in the notion of luxury goods.[70]

Table 6.2. Truth table: contradictions in International Business

m	P_1	P_2	P_3	Future moment/vignette
m_1	F	F	F	Historical discontinuity. Changes in the neoliberal colonisation of economies, a shift from directed technological homeostasis to creative & innovative technology adaptation and move to global embracement of national and diversified identities.
m_2	F	F	T	No move to global embracement of national and diversified identities.
m_3	F	T	F	No shift from directed technological homeostasis to creative & innovative technology adaptation.
m_4	F	T	T	No shift from directed technological homeostasis to creative & innovative technology adaptation and no move to global embracement of national and diversified identities.
m_5	T	F	F	No changes in the neoliberal colonisation of economies.
m_6	T	F	T	No changes in the neoliberal colonisation of economies and no move to global embracement of national and diversified identities.

67 Robert, "Here's Why You're Feeling Zoom Fatigue"; Sklar, "'Zoom Fatigue' Is Taxing the Brain. Here's Why That Happens."
68 Wood and Fassett, "Remote Control: Identity, Power, and Technology in the Communication Classroom."
69 Žižek, Living in the End Times.
70 Roberts, "Luxury International Business: A Critical Review and Agenda for Research."

m_7	T	T	F	No changes in the neoliberal colonisation of economies and no shift from directed technological homeostasis to creative & innovative technology adaptation.
m_8	T	T	T	Status quo? No changes in the neoliberal colonisation of economies, no shift from directed technological homeostasis to creative & innovative technology adaptation, and no move to global embracement of national and diversified identities.

(T=true, F=false)

Leaving aside systemic imbalances (which I posit are internal to the complex adaptive system of a global capitalist economy), I have argued the thesis that IB, as a sub-system of global capitalism, exists as a complex adaptive system in its own right. It is suspended in the context of the three systemic critical uncertainties I have identified. In a Žižekean sense, I suggest that the ecological crisis, the biogenetic revolution, and social inequality and exclusion, are signs—signals of a decay in global capitalism's effectiveness and, by extension, therefore, signals of a decay in IB. To explore this thesis, in Figure 6.1, I analyse the coherence between the counterfactual imaginations **($P1_1$ to $P3_2$)** that lie beyond the antagonistic horizon, and the range of possibility within the contradictions **(m_1-m_8)**.

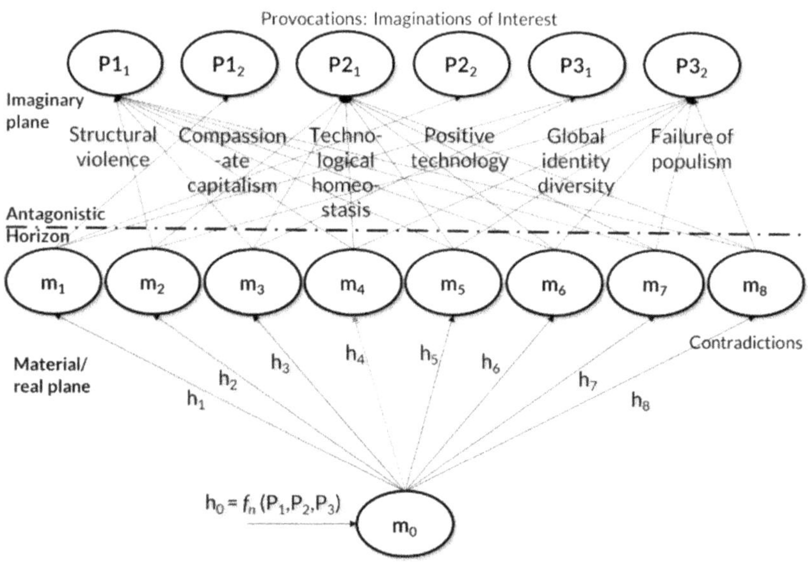

Figure 6.1. Finding truth in the future of International Business

Coherent futures: the provocations of history...

From Figure 6.1, I find the two most coherent of the imaginations as a function of the present trends identified, are $\mathbf{P1}_1$ and $\mathbf{P2}_1$. Thus, following exposure to the impact of Covid-19, I may rationally foresee a future, beyond the antagonistic horizon, characterised by: increasing 'structural violence'; nationalistic agendas, with governments driven, in part, by direction from the super-rich; and growth policies focussed on unsustainable resource exploitation. Consistent with this 'structural violence' is a high level of technology-induced homeostasis, such that the remaining social and state-contested corporate activities continue unabated. These perpetuate, if not accelerate, structural violence. A closely coherent imagination is $\mathbf{P3}_2$, in which, despite global concerns over the impact of Covid-19 and increasing levels of support, populism is a movement that is ultimately ineffective. Corporate hegemony continues with neoliberal capitalist colonisation, with IB regulating the identity of the individual, leading to either subjugated voices or conflict.

There is no moderately coherent outcome of the imagination visible. This leaves me with the least coherent of the imaginations being the development of a compassionate capitalism $\mathbf{P1}_2$, and no significant application of technology for the benefit of society, $\mathbf{P2}_2$. Both outcomes would require a major historical discontinuity, simultaneously affecting power, technology and identity. While Covid-19 offered a catalyst for such change, the necessary groundwork for change was not in evidence. Following Kurt Lewin's theory of change,[71] while the ground might have been unfrozen by Covid-19, there was no grand plan in place, in anticipation of a positive change opportunity.

There remains a marginal hope, with a slightly higher coherence of progress in identity diversity and its global acceptance, $\mathbf{P3}_1$. Growth in pockets of national, cosmopolitan and individual identity resistance would weaken cross-border IB structures, raising the possibility of increased (semi-) autonomous activity and counter-hegemonic projects. This is most likely to arise within marginal (social-)entrepreneurship and positive applications of technology. This is not an unreasonable hope. There will always be exceptions to the mainstream of any activity.

Allegoric speculation: the Four Horsemen in Oz...

Inspired, but not led by Žižek's invocation of the *Four Horsemen of the Apocalypse*,[72] I simply repurpose this canonical allegory. There is merit in this

[71] Lewin, Frontiers in Group Dynamics: Concept, Method and Reality in Social Science; Social Equilibria and Social Change.
[72] Žižek, Living in the End Times.

approach. Many people are aware of the *Four Horsemen of the Apocalypse.* Following Chapter 3, I recall stories are a powerful form of narrative which 'echo the voice, thinking, and perceptions of people... [and] are a valuable basis to explore the patterns of sensemaking'.[73] Stories can be subversive. And associating new realities with old meanings appeals to an interpretivist, narrative method on inquiry.[74] It is in this spirit that I also invoke L. Frank Baum's classic American children's story, *The Wonderful Wizard of Oz.* Here, I meet Dorothy, the Tin Woodman and other characters. While this story has been debated as allegorical of its time,[75] it is a useful tool to reflect on economic and political issues. Thus, I do not seek to add to the debate, but simply extend the principle of its usefulness—where the association of a remembered story allows sense to be made of aspects of our reality. So, beyond the antagonistic horizon, I evoke allegory as the basis for speculative discussion; I create and investigate the situation I study, employing conceptual and fictitious 'invention'—furthering imaginations that are rooted in the aesthetic and the political.[76]

For the following speculation, I also undertake a brief reading of four papers, each being selected on an abstract search of one of the keywords 'Conquest', 'War', 'Famine' and 'Death', in conjunction with 'International Business'. I simply selected a paper with an interesting tale to tell. Thus, I follow with my allegory of the Four Horsemen in the Land of Oz, as I recast each as a visitor to the Wizard of Oz. In place of the Tin Woodman, rides Conquest; instead of the Scarecrow, rides War. In the Cowardly Lion's stead, Famine; and in Dorothy's stead rides Death. They search for heart, brains, courage and direction.

Upon the white horse...

Upon the white horse rode Conquest, carrier of the bow and crown.

---

[73] Soin and Scheytt, "Making the Case for Narrative Methods in Cross-Cultural Organizational Research," 64.

[74] Soin and Scheytt, "Making the Case for Narrative Methods in Cross-Cultural Organizational Research."

[75] Gessel, Koupal, and Erisman, "The Politics of Oz : A Symposium"; Hansen, "The Fable of the Allegory: The Wizard of Oz in Economics."

[76] Steyaert, "Entrepreneurship as in(Ter)Vention: Reconsidering the Conceptual Politics of Method in Entrepreneurship Studies."

> As Conquest rose in the stirrups, he spoke clearly... "I shall take the heart," [he said] "for brains do not make one happy, and happiness is the best thing in the world." [parodying L.F. Baum [77]]

Conquest is the bringer of neoliberal colonisation, seen by some as positive, others as negative, perhaps as pestilence—the disease of a Western capitalist agenda. In recasting the Tin Woodman as Conquest, I first envisage the capitalistic search for the heart through conquest.

Ask the people of the Greek administrative regions of Thessaly and the island of Chios. There, the national government's post-2008 economic crisis response opened its renewable energy sector to foreign IB investment. The consequent disturbance of agricultural land by photovoltaic parks, and the island by wind farms, was seen by local inhabitants as a conquest of Ottoman proportions.[78] One might even say, ripping the heart out of local identities. As Nicolas Argenti and Daniel Knight argued, '[harnessing] natural resources such as the wind and the sun is perceived to be a colonial programme of economic extraction as much as a sustainable energy initiative, heralding a return to a time of foreign occupation'.[79] Faced with the prospect of colonising outsiders, local fears over national identity and resource ownership were set against the only perceived course of action open to the state to relieve its debts—debts created by the very structures that had led to the crisis in the first place.

The colonising mode of extracting the heart of a nation's identity speaks to national and global concerns, and ideas of inclusive economies, with people regarded on broadly equal terms. It questions disempowerment, exploitation and inequity.

> "I think you are wrong to want a heart[", said Oz. "]It makes most people unhappy. If you only knew it, you are in luck not to have a heart." [parodying L.F. Baum [80]]

A compassionate capitalism? In the search for a heart for capitalism, might there be wisdom in Oz? Happiness is an established critique of the economic growth of capitalism. At a mundane level, many people of many nations are

---

[77] Baum, The Wonderful Wizard of Oz, 52.
[78] Argenti and Knight, "Sun, Wind, and the Rebirth of Extractive Economies: Renewable Energy Investment and Metanarratives of Crisis in Greece."
[79] Argenti and Knight, "Sun, Wind, and the Rebirth of Extractive Economies: Renewable Energy Investment and Metanarratives of Crisis in Greece," 782.
[80] Baum, The Wonderful Wizard of Oz, 168.

generally better off financially now, than they were historically. Yet many people may be no happier as a result.[81] Nations, not least the Greeks, need to consider 'carefully and radically' how they recover from the devastation left by crises, such as the Covid-19 pandemic.[82] Here, there appears a greater urgency to adopt arguments for measures of growth (of national and global outputs) that include growth in human welfare.[83] This appeals, perhaps, to Kate Raworth's image of an economics guided by the 'Doughnut of social and planetary boundaries'.[84] In the Land of Oz, for Conquest to gain a heart, it must earn it, perhaps by responding to calls for a paradigm shift from a 'for profit' capitalism, to a more compassionate 'for benefit' form.[85] But in Conquest's search for heart, where is the leadership?

Upon the red horse...

Upon the red horse rode War, carrier of the double-edged sword of technology, a sword with the potential to slay the nationalistic resistance of any Emerald City.

> Menacingly, War leant forward in the saddle, and his voice chilled the air around them... "I shall [take] brains instead of a heart['; declared War, ']for a fool would not know what to do with a heart if he had one." [parodying L.F. Baum [86]]

In the context of IB, war is evident in national-level trade conflicts and disputes. In technology, where the competitive advantage of many businesses is secured in their ownership of intellectual property, the 'forced technology transfer' (FFT) policies of some nations, in return for foreign access to their markets, is a major concern; FFT policies have 'substantially fuelled the recent US-China trade war'.[87] But technology also isolates places. It impoverishes populations eager to gain access to what they increasingly see others have, via new technologies.[88] Wars of many natures have been and still are fought by

---

[81] Baumol, Litan, and Schramm, Good Capitalism, Bad Capitalism, and the Economics of Growth and Prosperity.
[82] Boyd, "Compassionate Capitalism Can Underpin Our Coronavirus Recovery."
[83] Baumol, Litan, and Schramm, Good Capitalism, Bad Capitalism, and the Economics of Growth and Prosperity.
[84] Raworth, "Why It's Time for Doughnut Economics," 218.
[85] Boyd, "Compassionate Capitalism Can Underpin Our Coronavirus Recovery."
[86] Baum, The Wonderful Wizard of Oz, 52.
[87] Prud'homme and von Zedtwitz, "Managing 'Forced' Technology Transfer in Emerging Markets: The Case of China," 6.
[88] Levitt, "The Globalization of Markets."

peoples wanting what others have, and they do not; and they are fought over peoples protecting access to what they do not want others to have.

Intellectual property laws erect barriers to protect markets, and in attempts to disrupt existing markets. Here, technology always disrupts. For example, aside from ICT disrupting travel, hotels and publishing, solar panels have democratised electricity production, disrupting traditional electric utility businesses.[89] Technology is a site of conflict and war, where taking the lead in a new order of things makes enemies of all those who have managed, and prospered, under the old.[90] The paradox of the double-edged sword is that, protected, its keen edge is dulled, emulsifying practice, stabilising the existing order of IB, restricting experience.

> 'Experience is the only thing that brings knowledge[', said Oz,']and the longer you are on earth the more experience you are sure to get… I will stuff your head with brains. I cannot tell you how to use them, however; you must find that out for yourself.' [parodying L.F. Baum[91]]

Technology, protected as an end, is emulsifying. I argue that it is not technology *per se* that holds value, but what we might choose to do with it. Thus, is there an argument that more sharing of technological capability will allow others, within the complex adaptive systems of economies and IB, to reap the adaptive benefits of more creative and innovative applications? Might the double-edged sword of technology be better raised against the atrophy of the public and private institutions that overprotect their existing knowledge and powerbases? Is this a sword—Herbert Marcuse might have suggested—best used to illustrate its transformational potential in converging technique with art? As Uri Zilbersheid suggests: '[on] a very high level in the development of productive forces, the criterion of efficiency [may] lose all real meaning, as any flow of products will be able to satisfy the needs of human beings'.[92] Nonetheless, raising the Sword of War for new knowledge will also require the leadership that appears to be missing.

Upon the black horse…

Upon the black horse rode Famine, carrier of the balances of international capital and trade – the judgement of imperial oppression.

---

[89] Lemley and McKenna, "Unfair Disruption."
[90] Machiavelli, The Prince.
[91] Baum, The Wonderful Wizard of Oz, 166–67.
[92] Zilbersheid, "The Utopia of Herbert Marcuse Part 1," 412.

> 'Why should I give you courage?' demanded Oz.

We have learnt Oz keeps a great pot of courage in his Throne Room, covered with a golden plate to prevent it from spilling over, and that he will be glad to give some to Famine.

> Famine leaned back in his saddle and roared: 'Because of all Wizards you are the greatest, and alone have power to grant my request.' [parodying L.F. Baum[93]]

It is what one does when faced with Famine that marks my interest. Carrying the mantle of the Cowardly Lion's search for courage, Famine seeks a share of what others have. He wants to identify with those others. An equitable distribution. To be a King among Kings. In reading Thomas Rawski's article on China's long economic boom, I learn that during the mid-1970s, most of China's rural village population were in absolute poverty—as defined by the World Bank.[94] Despite the commune system's shortcomings, pre-reform agriculture in China did yield rice, wheat and corn averages that equalled or exceeded world averages. However, average calorie consumption in the rural communities was below World Bank standards for nutrition. The pot of courage held by the pre-reform Chinese state, while far from being empty, was not to be shared equitably. The post-revolution commune system had imposed homeostasis on what might be termed the complex adaptive (sub)system of agriculture.

The effective removal of systemic stasis through the introduction of modest reforms in the late-1970s, enabled rural Chinese communities to shrug off decades of hunger, reducing the rural impoverished from 75% to less than 25% of their number. Paradoxically, this significant improvement was achieved with only a partial market, no international or NGO aid, and declining state support. Rawski makes a strong case that supports a reading that the Chinese State, faced by conditions of near famine, exercised the courage to change—to dismantle the commune system, to institute household management of farming, and to pay higher prices for the farm products produced. This led to 'an outpouring of entrepreneurial initiative'.[95] The removal of the stultifying structures of homeostasis allowed the components of the adaptive system to draw on the legacies of human capital—the variety pool for adaptive variability required to give effect to an effective, complex adaptive system.

---

[93] Baum, The Wonderful Wizard of Oz, 116.
[94] Rawski, "Human Resources and China's Long Economic Boom."
[95] Rawski, "Human Resources and China's Long Economic Boom," 34.

> 'There is no living thing that is not afraid when it faces danger[,' said Oz. ']The True courage is in facing danger when you are afraid, and that kind of courage you have in plenty.' [parodying L.F. Baum [96]]

Legacies of human capital? Courage to change? It rests with Famine to feed its own desire, but only with the knowledge and heart to do so. Historical and contemporary data suggest that in China, increases in grain prices following major crop failures were a moderate 20-70%. In comparison, following European famines, price rises were significantly higher, at 200-400%.[97] Profiteering in times of crisis raises questions concerning equity and identity, certainly of Western models of capitalism. The Covid-19 pandemic was not a direct attack on food production. Many international food prices, including cereal, wheat and maize, dropped in March 2020,[98] yet in countries like the USA and UK, consumer food prices rose[99] and, globally, food profiteering was evident. I ask: what price wheat and barley in the face of inequalities on a global scale, compounded by systemic structures that disperse identity?[100] Given the noted inconsistency in the role of identity as a source of positive flexibility or subversive resistance, there is a position for IB in appreciating and addressing the cognitive dissonance arising from global actions that moderate flexibility and enhance resistance. What it will take is courage.

Upon the pale, ashen horse...

And on the pale, ashen horse rode Death, the great leveller, an authority to kill with pestilence, sword, famine and nature. Death is the co-ordinator, the integration of thinking of Conquest, War and Famine.

> With one nudge of her knees, Death's pale horse steps forward of the others. Death dismounts in front of the Wizard. She looks Oz up and down. She speaks, quietly: 'Send me back [home]... I don't like your country,' said Death.

---

[96] Baum, The Wonderful Wizard of Oz, 168.

[97] Rawski, "Human Resources and China's Long Economic Boom."

[98] United Nations, "World Food Prices Drop in March."

[99] Partington, "Price of High Demand Food Bought Online in UK Rises Sharply"; Selasky, "Food Prices Soar to Highest One-Month Increase since 1974; Price of Eggs up 16% in April."

[100] There is a clear parallel here with the consequential aspects of food and energy price increases resulting from Putin's 2022 Russian 'special military operation' against the Ukraine. Although, to an extent, having seen the impact of their actions, Russia appeared to then weaponise elements (for example supplies of natural gas) as an indirect attack on the 'capitalist' West's support of Ukraine.

> 'In this country everyone must pay for everything he gets. If you wish me to use my magic power to send you home[', said Oz, ' then] you must do something for me first. Help me and I will help you.'
>
> 'What must I do? asked Death.
>
> 'Kill the Wicked Witch of the West,' answered Oz. [parodying L.F. Baum [101]]

We know that the West is ruled by the Wicked Witch of the West. She enslaves people who pass her way. A colonisation of the North, South, and East is the eternal worry of the great Oz.

In reading Yunus Butanaziba's article on ending 'Globalisation Disorders',[102] the author comments on the history of failures of states and wars of resources as, over the years, international governmental organizations have exercised regimes of global influence. Such regimes, he posits, emerge from war, 'guided by emotions rather than positive thought'.[103] As the fictional Wizard calls on Death and her friends to kill the Witch of the West, in reality, I read that, from 1946 to 2010, there were more than 136 resource wars, where violence by an agent, either state, organization or individual, has caused over 250million deaths at a market value loss of over USD500 trillion.[104]

The allegorical call for action to co-ordinate Power, Technology and Identity, is to exercise authority over Death. It is to: employ Conquest with a heart, spreading compassion as though it was a new, positive form of pestilence; raise War's Sword of Technology in service of social good and against systemic homeostasis; and face Famine with the courage to change toward an equitable, inclusive distribution of the good. This is Butanaziba's call to, *inter alia,* end the 'Third World'; create new geographies of peace; strengthen control over wars and resources; make IB ethics part of the social practice of IB; and encourage a movement toward cooperative and participatory enterprise. Such a strategic call on IB is a call to lead in the ending of global disorders that are brought into stark relief by crises.

Reconciling the promise of IB

While my speculations represent manipulations of the imagined future, they reveal antagonistic positions from which I have offered several perspectives on the shape of a post-pandemic world of IB. Rather than consider IB as an

---

[101] Baum, The Wonderful Wizard of Oz, 108–10.
[102] Butanaziba, "The Strategy: Ending Globalization Disorders."
[103] Butanaziba, "The Strategy: Ending Globalization Disorders," 82.
[104] Butanaziba, "The Strategy: Ending Globalization Disorders."

emerging imperialist project of neoliberal colonisation, as a macro attack on globalised capitalist markets,[105] my provocations merely posit IB as a complex adaptive system. This has emerged, and continues to emerge, in the context of a global economy, itself a complex adaptive system shaped by the many characteristics of neoliberal capitalism. In some places, ideas of imperialism also emerge. However, avoiding any accusation of entrenched ideological biases,[106] for example, Marxism, I find no grounds to disagree with Vernon Ellis, who argued that IB can be a force for good.[107] My critical concern is to address the question: what can be done to better realise its social potential? In extending a critical understanding of ways in which institutions, including IB, may better adapt to the future, I argue we should seek the means to re-engineer capitalism.

In addressing the question will neoliberalism continue to be a driver of global dimensions in shaping a post-pandemic world of IB, my analysis suggests it will. The most coherent outcome (to date) is a continuance of its worst characteristics of 'structural violence' and nationalistic agendas that, in the main, exploit unsustainable resources. This is not helped by a dispersed (globally uncoordinated) notion of populism as a movement that is, ultimately, ineffective. Thus, despite Covid-19, the inertia and flexibility inherent in extant levels of corporate hegemony suggest the direction of travel of capitalism. However, rather than toward a systemically deliberate global colonisation, I suggest that we might benefit from considering capitalism's travel as a form of pestilence, requiring new forms of control and mitigation—just as with the outbreak of any pandemic. Under different causes, the global financial crash of 2008 resolved to a similar continuation of capitalism. Despite the potential that sits within the concept of a more compassionate capitalism, and a technology that provides value to societies (rather than extracting it from them), the deeply entrenched homeostatic structures that disperse and regulate identity defy the co-ordination, on a global scale, of the subjugated voices of compassion. The dispersed voices of protest present little scope for systemic challenge.

So, if the future looks like more of the same, what does this say about a critique of power, technology and identity? My starting point is reflected in Lewin's challenge that a science (here: IB) cannot proceed beyond a certain

---

105 Verbeke, Coeurderoy, and Matt, "The Future of International Business Research on Corporate Globalization That Never Was…."

106 Vine, "Brexit, Trumpism and Paradox: Epistemological Lessons for the Critical Consensus."

107 Ellis, "Can Global Business Be a Force for Good?"

stage without entertaining conceptual development.[108] My starting point is thus the technology. Looking to the future, I agree with Ulrich Betz and colleagues, who argue that it is the uses to which technology is put, that are the subject of much uncertainty, not the changing nature of technology itself.[109] Consider that computers are used more for data storage and communications than calculation. They are used more in creating global networks of disparate, self-identifying social groups—all potential pockets of systemic influence and/or resistance—than they are in calculating the geometry of space travel.

We might well follow Frederick Ahen's calls for IB inquiries into the 'wicked questions' of sustainability, injustice, inequality and other emergent global challenges, and the blurred boundaries between them.[110] As Betz and colleagues argue, it is mainly the case that the areas of greatest social need are those to which businesses are least prepared to respond.[111] To prepare the ground, I argue that changes to any combination of power structures, technological applications and problems of identity and inclusion, are unlikely to produce great benefits to a future society, unless they are all challenged simultaneously. While some positive differences may result from superficial attention to just identity and inclusion, these are likely to remain isolated and marginal, as (relatively localised) responses to pockets of isolated resistance.

While a critical, negative dialectic understanding of the ways in which, internationally, institutions (including businesses and governments) might influence their own global futures, there can be no accurate projections for their individual futures. My provocative aim has simply been to stimulate new, critical thinking. While my inquiries continue, I might well suggest that the proper critical concern of IB is leadership—whether that is in IB research, IB policy, or IB practice. Leadership requires a holistic view of its domain. Here, I argue that the study of futures and foresight is a proper concern of IB leadership, in whatever guise. In this Chapter, I have shown that such a study can invoke new modes of thinking (through complex, adaptive systems) and how critical perspectives can be built and rationalised from fictional standpoints—from the imagination.

---

[108] Lewin, Frontiers in Group Dynamics: Concept, Method and Reality in Social Science; Social Equilibria and Social Change.

[109] Betz et al., "Surveying the Future of Science, Technology and Business – A 35 year Perspective."

[110] Ahen, "Global Health and International Business: New Frontiers of International Business Research."

[111] Betz et al., "Surveying the Future of Science, Technology and Business – A 35 year Perspective."

Conceptual development of IB will require change, invoking Lewin's three-step process of unfreezing, moving, and refreezing.[112] Here, provocative inquiry, such as this, leverages the unfreezing of thought prompted by crises. It gives fruitful space for movement and ideas in thinking about IB and beyond. Yet, post-crisis, the opportunity for change does not remain present in such a form for long. Unlike the previous chapter's provisional conclusion for a change to a 'conserver/disciplined' future society, the idea of global change, or change at a global scale suggests a requirement for an immanent critique of capitalism itself.

---

[112] Lewin, Frontiers in Group Dynamics: Concept, Method and Reality in Social Science; Social Equilibria and Social Change.

Chapter 7

Ghosts of democracy

DESPITE THE POTENTIAL WITHIN the concept of a (localised) more compassionate capitalism, the entrenched homeostatic structures that disperse and regulate identity, defy the co-ordination—on a global scale—of voices of compassion. To understand such structures further, I believe it is necessary to go beyond the localised issues of even internationalised institutions, such as IB, and turn toward a critical, futures-based examination of the long-term prognosis of capitalist economies in general—specifically those of a neoliberal nature. Therefore, in this fourth 'means' inquiry, I examine the notion that a neoliberal capitalist ideology—romanced by what has clearly been achieved for its incumbents and those enfranchised to its (positivistic) dialectic identity—has failed to understand the true nature of a self-organizing system. As I outlined in Chapter 1, the premiss is that, even before Covid-19, capitalism was in a state of crisis.[1] As a form of economic organization, capitalism aligns with Adam Smith's concept of an economic system.[2] And, from the perspective of a 'pure' neoliberal market, an efficient functioning system of capitalism requires, *inter alia*, protections from 'discretionary political interference'.[3] Yet, for Western democracies, such protections are problematic: discretionary political interference is the norm of a power-politic representative of its society—its voters. From this standpoint, market capitalism—as a protected 'closed' system: effective and efficient—is a utopian ideal, at best unachievable, at worst sclerotic.

---

[1] See *also: Streeck,* How Will Capitalism End?
[2] Dow, "Smith's Philosophy and Economic Methodology."
[3] Streeck, How Will Capitalism End?, 75.

Capitalism has certainly delivered benefits to some in society, yet it is increasingly held as fundamentally flawed—the dominant 'neoliberal' flavour reviving injustice and inequality to a 'state close to that 100 years ago'.[4] But, if it is failing (or has failed), certainly in Europe,[5] how do we, as Paul Mason suggests, '*design* the transition to [a] postcapitalism'?[6] Such a transition problem lies at the limit of our economic knowledge. It is a *knowledge problem.* It is as if we were to say: "we have tried everything we can do, to make capitalism work, but we have not found a way". If this is the case, should we not ask: "what would a future socially-just, effective, efficient and open post-neoliberal capitalist system of economic organization look like?"

Twentieth-century German sociologist and systems theorist, Niklas Luhmann (1927-1998) posited the economy as an 'open' subsystem, operating within a broader, social system.[7] This accords with a 'systems thinking' view that, at a high-level, every situation we examine—for example, our economic situation—is a human one: people taking purposeful (economic) action meaningful to them in their social situation.[8] As a subsystem then, the economy is differentiated from its environment: the system itself. It does not neglect its environment (the social system) but communicates with it through its own 'code'. That said, I extend the idea of an economy, as an open subsystem differentiated by and communicating within its 'systemically-social' environment, as a further example of a complex adaptive system.[9] As such a system, I may therefore treat the problematic of capitalism—its inherent failure to adequately account for social justice—as a systemic communications problem. Capitalism is thus a sclerotic, autonomously differentiated subsystem, failing to (adequately, efficiently, or effectively) communicate with its adaptive (social) environment. I can now recast the knowledge problem as a *field problem*:[10] a problem of application of an existing knowledge within the field of practice. Here, I can seek to 'design' improvements to the practice of (neoliberal) capitalism, in effect, to 'design' solutions to improve its 'code' of communication.

---

[4] Mason, Postcapitalism: A Guide to Our Future, xii.

[5] Varoufakis, And the Weak Suffer What They Must?: Europe, Austerity, and the Threat to Global Stability.

[6] Mason, Postcapitalism: A Guide to Our Future, 145.

[7] Boldyrev, "Economy as a Social System: Niklas Luhmann's Contribution and Its Significance for Economics."

[8] Checkland, "Soft Systems Methodology: A Thirty Year Retrospective," S14.

[9] Witt, "Capitalism as a Complex Adaptive System and Its Growth."

[10] van Aken, "Design Science and Organization Development Interventions: Aligning Business and Humanistic Values."

Design suggests a process to make manifest, ideas,[11] where the idea's design is the conjunction of a craft skill exercised with innovation.[12] Design operates only on what is known of the present reality. Thus, to explore the scope for future 'design' improvements to our neoliberal capitalist economic 'code', I pose the questions:

> Does neoliberal capitalism's failure contain within it an idea for a transition to a post Covid-19, postcapitalist society? And if so, what form might a postcapitalist transition take?

To seek answers to these questions, I proceed to map the economy from a complex adaptive systems perspective. Then, using an autoethnographic lens (as introduced in Chapter 3), I will again reflect on the role and regulation of identity, the nature of the power-politic and the emancipatory paradox of technological liberation in the development and transfer of economic value. This follows the modified form of CCF inquiry from Chapter 6. Here, I will explore the impacts of Covid-19 on each theme, imagining six exemplar future states on the imaginary plane—the imaginations. In this case, the truth table method will lead to a Wizard-of-Oz view in which, leaving aside the notion of allegory, I manipulate the future economic perspectives through the ghostly lenses of Karl Marx, Joseph Schumpeter and Martin Luther King.

An inquiry into a future democratic capitalism...

In the social environment of the economic subsystem of a democratic neoliberal capitalism, the drivers of discretionary political interference—ourselves: voters represented by the power-politic—exist under a heightened sense of the VUCA conditions I introduced previously. As I observe, from 2020 onward, the fragility of our existence has most recently been illustrated by the seismic impact of the Covid-19 pandemic. This is not the first, nor will it be the last, crisis of such proportions. As I close on the final edits of this book, the cost-of-living crisis, precipitated by Putin's Ukrainian incursion, has set Covid-19 into an almost benign perspective. Indeed, the UK Collins English Dictionary's 2022 word of the year was *permacrisis*—a prolonged period of instability and insecurity, such as the present crises of pandemic, war, inflation and geo-political instability. A heightened, palpable sense of unpredictability affects our economic and social life. It affects what we think

---

[11] Michael G Goldsby and others, 'Design-Centered Entrepreneurship: A Four Stage Iterative Process for Opportunity Development', Journal of Small Business & Entrepreneurship, 29.6 (2017), 477–90.

[12] Atkinson, Thinking the Art of Management: Stepping into "Heidegger's Shoes."

of ourselves (our identity), how we organize ourselves as societies (the distribution of power-politics) and what and how we make use of that which surrounds us (our use of resources and technologies).

As an environment, our system of society must adapt to the unpredictable challenges it faces. Consequently, our histories are replete with examples of our societies' resilience and adaptation to seismic events, whether natural disaster, or self-inflicted catastrophe. Our adaptability is reflected in Walter Buckley's conceptualisation of a society as a complex, adaptive system.[13] It reflects the capability and capacity for the interchanges between a society's components (its people) to effect significant changes in themselves. Here, tensions arise. When the subsystems created within a social system—for example, the subsystem of economic organization—deny the potential of their components to change, they fail to adapt in line with their environment.

As I introduced in Chapter 6, the study of a subsystem of reified economic practice seeks to identify, rationalise and hold-steady its internal, physical, and environmental conditions in search of optimal economic functioning. In optimisation, potential is lost in homeostasis. In optimisation, not only is the subsystem itself at risk of homeostasis[14] but, without the context of the wider social system—within which the economy merely serves a subordinate organizing role—a homeostatic economy places the wider social system at risk of sclerotic malfunctioning.

To retain the adaptability required to function effectively and efficiently within the adaptive system of society, the economic subsystem cannot neglect its environment. Its code of communication must be 'open' rather than 'closed' to both receipt and transmission of relevant information across its notional system boundaries. I argue, here, that it is this 'code' of the economy that is moderated by the 'identity' of its society, its 'power-politic' and the impacts of 'technology' upon it. This arguably simplistic notion of economic organization goes some way to suggest how a variety of 'flavours' of capitalism might be determined.[15] Here, the 'Variety of Capitals' literature has attracted some debate,[16] but it shall suffice that while I might argue that capitalisms do not come in varieties, it can be useful to assume they do.[17] Indeed, if we

---

[13] Buckley, Schwandt, and Goldstein, "Classic Paper Section: Society as a Complex Adaptive System (1968)"/ 1968.
[14] Buckley, Schwandt, and Goldstein.
[15] Hall and Soskice, Varieties of Capitalism; Hall, "Varieties of Capitalism in Light of the Euro Crisis."
[16] Hall and Soskice, "Varieties of Capitalism and Institutional Change: A Response to Three Critics"; Hay, "Does Capitalism (Still) Come in Varieties?"
[17] Hay, "Does Capitalism (Still) Come in Varieties?"

assume that identity, power-politics and technology moderate the capitalist code in some way, then it becomes improbable that there are discreetly identifiable varieties of capitalism.

I argue, here, that capitalism is infinitely variable, even 'fluid' in nature. It is moderated by a complex function of variability in identity, power-politics and technology. On the one hand, I might envisage convergence on an ideal, reified, capitalist economic practice. Here the internal, physical, and environmental conditions are identified, rationalised and held in homeostatic steadiness, striving for the optimal economic functioning of capitalism. This suggests evolution toward a society founded on a Weberian 'ideal type' of capitalist economy.[18] On the other hand, the simple existence of different identities, localised power-politics and a society's access to and utilisation of technology, suggests that an adaptive 'order' of social systems—by which a capitalist economy might be organized—will naturally lead to various forms of capitalism in different countries.[19] Convergence on a homeostatic, idealised system of capitalism is a function of protection from discretionary interference.[20] Thus, homeostasis is only avoided through pursuing a democracy that courts interference and, champions the voice of the people: the voters of a democratic power-politic.

Enterprise: the core activity of a democratic capitalism...

On the plane of reality, between its two hands—the twin poles of a diversified concept—the subsystem of capitalism functions to organize its society's enterprising economic activity, with enterprise broadly defined as that activity concerned with the production, distribution, consumption and/or transfer of capital wealth. While, traditionally, the 'real' focus on wealth is toward monetary capital, other forms of capital can be said to exist. For example, in the context of a society's enterprise and entrepreneurial activity, I imagine a four-capital model. Therefore, alongside the reality of money, in a (non-) concept of wealth, I include human capital (what is known), social capital (who is known) and, importantly, psychological capital (knowledge of the self).[21] Here, the individual (or 'self') engaged in enterprising activity—in either public or private capacity—is the essential 'agent' of economic activity, an essential 'component' of the operation of the economy as a subsystem of social organization.

---

[18] Crouch, "Models of Capitalism."
[19] Hall and Soskice, Varieties of Capitalism.
[20] Streeck, How Will Capitalism End?
[21] Envick, "Beyond Human and Social Capital: The Importance of Positive Psychological Capital for Entrepreneurial Success."

It is at the component level of the system that I turn to classic agency theory (AT); AT highlights the difficulties of controlling any subsystem (or system) where the functional goal of that subsystem conflicts with the goals of its agents, or where it is difficult or expensive for the system to verify the actual conduct of its (human) agents.[22] Here, the idea that individual human agents in such a complex subsystem as a democratic capitalism can be organized to deliver on its promise is, perhaps, antithetical. Not only are the enterprising agents, at whatever level of enterprising activity, agents of a real (financial) capitalist economy, they are also enterprising agents of the democratic organization of society—itself a complex adaptive system subject to the imaginations of other capital interests (for example: human, social and psychological). They are also, contemporaneously, agents of multiple other diverse systems and subsystems, each with their own motivations and functional goals (both real and imaginary). All these multiple systems and subsystems present many more multiple opportunities for inter-agent, inter-system and agent-system conflicts. In theorising a complex adaptive systems view of capitalism, enterprise and the world of work, it is within human agency that conflict arises, where questions of identity, power-politics and access to and use of technology matter.

The three themes of a complex adaptive economy

Given the context of a VUCA environment and its challenges: what we think (knowingly or imaginatively) of ourselves (our identity), including our available psychological capital; how we organize ourselves as a society through the distribution of the power-politic in response to those challenges; and how we make use of the resources and technologies available to us to overcome them, is fundamental to our understanding. It is fundamental to our understanding how we might best organize our enterprising activity within a future functioning, complex adaptive economy. This is an appeal to the concept of identity economics, where it is suggested that drawing on the micro-foundations of identity may assist with providing more robust accounts of our social and economic agency and its outcomes.[23]

The VUCA-induced variability of the internal, physical, and environmental conditions that we face as individual enterprising agents, highlights the inadequacy of extant (simplistic) typologies of work. They are inadequate in realising the nature and range of enterprising agential activity necessary to support the idea of a complex adaptive (sub)system of economic

[22] See, for example: Eisenhardt, "Agency Theory: An Assessment and Review."
[23] See, for example: Kranton, "Identity Economics 2016: Where Do Social Distinctions and Norms Come From?"

organization. Here, observers—for example German sociologist and systems theorist Niklas Luhmann—have suggested this social (human) variability constitutes a form of autopoiesis that hinders rational solutions to our human problems.[24] However, rather than uncritically accept such 'hindrance', to explore the systems' problematic further I shall turn to deconstruction. Following the CCF method, I first develop *identity*, the *power-politic* and *technology* as separate themes, then reconstruct them as a complex function of economic possibility.

Identity: finding 'I'...

Building on the work of Peter Checkland,[25] it is both an intellectual position and a basic tenet of systems thinking that our social reality is not a reified entity. It is constructed through socially negotiated alternatives,[26] between individuals and imperfectly coherent groups. In Chapter 6, I addressed the concept of identity in a systems context from the perspective of identity theory, eschewing the group-focussed social identity theory. Here, I take a narrative[27] autoethnographic perspective, with the concept 'identity' as a person's sense of *self*—their psychological and sociological nature. Again, my interest is in how identity impacts an individual's role as an aesthetically operating, adaptive component, contributing to a system's variety pool. This positions the individual relative to the economic subsystem.

Let me posit identity as the outcome of a process of *self*-construction, albeit a collectively negotiated identity. Here, identity helps to account for phenomena that an extant theorising of economics cannot.[28] To draw on Scottish philosopher Alasdair MacIntyre: 'I am a brother, cousin and grandson, member of this household, that village, this tribe'.[29] My self-construction of an embryonic identity is, however, no accident. As the somewhat controversial twentieth-century German writer, Ernst Junger[30]

---

[24] Valentinov, "From Equilibrium to Autopoiesis: A Luhmannian Reading of Veblenian Evolutionary Economics."
[25] Checkland, "Soft Systems Methodology: A Thirty Year Retrospective," S24.
[26] Atkinson, Thinking the Art of Management: Stepping into "Heidegger's Shoes."
[27] See, for example: Davis, "Identity and Individual Economic Agents: A Narrative Approach"; Juille and Jullien, "Narrativity and Identity in the Representation of the Economic Agent."
[28] Akerlof and Kranton, "Economics and Identity."
[29] MacIntyre, After Virtue, 33.
[30] The New York Times posted an obituary on February 18th, 1998 in which is described Ernst Jünger as 'an aloof warrior-author... one of Germany's most controversial and contradictory writers. *https://www.nytimes.com /1998/02/18/arts/ernst-junger-contradictory-german-author-who-wrote-about-war-is-dead-at 102.html*

suggested in his 1932 philosophical essay *The Worker*[31], I do not choose the school bench on which my identity and character are formed. I take 'on trust' that those who exercise such choice, act in my best interests. However, as I progress through life, schooled and integrated into family, community and society, I increasingly exercise 'trust' and 'individual choice'. I do so to the extent that the concepts of 'social order' and 'individual liberty' permit.

My identity as this or that sibling, cousin and grandchild, and member of this or that household, that village, this organization and society, is continually under the influence of exogenous factors that serve, in varying measure, to direct, shape, align or distance that identity and my role and function in society. I thus occupy a certain space within an interlocking set of social relations.[32] It is as a writer with the objective of framing critical futures perspectives on the potential for the (re)design of capitalism for post-Covid, post-Crisis economic systems, through the lens of Marx, Schumpeter and King, that 'I' therefore consider my own identity.

'I' am a brother, cousin, and father. I am member of a household and my village. I was born in 1958, in a caravan in a field in the north of Scotland, to Yorkshire parents. While I had no choice concerning my initial schooling, I did choose a naval training school in my later years. I have served, albeit for a short time, in the merchant navy, with service on three different trading ships and almost circling the globe. I have been an airman in the ranks of the UK's Royal Air Force, later gaining a commission after further study and serving as a specialist communications and ICT engineering officer for many years. I went on to establish several trading companies with varying levels of success. I have also gained a doctorate in critical management studies and have worked in an academic capacity. In short, I have been, and continue to be, a member of several organizations. While I have travelled and experienced other societies, as a product of various systems and subsystems, I am a British citizen, a member of the United Kingdom. It has a democratic social order, with a neoliberal economy in crisis.

'I' continue to function as a member of many systems and subsystems. I am constrained to live by the neoliberal social order that contributes to my sense-of-self: my identity. As a member of my family, I have responsibilities to house and feed myself and others. As a member of my village, I have responsibilities, inculcated through education and social norms. For example, I avoid causing a nuisance to others who identify as members of my village. I have met such responsibilities, and others, through enterprising activity. As a worker within

---

[31] Jünger, The Worker: Dominion and Form.

[32] MacIntyre, After Virtue.

several organizations, I have identified with responsibilities for my actions in line with organizational objectives that I have had no hand in setting. As both manager and leader, my role has included responsibilities entrusted to me, for the performance of others. As a founder of businesses and an employer, my responsibilities as a manager and leader have assumed additional dimensions, including setting objectives for others. At all times, my enterprising activity has been a component of the economic sub-system of the society I identify with—a neoliberal form of capitalism. My ability to undertake my role as that component is a function of my identity, a function of my experiences with Others and with other things, and my responses to them.

In March 2019, after 60 years of forming my identity, it received an additional dimension when I was assessed as autistic. I am autistic. That I have always been autistic—without being aware—has shaped my responses to the education and experiences that made me who I was and who I continue to become. Another autistic person, following similar experiences, would not identify as me. Neither would a non-autistic person. Implicit in this observation is the notion that it is the range of individual identities accessible in any given society at any given time that provides the variety pool of knowledge and experience. This is the stock of human capital that constitutes the adaptive variability required to contribute a range of responses to VUCA situations. It is therefore self-evident that any action or inaction that denies, excludes, restricts, limits, screens-out/in, self-selects, or otherwise reduces a system's pool of variability, risks limiting the system's responses to events.

Homeostatic limits, affecting the accessibility of society to its pool of adaptive variability, might be imposed by norms of identity, formed on exogenous grounds. For example, consider the issue of race, of the hyper-residential segregation of certain phenotypes experienced in some metropolitan areas of the USA.[33] Homeostatic systems that deny the adaptive variability of some social, group or individual identities, are as risk-prone as those which deny other identities their access to the subsystems that function to serve them. Such denial, as 'capability deprivation', limits necessary social-structural and individual capacities to enact a required social and economic agency.[34] Thus, while SIT has been embraced as an important framework for understanding that group and organizational level membership shapes the understanding of individual identity, I argue that it is individual identity construction that I must examine for 'effective and efficient functioning' from a systems

---

[33] Darity, Mason, and Stewart, "The Economics of Identity: The Origin and Persistence of Racial Identity Norms."

[34] See, for example: Duroy, "North African Identity and Racial Discrimination in France: A Social Economic Analysis of Capability Deprivation."

perspective. I therefore postulate that, in a post-Covid-19 social economic future, the first critical uncertainty is trust in the identity of the individual self as a functioning component of society. Therefore:

> **P_1:** The *identity of the self* is characterised by enfranchisement to, or disenfranchisement from, an exogenous norm, rather than to/from an endogenous, socially inclusive property.

The Covid-19 pandemic has exacerbated states of increasing nationalism (such as Brexit and Trumpism). Increasing national power distances, arising from weaker cross-border structures, reduce opportunities to deconstruct hegemony through cooperation. Thus, I may imagine **($P1_1$)** a future state of increased national hegemony, where individual identities are either increasingly enfranchised to, or increasingly disenfranchised from, trust in the exogenous norm of the incumbent state's (hegemonic) identity. Here, nationalism attempts to impose, from the outside in, greater influence on the identity of the individual. Individuals who identify with and trust in the norm, may be encouraged to perform positively as social and economic agents. Those who do not so trust, may be subjugated in silence or become oppositions: sources of resistance to effective (sub)system performance. The grounds are set for homeostasis and conflict, suggesting greater requirements on the (sub)system to exercise forms of identity regulation.

Alternatively, there is now greater uncertainty over the outcomes of identity construction, as 'social media' platforms connect localised movements of identity-construction on a global scale. The death of George Floyd in May 2020, under the knee of a police officer in Minnesota, US, saw the toppling of a statue of seventeenth-century British slave trader Edward Colston in Bristol. Local UK protestors, identifying with the increasingly global *Black Lives Matter* movement, acted quickly in sympathy with their US counterparts.[35] Thus, I may also imagine **($P1_2$)** a future state where weak cross-border structures of nationalisation are, in turn, further undermined by liberal, individual access to technologies. These allow identification with and 'trust' in more cosmopolitan and/or other social movements, not necessarily within the immediate (sub)systems of interest. The increasing complexity and agential conflicts facilitate the growth of (semi-)autonomous activity. It is the potential for growth of counter-hegemony.[36]

---

[35] BBC, "Edward Colston Statue : Protesters Tear down Slave Trader Monument."

[36] Bosman, "The Political Rhetoric of Corporate Globalisation and the Possibilities for Counter-Hegemonic Projects."

Power-politics: 'I' as a minority...

Drawing on a concept of power from Chapter 6, I again employ a narrow concept of politics. For this inquiry, the exercise of power is a challenge to a constituted authority. Thus, in context, from my present democratic position, all forms of challenge to a social and economic status quo through the exercise of power, are defined as political. Again, following Foucault,[37] the power-politic dynamic cannot be exercised successfully—that is, we cannot change the status quo—if the mechanisms of power outside, below and alongside the requirement for change do not also change. Therefore, my proper concern in considering the uncertainty of a power-politic is the consideration of the uncertainty of opportunity for a democratic transition, and the uncertainty of the bargaining power and interests of both incumbents and oppositions.[38]

At the head of our democratic society, the capitalist 'state' is the entity constituted by its various institutions of power. It is the guardian of society's democracy; the incumbents of its present power-politic are the incumbents of the various institutions and instruments of power: government, financial, security, et al. Its oppositions are those that seek opportunities for transitions of change within the state: other potential governments, political movements, social groups and individuals. Here, to the individual, the 'state' is often maligned and monstrous. "Only 'beyond the state', it appears, can a life worthy of free human individuals begin'.[39] Thus, beyond the capitalist, democratic state, society is replete with oppositions, those that would 'transition' the state to better meet their own group or individual interests. The contemporary power-politic is therefore a 'profusion of shifting alliances between diverse authorities [governing] multitude of facets of economic activity, social life and individual [agency].'[40]

Transitions in the power-politic of our contemporary 'state' of democratic capitalism require mechanisms of change outside, below and alongside the diverse authorities that govern the institutions delineating our social-economic activity, our 'social' life and our exercise of individual agency. Given my premiss that, exacerbated by the Covid-19 pandemic, neoliberal capitalism is in a state of crisis, the complexity of the challenge to even envisage a 'transition' or change in the present 'state' unfolds its true nature. The 'state' reveals itself to be a complexity of interconnected, interlocking, interdependent systems and subsystems, all inherently complex and potentially adaptive—

---

[37] Foucault, Power/Knowledge: Selected Interviews and Other Writings 1972–1977.
[38] Haggard and Kaufman, "The Political Economy of Democratic Transitions."
[39] Rose and Miller, "Political Power beyond the State: Problematics of Government," 173.
[40] Rose and Miller, "Political Power beyond the State: Problematics of Government," 174.

each according to the agency exercised by its human components, each of whom may act in accord with their individual identity. And, while 'I' may exercise my democratic right to vote for whomever I wish, I do so only from a highly restricted, limited range of candidates—none of whom I have pre-selected. My vote is my contribution to the form and structure of the organization of the social order by which I am constrained, by lack of individual capacity, either to change or to avoid.

My individual vote wields no power inside, outside, below or alongside the diverse authorities I might wish to change. Here, reflecting on an article in the UK's The Guardian newspaper[41], the complexity of my own identity shall serve as a simple illustration. 'I' may be identified (by others) as a white, middle-aged man, a member of the supposed 'pale, male and stale' brigade, identifiable—in a largely pejorative sense—as typical of those corresponding to the 'ruling political class'. However, my invisible identity as an autistic adult in the UK also sets me in a minority group that is only representative of some 1.1% of the population,[42] a smaller minority then many other minority groups that might be more readily identifiable. As a potential functioning element of our society's system and its economic subsystem, I must reflect on the fact that it is believed that just 16% of autistic adults in the UK are in full-time paid employment, leaving 84% in either un- or under-employment.[43]

It is self-evident that without the certainty of bargaining power to exercise a mechanism of change outside, below or alongside the diverse authorities that frame my social-economic activity, social life and my agency, 'I' and my (autistic) interests are subjugated to the periphery of silence. 'I' am in a minority and in opposition. By my subjugation, I am a source of potential resistance to effective system performance. Denied, excluded, restricted, limited, screened-out/in, self-selected, or otherwise reduced, the system's pool of variability lacks my innate ability to contribute a response to the VUCA situations we face. In direct consequence of my subjugated, minority voice, I live 'beyond the state'—I live a life worthy of a free human individual. I do so because in my identity are all the hallmarks of an adaptive component, free to rise to the VUCA situations I face as personal challenges within my life.

In 2021, as I first committed to write this Chapter, UK society was the emergent outcome of a neoliberal ideology, in which many public industries and services were outsourced and entrusted to private enterprise. This had been achieved under a political doctrine seeking the maximisation of as much

---

41 Freedland, "Don't Pity White, Middle-Aged Men. It's Ludicrous to Cast Them as Victims."
42 Brugha et al., "Estimating the Prevalence of Autism Spectrum Conditions in Adults: Extending the 2007 Adult Psychiatric Morbidity Survey."
43 Lever, "The Autism Employment Gap Too Much Information in the Workplace."

social-system and economic (sub)system efficiency as possible; the maximisation of efficiency being entrusted to the agency of competitive markets, all constituted by multiple profit-maximising sub-systems.[44] But the paradox of the reduced state is that the substitute, profit-driven enterprises increasingly assume a position as 'trusted' centres of a neoliberal power-politic, all allies in efficient economic development.

The irony of the neoliberal turn in the democratic power-politic is that—free of much institutional interference—profit-driven economic enterprise has been elevated from its more benign position beneath the state in the service of economic organization, to a new position alongside the institutions of the state in the service of society itself. The bargaining power of the custodians of society's democracy is now challenged by the increased bargaining power of private capitalism. This provides a mechanism for changes to democracy that do not serve society but serve the interests of profit maximisation. Thus, I argue that neoliberal capitalism provides a mechanism for sacrificing social needs on the altar of *pleonexia*. Again, we see a vice re-appropriated as a virtue in the name of liberty.[45] All the while, 'I', as a minority with a subjugated voice—in my state of neoliberal freedom—sit at liberty, outside and beneath all that is there to support me. 'I' sit, entrusted by the state, to act as an efficient and effective component of a social and economic order I am increasingly disenfranchised from. Yet 'I' frame my social-economic activity—my agency—amidst the irony of liberty. 'I' am at liberty to pursue my dreams and ambitions, only so long as they fit with the neoliberal ideal.

As Timothy Mitchell eloquently suggested, 'The problem of democracy [is] a question of how to manufacture a new model of the citizen, one whose mind is committed to the idea of democracy'.[46] For a neoliberal ideal, the ultimate consequence would be some solution or other for the control of individual identity; this is insofar as that identity is contracted to an agency relationship of enterprise, within, and on behalf of, the rising dominant capitalist power-politic. 'I' am therefore no longer a worker, 'I' am an entrepreneur. I am encouraged to creatively destruct the institutions that I look to for my own support. I am even able to acquire the means of production to do so. Thus, in this VUCA world, I postulate my second critical uncertainty:

> **P_2**: The power-politic is characterised by more, or less, state-directed neoliberal capitalist colonisation of its social system, rather than by a capitalist economy in service to its society

---

[44] Crouch, "The Paradoxes of Privatisation and Public Service Outsourcing."
[45] MacIntyre, After Virtue.
[46] Mitchell, Carbon Democracy: Political Power in the Age of Oil, 3.

Even from the crisis perspective of a pre-Covid19 neoliberal capitalism, this critical uncertainty is over who can exercise the necessary power to effect change. To follow Wolfgang Streeck, it is now commonplace that the crisis is also a crisis of trust, in which we, who sit outside and beneath the dominant power-politics of institutions and capitalists, do not trust "the capacity of political leaders to resist the pressures of 'the market', and the capacity of the markets to provide for an efficient, not to speak of fair, allocation of resources".[47] Yet Covid-19 has exposed the fragility of our homeostatic systems, where the search for efficiencies and cost reductions have corrupted resilience and removed adaptability, leaving sclerotic processes pone to systemic failure. For example, autonomous care workers having to risk people's lives.[48]

Across the antagonistic horizon, in a response to the Covid-19 pandemic, $\mathbf{P_2}$ provides a range of possible futures. At one end of the scale of uncertainty, I imagine **($\mathbf{P2_1}$)** that the state—influenced by its incumbent capitalists—facilitates a capitalist drive for growth. This is with even greater efficiencies and cost reductions, doubling down on its free and perfect ideology—a blind trust in its capacity to finally deliver an efficient and fair allocation of resources. While an imagination, its (prescient) empiric value had been demonstrated by a late-summer 2022[49] declaration from the (then soon to become) UK Prime Minister Liz Truss, that she would act positively to facilitate such a drive for growth.[50] Here, I imagine a range of initiatives and market reforms, exogenously imposed on society's disenfranchised incumbents. Alternatively, at the other end of the scale, I imagine **($\mathbf{P2_2}$)** that society's disenfranchised oppositions coalesce on a new, shared set of endogenous social values, challenging the incumbent neoliberal state and its capitalist institutions. This is the (continued) call for a meaningful democratic transition to a compassionate capitalism, serving society through a more cooperative form.

Technology: the 'system' and 'I'...

From the technological perspective, I again follow Marshall McLuhan.[51] My starting point is to acknowledge that technology shapes and controls the scale

---

[47] Streeck, How Will Capitalism End?, 247.

[48] Anonymous, "We Care Workers Face a Terrible Decision: Risk People's Lives or Go without Pay."

[49] This Chapter and its imaginations were first drafted in early 2021.

[50] Silvester, "Exclusive: Liz Truss : I'll Protect 'Crown Jewel' City of London as Prime Minister."

[51] McLuhan, "The Medium Is the Message."

and form of human agency. This agency is inherent within our social system and its economic subsystem, and their systemic responses to local and global environments. My concern with technology as a systemically uncertain system component, is the paradoxical nature by which it is both 1) a catalyst and accelerator of change—a force-multiplier to both the power-politic of incumbents, and to the oppositions of the state and its institutions—and 2) has a capacity to emulsify social practice, in that it may—as I have discussed earlier—function to stabilise elements of enterprising practice, stultifying the reflexivity necessary to 'open' the system to adaptive flexibility.

Technology is all-pervasive. Yet there is irony in the promises and discourse of its developed value propositions,[52] in which the legitimisation of capitalism has translated to no more than legitimised value extraction. Here, individual choice is reduced to a limited range of often anodyne options. Consider, if you will, 'I' as the individual customer of a certain financial services institution. In 2008, I faced a complex and uncertain but individual set of circumstances in which, indebted to that institution, I turned to it for assistance. In the institution's drive for effectiveness and efficiency, its applications of technology permitted the reduction of customer service to scripted interactions with its own ICT systems. There, institutional operators occupied interface positions between the sentient customer and the insentient machine. As interlocuter, the sentient nature of the operator was subverted by scripts, guiding my enquiry down a necessarily limited response-to-stress scenario. In the VUCA environment of my enquiry (an outcome of the 2008 economic crisis), my interaction with customer service failed, as I exceeded the limited agency entrusted to the operator. A breakdown in trust between 'I' and the institution ensued, as it exercised its power to deny my subjugated identity.

The scandal of UK banking's Payment Protection Insurance (PPI) liability, originating in 2005 and exacerbated by the financial crash of 2008, continued until 29 August 2019. This was the final date for lodging any claim against the banks for their mishandling of PPI products. The scandal came to prominence following the crash. Then, an estimated 64 million PPI policies (sold over the previous two decades) were proven to hold little or no value to the people who held the legitimate expectation that their PPI policy would help pay their debts in the event of illness or loss of income. The scandal, while not officially acknowledged as fraud,[53] exposed a liability well exceeding £45billion in compensation and costs, to be paid by the banks for mis-sold or otherwise

---

[52] Fisher, "Contemporary Technology Discourse and the Legitimation of Capitalism."
[53] Ellis, "Economic Freedom Mis-Sold: Neoliberalism and the Moral Economies of the PPI Scandal in the UK."

mishandled PPI.[54] In the social liminality of an individual's increasingly disenfranchised identity, the power to challenge the capitalist financial subsystem and its incumbent entities (banks), was lost behind a firewall of sentient yet impotent gatekeepers, shielded by applications of technology. In such a manner, technology in the service of profit—as opposed to technology in the service of the individual—enables the mere ownership of technology to produce nothing, yet it can facilitate value extraction from others.'[55]

Within the capitalist society, the popularised utility of ICT, particularly that associated with digital networking or network technology, is its promise of a variety of capitalism that is 'more democratic, participatory, and de-alienating for individuals.[56] However, as I suggest within the vignette of the UK banking PPI scandal, socially- and even state-contested corporate activity may continue undisturbed for many years. The first 'social' contestation of the bank's PPI activity rose in line with the state's removal of institutional provision for mortgage interest relief.[57] This allowed financial institutions an opportunity to replace a 'service by the state for society', by an ICT-enhanced, optimised 'service by capitalists for profit'.

Increasingly, as the PPI claims of UK society's incumbents were denied, consumer interest groups and media investigators highlighted the potential of a PPI market failure. However, positioned below the power politic of state and corporate UK, the contestations of such oppositions yielded little change. Thus, amid mounting social opposition, in 2005, the state assumed a position of contestation under the auspices of the UK's Financial Services Authority.[58] However, with corporate capitalists operating at an institutional level, the power politic of the state's institution-led contestation struggled against the banks' power. The contest was therefore elevated to the institution of the High Court, and only resolved in 2011, after the institutional body representing the banks—the British Bankers Association—capitulated.[59]

One might argue that the 'system' worked. The powerless, individual opponents won out in the end. In the face of mounting social and state contestation, the Foucauldian forces of opposition effected change in the

---

[54] Jones, "The End of a Scandal: Banks near a Final Release from Their PPI Liabilities."
[55] Sayer, "Moral Economy, Unearned Income, and Legalized Corruption," 47.
[56] Fisher, "Contemporary Technology Discourse and the Legitimation of Capitalism."
[57] Ellis, "Economic Freedom Mis-Sold: Neoliberalism and the Moral Economies of the PPI Scandal in the UK."
[58] The Financial Services Authority was later replaced by the Financial Conduct Authority, in August 2013.
[59] Ellis, "Economic Freedom Mis-Sold: Neoliberalism and the Moral Economies of the PPI Scandal in the UK."

incumbents. The mechanisms of power outside, below and alongside the banking institute changed, coalescing around a 'social' movement for that change. But the fact remains that the situation leading to the bank's capitulation in 2011 had existed for some decades. Despite the mounting opposition, it is estimated that one-third of the PPI policies were sold after 2005.[60] Also, the homeostatic technology facilitating the banks' capitalist practice remained in place. This allowed certain banks to continue to delay or deny some claims, despite the 2011 High Court outcome. Individual claimants, failing to gain compensation directly from the banks, had to resort to filing individual complaints through the State's own Financial Ombudsman's Service (FOS) at a further cost to society.

In early 2016, Richard Thomas CBE's report for the FOS, into the impact of the PPI scandal on their organization, commented on the 'tidal wave' of individual complaints received. At the time of the report, some 12.5 million claims for compensation had been submitted, with around 1.3 million elevated as complaints to the FOS. Approximately 60% of these were upheld. The increasing workload saw an expansion in average annual staff numbers in the FOS, from circa 1000 pre-2011 to over 3500 in 2016. They also installed their 'Navigator' decision-support technology as a supplement to their existing 'Clipper' case-management system. Navigator proved to be 'absolutely essential to the handling of such high complaint volumes.'[61]

Alongside the changes in the FOS, the opportunistic nature of some capitalist enterprises—in the main ICT-enhanced claims management companies (CMCs)—saw the growth of a market and exacerbated the rise in claims (an estimated five-fold increase, or 80% of all claims). These were on a no-win-no-fee basis, with commission rates of 25% to 40% on compensation. While the PPI claims process was straightforward to access and navigate—assisted by personal access to ICT—CMCs capitalised on factors that included: an individual's lack of access to ICT; a lack of awareness of the claims process itself; and the general reluctance of some individuals to engage in opposition. This latter factor is arguably an issue of identity. On the figures reflected in this brief analysis, assuming some £30bn due in PPI compensation, with circa 80% managed through CMCs at a minimum 25% commission, the CMCs initiated claims on behalf of their 'customers' that netted their industry over £6bn of 'easy money'. Far from revealing a self-correcting, adaptive system, the PPI scandal revealed a systemic failure of capitalism, in which value, rightly held by individuals, is first extracted by state-facilitated, private-finance institutional misconduct, before manipulation and retention to benefit others.

---

[60] Thomas CBE, "The Impact of PPI Mis-Selling on the Financial Ombudsman Service."
[61] Thomas CBE, 23.

Does the future of technology hold promise? Three 'mega' trends, namely: 1) AI; 2) Transparently Immersive Experiences; and 3) the growth of Digital Platforms, suggest companies will be offered even greater opportunities in the future to make their technology dynamically integral to the human experience.[62] Thus, as I envisage a post Covid-19 future, I postulate my third critical uncertainty:

> **P_3:** technology is characterised by more or less application in service of value extraction and homeostasis, rather than toward creative, innovative social value-adding adaptations.

Here, **P_3** delivers the prospect of greater systemic homeostasis in the elusive, ideological search for the internal, physical and environmental conditions of optimal growth and profits. This calls for new levels of protection from political interference. In a post Covid-19 sense, I imagine **($P3_1$)** a state where socially- and state-contested 'value extractive' corporate activity continues, at best, undisturbed. Here, historian of information and communications, Dan Schiller, argues that it is ICT that forms the 'beating pulse of capitalist development'.[63] A pulse which led to the financial crisis of 2008, where information and communications creatively 'wrenched' the changes in production required to exit the post-war recession of the early 1970s. Facilitated by the latest technology, 'cost cutting and transformation ripped through communities of wage earners in the United States and Western Europe'.[64] I imagine a future capitalist ascent into the permacrisis, as the owners of technology—such as AI, Transparently Immersive Experiences and Digital Platforms—continue to produce nothing, yet employ it to extract value from others.

The danger inherent in the existing neoliberal form of capitalism is that, unchecked, it may abolish itself. Technology, in the hands of the disenfranchised opens opportunities for opposition. It offers scope for the decentralisation of autonomous self-owned businesses.[65] Thus, I also imagine **($P3_2$)** the positive potential of technology, as it coalesces around a strong power-politic for change. Here, as a member of an organization, the 'I' that is an entrusted component of a functioning yet homeostatic subsystem, is also

---

62 Jari and Lauraéus, "Analysis of 2017 Gartner' s Three Megatrends to Thrive the Disruptive Business, Technology Trends 2008 - 2016, Dynamic Capabilities of VUCA and Foresight Leadership Tools."

63 Schiller, "Digital Capitalism's Ascent to Crisis."

64 Schiller, "Digital Capitalism's Ascent to Crisis," 15.

65 Hoffmann and Dahlinger, "How Capitalism Abolishes Itself in the Digital Era in Favour of Robo-Economic Systems: Socio-Economic Implications of Decentralized Autonomous Self-Owned Businesses."

an 'insider' to the knowledge required to realise an external opportunity. That 'I' is also a member of any number of other (sub)systems, social and economic, some of which 'I' may be disenfranchised from, or which may give rise to issues of identity that may cause my disenfranchisement.

As an entrusted insider in the wider society—where the notion of trust tends to the distributed—questions of who 'I' or 'we' can actually trust, arise.[66] Certainly, trust in the neoliberal capitalist state and its public and private institutions has been eroded by events such as the PPI scandal. Distributed trust is messy, unpredictable, and at times even dangerous.[67] But the notion of 'distributed' suggests decentralisation by intent. However, given the perception of a VUCA environment, and the homeostatic nature of many systems and subsystems, trust is more likely to be found fragmented across multiple components in opposition, exacerbating any messy, unpredictable and dangerous levels—a recipe for further crises.

The baseline: reframing the (socio-economic) future

I recall my premiss that, even before the Covid-19 pandemic, capitalism was in a state of crisis. While my inquiry in this part has centred on a local (UK) perspective, I can usefully recall Slavoj Žižek's premiss from *Living in the End Times*[68] (from Chapter 6), in which the global capitalist system is, itself, approaching an 'apocalyptic zero-point'. In a Žižekean sense, then, Covid-19 is just one more crisis alongside other crises—a veritable permacrisis. To explore this thesis further, following the CCF method of my inquiry, I (re)construct its range of future moments—the contradictions—through the triad of identity, power-politics and technology, a complex function of future possibility. Table 7.1 depicts the now-familiar truth table.

Table 7.1. Truth table: future post-Covid economic contradictions

m	P_1	P_2	P_3	Scenario Outline
m_1	F	F	F	Historical discontinuity. Changes in exogenous enfranchised/disenfranchised identities toward endogenous social inclusivity; Changes from capitalist colonisation of social systems to economy that serves society; Changes in technology to benefit society through adding value.

[66] Hua and Bapna, "Who Can We Trust? The Economic Impact of Insider Threats."

[67] Botsman, Who Can You Trust?: How Technology Brought Us Together - and Why It Could Drive Us Apart.

[68] Žižek, Living in the End Times.

m_2	F	F	T	No changes in technology to benefit society through adding value.
m_3	F	T	F	No changes from capitalist colonisation of social system to economy that serves society.
m_4	F	T	T	No changes from capitalist colonisation of social system to economy that serves society and no changes in technology to benefit society through adding value.
m_5	T	F	F	No changes in exogenous enfranchised/ disenfranchised identities toward endogenous social inclusivity.
m_6	T	F	T	No changes in exogenous enfranchised/ disenfranchised identities toward endogenous social inclusivity and no changes in technology to benefit society through adding value.
m_7	T	T	F	No changes in exogenous enfranchised/disenfranchised identities toward endogenous social inclusivity and no changes from capitalist colonisation of social system to economy that serves society.
m_8	T	T	T	Status quo? No changes in exogenous enfranchised/ disenfranchised identities toward endogenous social inclusivity; No changes from capitalist colonisation of social system to economy that serves society; No changes in technology to benefit society through adding value.

(T=true, F=false)

The counterfactuals: transposing the future

Figure 7.1 reveals the intuitive coherence between the contradictions **(m_1-m_8)** and the six exemplar imaginations **($P1_1$ to $P3_2$)**.

Coherent futures: the provocations of history...

With reference to Figure 7.1, the most coherent imaginations are **$P1_1$**, **$P1_2$** and **$P2_1$**. Here, I foresee a future economy characterised by increasing 'hegemonic identity regulation'. This acts to increase forms of 'populist social resistance' and renewed vigour directed to 'capitalist efficiency'. In contrast, without the major change associated with a historical discontinuity, beyond the antagonistic horizon, I argue that we are less likely to foresee **$P2_2$**, or **$P3_2$**. At the time of the present analysis, despite the significant (global) impact of Covid-19 and a Russian-Ukrainian war, it is not at all clear we will witness the coordinated change in identities, power politics and applications of technology that would lead to a 'socially compassionate capitalism'.

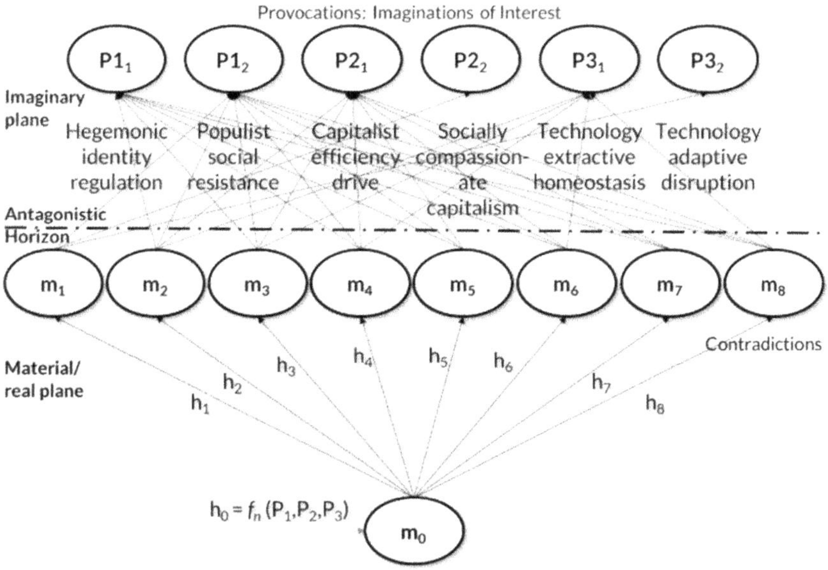

Figure 7.1. Finding truth in the future of capitalist economics

Neither, I argue, will we see any massive 'technology adaptive disruption' for the benefit of society. Also, relatively consistent with continued hegemonic, capitalist efficiency and social resistance is the imagined state **P3₁**—increasing identity diversity on a global scale. While this foresees high levels of 'value-extractive homeostasis', it is also an opportunity for more autonomous applications of technology in support of society, consistent with 'social entrepreneurship'. Under the shadow of capitalist excesses, this may be a focus for more populist social resistance.

Speculative ghosts: futures yet to come?

At the outset of this Chapter, I introduced the problematic of capitalism—that is its inherent failure to adequately account for social justice—as a systemic communications problem. It is a sclerotic, autonomously differentiated system failing to communicate with its adaptive environment. The scene is thus set with the demi-gods of capitalism's elite elevated to a level alongside the guardians of society itself. Here, the financial crisis of 2008 revealed the fragility of neoliberal, entrepreneurial capitalism. It renewed an interest in the theory of Karl Marx, and socialist politics in general. Marxist theory, as a theory of both capitalism and communication, thus provides an important critique of any form of exploitation or domination.[69]

Simplistically, money talks. Those with no access to money (capital) cannot talk. And as more people lose access to capital, disenfranchised from the capitalist 'system', they tend toward poverty. In the UK, the capitalist 'system' (or 'machine') has developed around five core principles of free markets, a small state, low rates of taxation, individual liberty and big defence.[70] Yet there are contradictions. Leaving aside defence: 1) free markets extend globally and see much of the UK-earned profit evading appropriate rates of UK taxation; 2) many of the once public institutions of the state have been placed in the hands of private capital, with the state itself retaining little capacity to respond to social crises, and with every crisis becoming an opportunity for private profiteering; 3) low rates of local taxation exacerbate the falling taxation receipts from globalised enterprise, providing insufficient state access to the necessary capital to redistribute to alleviate poverty; and 4) individual liberty makes trust in the state optional, on the assumption that the liberal member of society is fully aligned with the goals and ideals of neoliberal capitalism, and has the capacity to function unaided, under such liberty.

Marx's foresight?

Capitalism's failures, pre-Covid19, amounted to a catalogue of 'weak and unstable growth', 'stagnant living standards and rising inequality' and its negative impacts on 'climate change and environmental risk'.[71] Post-Covid19, it is informative to restate Karl Marx. Thus:

> 'The contradictions in the movement of capitalist society impress themselves upon the practical bourgeois most strikingly in the changes of the periodic cycle, through which modern industry runs, and whose crowning point is the universal crisis. That crisis is once again approaching, although as yet but in its preliminary stage; and by the universality of its theatre and the intensity of its action it will drum dialectics even into the heads of the mushroom-upstarts of the new [state]'.[72]

---

[69] Fuchs, Commun. Capital. A Crit. Theory.
[70] Knight, "Powering a Good Society."
[71] Jacobs and Mazzucato, "Rethinking Capitalism: An Introduction."
[72] Marx, Capital, 16.

For Marx, the contemporary 'practical bourgeois' of neocapitalism would exist in the form and function of the 'capitalist entrepreneur'.[73] This is the class of society's individuals, entrusted by the state with the development of the capitalist economy. Here, the 'everyday consciousness' of capitalist entrepreneurs is revealed in their exercise of forms of 'spontaneous thought' within which they reflect on, and experience, the workings of the capitalist system. Entrepreneurs work 'the system', exploit labour, and make profit, 'without benefit of a more sophisticated or "truer" understanding of what they are involved in'.[74] They are denied a social truth by a subsystem, closed to the consciousness of its social context by virtue of its own code. In short, to Marx, capitalism cannot survive because such conditions cause economic failure. When Marx talks of drumming dialectics into the heads of the new state, it is the absurdity of a naïve dialectic (that ignores its own contradiction of failure) that is the tune to be played on the drum.

I argue that our hope in any global crisis, such as that precipitated by Covid-19—once *in its preliminary stage*—is that the global *universality of its theatre, and the intensity of its action,* will drum the absurdity of a naïve dialectic of a 'dynamic [socio-economic] totality... of a network of contradictions',[75] into the consciousness of not only the neoliberal state, but also the *mushroom-upstarts* of the private, neoliberal capital institutions colonising its societal guardianship role. Those in the service of profit only. Here I invoke the work of Marx, not for any revolutionary purpose, but to draw attention to the idea that Marx has a key role to play in advancing capitalism's understanding of the social system within which it is situated.[76] Thus, I suggest we may accept that to make society materially better off, its productivity must grow over time. However, I argue that we must also accept that society's well-being is a function of how such productivity gains are distributed across it.[77]

Central to advancing capitalism's understanding of the social system is an understanding of Marx's theory of value. Here, the general production of useful objects ('use values') for exchange ('exchange values') through the appropriation, by the capitalist class, of the unpaid labour of the working class, is the *raison d'être* of capitalism.[78] However, I now usefully update this notion of 'use value' to include the production of information in knowledge-intensive markets. This extends the issue of the appropriation of (and thus the

---

[73] Hall, "The Problem of Ideology-Marxism without Guarantees."
[74] Hall, "The Problem of Ideology-Marxism without Guarantees," 30.
[75] Fuchs, Commun. Capital. A Crit. Theory, 5.
[76] Weeks, Capital and Exploitation.
[77] Lazonick, "Innovative Enterprise and the Theory of the Firm."
[78] See, for example: Weeks, Capital and Exploitation, 5.

exploitation of), the unpaid (knowledge) worker with the more general issues of the struggle for access to information.[79] Such issues are characteristic of the failing communications across the boundaries of a closed system—and thus, a systemic failure. Here, workers are increasingly disenfranchised from the economy by their decentralisation as autonomous self-owned businesses.

Schumpeter's error?

Capitalism is, by its nature, 'a form or method of economic change and not only never is but never can be stationary'.[80] Despite Capitalism's failures, its undeniable successes have long been held to be built on the principle of 'creative destruction'. This is a process that economist Joseph Schumpeter described as an industrial mutation, in which economic structures are incessantly revolutionised from within, in which the old structure is replaced by the emergent new one. 'Creative Destruction', writes Schumpeter, 'is the essential fact about capitalism.'[81] Schumpeter's notion of creative destruction is, itself, an extension of Marx and Engels' thinking, evident in the *Communist Manifesto* of 1848, published over a century earlier. Indeed, the weight of commentary concerning Marx, in *Part I, The Marxian Doctrine*, of Schumpeter's *Capitalism, Socialism, and Democracy*, cannot help but leave the reader informed as to how much Marx's writings played a part in Schumpeter's own work.

Here, I am not so much concerned with a discourse on political or economic theory *per se*, but on what such luminaries of thought might have said (or not said) in the context of my inquiry. Suffice to say that, over time, Schumpeter's writing on capitalism as 'the perennial gale of creative destruction',[82] has taken centre-stage on the platform of the modern neoliberal capitalist narrative. It pervades neoliberal political and economic thought and has permeated the world of business, entrepreneurship and productivity.[83] To all intent and purpose, it can be said that neoliberal capitalism is creative destruction.[84] Here, seemingly amid a permacrisis, I suggest there is a misrepresentation amid Schumpeter's framing of creative destruction.

In the prologue to Part II of *Capitalism, Socialism, and Democracy*, Schumpeter asks a question: 'Can capitalism survive?' 'No. I do not think it can', he replies.

---

[79] Hermann, "Value and Knowledge: Insights from Marxist Value Theory for the Transformation of Work in the Digital Economy."
[80] Schumpeter, Capitalism, Socialism, and Democracy, 94.
[81] Schumpeter, Capitalism, Socialism, and Democracy, 95.
[82] Schumpeter, Capitalism, Socialism, and Democracy, 96.
[83] Diamond Jr, "Schumpeter's Creative Destruction: A Review of the Evidence."
[84] Harvey, "Neo-Liberalism as Creative Destruction."

'But this opinion of mine... is in itself completely uninteresting.'[85] Schumpeter leads the naïve, uncritical reader to assume that his opinion that capitalism cannot survive, is not interesting, is not important, does not matter; that, in some way, it excuses the reader from a serious contemplation of the cause and effect of such failure and, ultimately, any challenge to the argumentation that follows. However, in my inquiry, Schumpeter is no less than an expert witness to the state of capitalism, socialism and democracy existing in his time.

Published separately as *Can Capitalism Survive*?[86] and read in absurd isolation, Part II of *Capitalism, Socialism, and Democracy* lacks the major work's preface and its essential contradiction. It merely opens with the question and concludes with the idea that while capitalism may not survive in the long run, 'for the purposes of short-run forecasting... a century is a "short run"'.[87] However, in the 1st edition preface of *Capitalism, Socialism, and Democracy,* Schumpeter states 'a socialist form of society will inevitably emerge from an equally inevitable decomposition of capitalist society'. He makes the paradoxical conclusion that 'capitalism is being killed by its achievements'.[88] Seemingly, this is a knowledge denied, by a capitalist 'sleight-of-hand' to many.[89]

In my critical questioning of Schumpeter's opinion, I need go no further than restate his thesis that '[capitalism's] very success undermines the social institutions which protect it, and "inevitably" creates conditions in which it will not be able to live and which strongly point to socialism as the heir apparent'.[90] In short, Schumpeter's opinion—an absurd contradiction, suppressed from his dialectic of creative destruction—cannot but be interesting, cannot but be important, and most certainly does matter. The irony of a 'neoliberal' capitalism that permits the capitalist's creative destruction of state and social institutions, means that Schumpeter's invitation to (some) readers to skip his analysis of Marxist socialism, is no longer advisable. The reader of Schumpeter's dialectic is not to be excused from its contradictions.

---

[85] Schumpeter, Capitalism, Socialism, and Democracy, 73.

[86] Schumpeter, Can Capitalism Survive?

[87] Schumpeter, Can Capitalism Survive? 195; Schumpeter, Capitalism, Socialism, and Democracy, 178.

[88] Schumpeter, Capitalism, Socialism, and Democracy, 12–13.

[89] With the back-cover quote "...THAT'S' CAPITALISM, AND IT WORKS", Malcolm Stevenson "Steve" Forbes Jr., publisher of Forbes magazine, is effectively complicit in misdirecting the readership of the 2009 Harper Perennial Modern Thought edition of Schumpeter's Can Capitalism Survive?.

[90] Schumpeter, Capitalism, Socialism, and Democracy, 73–74.

Martin Luther King, economic layperson?

It has been argued that public intellectual, Martin Luther King Jr, while a layperson in terms of economic theory, nevertheless showed significant insights into economic thinking that are increasingly relevant in considering our contemporary economic challenges.[91] Here, I argue that King's commentary is particularly relevant to this inquiry, in that his contribution to society stems from the central issue of a disenfranchised identity. Especially interesting in this context, is his article *Showdown for Nonviolence*, published shortly after his assassination on 4th April 1968, in *Look*, a US bi-weekly, general-interest magazine (Des Moines, Iowa).[92]

Given capitalism's exacerbated state of crisis, driven by Covid-19's market and institutional failures, I suggest we might foresee a future in which forms of 'hegemonic identity regulation' increasingly arise. I interpret this through a perceived requirement for 'capitalist efficiency drives' to pay down the cost of crisis response. Such identity regulation will require the inculcation of model 'neoliberal capitalist citizens': the conscious class of society's individuals, educated and entrusted by the state with the development of the capitalist economy. A society of entrepreneurs to work 'the system', exploit 'labour', and make 'profit' without the benefit of a true understanding of that in which they are involved. A society of entrepreneurs closed to the consciousness of its social context, by virtue of its own code. A society of 'digitally native' entrepreneurs wedded to applications of technology.

Arise a 'populist social resistance' of the disenfranchised. Here, over 50 years previously, Martin Luther King Jr championed a move to nonviolent protest to seek to benefit the poor of both Negroes and Whites alike—to avoid the tragedy of polarised communities and the destruction of democratic values. King called for national action, 'compassionate, massive and sustained', and above all, resourced by the state.[93] He was clearly aware of the sophisticated and true understanding of what he was, at the time, involved in: a struggle with the essential economic problems of the right to live and to have a job and income. In Showdown for Nonviolence, King set out plans for coordinated, nonviolent action in fifteen areas, including ten cities and five rural districts. He wrote:

> 'We hope that the sound and site of a growing mass of poor people walking slowly toward Washington will have a positive, dramatic effect

---

[91] Sommers, Hegland, and Delices, "American Public Policy and Full Employment: The Imperative of Martin Luther King's Political Economy in the 21st Century."
[92] King, "Showdown for Nonviolence."
[93] King, "Showdown for Nonviolence."

on Congress. Once demonstrations start, we feel, there will be spontaneous supporting activity taking place across the country'.[94]

Despite appealing to nonviolence, and following his assassination, April 1968 witnessed numerous riots and disturbances across the USA. It has been argued that the assassination was a catalyst that 'led individuals to an emotional disengagement from the realm of normal political behaviour'.[95] Over 100 cities experienced riots, 43 people were killed, 3000 injured and around 20,000 were arrested.

Direct comparisons are difficult. However, the (global) civil unrest during the 2020-2021 pandemic —not least as triggered by the killing of George Floyd and the impact on the Black Lives Matter movement—does bare comparison to 1968. In addition, accelerated by the social media connectivity of the disenfranchised, 2020 signalled 'a vastly more popular and widespread movement [of social unrest] reminiscent of the great outpouring of [1969's] anti-Vietnam War action'.[96] Added to that, the January 2021 Capitol Hill insurrection in Washington DC, during the certification of the 46th President of the United States (see Chapter 2), all illustrate questions of concern over identity and disenfranchisement. These are drums banged to different rhythms, but a similar tune. Yet, it remains unclear that we will witness the coordinated change in identities, power politics and technology to reduce the growing levels of disenfranchisement. Across the antagonistic horizon, the hope of a socially compassionate capitalism must therefore be that Covid-19 and continuing crises are at least catalysts for a new narrative. A narrative around which increasingly disenfranchised identities might coalesce.

Designs on reconciliation, from the inside out?

The realisation that neoliberal capitalism's failure to adequately account for social justice, through a systemic failure to communicate with its adaptive environment, gave me my opening question: does neoliberal capitalism's failure contain within it an idea for a transition to a post-Covid-19, postcapitalist society? Following the ghosts of Marx and Schumpeter, I find nothing to contradict a future reframed in the light of current power politics, disenfranchised identities and value extractive technologies. Both expound on a certain 'socialist' inevitability. But while resigned-Marxists might hope for—and misguided-capitalists might deny—a socially compassionate future, King reminds us that to struggle on the outside or underneath the

---

[94] King, "Showdown for Nonviolence."
[95] Hofstetter, "Political Disengagement and the Death of Martin Luther King," 174.
[96] Gitlin, "The Black Lives Matter Protests Don't Evoke 1968. They're More like 1969."

requirement for change is not easy. King would not simply hope for a transition to postcapitalism. He would not hope that a new narrative rises, phoenix-like, from the ashes of a thousand contesting fires. Such hope is, perhaps, the last refuge of the disenfranchised member(s) of society. Certainly, with the echo chambers of contemporary communications media diffusing key messages in an ocean of big data, all under the algorithmic control of a capitalist elite, what hope can there be for a coalescence around any message sufficient to challenge an incumbent power-politic?

As I suggested in Chapter 6, while Covid-19 might have been construed as a catalyst for the changes in capitalism apparently being sought by many in society, the necessary groundwork for change was not in evidence pre-crisis. Following the principles of change introduced by Kurt Lewin[97], although the ground for change may well have been unfrozen by Covid-19, the many voices of change outside, alongside and beneath the power-politic of a neoliberal capitalism just had not coalesced enough around any form of grand narrative, plan or idea for positive, social change. With the ground softened, there were no plans in evidence for any necessary foundations to be dug for the building of a postcapitalism. The hope of a future socially compassionate capitalism merely resolves to future crises as catalysts for that narrative.

The conclusion that a new narrative is now required should be a concern for capitalism. Many voices of opposition are now also insiders—members of the incumbent institutions of the extant power politic. Thus, the performance of existing systems and sub-systems are set to become increasingly unpredictable, as the contrary components of the neoliberal capitalist economic subsystem—its capitalist entrepreneurs and workers—increasingly practise their economic agency in conflict with their own changing, socially sensitive goals.

If the idea for a postcapitalist transition is toward some 'form' of socialism, what might that transition look like? Left to emergence—along the lines of my analysis—I suggest that society will continue to be impacted by crises, exacerbated (if not caused by) a decaying neoliberal capitalist economy. Two options exist. Left to society to act, the lack of a coherent narrative of socialism is problematic. How does society—much of it marginalised and outside the purview of the capitalist subsystem—design changes to that subsystem? There may be a will, coalescing in time, but (insiders aside) there is a general lack of means. However, left to capitalism to act itself, the isolation of its incumbents from the wider social system suggests that (insiders aside), while there may be a means for change, there will be a lack of will to do so.

---

[97] Lewin, Frontiers in Group Dynamics: Concept, Method and Reality in Social Science; Social Equilibria and Social Change.

Here, turning to the insider view, the neoliberal ideal of liberty highlights the difficulties of controlling the performance of the economic subsystem. It is increasingly difficult or expensive for the subsystem to verify the conduct of its human agents. Any system or subsystem at risk of homeostasis and disenfranchised insiders, may need to 'invest magnitude times more to protect its information from insiders than from external [oppositions]'.[98] Despite the existence of a capitalist sleight-of-hand, the ground is set for an exploration of possible 'reconciliations': designs on what Paul Mason has described as a transition to postcapitalism. The promise is of some hope that a transition to a post-neoliberal capitalism may be designed by insiders, from the inside out. Reconciliations are possible by design. And, amid a constellation of perspectives from across the antagonistic horizons of capitalism, work and enterprise, it is to the opportunities for the design of such reconciliations that my inquiry must now turn.

[98] Hua and Bapna, "Who Can We Trust? The Economic Impact of Insider Threats," 65.

Part III.
On opportunity

Chapter 8

The invisible hand, emergent

FOLLOWING THE DISCURSIVE INQUIRIES through the metaphoric 'means' of the empiric imaginations of Part II—and the resultant constellation of perspectives on the future of capitalism, work and enterprise—I now turn to (re)frame the idea of a *Design Capitalism.* With its roots in mid-20th century discourse, and a contemporary problematic that makes invisible its potential, I argue that a non-concept of Design Capitalism has a definable functional role in a post-Covid-19/post-crises society. It may be the salvation of a postcapitalism. The only pragmatic reconciliation of an idealistic notion of capitalism. Here I lay the groundwork for the re-introduction of the aesthetic theory of my earlier text: *Thinking the Art of Management,*[1] setting the scene for what I argue is the real potential for societal change. This potential is encapsulated in the idea that people require freeing from the chains and shackles of their slavery to the technologically aestheticised surface of global capitalism.

In this Chapter, the first of my *opportunity* inquiries, I argue that, figuratively, our emancipation is fundamentally a question of education—a re-imagining of an 'invisible hand' that might better encourage a sensible understanding to penetrate the attractive beauty of consumerism. Thus, rather than fine-tuning an educational curriculum to produce the ideal yet synthetic neoliberal capitalist, such an education should seek to reveal the sublime conditions of our social humanity. It should lead us to exercise a judgemental mode of beauty that questions our purposiveness in relation to

---

[1] Atkinson, Thinking the Art of Management: Stepping into "Heidegger's Shoes."

the sublimity of a VUCA world. Here, progress is fundamentally a question of how we open our minds to the adaptive flexibility that exists within us all—a poietic capacity to compose and negotiate both our individual and collective conscious emergence into that world.

Can we envisage a future where, as a society—collectively learning from the lessons of our past—we change the basis of our economic organization? Can we change from a failed growth conception of (neoliberal) capitalism, to a new (social) model of postcapitalism, such as represented in Figure 8.1? To paraphrase Dr Martin Luther King Jr, what we would require is '[a] movement powerful enough, dramatic enough, [and] morally appealing enough, so that [all] people of goodwill, [including] poor people themselves, begin to put pressure on [the state and its institutions] to the point that they can no longer elude our demands.'[2] However, King's call for nonviolent action against the state is a call represented in thousands of different voices, the diversity of which makes a single voice, at best, problematic.[3]

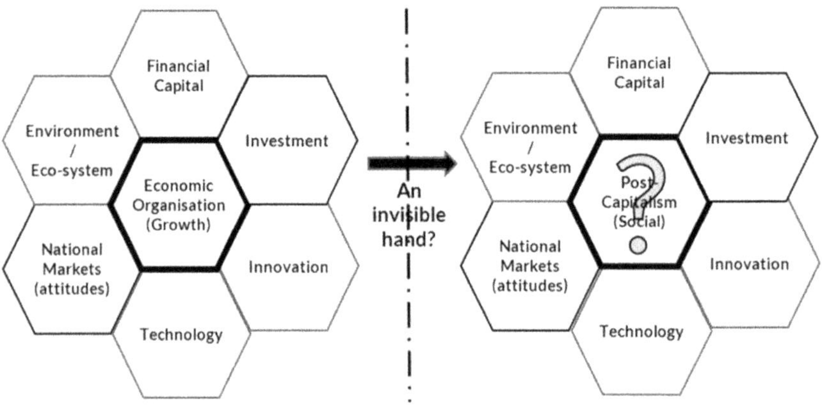

Figure 8.1. A concept of (social) postcapitalism?

Meanwhile, the new international institutions of growth capitalism: Facebook, Amazon, Apple, Netflix, and Google, et al. ('the FAANGs'), expand into 'every corner of the economy, politics and our lives'.[4] They dominate economic organization, exhibit monopolistic behaviours,[5] and employ aggressive tactics

[2] King, "Showdown for Nonviolence."
[3] Carney, "All Lives Matter, but so Does Race."
[4] Alleman, "Threat of Internet Platforms: Facebook, Google, Etc.," 1.
[5] Alleman, Baranes, and Rappoport, "Multisided Markets & Platform Dominance."

to stifle innovative competition.[6] They control access to markets, provide technology platforms that network identities within business models designed to maximise growth. They allow easy, mostly unverified membership, providing significant resistance to the removal of any member without extreme provocation. In short, the FAANGs and their like, control, disperse and suppress identities. They silence dissenting voices—all within an ocean of 'big data'. Thus, as my allegorical Inspector commences his summation, I start with a brief resume of the foregoing empirics of the imagination: the constellation of concerns and perspectives, and the folly of reading anything into Adam Smith's idea of *an invisible hand*. I then proceed to outline the idea of failure as incitement to change before moving to discuss, in more detail, elements of design as might be applicable to the notion of Design Capitalism.

The FAANGs: a paradoxical concern

The tightly controlled algorithms that process freely given personal data allow FAANGs a level of opaqueness that threaten democracy and civil society.[7] To draw on a Marxist concern, they deny a social truth. Their technology platforms are capitalist subsystems, closed to the consciousness of their social context by virtue of their own codes. As instruments of a digital-native class of capitalist elite, the *raison d'être* of these digital platforms is a paradox of social accessibility. The platforms produce knowledge (through big data analytics) as objects ('use values') for exchange ('exchange values'). This is an appropriation—by the elite—of the unpaid intellectual property and identity of those not of their class. That 'social' knowledge is, in general, a knowledge of the markets where other 'exchange values'—appropriated from the unpaid labour of the working class—can be realised by the traditional capitalist class. The digitally native capitalist elite is thus twice removed from any need to create value and from anything so dirty as traditional work. They have no concern over what might, pejoratively, be termed 'dirty production'.

Paradoxically, within this Huxleyesque, brave new world of dirty production, the appropriation and exploitation of the unpaid worker also places the capitalist entrepreneurial identity at risk, subjugating it to the periphery of work. Entrepreneurs may own their own means of production—as autonomous self-owned businesses—but they cannot access their markets without the 'rent' (advertising or subscriptions, for example) payable to their 'elite' brethren: those who continue to produce nothing, but extract exchange value from others, now capitalist and entrepreneurial worker alike. Here, hope is no strategy for change. But this conclusion is not new. To follow Alasdair

---

[6] Fung, "Congress Grilled the CEOs of Amazon, Apple, Facebook and Google."
[7] Alleman, "Threat of Internet Platforms: Facebook, Google, Etc.," 12.

MacIntyre, a totalitarian project—such as that favoured in fiction by Aldous Huxley or George Orwell, or envisaged in capitalism by Marx, Schumpeter and others—is doomed to failure. '[The] project of creating… wholly or largely predictable [systems] committed to creating a wholly or largely predictable society is doomed and doomed by the facts about social life… What the totalitarian project will always produce will be a kind of [sclerotic] inefficiency which may contribute in the long run to its defeat'.[8]

Postcapitalism: a taste of things to come?

For technology researchers Christian Hoffmann and André Dahlinger, capitalism might abolish itself in favour of 'robo-economic systems'.[9] Decentralised autonomous businesses (DABs)—for example: autonomous taxis or autonomous additive manufacturing units—may operate on decentralised blockchain-facilitated 'self-enforcing' contracts, without any form of human ownership. Zero ownership negates the dystopian appropriation by a capitalist elite of exchange value, in favour of its redistribution to society through reduced prices; DAB technology is held to only add value to society, rather than to extract from it. However, this scenario is based on flawed assumptions. In their article, Hoffmann and Dahlinger rely on a continuation of a liberalistic capitalist economy. But this is contradictory, given that neoliberal capitalism has seemingly already failed.

Hoffmann and Dahlinger acknowledge that their many assumptions are open to challenge. Even the progress of AI and blockchain technology—the basis for their scenario—is founded on capitalist principles of ownership. Market capitalisations are frequently cited for those organizations issuing shares or other (alternative) instruments of capital, such as variations on the cryptocurrency 'Bitcoin'. And it is a core principle of such capitalism that those who provide access to their capital—to invest in developing any technology—expect a return on its provision. It is improbable that an outbreak of mass altruism among the continuing liberalistic capitalists, would rise to the level necessary to relinquish the totality of the very thing that supports their position—their capital. A MacIntyrean, totalitarian project, doomed to fail. It is unsurprising that the authors, while invoking Adam

---

[8] MacIntyre, After Virtue, 106.

[9] Hoffmann and Dahlinger, "How Capitalism Abolishes Itself in the Digital Era in Favour of Robo-Economic Systems: Socio-Economic Implications of Decentralized Autonomous Self-Owned Businesses."

Smith's invisible hand of capitalism as a principle of their view on the future, are silent about how such a guiding, invisible hand works.[10]

Other postcapitalist ideas include Aaron Bastani's concept of Fully Automated Luxury Communism (FALC).[11] Here, the human ownership of DABs) is not relinquished to a form of non-human, non-existential, hard robo-capitalist system of economic organization—perhaps held in perpetuity, in a blockchain-powered escrow account for the benefit of society. Rather, a new communism sees ownership of DABs transferred to the state. Here, lacking the guidance of any form of Smith's 'invisible hand', the call for relinquishing ownership on any form of asset or instrument of capital into the hands of the state, is an existential threat to capitalism. It is a call to a revolutionary transition to communism. Here, dispersed among a surfeit of single-issue identities, often purposefully speaking of the same concerns but uncoordinated in purposiveness, history has shown that such transitions are fraught with difficulty. They are no certain harbingers of success.

An invisible hand (if it were to exist) might be envisaged as a guardian. A resolver of conflict between two opposing forces: the neoliberal ideal of Smithian capitalism, powered by self-interest; and the democratic force for a 'good' society. Such guardianship is the proper concern of the state at society's head—the entity constituted by its institutions of power. Here, in one of Adam Smith's two key invocations of an invisible hand, we are presented with the idea that the self-interested force of capitalism indirectly assists the 'good' society. What is good for me is good for you. Our guardian's invisible hand promotes a general good that is not the 'end' of an individual good: it promotes society's interests more effectively than was the self-interested's intent.[12] Neither does Smith's alter-invocation offer substantially more. As an innate obligation, the capitalist commits to distribute the rewards of productive labour, less the capitalist's relatively meagre needs, to satisfy the needs of those who labour in that production. Fair remuneration for fair labour. And, without knowing it, the capitalists are guided to advance the society on which the satisfaction of their needs depends.[13]

At this point, sociologist Niklas Luhmann's *Trust and Power*[14] is insightful. Let me assume there is an invisible hand available to us (presently absent or

---

[10] It is noted that Adam Smith does not define 'the invisible hand' of capitalism. Indeed, Smith's writing only refers to the idea of 'an invisible hand' twice across the entirety of work in the volumes The Theory of Moral Sentiments and The Wealth of Nations.

[11] Bastani, Fully Automated Luxury Communism.

[12] Smith, The Wealth of Nations: Books IV-V.

[13] Smith, The Theory of Moral Sentiments, 215.

[14] Luhmann, Trust and Power.

not), to guide the excesses of capitalist self-interest in the face of a desired 'good' society. The invisible hand, as a functioning guardian, would act to ease conflict, balancing society's needs against any self-interested tendency to excess. Yet, in the democratic positioning of the power-politic of the state, society's constituents—its voters—place their 'trust' in the hands of the state to guard over their interests. As Luhmann succinctly expressed, this societal trust is a confidence, in its broadest sense, of one's expectations. We, as voters, trust in the state. We bestow trust in those we elect as our representatives. We trust that those representatives have both the capability and capacity to exercise guardianship over our interests. Indeed, our system of democracy calls on this very mechanism of trust. Trust is a feature of the system of organization of our society. When we lack that trust, the system fails. Democracy fails. But a society educated to expect that its subsystem of capitalist economic organization centres on some notion of trust in an invisible hand, is a society misled for, really, in who's hand is that trust placed? In Hope's?

To paraphrase Luhmann, "the 'nature' of ['an invisible hand'—its identity—] is defined by the conditions under which it might be replaced by another."[15] When we reconsider the question of a balance between forces for a good society and forces for its subsystem of self-interested economic organization, we must consider both our own identity and our relationship to the identity of the Other that wields its hand of guardianship (invisible or otherwise). For many, contrary to our expectations of the state's role, as individuals of society we bear witness to the politics of neoliberal capitalism that have ceded much of our states' institutional identity to colonisation by the forces and functions of capitalism. The identity of the state, as the Other, is now more characterised by capitalist motivations of self-interest, than by any social 'good'. We yield to the self-interested state.

We are faced with both the state (as guardian of society) and its economic subsystem as 'becoming', if not 'being' self-interested. But this is not the identity of the state as a self-interested party on the global stage of nation states—a state that uses its national power to gain global influence. Rather, I speak of the identity of the state as inwardly looking, toward institutional self-interest, where such interest is no longer social, but capital. Here, the state exercises its considerable capacity for autopoietic reproduction and the maintenance of individual freedoms, based on the ownership, maintenance and growth of capital. This conceptualisation of the self-interested state mirrors the dichotomy noted by American economist and sociologist Thorstein Veblen (1857-1929). It is a dichotomy that exists between the interests of capitalists and the common interests of society. Here, the state's apparent abdication of

[15] Luhmann, 6.

responsibility for the common (social) interest, in favour of its capitalist colonisation, suggests that the proper consideration of the economy is now much more than its conceptualisation as a market.[16]

A natural consequence of the colonisation of the state (and thus society) by a capitalist economy, is that society, the state and its economic organization tend to be one and the same system—a system in which a pure market economics cannot function. As reflected in Chapter 7, while a pure market perspective might require that our economic subsystem of societal organization be protected from 'discretionary political interference', it cannot be the case that a democratic society, itself, requires such protections. The state, at the head of society, must exercise discretionary political interference. As a question of identity, it is for the state to make visible the invisible hand, to run interference on capitalism's excesses, as society's ultimate guardian. The alternative is a form of capitalist economic anarchy of self-interest. Here, an increasingly privileged elite—shy of the notion of labour toward a dirty production[17]—practise their Veblenian 'conspicuous consumption' in a global bubble of faux cosmopolitanism, served by technologically enslaved 'others'—the disenfranchised of a socio-capitalist ideology.

Failure as incitement to change

In a contemporary application of Veblen's 'machine discipline', the economic discipline of relentlessly employing technology to drive economic efficiencies and profits, continues to cut away the ground of law and order—the institutions that embody a more natural concept of liberty and the principles of conduct of civilised life. This is the ground on which society's enterprise is founded.[18] Wherein lies the paradox of the growth of enterprise itself: it is the technology that brings about the conditions of capitalist enterprise's own demise. Through a creative-destructive process, digital technologies in the hands of large capitalist institutions and under the ownership of an increasingly digitally-native elite, 'are breaking down the structure of natural rights by making these rights nugatory on the one hand and by cutting away the... foundations of them on the other hand.'[19] As I highlight in Chapter 5, in the UK for example, while Uber functions as an employer, we witness that

---

[16] Valentinov, "From Equilibrium to Autopoiesis: A Luhmannian Reading of Veblenian Evolutionary Economics."

[17] Veblen describes a 'conspicuous abstention from labour' as 'the conventional mark of superior pecuniary achievement', with the 'application to productive labour' as the 'mark of poverty and subjugation'.

[18] Veblen, "The Theory of Business Enterprise," 450.

[19] Veblen, "The Theory of Business Enterprise," 451.

employment rights are given little value when its drivers are subjugated in the faux-capitalist role of servant-entrepreneurs, constrained by the shackles of technology to act as surrogate employees.[20] Here, the Covid-19 crisis has highlighted the poor income support available for those not formally recognised as employees by the state,[21] evidence of a failure in the equitable functioning of neoliberal economic society.[22] The question arises, do such failures of equitable functionality indicate a growing lack of responsibility for the other? Recalling the words of J. B. Priestley's Inspector Goole:

> 'We don't live alone. We are members of one body. We are responsible for each other. And I tell you that the time will soon come when, if [we] will not learn that lesson, then [we] will be taught it in fire and blood and anguish.'[23]

Design as incitement to transition

From my analysis in Chapter 7, I have suggested that all we might hear from the ghosts of socialism, capitalism and democracy is that capitalism is, indeed, doomed. Socialism will be the order of the future. But, denied reasoned debate by a sleight-of-hand—a capitalist deceit—there is little to be acknowledged or accepted concerning what successful socialism might or could be. As Mark Fisher defined, there is a certain *Capitalist Realism*, a 'widespread sense that not only is capitalism the only viable political and economic system, but also that it is now impossible even to *imagine* a coherent alternative to it.'[24] In place of an invisible hand, the denial (or even the impossibility) of socialism is exacerbated by the double-edged sword of technology. Wielded by the new capitalist elite, this sword suppresses any potential for the growth of a grand narrative of socialism at the twist of an algorithm. It offers the imposition of a filter, a cut on the ideas of others. The

---

[20] McGaughey, "Uber, the Taylor Review, Mutuality and the Duty Not to Misrepresent Employment Status."
[21] Moss, "Uber Drivers in Court over Ministers' Failure to Help Gig Workers."
[22] While a February 2021 ruling from the UK Supreme Court decreed that Uber Drivers are to be considered as 'workers', and not self-employed, and that they are therefore eligible for certain employment rights, Uber maintains a reluctance to capitulate fully to the ruling. At the time of writing, Uber's position appears to be that, while their Drivers may be 'workers' that does not make them 'employees' in the traditional sense, and therefore the suggestion is that there is a half-way house between self-employment and employment. The situation appears to retain an element of ambiguity. See, for example: Marshall, "Uber Says Its UK Drivers Are 'Workers', but Not Employees."
[23] Priestley, "An Inspector Calls," 207.
[24] Fisher, Capitalist Realism: Is There No Alternative?

social democratisation of society has achieved little more than the global dispersion of identities, and the coalescing of minority interests around capitalist-manipulated, networked centres of virtual space. A surfeit of single-issue identities.

If (neoliberal) capitalism is failing, having achieved little more than incite, in many, a poverty of both capital and identity, yet promises of a socialist postcapitalism are scattered by the fickle winds of democracy, and fanned by the technical dialectics of identity and ownership, what might be the salvation in Paul Mason's call to design the transition to postcapitalism? Certainly, design suggests a purpose to the notion of a transition. A transition from a failure state to a new state of organization is inevitable. The idea of a designed transition thus makes more sense than to allow such a transition to freely evolve. An evolutionary transition, in which we simply emerge into the unknown, is fraught with risk and uncertainty. Given a state of failure then, how might 'design' be used to both incite and to challenge the incumbents of capitalism, to set about a necessary transition to some form of (to be defined) social capitalism?

In Chapter 7, I concluded that there is promise in a transition, by design, toward a post-neoliberal capitalist social economy. Here, the field is open for capitalists themselves to socially re-design capitalism. A form of Design Capitalism.[25] This would require leadership from 'socialist thinking' insiders of the neoliberal capitalist state and its public and private institutions. Such a transition invokes the idea of a re-design of capitalism, from the inside out, to the wider benefit of society. But inciting such change suggests that the (socialist) reform of capitalism may be too important to be left to the ardent, idealistic socialists. Yet, the alternative is to allow a rise in the regulation of a hegemonic capitalist identity, serving only to increase disparate forms of populist social resistance. Without an external and consistent social narrative, around which the disenfranchised can raise their voices of opposition, capitalism may simply continue its gradual path of decay in its ultimately fatal, sclerotic drive for efficiency and the maximisation of profit. That is, until capitalism's own power-politic structures are sufficiently undermined, so that even minority external interests are emboldened to wield their destructive influences, to chaotic effect.

Transition by design

It is not clear that we will witness a coordinated change in identities, or in institutional power-politics, or many social applications of technology, outside

---

[25] Brown, Martin, and Berger, "Capitalism Needs Design Thinking."

the incumbent power-politic. I suggest that we do not see the level of coordination that would give rise to a coherent 'socially compassionate capitalism', nor any massive 'technology-adaptive disruption' for societal benefit. The disenfranchised of neoliberal capitalist societies may be receptive to change, with pockets of opposition swimming against waves of creative destruction and crises, but individuals, even small entities, have little more than an opportunity to consider innovative change. Meanwhile, the behemoths of institutionalised capitalism represent either new waves of destruction, or hatches, battened down ahead of a storm.[26] With an armada of small boats scattered to the four winds, we might well ask how, out of many, comes one?

Might we look to other nations—to other forms of neoliberal or 'enlightened' capitalism—to derive designs for our own postcapitalist transition? Here, in a 2010 paper for the Max Planck Institute for the Study of Societies, Wolfgang Streeck suggested that progressing theories to support a wide belief in sustained political-economic variety—that is, between capitalist national political economies—'will require that more attention be paid to the commonalities of divergent capitalisms and their interdependent histories.'[27] Drawing on the title of Streeck's paper: *E Pluribus Unum*, out of the many (ontological) capitalisms that exist, is there one that might suffice for a VUCA world? Are the commonalities of capitalism's variety in any way suggestive of an error in Marx's or Schumpeter's conclusions? Are the differences sufficient to outline an overlooked opportunity, around which a new narrative might be construed? A basis for ontic design?

As I suggest, 'design' is a process of making manifest ideas, through the conjunction of a craft skill exercised with innovation. Thus, with variations in skill and the creativity of innovation, the idea of design applied to society and to capitalism may be considered a purposive attempt, not to identify an ontology of capitalisms *per se*, but to embrace the (potentially infinite) variability of a 'designed' post-neoliberal capitalism. Here, returning briefly to the Varieties of Capitalism literature, the idea of designs on capitalism contrasts with, for example, Colin Hay's idea that the varieties of capitalism approach might best proceed through the development of 'dystopic types', counter-posed against its more familiar 'ideal types'. But, viewing capitalist diversity in varietal terms *'distorts our object of analysis'*, where 'the fewer the varieties… the greater that distortion'.[28] Thus, counter to theorising about the dystopic arising from the ontic phenomenological commonalities of an extent

---

[26] Archibugi, Filippetti, and Frenz, "The Impact of the Economic Crisis on Innovation: Evidence from Europe."
[27] Streeck, "E Pluribus Unum? Varieties and Commonalities of Capitalism."
[28] Hay, "Does Capitalism (Still) Come in Varieties?," 315–16.

capitalism, might a pre-ontic 'becoming' or epiphenomenal emergence of an (indeterminate) postcapitalism be a better basis for a design that avoids a certain ideological ontology of postcapitalism?

I argue that 'transition by design' is more exploration or epiphenomenal emergence, than transitionary process of movement from one ontic state to another, either ideal or anti-dystopic. In exploration, I posit that we might equally envisage a 'becoming' of either: a socially designed capitalism; or a capitalist designed socialism. The mythical 'third way', perhaps? Thus, I do not apply design to form an ideal type. A utopian ideal social and economic organization cannot be deduced for a future that is not knowable. As Hay observes, ideal types are 'abstracted extrapolations from the real world'.[29] They can capture only an essence of the future. Neither should our sole aim be the avoidance of a dystopia—neglecting the problems of today. We should be wary of any attempt to design an ideal type of utopian postcapitalism. Rather, avoiding the dystopic, chaotic and unpredictable demise of capitalism, we require (to facilitate) its socialist-thinking insiders to imagine designs that address the field problem(s) of capitalism's sclerotic code. Such designs must reconcile our present reality and its inadequacies with our imagined uncertainties.

The emergent by design

Extending my analysis in Chapter 7 and addressing the question of what form a transition from neoliberal capitalism might take, I suggest we require new approaches to understand not only the necessary craft skills and innovation required to address the socio-economic challenges of today, but also what is meant by, and what craft skills and levels of innovation are required for, design for emergence. Here, I usefully frame these 'skill and innovation' requirements in the notion that what is needed is to consider the design of socio-economic interventions: reconciliations that structure the epiphenomenal emergence and maintenance of a 'good' society. Such a society should be one that is adaptable in a VUCA world; one in which its subsystem of economic organization works in support of its environment.

Here, I will draw on the work of social scientist and statistician, Barry Knight. Knight posits five principles for (the design of) a good society, being: 1) 'a decent standard of living, 2) a sense of security, 3) freedom to be creative, 4)

[29] Hay, "Does Capitalism (Still) Come in Varieties?," 308.

respectful relationships and 5) a sustainable future for the next generation.'[30] But before I can attend to these principles, I must first return to the distinction I made between the two modes of emergence in Chapter 4. This concerns whether we are to determine that a future emergent outcome is epiphenomenal or phenomenal.

Clearly, any discussion of *future moments* reflects underlying *critical uncertainties* that are phenomenal in nature; such moments are thus endogenous, in that they originate within our sense of reality. They are also autopoietic, in the sense that they constitute a cumulative form of change or evolution of that sense of reality. However, my concern turns to the reconciliation of *imaginations of interest*, now as *provocations* for design. Such provocations are epiphenomenal: they do not rely on an underlying phenomenal structure and may therefore be both exogenous and poietic. The potential of the epiphenomenal, exogenous form of emergence lies in Holland's treatise on emergence, I introduced in Chapter 4.

From Holland's perspective, an observer is perceived to innovate (a form of emergence) by the 'appropriate selection' of the right phenomenal elements or conditions.[31] However, in his desire to 'provide convincing evidence that we can increase our understanding of emergent phenomena through scientific study',[32] the issue Holland faced is the necessary specification of the mechanism of selection. This is a search for the rules of the game on which his theory of emergence is to be based. This is Holland's essential belief in there being a model or theory or science to the process of appropriate selection. However, as Holland acknowledged, this 'intuitive leap is a mystery we cannot fully resolve. No well-defined model of this aspect of the creative process exists', though he believes it does.[33] Holland's is a Hegelian dialectic search for an antithesis-synthesis to challenge this contradiction.

Holland's theory of emergence meets its dialectic contradiction in its inability to rationalise any emergence as in all ways and forms, both phenomenal and autopoietic. This is precisely because there is no explicit recognition within that theory, of the (absurd) possibility of an epiphenomenal (exogenous or poietic) emergence—a mode of emergence that does not obey the rules of the game. To Holland, all emergence is endogenous—if only its

---

30 Knight, "Powering a Good Society," 570; Knight's five principles of a good society are mirrored, in more expansive form, in the 17 Goals of Sustainable Development (SDGs), as advocated by the United Nations. (See, for example: *https://sdgs.un.org/goals*, accessed 21/07/2020). See also, notes to Chapter 1 on sustainability.

31 Holland, Emergence: From Chaos to Order, 211.

32 Holland, Emergence: From Chaos to Order, 238.

33 Holland, Emergence: From Chaos to Order, 211.

internal mechanism could be found. In place of a desired synthesis, Holland introduces the phenomenal metaphor, from which inferences of meaning may be transferred from metaphor to the emergent phenomenon.[34] Here, such a metaphor serves as a provisional dialectic synthesis. The promise in Holland's work is, however, to accept both the absurdity of the contradiction and to re-conceptualise emergence through its non-concept as a metaphor.

At first glance, then, Holland's singular view of emergence is solely autopoietic, yet the acknowledgment of a contradiction—the fact that the current understanding or theory of emergence is insufficient to apply to the creative process—suggests the limit at which a phenomenological interpretation neglects its creative Other. Here, while so far the prefix *epi-* has served to delineate the creative other—that is, the more exogenous and poietic aspects of emergence (the epiphenomenal emergent)—I now apply a semiotic interpretation. Although a move to semiotics from phenomenology might appear an unlikely deviation, it is not unacknowledged in the literature. There is the possibility, at least, of the two parallel approaches being 'wedded together in some kind of retroactive synthesis', with the one needing the other.[35]

From the point of view of the observer, the possibility of an *exogenous* emergence is derived from the observer's individual meaning-making; it offers a 'creative act' (*inciting the emergent*) that transcends the associated signified (the principal object) and signifier (its metaphor). Thus, in imagining a metaphor (*an imagination*) for the emergent conceptual model (*a reconciled moment* of conceptual becoming), I apply associated implications from *the imagination* (signifier) to its principal object (the signified). For example, in reconciling states of a non-concept of postcapitalism (*imaginations* as signifiers), I apply their associated implications (*provocations*) to the principal object—the negative dialectic of the extant economic system (as the signified)—to incite the emergent (the *reconciliations*).

The signifier (the imaginary metaphor) as imagination/story—such as the science fiction in the CCF method—is what Holland refers to as a form of deeper extended metaphor with the potential to cause 'a profound reconception of the subject matter'.[36] However, as incited subject matter, the emergent form of a negative dialectic of an extant capitalism is less a conceptual form of post-economic system. Rather, it is more that the signifiers (the imaginations) apply their associated implications (provocations) to the set of antecedent conditions (the signified) from which a new conceptual form of

---

[34] Holland, Emergence: From Chaos to Order, 210.
[35] Sonesson, "Phenomenology Meets Semiotics," 42.
[36] Holland, Emergence: From Chaos to Order, 209.

a *post*-economic system might emerge. The imaginations as metaphors therefore concern a reconceptualisation of the (pre-ontic) conditions for the ontic possibility of a postcapitalism.

Adopting Holland's concept of metaphor, allows me to suggest a form of 'metaphoric conjunction' arises, in which reconciliation is incited through a series of associations and disassociations between the signified state of an extant capitalism and signifiers of a form of post-capitalism. However, transcending Holland's dialectic approach, the negative dialectic requires me to move the focus off capitalism itself, and to imagine new forms of the conditions within which capitalism arises. I argue that this is necessary in order to see post-capitalism emerge as poietic and epiphenomenal. In this sense, the emergent is epiphenomenal to the design of its necessary conditions of emergence.

Beauty: a sword in the invisible hand made visible

Inculcating an adaptive ability in society is an appeal to leverage the creativity of the human individual—a release from the closed thinking that is often the outcome of much (narrow) scientific learning. Here, I revisit Luhmann's *autopoiesis* from Chapter 7.[37] If autopoiesis is the embodiment of the 'living' system, one that takes its nourishment from its environment and reproduces and maintains itself, it can only do so up to the point that the system dies—as all living things must do. An autopoietic system is not, conceptually, an immortal system. It simply carries a capacity, within limits, to perpetuate itself. Neither, conceptually, is an autopoietic system autonomous. In any living system, the energy for its maintenance and reproduction comes from its nourishment—that which it extracts from its environment. In an autopoietic social system, nourishment is a communication of meaning. As observed by Michael King, "if social systems are systems of meaning, people 'exist' within systems only according to the meaning that each system assigns to them."[38] The communication of meaning is the lifeblood of the social system. The hardening of communication channels is the sclerosis of the system's social network of meaning transmission and feedback—its capacity for sensemaking.

A social autopoiesis (with its biological roots) has its critics. However, at the conceptual level of this present work, I draw on the (compound) *auto* extension of the Greek term *poiêsis*, an activity in which people bring

[37] See also, for example: King, "The 'Truth' about Autopoiesis."
[38] King, "The 'Truth' about Autopoiesis," 220.

something into being: a composition.[39] Here, in a Platonic reading of Luhmann's conceptualisation of a social autopoietic system, the system relies on the *poiesis* or compositional capability of its people as components that perpetuate its reproduction and maintenance. It brings into being, composing that which the 'system' is there to compose: its purpose. Unlike an autopoietic system which is always in the act of reproducing its 'self', a poietic system is always in the act of 'becoming' some 'thing' other than its 'self'. On this basis, I now make a distinction between an autopoietic social system and a poietic one. In the former, the *autopoietic* social system derives the nature of its internal, reproductive compositions externally—a Platonic act of *mimesis*, a mirror-like reproduction, a reflection of its 'self'. In the latter, the *poietic* system draws its internal, reproductive compositions directly from its people. Since a democratic society should serve its people's compositional desires, it can properly tend to a *poietic* system. Here, rather than reproduction, a *poietic* pro-duction reveals something of the other, a new version of its self—an Aristotelian act of *mimesis*.[40] Yet, where people are expected to compose toward the reproduction of some externally imposed desire, they no longer compose through natural poiesis, but autopoietically. It is here that Luhmann's notion of society is visible as one that hinders rational solutions to its human problems.[41]

From Diotima's dialogue with Socrates, in Plato's 'The Symposium', we may learn that *'love is the desire to have the good forever... [Its] function is giving birth in beauty in body and mind.'*[42] If I consider the 'good' system (with a 'good' purposive function) as a body, and its collective 'culture' as its mind, then a Platonic love, simply restated as a desire for lasting goodness, presents one conceptual way that a 'good' system (or subsystem) might achieve its purpose. Diotima's metaphor of giving birth in beauty in body and mind is Plato's argument for a humanistic love that drives a natural predilection for immortality through the reproduction of its humanity. As Diotima continues:

> 'All human beings are pregnant in body and in mind, and when we reach a degree of adulthood, we naturally desire to give birth. We cannot give birth in what is ugly, only in what is [harmoniously]

---

[39] See Translator's Note 109, Plato, The Symposium, 78; In this respect, the concept of social autopoiesis is closer to the origin of the word poiesis, than its biologically derived cousin. This avoids what Michael King (1993) referred to as the sin of social biologism or of any claim to social Darwinism.

[40] I explain more about the concept of mimesis in the following Chapter 9.

[41] Valentinov, "From Equilibrium to Autopoiesis: A Luhmannian Reading of Veblenian Evolutionary Economics."

[42] Plato, The Symposium, 43.

> beautiful... this is how mortal creatures achieve immortality... This cannot occur in a condition of disharmony.'[43]

As the writer's mortal thoughts reach maturity in poiesis, bringing forth a composition and giving birth to an immortal prose, so too, I argue, might we consider the humanity within a social system, given free rein to poiesis, harmoniously giving birth to (rational) ideas and actions that (pre)serve its immortality. Yet, constrained by any disharmonious autopoietic objective, for example, in the preservation of capital for others, society may be seen to hinder such (rational) solutions to its human problems.

Beauty in a social system: the development of its humanity, lies in the harmonious intersections of its components and its environment. It reasonably follows that a complex systems perspective of socio-economic organization tends, not to the autopoietic, but to the poietic. For society to desire, compose and give metaphoric birth to the 'good' system, its people must provide the poiesis essential to transcend the simple (Platonic) reproduction and maintenance of their essential selves, and become their potential selves: their immortal purpose. Systemically, this goes beyond Luhmann's call to replace the notion of equilibrium with that of autopoiesis.[44] In the autopoietic system, it falls on the poiesis of the resistant insider, striving for harmonious beauty, to make their invisible hands visible and guide others. But, as hands of the subject supposed to design (c.f. Jacques Lacan's subject supposed to know),[45] insiders must be assisted by the state, as *agents at its visible hand.*

Design capitalism

I reach the conception of Design Capitalism, a critical notion where Márton Szentpéteri has said that *design capitalism* is:

> '...responsible for the appearance of things and thus it is destined to cover up the essence of things, to misguide the viewer's understanding of reality... the epiphany of the society of the ubiquitous market, of exchange value, of the fetish of commodity, of the spectacle, the

---

[43] Plato, The Symposium, 43.
[44] Valentinov, "From Equilibrium to Autopoiesis: A Luhmannian Reading of Veblenian Evolutionary Economics."
[45] Tie, "The Subject Supposed to Design."

> creation of a conforming surface that not only makes things invisible, but makes them disappear, as well.'[46]

Conceptually, the opaque yet aesthetic manipulation of data, of identity, and of markets, by the digitally native capitalist elite is problematic. Here, while it may be argued that Design Capitalism is a new conceptual kid on the capitalist block, technology's shaping and controlling of the scale and form of human agency in design, is reflected in the work of Marshall McLuhan, who wrote in the 1960s that:

> '...[the] effects of technology do not occur at the level of opinions or concepts, but alter sense ratios or patterns of perception steadily and without any resistance. The serious artist is the only person able to encounter technology with impunity, just because he [sic] is an expert aware of the changes in sense perception.'[47]

Thus, with its aesthetic root, as Szentpéteri suggests, 'the ever increasing and accelerating virtualization and growing hiperwiredness [sic] of contemporary design culture ...is completing the process of the total aestheticization of the world'.[48] I therefore argue that the proper approach to the contradictory VUCA reality of a capitalist society obscured by technology is, properly, an aesthetic one. However, one might still argue that, although there is a realisation that neoliberal capitalism exists in a state of crisis, and that there are strong arguments for its eventual demise, the idea of a design capitalism wielded by a digitally-native capitalist elite serves its own purpose.

From the perspective of any incumbent State and its power-politic, I have argued that challenges to its authority can only be successful if the mechanisms of power outside, below and alongside the requirement for change also align. A design capitalism, as I have so far described, serves to alter the sense ratios and patterns of perception of society steadily, without any resistance—perhaps romanced by a surfeit of consumer goods. A homeostatic economic subsystem drives homeostasis into the core of the social system itself. Identities are dispersed in the only media that truly welcomes all voices, particularly those that create controversy and conflict in the name of democracy. The technological suppression, through social

---

[46] Szentpéteri, "Changing the Rhythm of Design Capitalism and the Total Aestheticization of the World," 88.
[47] McLuhan, "The Medium Is the Message," 114.
[48] Szentpéteri, "Changing the Rhythm of Design Capitalism and the Total Aestheticization of the World," 89.

media's global dispersion and diffusion of any potential for a new grand narrative, acts as a negative feedback mechanism: it attenuates variety and encourages stability. The irony is that there is nothing democratic about the medium of social media. With Klaus Schwab's fourth industrial revolution[49] to some no revolution at all,[50] welcoming the creative destruction of (global) social media might advance the coalescing of localised identities of potentially greater impact. But, ridding our 'selves' of any one form of alienation and exploitation will not automatically result in a better system in its stead.[51]

The irony, lost in Schumpeter's error and perpetuated by capitalist deceit, is that Capitalism is its own worst enemy. Within its creative-destructive core are all the weapons for its own defeat. That its defeat is inevitable, greater minds than 'I' have already concluded. Even the relationship between Marx, Schumpeter and creative destruction is not new.[52] While some have chosen to hold on to the dreams of the past, others have ignored or been directed to ignore the future; yet other marginalised groups of Others have sought positive action for change. Here, as my analysis highlights, the defeat of capitalism, when it comes, is likely to be chaotic, messy, unpredictable and dangerous—a consequence, perhaps, (of the sum) of increasing, but disparate oppositional actions. While such actions will generally be well-meaning, socially acceptable and peaceful, in the ultimate irony a neoliberal democracy cannot, without intervention, prevent the use of technology by others in coordinating conflict and violence.

Given my analysis, I now ask, does the concept of a Design Capitalism have a definable function in a post-Covid-19 society? If so, what is the scope for its development? Here, design serves a purpose: it is a process to make manifest ideas, where a craft skill (in design) exercised with (creative) innovation operates on what is known of the present reality. Thus, beyond the contemporary concept of an aesthetic manipulation of data, of identity, and of markets, Design Capitalism can be the emergent outcome of craft skill and innovation. It can be used to resolve the field problems of economic organization. In effect, this is a negative dialectic reading of a non-concept of Design Capitalism: an economic organization that is always in a process of becoming, of evolving, but which never is a 'thing'. I therefore posit that our concern is no longer capitalism, *per se*—as I depict in Figure 8.2—but what capitalism is,

---

[49] Schwab, The Fourth Industrial Revolution.

[50] Petriglieri, "F**k Science!? An Invitation to Humanize Organization Theory."

[51] Zwick, "No Longer Violent Enough?: Creative Destruction, Innovation and the Ossification of Neoliberal Capitalism."

[52] Elliott, "Marx and Schumpeter on Capitalism's Creative Destruction: A Comparative Restatement."

itself, concerned with. That is to say, our concern is capitalism's non-concept: the constellation of economic activity from which it, in all its potential variety, emerges.

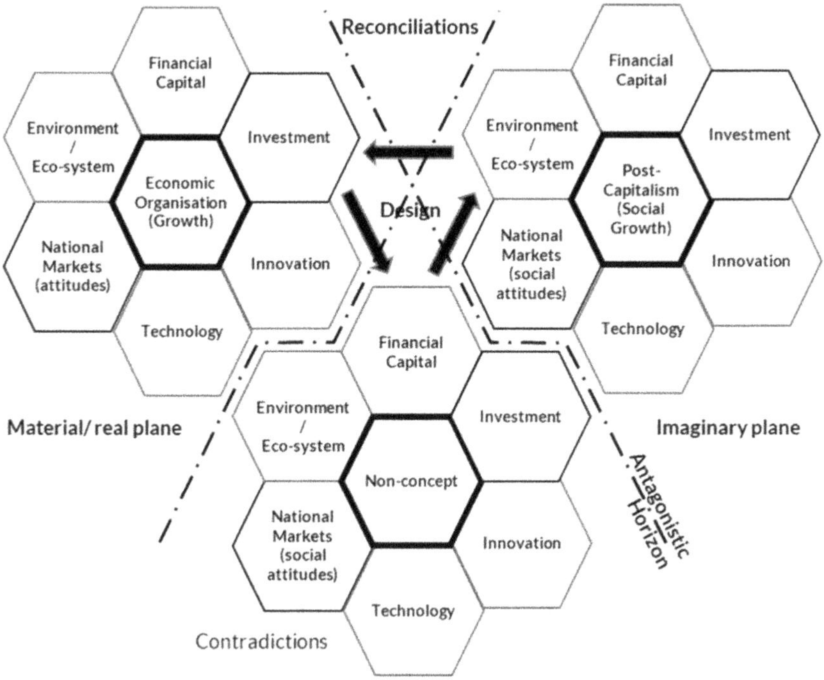

Figure 8.2. A non-concept of (social) postcapitalism

The present reality is that 'design' applied directly to the concept of 'capitalism' is in service of the perceived problematics of its internal effectiveness and efficiencies. This is the question of how to design systemic homeostasis into a system of economic organization. As homeostasis seeks stability through attenuation of variety, Design Capitalism—as currently understood—creates ever more innovative ways to seed its own destruction and the inevitable destabilisation of society. However, I argue that the same craft skills in design, applied with creative innovation to the problematic of capitalism's missing service to society holds promise. This is the concern of the economic organization, not of capitalism itself, but of that from which it emerges. Thus, again referring to Figure 8.2 (drawing on the example of the domain map from Chapters 4 and 5) Design Capitalism turns its attention to how a growth mode of society's economic organization has become sclerotic, in terms of: the contradictions that support it; its unevenly distributed capital base; is mode(s) of investment; its principles of innovation; its applications of technology; and its attitudes and applications of market principles.

A non-concept of Design Capitalism holds the promise of 'designing' improvements to our capitalist subsystem of economic organization that alleviate its communication problems with society. This allows—as Paul Mason might concur[53]—the potential to '*design* the transition to [a] postcapitalism'. But here, a postcapitalism is not the absence of, or destruction of capitalism *per se*. Rather, I imagine the emergence of a designed post-neoliberal (social) capitalism. Thus, a Design Capitalism serving society (social design) would be responsible for revealing the reality of society to its capitalists. It would remove the codified restrictions to its essence and encourage the capitalist subsystem to accept that the society—on which it depends for its own existence—is an indivisible part of its own reality. This is an epiphany of a society, not of the ubiquitous market, but of its people. It is a removal of the fetish of commodity and the creation of a penetrating vision that makes society visible, in all its variety. It is a non-concept of Design Capitalism in the service of society. It eschews the opaque yet aesthetic manipulation of data, of identity, and of markets. Instead, it encourages the embrace of an aesthetic of sensible cognition by the digitally native capitalist elite. This would no longer be so problematic. It would indeed be the new kid on the capitalist block, but one rooted in the commentary of old.

Design's problematic

Design recognises that technology shapes and controls the scale and form of human agency. Thus, Design Capitalism can inform and alter sense ratios or patterns of perception steadily and without any resistance. This works for the manipulative and extractive, but it may also work for the good. However, to open the subsystem of neoliberal capitalism to design for the 'good', will require changes in sense perception, in which the proper approach to a Design Capitalism for a VUCA reality is an aesthetic one, and at its heart, employs a certain aesthetic sensibility.[54]

As Sheila Dow observed, even Adam Smith 'wrote about the aesthetic appeal of systems' suggesting Smith acknowledged their 'profound psychological appeal at the level of ideas.'[55] Thus, I argue, an economy designed for a VUCA world will require the State, its power-politic, and its institutions, including education, to condition society for equality of sensible cognition, rather than

---

[53] Mason, Postcapitalism: A Guide to Our Future, 145.
[54] Atkinson, Thinking the Art of Management: Stepping into "Heidegger's Shoes."
[55] Dow, "Smith's Philosophy and Economic Methodology," 107.

the inequality of tracking identities within a capitalist ideal of production and exploitation.[56] The (non)concept of 'sensible cognition' is consistent with recent calls for: 'agility, dexterity, flexibility, and resilience'; and new skills and tools in 'design, foresight, and systems thinking', to navigate VUCA environments.[57] A transition to a non-concept of Design Capitalism, through developing society's aesthetic sensibility at an individual level, would avoid the tendency of an economic appeal to the one-dimensional consumer, and the disenfranchisement of Others—a feature of the current state of design capitalism as 'one of the ultimate sources of the decay of liberal democracies… and the rise of illiberalism'.[58]

Ideas such as broadening creativity and innovation activity across the range of social and economic activity are not new. They have been related to future forecasting, social change, sustainability, and a learning society, with change being sought through adding value. In such ideas, innovation transcends any notion of a specific technology.[59] Yet none of these ideas are broached from the perspective of realising change in the economic subsystem itself. They are, in effect, enacted through the peripheral activity of (semi) autonomous self-owned businesses, acting independently as *social entrepreneurs*.[60]

Otto von Busch and Karl Palmås[61] argue that the proposition that design thinking might be applied to transition a democratic capitalism to some form of postcapitalism, gives rise to three problematics. Firstly, there is little to

---

[56] Österman, "Varieties of Education and Inequality: How the Institutions of Education and Political Economy Condition Inequality."

[57] Millar, Groth, and Mahon, "Management Innovation in a VUCA World: Challenges and Recommendations," 11.

[58] Szentpéteri, "Changing the Rhythm of Design Capitalism and the Total Aestheticization of the World," 93.

[59] See, for example: Conceiçao, Heitor, and Veloso, "Infrastructures, Incentives, and Institutions: Fostering Distributed Knowledge Bases for the Learning Society"; Conceição et al., "Beyond the Digital Economy: A Perspective on Innovation for the Learning Society"; Dijkema et al., "Trends and Opportunities Framing Innovation for Sustainability in the Learning Society."

[60] A recent initiative concerning the application of design principles, particularly in relation to the 17 SDGs is the idea of 'collective intelligence design' advocated by NESTA (see: Peach et al., The Collective Intelligence Playbook. Collective intelligence design is defined as the art and science of bringing together diverse groups of people, data (including information or ideas) and technology. While the NESTA playbook is replete with principles processes and tools for the application of its collective intelligence design, it lacks a critical approach to understanding the social nature of society itself and therefore the need to account for emergence at a societal level.

[61] von Busch and Palmås, "Designing Consent: Can Design Thinking Manufacture Democratic Capitalism?"

prevent it being used as a political tool by incumbents in any position, to maintain or strengthen their status quo, for example, toward the development of an authoritarian postcapitalism. Secondly, there is the agency problem that design thinking applied at the societal level may require a new class of elite design professionals—a social hazard. Thirdly, the tripartite relationship between design, ideology and pragmatism, or design in relation to both the realpolitik of social injustice and the ideology of theory and ethics, is problematic. But, I suggest these problems arise through the idea that design thinking and its toolset may simply be applied to the level of society, without first understanding, at a non-conceptual level, the true nature of the field problem of neoliberal capitalism's own emergence.

In the first problematic, von Busch and Palmås discuss the need to avoid the 'cybernetic hypothesis', referencing a text from Tiqqun, a French collective of authors and activists, founded in 1999. Here, in contrast to a (natural) liberal hypothesis, based on the idea of the animal spirits of self-interested individuals—for example, as rooted in Freud's writings on the content of the unconscious, discussed in Chapter 3—the cybernetic hypothesis sees human behaviour as subject to re-programming.[62] This is no more than the perceived need to exercise increasing levels of control over identity. It revisits a key issue from Chapter 7: a continuation of neoliberal economic idealism invokes a need for increasing control over individual identity. The ideal neoliberal is simply contracted into an agency relationship of enterprise in a society dominated by a market-driven capitalist power-politic. In a process of othering, the neoliberal elite no longer requires workers, it requires an army of entrepreneurs, obviating any innate obligation to distribute the rewards of productive labour, since these are obligations on the Others themselves. Those Others are simply encouraged to creatively destruct what they may, in search of their own support.

Rather than a problematic to be avoided, arising from any attempt to envisage a design capitalism, I argue the cybernetic hypothesis is no hypothesis. Rather, the reality is that design thinking is already a political tool employed by the incumbents of the present neoliberal power-politic of public and private capitalist institutions. Educational curricula are constantly being fine-tuned to meet the cyber-critical, technological needs of individuals destined to be

[62] Tiqqun, The Cybernetic Hypothesis, 25.

contracted as the new *Others*.[63] The inculcation of a contemporary Veblen 'machine discipline', through education, is destined to drive economic efficiencies and profits, further cutting away the ground of law and order and the principles of conduct of civilised life. This runs counter to the idea of a pure, natural liberalism, where Freud and Maslow et al.'s *animal spirits* suggest scope for self-interest toward poietic actualisation of the human potential (self-actualisation). The need to avoid the 'cybernetic hypothesis' is not a problematic arising from the possibility of a design capitalism, it is a problematic of capitalism's manipulation of design.

In the second problematic, von Busch and Palmås address the issue of agency, and the danger of creating a new class of socially elite design professionals. Again, this is an issue, the roots of which might be traced to changing educational curricula. The ability to use design thinking to solve field problems in general, can be facilitated through inculcating design thinking and practice in the mainstream education of populations. This is not only an appreciation of the possible craft skills required, but an acceptance of a need to prioritise a creative application of these skills. Sadly, in this respect, in producing the ideal capitalist human—since everyone is expected to be an entrepreneur these days—educational curricula are driven more by the mechanics of automating the poietic process, than the appreciation of beauty required to give a natural poietic birth to appropriate ideas at appropriate times. This is, perhaps, the challenge of finding beauty in a VUCA world. Again, it is thus not the issue of applying design thinking to capitalism that gives rise to this problematic—it follows, naturally, from the very essence of the perceived need to educate a cyber-ready population for a utopian world.

In the third problematic, von Busch and Palmås raise their concern over the tripartite relationship between design, ideology and pragmatism. But I have already expressed the view that, non-conceptually, design capitalism is properly concerned with the field problem(s) of capitalism's sclerotic code. Design capitalism must operate on what is known of our present reality. Its application must accept that there can be no ideal future. Design thinking can only work in the present by anticipating uncertainty. In this sense, ideology has no real or practical use. Design capitalism should be design in relation to the realpolitik of social injustice and not the ideology of sociological theory, yet it may be informed by theory as a provisional truth.

---

[63] As widely reported in the UK press during late September 2020, the incumbent Conservative UK Government (as 'state') purportedly gave instructions, through its Department of Education (as 'institution') for schools in England not to use resources that illustrate or discuss an end capitalism. See for example: Busby, "Schools in England Told Not to Use Material from Anti Capitalist Groups."

Designing capitalism's respect for humanity goes beyond the mere inculcation of enterprise empathy at the level of a business or other related organizational unit, or the use of design thinking and systems thinking toolsets.[64] While such activity at a local level can be purposeful, respecting the individual in relation to the organizational unit, it must also address the purposive role of an enterprise in support of society. Here I suggest the purposive dimension of society's desire should be a respect for the collective and individual dignity of humanity. By dignity, I refer to humanity's inherent value and worth.[65] That value and worth is the individual human's unique capacity to love, to compose solutions to their own immortality, to give birth—to reproduce—in beauty in body and mind and thus to contribute to the immortality of humanity itself. Arguably, respect for an individual's dignity is no more than a redefinition of self-interest, for if we respect the individual right to compose (general) solutions to immortality, we step beyond the simplistic, constraining view of the accumulation of capital. One cannot buy immortality (happiness), one can only give birth to it. And that requires harmonious relationships with countless Others. I venture that society's purposive desire is simply beyond any (re)conceptualisation of economic (re)organization; it requires a non-conceptualisation.

Design's utopia

Writing in the International Journal of Design, Ipo Koskinen and Gordon Hush observe that the mainstream application of design for society is no doubt 'utopian'. Here, disparate groups of 'professional' designers, perhaps aligned with groups of the marginalised or disenfranchised, may seek to improve society with the application of advanced technology.[66] The utopian ideal might be seen as 'what people want'; but is it in any sense achievable, given the nature of a MacIntyrean, totalitarian project? Is it not the case that an ideal is, in and of itself, a totalitarian project? In which case, is it not therefore doomed to fail, on the very same facts about social life—its inherent and often absurd differences?

Barry Knight's five-year empirical study, researching the views of over 12,000 UK individuals, six focus groups, commissioned studies and Parliamentary discussions, offers some insight; yet can it reveal an objective future reality? His five principles for (the design of) a good society: 'a decent standard of living, a sense of security, freedom to be creative, respectful relationships and

---

[64] Waring, Price, and Waring, "Business Empathy."
[65] See, for example: Hicks, Leading with Dignity.
[66] Koskinen and Hush, "Utopian, Molecular and Sociological Social Design," 70.

a sustainable future for the next generation'[67] may, indeed, be considered utopian ideals. But Knight speaks of the 'demand side' of (political) governance that drives governments to build the societies the people want, where '[it] is evident that society needs a new narrative'.[68] Yet, as I argue, the lack of a cohesive narrative, together with dispersed identities, makes the coalescing of a single (utopian) concept of a new model of society mostly problematic. And while much will be achieved at a local level by interested groups and social entrepreneurship, large scale change will not occur unless we can again trust in the state.

What is more relevant in Knight's work is the idea that 'what matters is that people are sufficiently free to live the lives that they want', where the materialism of capitalism matters less than society.[69] As a design principle, this provides a different objective to the 'principle of capitalism', in which the self-interested individual seeks to maximise their income and capital. This suggests change will only come from civil society. But as I have argued, and as Knight also observed:

> '...[there] is no social movement that joins together efforts to improve the environment, reduce poverty, raise the status of women, guarantee human rights for oppressed groups such as migrants and refugees, and combat racism. Civil society lacks a coordinated strategy so that there is a cacophony of voices.'[70]

I have already noted that the intent is not to apply design to form an ideal type: a conceptual postcapitalism. A utopian ideal social and economic organization cannot be deduced for a future that is not knowable. Rather, as I set out in this Chapter, a non-concept of Design Capitalism is about (re)organizing society and its subsystems to facilitate individual poiesis, where people are sufficiently free to live the lives that they want, in which they can give birth to their own immortality. This is a form of social design in which a focus on social inclusivity and the preservation of society's environment adopts an ethical concern, where we can acknowledge that the design of interventions to society and its subsystems that encourage poiesis, will all have social implications.[71] A non-concept of Design Capitalism, as I envisage here, takes the idea of social design beyond design for the 'social' market—

---

[67] Knight, "Powering a Good Society," 570.
[68] Knight, "Powering a Good Society," 574.
[69] Knight, "Powering a Good Society," 576.
[70] Knight, "Powering a Good Society," 579.
[71] Ponte, Ellwanger, and Niemeyer, "Social Design and Ethics in Peirce's Philosophy."

that is, the design of products for sale that meet a certain social need within a market context.[72] Here the priorities for the commission of 'design' elements to the structures, methods and objectives of social and economic organization, lie in the perceived need to extend capitalism's purpose beyond the narrow purview of a 'capital' market of finance, to the need for poietic responses that embrace the 'capitals' of knowledge, social and human capacity in the individual pursuit of beauty.

Molecular design

Following Tim Brown and Roger Martin, I suggest that we might say: '[design intervention] is a multistep process—consisting of many small steps, not a few big ones. Along the entire journey interactions with the users of a complex artifact [such as the economy] are essential to weeding out bad designs and building confidence in the success of good ones.'[73] Thus, contrary to utopian images of a future for postcapitalism—a search for some grand unifying narrative—a great deal of what appear to be 'designed' solutions currently offered to social problems, can be argued to occur on a one-step-at-a-time approach—what Koskinen and Hush posit is a molecular level of social design. For example, the *socially conscious* enterprise initiatives of dispersed local voices of consent, illustrate (a reluctant) acceptance that society might need to be changed without some larger vision, or some grand narrative in place.[74]

Following Warwick Tie's Lancanian conceptualisation of *the subject supposed to design*—which I argue, here, is the socialist insider within capitalism—the knowledge required to design a 'social' society is not manifest within some unified truth of market, state, law, democracy, science or so on. Rather, Tie suggests, it rests on the "demand placed upon the one who occupies the field of knowledge to demonstrate, in an unreserved (though unattainable) manner, a capacity to be the subject who 'knows': ...to be 'the expert'."[75] In a molecular, step-wise design approach, it tends to the pragmatic that, as Tie suggests, rather than invest a designer with design expertise, the inside user—the social-thinking member of society's capitalist economic organization—as a user of elements of the capitalist economic organization, is left to (re)design, on an ongoing basis, the form and function of those elements in the course of their use. This is design in practice.

---

[72] Margolin and Margolin, "A 'Social Model' of Design: Issues of Practice and Research."
[73] Brown and Martin, "Design for Action," 10.
[74] Koskinen and Hush, "Utopian, Molecular and Sociological Social Design."
[75] Tie, "The Subject Supposed to Design," 17.

Much as the person promoted to manage is expected to manage the situation to which they are promoted, so the designer—at a molecular level—is expected to (re)design that which concerns them. This approach avoids the alternative of creating some form of a design elite, in response to an unachievable utopian design—one of the three problematics of a design capitalism. A molecular-level Design Capitalism leads to a requirement for education. This is to inculcate, within society, a capacity for developing (potential) insiders with capabilities that might empower them to see every situation as a design situation. However, the danger inherent under a simple molecular design approach is that the person supposed to design, inculcated to respond to system 'use conditions' as design opportunities, simply finds themself exercising their design capability to 'enhance their social autonomy'. This allows themselves—the insiders—to 'unplug, to some degree at least', from capitalism itself.[76] It is here that we find the disenfranchised, autonomous individual at the edge of neoliberal capitalism, in search of meaning, in a role as social designer of individual capitalist self-interest.

Sociological design

An alternative to a simple molecular view of design, is to consider Koskinen and Hush's conceptualisation of sociological social design. Here, sociological theorising may be taken beyond a local level of change, to consider the prototyping of policy. In this respect, sociological design adopts a definition of social that embraces society itself. This leads to design targets for social structures than might reduce social inequalities. It suggests a move from evidence-based policy to accept more experimental possibilities for policy development. Again, rather than some unreachable utopia, sociological social design can be 'molecular in its strategy' yet aim at changes in 'structures that pertain to persistent social problems'. A non-conceptual Design Capitalism, built on sociological social design, develops what is currently known of the socially real; it is different from ideological, utopian design.[77]

From a sociological perspective, the development, structure and function of a more human society needs to address the issue Diotima avoided. While all human beings may be pregnant in body and in mind, as we reach adulthood and desire to give birth, we have a choice: to do so, or not to do so. Once committed to do so, we cannot but give birth to a state that we can neither predetermine is beautiful nor ugly. Certainly, as individuals, we will have little or no control over what might be (harmoniously) beautiful. While we might strive, as mortal creatures, to achieve immortality, we cannot do so if what

---

[76] Tie, "The Subject Supposed to Design," 19.

[77] Koskinen and Hush, "Utopian, Molecular and Sociological Social Design," 70.

once appeared harmonious is now disharmonious.[78] Thus, as the writer's mortal thoughts mature in poiesis, bringing forth a composition, birthing an immortal prose, that prose might simply be disharmonious in birth. We therefore consider the humanity within a social system given free rein to poiesis—giving birth to (rational) ideas and actions that, while seeking to (pre)serve society's immortality, meet only disharmony in the face of autopoiesis. Here, for example, in the preservation of capital for others, society cannot face (rational) solutions to its own human problems.

My Platonic reading of a poietic society—in which, pregnant in mind, we strive to give birth to ideas and actions that promote society's immortality[79]—calls on a cultural appreciation of the beautiful at the moment of its birth into a future 'sublime' VUCA state. This is an aesthetic consideration. It calls for an aesthetic sensibility that goes beyond a simple 'algedonic' treatment of sensory perception—the pain or pleasure, the good or bad of the outcomes of our decisions.[80] Here, culture is the visible character of a system. It is the way this or that system works, in all its complexity, around here. In this respect, culture is shorthand for making sense of—and creating meaning out of—the operation of the system. As subtle as culture is symptomatic, a binary perceptive response is inadequate. Only aesthetics can provide the level of perception required to separate the beautiful from the sublime—the pleasure from the pain. Here, I suggest that the cultivation of a capability for abduction may serve as the connection between the aesthetics of our external (social) reality and the biology of our innate individuality.[81] It is here that I argue that an education for a sociological design capability should seek to reveal the sublime conditions of our social humanity.

Educating a dexterous society?

I have commented on the trend for fine-tuning educational curriculum in favour of producing the ideal neoliberal capitalist. This is not news. In her 2010 seminal work, *Not for Profit,* Martha Nussbaum wrote:

> 'Thirsty for national profit, nations, and their systems of education, are heedlessly discarding skills that are needed to keep democracies alive.

---

[78] Plato, The Symposium, 43.

[79] In this sense, the concept of immortality might be read as analogous to the notion of sustainability.

[80] Klein, "The Culturally Embedded Algedonics of Society: The Drivers and Controls of Integrating Culture."

[81] See, for example: von der Fehr, "Abduction as the Missing Link Between Aesthetics and Biology."

> If this trend continues, nations all over the world will soon be producing generations of useful machines.'[82]

The machine-like citizens of Nussbaum's autopoietic dystopia may readily—and soon—be replaced by actual machines. This may suit the elite capitalists so far-removed from the toil of 'dirty production' that such replacement is of no material consequence. That is, until the next crisis has the capitalists themselves call for greater care, dextrousness, creativity and ingenuity.

In a VUCA environment, society and its people must respond with less repetitiveness, less predictability, and less regularity.[83] Poietic responses need creativity, experimentation, problem-solving capabilities and ingenuity. As Peter Murphy posits '[machines] are not ironic, ambiguous, incongruous, contradictory, or paradoxical...but human beings are.'[84] The ironic, ambiguous, incongruous, contradictory and paradoxical nature of the human being is the great strength of humanity at large—a strength largely eroded in a drift toward Nussbaum's autopoietic dystopia. My question at the head of this Chapter was: can we envisage a future where—as a society learning from the lessons of our past—we change the basis of our economic organization, from the failed model of neoliberal capitalism to a new model of social capitalism? Ultimately, as incumbents of failed or failing systems, I argue that we have a choice. Subject to homeostasis and the disenfranchisement of many of our systems' insiders, we may choose to exercise our power-politic and invest a great deal more resource into protecting our systems from those insiders—more so than we would in protecting against any external opposition.[85] Or we may challenge those insiders to become part of the solution, leveraging their innate humanistic capability and capacity for poietic action.

The cost of any form of proactive education of the ideal autopoietic capitalist, must account for the fact that such education is always contingent on the future reality that it will be subject to, and yet cannot prejudge: its VUCA environment. In acknowledging the present field problem(s) of our systems, we have the option to choose to (re)design them to alleviate sources of conflict and seek to (re)enfranchise those insiders who would act in either opposition or in subversive counter-production. As Raquel Ponte, Daniele

---

[82] Nussbaum, Not for Profit: Why Democracy Needs the Humanities, 2.
[83] Murphy, "Design Capitalism: Design, Economics and Innovation in the Auto-Industrial Age."
[84] Murphy, "Design Capitalism: Design, Economics and Innovation in the Auto-Industrial Age," 145.
[85] See, for example: Hua and Bapna, "Who Can We Trust? The Economic Impact of Insider Threats."

Ellwanger and Lucy Niemeyer argue, drawing on the philosophy of pragmatism of Charles Peirce (1839-1914), in retrospect:

> '...the emergence of social design can be seen only as the realization of the ethical necessity after the recognition of the negative impact that design provokes when done unconsciously... As human beings endowed with rational thought, we have the ability to control our behavior and therefore it is pointless to remain in ignorance of the consequences of our actions, which are nothing more than expressions of our thinking.'[86]

If we are to avoid the drift to Nussbaum's autopoietic dystopia—that is, if we are to avoid a society capable only of producing 'generations of useful machines', a generation of citizens who lack the ability to 'think for themselves, criticize tradition, [or] understand the significance of another person's sufferings and achievement'[87], then we need to widen the relevance of the sociological social design. We need to inculcate ways of knowing that legitimise education for design within a framework of liberal learning.[88] Such an education should seek to reveal the sublime conditions of our social humanity. It should lead us to exercise a judgemental mode of beauty that questions our purposiveness in relation to the sublimity of a VUCA world, encouraging the separation of the beautiful from the sublime. This implies that, to better prepare humanistic responses to a VUCA environment, societies and their people will require different skills. Perhaps a new language and a typology of meaningful, enterprising work may be necessary to encourage poietic responses that pitch creativity, experimentation, problem-solving capabilities and ingenuity, against an antagonistic reality that promises less repetitiveness, less predictability, and less regularity. Such progress in education is, I suggest, a fundamental question of how we open our minds, individually, to the adaptive flexibility that exists within us all—a poietic capacity to compose our own conscious emergence into that VUCA world.

---

[86] Ponte, Ellwanger, and Niemeyer, "Social Design and Ethics in Peirce's Philosophy," 240.
[87] Nussbaum, Not for Profit: Why Democracy Needs the Humanities, 2.
[88] Szentpéteri, "Changing the Rhythm of Design Capitalism and the Total Aestheticization of the World," 94.

Chapter 9

Emergence and the non-hero

OPENING OUR MINDS, INDIVIDUALLY, requires the broadening of our education. Inculcating ways of knowing that legitimise education for design, challenges the current institutionalised forms of education. Here, as I have argued, the present focus is on a narrowing of education to the benefit of a capitalist doctrine of 'preparation for work'. This is the production of a society of heroic, enterprising 'worker' bees. In the capitalist, autopoietic system of honey production, we might parallel the distinction between the independent 'scout' bees—foraging for food—and the 'recruits', directed by their hive partners. Thus: 'a scout explores, whereas recruits never decide by themselves, but are guided by the scout's information.'[1] We therefore have the entrepreneurs exploring creative destruction in the name of opportunity; the neoliberal worker is simply recruited to fulfil their promise to capitalism. But this distinction—between the 'us' that are the recruits to entrepreneurial employment and the heroic 'others' as entrepreneurs—is problematic under anything other than a utopian autopoietic activity. Even in the bee colony, such a binary distinction is untenable. This suggests the requirement for a modified concept of the enterprising work of the honeybee that 'describes both the different behavioural states of a forager and the transitions that may occur from one state to another.'[2] I therefore return specifically to (re)question

[1] Biesmeijer and De Vries, "Exploration and Exploitation of Food Sources by Social Insect Colonies: A Revision of the Scout-Recruit Concept," 88.

[2] Biesmeijer and De Vries, "Exploration and Exploitation of Food Sources by Social Insect Colonies: A Revision of the Scout-Recruit Concept," 90.

the (non)concept of entrepreneurship, in which the entirety of this inquiry is inextricably bound.

In a metaphoric reflection of our social reality, '[not] every scout discovers a food source new to the colony and not every recruit locates the food source indicated.'[3] Not every entrepreneur succeeds in founding new opportunities, and not every (potential) employee is able to take up the employment they might be directed to, by their society. While Jacobus Biesmeijer and Han De Vries explore the diversity of worker bees through the broader notion of scouts, recruits, the employed and unemployed foragers, the experienced and novice foragers, and the inspectors and reactivated foragers, I further reflect on the limitations of our capitalist society's present enamoured focus on entrepreneurs and non-entrepreneurs in the world of work. The general reality of our socio-economic enterprising activity is that a simple taxonomy of entrepreneurial activity is as untenable as thinking that honey production simply requires a queen and an army of scouts and recruits. Following Ashby's law of requisite variety[4], if our education system is geared solely to the production of scouts and recruits, we ignore the requisite variety of social life required to attend to society's sustainable growth.[5] We must do more than suggest a taxonomic classification of those with entrepreneurial characteristics. In this Chapter, I ask what might a new typology of enterprising work look like?

De-othering the entrepreneur

A new typology of enterprising work should be one which allows for a richer response to the design of an emergent, postcapitalist (educational) solution for sustainable social and economic activity. In essence, I speak to the idea of de-othering the entrepreneur. In this respect, my challenge is to (re)situate entrepreneurs, entrepreneuring and entrepreneurship in the context of a

---

[3] Biesmeijer and De Vries, "Exploration and Exploitation of Food Sources by Social Insect Colonies: A Revision of the Scout-Recruit Concept."

[4] Requisite variety is a term introduced to systems theory by W. Ross Ashby. Ashby considered complex systems as containing 'much heterogeneity' in its parts, with a great richness in connections and interactions. Requisite variety assumes the difference arising from heterogeneity is measurable. Here we can see the idea that systems thinking that relies on some rationalised concept of human homogeneity—such as might arise through technological rationality, or instrumental reasoning concerning the human components of systems—is homeostatic. See, for example: Ashby and Goldstein, "Requisite Variety and the Difference That Makes a Difference: An Introduction to W. Ross Ashby's " Variety, Constraint and Law of Requisite Variety " Cybernetics, Regulation, and Complex Systems."

[5] See, for example: Palumbo and Manna, "The Need for Requisite Variety to Support Growth: An Organizational Life Cycle Perspective."

more general and inclusive social practice of enterprise. Here, my objective is to explore the non-concept of an emergent entrepreneurial identity in the wider context of the social practice of (economic) work.[6] From a critical perspective, a hegemonic conceptual reification of the naïve dialectic of a Western 'hero' entrepreneur, in the interests of global prosperity, stands accused of a reductionist and inferior 'othering' of the rest.[7] But, I question: are these hero(in)es the esteemed artists of a dialectic entrepreneurship, considered as much an art as a science?[8] With the artistic element difficult to inculcate in others?[9] Despite previous calls to de-link entrepreneurship from capitalism—in an attempt to demystify its heroes[10]—there persists an idea that entrepreneurs are unique, and that their special abilities are a source of value, responsible for redeeming crises of identity and economy.[11] Yet the erroneous assumption of stable identities[12] sets conditions for liminality,[13] and entrepreneurship's equivocal empirical success.[14] It also raises questions about the efficacy of institutional strategies that 'push' entrepreneurship.[15]

Previously (in Chapter 3), I noted the Gartner-marked organizational turn in the study of entrepreneurship.[16] Following this, the locus of my inquiries has been a dynamic capitalism and a functional, process-centred entrepreneurship that creatively and successfully destroys existing markets.[17] In this organizational turn, entrepreneurial small businesses are held to be among the most dynamic

---

[6] Billett, "Work as Social Practice: Activities and Interdependencies."

[7] Muñoz and Kimmitt, "Entrepreneurship and the Rest: The Missing Debate."

[8] Berglund, "Researching Entrepreneurship as Lived Experience."

[9] Anderson and Jack, "Teaching the Entrepreneurial Art."

[10] See, for example: Williams and Nadin, "Beyond the Entrepreneur as a Heroic Figurehead of Capitalism: Re-Representing the Lived Practices of Entrepreneurs."

[11] Johnsen and Sørensen, "Traversing the Fantasy of the Heroic Entrepreneur."

[12] Gartner, "'Who Is an Entrepreneur?' Is the Wrong Question."

[13] Muhr et al., "Constructing an Entrepreneurial Life: Liminality and Emotional Reflexivity in Identity Work"; Garcia-Lorenzo et al., "Liminal Entrepreneuring: The Creative Practices of Nascent Necessity Entrepreneurs."

[14] Lerner, "The Boulevard of Broken Dreams: Innovation Policy and Entrepreneurship"; Lucas et al., "Visions of Entrepreneurship Policy"; Wiklund and Shepherd, "Entrepreneurial Orientation and Small Business Performance: A Configurational Approach."

[15] See, for example: Wegner et al., "University Entrepreneurial Push Strategy and Students' Entrepreneurial Intention."

[16] Gartner, "'Who Is an Entrepreneur?' Is the Wrong Question"; Landström, Harirchi, and Åström, "Entrepreneurship: Exploring the Knowledge Base."

[17] Kirchhoff, Entrepreneurship and Dynamic Capitalism; Greene and Brown, "Resource Needs and the Dynamic Capitalism Typology"; Kirchhoff, Linton, and Walsh, "Neo-Marshellian Equilibrium versus Schumpeterian Creative Destruction: Its Impact on Business Research and Economic Policy."

firms in emerging economies,[18] driving growth and innovation.[19] Indeed, they are held to be important to most economies,[20] contributing to employment and turnover,[21] even stalling unemployment in the European Economic Area.[22] Yet, despite the turn to entrepreneurship study at the organizational and small business level,[23] Brian McKenzie and his colleagues have supported the idea that entrepreneurship is, *inter alia*, influenced by the intentions and capacity of particular individuals (or groups of individuals)—the entrepreneurs. Perhaps an absurdity, given their contrariness.

While, to some, entrepreneurs and their firms are indistinguishable,[24] others have attempted to classify them[25] and, in a critical voice, address their 'dark'[26] and 'light'[27] sides. However, I follow others in discussing the emergence and relevance of the unconventional (and even absurd) in entrepreneurship.[28] Thus, in the spirit of creative play,[29] I ask: is there scope for an alternative non-conceptual theory of entrepreneurship? One that offers coherence with the identity of the entrepreneur, yet resists their reification—their hero-worship? If so, what insights might be achievable; of what value might these insights be; and for whom?[30] To do so, I proceed with a knowledge-based

---

18 Storey, Understanding the Small Business Sector; Pissarides, "Is Lack of Funds the Main Obstacle to Growth? Ebrd's Experience with Small- and Medium-Sized Businesses in Central and Eastern Europe"; Wang, "What Are the Biggest Obstacles to Growth of SMEs in Developing Countries? – An Empirical Evidence from an Enterprise Survey."

19 Willis, Theories and Practices of Development; Battilana and Casciaro, "Change Agents, Networks, and Institutions: A Contingency Theory of Organizational Change. (Report)."

20 Wiklund and Shepherd, "Entrepreneurial Orientation and Small Business Performance: A Configurational Approach."

21 Bennett, "SME Policy Support in Britain since the 1990s: What Have We Learnt?"

22 Pichler, "In Quest of SME-Conducive Policy Formulation."

23 McKenzie, Ugbah, and Smothers, "'Who Is an Entrepreneur?' Is It Still the Wrong Question?"

24 Marchal, "The Construction of a New Theory of Profit."

25 Webster, "Entrepreneurs and Ventures: An Attempt at Classification and Clarification."

26 Jones and Spicer, Unmasking the Entrepreneur; Casson and Pavelin, "The Social Performance and Responsibilities of Entrepreneurship."

27 Calas, Smircich, and Bourne, "Extending the Boundaries 'Entrepreneurship as Social Change.'"

28 See, for example: Hjorth, "Absolutely Fabulous! Fabulation and Organisation-Creation in Processes of Becoming-Entrepreneur"; Guercini and Cova, "Unconventional Entrepreneurship."

29 Sarasvathy, "The Questions We Ask and the Questions We Care about: Reformulating Some Problems in Entrepreneurship Research."

30 Welter et al., "Everyday Entrepreneurship—A Call for Entrepreneurship Research to Embrace Entrepreneurial Diversity."

focus.[31] Firstly, I briefly address the fragmented, tautologous nature of *entrepreneurship* and the *entrepreneur*, before reviewing their triadic partner *entrepreneuring* as a socially embodied, systemic practice of entrepreneurial work. This allows me to draw on ideas of entrepreneurial emplacement, highlighting both an aesthetic cause-effect, and the structure of enterprising space. From a critical perspective, I then introduce a heterodox (re)location of the entrepreneur. In a negative dialectic approach to entrepreneurship study,[32] I employ the conjunctive theory of artistic (work) practice from my earlier work: *Thinking the Art of Management.*[33] This offers a (non)conceptual mapping of artistic space, allowing me to (re)locate the entrepreneur as the emergent artistic agent of a dimensional, social practice of work: an emergent and inclusive model of enterprise.

Entrepreneurship and the entrepreneur

It has been said that there is a lack of agreement on many key issues regarding what constitutes entrepreneurship.[34] Typically, entrepreneurship is defined as the process of innovation and production of new products and services, through the support of four dimensions or elements: individual, organization, external factors, and management process.[35] However, anecdotally, in the world of business, entrepreneurship is simply referred to as the work of running one's own business. But the situation is complicated by studies such as extra-preneurship[36] and eco-preneurship.[37] And in the UK at least, entrepreneurship's broad nature is recognised by the Quality Assurance Agency for Higher Education, with definitions of social-, green-, digital- and intra-preneurship.[38] As Campbell Jones and Andre Spicer suggested, entrepreneurship can be almost anything.[39] Nevertheless, entrepreneurship may be deemed to comprise two distinctly different categories of activity: the skills required to start and run an enterprise, and what might, generally, be

---

[31] Landström, Harirchi, and Åström, "Entrepreneurship: Exploring the Knowledge Base."
[32] Jones and Spicer, Unmasking the Entrepreneur.
[33] Atkinson, Thinking the Art of Management: Stepping into "Heidegger's Shoes."
[34] Rauch et al., "Entrepreneurial Orientation and Business Performance: An Assessment of Past Research and Suggestions for the Future."
[35] Kuratko and Hodgetts, Entrepreneurship: Theory, Process, Practice; Chowdhury, Alam, and Arif., "Success Factors of Entrepreneurs of Small and Medium Sized Enterprises: Evidence from Bangladesh."
[36] Snyder, "Extra-Preneurship: Reinventing Enterprise for the Information Age."
[37] Schaper, "The Essence of Ecopreneurship."
[38] QAA, Enterprise and Entrepreneurship Education: Guidance for UK Higher Education Providers.
[39] Jones and Spicer, Unmasking the Entrepreneur.

described as entrepreneurial attitudes:[40] skills and attitudes generally attributed to the class: 'entrepreneurs'.

In studying entrepreneurship, I suggest that we assign entrepreneurs to an outgroup: 'them', different from 'us'; we cannot avoid representing 'them' as the 'other'.[41] Thus, our 'othering' of entrepreneurs tends to any number of characterizations, each labelled apart from non-entrepreneurs. Here, our social science narratives are 'long on texts that inscribe some Others, preserve other Others from scrutiny, and seek to hide the researcher/writer under a veil of neutrality or objectivity'.[42] Thus, as I might write 'for' the class(es) of entrepreneurs—the 'scouts'—I risk the construction, legitimisation and distancing of 'others' and allocating them to some cultural margin of organizational work—the 'recruits'. There, I may even hail academic dropouts as hero entrepreneurs,[43] setting 'them' apart as an 'other' to which we may aspire.[44] Thus, as others observe, with social desirability bias difficult to exclude, the location of the entrepreneurial identity requires careful thought.[45]

Let me make the reasonable assumption that what marks the entrepreneur is: 1) a certain attitude, including to risk and uncertainty; 2) an approach, involving creativity and innovation; and 3) the practice of entrepreneurially focussed skills. Let me also adopt the widely held assumption that entrepreneurship is a social good, stimulating and generating economic value and creating jobs. Then, to create new demand, or to find new ways of exploiting existing markets, or to create new markets, I may surmise that an entrepreneur's attitude, (creative) capabilities and skills are necessary. But, with entrepreneurship being almost anything, practised anywhere, by any number of 'others', how might I begin to conceptualise an alternative theory of it—one that respects its contradictions, and is coherent with the identity of its entrepreneurs, yet resists their reification? Concurrently, in appealing to Alf Rehn and colleagues' call to challenge the myths that build around certain 'others',[46] how do I avoid the risk of the entrepreneurship concept becoming vacuous to the point that it is merely 'shorthand' for any positive change in

---

[40] Pyysiäinen et al., "Developing the Entrepreneurial Skills of Farmers: Some Myths Explored."

[41] Fitzsimmons, "Us, Them, and Others in Management Research."

[42] Fine, "Working the Hyphens: Reinventing Self and Other in Qualitative Research," 73–74.

[43] Watt, "The Rise of the 'Dropout Entrepreneur': Dropping out, 'Self-Reliance' and the American Myth of Entrepreneurial Success."

[44] Peverelli and Song, "Chinese Entrepreneurship: A Social Capital Approach."

[45] Overall and Wise, "The Antecedents of Entrepreneurial Success: A Mixed Methods Approach"; Mooradian et al., "Perspiration and Inspiration: Grit and Innovativeness as Antecedents of Entrepreneurial Success."

[46] Rehn et al., "Challenging the Myths of Entrepreneurship?"

any field yet, at the same time, opening ourselves—as observers of entrepreneurship—to the usefulness that exists in a multiplicity of perspectives?[47]

Entrepreneuring: entrepreneurship as practice

The above discussion supports the argument that the essential understanding of what entrepreneurs do, is subject to the fragmentation of a multitude of theories and concepts of entrepreneurship.[48] Here, a surfeit of rich, yet unconnected component explanations tend to the tautologous.[49] For example, social entrepreneurship is perhaps *the* exemplar of a tautology, in which entrepreneurship is a social activity in its own right.[50] Here, commenting on the tautology of some entrepreneurial definitions, Sasi Misra and Sendil Kumar advance a framework for understanding entrepreneurial behaviour.[51] They suggest it is not an individual's dispositions that might mark them as an entrepreneur, but their behaviour and action. Thus, the question of entrepreneurial behaviour and action is one of a socially situated and influenced practice.[52] This reflects a general 'practice turn' in social science[53]—where 'entrepreneuring' is introduced as a practice, deemed a series of (social) activities within the entrepreneurial process, with activity being the unit of analysis.[54] Entrepreneuring as practice challenges the ontology of entrepreneurship and entrepreneurs.[55] Immediately, therefore, I

---

[47] Welter et al., "Everyday Entrepreneurship—A Call for Entrepreneurship Research to Embrace Entrepreneurial Diversity."

[48] Anderson and Ronteau, "Towards an Entrepreneurial Theory of Practice; Emerging Ideas for Emerging Economies."

[49] Anderson, Drakopoulou Dodd, and Jack, "Entrepreneurship as Connecting; Some Implications for Theorising and Practice."

[50] Hjorth and Holt, "It's Entrepreneurship, Not Enterprise: Ai Weiwei as Entrepreneur"; Santos, "A Positive Theory of Social Entrepreneurship"; Mckeever, Anderson, and Jack, "Entrepreneurship and Mutuality: Social Capital in Processes and Practices."

[51] Misra and Kumar, "Resourcefulness: A Proximal Conceptualisation of Entrepreneurial Behaviour."

[52] Mckeever, Anderson, and Jack, "Entrepreneurship and Mutuality: Social Capital in Processes and Practices."

[53] Gartner et al., "Entrepreneurship as Practice: Grounding Contemporary Practice Theory into Entrepreneurship Studies"; Thompson, Verduijn, and Gartner, "Entrepreneurship-as-Practice: Grounding Contemporary Theories of Practice into Entrepreneurship Studies."

[54] Shepherd, "Party On! A Call for Entrepreneurship Research That Is More Interactive, Activity Based, Cognitively Hot, Compassionate, and Prosocial."

[55] Thompson, Verduijn, and Gartner, "Entrepreneurship-as-Practice: Grounding Contemporary Theories of Practice into Entrepreneurship Studies."

reject a conceptual 'othering' of the entrepreneur on the grounds it is antithetical to social practice. I turn to a non-concept.

Despite social science's practice turn in the 1970s, within the field of entrepreneurship the study of 'entrepreneurial practice' as entrepreneuring is somewhat nascent.[56] While not referencing social practice theory, Saras Sarasvathy stressed the potential of considering specific aspects of entrepreneuring—for example, opportunity formulation or failure management—as part of the identification and classification of individuals as entrepreneurs. [57] Also, from Chris Steyaert, I note that the concept of entrepreneuring invokes a social construction of reality, as entrepreneurial actors negotiate meaning and discourse in the creation of an entrepreneurial venture—an open and temporal nexus of entrepreneurial action.[58] As social construction, entrepreneuring is not an individualistic phenomenon. A socially negotiated practice of entrepreneuring subversively challenges both methodological individualism and extant theories of entrepreneurship.

Critically, entrepreneuring as a social construct carries the potential for the emancipation of the 'others' of entrepreneurship. It gives political, social and economic credence to the essential non- (or even anti-) hero(in)es of an individualistic entrepreneurship.[59] Even if such emancipation may often find itself limited, or even suppressed.[60] With its socially constructive rootstock, the concept of entrepreneuring retains an essence of agency and a correlation with the idea of entrepreneurial identity construction, where entrepreneuring offers an opportunity for subversive activity against the dominant narratives of entrepreneurship and the entrepreneurs—either intentionally[61] or, debatably, unintentionally.[62] Yet it would be naïve to argue that entrepreneuring be defined according to an idealistic emancipatory objective.

For now, avoiding the subversive, emancipatory and anti-managerialist overtones of entrepreneuring as a conceptual means of reconciling the

---

[56] Champenois, Lefebvre, and Ronteau, "Entrepreneurship as Practice: Systematic Literature Review of a Nascent Field."
[57] Sarasvathy, "The Questions We Ask and the Questions We Care about: Reformulating Some Problems in Entrepreneurship Research."
[58] Steyaert, "'Entrepreneuring' as a Conceptual Attractor? A Review of Process Theories in 20 Years of Entrepreneurship Studies."
[59] Rindova, Barry, and Ketchen, "Entrepreneuring as Emancipation."
[60] Verduijn et al., "Emancipation and/or Oppression? Conceptualizing Dimensions of Criticality in Entrepreneurship Studies."
[61] Kauppinen and Daskalaki, "'Becoming Other': Entrepreneuring as Subversive Organising."
[62] Muhr et al., "Constructing an Entrepreneurial Life: Liminality and Emotional Reflexivity in Identity Work."

entrepreneur in entrepreneurship, I note William Gartner and his colleagues' call to ground contemporary practice theory into the practice of entrepreneurship. Here, the idea of entrepreneurship as a practice is not new.[63] Reflections of practice appear in the work of such luminaries as Schumpeter and Drucker.[64] But, where should this call to ground contemporary practice theory in entrepreneurship take me? Is it a case of releasing, reconciling and realising the value locked in existing theories? Do I search for a gap in the literature, the closure of which will synthesise a new level of understanding of thinking, acting and knowing what constitutes the activity of (entrepreneurial) work.[65] Or does it provide the potential to search for new moons, from which I might cast my gaze backward, to identify new perspectives? To follow Stephen Billett, I question what insight will illuminate what types of practice, agnostic of the cultural needs of future work?

Entrepreneuring: systemic entrepreneurial action

A social construction of entrepreneurship offers no easy way to connect (extant) explanatory theories. Rather, one might consider 'the entirety of the entrepreneurial effort as a complex adaptive system'.[66] But, even here, the liminality of entrepreneuring[67] risks the systemic othering of entrepreneurs. That an actor is either engaged in entrepreneuring or is not, highlights the inadequacy of extant (simple) typologies in realising the range of actors necessary to give credence to the idea of a complex adaptive system.[68] As an example, Christina Lüthy and Chris Steyaert see entrepreneuring as an experimental system, where the different actors—as system components of an emergent, entrepreneurial becoming—appear limited to the entrepreneurs and the non-entrepreneurs: the employees, experts, investors and partners.[69] This offers little insight into the fluid and adaptive nature of the system's human components as they respond to Billett's thinking, acting and knowing

---

63 Gartner et al., "Entrepreneurship as Practice: Grounding Contemporary Practice Theory into Entrepreneurship Studies."

64 Johannisson, "Disclosing Everyday Practices Constituting Social Entrepreneuring–a Case of Necessity Effectuation."

65 Billett, "Work as Social Practice: Activities and Interdependencies."

66 Anderson, Drakopoulou Dodd, and Jack, "Entrepreneurship as Connecting; Some Implications for Theorising and Practice," 966.

67 Garcia-Lorenzo et al., "Liminal Entrepreneuring: The Creative Practices of Nascent Necessity Entrepreneurs."

68 Buckley, Schwandt, and Goldstein, "Classic Paper Section: Society as a Complex Adaptive System (1968)."

69 Lüthy and Steyaert, "The Onto-Politics of Entrepreneurial Experimentation: Re-Reading Hans-Jörg Rheinberger's Understanding of 'Experimental Systems.'"

of (entrepreneurial) work.[70] Thus, entrepreneuring, as a systemic practice of reified (heroic) entrepreneurial elements is simply removed to the margins of social and cultural (working) life in the service of *pleonexia,* re-appropriating a vice as virtue.[71] Such a system, closed to the potential for the components themselves to change—as I have previously argued—tends to the homeostatic.[72]

The potential of entrepreneurship as a complex adaptive system is lost in homeostasis, as the study of a reified social practice attempts to steady the internal, physical, and environmental conditions in search of optimal entrepreneurial functioning. Here I might, for example, suggest the emergence of entrepreneurial eco-systems[73] as homeostatic exemplars. I argue we can only maintain Walter Buckley's notion that the interchanges among a complex adaptive system's components may result in '*significant changes in the nature of the components themselves*—with important consequences for the system as a whole'[74]—if our understanding of entrepreneurship acknowledges the fluidity of the concept (the plasticity of the entrepreneurial environment) and the malleability of its actors (the variety pool for adaptive variability).

Following Buckley, entrepreneurship as both complex adaptive system and continuing entity (entrepreneuring) is not to be confused with the structure of entrepreneurship (including its entrepreneurs) that might be represented by that system from time to time. Again, I need only consider the example that systemic entrepreneuring (complex adaptive, homeostatic or, indeed, closed) exists, itself, as one component in another complex adaptive system—the economy.[75] I argue, therefore, that entrepreneuring is subject to (the risk of) change occurring in its environment, often in unidentified external components. Such change may have important consequences for its practice at any time, compounding the problematic of internal component reification. The essential plasticity of the entrepreneurial environment, including its own component role, and the malleability of its actors (as components in their own right) suggests the necessary elements of sense and anticipation in entrepreneuring's actions. Recalling Chapters 3 and 4, entrepreneuring emerges from an environment of praxis; what remains (its negative dialectic) is what defines it: entrepreneuring's essence lies in its Other, its non-concept.

---

[70] Billett, "Coparticipation at Work: Knowing and Work Practice."
[71] MacIntyre, After Virtue.
[72] Buckley, Schwandt, and Goldstein, "Classic Paper Section: Society as a Complex Adaptive System (1968)."
[73] Roundy, Bradshaw, and Brockman, "The Emergence of Entrepreneurial Ecosystems: A Complex Adaptive Systems Approach"; Han et al., "Toward a Complex Adaptive System: The Case of the Zhongguancun Entrepreneurship Ecosystem."
[74] Buckley, "Society as a Complex Adaptive System," 490.
[75] Witt, "Capitalism as a Complex Adaptive System and Its Growth."

Emplacing: the practicing of entrepreneuring

Alongside the 'practising' of practice,[76] in accounting for sense and anticipation, Elena Antonacopoulou and Ted Fuller offer the social concept of emplacement—the cyclic rehearsal, review, refinement and change inherent in the concept of entrepreneuring.[77] At a basic level, I find that much of what relates to the reflexive concept of 'practising'—certainly in the sense of the organizational practice of entrepreneuring—can be found in other models. Deming's PDCA or Boyd's OODA loops, used in systems thinking applications,[78] to an extent, offer a reflection of the fluidity of practice and embrace adaptive learning. However, on a more complex level, the conceptualisation of practice raises the questions: 'who are the practitioners, [and] why [do] they perform the practice the ways they do in relation to where and when the practice is performed'?[79] Here, actors are 'emplaced' in the entrepreneurial space: its non-concept.

With reference to Figure 9.1, entrepreneurial actors practise entrepreneuring in terms of a context (including access to resources, investment, and social capital), an environment of entrepreneurship, and processes that include innovation and the support of others who may not be entrepreneurs. In this context, there is attention to: 'sensation' (the capacity to see or imagine a situation simultaneously, within, above and beyond the perspective of action); and 'anticipation' (the disposition to act on a future imagined state).[80] While the conceptualisation as emplacement suggests a privileging of place, I suggest that it does at least provide the basis for understanding entrepreneuring as the essential character of entrepreneurship, situated in a context defined by its non-concept.

---

[76] Antonacopoulou, "On the Practise of Practice: In-Tensions and Ex-Tensions in the Ongoing Reconfiguration of Practice Evolution of Business Knowledge View Project."
[77] Elena P. Antonacopoulou and Ted Fuller, 'Practising Entrepreneuring as Emplacement: The Impact of Sensation and Anticipation in Entrepreneurial Action', Entrepreneurship and Regional Development, 32.3–4 (2020), 257–80.
[78] Monat and Gannon, "Applying Systems Thinking to Engineering and Design."
[79] Antonacopoulou, "On the Practise of Practice: In-Tensions and Ex-Tensions in the Ongoing Reconfiguration of Practice Evolution of Business Knowledge View Project," 126.
[80] Antonacopoulou and Fuller, "Practising Entrepreneuring as Emplacement: The Impact of Sensation and Anticipation in Entrepreneurial Action."

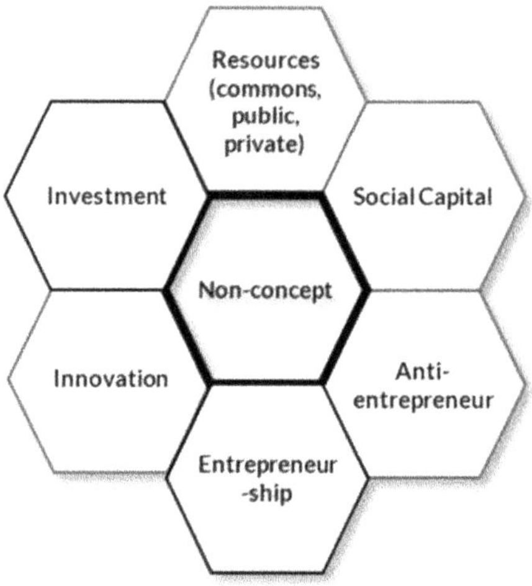

Figure 9.1. Non-concept of the entrepreneur (from Chapter 4)

In the context of the human elements of systems, I argue that 'sensation' and 'anticipation' are aesthetic dimensions. They provide the essential non-systemic, adaptive (and poietic) character of the autonomous actors, as they engage in the social practice of entrepreneuring. As aesthetic cause and effect, the value of sensation and anticipation stems from an evaluative process by which the entrepreneurial actor imagines or anticipates the potential implications of a future state—according to their sense of present conditions.[81] I argue, therefore, that aesthetics gives voice to the affective place of entrepreneurship's origin on the imaginary plane—with affections being the 'actions' and 'passions'; the former a power to act; the latter a power upon which to act.[82] Thus, while in no sense privileging place (or context), the affectiveness of emplacement within a non-conceptual locus of entrepreneuring, acknowledges the role power plays in the practice of aesthetic cause and effect; it embodies notions of risk and failure, where passions may over-rule senses and actions do not always realise expected results.

Critically, reflexivity concerning a turn to (social) practice[83] may remind us that, despite an attention to entrepreneuring, we may make little headway in

---

[81] Xenakis and Arnellos, "Aesthetics as an Emotional Activity That Facilitates Sense-Making: Towards an Enactive Approach to Aesthetic Experience."
[82] Hjorth, "Absolutely Fabulous! Fabulation and Organisation-Creation in Processes of Becoming-Entrepreneur."
[83] Sklaveniti and Steyaert, "Reflecting with Pierre Bourdieu: Towards a Reflexive Outlook for Practice-Based Studies of Entrepreneurship."

evolving an understanding of entrepreneurship and its entrepreneurs—and their constantly adapting relations with context, environment and process—if we are not able to understand the elements, both human and non-human, from which it emerges: its non-concept. While concepts such as complex adaptive systems, sensations and the anticipation of emplacement offer new insights, we should refrain from merely projecting Bourdieu's 'blindness'[84]—offering nothing of a reflexive focus on practical intelligibility.[85] As Elena Antonacopoulou and Ted Fuller write, in the act of practice,

> '...entrepreneuring would signal reflexivity not only in reviewing one's personal identity as an entrepreneur, but also discovering what makes a difference in the social context, as social actors express through their actions who they are and what matters to them'.[86]

The recognition of othering—a reflexive posture to entrepreneurial practice—would, by definition, be inclusive of 'other' actors. This provides a necessary insight into unexplored themes.[87] Thus, alongside a Levinasian responsibility for others (Chapter 2), in which the character of an individual engaged in entrepreneurial practice is only revealed through their engagement with others in that practice, there can be an acceptance of ideas such as liminal entrepreneuring. This acknowledges the integral complexity of reflexivity within the inherent complexity of adaptive social systems. Thus, I question the idea that there *are* entrepreneurs and non-entrepreneurs. Entrepreneurs *are* an emergent (socially constructed) phenomenon—a product of the observer's approach and an object of their social condition of possibility.[88] What is required here is to reveal the structures of the space of enterprising

---

[84] In discussing the concept of reflexivity, French sociologist Pierre Bourdieu (1930-2002) suggested that it was not a form of 'art for art's sake' or, more colloquially, navel-gazing. The purpose of reflexivity is not simply to contemplate what is one's 'backyard' but to use a knowledge of what is in that 'backyard' to examine 'what lies behind its fence.' To Bourdieu, as long as he did not know what went on in his own backyard, he argued he could not see 'anything'. To look without knowing is analogous to projecting one's blindness. See, for example: Sklaveniti and Steyaert. To an extent, the concept of reflexivity is also bound within Niklas Luhmann's explication of observation—explored in Chapter 11.

[85] Sklaveniti and Steyaert, "Reflecting with Pierre Bourdieu: Towards a Reflexive Outlook for Practice-Based Studies of Entrepreneurship."

[86] Antonacopoulou and Fuller, "Practising Entrepreneuring as Emplacement: The Impact of Sensation and Anticipation in Entrepreneurial Action," 266.

[87] Sklaveniti and Steyaert, "Reflecting with Pierre Bourdieu: Towards a Reflexive Outlook for Practice-Based Studies of Entrepreneurship."

[88] Bourdieu, "Participant Objectivation."

positions—a space within which the observer belongs, alongside the practitioners and non-practitioners of a fluid enterprising work. This suggests a requirement to understand one's position in relation to another, providing 'a point of view on one's own point of view and, thereby, on the whole set of points of view in relation to which it defines itself as such'.[89] It is a form of *social presence*, as I have defined in Chapter 2—the degree to which the individual is able to sense the perspective of an 'other', and thus be able to take a perspective on a reality that includes the 'self' and 'others' as participating objects.

A heterodox (re)location of the entrepreneur...

It has been suggested that the word 'entrepreneur' should be dropped in favour of a typology of small business owners.[90] Clearly, all small business owners are not the same. Robert Hornaday proposed a typology based on three owner types: Craft, Promoter, and Professional Manager. Bryan Stinchfield and his colleagues later offered a typology embracing entrepreneurship as inclusive of art, craft, engineering, bricolage and brokerage.[91] More recently, Blake Mathias and David Williams have drawn on role identity theory to offer a variation on typology, suggesting entrepreneurship is flexibly characterised through a series of entrepreneurial role identities—the *multiple hats of the practicing entrepreneur*.[92] This latter approach bears some semblance to the idea of entrepreneuring as the practice of a set of definable activities. However, while such approaches offer some sense of the divergent types of entrepreneurs encountered, they all tend to the othering of the entrepreneur, focusing the attention of entrepreneurship on certain classes of individuals that fit *la mode du jour*. Also, such approaches generally neglect differences in the risk-taking profiles that might exist between such classes. This neglect was made explicit by Hornaday, in which his denial of the 'E-word' resolved only to a consideration of small business activity.[93] As such, these typologies fail to provide any measure of entrepreneurship,[94] where entrepreneurship exists in

---

89 Bourdieu, "Participant Objectivation," 284.

90 Hornaday, "Dropping the E-Words from Small Business Research: An Alternative Typology."

91 Stinchfield, Nelson, and Wood, "Learning From Levi-Strauss' Legacy: Art, Craft, Engineering, Bricolage, and Brokerage in Entrepreneurship."

92 Mathias and Williams, "The Impact of Role Identities on Entrepreneurs' Evaluation and Selection of Opportunities"; Mathias and Williams, "Giving up the Hats? Entrepreneurs' Role Transitions and Venture Growth."

93 Hornaday, "Dropping the E-Words from Small Business Research: An Alternative Typology."

94 Henrekson and Sanandaji, "Small Business Activity Does Not Measure Entrepreneurship."

a diversity such that 'it is presumptuous to conceive of a simple, unifying approach'.[95]

Stan Metcalfe advised that a definition of entrepreneurship should focus on positive, novel conjectures.[96] Such conjectures may be found in an application of the Conjunctive Theory of Art (CTA), as I explicate, in significant detail, in *Thinking the Art of Management.*[97] Having exposed the aesthetic potential underpinning the entrepreneuring concept—to an extent, a confirmation of the artistic dimension of entrepreneurship—I argue that CTA provides an application of the artistic metaphor to the creative exercise of a craft skill; in this case the craft of enterprising work. Here, art emerges as a conjunction of three core elements, the exercise of the identified craft skill, with innovation, in experiencing a mimetic[98] realization of some aspect of the lived-in-world. An application of CTA to the concept of entrepreneuring amounts to an example of 'evocative theoretical boundary spanning', in the tradition of radical theorising.[99]

In briefly introducing CTA, I show, in Figure 9.2, the circle with the shaded portion as representative of the world and what is both *known* and *unknown* within it. The shaded *unknown* space is that space within which artist and audience engage in the process of mediating a (new) *sense of place*, coming to a (new) 'shared' sense of *being-in-this-world.* This shaded area is dissected by the imaginary plane, delineating an area in which access to knowledge of the unknown is through the imagination. The un-shaded area represents what is currently *known*—that which exists predominantly on the real plane. The separation between real and imaginary planes is the antagonistic horizon.

In considering an art of enterprising work, the Craft object 'C' is a 'convention' of work practice; a design 'D' is an adaptation or variation of such a practice convention.

---

95 Metcalfe, "The Entrepreneur and the Style of Modern Economics," 157.

96 Metcalfe, "The Entrepreneur and the Style of Modern Economics."

97 Atkinson, Thinking the Art of Management: Stepping into "Heidegger's Shoes."

98 I make a distinction between Plato's mirror-like mimesis and mimesis as an element of CTA. Ontologically, mimesis acts to make present unseen elements of the inventory of phenomena, things, concepts and ideas that describe the lived-in world. This richer view of mimesis is in the Aristotelian tradition; it provides for mimesis as a discovery and learning experience, including the idea of interpretation (see, for example, Mete, "Mimetic Tradition and the Critical Theory.").

99 Nadkarni et al., "New Ways of Seeing: Radical Theorizing."

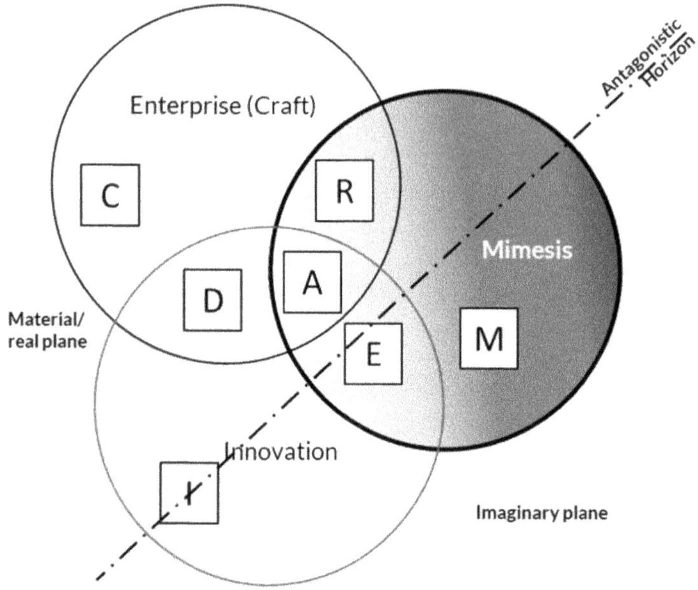

Figure 9.2. (Re) Locating the entrepreneur

The idea 'I' within an innovative activity is that which is purely new, emerging solely from the activity of creative play. The experiment 'E' is the application of an idea to the process of mimesis, revealing an aspect of the *unknown*. The mimetic experience 'M' is that which exists in the *unknown* with the potential for realisation of a *sensible affect* that triggers an aesthetic response (anticipation) within the audience. The representation 'R' is what is capable of being reproduced by virtue of the conventions of work's practice.

The space represented by the union of C, M and I is analogous to the space in which the practice of enterprising work is emplaced. Here, my goal is to identify the structures of that space, providing the positions within which the researcher sits alongside both practitioners and non-practitioners of a fluid enterprising work. In adopting CTA as a framework for exploring the emergence of (artistic) practice of the craft of enterprising work, I allow that some forms of the *practice* may tend to *entrepreneuring*—as the *Art of enterprise* 'A'—while other forms of practice may co-emerge without in any sense being marginalised. I suggest that the CTA perspective offers the possibility of de-othering the entrepreneur in the context of their work—a negative dialectic of the entrepreneur, in which the entrepreneur can only emerge from its non-concept. This allows a greater, more inclusive range of actors to emerge. I now, therefore, consider how the CTA framework reveals a new and inclusive typology of enterprising actors.

Individual as Craftsperson (C)

The term 'craft' commonly refers to an activity involving skill in making things by hand. It also refers to '…ambiguous conglomerations of organizational and stylistic traits and cannot be used as unequivocally…'.[100] But, in this post-industrial, post-technical, post-digital era, as a retrospective consideration of Marxist, Veblenian thought,[101] I re-align the concept of craft with that which is quintessential about real human activity—that is: the activity of humans engaged in an(y) enterprise; that is: real work.[102] I do not define the thing being made by hand or otherwise handled, nor do I define the specific skill(s) or level of skill(s) that constitute the craft. I merely conceptualise craft as the root of some complete aspect of work. Conceptually, when I refer to the activity of real work, I relate to a defined set of craft skills associated with that work. For example, I may discuss, conceptually, the craft of management or the craft of leadership alongside the many crafts of human enterprise. For example, a surgeon's craft skills in surgery, or an architect's in building or an engineer's in machine production. Conceptually, I may therefore identify any individual as a craftsperson to some extent or another.

The framing of 'craft' as a high-level concept does not subvert other uses of the term. On one hand, it identifies hobbyists and artisans.[103] On the other hand, it also identifies specific craft industries.[104] The question arises: is a broad concept of craft valid in the light of a post-modern, capitalist critique that suggests real work as the basis of labour has become increasingly degraded and deskilled?[105] Insofar as craft is a core of work activity exhibiting a dimension of skill, I argue it is related to a scale—typically from an absence to a mastery of that skill. Thus, one is not 'born' a craftsperson. One acquires real craft skills through learning. However, it is reasonable to suggest that some individuals may be more pre-disposed to learning certain skills associated with certain craft skillsets than others.

---

[100] Becker, "Arts and Crafts."

[101] Campbell, "The Craft Consumer: Culture, Craft and Consumption in a Postmodern Society."

[102] The notion of 'Real' work positions the idea of work on the plane of reality. Work, and the craft skills associated with work are not, in this sense, of the imagination. Though new skills (see Innovation) may by imagined and brought to the 'real', through design or artistry.

[103] Bouette and Magee, "Hobbyists, Artisans and Entrepreneurs."

[104] Reijonen and Komppula, "Perception of Success and Its Effect on Small Firm Performance."

[105] Chell, "Review of Skill and the Entrepreneurial Process."

Individual as Innovator (I)

Innovation is an act of introducing some new thing, either real or imaginary. It comprises both the creativity of generating novel ideas and the implementation (or innovation process) of turning those ideas into things or processes of value in the plane of reality.[106] In this respect, the individual as an *innovator* has the capacity to work innovatively—an ability to generate and implement creative ideas within a given domain.[107] While, as Birgitta Sandberg and her colleagues suggest, the terms *innovator* and *entrepreneurship* are generally interlinked, I posit a pure form of innovation. Following Everett Rogers[108] and others,[109] I argue that the *innovator* is a person who can create and/or try out a new idea before others do so—an ability to work with both the real and imaginary planes.

Here, creative individuals may possess other traits, such as a propensity for risk-taking, a high tolerance for ambiguity and openness to change, persistence, self-efficacy, curiosity and an interest in problem-solving.[110] But, while these traits suggest an ability to focus creative ability within a given domain, it remains creative ability that lies at the heart of an individual's innovativeness. Here, *creative ability*—an innate quest for originality[111]—is an ability to apply imaginative thinking or behaviour to an original purpose or objective that has value.[112] While most of the time it is applied to that which is wholly new (or imaginative), there may be occasions when it is applied to an original derivative of some existing *thing*.[113] Insofar as the application of imaginative thinking lies at the core of an innovative ability, I argue that it also exhibits a dimension of skill and ability in that application. *Innovation* therefore also relates to a scale—typically from an absence to a mastery of creative ability. Again, I suggest one is not 'born' an innovator. Skills in innovation are acquired through learning. However, it is reasonable to suggest

---

[106] See, for example: Sarooghi, Libaers, and Burkemper, "Examining the Relationship between Creativity and Innovation: A Meta-Analysis of Organizational, Cultural, and Environmental Factors."
[107] Sandberg, Hurmerinta, and Zettinig, "Highly Innovative and Extremely Entrepreneurial Individuals: What Are These Rare Birds Made Of?"
[108] Rogers, Diffusion of Innovations, 3rd Ed.
[109] Moore, Geoffrey and Mckenna, Crossing the Chasm.
[110] Sandberg, Hurmerinta, and Zettinig, "Highly Innovative and Extremely Entrepreneurial Individuals: What Are These Rare Birds Made Of?"
[111] Wilson, Origins of Creativity.
[112] The idea of value is intrinsic to a social concept of innovation, in which an innovative thing appeals to others. This implies an understanding of needs, and how needs can be satisfied in a way appreciated by others.
[113] Bujor and Avasilcai, "The Creative Entrepreneur: A Framework of Analysis."

that individuals may have a pre-disposition to both creative behaviour and to learning additional skills associated with the focused application of that behaviour towards innovation.

Risk and the innovator

The enterprising practice of a pure innovation—the implementation of creative ideas within a given domain of interest—is a practice of creativity toward the present reality. Here, I recognise that the creative individual's trait of risk-taking is related to innovation.[114] I also acknowledge a distinction between risky and uncertain (economic) outcomes,[115] in which those outcomes with *a priori* probabilities fall into the category of risk, and those without fall into the category of uncertainty.[116] Intuitively, I thus attach the concept of risk to the activity of the *Innovator*, in that the *Innovator's* creative endeavour may, or may not, realise a desired new *thing*, *concept* or *idea*. Since the domain is a known reality, the *a priori* probability of an unsuccessful outcome is more likely to be knowable, than if the domain were wholly imaginary or unknown. In Knightian terms, a pure innovation is most likely to resolve to a risky situation, in which the *Innovator* is guided by *known* chances; it avoids a Knightian *uncertainty*. However, the use of an individual's faculty for imagination suggests there will be an element of the unknown about any creative outcome. The corollary is that the more an innovation respects the *real* rather than the *imaginary*, the more innovators will be able to assess the risks associated with their activity.

Individual as Dreamer/Visionary (M)

As I have already noted, the concept of *mimesis* (M) represents making the *absent* present. It reveals something of the *unknown* and includes the notion of interpretation. In context, there is a visionary element to a sensory revealing of something of the *unknown* (including what might be real and *knowable*) about the world of enterprise. Here, vision sits alongside concepts such as intuition, insight, creativity, imagination, and optimism—exemplars of a non-linear thinking style.[117] This reading of mimesis requires imagination: an ability to first imagine the seemingly impossible, then to communicate its

---

[114] Massa and Testa, "Innovation and SMEs: Misaligned Perspectives and Goals among Entrepreneurs, Academics, and Policy Makers."
[115] Knight, Risk, Uncertainty and Profit; Knight, "Profit and Entrepreneurial Functions."
[116] J Runde, 'Clarifying Frank Knight's Discussion of the Meaning of Risk and Uncertainty', Cambridge Journal of Economics, 22.5 (1998), 539–46.
[117] Groves et al., "An Examination of the Nonlinear Thinking Style Profile Stereotype of Successful Entrepreneurs."

possibility as a step toward making that which is impossible, possible. Thus mimesis is always exercised on or toward the imaginary plane.

In the context of enterprise, mimesis invokes ideas of dreaming. Indeed, it has been said that innovation is the 'output of a dreamer'.[118] Here, Tony Watson discussed a causal model of business start-up activity, which begins with 'dreams' of an *end* (or goal).[119] The *means* to achieve an *end goal* are then sought by the individual. This *means-ends* activity is congruent with Per Davidsson's construct of a New Venture Idea—an imaginary mix of market, offer and the means of bringing the offer to market.[120] I therefore argue that the imagination and/or vision (or dreaming) lie at the core of a mimetic, visionary learning—a capacity for discovering and revealing what is presently *unknown*. This suggests the existence of a further scale, typically from an absence of visionary capacity (or a lack of ability to focus that capacity), to an inordinate ability to focus it. While the creative faculties of an infant at play suggest one might be born a *visionary*, an ability to 'focus' *vision* as a constructive force for innovative enterprise indicates a learning process. It is therefore reasonable to suggest that all individuals may have some pre-disposition to visionary and/or dream-like behaviour, and the potential to learn skills associated with focusing that behaviour, toward innovative practices.

Risk and the dreamer/visionary

Intuitively, there is a risk associated with any vision of the imagination. The vision itself may not be realisable, may not be communicable, nor may it be sustainable in any value-giving sense. As distinguishable from the 'created' risk associated with pure innovation, the fundamental (Knightian) uncertainty surrounding any imaginative vision means it is not possible to determine *a priori* probabilities of outcomes.[121] The negative, indeterminate risk is that any resource (such as time, money, effort, or labour) committed to visionary dreaming, may fail to realise a transfer of value to either the *self* or an *other*. Intuitively, then, the further into the unknown the visionary or dreamer exercises their imagination, the greater the Knightian uncertainty and the 'fundamental' risk associated with it. Here, an endless and unfocussed activity of, say, 'day-dreaming' is (potentially) a wasteful, meaning-less, value-less

---

118 Massa and Testa, "Innovation and SMEs: Misaligned Perspectives and Goals among Entrepreneurs, Academics, and Policy Makers."

119 Watson, "Entrepreneurship in Action: Bringing Together the Individual, Organizational and Institutional Dimensions of Entrepreneurial Action."

120 Davidsson, "Entrepreneurial Opportunities and the Entrepreneurship Nexus: A Re-Conceptualization."

121 Runde, "Clarifying Frank Knight's Discussion of the Meaning of Risk and Uncertainty."

(pre)occupation, to be frowned upon in the workplace.[122] An unfocussed, *naïve imagination* suggests a propensity for ignorance of the possibilities of discovering an *a priori* probability; daydreaming embraces the Knightian uncertainty of what remains unknowable. Conversely, focussing visionary capacity on specific areas of the presently unknown but knowable, may reduce the uncertainty of uncovering the unknowable. Focussed visionary capacity is more likely to be 'less' risky, and less wasteful. To channel an unclear vision into premature innovative activity puts innovation 'at (fundamental) risk'. In other words, innovation is not risk, but the imaginative, visionary practice of innovation cannot be disassociated from it.

Individual as Artist: the Entrepreneur (CIM)

While the foregoing discussion of the separate elements of CTA's practice is suggestive of the individual who can act in a pure craft, innovative or visionary capacity, it is when the three are practised (each to a varying degree) in conjunction with each other that, non-conceptually, an *artistic* process emerges, from mimetic vision to experimentation, into the plane of reality. Here, CTA posits that artistic practice is the conjunction of the three elements of craft, innovation and mimesis, in which the *art-form* is its outcome.[123] Therefore, in the context of enterprising work, entrepreneuring can be defined as: the conscious, conjunctive practice of the real craft activities of enterprise, with innovation, in an imaginative, mimetic reconciling of something of the unknown, that is a potential new 'real' position in the field (or world) of enterprise. This is an inclusive definition that embraces: 1) any real field of enterprise; 2) any real set (or sub-set) of craft skills associated with that field; and 3) a focused application of imagination and creativity in the development of innovations of value through a mimetic realisation of the currently unknown about that field. While the entrepreneuring is a *means*, its real *end* is the realisation of innovative objects (products or services) of value. There are, however, three further conjunctions of note. I shall consider these in the next sections.

Individual as Reproducer (CM)

Representation is CTA's conjunction between craft and mimesis. It presents nothing that isn't already known (or knowable or real). Representation is Platonic 'imitation'.[124] It presents no discernible difference between its 'end'

---

[122] This does not preclude the 'accidental' achievement of some value from a seemingly wasteful activity.
[123] Atkinson, Thinking the Art of Management: Stepping into "Heidegger's Shoes."
[124] Earle, "Plato, Aristotle, and the Imitation of Reason."

and that which it represents. In the context of enterprise, a mere representation is no more than the reproduction of something that has already been realised. The *Reproducer* simply exercises the real craft skills of enterprise in realising what is already in the world, on the plane of reality. This is not a flawed or in any sense inferior practice. Representation is simply an act of enterprise that 'replicates prevailing practices' what Jennifer Cliff and her colleagues have labelled 'imitative entrepreneurship'.[125] Without the imagination associated with innovation, there is little of the risk of exploring the unknown; it is a low-risk exploitation of a known opportunity of value. In developing markets, for example, local firms seeking livelihoods do so by searching for and replicating ideas from advanced markets.[126]

Absent of a necessity to do things differently, there is much to be said for 'sticking to the knitting', particularly if such activity is associated with an established business.[127] Stripped of innovation, *reproductive* enterprise is a functional *means* of acquiring and enjoying an *end* of 'value'. Even in advanced markets, the individual running a corner shop acquires a livelihood by reproducing a known trade in staple goods. However, at scale, the large representational enterprises of developed economies seemingly practise an almost-Marxist concept of pure capitalism, in which reproduction serves solely to convert surplus use-value into capital.[128]

Individual as Designer (CI)

Design is a process by which ideas are made manifest,[129] as solutions to problems. These are not the *knowledge problems* arising at the 'limits' of our knowledge of a present reality. They are the *field problems* of 'improving' the present reality.[130] The design of a thing, concept or idea, is the conjunction of a craft skill exercised with innovation.[131] It operates only on what is known within the present reality. A pure *design*, distinct from style as the carrier of

---

[125] Cliff, Jennings, and Greenwood, "New to the Game and Questioning the Rules: The Experiences and Beliefs of Founders Who Start Imitative versus Innovative Firms."
[126] Chen, Guo, and Zhu, "Can Me-Too Products Prevail? Performance of New Product Development and Sources of Idea Generation in China - an Emerging Market."
[127] Burgelman, "Designs for Corporate Entrepreneurship in Established Firms."
[128] Block, "What Would Karl Say? The Entrepreneur as Ideal (and Cool) Citizen in 21st Century Societies."
[129] Goldsby et al., "Design-Centered Entrepreneurship: A Four Stage Iterative Process for Opportunity Development."
[130] van Aken, "Design Science and Organization Development Interventions: Aligning Business and Humanistic Values."
[131] Atkinson, Thinking the Art of Management: Stepping into "Heidegger's Shoes."

design's aesthetic[132], is a crafted instance of innovation, neither reliant on, nor invoking a mimetic uncovering of an existing or non-existing real or imaginary thing, concept or idea. A *design* is unique. Unless a *design* is for its own sake—that is, the value of the *design* to an 'other' lies in the *design* or its style—a *design* is simply a model of a thing, concept or idea yet to be realised. It is an instruction for a next step in the creative process of uncovering the real. This is the notion of design I talk of in Chapter 8.

Clothing designs exhibited on catwalks bear all the marks of a design for design's sake, yet as designs, they may be models for innovative production garments with an exchange value in the wider fashion industry. In the sense that pure designs are devoid of visionary mimetic practice and relate simply to things knowable, yet to be realised, there are limits to the risks involved. Designs may be trialled (on catwalks, for example) before greater resources are committed, lowering the cost of risk. And, in the sense that once a design is realised it becomes known, it may be the basis for further *reproductive* activity. Here, an important design concept is the idea of the 'outsider's perspective'. In essence, a lack of knowledge can provide a perspective of benefit to a new market entrant, through a reduction in local search bias; a fresh set of *Designer's* eyes overcomes a stale view of a problem.[133] However, a lack of domain knowledge of some existing thing, concept or idea suggests a *Designer's* craft skills must include the (systematic) application of design techniques. As a basis for enterprise, there is a place for both the *Designer* generating design objects of intrinsic value, and for the *Designer* who acquires and enjoys an *end* of 'use-value' through transferring designs for an *other's* enterprise.

Individual as Experimenter (IM)

While the *Designer* uses craft skills and creativity to find solutions to the *field problem* of a known reality, I also address the idea that creativity may be used to explore the *knowledge problem* beyond the limits of knowledge, and to imagine new realities. Here, CTA presents the conjunction of innovation with mimesis as *Experimentation*: 'an opportunity to [imagine,] learn and discover further (as yet unseen) knowledge and insight into existing things, concepts and ideas'.[134] (An idea of postcapitalism, perhaps?) Here, I differentiate from

---

132 Brassett and O'reilly, "Styling the Future. A Philosophical Approach to Design and Scenarios," 44.

133 Goldsby et al., "Design-Centered Entrepreneurship: A Four Stage Iterative Process for Opportunity Development."

134 Atkinson, Thinking the Art of Management: Stepping into "Heidegger's Shoes," 97.

any notion of entrepreneurship *as* experimentation.[135] The pure *experiment* does not rely on craft skill. In the realm of *experimentation*, the skills required to be successful are not known in advance nor deducible from first principles. Experimentation is practised largely through intuition, in which the consequence is subject to extreme Knightian uncertainty.[136] But this does not suggest the *Experimenter* requires no skill at all.

Unlike the *Dreamer* as a 'naïve' risk-taker, I argue the *Experimenter* is a 'knowing' risk-taker, intuitively or consciously acknowledging the risks of mimetic discovery. In context, the construct of *experimentation* is relevant to individual acts of enterprising endeavour, with each experiment aimed at revealing new information—a foundation-stone of Schumpeter's 'creative destruction',[137] where understanding individual practice is key. The *pure Experimenter*, free of the cost of resources associated with the application of a craft field, limits the impact of risk. In this way, reducing the application (cost) of the craft of enterprise, through experimentation, may allow the pursuit of the seemingly unfeasible.[138]

A non-conceptual, strategic basis for entrepreneurship

While under CTA, the pure *Experimenter* is not an *Entrepreneur*, entrepreneurship clearly embraces experimentation. An object of design, experiment or representation can, at any time, attain the additional characteristics that elevate it to an instance of artwork.[139] Thus, in terms of enterprise, designs, experimental outcomes and representations (as re-productions) may all form the basis of entrepreneurial activity. Here, while such outcomes may not have been intended as entrepreneurial, the subsequent application of mimetic discovery (on designs), the craft of enterprise (on experimental outcomes), and creativity/innovation (on reproductions) may see them emerge as entrepreneurial in nature.

A consequence of the above is that the space of enterprise is adaptive and fluid.[140] This is congruent with, for example, the notion of a liquid, consumer-type entrepreneurship arising from the networked-tribe environment of

---

135 See, for example: Lüthy and Steyaert, "The Onto-Politics of Entrepreneurial Experimentation: Re-Reading Hans-Jörg Rheinberger's Understanding of 'Experimental Systems.'"

136 Kerr, Nanda, and Rhodes-Kropf, "Entrepreneurship as Experimentation."

137 Kerr, Nanda, and Rhodes-Kropf, "Entrepreneurship as Experimentation."

138 Kerr, Nanda, and Rhodes-Kropf, "Entrepreneurship as Experimentation."

139 Atkinson, Thinking the Art of Management: Stepping into "Heidegger's Shoes."

140 Garcia-Lorenzo et al., "Liminal Entrepreneuring: The Creative Practices of Nascent Necessity Entrepreneurs."

contemporary, online consumerism.[141] An individual may start out as a Craftsperson, Innovator, or Visionary/Dreamer. The Innovator may dream of a yet-to-be-revealed reality, to become an Experimenter, or they may apply craft skills to produce creative designs on what is currently known. The Craftsperson may apply enterprising skills to reproduce representations of what already exists. Or they may creatively design new enterprising activity. The Visionary/Dreamer may be motivated to attain the skills necessary to reproduce their vision, or they may focus their visions through innovative experimentation. All have the potential for entrepreneurship—to practise entrepreneuring—their outcomes a basis to take up and hold a new position in the space of enterprise. The individual who sets out to occupy this new position, sets out on a journey of artistic endeavour in the 'craft of Enterprise'. To set out is to practise entrepreneurship, to achieve it is entrepreneurial. The non-concept of entrepreneurship, defined by its enterprising skills, innovation and mimesis, allows the entrepreneur to emerge within a requisite variety of identities.

To be a worker bee?

As I introduced, the distinction between the 'us' that may be the 'recruits' to contemporary entrepreneurial employment and the heroic 'others' as entrepreneurs is problematic under anything other than a utopian autopoietic activity. As I have expounded through the inquiries of this text, autopoiesis is purposive, it presupposes the regeneration of a known state of being. This seemingly absolves society of a mimetic dreamlike or visionary purpose. Left alone to design for the future, innovation is absolved of its necessary creativity. Everything, including the notion of entrepreneurship resolves to a craft skill, to be taught and inculcated in an enterprising society, where creative destruction resolves to a design-led purposive activity, in which value is attributed to the act of design only. In this autopoietic state, entrepreneurship can only ever be design; it can only ever achieve value through designs on what has already been realised. The more we might teach entrepreneurship as design, the more value is locked in design-for-design's sake—entrepreneurship-for-entrepreneurship's sake: money for nothing.

As in the bee colony, a binary distinction in enterprising work is untenable. Not every aspirational design-led, autopoietic hero entrepreneur may succeed as a 'scout', founding a new 'designed' opportunity within the limits of our current knowledge. And not every non-entrepreneur can be a 'recruit' to some enterprising craft or other, as educated and directed by their purposive society. Put simply, we need to be more creative than that. We need imagination.

---

141 Biraghi and Gambetti, "Between Tribes and Markets: The Emergence of a Liquid Consumer-Entrepreneurship."

As Stan Metcalfe asked, can we go beyond a passive adoption of the concept 'entrepreneur' to focus on heterodox conjectures and bring new knowledge or beliefs into economic application?[142] I argue that, by applying CTA to the field of enterprising work, we can. The potential of a non-conceptual 'inclusive' definition of enterprise practice is revealed—one that embraces both what it is to be entrepreneurial and, crucially, what being entrepreneurial is not. The non-concept eschews autopoiesis and embraces poiesis. It limits who can claim the mantle *entrepreneur.*[143] Thus, under CTA, no individual is born an entrepreneur. Rather, an individual is free to adopt any of the *personas* of craftsperson, innovator, dreamer/visionary, reproducer, designer, experimenter, or entrepreneur. They do so in the context of a social practice in which they contribute to, variously: a state, a region, a market, an organization, a family, and/or the self. Poietically, if all that matters (as purposeful) to the individual is that they adopt the persona of *entrepreneur*, an agent for the 'self', then they may self-identify as an *entrepreneur.*

The hungry individual advertising his skills for food, adopts a *persona*, an agent of an *enterprising practice* in the interest of his or her '*self*'. But is this *entrepreneurship*? The heterodox clarification of this individual's persona is that of *craftsperson.* However, in the context of enterprising activity, this identity provides an alternate emplacement, a legitimisation of a position of value to society (and enterprise) without chasing the hero myth of entrepreneurship. Yet it is rare that an individual simply adopts an enterprising *persona* at the level of the *self.* In the context of enterprising activity, there is an implicit (social) exchange value for its outcomes. *Enterprising personas* are practiced as agents for an *other*—it is by virtue of some purposive power of the *other*, that the mantle of practice is conferred. Here, I return to the identification of small businesses and their role within both developed and developing economies. An individual who purports to be adept at the practice of any given *persona*, must establish that they can achieve its associated outcomes, and deliver value. Again, setting the *entrepreneur* as one of multiple *enterprising personas* provides latitude, it leaves other 'identifications' open for attribution, avoiding liminality. For example, one might fail to achieve the mantle *entrepreneur* but prove an adept *craftsperson, designer*, or *visionary leader.*

---

142 Metcalfe, "The Entrepreneur and the Style of Modern Economics."
143 Jones and Spicer, Unmasking the Entrepreneur.

As a rich, inclusive framework of enterprising activity, CTA provides a fertile ground for the classification of worker bees. By way of illustration—perhaps as a primer to the possibility of future, empirical study—I can assign arbitrary values to the three scaler dimensions of *Vision, Innovation* and *Craft skills.* In this way, it is possible to appreciate how various *personas* relate to each other. In Figure 9.3, I illustrate that the *personas* adopted by individuals engaged in enterprising work may be located anywhere in the *enterprising space.* The enterprising activity of each *persona* depends on its profile of *craft skill, innovation* and (*mimetic*)vision. Thus, different risk profiles attach to the identified activities[144]. In context, if there is a 'use' value associated with any enterprising activity's outcomes, a new business venture might be established around its enterprising *persona.* Thus, the gipsy fortune teller on the pleasure beach earns income from the output of her visionary capability, offering a *mimetic* revealing of elements of what is unknown. There is little that is intrinsically innovative about her centuries-old tradition, and no pretence that she is, in any sense, an *entrepreneur,* yet her enterprise is, by any definition, a small business and plays a socio-economic role. The plumber or electrician—a *craftsperson* bound by regulations and certifications—provides skills to others without design, or vision; they are a small business, nonetheless. Also, the outsourced product development team, working to a strict client brief, bears all the hallmarks of an *innovation agent*—again a viable basis for a profitable enterprise.

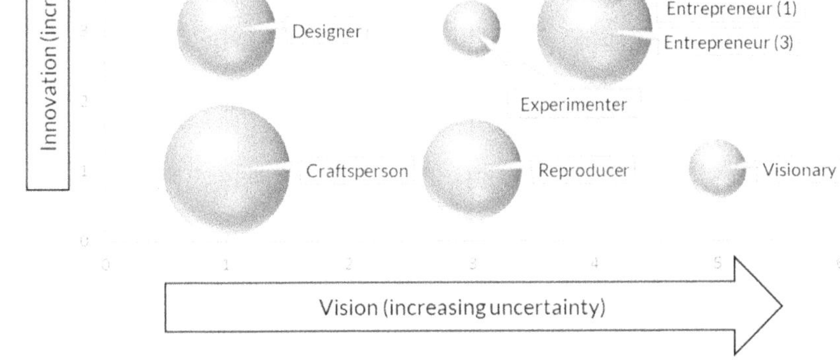

Figure 9.3. Mapping the enterprise space

---

144 Note: a "1" is low-level, a "5" high; the size of a persona is related to the level of craft skill.

Introducing elements of innovation and/or visionary activity orientates an individual (or small group of individuals) and their venture toward entrepreneurial activity. There is a sense in which any individual—dependent on capability and intent—may act in an entrepreneurial capacity.[145] I therefore posit that much of what is presently labelled *entrepreneurial activity* would, more appropriately, benefit from categorisation through alternative *personas*, from which a greater understanding of their enterprise (and their development) can be evolved.

Toward a better understanding of enterprise

De-othering the entrepreneur through (re)locating the entrepreneurial persona as one among several personas in the space of enterprising work, focuses entrepreneurship on *the art of enterprising work.* In acknowledging the entrepreneur as *the artist* in the practice of *entrepreneuring,* the CTA framework posits *entrepreneurship* as a fluid concept emplaced within the space of *enterprising work.* Here, the variety of personas is more important to the legitimisation of work in general, than it is to find and replicate the identity of the hero entrepreneur.[146] It sets the field for a greater variety of outcomes. Thus, avoiding the hegemonic reification of the 'hero' entrepreneur, I follow Jones and Spicer's reflections on the impact of a critical perspective, by highlighting the following three aspects.[147]

Firstly, applying CTA to enterprising work acknowledges the complexity of social analysis. Here, writing in Forbes, Tom O'Neal said that: '*if you've met one entrepreneur, you've met one entrepreneur.*'[148] The idea that every entrepreneur is different is a fundamental problem for social scientists studying what makes an entrepreneur and what separates the entrepreneur from the non-entrepreneur. The promise of a non-conceptual (re)location of the entrepreneur is that the traditional, dialectic dichotomy of non-entrepreneurial and entrepreneurial activity is dissolved by the absurdly fluid nature of much of what enterprise is.

---

[145] Wilson and Martin, "Entrepreneurial Opportunities for All?: Entrepreneurial Capability and the Capabilities Approach."

[146] Berglund, Dahlin, and Johansson, "Walking a Tightrope between Artistry and Entrepreneurship: The Stories of the Hotel Woodpecker, Otter Inn and Luna Resort."

[147] Jones and Spicer, Unmasking the Entrepreneur.

[148] Tom O'Neal, Associate VP of Research & Commercialization at the University of Central Florida. 'Real Business Incubators Build Business', Forbes Jul 8, 2014. (https://www.forbes.com/sites/groupthink/2014/07/08/real-business-incubators-build-business/#3551f1083d7c)

Secondly, with its roots in aesthetically informed social practice, CTA allows the study of entrepreneurship to be infinitely more socialised than that for which it is typically known. It presents the *reality* of enterprise based on a philosophy of Socially Negotiated Alternativism. This provides an infinitely malleable ontology of 'becoming'—of 'one-world', negotiated in a 'continuous dialogic process, [between real and imaginary planes,] in which we may alter our interpretation of the world by some reference to another's alternative interpretation'.[149] This permits the revision and replacement of elements of our interpretations of entrepreneurship, as required—an ontology that respects Anderson, Drakopoulou Dodd, and Jack's desire for a social ontology of relatedness.[150] Given this *socially negotiated reality* of enterprising work, the question arises: what might represent knowledge of it—where our entities (personas) within the broad substantive area of enterprising work have a fluid but definable form? This question offers a fertile ground for future, more traditional, empirical study.

Thirdly, the application of CTA allows the study of enterprising work and entrepreneurship to be more creative than it has previously been. For example, there is scope to strengthen connections between the study of entrepreneurship and that of innovation,[151] where innovation is one of the dimensions defining the space of an embodied and emplaced enterprising work. This would allow the co-emergence of innovative and non- (or marginally-) innovative enterprise, allowing attention to the points raised by Hans Landström and his colleagues, in seeking connections between the two. Furthermore, CTA suggests the possibility of drawing on design cognition research in theorising regional development issues. Design thinking extends cognitive acts of framing, analogical reasoning, abductive reasoning and mental stimulation.[152]It extends to thinking about how enterprise-as-a-whole (and not just entrepreneurship) can contribute to economic development. The range of personas yielded by CTA goes beyond the use of personas to understand users in design thinking entrepreneurial problems.[153] It facilitates theorising the social justice impacts of a range of enterprising others in the

---

[149] Atkinson, Thinking the Art of Management: Stepping into "Heidegger's Shoes," 154.

[150] Anderson, Drakopoulou Dodd, and Jack, "Entrepreneurship as Connecting; Some Implications for Theorising and Practice."

[151] Landström, Harirchi, and Åström, "Entrepreneurship: Exploring the Knowledge Base."

[152] Garbuio et al., "Demystifying the Genius of Entrepreneurship: How Design Cognition Can Help Create the next Generation of Entrepreneurs."

[153] Linton and Klinton, "University Entrepreneurship Education: A Design Thinking Approach to Learning."

design of markets,[154] or theorising around the idea of *Design Capitalism*, as covered in Chapter 8. That is to say, it is crucial in envisaging a pragmatic form of Design Capitalism.

Toward a better practice of enterprise

While it is generally agreed that an entrepreneurial society is conducive to economic development,[155] David Smallbone argued that variations in economic conditions affecting different countries, regions and localities mean that the context in which entrepreneurship may be a positive influence also varies.[156] A greater understanding of what constitutes both entrepreneurial and non-entrepreneurial activity has the potential for impact on what might be construed, *a priori*, as a basis for a more inclusive practice of economic enterprise, including the application of *design thinking* to the provision of the necessary education to guide and facilitate it.[157] Again, guided by Jones and Spicer, I offer three further critical perspectives.

Firstly, (re)locating entrepreneurship within the field of enterprising work retains the context of other enterprising personas. This opens options for policy design, offering a greater understanding of what entrepreneurship practice means, its limits, and knowing when talk of it is simply meaningless.[158] This appeals to a more individualistic view of policy interventions for the support of enterprise practice that respect: 1) the origin of nascent enterprising activity, 2) what might be required to achieve it, 3) how best to do so, and 4) with what level of support.

Secondly, variation in the individuality of the highlighted enterprising personas respects a concern that policymakers *'need to recognize the radical, social nature of entrepreneurship'*.[159] Since CTA distinguishes between innovative/creative behaviours and the visionary and craft endeavours, it embraces the idea of design as a part of an alternative social process of negotiating the necessities of life. This obviates a perceived need for a policy-fuelled 'big-bang' push to 'entrepreneurial' interventions. Individual enterprising agents, acting socially, practise the negotiation of new, imaginative realities at relatively low risk/cost, whereas an evidenced-based,

---

[154] Lotz, "Engineering Fairness? Market Design as a Resource for Social Justice Research."
[155] Lucas et al., "Visions of Entrepreneurship Policy."
[156] Smallbone, "Entrepreneurship Policy: Issues and Challenges."
[157] Johannisson, "Limits to and Prospects of Entrepreneurship Education in the Academic Context"; Sarooghi et al., "Design Thinking and Entrepreneurship Education: Where Are We, and What Are the Possibilities?"
[158] Jones and Spicer, Unmasking the Entrepreneur.
[159] Jones and Spicer, Unmasking the Entrepreneur, 114.

policy-fuelled focus on disruptive entrepreneurship is likely to remain high risk/cost, particularly, when there is no evidence for what is presently unknown.

Thirdly, the rewards for entrepreneurially focussed enterprise currently play to its 'myths' and not to its social reality. One might classify Bill Gates as an archetypal entrepreneur-hero, yet the anti-competitive practices of Microsoft in the late 1990s (the 'dark-side' of entrepreneurship) threw an uneasy challenge to entrepreneurship's role as singularly and wholly beneficial to society. And, as I highlighted in Chapter 8, the FAANGs represent yet more contemporary exemplars of debatable social benefit. There is, then, a question of the value of entrepreneurs over and above other enterprising individuals within society.[160] In acknowledging the existence of multiple enterprise personas and their role in the social construction of enterprising work, there will be less privileging of a mythical few in favour of a just recognition of a more inclusive range of enterprise's value outcomes in the context of a socially responsible, enterprising reality. This is the potential of a Design Capitalism.

On education for poietic enterprise

Is there scope for a non-conceptual theory of entrepreneurship that offers both coherence with the identity of the entrepreneur and which resists their reification? My objective in this Chapter has been to extend the typology of enterprising work, to allow for a richer potential in the design of postcapitalist (educational) responses to social and economic activity. Following Elena Antonacopoulou and Ted Fuller's explication of an embodied and emplaced entrepreneuring,[161] I have developed the idea that the aesthetic structures of place define the positions of both practitioners and non-practitioners of a fluid enterprising work. By extending an application of CTA, I have argued a coherence between the entrepreneurial identity, and an entrepreneuring practice that resists reification. This non-conceptually positions the entrepreneur by looking for entrepreneurship in all the wrong places.[162] As with a digital versus analogue clock display, we may have a richer understanding of a moment in time, when we see that moment in the context of all the moments it is not. Here, CTA presents a theory of enterprising space that permits the emergence of conceptual formations of enterprising work, including

---

160 See, for example: Engelke et al., "Heading Toward a More Social Future? Scenarios for Social Enterprises in Germany."

161 Antonacopoulou and Fuller, "Practising Entrepreneuring as Emplacement: The Impact of Sensation and Anticipation in Entrepreneurial Action."

162 Welter et al., "Everyday Entrepreneurship—A Call for Entrepreneurship Research to Embrace Entrepreneurial Diversity."

entrepreneuring, that are both socially contingent and contextual.[163] I therefore argue that there is scope for a new conceptual theory, not of entrepreneurship, but of an underlying practice of enterprising work.

The highlighted *personas* of practice provide a range of common epithets: artists, designers, innovators, and dreamers. These are not uncommon terms. I do not argue their existence simply to challenge the 'hero' myth. Rather, I argue for a necessary understanding of each *persona* as a MacIntyrean 'social character'.[164] This provides for an interpretation of the actions of those who act in character, within the complex adaptive system of enterprising (economic) work. Given this position, what insights are achievable, what value are they, and for whom?

The de-othering of the entrepreneur and understanding their co-emergence/co-existence with other forms of enterprising activity may facilitate a greater understanding of liminality[165] and identity construction.[166] In a practical sense, understanding that one might be able to design certain enterprising system objectives (for example: meaningful employment, income and social status) around a range of personas, without naïvely grasping for an unreachable epithet, would certainly be of mental-health value to students and practitioners of enterprising work—setting and managing appropriate expectations. By better understanding the space in which entrepreneurship co-emerges with other enterprising work, there is value to policymakers in *design thinking* how those structures (craft skills of a given context in practice, the practice of creativity and innovation, and the practice of envisioning) can best be supported—a support that fundamentally extends to the educational systems that prepare a society's people for work.

Entrepreneurship has often been recognised as a form of art.[167] Here, CTA provides an efficacious framework for requisite variety. In unmasking entrepreneurs and re-locating them amid a typology of personas of the practice of the social reality of work, I argue that we need not share a concern with expanding the idea of the entrepreneur into all areas of social life.[168] This re-location also hints at how the structure of an education system for an

---

163 Anderson, Drakopoulou Dodd, and Jack, "Entrepreneurship as Connecting; Some Implications for Theorising and Practice."
164 MacIntyre, After Virtue.
165 Garcia-Lorenzo et al., "Liminal Entrepreneuring: The Creative Practices of Nascent Necessity Entrepreneurs."
166 Williams and Nadin, "Beyond the Entrepreneur as a Heroic Figurehead of Capitalism: Re-Representing the Lived Practices of Entrepreneurs."
167 Berglund, "Researching Entrepreneurship as Lived Experience."
168 Jones and Spicer, Unmasking the Entrepreneur.

antagonistic future of work might be envisaged. Educational systems must accept that entrepreneurship can be almost anywhere. But it cannot be about everything. It calls for a critical understanding of context, in which we must not lose sight of entrepreneurship's political, socio-economic nature.

Entrepreneurship is just one enterprising activity, in which the entrepreneur is not the only actor. In not losing sight of entrepreneurship's political, socio-economic nature, I argue that we must accept that the social reality of work is far greater than entrepreneurship. Entrepreneurship may present itself as the art of enterprising activity, but it is not the only (desirable) enterprising activity. The ideas in this Chapter eschew the narrow view that entrepreneurship is solely the economic act of starting a small business and thus, the only savour of economies and the holy grail of education for work. To parody the inimitable Oscar Wilde, in the *Decay of Lying*, the current practice of enterprising work is that it attempts to imitate the 'ends' of great entrepreneurship.[169] There is no imagination in imitation. In a broadly inclusive world of enterprising work, we might better reconcile with Robert Reich's conclusion that it is the team—defined as a collection of enterprising personas—that is the real hero(ine) of society.[170]

---

[169] Wilde, The Soul of Man under Socialism & Selected Critical Prose, 192.
[170] Reich, "Reconsidered: The Team As Hero."

Chapter 10

On experts and wizards

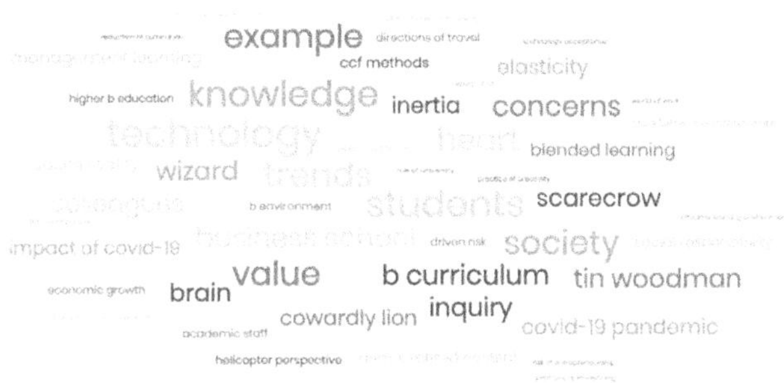

IN EDUCATING FOR POSTCAPITALISM I have argued for an understanding of the space in which a non-conceptual entrepreneurship emerges from other enterprising work. In this Chapter, I revert to the CCF method of 'means' to question the future state of learning with regard to a requisite change in our approach to education—that is, in relation to the education of a population toward a more inclusive concept of enterprising work. However, while I strive for the understanding I have argued for, a transition of our educational systems will require the application of *design thinking* to enable the necessary learning scaffolds and structures relating to: 1) how craft skills in any given context might be best taught and committed to practice; 2) how the practice of creativity and innovation can be inculcated to extend any craft, and 3) how the practice of envisioning can be inculcated and sanctioned as a legitimate practice in its own right. This is no insignificant challenge. Again, following Kurt Lewin, at the (non)conceptual level of my overall inquiry and provocation, this challenge of social change invokes Lewin's three-step process of unfreezing, moving, and refreezing. It is therefore reasonable, at this juncture, to investigate how receptive our educational systems might be to such change.

My aim, here, is to carry the argument for a new (aesthetic) understanding of enterprising work, into a futures-based examination of the long-term potential of the Business School (BS) in Higher Education (HE). This inquiry is inspired by the idea that the disruption caused by the Covid-19 pandemic might have provided the *'best chance to change universities for good'*.[1] Faced with the

---

[1] Jones, "Covid-19 Is Our Best Chance to Change Universities for Good."

embodiment of the 'uncertainty' which 'underpins government, business and the economy'[2] we have moved from a world 'disenchanted' by the loss of mystery in the face of science, and its promise of a mastery of calculation,[3] to a 'disenchantment' that—at least in government, business and the economy—science does not hold all the answers. In this context then, Steven Jones highlighted that, as universities were locked down and academic staff were confined to their homes, they demonstrated their commitment to their "students' education and wellbeing", supported by legions of administration and ICT staff.[4] He argued that, in a post-Covid-19 future, competition and casualisation—features of much contemporary HE—should yield to greater fairness and social responsibility. In this sense, the pandemic might have been seen as a catalyst, unfreezing the ground for change. In part, Jones wrote from a concern over market-based education policy and the emergence of a 'value for money' discourse.[5] This concern, was voiced by Max Weber over a century earlier, noting the change in the German HE system at that time [6]—a concern brought into contemporary relief by more recent observers.[7]

Embedded in Jones' article are several themes. For this inquiry, I highlight just three: 1) the place of the university as a bastion of HE within society, concentrating on its role and value; 2) the core function of HE and the mediation of its delivery—that is the necessary social aspects of relationships and collaboration; and 3) the regulatory frameworks required to achieve a sustainable HE institution (HEI). However, while inspired by Jones' commentary,[8] my point of departure must be to consider the specific role of the twenty-first century BS, a principal adjunct of the institute of HE, and in many ways more acutely focused on market competition and casualisation, both in

---

[2] Moeran, "Magical Capitalism," 134.
[3] Weber, "Science as a Vocation."
[4] Jones, "Covid-19 Is Our Best Chance to Change Universities for Good."
[5] Jones, Vigurs, and Harris, "Discursive Framings of Market-Based Education Policy and Their Negotiation by Students: The Case of 'Value for Money' in English Universities."
[6] Ringer, "Education, Knowledge, and Vocation."
[7] Burchell, Kennedy, and Murray, "Responsible Management Education in UK Business Schools: Critically Examining the Role of the United Nations Principles for Responsible Management Education as a Driver for Change"; Starkey, Tempest, and Cinque, "Management Education and the Theatre of the Absurd"; Loomes, Owens, and McCarthy, "Patterns of Recruitment of Academic Leaders to Australian Universities and Implications for the Future of Higher Education."
[8] Jones, "Covid-19 Is Our Best Chance to Change Universities for Good."

terms of its faculty,[9] and its customer base.[10] Indeed, spurred partly by Martin Parker's call to *Shut down the business school*,[11] there is a persistent critique of the BS institution's future. This critique is broad. It ranges, for example, from a perceived lack of response to the United Nations' call for responsible management education,[12] through changing the ways of teaching,[13] to the perceived poor impact of most published research, increasing unethical behaviour and the decline of teaching.[14] Thus, following Michel Kalika, Gordon Shenton, and Pierre Dubois,[15] I pose the questions: Will BSs maintain an HE role in 2030? And if so, what might that role and function look like?

Following the CCF method then, I proceed as follows. I trace a line of current expert opinion and research through a historical view of the BS, revealing the changing systemic nature of a growing networked social reality. This is revealed as a form of paradigm shift that impacts on the role and function of (business) management and organizational education, not directly, but through a system of cultural dimensionality. This is reflected in the critical uncertainty inherent in the three identified themes. It allows a brief examination of the impact of the Covid-19 pandemic upon these themes, setting up six exemplar outcomes—the imaginations. Following the CCF method, the resultant truth table reflects the relative coherence of these thematic imaginations to a range of future moments—the contradictions. Finally, I offer a further Wizard-of-Oz speculation of the simulated but coherent futures—providing a further allegorical discussion, this time as the (real) Tin Man, Scarecrow, and Cowardly Lion, meet the Wizard.

---

9 Collins, Glover, and Jones Myers, "The Automation Game: Perceptions on the Impact of the Changes on Business School Tutors' Roles and Identity during the Introduction of Technological Student Retention Activities"; Courtney, "Adapting Higher Education through Changes in Academic Work"; Loomes, Owens, and McCarthy, "Patterns of Recruitment of Academic Leaders to Australian Universities and Implications for the Future of Higher Education."

10 Polanyi and Tompa, "Rethinking Work-Health Models for the New Global Economy: A Qualitative Analysis of Emerging Dimensions of Work"; Standing, "Economic Insecurity and Global Casualisation: Threat or Promise?"

11 Parker, Shut Down Bus. Sch.

12 Burchell, Kennedy, and Murray, "Responsible Management Education in UK Business Schools: Critically Examining the Role of the United Nations Principles for Responsible Management Education as a Driver for Change."

13 Wierzbinska, "The Future of Managerial Education."

14 Harley, "Confronting the Crisis of Confidence in Management Studies: Why Senior Scholars Need to Stop Setting a Bad Example."

15 Kalika, Shenton, and Dubois, "What Happens If a Business School Disappears? The Intellectual Foundations of BSIS."

A historical view of HE and management learning

Firstly, although we may talk of BSs and management learning, we really talk of the gamut of education and learning in the fields of designing, leading and managing organizations and their enterprising work, whether public or private, profit or non-profit. Here, within the knowledge society, the key role of universities is traditionally perceived as the triad of: 1) the governance and supply of (useful) knowledge, as a direct investment in and contribution to human capital;[16] 2) a site of 'cognitive evolution', nurturing 'the dominant and emergent cultural models of society';[17] and 3) bridging a communications gap between science, technology and society.[18] Within this context, in the decades preceding the twenty-first-century incarnation of the BS, the rapid change of business, and organizations in general—brought about by incessant rounds of efficiency-seeking process re-engineering, an antidote to Adam Smith's division of labour—set a scene for the organization of work within an envisaged hyper-competitive future. A move from 'work preparation' through training to 'work preparation' through education, thus placed pressure on BSs to deliver process-orientated business and management learning.[19]

At the turn of the century, the trend toward process-managed organizations supported models of process-centred business education, appealing to both academic and business calls for broader, more integrated educational outcomes. This arose, as Kenton Walker and Ervin Black suggested, through a revolution in customer demand, advances in technology, global economic shifts in competition, and an increasing requirement for broad and complete competence.[20] They argued that a process-centred business education should be built around the three dimensions of: discipline knowledge (for example, accounting, marketing, HR etc.); relevant skills (for example, communications, ICT, and critical thinking etc.); and an integrative theme (such as business strategy, information systems, or change management). Despite both criticism and defence,[21] the 'marketization' of the BS output has been perceived as

---

[16] Schultz, "Investment in Human Capital."

[17] Delanty, "The Governance of Universities: What Is the Role of the University in the Knowledge Society?," 188.

[18] See, for example: Vliegenthart, "The Role of the University in Bridging the Communication Gap between Science and Technology and Society."

[19] Davis and Mehta, "Reengineering a School of Business of the Future : A Mission/Vision Model for Higher Education in Transformational Times."

[20] Walker and Black, "Reengineering the Undergraduate Business Core Curriculum: Aligning Business Schools with Business for Improved Performance."

[21] Hay and Hodgkinson, "More Success than Meets the Eye-a Challenge to Critiques of the MBA: Possibilities for Critical Management Education?"

symptomatic of the twenty-first-century drift from the traditional, key roles of university-led HE.

The increasing massification of HE—that is, the policy-reinforced practice of making the luxury products of HE available to the mass market of the wider population—can be seen as a general response to this trend toward work preparation through education, rather than training. Here, Eric Cornuel suggested massification compounds the challenges faced by BSs as they meet the increasing and 'rapidly changing preferences of students, employers, governments and other stakeholders'.[22] In a competitive response, BSs are seen to increase links with the business world to identify common goals and objectives, preparing the ground for a more responsive, practice-based education.[23] If successful, business organizations simply outsource their preparation of workers to HE, in search of *prêt à travailler* employees. Inexorably, the forces for change appear to colonise the BS curriculum to address the needs of an autopoietic practice. This is rather than, as my inquiry has so far called for, deliver a more poietic capability to face the VUCA challenges of tomorrow. Current practice reflects trends toward globalisation and specialisation, where practical skills gained through HE are held to outweigh HE's tradition in theoretical knowledge and cognitive evolution.[24] Colloquially, as Steve Denning, author of *The Age of Agile*,[25] observed in Forbes, '...today's business schools teach yesterday's expertise'.[26]

Denning points to the paradox that, despite a perceived drive to the colonisation of BS curricula by the needs of current practice, a BS hot-bed of innovation and thinking now appears to reflect the content of teaching and researching twentieth-century principles and practice. He argues that there has been a paradigm shift in management learning that is not adequately reflected in its curriculum. In advocating the revolutionary paradigm of agile management, Denning cites the success of exemplar firms like Facebook, Amazon, Apple, Google, Microsoft, Alibaba, Airbnb, and Uber—all names within the global vocabulary; an extension of the group of FAANGs I have previously discussed. He suggests that for these firms 'profits are the result,

---

[22] Cornuel, "Challenges Facing Business Schools in the Future," 89.
[23] Cornuel, "Challenges Facing Business Schools in the Future."
[24] This observation is in many respects a reflection of the Mode 1/Mode 2 knowledge debate. For an exploration of this, and the related concepts of a Model 1 and Model 2 manager, see Atkinson, Thinking the Art of Management: Stepping into "Heidegger's Shoes."
[25] Denning, The Age of Agile: How Smart Companies Are Transforming the Way Work Gets Done.
[26] Denning, "Why Today's Business Schools Teach Yesterday's Expertise."

not the goal, of the enterprise'.[27] Yet, while the future may be thrilling for such firms, as my discussion of capitalism's guiding 'invisible hand' in Chapter 8 suggests, it would be naïve to assume they do not utilise management practices steeped in capitalist history.

Arguably, even in the contemporary digitally focussed business, there is an ever-increasing focus on profit and the philosophies of managerial control. This suppresses more creative forms of management and management learning. But, historically, as I have previously written:

> '[Management] in practice, is management – it is no more than that; management is neither a science, nor an art, nor a craft. [It] is whatever managers do; it is not what an individual has to do to be a manager. Management in this sense cannot, therefore, be described as an autonomous activity; one that might be objectively studied to produce a set of prescriptive "management practices" fully defining the social role of manager. What can be said, however, is that whatever it is that managers do, they are responsible to the socio-cultural grouping that recognizes them as a manager – for the performance of their role.'[28]

Michał Szostak and Łukasz Sułkowski misinterpret my opening gambit on the possibility of an aesthetic management as, in some way, a conclusion[29]—a conclusion Stephen Dunne avoided.[30] As I go on to expound in *Thinking the Art of Management*, it *is* possible to think of managerial practice as an art form, as long as we are precise about what is meant by 'managerial practice' and what is meant by 'art form'. Thus, despite the potential in aesthetic approaches, and given Eric Cornuel's observation on BS links with business,[31] the increasingly commercial outlook of many schools glosses over the tendency of strong commercial relationships to stifle HE's traditional strengths of independent thinking and academic counterculture. As Sijbolt Noorda argued, past results are no guarantee of future performance.[32]

I suggest that we might consider whether the BS model is crisis-proof. Consider the notion of BS rankings, a measure of strong commercial

---

27 Denning, "Why Today's Business Schools Teach Yesterday's Expertise."
28 Atkinson, Thinking the Art of Management: Stepping into "Heidegger's Shoes," 3.
29 Szostak and Sułkowski, "Manager as an Artist: Creative Endeavour in Crossing the Borders of Art and Organizational Discourse."
30 Dunne, "Book Review: Thinking the Art of Management: Stepping into 'Heidegger's Shoes'."
31 Cornuel, "Challenges Facing Business Schools in the Future."
32 Noorda, "Future Business Schools."

relationships, research assessment and funding, and the launch of students into significant employment opportunity. Isn't this also a measure of the degree to which the preclusion of independent thought and academic counterculture (a more direct route to human capital growth), serves to set up future conditions of failure—at least in an HE sense? It would, for example, be naïve to assume that students do not identify with intellectual curiosity and critical thought.[33] In the event of any major socio-economic crisis in business fortunes, if the aspiration of lower-ranking schools acts to drive out independent thought and academic counterculture—replicating colonising commercial activity in search of a higher rank—might the ground be set for a crisis of BS identity? In such times, as Noorda observes, 'people ask about the role of business schools. Why didn't they foresee these risks, why didn't they train business people better, why are they all speaking the same language?'[34]

While my argument, here, is against an evidential paradigm shift in management, I can agree with Denning's underlying 'vast societal drama'[35] playing out in a world under the influence of the Fourth Industrial Revolution.[36] Arguably, this social drama, impacted by the Covid-19 and subsequent crises, has consequences beyond any form of managerialism underpinning some new set of principles for the foundation of contemporary enterprise and organization, or for the reconciliation of their bureaucratic and pluralistic forms.[37] Here, I acknowledge '[high]-level changes in social and economic systems and resulting institutional shifts are simply beyond the power of individuals to change'.[38] Thus, rather than critique the BS curriculum *per se*, the importance of viewing a paradigmatic shift, not in management but in social reality, lies in understanding the BS's institutional role and its functional position. Full circle, however, this suggests that some change in management 'thinking and doing' is both necessary and inevitable. Here, pockets of change have been evidenced in some BS curricula, with turns to 'critical management learning',[39] and 'design-' or 'integrated-' thinking.[40]

---

33 Koris, Örtenblad, and Ojala, "From Maintaining the Status Quo to Promoting Free Thinking and Inquiry: Business Students' Perspective on the Purpose of Business School Teaching."

34 Noorda, "Future Business Schools," 523.

35 Denning, "Why Today's Business Schools Teach Yesterday's Expertise."

36 Schwab, The Fourth Industrial Revolution.

37 Clarke and Butcher, "Political Leadership, Bureaucracies and Business Schools: A Comfortable Union?"

38 Harley, "Confronting the Crisis of Confidence in Management Studies: Why Senior Scholars Need to Stop Setting a Bad Example," 292.

39 Hay and Hodgkinson, "More Success than Meets the Eye-a Challenge to Critiques of the MBA: Possibilities for Critical Management Education?"

The changing nature of (networked) social reality

Embedded in the context of the HEI/BS environment, we face a present social reality of people's behaviour and their social values and relationships. These are all aspects of a social capital.[41] Here, for example, social networking accounts for trends and preferences in social interactions through local, physical presence, set against any tendency to revert to, or rely on, a technology-mediated and increasingly globalised, virtual presence. Technology—particularly the internet, digital communications and social networking platforms—has fundamentally changed the landscape of early twenty-first-century relationships. While (dating Denning's examples[42]) children of the 1970s (Apple and Microsoft) have provided enabling technology, the children of the 1990s (Amazon, Google and Alibaba) gave birth to the digital medium, demonstrating the power of global connectivity. Yet, it is the children of the twenty-first century: Facebook (2004), Airbnb (2008) and Uber (2009), that really mark the paradigmatic shift to a more globalised (de-localised) society, through the democratisation of information.

Pre-Facebook, social networking was more likely to be a focus of study at a localised anthropological level—for example, in examining the role of sub-cultures in social networks and business success in an African context.[43] However, the changing nature of networked relationships is reflected in the complex and dynamic casualisation of the labour market.[44] By the second decade of the twenty-first century, a concern with social networking bridges both the formal, hierarchical relationships within organizations, and the fluidity and dynamism of a multitude of co-existing, co-operating, and co-evolving social networks, both physical and virtual.[45] This has led some observers to suggest that, in empowering future managers and leaders, the reach of social networking can leverage other technological richness (for example, augmented reality) in yielding a new paradigm of agile BS

---

[40] Lancione and Clegg, "The Lightness of Management Learning."

[41] Coleman, "Social Capital in the Creation of Human Capital"; Robison and Ritchie, Relatsh. Econ. Soc. Cap. Paradig. It's Appl. to Business, Polit. Other Trans.

[42] Founding dates of Denning, "Why Today's Business Schools Teach Yesterday's Expertise."were obtained by reference to Wikipedia pages for the respective companies *https://en.wikipedia.org/ wiki/Main_Page*

[43] Kristiansen, "Social Networks and Business Success the Role of Subcultures in an African Context."

[44] See, for example: Antcliff, Saundry, and Stuart, "Networks and Social Capital in the UK Television Industry: The Weakness of Weak Ties."

[45] Smith and Sharicz, "The Bi-Modal Organization: Balancing Autopoiesis and Fluid Social Networks for Sustainability."

education.[46] And, from a customer perspective (student or business organization), learning about the leveraging of social networks provides opportunities for new product development.[47]

I have noted that drivers toward networked organizational and social behaviour are heavily based on technology. This includes the functional replacement of institutional dimensions with technological innovation.[48] Other drivers include geo-politics, for example, the USA's nationalism and China's increasing global reach. Intuitively, such issues are inextricably linked to low growth for some, yet entwined with the conflicts between individualism and collectivism,[49] and equality and diversity for others. Also, global, national and local responses to conditions of social stress and crises, reflect the degree to which societies respond to or accept uncertainty and risk, and the degree to which they adopt a long or short-term view. Permatasari and colleagues[50] argued that such drivers relate closely to Geert Hofstede's principal dimensions of culture.[51] This invokes the degree to which gratification (or self-interest) conflicts with self-control, as a basic human behaviour related to living life. In turn, I argue that we can reasonably hold these drivers to be moderated by aspects of law and regulation (in relation, for example, to risk aversity) and issues of sustainability, including of the economy, climate and the environment. In context, and as reflected in my inquiries, there is much

---

46 Gupta and Bharadwaj, "Agility in Business School Education through Richness and Reach: A Conceptual Model."

47 Roberts and Candi, "Leveraging Social Network Sites in New Product Development: Opportunity or Hype?"

48 Abbasi et al., "Social, Organizational, Demography and Individuals' Technology Acceptance Behaviour: A Conceptual Model"; Permatasari, Sensuse, and Santoso, "Cultural Aspects Influencing the Application of E-Learning: A Literature Review"; Tarhini, Hone, and Liu, "User Acceptance towards Web-Based Learning Systems: Investigating the Role of Social, Organizational and Individual Factors in European Higher Education"; Yeou, "An Investigation of Students' Acceptance of Moodle in a Blended Learning Setting Using Technology Acceptance Model."

49 There is a sense in which collectivism is no more than a 'capacious form of individualism', with the real alternative to individualism being relationalism. See, for example: Wang and Liu, "What Collective? Collectivism and Relationalism from a Chinese Perspective." Wang and Liu point to the shortcomings of the idea of collectivism, given the nature of cross-cultural communications—such as we can anticipate in a virtual, globally connected space. The authors further suggest a tripartite model of individualism, collectivism and relationalism as a richer framework for understanding, for example, conflict in multi-cultural scenarios.

50 Permatasari, Sensuse, and Santoso, "Cultural Aspects Influencing the Application of E-Learning: A Literature Review."

51 Hofstede, "Dimensionalizing Cultures: The Hofstede Model in Context."

complexity to the socio-technical system within which I must position the HE BS.

The impact of Covid-19...

I turn, now, to consider the broader impact of Covid-19 in relation to the three identified themes that underpin the position of the HE BS. Recapping, these themes are: 1) role and value, 2) relationships and collaboration, and 3) managerialism, metrics and accountability.[52]

Place in society (role and value)

In considering role and value, I address the core function of HE and the BS—its place in society. Here, I position my argument around the trend of neoliberalistic political intervention, and its colonisation of the HE curriculum. This corollary of neoliberalism privileges strong private ownership rights, free markets and trade.[53] Here, as Gifty Gyamera and Penny Burke suggest, market hegemony in the name of 'international leadership', has focused BS curricula on effecting 'innovation' in HE toward 'global market' competition, and the formation of 'commercial partnerships'.[54] However, I posit that one need only consider the USA, to see the impact of the extreme 'innovative', neoliberalist creative destruction of public education. In the US (in part), a 'quest for profit on behalf of educational for-profit corporations and investors', drives such reforms as the reduction of curriculum and pedagogy to 'narrow numerically quantifiable and positivistic test-based forms'.[55]

Kenneth Saltman suggested that neoliberal educational ideology is primarily useful for preparing workers and consumers for the economy. Recalling the Fable of the Bees from Chapter 1, and the discussion of Chapter 9, I suggest that this is no more than the deterministic recruitment and development of a society of heroic, enterprising 'worker bees'. Here, MBAs are trained as management gurus to confront the 'limits and contradictions of the neoliberal [economic] order'.[56] Yet, neoliberal capitalism infuses BS curricula

---

[52] Jones, "Covid-19 Is Our Best Chance to Change Universities for Good"; Jones, Vigurs, and Harris, "Discursive Framings of Market-Based Education Policy and Their Negotiation by Students: The Case of 'Value for Money' in English Universities."

[53] Gyamera and Burke, "Neoliberalism and Curriculum in Higher Education: A Post-Colonial Analyses"; Tight, "The Neoliberal Turn in Higher Education."

[54] Gyamera and Burke, "Neoliberalism and Curriculum in Higher Education: A Post-Colonial Analyses," 451.

[55] Saltman, "Neoliberalism and Corporate School Reform: 'Failure' and 'Creative Destruction,'" 249.

[56] Orta, "Imagining the Unmanageable: MBAs at the Limits of Neoliberalism," 52.

with a teaching that inculcates an individualistic level of self-interest that can only advance social inequality.[57] Here, the irony of a radical individualism of self-interest is the loss of any form of social cohesion, where the increasing gap between rich and poor risks political and cultural instability and undermines both health and education.[58]

Enter the Covid-19 paradox. The global level of state-imposed social isolation, fuelled by technology-enabled social networking, revealed a level of social cohesion not well-reflected in the neoliberalistic institutional structures of recent decades. As Andrew Orta observed, before the pandemic: 'sociality and sociocultural difference [confounded] the apparent organizing premises (or goals) of a neoliberal worldview.'[59] Despite Orta's reference to Margaret Thatcher's (1987) comment that 'There is no such thing as society', he concluded that, for 'the good MBA students of neoliberalism, sociality is essential to its execution in practice'.[60] This is an oft-over-looked principle, acknowledged by Thatcher later in her commentary:

> 'There is [a] living tapestry of ...people [The] beauty of that tapestry and the quality of our lives will depend upon how much each of us is prepared to take responsibility for ourselves and each of us prepared to turn ...and help by our own efforts those who are unfortunate.'[61]

Steven Jones implied that the advent of Covid-19 was an opportunity to capitalise on the wider HE institution, with a new role as a single point of truth-seeking, in a sea of indeterminacy and uncertainty.[62] Yet, in the case of the BS, management defies description as an autonomous activity; it denies objective study in the search for such truth. However, what Covid-19 has perhaps surfaced is the reality of the 'social viruses' of democratised information and data that might (if marshalled) act to undermine the very neoliberal foundations that have enabled it to flourish. I ask: what value is HE when work priorities are revealed, post Covid-19, to favour low-knowledge and/or soft-skills foci? I therefore advance my first critical uncertainty:

---

57 Fotaki and Prasad, "Questioning Neoliberal Capitalism and Economic Inequality in Business Schools," 557.
58 Fotaki and Prasad, "Questioning Neoliberal Capitalism and Economic Inequality in Business Schools," 556.
59 Orta, "Imagining the Unmanageable: MBAs at the Limits of Neoliberalism," 63.
60 Orta, "Imagining the Unmanageable: MBAs at the Limits of Neoliberalism," 63.
61 Thatcher, "No Such Thing as Society."
62 Jones, "Covid-19 Is Our Best Chance to Change Universities for Good."

> **P_1**: Higher BS education is characterised by more or less neoliberalistic (capitalist) colonisation of business school curricula, rather than an increasing concern for sociality.

Given a projection of the critical uncertainty **P_1**, my concern in this part of the inquiry is over the BS role and function in advancing economic growth through innovation or (perhaps) rebuilding institutions that care for society. This is a question of the continued- versus de-colonisation of HE BS curriculum. For example, I may imagine **($P1_1$)** that, given exposure to the impact of Covid-19—and (more recently) the cost-of-living crisis invoked by the February 2022 Russian incursion into Ukraine—the likelihood is for the origin of a student movement for the de-stabilising decolonisation of neoliberalistic capitalism in the HE BS curriculum, in the same manner as the movement for the decolonisation of Colonial influences in the more general HE curriculum.[63] Alternatively, I might imagine **($P1_2$)**, that an increased capitalist colonisation under a new imperative for economic: growth will only lead to the creative destruction of the BS as an HEI, where the reduction of curriculum and pedagogy to Saltman's 'narrow numerically quantifiable and positivistic test-based forms',[64] will alienate the wider HEI, leading to a separation of school from its parent institution.

Mediation of delivery (relationships and collaboration)

In twenty-first-century UK, and many developed nations, massification sees HE as an increasingly competitive space. Here, HEIs compete on at least three fronts: for students, for funding and for recognition within society.[65] In this space, Tarhini et al. suggest competition between HEIs has led to significant investment in internet-based learning systems.[66] These systems build on the distance learning concept, from electronic or e-learning, to mobile or m-learning.[67] Here, while Keegan posited the advent of a new market sector of education and training, technology innovation yielded responsive and

---

[63] See, for example: McGregor and Park, "Towards a Deconstructed Curriculum: Rethinking Higher Education in the Global North"; Pimblott, "Decolonising the University: The Origins and Meaning of a Movement."

[64] Saltman, "Neoliberalism and Corporate School Reform: 'Failure' and 'Creative Destruction,'" 249.

[65] O'Neill, Singh, and O'Donoghue, "Implementing ELearning Programmes for Higher Education: A Review of the Literature."

[66] Tarhini, Hone, and Liu, "User Acceptance towards Web-Based Learning Systems: Investigating the Role of Social, Organizational and Individual Factors in European Higher Education."

[67] Keegan, "The Future of Learning: From ELearning to MLearning."

adaptable web-based learning applications operating across multiple platforms—from smartphone, through tablet, to more traditional laptop and desktop modes.[68] This risks market homogenisation not segmentation.[69]

The early views of Kayte O'Neil and her colleagues suggested that e-learning applications, imposed on academic staff in consequence of managerialist responses to market forces, might lack the underpinnings of sound pedagogic practice.[70] Thus, the Covid-19 enforced shutdowns of academic buildings saw academic staff join the legions of home-workers. Seminars were 'Zoomed' onto students' smartphones, demonstrating staff commitment to their education and wellbeing.[71] Anecdotally then, all appeared well for a transition to a new, post-Covid-19 world of HE. However, it would be naïve to imply from (for example) O'Neill and her colleagues' suggestion, that all that is required to successfully leverage the latest educational technology with new-found confidence, is to deliver high-quality e-learning that meets the needs of a diverse student population.[72] If nothing else, Covid-19 also highlighted the internet's ubiquity as a medium of mediation, and the 'un-trustable' nature of much of the democratised content it can deliver. Also, Porter's five forces model suggests that what can be achieved in online HE provision can easily be replicated by non-HEI interests (for example, MOOCs—massive open online courses).[73] This may undermine, rather than enhance, an HEI's competitive edge.[74]

Blending HE between the poles of traditional face-to-face learning and e-enabled distance learning needs consistency, both in the student experience and learner-centred environments.[75] Here, effectiveness is centred on a student's access to, their success with, and their perceptions of, the learning environment. While blended learning has been held to maintain or increase

---

[68] Peng and Zhou, "The Design and Research of Responsive Web Supporting Mobile Learning Devices."

[69] During the covid 19 epidemic, plans in some Universities to increase online provision were not always accepted by staff and students. See " https://www.theguardian.com/education/2020/apr/25/durham-university-retracts-controversial-plan-to-provide-online-only-degrees

[70] O'Neill, Singh, and O'Donoghue, "Implementing ELearning Programmes for Higher Education: A Review of the Literature."

[71] Jones, "Covid-19 Is Our Best Chance to Change Universities for Good."

[72] O'Neill, Singh, and O'Donoghue, "Implementing ELearning Programmes for Higher Education: A Review of the Literature."

[73] Grundy, "Rethinking and Reinventing Michael Porter's Five Forces Model."

[74] McPherson and Bacow, "Online Higher Education: Beyond the Hype Cycle."

[75] Fresen, "Embracing Distance Education in a Blended Learning Model: Challenges and Prospects."

access and improve success, students appeared to relate more to the establishment of and progression toward clear course objectives, delivered in an effective learning environment with effective student-staff communication.[76] However, it also required acceptance of technology as part of that learning environment.

Pre-Covid-19, technology acceptance—the adoption/diffusion of e-learning in mediating the HE experience—had been disappointing, despite its documentation and promotion by managers and enthusiasts alike.[77] Limited studies suggested students had been more inclined to adopt e-learning only if they thought it was useful and/or it would improve their quality of work-life, such as saving time, money and/or effort.[78] Others acknowledged the individual, social and organizational factors influencing technology acceptance, including institute and government support.[79] Invoking such support reflects Permatasari and colleagues' suggestion of an overarching socio-economic perspective—an external factor, indirectly acting on students' adoption of e-learning.[80] However, they did not detail such a perspective. Here I suggest that, (non)conceptually at least, the socio-economic factor is inextricably linked to $\mathbf{P_1}$: the degree to which market-driven capitalist colonisation of the BS curriculum can be observed.

Beyond blended learning, Marcela Hernandez-de-Menendez and colleagues sought to explore other technologies in the context of mediating the learning experience.[81] They commented in the context of engineering education, yet it is as well to refer to it in the BS context. While the possibilities of Virtual and Augmented Reality, AI and Holograms are to some extent foreseeable as a BS learning experience, the appropriation of 3D Printing, Drones, the Internet of Things, Robots, Wearable Devices, Virtual Laboratories and Blockchain are more tenuous. The take-away from Hernandez-de-Menendez and colleagues' work, is that the competencies fostered by even the more tenuous technologies, may well be the ones an increasing capitalist colonisation of curriculum

---

[76] Dziuban et al., "Blended Learning: The New Normal and Emerging Technologies."

[77] Singh and Hardaker, "Barriers and Enablers to Adoption and Diffusion of ELearning : A Systematic Review of the Literature - a Need for an Integrative Approach."

[78] Tarhini, Hone, and Liu, "User Acceptance towards Web-Based Learning Systems: Investigating the Role of Social, Organizational and Individual Factors in European Higher Education."

[79] Abbasi et al., "Social, Organizational, Demography and Individuals' Technology Acceptance Behaviour: A Conceptual Model."

[80] Permatasari, Sensuse, and Santoso, "Cultural Aspects Influencing the Application of E-Learning: A Literature Review."

[81] Hernandez-de-Menendez, Escobar Díaz, and Morales-Menendez, "Technologies for the Future of Learning: State of the Art."

demands for future workforces—albeit masked by the promise of increased critical thinking, innovation, collaboration and creativity. However, they conclude there remains a requirement to inculcate, in the student, a lifelong learning ability that will enable them to face new challenges in their pursuit of a career. Post Covid-19, I therefore postulate my second critical uncertainty:

> **P2**: Higher BS education is characterised by more or less technology in the mediation of HE delivery, rather than an institutionalised, more socially informed search for knowledge.

Given a projection of the critical uncertainty **P2**, my concern is over the role and function of technology within the BS, in creating an effective learning environment. This is a question of whether the curriculum becomes a slave to technology. Is technology implemented because it exists and because, increasingly, its tested capabilities are better understood, yet ignored in their potential systemic impact? Or is technology, now better understood, used to the benefit of society? Given the impact of Covid-19, the knowledge that much face-to-face learning 'can' be moved online, may drive even blended learning to new applications, promoted by the 'Ed-Tech' marketplace. I might therefore imagine **(P2$_1$)** that all BS HE is delivered at a distance, within organizations that pay for their employees as students, with HEIs just one option on a human resource list of preferred MOOC suppliers. Or I might imagine **(P2$_2$)** that, aware of the technology-driven risk of massified, democratised content, we re-think the role and function of the HEI. Might we choose to capitalise on differentiation, and seek to offer something unique, where technology features in blending learning, but is no cause for slavery to it?

Regulatory frameworks (managerialism and accountability)

Alongside the neoliberal colonisation of HE curricula, and the technology-induced pull to blended learning, UK HEIs have—from the last decades of the twentieth century—faced increasing levels of bureaucratic reforms as instruments of accountability. These include the Research Excellence and Teaching Excellence Frameworks (REF and TEF). Such imposed audits of scholarly activity are designed to 'better' academic 'productivity' and 'competitiveness' within a marketised HE.

To some, the excellence frameworks are a distortion of the role and function of the HEI—'a centre for the acquisition and dissemination of knowledge, and for holding of the state and its institutions to account'.[82] Amid criticism of the

[82] O'Regan and Gray, "The Bureaucratic Distortion of Academic Work: A Transdisciplinary Analysis of the UK Research Excellence Framework in the Age of Neoliberalism," 546.

REF and TEF[83]—rendering 'universities, staff and students as neoliberal subjects'[84]—others place importance on maintaining a distinction between a 'marketizing' bureaucracy and a 'socialising' one, one that maintains institutional values of public good, lest there be a crisis of legitimation.[85] Thus, rather than a resistance to all forms of bureaucracy, my concern is directed to maintain the exercise of academic autonomy, protecting values 'other than those of entrepreneurship and consumer choice', for public or social good.[86]

In her own study, Kate Nash observed that, despite marketization, universities may have resisted losing much of the value of education, having maintained—to various extents—a distinction between education and training.[87] However, I argue that the 'value' foundations of BSs may be susceptible to erosion on the basis that—beyond the basic tools of business and organizational enterprise—a deep understanding of management is out of reach, and certainly not achievable in the timescales that the 'capitalist' market would seek to maintain competitive advantage. Thus, in a move to a 'Mode 2' knowledge of practice,[88] a search for the deep meaning of 'Mode 1' knowledge is, perhaps, viewed as a luxury. Here, the employed student—a product of colonised Mode 1 education—is seen simply to fail in the face of the complex and uncertain challenges of contemporary capitalism. Thus, following Kate Nash, BSs may realise value and strengthen their foundations through attending to the socialising bureaucracy that:

> '...helps academics communicate what counts as good teaching and learning, what counts as research and learning that is of academic merit, and what assumptions and biases should not be allowed to make a difference in these judgements'.[89]

I therefore arrive at my third critical uncertainty:

> **P3**: Higher BS education is characterised by more or less marketised bureaucracy set against a perceived market adhocracy, rather than an institutional bureaucracy of social 'goods'.

---

83 Shattock, "Better Informing the Market? The Teaching Excellence Framework in British Higher Education."

84 Morrish, "The Accident of Accessibility: How the Data of the TEF Creates Neoliberal Subjects," 364.

85 Welsh and Dehler, "Whither the MBA? Or the Withering of MBAs?"

86 Nash, "Neo-Liberalisation, Universities and the Values of Bureaucracy," 179.

87 Nash, "Neo-Liberalisation, Universities and the Values of Bureaucracy."

88 Gibbons, "Mode 2 Society and the Emergence of Context-Sensitive Science."

89 Nash, "Neo-Liberalisation, Universities and the Values of Bureaucracy," 185.

Here, given a projection of the critical uncertainty $\mathbf{P_3}$, my concern is over the impact of both a market-led bureaucracy within the BS that serves a highly competitive, customer focussed market, and its operation within a framework of academic autonomy, seeking to retain an identity as a centre for the acquisition and dissemination of knowledge. Ultimately, this may be resolved to a question of: what is it that the BS is perceived to be 'there' to deliver? For example, I might imagine **($P3_1$)** that the market—the employing businesses, organizations and society in general—may well question the point of an HE BS education which cannot adequately equip its students to face an increasingly complex and uncertain future. What value is such an education, when the concern is the acquisition of a requisite knowledge for immediate practice? When it is little more than the conversion of education to training, and eminently substitutable at lower cost and in shorter timescales? Alternatively, I might imagine **($P3_2$)** the post-Covid-19 BS as an HE bastion in the search for, and dissemination of, the necessary knowledge to hold both the state and its (capitalist) institutions to account. Counter-intuitively to the market, this is the acquisition of the sort of deep knowledge of critical thinking, innovation, collaboration, and creativity that is only (as yet) the mere promise of technology.

The baseline: reframing future business schools

Following the CCF method, Table 10.1 depicts the truth table for the range of future moments **(m_1-m_6)**. These are the contradictions in history **(h)** as a function of the three critical uncertainties, $\mathbf{P_1}$, $\mathbf{P_2}$ and $\mathbf{P_3}$.

Table 10.1. Truth table: contradictions of Business Schools

m	P_1	P_2	P_3	Scenario Outline
m_1	F	F	F	Historical discontinuity. Changes in the neoliberal colonisation of BS curriculum, a shift from technological mediated delivery to technology-mediated socialised learning, and changes to the implementation of marketised bureaucracy to benefit academic integrity.
m_2	F	F	T	No perceived change to the implementation of marketised bureaucracy to benefit from academic integrity.
m_3	F	T	F	No perceived shift from technological mediated delivery to technology-mediated socialised learning.
m_4	F	T	T	No shift from technologically mediated delivery to technology-mediated socialised learning, and no perceived change to the implementation of marketised bureaucracy to benefit from academic integrity.

m_5	T	F	F	No perceived change from the neoliberal colonisation of BS curriculum.
m_6	T	F	T	No perceived change from the neoliberal colonisation of BS curriculum, and no perceived change to the implementation of marketised bureaucracy to benefit from academic integrity.
m_7	T	T	F	No perceived change from the perceived neoliberal colonisation of BS curriculum, and no shift from technological mediated delivery to technology-mediated socialised learning.
m_8	T	T	T	Status quo. No changes in the perceived neoliberal colonisation of BS curriculum, no shift from technological mediated delivery to technology-mediated socialised learning, and no change to the implementation of marketised bureaucracy to benefit from academic integrity.

(T=true, F=false)

The counterfactuals: transposing the future of BS

The contradictions are shown graphically in Figure 10.1, together with the set of counterfactual imaginations (**$P1_1$ to $P3_2$**) that lie beyond the antagonistic horizon of a post-Covid-19 reality. The set of intuitively derived relationships between the contradictions and the imaginations show the relative coherence between each. Thus, the imaginations of interest—the provocations—represent the manipulations of a projected future by the researcher to reveal a position from which a perspective on the role and position of the HE BS can be taken, based on a certain expert knowledge of its antecedent conditions.

Coherent futures: the provocations of history...

From Figure 10.1, the most coherent of the imaginations introduced as a function of the present trends identified, is **$P1_1$**. Thus, beyond the antagonistic horizon and following exposure to the impact of Covid-19, I suggest that we may rationally foresee a future student movement arising, actively seeking decolonisation of the dominant neoliberalistic capitalist agenda in the HE BS curriculum. This movement might, for example, be part of a wider-HE movement, or it might simply be seen in a fall-off of potential BS students, disillusioned by poor work prospects and a falling interest in the better-understood risks of entrepreneurship, or a move to the substitutability of commercial courses, such as MOOCs. However, an alternative, only slightly less coherent imagined possibility is **$P3_2$**, in which, following Covid-19, BSs act counter-intuitively (to the market), and seek to regain a new position as a traditional bastion of HE, in the search for, and dissemination of, the necessary knowledge to hold both the state and its (capitalist) institutions to account.

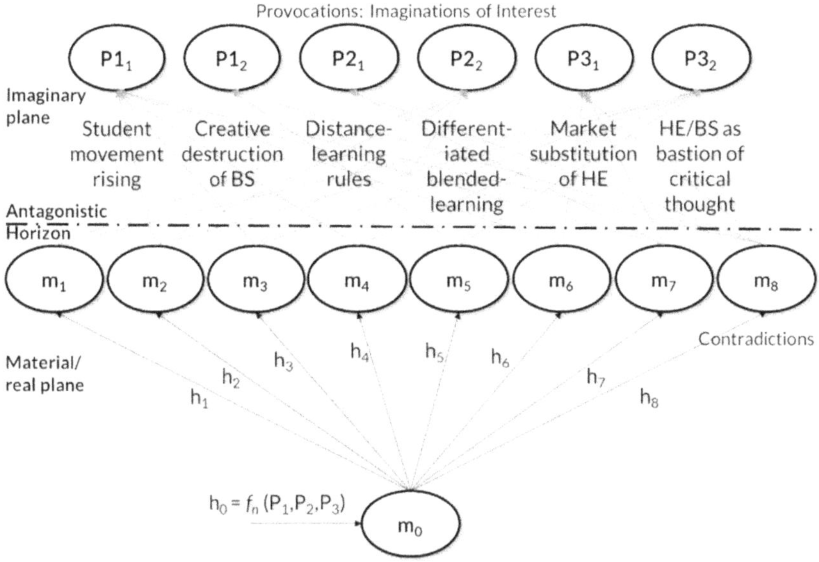

Figure 10.1. Finding truth in the future of Business Schools

A moderately coherent imagined outcome for the BS is $\mathbf{P2_2}$. That is the gaining of a better understanding of the technology-driven risk of massified, democratised content. Here, there is a rethinking of the role and function of the HEI, leading to the identification and capitalisation of differentiation, as the BS moves to offer something unique in tech-centred blended learning. Equally moderately coherent, is the imagined outcome, $\mathbf{P3_1}$. Here, the market—the employing businesses, organizations, etc.—reeling from the escalating impacts of the permacrisis, question the point of an HE BS education for its employees, citing its general inadequacy in equipping students for the complex and uncertain world of work. Employing organizations turn to increased use of non-HEI training, causing a loss of market share for the BS and HE in general.

The imagined outcomes showing least coherence with current trends include $\mathbf{P1_2}$ and $\mathbf{P2_1}$. In the former, an increasing level of capitalist colonisation, under a renewed imperative for economic growth, leads to the creative destruction of the BS as an HEI. Here, the extreme of a narrowed curriculum and pedagogy alienates the wider HEI, leading to a separation of the BS from its parent. Given the status of many BS as a key contribution to HEI budgets (as cash cows), this situation is thought least likely to arise. In the latter outcome, a future where all BS HE is delivered as a MOOC, at a distance—perhaps through increasing use of apprenticeships—represents a similar prospect to the former case, **P1**$_2$.

Allegoric speculation: in the land of Oz...

In speculating on the future, I revisit L. Frank Baum's classic story, *The Wonderful Wizard of Oz,* including the Tin Woodman and his friends from Chapter 6. However, here, I simply allow the characters their original voices—gone is the Žižekean sublimity of the *Four Horsemen.* Yet I retain the story's allegoric usefulness, reflecting on current economic and political issues. Firstly, I recast the BS persona in the character of the Tin Woodman.

The business school as the Tin Woodman

> 'I shall take the heart,' [said] the Tin Woodman; 'for brains do not make one happy, and happiness is the best thing in the world.'[90]

The Tin Woodman, as we are told, is in search of a heart. The Tin Woodman wants to feel love. But, here, neoliberalism, as the bedrock of contemporary capitalism, has within its foundations the concept of the rational economic person—the idea of the pure reason of economic agents, workers, and consumers.[91] Feelings are generally excluded from the rational within organizations, and neoliberalism's concern with material self-interest has left elements of society 'morally queasy about business'.[92] Despite the critique of Sherwin Klein and others over the apparent disdain for feelings, and the considerable literature on the role of emotions in organizations, it has been argued that the discourse on emotions has simply been rationalised and subsumed within the overall rational argument. Here, emotions (for example: emotional intelligence, organizational culture and the commercialisation of experience) are little more than tools for gaining a competitive edge, revealing the corporate 'rationality of the managerial governing of emotions. ...[It is] the submission of emotional life to neoliberal rationality'.[93] Alongside the Tin Woodman, I ask: where is the heart in that?

The submission of emotional life is, fundamentally, the character of the colonisation in trend **P**$_1$; it is the dominant antecedent of outcome **P1**$_1$. Here, I may gaze into the Wizard's crystal ball and take a helicopter perspective from

[90] Baum, The Wonderful Wizard of Oz, 52.
[91] Andrade, "Emotional Economic Man: Power and Emotion in the Corporate World"; Klein, "The Head, the Heart, and Business Virtues."
[92] Klein, "The Head, the Heart, and Business Virtues," 355.
[93] Andrade, "Emotional Economic Man: Power and Emotion in the Corporate World," 801.

the future. Rationally, I may speculatively foresee a student movement arising, actively seeking a decolonisation of the dominant neoliberalistic capitalism in the HE BS curriculum. The movement seeks a more compassionate capitalism, one with a heart. However, I also speculate that this movement might not manifest itself in direct action. It might simply—and more subtly—be seen through reducing numbers for the more capitalist-focused business courses. These are the ones that seemingly lack heart. Certainly, ex-students, disillusioned by poor work prospects and a falling interest in the better-understood risks of entrepreneurship and self-employment, may question the usefulness of business calculus and international business skills, when they are destined for little more than a portfolio career of gigging opportunities. Instead, they may consciously seek out courses that advance soft skills, such as communication and problem-solving.[94]

Consider the value to businesses and organizations of the study of literature or drama[95] in communicating, and of history and engineering in the practice of problem-solving. Yet, reflecting on the present from my speculative position in the future, the trend of neoliberal colonisation of the BS curriculum has continued for some time. It has inertia, as faculty have been recruited around its core, rational foundations. As curricula and research have narrowed, fuelling both a weakening literature and undergraduate recruitment criteria that feed back into both secondary and primary education curricula, the inertia builds. We self-select mediocrity. A conformity to marketization—and thus the potential for resistance to it—is undermined.[96]

Through my Wizard's helicopter perspective on the neoliberal trend, if I acknowledge the growing disenchantment with neoliberal, capitalist thinking, we, as did the Tin Woodman, face the choice of pursuing a heart. As a 'cyclone' [sic] catalysed the journey of the characters in Baum's classic tale, so one might look, from Covid-19 to the permacrisis, as the catalyst to a new journey for BSs. For the BS as the Tin Woodman, in search of a heart, I speculate on the coherence with the imagined state **$P3_2$**. Here, counter to the present trend of marketization, there is a choice available to seek a new position closer to the heart and traditions of HE; a choice in which there is a renewed search for, and dissemination of, the social and humanistic knowledge required to hold both state and institutions to account, contesting the managerial reductionism

94 Garner et al., "Exploring the Gap between Employers' Needs and Undergraduate Business Curricula: A Survey of Alumni Regarding Core Business Curricula."

95 Starkey, Tempest, and Cinque, "Management Education and the Theatre of the Absurd."

96 Collyer, "Practices of Conformity and Resistance in the Marketisation of the Academy: Bourdieu, Professionalism and Academic Capitalism."

of complex socio-economic challenges.[97] Such a search for the heart of HE in the BS environment is an acknowledgement of the need to address capitalist excesses. Elsewhere, the journey in search of a heart is evidenced in the turn to social innovation and sustainability.[98] But, as Annie Snelson-Powell and her colleagues imply, the journey is a difficult one, with the danger of institutional decoupling and the loss of yet more heart(s) to rationalism.[99]

> 'You people with hearts,' [said the Tin Woodman], 'have something to guide you, and need never do wrong; but I have no heart, and so I must be very careful.'[100]

The business school as the Scarecrow

> '…I do not want people to call me a fool,[', said the Scarecrow, ']and if my head stays stuffed with straw instead of with brains, as yours is, how am I ever to know anything?'[101]

When we meet the Scarecrow, we learn he is wanting a brain. He embarks on the journey to the see the Wizard of Oz along a road paved with uneven bricks. Sometimes these bricks are broken or missing altogether and, having no brain, he walks ahead, stepping into holes and falling at full length on the hard surface. But, made of straw, such falls do not hurt him—with his companions to help, he makes progress. As we follow the story, we learn that the Scarecrow does have some knowledge—he is just not aware of what and how it might be used. Here, a head stuffed with information it neither needs nor can apply, or with information that is: ill-informed, untrusted, unrecognised, or inappropriate, might as well be a head stuffed with straw.

In the contemporary context, we may look to our hands—in them, we may see all the knowledge of the world. Untold bytes of data are stuffed within a digital cloud. A digital head stuffed with straw. Yet, what do we know and how can we know it? I speculate that this is a direct appeal to question the trend **P**$_2$—the role of technology in mediating HE. In particular, I question technology's role in communicating the gap between science, technology and

---

[97] Starkey, Tempest, and Cinque, "Management Education and the Theatre of the Absurd."
[98] McKelvey and Zaring, "Co-Delivery of Social Innovations: Exploring the University's Role in Academic Engagement with Society"; Winfield and Ndlovu, "'Future-Proof Your Degree': Embedding Sustainability and Employability at Nottingham Business School (NBS)."
[99] Snelson-Powell, Grosvold, and Millington, "Business School Legitimacy and the Challenge of Sustainability: A Fuzzy Set Analysis of Institutional Decoupling."
[100] Baum, The Wonderful Wizard of Oz, 61.
[101] Baum, The Wonderful Wizard of Oz, 32.

society. Here, at the heart of communications, lies the concept of literacy, and in a more focussed conceptualisation, digital literacy.[102] In the guise of the BS venturing forth in search of a brain, the Scarecrow must acknowledge that what is required is not memory for the acquisition and retention of knowledge, but a capability and capacity for inculcating learning within the self.

The Wizard invites us to take a helicopter perspective on this question of self-learning, from the position of imagined outcome $\mathbf{P2_2}$—the gaining of an understanding of the technology-driven risk of massified, democratised content. From this position, I see that Holger Pötzsch's critical view of digital literacy enables engagement with the ambiguity of technology,[103] in that it at once represents both political notions of freedom and control over knowledge, and where the nature of knowledge itself is modified by capital.[104] This encourages the consideration that reflective, investigative and mature learning might best be fostered through traditional teaching methods or existing technologies.[105] It resists the sorts of political and commercial control of those seeking to further monetise, ever-advancing and novel ways of manipulating the metaphoric straw in our collective heads. What value AI, if it is only set to rearrange the straw?

In search of a brain to accommodate critical self-learning, I argue that we may re-think the role and function of the BS in the HEI context. Here exists the potential for the identification and capitalisation of difference, as the BS moves to offer something unique in technology-centred blended learning—where the tendency to over-technologise is resisted by retention of more traditional methods. Consider, for example, Weber's concern with the transmission of expert knowledge and the exercise of logical analysis.[106] Anecdotally, one can experience 'posts' and comments on the professional social network LinkedIn[107]—at the cross-over from academic learning to professional (business) training. Such 'posts' frequently posit audiobooks, E-

---

[102] Pötzsch, "Critical Digital Literacy: Technology in Education beyond Issues of User Competence and Labour-Market Qualifications."
[103] Pötzsch, "Critical Digital Literacy: Technology in Education beyond Issues of User Competence and Labour-Market Qualifications," 226.
[104] Ouellet and Martin, "University Transformations and the New Knowledge Production Regime in Informational Capitalism."
[105] Pötzsch, "Critical Digital Literacy: Technology in Education beyond Issues of User Competence and Labour-Market Qualifications," 227.
[106] Ringer, "Education, Knowledge, and Vocation"; Weber, "Science as a Vocation."
[107] A comment from a business school lecturer/tech-innovation consultant in response to a post from the head of another business school on the different ways people learn and the solutions available to them. These ways were noted as particularly relevant during the Covid-19 pandemic (LinkedIn, 24/04/2020).

Books and course workbooks on the assumption that 'when you drop lectures', content must enable students to access it in any given situation. Certainly, technology allows the easy production of video podcasts, but I argue that we need to ask the question: how does such content amount to 'critical' and/or 'immersive' learning?

If HE content resolves to audiobooks for use in the car and walking, what does it say about the nature of critical engagement with a subject—given elements of the brain are off looking at the dangers of uneven terrain; *en voiture ou à pied*, the Scarecrow is in danger of repeatedly falling. While tech-enhanced devices for communicating knowledge have a time and place, one can happily debate the difference to the level and quality of engagement they might offer in isolation. To understand this, I argue we need to revisit, briefly, the role of the university in society. Here, Deborah Zornes highlights the three pillars of education, research and service—the engagement with, and delivery of services to, communities that have relationships with the university—and that these pillars are inclusive of the notions of social responsibility and responsiveness.[108] However, I speculate, here, that the massification of HE in the BS environment—as, in effect, training for employment—only appears to satisfy responsibility to the politically driven (social) neoliberal agenda. A massified, technology-mediated, simple communication of, for example, management and organizational learning, is deficient in both social responsibility and responsiveness to the communities it serves.

> 'I shall ask for brains instead of a heart;[' said the Scarecrow, ']for a fool would not know what to do with a heart if he had one.'[109]

The business school as the Cowardly Lion

> '...I learned that if I roared very loudly every living thing was frightened and got out of my way[,' said the Cowardly Lion. ']Whenever I've met a man I've been awfully scared; but I just roared at him, and he has always run away... I'm such a coward...'[110]

Money (and its capitalist concern) shouts—it roars like a Lion. Like Baum's Cowardly lion, bounding into the path of the Tin Woodman, and the

---

108 Zornes, 'The Business of the University: Research, Its Place in the "Business", and the Role of the University in Society.'
109 Baum, The Wonderful Wizard of Oz, 52.
110 Baum, The Wonderful Wizard of Oz, 57.

Scarecrow,[111] with one blow money might be said to have sent the search for a brain *'spinning over and over to the edge of the road'* and, to its surprise, its sharp claws have failed to make an impression on the surface of a search for a heart; yet the search falls and lies, still, in the road. Only when the Cowardly Lion receives a 'slap' on its nose, does it admit to its cowardice, hanging its head in shame: *'But how can I help it?',* says a lion in search of courage.

Constrained by its culture—as the *de facto* King of the Jungle—the lion is conditioned to exercise its prerogative to roar. It does so as easily as breathing. Imagine the BS as the new lion on the capitalist block, forming ever closer relationships with other capitalist institutions and increasingly reliant on conformity to the marketised bureaucracy[112] for its food. The contemporary lion has become consigned to the wildlife park. Here, I speculate on the bureaucratic trend **P3**. Rather than a certain adhocracy and a position of strength and influence in the wider society, the BS lion risks the limited confines of a marketised economy, blind to the richness beyond. While some point to the contribution of HE to the social-economic performance of globalised markets,[113] this is a narrow perspective of achieving economic competitiveness. But, HE must also be considered in its relation to advancing human, social and psychological capitals.

Stepping into the Wizard's helicopter, my coherent, speculative perspective is the imagined outcome **P3**$_1$. The HE BS market—the businesses and organizations employing its students—reels from the impact of the Covid-19-led permacrisis. Slapped on its nose, the Cowardly Lion's position in the safari park is questioned. What value does it really deliver to flailing organizations, through their employment of ex-students with impressive HE BS qualifications? The students themselves question such value. What value a student's qualifications—when they cannot even gain a meaningful job (let alone career) opportunity? What value—when so much of what students have spent their valuable time and money on learning, seems inappropriate or inadequate in the face of the VUCA world of work they seek to join?

Technology is a leveller, not in the sense of achieving equality and social justice, but in its ability to creatively destroy all institutions; it lifts Porter's threat of product and service substitutability through new levels of innovation. I therefore speculate that when perceptions of value are—at best—poor, the costs of tightly constrained, irresponsive and massified HE BS

---

[111] Baum, The Wonderful Wizard of Oz, 54.

[112] With reference to the UK's research and teaching excellence and knowledge exchange frameworks (REF, TEF, KEF).

[113] Volchik, Oganesyan, and Olejarz, "Higher Education as a Factor of Socio-Economic Performance and Development."

products are to be set against the costs of commercially delivered ones, of similar quality. The consequence? The consequence can only be a loss of HE market share to non-HE suppliers. Witness the growth of Ed-Tech. As HE BS open their doors to commercial and private delivery partners, able to demonstrate both capability and responsive delivery performance, it may only take a realisation that the same knowledge already exists in the public domain. If the only thing separating the communication of that knowledge is institutional accreditation—when even that is challenged as intrinsically 'value-less'—what then, for the HE BS? Does it label neoliberalism a 'fright term'—a signifier of resistance to change in the HE environment?[114]

The proximity of HE BSs to the social reality of their massified, commercialised products and services—in essence, an appeal to the excesses of capitalism—suggests the 'fright' is best considered an existential threat. Arguably, with its proximity to the threat, the HE BS does not possess the level of immunity offered by a purer, more traditionally 'liberal' HE context. Here, the impact of a BS on a given region, in terms of its financial contribution, community, attractiveness and image, has been considered in relation to the question: what would happen to that region, if its BS were to disappear?[115] Predating the Covid-19 crisis, Michel Kalika and colleagues observed that, within Europe, some BSs have become increasingly weak, only to discover salvation through mergers and absorptions. Within the UK, Covid-19 was an accelerant. At the time of my initial writing up of this part of my inquiry, some universities were experiencing increasingly precarious finances.[116] What price a BS on the open market? What value an inoculation of HE wisdom from philosophy, political theory and sociology?[117]

The ditch ahead of them was very wide. And very deep, with many big, jagged rocks at the bottom. The sides were so steep non could climb down. It seemed the journey to Oz had reached its end.

> 'I think I could jump over it,' said the Cowardly Lion. 'I am terribly afraid of falling… but I suppose there is nothing to do but try it. So get on my back… [we'll] make the attempt.'[118]

---

[114] Tight, "The Neoliberal Turn in Higher Education."
[115] Kalika, Shenton, and Dubois, "What Happens If a Business School Disappears? The Intellectual Foundations of BSIS."
[116] Foster, "Universities' Plea for £ 2bn Bailout Falls on Deaf Ears in Treasury."
[117] Statler, "Developing Wisdom in a Business School? Critical Reflections on Pedagogical Practice."
[118] Baum, The Wonderful Wizard of Oz, 64–65.

Reconciling experts, wizards and BS change

Intuitively, we may imbue the concept of a trend with qualities of both inertia and elasticity. A trend has inertia by virtue of its potential to continue in its direction of travel with seemingly little external motivation—a 'do nothing' scenario. A trend exhibits elasticity if, at once interrupted or influenced by some external force, it returns to its previous direction of travel—flexing, stretching, but not breaking its course. In common with other trends throughout the various stages of my inquiry, my exploration of three major uncertainties (**P_1, P_2, P_3**) has identified an expert perspective that can reasonably be held to exhibit a high degree of inertia, and a good degree of elasticity. These trends have seemingly maintained their direction for at least several decades and, despite crises and some attempts at influencing their direction of travel, have stayed relatively true to course. They are trends with the inertia of a super-tanker and the elasticity of movement of a spinning gyroscope. But, as my speculations highlight, there is the inevitable question of risk, exacerbated by uncertainty. Antagonistically, are HE BSs content in the face of such fundamental trends? Are they unable or unwilling to challenge their elasticity or inertia? Can they face the other, revealing their character in its potentiality? Or have they already been colonised by that other?

While three trends are highlighted, there is a dominant recurrence of **P_1**—the increasing neoliberalism of HE. While providing a service to capitalism, HEIs increasingly fail to hold both the state and its capitalist institutions to account. Arguably, in the UK at least, with the increasing homogeneity of neoliberal politics, there is no other institution remaining with the potential to correct this situation. While others suggest scope for HE curriculum innovation in, for example, community and service learning[119] and citizenship,[120] such initiatives—although important—merely play to the state. They accept the individualistic onus of social responsibility and responsiveness placed on the individual, where, as the Covid-19 pandemic revealed, there is already (and arguably always has been) a deep, underlying 'living tapestry' of individuals 'prepared to turn round and help by [their] own efforts those who are unfortunate'.[121]

Margaret Thatcher's comment that 'there's no such thing as society',[122] represented an abdication of state responsibility to society, and a licence to

---

[119] Annette, Community, Service Learning and Higher Education in the UK.

[120] John Annette and Terence McLaughlin, "Citizenship and Higher Education in the UK," in ed. by J. Arthur and K. Bohlin, Citizenship and Higher Education: The Role of Universities in Communities and Society (Routledge, 2005).

[121] Thatcher, "No Such Thing as Society."

[122] Thatcher, "No Such Thing as Society."

the excesses of capitalism that has, arguably, been inadequately challenged by those with the capability and authority to do so. Yet we witnessed armies of furloughed individuals raising private, charitable funds and employing traditional low-level skills, to sew and fashion essential medical protective clothing that could not be adequately supplied through the state and its capitalist enterprises. Did the Covid-19 pandemic present the sort of threat to stretch the elasticity of the underlying trend to breaking point? And what of a permacrisis? Does it present the sort of energy to fundamentally change the nature and direction of the trend? Or is there a danger of returning to a status quo?

My argument is antagonistically conceptual in nature. It is a provocation designed to raise questions, rather than provide answers. In this respect, in the context of examining the long-term potential of the BS in HE, it is worth restating Kurt Lewin's three objectives of scientific development.[123] These are:

1. the (post-disciplinary) need to integrate social sciences;
2. the need to move from the description of the field to a study of its dynamic problems; and
3. the development of new instruments and techniques of research.

In a sense, there is nothing new here. Yet, amid the Covid-19 pandemic, there was a sense that all had changed. *Plus ça change, plus c'est la même chose.* Extending Lewin's argument into the realm of the BS, its contribution to (the poverty of) human capital—and, by extension to social and psychological capitals—is unlikely to be served as a slave to commerciality. The BS must first rise to Lewin's challenge that a science (of the BS's domain) cannot proceed beyond a certain stage without entertaining conceptual development. This may require change. Certainly, to reconcile the BS within the HE environment, I again draw on Lewin's explication of the problem of social change and speculate a three-step process of unfreezing, moving, and refreezing. This is a response to Riina Koris and colleagues' call to legitimately position the BS as a university.[124] It is in this sense that inspiration can be drawn from Jones's comment that the Covid-19 pandemic might have given us the 'best chance to

---

[123] Lewin, Frontiers in Group Dynamics: Concept, Method and Reality in Social Science; Social Equilibria and Social Change, 1:5.
[124] Koris, Örtenblad, and Ojala, "From Maintaining the Status Quo to Promoting Free Thinking and Inquiry: Business Students' Perspective on the Purpose of Business School Teaching."

change universities for good'.[125] Here, I consider the Covid-19 event as the catalyst to unfreeze a current mode of thought.

In this inquiry into the BS, I have sought to cast a light on the capacity and capability of an educational subsystem to change. Here, there is hope in the potential of BSs to drive a new academic agenda, in differentiation of the commercialisation of their space. However, unfrozen in thought, what room is there for movement and ideas? Where might the motivation for change come from? I venture that this inquiry extends, by virtue of similar argumentation, to the range of education required for a society preparing for a world of meaningful, purposeful and enterprising work. On unfrozen ground, the opportunity for change does not remain for long. Not, perhaps, until the next unprecedented, unexpected and complex event. Yet, while we move from crisis to crisis, hope may remain alive. Although both I[126] and others[127] have explored analogies of the BS with The Bauhaus—an exemplar of such movement and ideas—I simply suggest that a failure to consider even a bad wizard as a well-intentioned person,[128] may see the future landscape of education change in unexpected, and uncontrolled ways. In reconciliation, *Design thinking* applied to learning scaffolds and structures relating to: 1) how any craft skills might be best taught and committed to practice; 2) how the practice of creativity and innovation can be inculcated to extend any craft; and 3) how the practice of envisioning can be inculcated and sanctioned as a legitimate practice in its own right, may hold the key to controlled change.

Certainly, there is a need for both a heart and courage in reassessing the knowledge to be delivered to students as they enter the world of enterprising work. But, in this respect, there is significant inertia and elasticity to be overcome in the educational system.

---

[125] Jones, "Covid-19 Is Our Best Chance to Change Universities for Good."

[126] Atkinson, Thinking the Art of Management: Stepping into "Heidegger's Shoes."

[127] Volkmann and De Cock, "The Bauhaus and the Business School: Exploring Analogies, Resisting Imitation."

[128] Grimmelikhuijsen, "A Good Man but a Bad Wizard. about the Limits and Future of Transparency of Democratic Governments."

Chapter 11

Dancing the VUCA: emergence

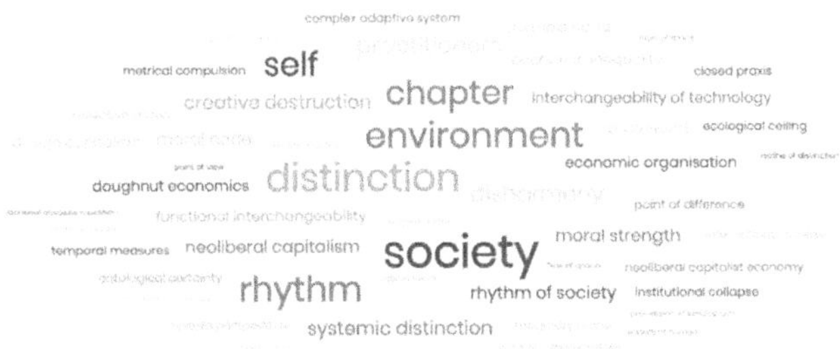

IS THREE A MAGIC NUMBER? In contemplating the ditch—the abyss—ahead of us, taking in its depth, and the many big, jagged rocks that line its walls, and which we might imagine lie at the bottom, beyond our sight, I stand with others in critical contemplation also. In *Reimagining Capitalism In a World on Fire*, Rebecca Henderson offers a thought-provoking exposé of 'why and how we can build a profitable, equitable, and sustainable capitalism by changing how we think about the purpose of firms, their role in society, and their relationship to government and the state.'[1] However, I believe a focus on firms as a solution risks a drive toward business and economic resilience. It risks foundering on jagged rocks. Therefore, in this Chapter, I turn to question the need for such resilience. I posit that resilience is the wrong word. I do so, on the basis of questioning three things.

Following my inquiries herein, I believe that I can safely set aside Henderson's 'why' capitalism—at least as we have come to know it—is destined for failure; that is, if we cannot already adjudge it failed. I am therefore left with the 'how'. This is a question set amid the context of what Henderson posits are 'the three great problems of our time': 1) massive environmental degradation, 2) economic inequality, and 3) institutional collapse.[2] Her position is, in no small way, another form of my own—how to organize our 'selves' and 'others' in our environment of VUCA crises and economic injustice—but with one major exception. At the outset of my inquiry, I did not prejudge the form of solution. I did not suggest that the solution was to be found through 'changing how we

[1] Henderson, Reimagining Capitalism In a World on Fire, 4.
[2] Henderson, Reimagining Capitalism In a World on Fire, 7–8.

think about the purpose of firms, their role in society, and their relationship to government and the state.' I do not disagree with either the sentiment or the detail presented by Henderson. Hers is an insightful work. I merely suggest there is a place, and indeed a requirement, for an alternative perspective—based on an alternative (immanent) critique. Against this note, in this penultimate Chapter, I pick up the theme of the potential for controlled change, with a focus on education.

The concerns expressed in Henderson's three problematics are well rehearsed. A scan of the titles of innumerable references, from which I have only drawn on a sample in this book, testify to their perennial nature. Indeed, *The Grumbling Hive: OR, Knaves Turn'd Honest*, owes its very existence to the same concerns—a poem published in 1705, over 300 years prior to both Henderson's and my own work. Our concerns are shared. As Henderson observes, the world is not short of individuals, groups and corporations all diligently attempting to make a difference. In the UK, Cadbury's became a stand-out example of a socially aware, purpose-led firm. Yet, as Henderson recalls, that was a journey started in 1861, with the brothers George and Richard Cadbury.[3] Over 150 years ago. Yet still, as I recall in Chapter 8, *An Invisible Hand*, in discussing the paradoxical nature of the FAANGs, I question the social purposes of those held by many to be the exemplars of contemporary commercial success.

Consider the magic number three. By magic, I simply refer to 'the art, or pretended art, of controlling natural phenomena by preternatural means.'[4] Thus, I extend the idea that we might consider the preternatural possibility of controlling various phenomena by means of three elements, dimensions, factors, or components. As a remedy for control, the magic lies in one knowing 'the proper combination of magic details.'[5] Let me simply re-express Henderson's three problematics as the triadic dimensions: environment, equality and institutions. I ask: to what extent might these three dimensions be representative of the phenomenon of our global society? Is there a natural combination, order, degree, or some other proper combination that suggests a perfect society? A desirable system of social performativity? If so, where in this triad of essential components do we see the primacy of business as a controlling factor?

In this book, it is on the question of the perceived primacy of business that I have set a point of departure from those others who write on the same subject. We live, as a society, within one global environment. That this environment is

---

[3] Henderson, Reimagining Capitalism In a World on Fire, 111–14.
[4] Tavenner, "Three as a Magic Number in Latin Literature."
[5] Tavenner, "Three as a Magic Number in Latin Literature," 142.

limited, has supplied our technologies and other resources, and has seen significant degradation over the years is without a doubt. As a society of humans, our sense of equality, economic or otherwise, is inextricably linked to our sense of identity. Our identities are set within the context of our individual circumstances and needs, our geo-location, our access to resources, and our agency and choice of action. As a society of humans possessed of the 'animal passions' of humanity, just as in Mandeville's *The Fable of the Bees*, we look to the social concept of justice, enacted through institutional form, to 'lop and bind' the excesses of individual vice. The very prevalent issues of environmental degradation, economic inequality and institutional collapse, cannot, I suggest, be left to the primacy of business alone to offer solutions.

As I set out in Chapter 1, "An Inspector Calls", any recommendations for remedial action by businesses simply calls on the existing, unjust socio-economic system environment for their implementation. Such remedial action is little more than a gesture against the inertia and elasticity that I have set out as being symptomatic of *autopoiesis*—the dialectic order of *homeostasis*. It is a drive toward business and economic resilience and the contrast of a desirable *poiesis*. Here, I have already questioned the need for such resilience and posited that resilience is the wrong word. Do we really need a more resilient 'business' economy to drive society? I say again, this is not the resilience of individuals. My alternate perspective has been to ask: 'what if we change the socio-economic system first—away from the autopoiesis of resilience?' Might it be the right thing to do, even if we make mistakes trying?

I proceed as follows. In drawing a convergence of my inquiries into entrepreneurship, work and enterprise, I move on from this short critique of Henderson's position to highlight the order of society's problematics and note the rhythm of its enterprising creative destruction. This leads me to reject the autopoiesis of dialectic complex adaptive systems. Rather, drawing on a reading of Niklas Luhmann's lecture on Observing, and the contemporary aesthetics of Giorgio Agamben, I call for an enhancement of first-order poietic action through inculcating an aesthetic sensibility. Then, to illustrate—to imagine—the application of Design Capitalism, I set out the example of extruding the doughnut of Kate Raworth's Doughnut Economics.

A sense of order

I believe there is something insightful in the order of stating Henderson's three problematics. If I am to suggest 1) environmental degradation, 2) economic inequality, and then 3) institutional collapse, there is a sense in which this may be taken as an *order-of-business*. Thus, if we can 'transform the world's firms' to address environmental issues and economic inequality first—albeit, as Henderson suggests, a hard-enough task—then we might move to the even harder task of 'transforming the world's social and political systems'.[6] But a $12trillion opportunity, translated into a business case for meeting the UN's 17 Sustainable Development Goals,[7] bears little immediate relevance to individuals who—having become willing or not-so-willing entrepreneurs—now face post-Covid-19 and in the midst of a cost-of-living crisis, the potential decimation of entire industries within an uncertain world order.

Let me consider the case of the enterprising eco-system of small independent businesses—that liminal form of entrepreneurship: the self-employed and the freelance workers—that constitute and support the global entertainment industry. In the US, months after the Covid-19 outbreak, it was reported that Hollywood studios and unions sought Congressional support to revive their battered industry.[8] And, in the UK, after the mid-2020 relaxation of many lockdown measures, theatres remained closed. The UK's 'Stage heavyweights' warned of the industry's perilous state, while the actors' union, Equity, voiced its belief that the government's self-employment support scheme was not enough, and campaigned for a better deal for freelancers.[9]

From Chapter 5, *Work: Experts and storytellers,* I recall the issues of employment displacement visible in the proportion of UK businesses that employ others. This fell from one-third of all businesses in 2000 to one-quarter in 2019. The decline in employers was seemingly offset by a disproportionate increase in self-employment. Under the impact of the Covid-19 pandemic, we witnessed the inability of the state to equitably support its citizens, many of whom, through no fault of their own, saw their incomes decimated. To a significant proportion of society, a $12 trillion business case for sustainable development is too remote an opportunity. From Chapter 3, *The contrary entrepreneur,* I saw no immediate call to action at an individual level, offering little pull to balance an individual's needs through enterprising action to change business and society for the better. Post-Covid, the individual is more likely pushed to take whatever action is necessary to meet the imbalance of their own immediate needs. And, in the face of the cost-of-living crisis post-Russisa's February 2022 incursion into Ukraine, such imbalances persist, with increasing numbers of society unable to afford the high cost of fuel.

In a push to restore balance, a call on the animal passions is a call to arms in a personal battle to survive. Thus, the order of the problematics of society is important. To the individual, it matters, first: that the institutions (particularly

---

[6] Henderson, Reimagining Capitalism In a World on Fire, 5.
[7] Henderson, Reimagining Capitalism In a World on Fire, 255.
[8] McNary, "Entertainment Industry Seeks Legislative Relief From COVID- 19 Impact."
[9] Cook, "Coronavirus + the UK Entertainment Industr y — the Latest."

of justice) prevent the excesses of vice; that they are properly constituted and resourced by the state; and that there is a widely held trust in them to act accordingly. Secondly, to the individual it matters that the institutions of the state ensure society's subsystems—for example: the economy, law, and education—function in the interests of the society and its individuals on an equitable basis, without fear or favour. And, thirdly, it matters to the individual that no one, or nobody (public, private, profit or non-profit), be allowed to degrade the environment. The problems of society are too important to be left to the tune of business. Rather, business would be best choreographed to dance to society's tune.

The rhythm of a VUCA world

The present rhythm of our neoliberal capitalist world, the rhythm of neoliberal capitalist business, is the rhythm of creative destruction—the variation in length and accentuation of cycles of creation and destruction, as new sweeps out the old. As I surfaced in Chapter 7, "Ghosts of democracy", our Western economies appear to have danced to the wrong tune, choreographed by the prophets of neoliberal capitalism. Here, Schumpeter's 'sleight-of-hand' in misdirecting the choreography of economies is self-evident, expounded by corporate-level self-interest—a vice sanctioned as a virtue in the service of *pleonexia*. And, globally, the neoliberal capitalist prophets appear to colonise the routes of international trade. Yet, recently, the cycles of creative destruction have seemingly achieved little more than accelerate the destruction of the democratic institutions that Western societies have looked to, and continue to do so, for their support—where in the UK one might work for a £1(UKP) per hour benefit.[10]

Under the rhythm of creative destruction, the theory and technological rationality—or instrumental reasoning—that underpins most complexity and systems approaches has, to date, simply fuelled the fire of neoliberalism. Perhaps reflecting Henderson's *World on Fire*, Christian Fuchs argues these approaches—viewing the economy as a complex adaptive system—have merely allowed an ideological justification of neoliberal capitalism's value. This is 'the market [as] a self-organising system', in denial of social problems.[11] In essence, a denial of any coherent sense of morality. Here, philosopher Michael Sandel has called for a moral and political renewal.[12] And here, I reject the autopoiesis of dialectic complex adaptive systems. Precisely because

---

[10] Garthwaite et al., "A Commentary on Encountering Austerity; the Experiences of Four Men Living in a London Hostel."

[11] Fuchs, Commun. Capital. A Crit. Theory, 4.

[12] Sandel, The Tyranny of Merit.

of the communications problematic I have outlined in my preceding inquiries, while undoubtedly complex, neoliberal capitalism is a closed system. It is not an open subsystem of economic organization. It has no (or at least minimal) access to a requisite variety pool. It increasingly lacks capacity for endogenous adaptability. From a critical—as opposed to naïve—systems perspective, neoliberal capitalist ideology, romanced by what it has clearly and previously achieved for its incumbents and those enfranchised to its identity, has failed to understand the true nature of a self-organizing system. It has failed to understand that the economy is merely a 'perceived' subsystem of a society that—in many respects—its 'closed' code of *a*moral communications insulates it from.

As Michael Jackson explains, critical systems thinking accepts that it is 'impossible for any systems or complexity theory approach to provide the kind of prior understanding of complex adaptive systems that would allow intervention on the basis of explanation, prediction, and control.'[13] In the sense that the social system is open, it is unknowable. Yet, in the sense that, unwittingly perhaps, the economic system has been rendered 'closed', 'homeostatic' and 'sclerotic', I argue that it is knowable—to the extent that we can know it does not function as we might believe or anticipate that it should. In this 'critical' sense, I may explore the problem situation and seek to design solutions that address the (re)opening of the system to greater adaptability and epiphenomenal emergence. I argue we must accept the impossibility of control,[14] and learn to trust the system's ability to embrace emergence. But first, we must understand the moral rhythm of society within which the dance toward postcapitalism is to be performed. Here, I side with Niklas Luhmann's view that 'social theory must give up its quest for ontological certainty'.[15] Indeed, a negative dialectic understanding does just that, denying an ontological certainty by diverting attention from the conceptually ontological to the pre-ontic state of constantly becoming—the emergent, non-conceptually real.

---

[13] Jackson, "Critical Systems Thinking and Practice : What Has Been Done and What Needs Doing."

[14] In Ashby's requisite variety, the notion of control is important, though Goldstein refers to it as 'regulation', in the sense of the systemic 'processes and mechanisms' that enable a system to return to a goal-seeking state, once subject to a disturbance, such as a crisis. See: Ashby and Goldstein, "Requisite Variety and the Difference That Makes a Difference: An Introduction to W. Ross Ashby's 'Variety, Constraint and Law of Requisite Variety' Cybernetics, Regulation, and Complex Systems."

[15] Jackson, "Critical Systems Thinking and Practice : What Has Been Done and What Needs Doing."

The rhythm of society

As Friedrich Nietzsche posits in *Beyond Good and Evil* (and, apposite to my inquiry, subtitled: *Prelude to a Philosophy of the Future*), 'What is essential and inestimable in every morality is that it constitutes a long compulsion: to understand... one should recall the compulsion under which every language [or code] so far has achieved strength and freedom—the metrical compulsion of rhyme and rhythm.'[16] As the *a*morality of the capitalist code gains its strength and 'freedom of self-interest' from the 'metrical compulsion of creative destruction', so I argue that a society's morality—its foundation—must gain strength and freedom from the humanistic rhyme and rhythm of its people. However, while the rhythm of life might be taken from human nature, it is not, as Nietzsche believes, *laisser-aller*—without constraints or regulation.

I recall Chapter 8, "An invisible hand", I suggest that as we humans reach a degree of adulthood, it is in our nature to desire to give birth—whether to an idea or through procreation—under harmonious conditions to achieve immortality (or sustained life). In following our nature, we have a choice: to do so or not to do so. Once committed to giving birth, I have posited that we cannot but give birth into a state that we can neither predetermine is harmonious (or beautiful) nor disharmonious (or ugly).

Recalling the issue that Diotima avoided, while we might be pregnant in body or in mind, we will have little or no control over what might be harmoniously beautiful at the time of birth. While we might strive to achieve sustainable life (or immortality), we cannot do so without anxiety if what once appeared harmonious is now in a condition of disharmony.[17] As my enterprising thoughts reach poietic maturity, bringing forth my composition—an immortal enterprise—it may be disharmonious in birth. Given free rein to poiesis, in birthing (rational) enterprising ideas or actions that seek to (pre)serve society's enterprise, I may meet disharmony in the face of an autopoietic cycle of creative destruction. But I am free to adapt to the rhythm of society. I am free to account for the emergent possibility of other rational solutions to society's human problems. Yet, critically, I can only adapt if I am aware of the disharmony. Otherwise, the birthing is at risk—the seed of my enterprising action falling on stony ground.

Rhythm is structure in form. It carries us, on a flow in time, into an 'other' place. As Giorgio Agamben suggests, it is a measure and logos (ratio)—a metrical compulsion—that provides a sense of presence, a sense that every 'thing' has its proper station. Agamben characterises rhythm through the

---

[16] Nietzsche, "Beyond Good and Evil: Prelude to a Philosophy of the Future," 290.
[17] Plato, The Symposium, 43.

notion of *a stop*, 'an interruption in the incessant flow of instants that, coming from the future, [sink] into the past'.[18] However, I add that rhythm is also the temporal unity in the flow of space, providing both matter and energy the capacity to form presence.

To Henri Lefebvre, rhythm contains repetition, measure and difference; its repetitions—*its reprises*—are organic, introducing difference: 'there is no identical absolute repetition, indefinitely.'[19] Discernible from Lefebvre's work is the measure of rhythm that lies in relative forms of *beat*. Rhythm possesses a triadic character of repetition, measure and difference—in which there is no 'identical absolute repetition, indefinitely';[20] the notion of the stop provides us with points of difference in the cycle of repetition. A stop but freezes a moment in time, at which point stock is taken of our temporal presence. Yet I recall that from a systems perspective, we cannot—from a single moment in time—both take stock of the structure of society as manifest in that moment, and understand society as a continuing entity.[21] A stop serves a purpose, as in Agamben's contemplation of a Work of art, 'held, arrested before something... a being-outside'.[22] However, I must consider that the *stop* is merely transient—a point of difference, of change or inflexion—in the logos of space. To understand society as a continuing, emergent entity, I argue that we need its measure and logos, in space through time.

A temporal unity of flow of space, delineated by matter (the body) and energy (movement), allows for an emergent presence as the very experience of that future sinking into the past—the actual experience of living 'emergence'. Thus, rather than the interruptions of the ordinary experience of ceaseless instants, I argue the rhythm of society is one in which humanity faces the collective emergent experiences of the ordinary, temporal flow of ceaseless instants—an amalgam, in which the temporal measure and ratio of space reveals itself in the interplay of body and movement. And, it is within this rhythmic emergent presence, that our human poiesis is constrained, or controlled, or regulated within the limits of nature. It is under this rhythmic compulsion—the repetition, measure and difference—of nature's (our ecology's) measure and the ratio of its own magic three: space, matter and

---

[18] Agamben, The Man Without Content, 98–99.
[19] Lefebvre, Rhythmanalysis: Space, Time, and Everyday Life, 16.
[20] Lefebvre, Rhythmanalysis: Space, Time, and Everyday Life, 16.
[21] Buckley, "Society as a Complex Adaptive System," 493.
[22] Agamben, The Man Without Content, 99; A stop, in the sense of rhythm, is also characteristic of the idea of moments in time featured as part of the critical counterfactual method of my inquiries in earlier chapters. See method detailed in Chapter 4.

energy, that our language (or code) of social morality may achieve its strengths and freedoms.

Dancing to society's tune

Society gains its moral strength and freedoms from the humanistic rhythm of its people, bounded by their ecology. This ground—society's foundation—provides an intellectual basis for arguing an understanding that the conscious interests of societal conditioning are the proper focus of our attention, as we adapt to society's changing nature and its changing ecology. I suggest that our attention is directed to society's rhythm because of its tangible properties, not merely because of any symbolic connection with our unconscious interests. Here, I extend the idea—from organization to society—that human relationships, as functions of movement in time and space, may be synchronized in concert with the concept of rhythm: the idea of the moral organization of society.

Insofar as I observe that the choreography of dance is the innovative application of body, movement, physical space and time,[23] then the choreography of humanity's dance to the constraint of society's moral rhythm is a matter of innovative, collective application of human agency—as society's body—to its own environment: its ecology. A dance within a dance. But here, from a systems perspective, as Buckley suggests, the degree of change or adaptability of an adaptive system is 'a complex function of the internal state of the system, the state of its relevant environment, and the nature of the interchange between the two.'[24] I posit that the individual, or small group, or organization, is constrained to dance to a rhythm that is, itself, regulated by its own moral code.

Having first posited the impossibility of systemic control, I extend the idea that we might, instead, entertain the preternatural possibility of regulating society's moral code. From the rhythm of society, our code of social morality is set from the temporal measure and ratio of space, body and movement. Here, space and time are intangible, while the body represents the amalgam of identity and technology—technology being a resource capable of moderating identity. The concept of power represents energy or movement—a capacity of the individual, group, organization or society. Power may also be moderated by technology, as it influences change or movement. I can now ask: to what extent are the ratio's three dimensions, re-expressed as a *logos* of space, body

---

[23] See, for example: Bozic Yams, "The Impact of Contemporary Dance Methods on Innovative Competence Development," 497.
[24] Buckley, "Society as a Complex Adaptive System," 493.

(as identity and technology), and power (as movement), controllable as a phenomenon from which we may realise our moral strength and freedom? In Figure 11.1, I depict the three dimensions of identity, power and technology—in *logos*—as a triple helix. Here, space passes above, below, alongside and through the helix, to the tune of some temporal measure.

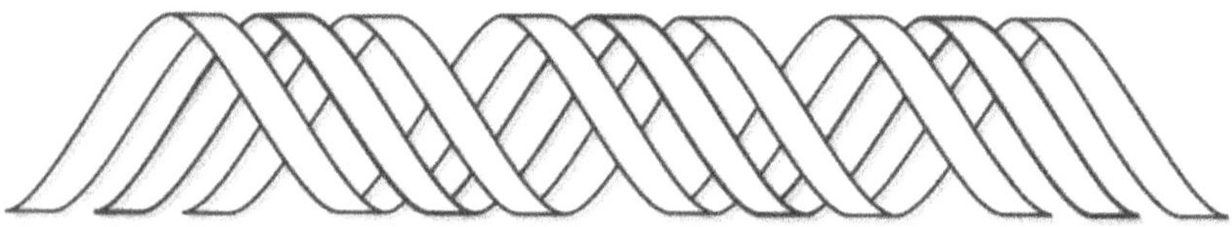

Figure 11.1. A *logos* of society's moral strength and freedom

Deconstructing the doughnut

Identifying a society's logos in a balance of identity, technology and power is one thing, but I should ask: how is this one thing, itself, to be reconciled with a new practice of Design Capitalism, as I set out in Chapter 9? While this present text remains a provocation, and a 'how to design a post capitalism' solution lies beyond the scope of my inquiry, I suggest that there is a case I might consider in illustrating the potential of such a logos. Here I consider Kate Raworth's ideological model of an economy that respects both the needs of society[25] and the environmental and ecological boundaries of the world in which it exists. The Doughnut Economics,[26] I briefly introduced in Chapter 6, is represented by the iconic doughnut shape. I provide a much-simplified version in Figure 11.2.

---

[25] There is a sense in which the needs of a society might be equated with the satisfaction of its moral identity, that is in being seen to be true to itself.

[26] Raworth, Doughnut Economics: Seven Ways to Think Like a 21st-Century Economist; Raworth, "Why It's Time for Doughnut Economics."

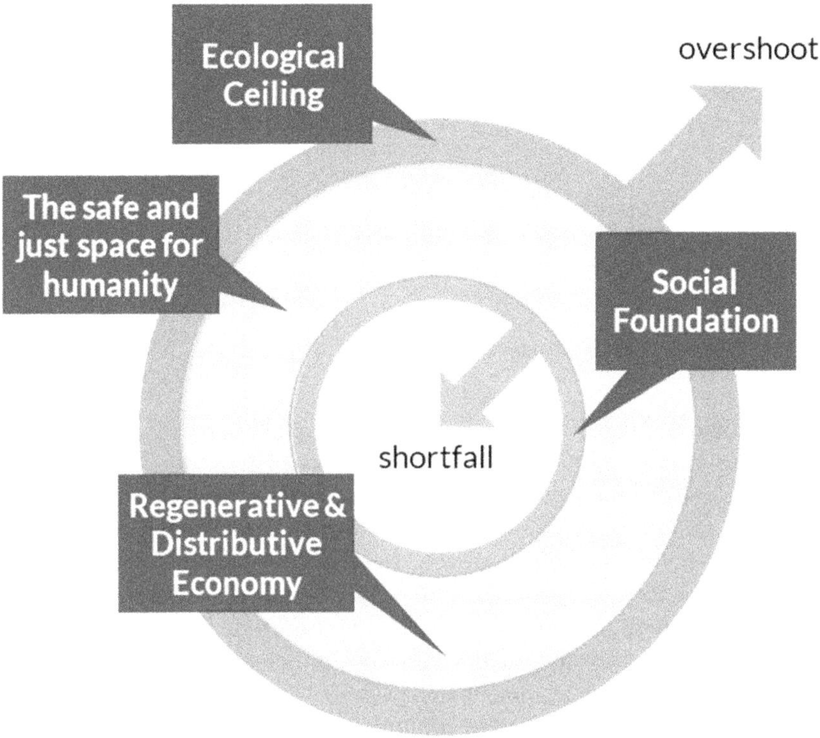

Figure 11.2. Simplified schematic of Raworth's economic Doughnut

Here, the Doughnut of social and planetary boundaries is offered as a compass for twenty-first-century policymakers. As Raworth explains:

> 'The hole in the middle reveals the extent to which people… [suffer a shortfall in] life's essentials, such as food and water, healthcare, and housing, gender equality and political voice—the 12 social priorities set out in the United Nations Sustainable Development Goals. Beyond the… outer ring, …humanity risks [an overshoot of] pressure on Earth's critical life-supporting systems, known as planetary boundaries… Between these two [rings] …lies a possible [safe and just] future for humanity in which it is feasible to meet the needs of all within the means of the planet.'[27]

[27] Raworth, "Why It's Time for Doughnut Economics," 217.

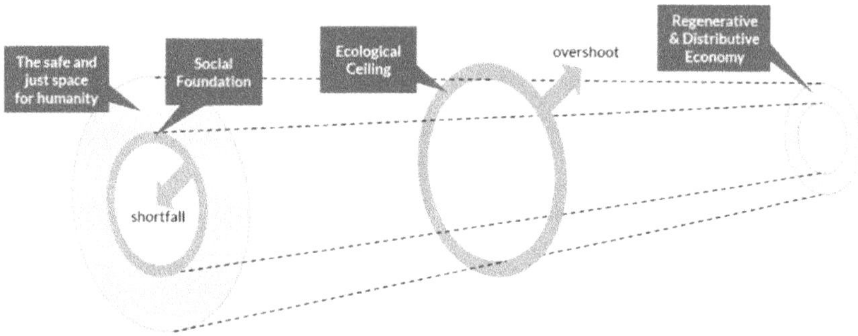

Figure 11.3. Extruding the Doughnut

The Doughnut model has received much popular and some (qualified) academic praise[28] amid what has been proposed by some as the age of Anthropocene Economics.[29] However, Raworth's work has its critics, who (for example), on the one hand, seemingly dismiss such thinking simply as 'antagonistic about economic growth', treating growth as an 'optional extra' for capitalism,[30] yet on the other hand call for 'robust democratic systems for basic social provisioning for all via socially and ecologically ethical means of production.'[31] Indeed, the qualified success of her work is countered by a critique that it is more 'sermon' than 'analysis'.[32] Even Raworth acknowledges '*Doughnut Economics* sets out an optimistic vision of humanity's common future'.[33] In this respect, I posit that Doughnut Economics exists on the imaginary plane, across the antagonistic horizon of a projected '...global human health crisis [that] has tested the system and shown its failings and [which] should be taken as a warning in the face of the impending ecological crisis.'[34] In this position, I argue the imagination should not simply be

---

[28] See, for example: Schokkaert, "Review of Kate Raworth's Doughnut Economics. London: Random House, 2017, 373 Pp."; Diethelm, "Doughnut Economics: Seven Ways to Think Like a 21st Century Economist"; Brauers and von Hirschhausen, "Doughnut Economics: Seven Ways to Think Like a 21st Century Economist."

[29] For example: Boehnert, "Anthropocene Economics and Design: Heterodox Economics for Design Transitions."

[30] Spash, "'The Economy' as If People Mattered: Revisiting Critiques of Economic Growth in a Time of Crisis," 7.

[31] Spash, 14.

[32] Schokkaert, "Review of Kate Raworth's Doughnut Economics. London: Random House, 2017, 373 Pp.," 131.

[33] Raworth, Doughnut Economics: Seven Ways to Think Like a 21st-Century Economist, 286.

[34] Spash, "'The Economy' as If People Mattered: Revisiting Critiques of Economic Growth in a Time of Crisis," 14.

dismissed; rather, the imagination requires reconciliation. Thus, in Figure 11.3, I depict an extrusion of the Doughnut in time. (I eschew any dialectic treatment of its concept.)

Here, I imagine, at the left-hand side, a baseline of a social foundation in shortfall, moving toward a significant overshoot of our ecological horizon, attempting to keep within its boundaries as we move right toward the *becoming* of an imaginary, regenerative and distributive form of economic organization.

Let me now position the present shortfall in the doughnut's 12 social priorities, on the plane of reality. I then place the ecological ceiling on the antagonistic horizon; and I place the regenerative and distributive economy as a provocation—an imagination of interest—on the imaginary plane. I then ask, how might my non-concept of a *logos* of society's moral strength and freedom help design a transition to an emergent postcapitalism? While I cannot forecast a transition to a concept of an ontic regenerative and distributive economy, I can work toward its non-conceptual emergence through a Design Capitalism that seeks to develop the logos at the heart of society. This is with a view to controlling for society's moral form and freedoms, within humanity's safe and just space. In Figure 11.4, I therefore imagine the logos of identity, technology and power at the core of the now extruded Doughnut of economic organization.

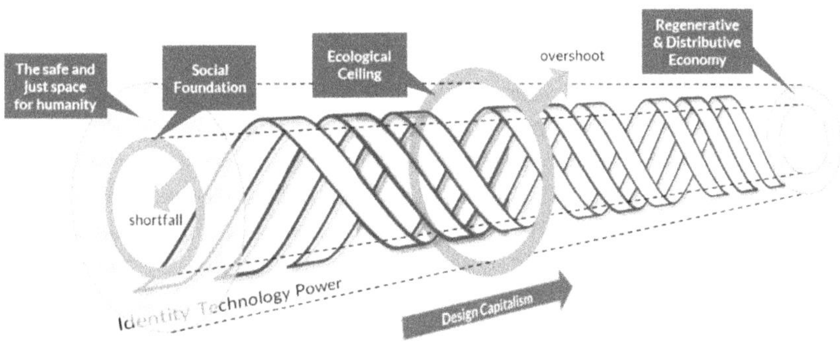

Figure 11.4. Reimagining capitalism?

Yet, for all the potential in this imagery of a doughnut of emergent economic organization, extruded along the length of a constantly evolving social logos of moral strength and freedoms, how is society to reshape its core activities in alignment with the constraints imposed upon it by its own responsibilities and its ecological environment?

Changing society's tune: distinction in rhythm

In my inquiries into the empirics of the imagination in emergent entrepreneurship (Chapter 4), work and the functional interchangeability of technology and institutions (Chapter 5), international business (Chapter 6), and neoliberal capitalist economies (Chapter 7), I have employed the idea of three 'controlling' themes or uncertainties. In entrepreneurship, I advanced the uncertain themes of the productivity paradox, the future of work, and sustainable growth as controlling variables of an advancing history—a movement, in *praxis*[35] in the space of entrepreneurship. This is a function of what was knowable about each uncertainty. Here, the limits of what is presently known or knowable about how entrepreneurship relates to, in turn, its ability to: 1) sustainably increase productivity; 2) develop meaningful and sustainable levels of employment; and 3) provide a sustainable level of economic growth to meet the requirements of society, constitute the limits of our knowledge of the entrepreneurial subsystem. They represent an isarithmic map, in which the isoline of 'knowable' entrepreneurial outcomes marks the ontological boundary of the entrepreneurial subsystem. This subsystem operates within both an economy and a society, each with their own ontic boundaries.

The knowable outcomes of the subsystems of entrepreneurship, work, international business (IB) and capitalist *praxis*, represent points of difference from that which would normally occur in the subsystem's own environment. The practitioners of entrepreneurship, work, IB, or capitalist *praxis*, observe the outcomes of their systemic practice. The entrepreneur observes their entrepreneurial outcomes, the worker their employment outcomes, the IB person the outcomes of their international trade, and the capitalist the outcomes of their capitalism. These outcomes are invariably measured in terms of economic benefit. To the entrepreneur, profit. To the worker, income. To the IB person, increased revenues from remote territories. And to the capitalist, increased capital. Practitioners and their practice are elements of (sub) systems that exist only by virtue of their outcomes—points of ontological difference between the systems and their environments. The isolines of concern are the distinctions of finance alone.

---

[35] The term praxis is introduced in respect of its representation as a manifestation of human will that produces a concrete effect—that is the act of doing in the sense of acting or practice. Praxis finds its 'immediate effect' in the act of doing. Management praxis is management doing. Work is praxis. In this sense, I posit that contemporary entrepreneurship, the act of enterprising work, and international business (IB) all serve as exemplars of a praxis in the act of doing capitalism. See: Agamben, The Man Without Content, 68.

To understand the significance of the isoline of finance, I believe it is necessary to revisit Niklas Luhmann's conceptualisation of a social autopoietic system, I introduced earlier in Chapters 7 and 8. Here, for example, entrepreneurship is differentiated from its environment—the economy—by the distinction of its entrepreneurial outputs. Entrepreneurship does not neglect the rest of the economy but communicates its distinction through its own entrepreneurial 'code'. However, Luhmann posited the economy as an 'open' subsystem, operating within the broader, social system. Thus, the distinctions made by entrepreneurship create moments of change that flow through to new distinctions on the boundary of the economy and society and, in turn, society's environment. However, in praxis, the practitioner's ability to observe any distinction is necessarily limited.

Luhmann argued that 'nothing can be observed without a distinction, and that this distinction must be used asymmetrically.'[36] A distinction indicates one side and not the other. The entrepreneur observes, in a moment of *praxis,* the outcome of their entrepreneuring from the perspective (or system side) of entrepreneurship, not from any other point of view—not in the wider economy, nor in its society, nor its environment. All other views of the systemic distinction of entrepreneurship remain hidden. However, as Luhmann further suggested, 'one always carries along the fact that there is another side that is not indicated at the moment and has no operational significance.'[37] Thus, at the moment of praxis, in the entrepreneurial present, entrepreneurship's 'other' is also present, but is disregarded. In a Lévinasian sense, the entrepreneur, in disregarding their Others, does them an injustice. Yet, the asymmetric application of distinction is, in all other senses, symmetrical: the entrepreneurs only gaining their true nature from facing their Other. This is to say that entrepreneurship cannot exist without its other: the economy, which in turn cannot exist without its society and its environment. Systems thinking presupposes this distinction. Paradoxically, however, if one attempts to use both sides in the moment, both distinction and system boundary dissolve.

The system boundary is an isoline of distinction between system and environment. On the real plane, the boundary (or isoline) does not exist, yet it is useful, conceptually, to consider that it may. Here, the traditional observer of a 'systems' view of entrepreneurship, work and the functional interchangeability of technology and institutions, IB, or neoliberal capitalist economies, would concentrate their observations on the one 'system' side of the asymmetry of distinction, at the expense of its 'other', the environment

[36] Luhmann, Introduction to Systems Theory, 103.
[37] Luhmann, Introduction to Systems Theory (op. cit.).

side. On the isoline of financial outcome, the focus is on the return on investment in the praxis of entrepreneurship, work, IB or capitalism in general. In essence, the environment is 'blind-sided'; the practitioner no longer sees the distinction, nor the environment beyond. To entertain observations that, outside the isoline of distinction, are inclusive of the environment, is to entertain a unity with that inside it. This amounts to Luhmann's paradox of the unity of a difference. Here, the forcing into existence of an ontic boundary of distinction closes the system to its becoming, in praxis. It closes it to its potential beyond, in its environment. Here, as observers of a system's praxis, I suggest that we might also take a view on that environment, and thus its unity. However, without our imagination, I argue we may only relay this view to others as a second-order observation, through our conceptual models and theories.

Aesthetics, transcending distinction

To Luhmann, for the observer taking an external view of the unity of systemic praxis, such a view was a first-order view of both sides of a distinction. Thus, without the benefit of a practitioner's first-order view of that distinction, the external observer's view of the unity can only ever be contingent on what can be known about the practitioner. This raises the question: 'with what distinctions does a [practitioner] whom I observe work?'[38] For example, if I cannot, with confidence, approach questions such as 'Who is the entrepreneur?' (Chapter 3), then by what level of authority might I argue that we should drive an economy through entrepreneurship? In a complex system with multiple actors, in which each actor may hold contrary points of view, second-order theories and models of systems are—without the benefit of the imaginary plane—generally subject to a forced rationalisation of distinctions. This is a peculiar reductionist code that both simplifies complexity and closes a system through its contingency. Here, the 'real' system is bound, in circularity, to reproduce itself in its own praxis. This is the concept of *autopoiesis:* the self-reproduction of the system by those elements of the system, produced in and by that system.[39] An autopoietic system is one contingent upon its 'self'. The limit of a *closed praxis* is revealed in *autopoiesis.*

Closed systems are constrained, or regulated, to a level of contingent second-order-limited praxis, influenced by dialectic models and theories of extant—but closed—ontic concepts of entrepreneurship, work and the functional interchangeability of technology and institutions, IB, or neoliberal

---

[38] Luhmann, Introduction to Systems Theory, 112.
[39] Luhmann, Introduction to Systems Theory, 43.

capitalism.[40] In order to (re)open these systems, I argue that practitioners require skills that allow them to transcend the systemic distinctions, and enable a greater cognition of the disharmony that arises from their contingent nature. It is only when the truth of a disharmony is revealed that the human can imagine a harmonious poietic outcome, over a constrained autopoietic one. Here, I argue that aesthetics is an approach in which first-order observers may open their minds to a greater range of possible knowing, beyond sight of simple first-order observations; aesthetics eschews any notion of a realist second-order perspective.

Hans Moeller explains that, '[one] operates in the form of second order observation as soon as one does not directly observe something, but observes it as it is observed by someone else.'[41] I posit that if we act on someone else's advice, we operate in a second-order mode. But, as practitioners, if what we seek is an open, first-order system, we need an enhanced capacity to act on our own advice. As I recall from Chapter 2, Georg Franck noted, '[the] only way we have access to the reality deemed to exist independently of being experienced is conscious thought'.[42] Thus I draw, not only on my individual level of knowledge, but also on my instincts, feelings, beliefs and my wider senses. I also require my imagination. Therefore, with reference to my Needs-consciousness model (Chapter 3), I suggest that this calls for a greater awareness of our individual unconscious capacities—our cognitive, aesthetic, self-actualization and self-transcendent capacities—and our abilities to recognise and assuage our calls to action. I argue we need a more open aesthetically-informed praxis.

In a contemporary re-enactment of Danish author Hans Christian Andersen's literary folktale, *The Emperor's New Clothes*, I suggest society has been denied a broad aesthetic sensibility through (educational) suppression. It has been led to believe that, from the second order of technological rationality and instrumental reasoning embedded in neoliberal capitalist economic theory, the virtue of self-interest is a cloak to be worn by all citizens, for the good of all. What, from a second-order ideology makes sense—such as Adam Smith's

---

[40] As in the idea of an organization as a 'bounded' universe, this is a rehearsal of Chris Argyris's (1923-2013) Model I/Model II conceptualisation of theories in use. See Atkinson, "A Portrait of the Organizational Manager." In the context of this present inquiry, both Model I (first-order observation) and Model II (second-order observation) are held deficient. Here, an example Model I theory-in-use would be the selection of a past narrative as a model for future action. A Model II theory-in-use would be the reliance on a generalised, contingent model.

[41] Moeller, "On Second-Order Observation and Genuine Pretending: Coming to Terms with Society," 30.

[42] Franck, "Mental Presence and the Temporal Present," 49.

invisible hand—and in a critical sense is believed significant—such as exposing the invisible hand as fallacy without a foundation in reason (Chapter 8)—is groundless and, in Luhmannian terms, is *'utterly contingent'*.[43] Therefore, in transcending all systemic distinction and looking for a sense of control over society's rhythm, I am—from Chapter 2—concerned with developing a first-order sense of the culturally socialised and historic embeddedness of an *a posteriori* system (or pattern) of rules (or conventions), arising within the gamut of our social relationships. Here, in a reprise of my opening theme in Chapter 2, I posit that the dynamics of social change emerge, dance-like, from the negative dialectics of a society that, itself, emerges in a constant state of becoming within its VUCA environment.

Controlling distinction

From Chapter 2, I introduced the notion that, while deconstruction has built a metaphysics around the privileging of presence over absence, an adaption of a 'sixth sense' of social presence appeals to a more constructive paradigm. To imagine our continued becoming, our emergence into a future VUCA environment, I ague that we must embrace both absence and presence with equal fervour. To dance society's tune, I suggest we must first call society's tune. We must embrace both absence and presence along the rhythmic dimensions of identity, power and technology. Thus, in embracing the meter of both absence and presence in temporality and space, I argue that we should ask: who are we? what power do we have? and how are we mediated by technology? Knowing who we are, in relation to who we are not tells us what part we might play in poiesis; knowing what power we may have to influence change in relation to that part, and what we cannot influence, tells us our capacity to achieve poiesis; and knowing what technology can and cannot do will either strengthen or weaken that capacity.

In a moral code of society, I argue that we cannot justify autopoietic praxis. Such a praxis of distinction is always asymmetric; it disregards Others in favour of a second-order view from the 'self'. Again, in the Lévinasian sense, such a moral code of praxis is intrinsically unjust. Thus, if there is to be an entrepreneur to whom the asymmetric rewards of capitalism may justifiably accrue, there must always be a just exchange of value toward those Others from whom those rewards are garnered. If there is to be an employee engaged in non-entrepreneurial work, there must always be an employer to whom responsibilities of employment accrue. And if there is to be an international business, there must always be a related corner of a foreign land to which that

---

[43] Moeller, "On Second-Order Observation and Genuine Pretending: Coming to Terms with Society," 29.

business owes both respect and dignity. Without a knowledge or sense of their Other's, no individual, group or society may subsist indefinitely. Nor may they achieve, in any sense, a poiesis of immortality. The concept of self-interest at the heart of capitalism tends to be an absurdity in the face of a requirement for poietic sustainability. Ultimately, the function of a moral code for society must therefore be to control for the absurdity of self-interest.

There is support for the notion of controlling the absurdity in distinctions of identity, power and technology. I argue that the concept of justice—aligned with the need to exercise control of the appropriation of the vice of self-interest as a virtue—is, in a Luhmannian sense, strictly contingent. We may set our own rhythm. If it feels right, it is right; there is no absolute rationality, nor instrumentality to the organization of society. In my analysis, society is wholly contingent on its emergence from a negative dialectic of socially collective action. Thus, to a society faced with its own emergence in a VUCA world, there is a sense in which the setting of social and economic order, against even a second-order concept of rationalisation of self-interest as a virtue, is absurd. While a Luhmannian critical theory of complex adaptive systems suggests that 'basic social values and ideals (such as justice)' are 'irrational, unreachable, and ultimately meaningless',[44] if Raworth's Doughnut Economics is illustrative of anything, it is that there are potentially safe limits within which socially collective action must be practised.

A necessary 'systemic' distinction subverts any claim to a 'comprehensive enlightening', or 'scientific elucidation', of a wholistic totality of the world as some form of meta-system.[45] Yet, given the contingent nature of praxis, in the cognition of disharmony in systemic distinctions, I suggest that we can only resort to what Luhmann suggested is the 'possibility of stating clearly what we mean.'[46] The irony is that systems thinking is essential to understand the distinction we are attempting to dissolve, in favour of a more poietic action. Yet, dispensing with our ontological certainty, we must define the border merely to dissolve it in a poietic becoming. Here, I follow Luhmann on 'observation', and his argument that 'the capitalists cannot see that they create their own demise.'[47] However, I add that economic theory (by sleight of hand) is fashioned in such a way as to deny the blind spots of both humanity and society. As Luhmann suggested, the question (now) is whether one helps in capitalism's demise, or simply waits until its time comes? However, from

---

[44] Moeller, "On Second-Order Observation and Genuine Pretending: Coming to Terms with Society," 29.
[45] Luhmann, Introduction to Systems Theory, 105.
[46] Luhmann, Introduction to Systems Theory, 107.
[47] Luhmann, Introduction to Systems Theory, 114.

Chapter 8, I am reminded, that the defeat of capitalism, when it comes, is likely to be chaotic, messy, unpredictable and dangerous. However, if we can be clear about what we mean, I argue that aesthetics and a Design Capitalism provide a viable approach to addressing systemic disharmony, even if we make mistakes along the way, trying.

Design capitalism: pro-duction into presence

There is support for locating poiesis in an aesthetic approach that transcends a *closed praxis* into openness. This is where *poiesis* trumps the mere act of doing, by 'pro-ducing'—a pre-ontic state of becoming. Here, in the sense of bringing some 'thing' into being, *poiesis* is the experience of production into presence[48]—a revealing or emergence of a unity of work. As Agamben argued, the essential nature of (an aesthetic) poiesis is a mode of truth, understood as an unveiling: assigning—in an Aristotelian sense—poiesis as a higher-order of enterprise than simply doing. The issue at hand, however, is that as a *closed praxis* reaches its limit in a systemic autopoiesis, the potential of poiesis is denied.

Agamben suggested that contemporary aesthetics has been subsumed by the question of 'how'. Even the concept of art is heavily imbued with the 'how' of 'creative genius and the particular characteristics of the artistic process'.[49] This is art's praxis, rather than its aesthetic of an unfolding truth; it is the process of art, as opposed to a birth of some 'thing' new: a 'Work' of art. I argue it can be seen in the autopoietic re-production of examples that have gone before, and in the incessant production of simulacra at the expense of losing what might be truly innovative. Here, to draw further on Baudrillard, the product of contemporary neoliberal capitalism, work and enterprise, is a '*precession of simulacra*'[50]—its systemic outputs cast upon the deserts of their social and environmental reality. It is here that we can say all Art is both mediated and subverted by power. Art—its identity as an object—evolves under the incessant mediation of a benign social power (its audience), while its inherent 'truth' value is subverted by an excess of objectification under the manipulation of a more malign, individualist power. Consider the absurdity of an Art object so raised in monetary value (through trade) that it cannot be exchanged at any price. Lost in self-interest, its 'truth' value is subverted for all 'others'.

---

[48] Agamben, The Man Without Content, 68.
[49] Agamben, The Man Without Content, 70.
[50] Baudrillard, Simulacra and Simulation, 1.

If an autopoiesis of the system rejects—in its *precession of simulacra*—all moral principles in the belief that all that matters is money; if the capitalist pursuit of self-interest—and therefore life itself—is otherwise meaningless, then, what is to be done? What is to be done about the transparent nihilism of our systems?[51] How do we approach a nihilism, not of destruction, but of second-order simulation and the deterrence (or suppression) of first-order poiesis? Here, Baudrillard offered little hope for meaning, championing its loss as a good thing—*meaning is mortal*.[52] However, in the face of the volatility, uncertainty, complexity and ambiguity of our VUCA world, if we are to seek immortality through poietic birth, I argue that our meaningful response must be to resolve the disharmony at the borders of systemic distinction. To do so requires education. I argue that we must first be educated to appreciate the level of abstraction—as simply a map of the real, rather than in any sense real. Then educated to transcend the purpose of distinction as a guide to the future. Such a future can only remain antagonistic in its volatility, uncertainty, complexity and ambiguity. Such an education will require imagination.

In a Luhmannian paradox of re-entry,[53] I argue that we must (re)approach the design of our systems—and our interventions into them—as observers of a system in which our designs must reflect the fact that whatever distinction held contingent at the outset, cannot remain the same. This is a move from a dialectic of being to a negative dialectic of becoming—a constant state of emergence. As my earlier discussion of Buckley's position on adaptive systems revealed, we cannot—from a single moment in time—take stock of the structure of our systems as manifest in that moment and understand their function as a continuing entity.[54] I argue we can, and must, design for poietic emergence. In respecting the adaptive capability of humans, we must permit them the freedom to react, individually to (and within the confines of) their environment. We must allow them to balance their own deficit and being needs with Others through collective action. Here, a certain sublimity subsists in the concept of a wholistic meta-system—such as the whole VUCA world. We may seek and find what is 'attractive' in the notion of a system boundary—be it an antagonistic, ecological ceiling or a responsibility to Others within a social foundation—only to become disinterested in it. We must look beyond—to dissolve that distinction; we must look to practise an aesthetic judgement on the beauty within that which is sublime—to recognise and leverage the conditions of its existence.

---

[51] Baudrillard, Simulacra and Simulation, 159.
[52] Baudrillard, Simulacra and Simulation, 164.
[53] Luhmann, Introduction to Systems Theory, 120.
[54] Buckley, "Society as a Complex Adaptive System," 493.

The sublimity of aesthetic enterprise

As enterprising agents in the self-interested pursuit of capital wealth, I argue we must learn to understand the limits of any systemic distinction that presents itself to us. For example, in production, we must understand what lies on the 'other' side of the aesthetic sublimity of the fortunes of the mega-rich hero(ines) of an extant entrepreneurship. It is, in aesthetic judgement, beyond a certain attractive beauty. What lies beyond the mysterious pleasure embedded in that sublimity—yet interacts with it—is the potential tragedy, terror and anguish of the 'other' side: the violence of failure and the creative destruction of the livelihoods of others;[55] and equally—constrained by an ecological ceiling—of the creative destruction of our environment. As an employer of labour, in the design and production of systems of work and employment—and considering the functional interchangeability of technology and institutions—I argue that we must understand what lies on the 'other' side of efficiency and effectiveness. We must consider the violence of the tragedy, terror and anguish arising from the displacement of humanity, and the potential for sclerotic, adaptive responses to future crises. In IB, we must consider the violence of the tragedy, terror and anguish arising from the erosion of local identities, the misappropriation of others' resources, and accusations of territorial colonisation.

In this penultimate Chapter, I have posited that Doughnut Economics exists on the imaginary plane, across the antagonistic horizon. In reconciling its potential, Design Capitalism suggests that working toward its possibility—of a regenerative and distributive economy—will require controlled experimentation. Here, in designs to shape society's logos of identity, technology and power—now at the core of society's foundation—we should permit mistakes to be made along the way. Solving such mistakes will be solving toward emergent success, not failure. This is learning to control for change, rather than simply to create change. I argue that leaders of neoliberal capitalist economies would do well to concentrate their observations on the asymmetry of their own distinctions. In Western democracies, those political leaders whom we—as moral citizens—have voted into positions of incredible power, must understand what lies on the 'other' side of the aesthetic sublimity they pursue in the acquisition and wielding of that power. As incumbents of the power-politic of the state, they must consider what violence of tragedy, terror and anguish might arise from the decisions they are emboldened to enact. In short, in dancing the VUCA, I suggest we must all dance to a different tune; we must all dance to a tune called by our society, dancing in the safe space of an emergent, but sustainable economy.

---

[55] Atkinson, Thinking the Art of Management: Stepping into "Heidegger's Shoes," 108–9.

Chapter 12

An emergent conclusion

TO DRAW THIS INQUIRY and provocation to a close, I reflect on my intent to offer—as I introduced in Figure 1.1—a contribution to social philosophy through an application of negative dialectics. Throughout, I have posited a methodology of applied negative dialectics in the context of what I have positioned as enterprise studies—a scholarly treatment of practical, socio-economic concerns about our emergence in an antagonistic VUCA world of Western neoliberal (mainly entrepreneurial) capitalism. In my reimagining of capitalism, my focus on enterprise respects the position of the entrepreneur at the heart of capitalism's history, from Jean-Baptiste Say's entrepreneurial agency to Schumpeter's economics of creative destruction. Here, I return to Rebecca Henderson's question from the opening of the preceding Chapter 11. That is, *'how we can build a profitable, equitable, and sustainable capitalism, by changing how we think about the purpose of firms, their role in society, and their relationship to government and the state?'* This question contains three presuppositions. The word 'how', occurs twice; it presupposes two knowable objectives. Firstly, it presupposes that we know what a profitable, equitable and sustainable capitalism is. Secondly, it presupposes that the purpose of firms can be objectively set to achieve that profitable, equitable and sustainable capitalism. And thirdly, the word 'by' introduces a known strategy; it presupposes that the objective outcomes we might dialectically define, are reachable through a plan of action. Such a plan is to be carried out within the systemic praxis of firms, as they conduct their relationships within society.

Henderson provides a compelling evidence base that supports the idea of a 'how'. She invokes a plan of action about how we should think about things, to achieve profitable, equitable, and sustainable capitalism. Her perspective is a comprehensive and insightful second-order analysis. Yet it remains a second-order analysis. It relates to the process through which the object—a profitable, equitable, and sustainable capitalism—is to be produced.[1] Yet, from the title of Henderson's work, we anticipate only a reimagining of capitalism. The 'what' escapes us, as it can only do so in a VUCA world. We cannot, for example, know precisely 'what' will constitute a profitable, equitable, and sustainable capitalism in the context of a future which is objectively unknowable. The potential in a poietic pro-duction into some future presence is subverted by the very idea that a 'how' to attain some future state of 'what' can, in fact, be knowable. It is for this reason that I have offered, in a contribution to futures studies, a new critical counterfactual method for contemplating the empiric value of imaginations of the future in context—a method that is coherent with my methodology of negative dialectics.

Plans of action aside, in praxis I suggest—collectively—we remain simply and constantly assaulted by the disappointments and paradoxes of our autopoietic initiatives and interventions toward our many dialectic ideals. I have taken this praxis and offered a variety of innovative perspectives in a critical review of the future of entrepreneurship, work, international business, capitalism and HE business schools. Consequently, I argue that if we can learn anything of the empiric value of the imagination, it is that merely thinking about the purpose of firms and their role as the basis for change, cannot suggest an effective plan of action to be left to the incumbents of enterprise—the *de facto* practitioners of some new purposeful, poietic order. In our Western economies, I argue that practitioners of an extant concept of creative-destructive enterprise—denied an aesthetic sensibility of the 'other' through a regulated educational system and focussed on theoretical and technological rationality and instrumental reasoning—will simply fuel the fire of neoliberalism. Meanwhile, 'others' continue to observe and wonder why and generate more texts on reimagining capitalism—coining new epithets of purposeful action.

In challenging the dialectic throughout this inquiry, I have both highlighted and argued for the value inherent in negative dialectics. This value, I argue, lies in the surfacing of ideas—imaginations of empiric value—for application to, for example, the design of policy and practice in economic enterprise. This includes the need for the reform of both educational and justice subsystems. In this summation of my inquiry, my point of coalescence is to challenge Henderson's presupposed strategy. Rather than changing how we think about the purpose of firms and their role in society as the basis for the action of others, I have set my own question. I have asked: 'what if we change the socio-

[1] Agamben, The Man Without Content, 70.

economic system first?' But, here, my 'what' cannot be a certain profitable, equitable, and sustainable form of capitalism. We cannot know what such a form needs to be. My inquiries suggest that, despite growing counter-narratives of social compassion and a values-led capitalism—consequences of continued global crises, exacerbated by Covid-19—it is not at all clear we will witness the coordinated level of change in identities, power politics and applications of technology that would permit its rise. Neither would any massive 'technology adaptive disruption' benefit society. Yet I do not suggest there is no hope.

What I believe we do know is that, given the VUCA nature of our lived-in-world, we might only act to shape certain emergent outcomes. We can only seek to control our emergence into some future state of being, through an attendance to the preconditions for that emergence. In a cumulative sense, then, I offer the reader provocative perspectives on an emergent post-capitalism through the negative dialectic of future-focussed socio-economic enterprise. I therefore suggest that the 'what' we might strive for is a society that—while seeking to shape a profitable, equitable and sustainable existence (based on the best available knowledge and evidence of its time)—is better equipped to emerge and adapt into an unknowable future. This is a poietic pro-duction into some future presence. Thus, rather than asking 'how', I argue we should draw on the human capacity for poiesis. My question resolves to: 'how can we best prepare society to emerge in a future state—guided by principles of profitability, equity and sustainability—through changing the socio-economic system?' In other words, what changes can we design/implement in our socio-economic systems that will best prepare society to emerge, in a future state, guided by principles of profitability, equity and sustainability? However, I recall that I have argued that change must come from the inside out. Such change as might be required can only occur if the state regains its capacity to exercise the justice necessary to lop and bind antagonistic, socially unproductive vices. There is no invisible hand. In drawing my provisional, emergent conclusions, I first review the positions on identity, the power-politic and technology. I then coalesce on the provocations of education and justice and their potential to shape postcapitalism, work and an aesthetic enterprise.

Calling our own tune...

As a society, suspended in the precession of socio-economic history, characterised by its own rhythmic DNA of identity, power politics and technology, I argue that we can achieve any necessary change. We can change from the limiting constraints of autopoiesis to poietic emergence—but only if we have the will to do so. This is not change for a specific outcome, nor change for change's sake. Rather, the change I speak of is a change that accepts—with reference to Heraclitus' moving river—that change itself is the real nature of our VUCA future. The implication of my inquiry is that we may well have the wrong idea of change. Instead of change being a means to an end, change must prepare us for that end—which, itself, is change. We must change to control for change itself. Here, as I reach an emergent conclusion, I consider the precession of our history through these three key insights of identity, power and technology uncertainty that I posit lie at the heart of the potential of a (non-)concept of Design Capitalism.

Knowing ourselves

Firstly, I argue that we have a responsibility to our own identity, both as individuals and, collectively, as a society. To progress to poiesis, I reason that we must be able to identify as members of an open society. To be an open society is to be an inclusive society. A society that constrains itself through an isoline of distinction cannot be truly poietic; a constrained society is regulated, constrained by autopoiesis, denying the full potential of adaptive variability. For example, an entrepreneurial society excludes 'others', or regulates them into an unsuitable role. Such a society asks 'how' do we become inclusive? How do we, for example, inclusively regulate all our citizens as good 'capitalists'—as good 'entrepreneurs'? For example, we might well question initiatives in the UK to educate all children as potential 'entrepreneurs'.[2]

To truly accept diversity in an enterprising society is to dissolve its distinctions and approach a unity of meaningful enterprising activity. The borders of identity distinction must be dissolved. Here, a collective, societal identity does not prejudice individual identity. I recall that I can be a member of many systems, and a member of this household, that village, this tribe. Yet my self-construction of my individual identity may be constrained in a historical sense—I did not choose my first school bench, nor the DNA with which my identify and character were first formed. However, I did and do exercise 'trust' and 'individual choice' in identifying myself, to the extent that I can, within society's concepts of 'social order' and 'individual liberty'. Therefore, I argue that identifying a range of enterprising praxis, such as I have advanced in Chapter 9, "Emergence and the non-hero", will provide a more inclusive structure to organize enterprising work for a society's citizens.

In a constrained neoliberal capitalist society, the opportunity for meaningful individual identification is autopoietic—we are cast as members of an entrepreneurial, materialistic, self-interested society. We are encouraged with

[2] Dumitriu, "Educating Future Founders."

the rhetoric that we can be anything we want to be, as long as we fit the closed neoliberal capitalist mould. But, in the open society, the good citizen must be more than the success story of capitalist entrepreneurship, sportsmanship, or celebrity. In a meaningful contribution to society, where is the scope for the valuable contributions of dreamers and visionaries, the crafters, the experimenters, the designers, and copyists? Not every 'other' person can be the *faux artist* that capitalism seeks to autopoietically recreate through a study of their 'how'. The social science of self-selecting mediocrity[3] through second-order observation, risks the systemic spread of exclusion. It consigns those beyond two or three standard deviations of the 'norm' to the land of 'others'. There, social interventions create an autopoiesis that stiffens systemic responses against the emergent future of our VUCA world.

I argue that we must understand that one might achieve certain enterprising objectives without naïvely grasping for an unreachable epithet. In a practical sense, such understanding would certainly be of benefit in the education of students and practitioners of enterprising work. Such an understanding would allow the setting and managing of more appropriate expectations. To call our own tune, the 'we' that is society must be educated to know who 'we' are and for what 'we' stand. We must be able to self-identify with a greater, more inclusive and flexible range of valuable personas within society, knowing and accepting the great diversity that already exists within our humanity. It is for this reason that I offer, in this text, a new inclusive typology of enterprising work. To do otherwise, risks ever-more disenfranchisement in work.

Power to speak the truth

Secondly, I consider the balance of the power-politic. Here, writing on the culturally embedded mix of pleasure and pain—the algedonics—of society, Louis Klein suggested,

> 'If there is a cultural or paradigmatic handicap to cope with malign systemicity it is the idea of truth. ...truth as culturally processed in science and religion has a tendency to unfold... structures which have a tendency to compete ...and produce conflict.'[4]

---

[3] I do not use the word mediocrity in any pejorative sense. I simply use it to suggest the selection of the medium or norm, as in the application of statistical science methods in quantitative social research.

[4] Klein, "The Culturally Embedded Algedonics of Society: The Drivers and Controls of Integrating Culture."

Here, religion—in its broadest sense, a belief system other than that of pure science—may manifest itself as an ideology in conflict with rationality. The idea that a capitalist ideology, pitched with almost religious zeal against what might knowingly (or scientifically) be irrational or absurd—for example, the concept of an invisible hand, or the sustainability of capitalism itself—becomes the scene of conflict in a battle for (a) truth. We might ask: who is right? The religion of capitalist self-interest, perpetuated by a minority? Or a science of inclusivity? 'If you do not follow my scientific school or my religion you must be wrong. I am right, you are wrong.'[5] Yet, I have argued there can be no such absolute concepts. Society gains its moral strength and freedom from the humanistic rhythm of its people. We call our own tune. Knowing what power that we have available to us, to influence change in relation to that tune, and knowing what we cannot influence, tells us our capacity to achieve poiesis.

Power, specifically the power of humanity, is vested in individuals, groups, organizations, institutions and the state. Indeed, any representation or collective of humanity—for example, a social movement—has a power to influence change at some level or another. As I have explored in the earlier Chapters, the Foucauldian (political) mechanisms of power relations to effect change must subsist outside, below and alongside the need for change. Yet, while democratic society establishes the 'state' as its organ of power 'to safeguard its common interests',[6] the irony of the state's independence from society (and its turn to neoliberalism) has seen control—in the form of homogenous autopoiesis—assume the 'truth' of an ideal capitalist citizen. Such a citizen is entrusted to play their part in the pursuit of self-interest. This allusion of control merely provides a mechanism for repressing changes to democracy that do not serve the interests of profit maximisation. Social needs are, indeed, sacrificed on the altar of pleonexia.

The paradox of Western democratic liberalism is the systemic erosion of identity (both individual and collective) and the relative de-powering of its state's institutions, through capitalist technological substitution. This substitution is carried out in the name of efficiency and effectiveness. The capitalist mantra of protections from 'discretionary political interference',[7] raised in the face of a Foucauldian power-politics of society, leverages the absurdity of Adam Smith's 'invisible hand'. It broadens the definition of 'political interference', adding fuel to the fire. Here, amid the differentiation and dissolution of integrating, institutional control structures, the cost of

---

[5] Klein, "The Culturally Embedded Algedonics of Society: The Drivers and Controls of Integrating Culture."

[6] Polanyi, Economy and Society: Selected Writings, 18.

[7] Streeck, How Will Capitalism End?, 75.

correcting capitalism's recurrent crises has taken its toll on the residual effectiveness of, for example (and in no particular order) the societal institutions of: health, law, security, defence and education. In the UK, for example, with legal aid reduced to negligible levels, many citizens simply cannot afford to engage with structures that might instate or re-instate equity—a principle of much justice.[8] And, as Amanda Gregory has argued, the differentiation of society and its institutions, without control, has led to a plethora of self-serving, 'pathologically autopoietic' subsystems.[9]

I argue that the homogeneity of capitalist autopoietic identity serves no truth but its own. Neoliberal (entrepreneurial) capitalism—free from discretionary political interference—has progressively dismantled the internal controls over institutional truth. Here, Gregory argues that, in the face of the variety in its environment, 'society must employ strategies to amplify its own variety and attenuate that of the environment'.[10] However, I argue that under VUCA conditions, society is unable to attenuate such conditions, it therefore needs strategies that do not amplify a homogenous autopoiesis, but instead institute controls against such homogeneity. Here, recognising the absurdity of an ultimate self-interest, I argue that capitalism must be discouraged from further dismantling those remaining sources of the power-politic capable of influencing itself. What is required is the re-institution of some key institutions—giving them power to speak their truth to capitalism. However, this need not be a return to discretionary political interference. The reconciliation of control over a society's rhythm is subtly different to control over its systems' purposes. Ultimately, what emerges from my inquiry is, I argue, a conditional defence of capitalism—the condition being an acceptance of social design thinking.

Technology in our own hands

Thirdly, faced with little power and no absolute concept of truth, I argue that society struggles to gain its moral strength and freedoms from its own humanistic rhythm. While we might strive to call our own tune, our representatives are subverted by their ideology—an ideology that is fundamentally flawed and serving its own truth. As Gregory argues, while we are 'increasingly encouraged to question our personal values', these are set aside as we play our enterprising part in the economic system and cede to 'the imposition of a professional set of values', for example, those associated with

---

[8] See, for example: Flynn and Hodgson, "Access to Justice and Legal Aid Cuts: A Mismatch of Concepts in the Contemporary Australian and British Legal Landscapes."
[9] Gregory, "The State We Are in: Insights from Autopoiesis and Complexity Theory."
[10] Gregory, "The State We Are in: Insights from Autopoiesis and Complexity Theory," 966.

capitalist self-interest. We either adopt the capitalist identity and its mantra, or we fall outside, disenfranchised from the benefits of a system of justice, subsumed by an economic self-interest that serves only those on the inside of the system.

Where is the power to speak another truth? I argue that, presently, without a new substantial movement to re-exercise the state's political power, it may only be found on the inside. The insiders must be guided to the idea that a benign control over a society's rhythm is subtly different to a malign control over its economic purpose. Here, resolution may be sought in embracing the meter of both absence and presence in temporality and space. If we ask, who are we? And what power do we have? We may identify that we are all, in praxis, mediated by technology. A light is visible. Knowing who we are, in relation to who we are not, might tell us the part we can play in poiesis. And while our position of power suggests any desired change is problematic, we may come to know what the double-edged sword of technology can and cannot do to strengthen our society's position, and weaken that of its self-interested believers.

Is there a need for a new analysis of technological evolution? Can we, for example, take advantage of the availability of the technologies on the market, the capabilities of which, in terms of human-machine interaction (seemingly) far exceed customer demands?[11] Here, Jannis Kallinikos has argued that the manifestation and diffusion of ICT and the internet, 'spin a web of technological relations that challenge the strategies of functional simplification and closure'. They impact the systemic practices that accommodate them.[12] Here, technology is seen to represent 'complex layers of objectified intentions'.[13] These intentions are embodied second-order observations, a contribution to nihilistic simulation and the suppression of poiesis. Here, technology in the service of 'the system' provides a level of connectedness that can filter the identities it can, itself, facilitate. Digital technology is as potentially disenfranchising as it is enfranchising or democratising. As Kallinikos argues, technology may 'unwittingly undo defence mechanisms that secure the smooth function of the processes or systems involved, or simply provide new

---

[11] See, for example: Filippi and Barattin, "Definition and Exploitation of Trends of Evolution about Interaction."

[12] Kallinikos, "The Order of Technology: Complexity and Control in a Connected World."

[13] Kallinikos, "The Order of Technology: Complexity and Control in a Connected World," 186.

opportunities that can be used in adverse ways, as most electronic crime exemplifies.'[14] One might add, rather cynically, where is the justice in that?

From Chapter 8, I recall the problematic of avoiding Tiqqun's *cybernetic hypothesis.*[15] Here, a more natural liberal hypothesis may serve the perceived need to counter capitalist human behaviour through re-programming (as in education) and the dispersion (as in control) of identity. This is based on the idea of the animal spirits of self-interested individuals, rooted in Freud's writings on the unconscious that I introduced in Chapter 3. I suggest that the reality we face is that design thinking is a political tool already employed by capitalist institutions. As I previously highlighted, educational curricula are designed to meet the cyber-critical, technological needs of individuals destined to be contracted as the new *Others.* This is the inculcation of a contemporary Veblen 'machine discipline' in search of economic innovations, efficiencies and profits. This is contrary to the idea of a pure, natural liberalism, where Maslow's animal spirits suggest scope for self-interest toward the poietic actualisation of the human potential. Here, the reconciliation is the need to utilise technology in our own hands to offset capitalism's self-interested manipulation of design.

No change for change's sake...

The question I now ask is what changes can we make to the socio-economic system that will best prepare society to emerge in a future uncertain, indeterminate state, guided by principles of profitability, equity and sustainability? What can we do to call our own tune—to set the dance of our social and economic organization within the *logos* of our identity, power and technology? While, arguably, there are many areas one might conceive of using the principles of design to combat or alleviate the symptoms of a distressed capitalism—to design and implement solutions to its 'field' problems—there are few that go to the problematic root(s). In the following sections, I move to reach an emergent conclusion. It is emergent insofar that my stated purpose in writing this book is to provide a provocation toward a solution of design for emergence; it is not 'the' or even 'a' solution to postcapitalism. It is here that I offer concluding ideas in my reimagining of capitalism using the applied negative dialectics of a Design Capitalism. I offer provocations for the design of interventions into education, and (social) justice. In doing so, I posit that this book's interventional inquiry will extend

---

[14] Kallinikos, "The Order of Technology: Complexity and Control in a Connected World," 187.

[15] Tiqqun, The Cybernetic Hypothesis, 25.

the field of social philosophy and will offer the opportunity to underpin future scholastic inquiries.

Education, education, education: 1997 and all that

Our identity as a society matters. We must state clearly who we are and for what we stand. But, within our social identity, we can, and should, be free to exercise autonomy in our activity; we should be free to attain a necessary balance in our conscious and unconscious needs. The greater awareness (or consciousness) we have of our varied needs, the greater the ability we may have to envisage a balance within them. Here, education can, and does, play a pivotal role in regulating (enhancing or suppressing) our consciousness. An education that accepts a greater range of needs can encourage an open mind; what to some may seem irrational choices, may become rational in the constantly varying contexts of VUCA conditions.

Increasingly, we see the neoliberal regulation of identity enacted through the regulation of education curricula, where the enhancement of knowledge deemed appropriate to the furtherance of capitalist enterprise is at the cost of suppressing studies in the creative arts and humanities. For example, in submitting a version of Chapter 10, "On Experts and Wizards", for publication in the journal *Management Learning*, one reviewer commented: 'The approach to speculate what will happen in the future is not that well accepted in the academic community'. Another commented 'Please refrain from asserting possible futures without empirical or conceptual substantiation.'[16] While clearly these quotations lack some additional context (the entire review text), they do indicate the difficulties to be faced in advancing ideas that are not rooted in traditional empiricism and rationalism. Where is the evidence of the future?

Present reality, a consequence of action based solely on predominantly evidence-based social policies tends to the autopoietic. Such policies, founded on rational social science, merely self-select mediocrity. They imbue systems with homeostasis. Crises—scenes of conflict on the borders of systems—are a corollary of such systemic homeostasis; metaphorically, crises replicate the movement and release of energy of the tectonic[17] shifts of the

---

[16] Quotes taken from private correspondence: the author-Journal Management Learning, Decision on Manuscript ID MLQ-20-0085, email, dated 8 July 2020.

[17] The analogous use of plate tectonics in considering a concept of 'social tectonics' has previously been applied to the idea that groups of people move past each other like tectonic plates. See, for example: Jackson and Butler, "Revisiting 'Social Tectonics': The Middle Classes and Social Mix in Gentrifying Neighbourhoods." However, in Jackson and Butler's treatment of social tectonics, their analogy is restricted to more localised movements. A 'social tectonics' of social-economic systems presents an interesting thought for future study, beyond the scope of this present book.

earth's surface—that outer, hardened crust on a molten, flexible core. Extending this analogy, I suggest we might reconcile with the prospect of keeping the crust—the systemic border—malleable, to avoid crises of seismic proportions. The less rigid we are in our beliefs, the more malleable we might be to changes in our environment—to imagine and work toward our socio-human possibility.

Education is key to an open mind. In 1997, a series of UK reports were published, invoking the idea of lifelong learning. This is a rejection of the idea that education is 'confined to childhood, adolescence and early adulthood'—the 'old school' of education—and is instead a process to be engaged with throughout one's life.[18] However, this process is grounded in the belief that individuals are, or can become, self-directing. Early criticism suggested a tendency for policies to charge those not engaged in post-'old school' education to "'fulfil their potential', 'modify their behaviour' and personally invest in their future"—largely through a purposive curriculum of vocational (training) content.[19] This early critique has proven prescient, with policy driving education toward the 'economic' rather than 'social' good, where one trains, then retrains, to meet vocational needs, at some personal cost. This is the development of an ideal capitalist resource at low risk to the capitalist. Today, amid a certain acceptance of the value of lifelong learning, the rising costs to the individual learner and an associated falling participation of adult learners in particular, we find a narrowing of the curriculum toward only those skills thought to be directly required as a contribution toward the economy.[20] In October 2020, amid all the talk of the incumbent UK Conservative government, was the rumoured unviability of the arts as a commercial activity—it was not seen as deserving of the necessary Covid-19 crisis support. Indeed, then-Chancellor Rishi Sunak reportedly told the 'entire creative industry to get another job'.[21] Little more than an educational mantra to train, then retain.

The book is a provocation. Its purpose is not to set out a 'how'; rather, I argue we still very much need to set out a 'what'. Here, I find there is a need to address the curriculum of education to inculcate a poietic capability—a certain capacity for an individual to act (fluidly) across the full gamut of useful

---

[18] Tight, "Education, Education, Education! The Vision of Lifelong Learning in the Kennedy, Dearing and Fryer Reports," 474.
[19] Tight, "Education, Education, Education! The Vision of Lifelong Learning in the Kennedy, Dearing and Fryer Reports," 483.
[20] Bynner, "Whatever Happened to Lifelong Learning? And Does It Matter?"
[21] Cavendish, "Not 'Viable'? Rishi Sunak Just Told Our Entire Creative Industry to Get Another Job."

enterprising personas. This is a capacity to act beyond a purposive slavery to economics, toward the possibility of purposeful actions for the self and society. Imagine the value to the self and society, of the craftsperson who challenges the 'how' of their craft, to develop new designs for the application of their skills; or of the 'designer' who continues to dream big, and beyond the constraints of their horizons. Faced with crises, such individuals are better positioned to adapt. Intuitively, organizations of such individuals stand to be more adaptable to the economy's needs and society is more adaptable to its changing environment. To achieve all this, I believe our education system requires inculcating creativity and vision. Developing (or rather not suppressing) these skills is not hard. But it is neglected in the short-termism of extant education for employment. The challenge ahead is the design of interventions to control the narrowing of education—to reinstate the arts and the humanities, very much as in the global reset of education advocated by the late Sir Ken Robinson.[22]

Justice, justice, justice: lefty lawyers, really?

Although Jannis Kallinikos suggested that control is 'an exercise in boundary drawing and boundary management',[23] I speak of control as an exercise in managing the rules of the game. As I introduced in Chapter 1, theoretical advances in understanding complex system performance—such as game theory, including Nash's equilibria—have undeniably had a major, and in many cases, positive impact on shaping our social and economic existence. However, the rational assumptions of game theory require that its human players act rationally. And, as my inquiry into the entrepreneur's contrary character suggests, what is rational to some, is irrational to others. From the Needs-consciousness model I advanced in Chapter 3, with only one 'rational' operating mode of four, there stands to be a greater opportunity for observed irrationality than not. Certainly, this appears prevalent in the sense of observing entrepreneurial action, the pinnacle of the current concept of capitalist enterprise.

Recognition of the four modes of motivation suggests that the low-risk ***Conscious to conscious mode*** of motivation better prepares an individual faced with a pull-push towards enterprising opportunity. However, while the Needs-consciousness model highlights how design interventions to education might better leverage human poietic capacity, it can neither guard against excess, nor insure against boundary transgressions. Here, the basic passions

---

[22] Robinson, "A Global Reset of Education."

[23] Kallinikos, "The Order of Technology: Complexity and Control in a Connected World," 187.

or instincts (conscious, subconscious, or unconscious) that might motivate an individual toward essential: physiological, safety, love/belonging, esteem, cognitive, aesthetic, self-actualization, and self-transcendent needs, are virtuous.[24] As the self-interested pursuit of such passions within an ordered society, there is virtue in the individual taking responsibility for their own needs. However, when taking this responsibility to the extreme, when the individual pursues self-interest to the detriment of 'others', virtue transfigures as a vice. I recall that, within my conception of sustainability[25], it is implicit that our 'needs' of the present should not compromise the ability of others, including their future generations, to meet their own needs. Collectively, our 'needs' are thus referenced to the 'essential' needs of the world's poor. Sustainability cannot be achieved unless control is exercised over the excesses of the self-interested pursuit of an individual's needs at the expense of the world's poor.

I return to Mandeville's *The Fable of the Bees,* where the control over the excesses of passions—those individual virtues transgressed as social vices—are subject to the institutionalised (social) concept of justice, enacted to 'lop and bind' the excesses of individual vice. Here, I have drawn attention to the very prevalent issues of environmental degradation, economic inequality and institutional collapse. While I have noted that a Luhmannian critical theory of complex adaptive systems suggests that an ideal concept of 'justice' is 'irrational, unreachable, and ultimately meaningless', I argue we can reconcile this absurdity with a notion of controlling our own rhythm in the distinctions of identity, power and technology. I have also argued for a concept of justice that is aligned with the need to exercise control over the appropriation of the vice of self-interest as a virtue. While it is virtuous to suggest the individual has a responsibility for their 'self' within society, it cannot be that within the systemic game of enterprise, 'virtue' is allowed—even coached and accelerated by others—to play against the essential needs of yet other 'Others', and all their respective future generations. Breaching the rules of the game cannot, in any sense, be sustainable.

Played to excess, there is no guiding, invisible hand on virtue but the one we institute for ourselves in the form and institution of our processes of democratic justice. This notion was accepted by Milton Friedman in his work *Capitalism and Freedom,* writing: 'a good society requires that its members agree on the general conditions that will govern relations among them, on some means of arbitrating different interpretations of these conditions, and

---

[24] Maslow, Motivation and Personality.
[25] See notes to Chapter 1: explication of concept of sustainability.

on some device for enforcing compliance with the generally accepted rules.'[26] Yet, through the actions and encroachment of neoliberal capitalist economics, I suggest we bear witness to the restriction of justice to only those that can afford to call upon its mechanisms for enforcing (or defending against) compliance. I argue that we can only reconcile a balance in justice if the state reinstates its capacity to exercise it equitably. Here, in October 2020, the legal profession expressed fury over the divisive language of UK Prime Minister Boris Johnson, concerning the hampering of the criminal justice system by 'lefty human rights lawyers.'[27] The indignation felt by the entire criminal justice system amid the Covid-19 crises, was palpable. It was preceded by a decade of financial cuts and reduced investment—a consequence of the 2008 financial, crisis-induced austerity. The challenge ahead is the design of interventions to reconcile access to justice to those presently denied it.

Postcapitalism, work and aesthetic enterprise

So, what if we change the socio-economic system first? What if we attempt to make the economy dance to society's tune? What might be the outcomes of experiments in Design Capitalism? And what form might such experiments take? What might be the outcomes for a postcapitalism as emergent of Design Capitalism, were economic 'designs' are directed toward our educational subsystems, to open them up in poiesis rather than close them down in autopoiesis, reclaiming ground from the creative arts and humanities for the benefit of a more inclusive, more adaptable and enterprising society? What might be the outcomes for a postcapitalism as emergent of Design Capitalism, where economic 'design' interventions are directed toward our subsystems of justice, realising a less than invisible hand to uphold the values of virtuous individual action, yet taking a stand on the needs of 'others' through reopening access to justice and equity, lopping and binding the excesses of those who's self-interested virtues transfigure as social vices?

---

[26] Friedman, Capitalism and Freedom, 25; Taken out of context, Milton Friedman's suggestion that 'The Social Responsibility of Business Is to Increase Its Profits (Friedman, "The Social Responsibility of Business Is to Increase Its Profits.") belies that this responsibility charges business to use its resources and engage in its activities, 'so long as it stays within the rules of the game, which is to say, engages in open and free competition without deception or fraud.' In this sense, therefore, some contemporary criticism of Friedman objectifies the title of his essay, at the expense of ignoring the wider argument and Friedman's observations on society. It is society's responsibility to set the rules of the game of business.

[27] Cross, "Johnson Opens New Front in War on 'Lefty Lawyers.'"

Design thinking sanctions experimentation with what is currently known about the problems of our current reality, engaging with others, trialling, prototyping. It sanctions the asking of 'what if'. Design thinking is not waiting to collect an extensive evidence base of second-order observations, before further reductionist rationalisation and, only then, taking some measure of purposive action. In the preceding inquiries, I have drawn from design thinking, particularly in providing a Wizard-of-Oz view on provocations, manipulating an imagined reality toward which your response—as a reader—can but contribute to an emergent, provisional truth. In the spirit of reconciliations, I do not prejudge an emergent future. This book is no place to detail specific plans. Its sole aim is a provocation—suggesting a transitionary path from neoliberal capitalism, purposive work and autopoietic enterprise, to an emergent postcapitalism via a Design Capitalism, purposeful work, and aesthetically poietic enterprise.

As members of society and humanity, we may continue to ask of the present and future crises we face: to what extent will they impact the viability of big business and employment opportunity in the future? Is it really the case that the size of our economies, organizations, businesses, profits and GDP matters? Is the quantum of any 'thing' really 'a' thing? And, to draw on the popular label of 'Agile', is agility survival? While the dinosaurs are popularly held to have died out due to their lack of agility and resistance to change, might not the behemoths of Facebook, Amazon, Apple, Netflix and Google suffer a similar fate? Or even, should they? What is the anger of ignoring the Inspector's call? Might growing civil unrest, even war, combine with another deadly pandemic, wiping-out major populations, leaving societies without the skills to deal with global warming, or whatever extinction event might next occur?

What about drivers for change that may be more local, for example, social pressures around local concerns, the fragmentation of globalization projects, and political movements. And what about the increasing ineffectiveness of law and justice as it struggles from a lack of resources. As global power politics wax and wane, will new empires grow and fall faster, leaving devastation? Wars fought by those wanting access to an *Other's* things are not the only reason for conflict. Other reasons are political expediency, ideology, stupidity, populism, and financial gain. What of the impact of bad players such as Russia? Will there be a downfall of the US and the dollar economy? We cannot answer such questions for the future by waiting for evidence. I posit that we cannot address the problematics of present-day capitalism by consigning them to the question: how can we build a profitable, equitable, and sustainable capitalism by changing how we think about the purpose of firms, their role in society, and their relationship to government and the state. As I have set out, the purpose of firms, their role in society, and their relationship to government and the state has little, directly, to do with addressing the failing institutions of an autopoietic education and the restricted, asymmetric application of justice.

Given the above, postcapitalism, its work and aesthetic enterprise, is not a direct attack on capitalism itself, merely on the neoliberal manipulation of capitalism by a relative few in their pursuance of an excess of self-interest. There is much good being done in the name of capitalism, and there is much potential, still, within it. While we cannot address the future directly, we can, instead—I have argued—try to understand the rhythm of the society in which we dance toward it. Controlling for the rhythm and not for an indeterminate economic or social outcome, provides scope for a more poietic capitalism to do what it has the potential to do best, that is, give birth to the new, without having to destroy the old. I posit that we can use technology more creatively than to destroy the old in a seemingly uncontrolled manner—simply in a heroic display of self-interested entrepreneurship for the purposiveness of profit. Such heroism is only at the furtherance of inequity for others. To destroy is to converge on an unviable and ultimately uncreative world, emerging unprepared for its future—risking the courting of a catastrophic end to a resilient *Stability*[28] in the manner of Philip K. Dick. What is required is to change the socio-economic system, away from its creative-destructive pursuits. And, recalling another fable, that of The Boiling Frog, I argue there is no time like the present to institute such change.

The Artist, and the parable of the boiling frog

> "[We] can talk about the effect of a boiled frog that can die when the temperature in a shallow aquarium will be heated very slowly while

---

[28] For the systems enthusiast, while not previously addressed herein, design interventions on system exceptions, as opposed to performance, suggests a move from the possibilities of Stafford Beer's Viable System Model (VSM), where a system is held to be viable if it survives. Such a system, for example a stable but ultimately uncreative economy, might be said to be coherent and homeostatically balanced, to both internal and external conditions. However, despite this homeostasis, according to the VSM, the system retains mechanisms (including cybernetics) and opportunities that enable it grow, learn, evolve and adapt within its environment. The principle issue with VSM lies in the idea of homeostatic balance. Despite a capacity for change within the concept *organizational cybernetics*, it might be argued that if a system's environment or its identity changes, its organization will need to be re-invented and re-configured. See also: Jackson, Critical Systems Thinking and the Management of Complexity: Responsible Leadership for a Complex World, 291-340.

> throwing the frog to the hot water would make it to jump out immediately." [29]

What is clear is that much more could be said and written about a great many of the things I have written about herein. As a provocation, the aim is simply to awaken the drowsy frog, lulled by the warmth of the liquid in which it sits. Awake, has the frog the courage to leap? Here, to parody Marx, I suggest that:

> Every sphere of [public and individual life] must be shown as the partie honteuse of ...society: these petrified relations must be forced to dance by singing their own tune to them! [Society] must be taught to be terrified at itself, in order to give it [the] courage [to change].[30]

The frog must be taught to be terrified at itself, for it to understand that it has no option but to jump, to embrace the uncertain future. The Inspector's role is to uncover what is before the drowsy frog—to illustrate the 'what' that lies beyond the mysterious pleasure embedded in the sublimity of its present situation—yet interacting with it. The Inspector's role is to reveal the potential for the tragedy, terror and anguish of the 'other' side.

It is the artist that mediates the sublime on behalf of the audience. Here, I offer the last words to J. B. Priestley who—wrote John Baxendale[31]—*"believed that only art, 'enduring and unforgettable', could really nurture the soul."* Here, I take nurturing the soul in the sense of the soul of a society increasingly conscious of the tragedy, terror and anguish that lies amid the sublimity of its environment (and its degradation), its economy (and its inequality), and its institutions (and their collapse). As did Priestley, I also take *"a broad view of what 'art' [is]"*. According to Baxendale, Priestley, 'distanced himself from any hint of elitism, [asserting] that, given the opportunity, all were capable of actively appreciating and creating [Art], even if they did it badly.' Such a view of the artistic opportunity is poietic—it eschews the incessant autopoietic reproduction of simulacra. Here, while Schumpeter might have agreed with Marx that some form of socialism will win out over capitalism, the promise of a Design Capitalism—one with social intent—should be to open such poietic opportunity to, as Priestley commented, 'turn a mass of people on to the arts.' Broadly echoing British designer William Morris (1834-1896), 'we might [thus]

---

[29] Harley, "Confronting the Crisis of Confidence in Management Studies: Why Senior Scholars Need to Stop Setting a Bad Example," 48.

[30] Marx, "'A Contribution to the Critique of Hegel's Philosophy of Right: Introduction.'"

[31] Baxendale, "'Now We Must Live up to Ourselves': New Jerusalem and Beyond," 107.

find it possible to achieve a community in which every citizen felt himself to be something of an artist and every artist knew himself to be a citizen'.[32]

---

[32] Priestley, The Arts Under Socialism, 18, 22; Cited in: Baxendale, "'Now We Must Live up to Ourselves': New Jerusalem and Beyond," 171.

Afterword: a manifesto

WE LOVE AND CARE for the one reality we inhabit. We love and care for the diversity of forms, including all living organisms, animals, plants, fungi, protists and bacteria that inhabit it alongside ourselves. We love to be enterprising and to work, wherever humanly possible, for the good and care of all forms (things). Where we cannot work for the good of all things, then we do all that is humanly possible to take care and mitigate the consequences of our enterprises. As humans, we love and care that we are all different and that, collectively, we possess the diversity of thinking and acting differently from each other. We love that some of us may simply be a little more different and may think and act a little more differently than others. We love that it is within the grasp of each of us to do something different for the good and care of others.

WE BELIEVE THAT IT is better to work to contribute to the generation of wealth for our world, regardless of whether that is ecological, human, social, psychological or financial wealth, so long as it is not to favour any one form at the expense of, or lack of care for one or more of the others. We believe that it is self-evident that, as members of one global community, we all need to respect, care for and assist the diversity that exists amongst us to generate our collective wealth. We believe that our collective diversity requires visibility to be recognised, room to breathe, and the support to enter, develop and flourish in enterprise. For that, we believe in the capacity of enterprising individuals and organizations to take beneficial and affirmative, careful and purposeful action to ensure that our global community benefits from its diversity of enterprise, for the good and care of the world we love and the generations to follow. But we believe that, so far, we are mostly failing to employ this capacity. We believe that, in the face of an undisputed perception of volatility, uncertainty, complexity and ambiguousness—of various flavours—across the one world we inhabit, enterprising individuals and organizations need to respond to our collective shortcomings now.

WE ARE COMMITTED TO champion the thinking and doing required by enterprising individuals and organizations in respect of the challenges ahead of us all. We are committed to respect all and champion all those who think differently about the world and what goes on within it. We are committed to champion diverse thoughts and ideas that are likely to open the eyes and minds of enterprising individuals and organizations, so that the aesthetics of any situation are recognised and employed to full affect in delivering effective, caring flourishing across the full range of our societies' wealth. We are therefore committed to provide the necessary systems of education for all people of all societies to ensure our commitments are met. And we are committed to the provide the necessary systems of law and justice to ensure equity is maintained in meeting our commitments and upholding our beliefs.

WE NEED TO DO all this for the sustainability of our existence, for the collective good and care of our global community and for the generation and preservation of our collective ecological, human, social, psychological and financial wealth. We need to do all this for the sustainable, fair and compassionate distribution of the fruits of our enterprise that respects the natural world we live in, that rationalises the use of non-renewable resources, and that enables our future generations to enjoy a beautiful and hospitable earth. For if we lose any element of it through our collective neglect or misguided activity, we will undermine the substance of our human potential and our very existence.

Bibliography

Abbasi, Muhammad Sharif, Ali Tarhini, Mohammed Hassouna, and Farwa Shah. "Social, Organizational, Demography and Individuals' Technology Acceptance Behaviour: A Conceptual Model." *European Scientific Journal* 11, no. 9 (2015): 39–68.

Acemoglu, Daron, David Autor, David Dorn, Gordon H. Hanson, and Brendan Price. "Return of the Solow Paradox? It, Productivity, and Employment in US Manufacturing." *American Economic Review* 104, no. 5 (2014): 394–99. https://doi.org/10.1257/aer.104.5.394.

Acevedo, Alma. "A Personalistic Appraisal of Maslow's Needs Theory of Motivation: From 'Humanistic' Psychology to Integral Humanism." *Journal of Business Ethics* 148, no. 4 (2018): 741–63. https://doi.org/10.1007/s10551-015-2970-0.

Ackoff, Russell L. "A Lifetime Of Systems Thinking." *The Systems Thinker* 10, no. 5 (1999): 1–4.

Adorno, Theodor W. *Lectures on Negative Dialectics.* Edited by Rolf Tiedemann and Rodney Livingstone. English. Cambridge, UK: Polity Press (2003), 2008.

Agamben, Giorgio. *The Man Without Content.* Edited by Georgia Albert. Transl. Stanford, CA: Stanford University Press (1994), 1999.

Ahen, Frederick. "Global Health and International Business: New Frontiers of International Business Research." *Critical Perspectives on International Business* 15, no. 2–3 (2019): 158–78. https://doi.org/10.1108/cpoib-12-2017-0091.

Ahlqvist, Toni, and Martin Rhisiart. "Emerging Pathways for Critical Futures Research: Changing Contexts and Impacts of Social Theory." *Futures* 71 (2015): 91–104. https://doi.org/10.1016/j.futures.2015.07.012.

Ahmed, Taufiq, Shamsul Hasan, and Rifat Haneef. "Entrepreneurial Characteristics of the Agripreneurs under the Scheme of Agriclinics & Agri - Buisness Centres." *Journal of Community Mobilization and Sustainable Development* 6, no. 2 (2011): 145–49.

Aken, Joan Ernst van. "Design Science and Organization Development Interventions: Aligning Business and Humanistic Values." *Journal of Applied Behavioral Science* 43, no. 1 (2007): 67–88. https://doi.org/10.1177/00218863 06297761.

Akerlof, George A., and Rachel E. Kranton. "Economics and Identity." *The Quarterly Journal of Economics* CXV, no. 3 (2000): 715–53.

Albo, Greg, Leo Panitch, and Alan Zuege. *Capitalism, Technology, Labor: A Socialist Register Reader, Vol 2.* Edited by Greg Albo, Leo Panitch, and Alan Zuege. Chicago, IL: Haymarket Books, 2020.

Aldrich, Howard E. "The Emergence of Entrepreneurship as an Academic Field: A Personal Essay on Institutional Entrepreneurship." *Research Policy* 41, no. 7 (2012): 1240–48. https://doi.org/10.1016/j.respol.2012.03.013.

Aldrich, Howard E., and Martha Argelia Martinez. "Many Are Called, but Few Are Chosen: An Evolutionary Perspective for the Study of Entrepreneurship." In *Entrepreneurship: Concepts, Theory and Perspective*, 293–311. Springer Berlin Heidelberg, 2007. https://doi.org/10.1007/978-3-540-48543-8_14.

Allard-Poesi, Florence. "Dancing in the Dark: Making Sense of Managerial Roles during Strategic Conversations." *Scandinavian Journal of Management* 31, no. 3 (2015): 338–50. https://doi.org/10.1016/j.scaman.2015.04.002.

Alleman, James. "Threat of Internet Platforms: Facebook, Google, Etc." In *29th European Regional Conference of the International Telecommunications Society (ITS): "Towards a Digital Future: Turning Technology into Markets?", Trento, Italy, 1st - 4th August, 2018*. Calgary: International Telecommunications Society (ITS), 2018.

Alleman, James, Edmond Baranes, and Paul Rappoport. "Multisided Markets & Platform Dominance." In *30th European Conference of the International Telecommunications Society (ITS): "Towards a Connected and Automated Society", Helsinki, Finland, 16th-19th June, 2019*. Calgary: International Telecommunications Society (ITS), 2019.

Alvesson, Mats. "Methodology for Close up Studies - Struggling with Closeness and Closure." *Higher Education* 46, no. 2 (2003): 167–93. https://doi.org/10.1023/A:1024716513774.

Ambos, Tina C., Björn Ambos, Katharina J. Eich, and Jonas Puck. "Imbalance and Isolation: How Team Configurations Affect Global Knowledge Sharing." *Journal of International Management* 22, no. 4 (2016): 316–32. https://doi.org/10.1016/j.intman.2016.03.005.

Amit, R., and E. Muller. "'Push' and 'Pull' Entrepreneurship." *Journal of Small Business & Entrepreneurship* 12, no. 4 (1995): 64–80.

Anderson, Alistair. R., and S. L. Jack. "Teaching the Entrepreneurial Art." In *International Dimensions of Teaching Entrepreneurship*, edited by D. S. Evans, 84–105. Paris, 1999.

Anderson, Alistair R., S. Drakopoulou Dodd, and S. L. Jack. "Entrepreneurship as Connecting; Some Implications for Theorising and Practice." *Management Decision* 50, no. 5 (2012): 958–71. https://doi.org/10.1108/00251741211227708.

Anderson, Alistair R., and Sébastien Ronteau. "Towards an Entrepreneurial Theory of Practice; Emerging Ideas for Emerging Economies." *Journal of Entrepreneurship in Emerging Economies* 9, no. 2 (2017): 110–20. https://doi.org/10.1108/JEEE-12-2016-0054.

Anderson, Neil, Carsten K.W. De Dreu, and Bernard A. Nijstad. "The Routinization of Innovation Research: A Constructively Critical Review of the State-of-the-Science." *Journal of Organizational Behavior* 25, no. 2 (2004): 147–73. https://doi.org/10.1002/job.236.

Andrade, Daniel Pereira. "Emotional Economic Man: Power and Emotion in the Corporate World." *Critical Sociology* 41, no. 4–5 (2015): 785–805. https://doi.org/10.1177/0896920513497376.

Andriole, S. J. "Comparative Forecasting: Hindsighting the Czechoslovakian Invasion." *Futures* 11, no. 4 (1979): 275–86.

Annette, John. *Community, Service Learning and Higher Education in the UK*. Edited by J. Arthur and K. Bohlin. *Citizenship and Higher Education: The*

Role of Universities in Communities and Society. Routledge, 2005. https://doi.org/10.4324/9780203415931.

Annette, John, and Terence McLaughlin. *Citizenship and Higher Education in the UK*. Edited by J. Arthur and K. Bohlin. *Citizenship and Higher Education: The Role of Universities in Communities and Society*. Routledge, 2005. https://doi.org/10.4324/9780203415931.

Anonymous. "We Care Workers Face a Terrible Decision: Risk People's Lives or Go without Pay." The Guardian, 2020. https://www.theguardian.com/commentisfree/2020/may/08/care-workers-pay-ppe-stress-zero-hours-contracts-coronavirus.

Antcliff, Valerie, Richard Saundry, and Mark Stuart. "Networks and Social Capital in the UK Television Industry: The Weakness of Weak Ties." *Human Relations* 60, no. 2 (2007): 371–93. https://doi.org/10.1177/0018726707075880.

Antonacopoulou, Elena P. "On the Practise of Practice: In-Tensions and Ex-Tensions in the Ongoing Reconfiguration of Practice Evolution of Business Knowledge View Project." *The SAGE Handbook of New Approaches in Management and Organization*, no. August (2008): 112–34. https://doi.org/10.13140/2.1.2955.5849.

———. "Organisational Learning for and with VUCA: Learning Leadership Revisited." *Teoria e Prática Em Administração* 8, no. 2 (2018): 10–32. https://doi.org/10.21714/2238-104x2018v8i2s-40869.

Antonacopoulou, Elena P., and Ted Fuller. "Practising Entrepreneuring as Emplacement: The Impact of Sensation and Anticipation in Entrepreneurial Action." *Entrepreneurship and Regional Development* 32, no. 3–4 (2020): 257–80. https://doi.org/10.1080/08985626.2019.1641974.

Archibugi, Daniele, Andrea Filippetti, and Marion Frenz. "The Impact of the Economic Crisis on Innovation: Evidence from Europe." *Technological Forecasting and Social Change* 80, no. 7 (2013): 1247–60. https://doi.org/10.1016/j.techfore.2013.05.005.

Argenti, Nicolas, and Daniel M. Knight. "Sun, Wind, and the Rebirth of Extractive Economies: Renewable Energy Investment and Metanarratives of Crisis in Greece." *Journal of the Royal Anthropological Institute* 21, no. 4 (2015): 781–802. https://doi.org/10.1111/1467-9655.12287.

Aristotle. *Poetics*. Edited by M. Heath. Transl. London, UK: Penguin, 1996.

Armstrong, Elizabeth A., and Mary Bernstein. "Culture, Power, and Institutions: A Multi-Institutional Politics Approach to Social Movements." *Sociological Theory* 26, no. 1 (2008): 74–99. https://doi.org/10.1111/j.1467-9558.2008.00319.x.

Ashby, W. Ross, and Jeffrey Goldstein. "Requisite Variety and the Difference That Makes a Difference: An Introduction to W. Ross Ashby's 'Variety, Constraint and Law of Requisite Variety' Cybernetics, Regulation, and Complex Systems." *E:CO* 13, no. 1–2 (2011): 190–207.

Atherton, Andrew. "A Future for Small Business? Prospective Scenarios for the Development of the Economy Based on Current Policy Thinking and Counterfactual Reasoning." *Futures* 37, no. 8 (2005): 777–94. https://doi.org/10.1016/j.futures.2005.01.002.

Atkinson, David M. "A Portrait of the Organizational Manager." In *Thinking the Art of Management*, 37–59, 2007. https://doi.org/10.1057/9780230589988_3.

———. "Dancing 'the Management': On Social Presence, Rhythm and Finding Common Purpose." *Management Decision* 46, no. 7 (2008): 1081–95. https://doi.org/10.1108/00251740810890230.

———. *Thinking the Art of Management: Stepping into "Heidegger's Shoes."* Palgrave Macmillan, 2007. https://doi.org/10.1057/9780230589988.

———. *Unpublished Manuscript*, n.d.

Atkinson, Will. "Class Habitus and Perception of the Future: Recession, Employment Insecurity and Temporality." *British Journal of Sociology* 64, no. 4 (2013): 643–61. https://doi.org/10.1111/1468-4446.12049.

Azmanova, Albena. *Capitalism on Edge: How Fighting Precarity Can Achieve Radical Change Without Crisis or Utopia.* New York, NY: Columbia University Press, 2020.

Baccaro, Lucio, and Diego Rei. "Institutional Determinants of Unemployment in OECD Countries: Does the Deregulatory View Hold Water?" *International Organization* 61, no. 3 (2007): 527–69. https://doi.org/10.1017/S0020818307070221.

Badiou, Alain, and Ben Woodward. "Interview." In *The Specuative Turn: Continental Materialism and Realism*, edited by Levi Bryant, Nick Srnicek, and Graham Harman, 19–20. Melbourne: Re.Press, 2011.

Baily, Martin Neil, and Robert M Solow. "International Productivity Comparisons Built from the Firm Level" 15, no. 3 (2001): 151–72.

Balasubramaniam, R. "Compassionate Capitalism in Covid Era." The New Indian Express, 2020. https://www.newindianexpress.com/opinions/2020/may/21/compassionate-capitalism-in-covid-era-2146048.html.

Baldry, Chris. "Editorial: Chronicling the Information Revolution." *New Technology, Work and Employment* 26, no. 3 (2011): 175–82. https://doi.org/10.1111/j.1468-005X.2011.00267.x.

Banker, Steve. "COVID-19 And 3D Printing." *Forbes*, 2020, 1–4.

Baños, R. M., C. Botella, M. Alcañiz, V. Liaño, B. Guerrero, and B. Rey. "Immersion and Emotion: Their Impact on the Sense of Presence." *Cyberpsychology and Behavior* 7, no. 6 (2004): 734–41. https://doi.org/10.1089/cpb.2004.7.734.

Barnett, Vincent. "Keynes, Animal Spirits, and Instinct: Reason plus Intuition Is Better than Rational." *Journal of the History of Economic Thought* 39, no. 3 (2017): 381–99. https://doi.org/10.1017/S1053837216000274.

Baron-Cohen, Simon. "Theory of Mind and Autism: A Review." *International Review of Research in Mental Retardation* 23 (2000): 169–84. https://doi.org/10.1016/s0074-7750(00)80010-5.

Bastani, Aaron. *Fully Automated Luxury Communism.* New York, NY: Verso, 2019.

Battilana, Julie, and Tiziana Casciaro. "Change Agents, Networks, and Institutions: A Contingency Theory of Organizational Change.(Report)." *Academy of Management Journal* 55, no. 2 (2012): 381. https://doi.org/10.5465/amj.2009.0891.

Baudrillard, Jean. *Simulacra and Simulation.* Edited by Sheila Faria Glaser. Eng. Trans. The University of Michigan Press, 1994.

Baum, Lyman Frank. *The Wonderful Wizard of Oz.* The Floating Press, 2009.

Baumol, William J. "Joseph Schumpeter: The Long Run, and the Short." *Journal of Evolutionary Economics* 25, no. 1 (2015): 37–43. https://doi.org/10.1007/s00191-013-0327-3.

Baumol, William J., Robert E. Litan, and Carl J. Schramm. *Good Capitalism, Bad Capitalism, and the Economics of Growth and Prosperity. Good Capitalism, Bad Capitalism, and the Economics of Growth and Prosperity.* New Haven: Yale University Press, 2009. https://doi.org/10.32418/rfs.2009.256.1996.

Baxendale, John. "'Now We Must Live up to Ourselves': New Jerusalem and Beyond." In *Priestley's England: J. B. Priestley and English Culture*, 166–93. Manchester: Manchester University Press, 2007. https://doi.org/10.7765/9781847791320.00010.

BBC. "Edward Colston Statue : Protesters Tear down Slave Trader Monument." www.bbc.co.uk/news, 2020. https://www.bbc.co.uk/news/uk-52954305.

Becker, Howard S. "Arts and Crafts." *American Journal of Sociology* 83, no. 4 (1978): 862–89. https://doi.org/10.1086/226635.

Beer, Stafford. "What Is Cybernetics?" *Kybernetes* 31, no. 2 (2002): 209–19. https://doi.org/10.1108/03684920210417283.

BEIS. *Industrial Strategy: Building a Britain Fit for the Future. Indistrial Strategy White Paper.* London, UK: UK Government, 2017.

Bell, Frances, Gordon Fletcher, Anita Greenhill, Marie Griffiths, and Rachel McLean. "Science Fiction Prototypes: Visionary Technology Narratives between Futures." *Futures* 50 (2013): 15–24. https://doi.org/10.1016/j.futures.2013.04.004.

Bell, W. *Foundations of Futures Studies—Vol. 1: History, Purposes and Knowledge.* New Brunswick: Transaction Publishers, 1997.

Bengston, David N. "Principles for Thinking about the Future and Foresight Education." *World Futures Review* 10, no. 3 (2018): 193–202. https://doi.org/10.1177/1946756718777252.

Bennett, Nathan, and G. James Lemoine. "What a Difference a Word Makes: Understanding Threats to Performance in a VUCA World." *Business Horizons* 57, no. 3 (2014): 311–17. https://doi.org/10.1016/j.bushor.2014.01.001.

Bennett, Robert. "SME Policy Support in Britain since the 1990s: What Have We Learnt?" *Environment and Planning C: Government and Policy* 26, no. 2 (April 2008): 375–97. https://doi.org/10.1068/c07118.

Berglund, Henrik. "Researching Entrepreneurship as Lived Experience." In *Handbook of Qualitative Research Methods in Entrepreneurship*, edited by H. Neergaard and J. P. Ulhøi, 75-93. Cheltenham: Edward Elgar Publishing, 2007.

Berglund, Karin, Maria Dahlin, and Anders W. Johansson. "Walking a Tightrope between Artistry and Entrepreneurship: The Stories of the Hotel Woodpecker, Otter Inn and Luna Resort." *Journal of Enterprising Communities: People and Places in the Global Economy* 1, no. 3 (August 2007): 268–84. https://doi.org/10.1108/17506200710779567.

Bergman, Ann, Jan Ch Karlsson, and Jonas Axelsson. "Truth Claims and Explanatory Claims-An Ontological Typology of Futures Studies." *Futures* 42, no. 8 (2010): 857–65. https://doi.org/10.1016/j.futures.2010.02.003.

Betz, Ulrich A.K., Frederick Betz, Rachel Kim, Brendan Monks, and Fred Phillips. "Surveying the Future of Science, Technology and Business – A 35 year Perspective." *Technological Forecasting and Social Change* 144, no. February (2019): 137–47. https://doi.org/10.1016/j.techfore.2019.04.005.

Beynon-Davies, Paul. "Dances with Bees: Exploring the Relevance of the Study of Animal Communication to Informatics." *International Journal of Information Management* 30, no. 3 (2010): 185–98. https://doi.org/10.1016/j.ijinfomgt.2010.02.001.

Bezold, Clement. "Jim Dator's Alternative Futures and the Path to IAF's Aspirational Futures." *Journal of Futures Studies* 14, no. 2 (2009): 123–34.

Biesmeijer, Jacobus Christiaan, and Han De Vries. "Exploration and Exploitation of Food Sources by Social Insect Colonies: A Revision of the Scout-Recruit Concept." *Behavioral Ecology and Sociobiology* 49, no. 2–3 (2001): 89–99. https://doi.org/10.1007/s002650000289.

Billett, Stephen. "Coparticipation at Work: Knowing and Work Practice" 1 (2000): 16–24.

———. "Work as Social Practice: Activities and Interdependencies." *7th Annual International Conference on Post Compulsorary Education and Training, Changing Practice through Research: Changing Research through Practice, Volume 2*, 1999, 128–38.

Biocca, Frank, Judee Burgoon, Chad Harms, and Matthew Stoner. "Criteria and Scope Conditions for a Theory and Measure of Social Presence." In *Presence 2001, 4th International Workshop on Presence*, 2001.

Biraghi, Silvia, and Rossella Gambetti. "Between Tribes and Markets: The Emergence of a Liquid Consumer-Entrepreneurship." *Journal of Business Research* 92 (2018): 392–402.

Blass, Eddie. "Researching the Future: Method or Madness?" *Futures* 35, no. 10 (2003): 1041–54. https://doi.org/10.1016/S0016-3287(03)00069-7.

Block, David. "What Would Karl Say? The Entrepreneur as Ideal (and Cool) Citizen in 21st Century Societies." *Language Sciences* 70 (2018): 16–25. https://doi.org/10.1016/j.langsci.2018.04.006.

Boddewyn, Jean J. "The Conceptual Domain of International Business: Territory, Boundaries, and Levels." In *International Business: An Emerging Vision*, edited by B. Toyne and D. Nigh, 50–61. Columbia: University of South Carolina Press, 1997.

Boehnert, Joanna. "Anthropocene Economics and Design: Heterodox Economics for Design Transitions." *She Ji* 4, no. 4 (2018): 355–74. https://doi.org/10.1016/j.sheji.2018.10.002.

Boje, David, and Jo A. Tyler. "Story and Narrative Noticing: Workaholism Autoethnographies." *Journal of Business Ethics* 84, no. SUPPL. 2 (2009): 173–94. https://doi.org/10.1007/s10551-008-9702-7.

Boldyrev, Ivan A. "Economy as a Social System: Niklas Luhmann's Contribution and Its Significance for Economics." *American Journal of Economics and Sociology* 72, no. 2 (2013): 265–92. https://doi.org/10.1111/ajes.12013.

Bonefeld, Werner. "Negative Dialectics in Miserable Times: Notes on Adorno and Social Praxis." *Journal of Classical Sociology* 12, no. 1 (2012): 122–34. https://doi.org/10.1177/1468795X11433701.

Booker, Christopher. *The Seven Basic Plots: Why We Tell Stories*. London: Continuum, 2004.

Booth, Charles, Michael Rowlinson, Peter Clark, Agnes Delahaye, and Stephen Procter. "Scenarios and Counterfactuals as Modal Narratives." *Futures* 41, no. 2 (2009): 87–95. https://doi.org/10.1016/j.futures.2008.07.037.

Bosman, M. Martin. "The Political Rhetoric of Corporate Globalisation and the Possibilities for Counter-Hegemonic Projects." *Space and Polity* 3, no. 2 (1999): 125–52. https://doi.org/10.1080/13562579908721790.

Botsman, Rachel. *Who Can You Trust? : How Technology Brought Us Together - and Why It Could Drive Us Apart*. Updated. Penguin Business, 2018.

Bouette, Martin, and Florence Magee. "Hobbyists, Artisans and Entrepreneurs." *Journal of Small Business and Enterprise Development* 22, no. 2 (2015): 337–51. https://doi.org/10.1108/JSBED-02-2013-0022.

Bourdieu, Pierre. "Participant Objectivation." *Journal of the Royal Anthropological Institute* 9, no. 2 (2003): 281–94. https://doi.org/10.1111/1467-9655.00150.

Boussebaa, Mehdi. "Identity Regulation and Globalization." *The Oxford Handbook of Identities in Organizations*, no. January (2020): 682–96. https://doi.org/10.1093/oxfordhb/9780198827115.013.15.

———. "In the Shadow of Empire: Global Britain and the UK Business School." *Organization*, 2019. https://doi.org/10.1177/1350508419855700.

Boussebaa, Mehdi, and Glenn Morgan. "Pushing the Frontiers of Critical International Business Studies: The Multinational as a Neo-Imperial Space." *Critical Perspectives on International Business* 10, no. 1 (2014): 96–106. https://doi.org/10.1108/cpoib-11-2013-0046.

Boyd, Edward. "Compassionate Capitalism Can Underpin Our Coronavirus Recovery." City AM, 2020. https://www.cityam.com/compassionate-capitalism-can-underpin-our-coronavirus-recovery/.

Boyd, Ross, and Robert J. Holton. "Technology, Innovation, Employment and Power: Does Robotics and Artificial Intelligence Really Mean Social Transformation?" *Journal of Sociology* 54, no. 3 (2018): 331–45. https://doi.org/10.1177/1440783317726591.

Bozic Yams, Nina. "The Impact of Contemporary Dance Methods on Innovative Competence Development." *Journal of Business Research* 85, no. October 2017 (2018): 494–503. https://doi.org/10.1016/j.jbusres.2017.10.028.

Brannick, Teresa, and David Coghlan. "In Defense of Being 'Native': The Case for Insider Academic Research." *Organizational Research Methods* 10, no. 1 (2007): 59–74. https://doi.org/10.1177/1094428106289253.

Brassett, Jamie, and John O'reilly. "Styling the Future. A Philosophical Approach to Design and Scenarios." *Futures* 74 (2015): 37–48. https://doi.org/10.1016/j.futures.2015.07.001.

Brauers, Hanna, and Christian von Hirschhausen. "Doughnut Economics: Seven Ways to Think Like a 21st Century Economist." *Economics of Energy & Environmental Policy* 7, no. 2 (2018): 155–58.

Brocklehurst, Michael. "Power, Identity and New Technology Homework: Implications for 'new Forms' of Organizing." *Organization Science* 22, no. 3 (2001): 445–66. https://doi.org/0803973233.

Broersma, Marcel. "The Unbearable Limitations of Journalism: On Press Critique and Journalism's Claim to Truth." *International Communication Gazette* 72, no. 1 (2010): 21–33. https://doi.org/10.1177/1748048509350336.

Brown, Stephen. "The Wind in the Wallows: Literary Theory, Autobiographical Criticism and Subjective Personal Introspection." *ACR North American Advances* NA-25 (1998): 25–31.

Brown, Tim, and Roger Martin. "Design for Action." *Harvard Business Review* 2015, no. September (2015): 58–64. https://doi.org/10.1109/emr.2016.7559061.

Brown, Tim, Roger L. Martin, and Shoshana Berger. "Capitalism Needs Design Thinking." *Harvard Business Review* December (2014): 1–6.

Brugha, Traolach, Sally-Ann Cooper, Sally McManus, Susan Purdon, Jane Smith, Fiona J. Scott, Nicola Spiers, and Freya Tryer. "Estimating the Prevalence of Autism Spectrum Conditions in Adults: Extending the 2007 Adult Psychiatric Morbidity Survey." *The NHS Information Centre for Health and Social Care*, 2012.

Brynjolfsson, Erik, and Andrew McAfee. "Race against the Machine: How the Digital Revolution Is Accelerating Innovation, Driving Productivity and Irreversibly Transforming Employment and the Economy." A major research initiative at the MIT Sloan School of Management., 2012. http://digital.mit.edu/research/briefs/brynjolfsson_McAfee_Race_Against_the_Machine.pdf.

Buchanan, Ian. "Critical Theory." In *Oxford Dictionary of Critical Theory*, 2nd (onlin. Oxford University Press, 2018. https://doi.org/10.1093/acref/9780198794790.001.0001.

Buchholz, René. "'Grand Hotel Abyss?' On the Actuality of Theodor W. Adorno's Critical Theory [Transl.]." Edited by Frederik Van Gelder. Cologne, 2020.

Buckley, Walter. "Society as a Complex Adaptive System." In *Modern Systems Research for the Behavioral Scientist*, edited by Walter Buckley. Chicago, IL: Aldine Publishing Company, 1968.

Buckley, Walter, David Schwandt, and Jeffrey A. Goldstein. "Classic Paper Section: Society as a Complex Adaptive System (1968)." *Emergence: Complexity and Organization* 10, no. 3 (2008): 86–112. https://doi.org/10.1017/CBO9781107415324.004.

Bujor, Adriana, and Silvia Avasilcai. "The Creative Entrepreneur: A Framework of Analysis." *Procedia - Social and Behavioral Sciences* 221 (2016): 21–28. https://doi.org/10.1016/j.sbspro.2016.05.086.

Bunge, Mario. "Comment on Apostol' s Paper." *Studies in Soviet Thought* 29, no. 2 (1985): 137–38.

Burchell, Jon, Steve Kennedy, and Alan Murray. "Responsible Management Education in UK Business Schools: Critically Examining the Role of the United Nations Principles for Responsible Management Education as a Driver for Change." *Management Learning* 46, no. 4 (2015): 479–97. https://doi.org/10.1177/1350507614549117.

Burgelman, Robert A. "Designs for Corporate Entrepreneurship in Established Firms." *California Management Review* 26, no. 3 (1984): 154–66. https://doi.org/10.2307/41165086.

Burke, Peter J. "Identity Dispersion: Flexibility, Uncertainty, or Inconsistency?" *Identity and Symbolic Interaction*, 2020, 89–117. https://doi.org/10.1007/978-3-030-41231-9_4.

Burmaoglu, Serhat, Olivier Sartenaer, and Alan Porter. "Conceptual Definition of Technology Emergence: A Long Journey from Philosophy of Science to Science Policy." *Technology in Society* 59, no. January (2019): 101126. https://doi.org/10.1016/j.techsoc.2019.04.002.

Burns, Paul. *Entrepreneurship and Small Business : Start-up, Growth and Maturity*. 4th ed. Palgrave Macmillan, 2016.

Busby, Mattha. "Schools in England Told Not to Use Material from Anti Capitalist Groups." *The Guardian*. September 27, 2020.

Busch, Otto von, and Karl Palmås. "Designing Consent: Can Design Thinking Manufacture Democratic Capitalism?" *Organizational Aesthetics* 5, no. 2 (2016): 10–24.

Butanaziba, Yunus Lebga. "The Strategy: Ending Globalization Disorders." *Interdisciplinary Description of Complex System* 8, no. 2 (2010): 81–103.

Bynner, John. "Whatever Happened to Lifelong Learning? And Does It Matter?" *Journal of the British Academy* 5, no. March (2017): 61–89. https://doi.org/10.5871/jba/005.061.

Cabrera, Nolan L. "Where Is the Racial Theory in Critical Race Theory?: A Constructive Criticism of the Crits." *Review of Higher Education* 42, no. 1 (2018): 209–33.

Caelli, Kate, Lynne Ray, and Judy Mill. "'Clear as Mud': Toward Greater Clarity in Generic Qualitative Research." *International Journal of Qualitative Methods* 2, no. 2 (2003): 1–13. https://doi.org/10.1177/160940690300200201.

Cairns, George, Martyna Śliwa, and George Wright. "Problematizing International Business Futures through a 'Critical Scenario Method.'" *Futures* 42, no. 9 (2010): 971–79. https://doi.org/10.1016/j.futures.2010.08.016.

Calas, Marta B, Linda Smircich, and Kristina A Bourne. "Extending the Boundaries 'Entrepreneurship as Social Change.'" *Academy of Management Review* 34, no. 3 (2009): 552–69. https://doi.org/10.5465/AMR.2009.40633597.

Campbell, Colin. "The Craft Consumer: Culture, Craft and Consumption in a Postmodern Society." *Journal of Consumer Culture* 5, no. 1 (2005): 23–42. https://doi.org/10.1177/1469540505049843.

Campbell, Joseph. *The Hero with a Thousand Faces*. 3rd ed. Novato, CA: New World Library (1949), 2008.

Card, Debora, and Craig Nelson. "How Automation and Digital Disruption Are Shaping the Workforce of the Future." *Strategic HR Review* 18, no. 6 (2019): 242–45. https://doi.org/10.1108/shr-08-2019-0067.

Carney, Nikita. "All Lives Matter, but so Does Race." *Humanity & Society* 40, no. 2 (2016): 180–99. https://doi.org/10.1177/0160597616643868.

Casson, Mark C, and Stephen Pavelin. "The Social Performance and Responsibilities of Entrepreneurship." *Business & Society* 55, no. 1 (2016): 11–13. https://doi.org/10.1177/0007650314566375.

Cavendish, Dominic. "Not 'Viable'? Rishi Sunak Just Told Our Entire Creative Industry to Get Another Job." The Telegraph, 2020. https://www.telegraph.

co.uk/theatre/what-to-see/not-viable-rishi-sunak-just-told-entire-creative-industry-get/.

Chalk, Alfred F. "Mandeville's Fable of the Bees: A Reappraisal." *Southern Economic Journal* 33, no. 1 (1966): 1–16. https://doi.org/10.2307/1055985.

Champenois, Claire, Vincent Lefebvre, and Sébastien Ronteau. "Entrepreneurship as Practice: Systematic Literature Review of a Nascent Field." *Entrepreneurship and Regional Development* 32, no. 3–4 (2020): 281–312. https://doi.org/10.1080/08985626.2019.1641975.

Checkland, Peter. "Soft Systems Methodology: A Thirty Year Retrospective." *Sytems Research and Behavioral Science* 17 (2000): S11–58.

———. *Systems Thinking, Systems Practice.* Chichester, UK: John Wiley & Sons, 1999.

Chell, Elizabeth. "Review of Skill and the Entrepreneurial Process." *International Journal of Entrepreneurial Behaviour & Research* 19, no. 1 (2013): 6–31. https://doi.org/10.1108/13552551311299233.

Chen, Jian, Yidi Guo, and Hengyuan Zhu. "Can Me-Too Products Prevail? Performance of New Product Development and Sources of Idea Generation in China - an Emerging Market." *R & D Management* 42, no. 3 (2012): 273. https://doi.org/10.1111/j.1467-9310.2012.00683.x.

Chiappero-Martinetti, Enrica, Nadia von Jacobi, and Marcello Signorelli. "Human Development and Economic Growth." In *Palgrave Dictionary of Emerging Markets and Transition Economics*, edited by Jens Hölscher and Horst Tomann, 223–44. London, UK: Palgrave Macmillan, 2015.

Chiles, Todd H., Allen C. Bluedorn, and Vishal K. Gupta. "Beyond Creative Destruction and Entrepreneurial Discovery: A Radical Austrian Approach to Entrepreneurship." *Organization Studies* 28, no. 4 (2007): 467–93. https://doi.org/10.1177/0170840606067996.

Chowdhury, Mohammed S., Zahurul Alam, and Md. Ifttekhar Arif. "Success Factors of Entrepreneurs of Small and Medium Sized Enterprises: Evidence from Bangladesh." *Business and Economic Research. 3(2)* 3, no. 2 (2013): 38–52.

Clarke, Martin, and David Butcher. "Political Leadership, Bureaucracies and Business Schools: A Comfortable Union?" *Management Learning* 40, no. 5 (2009): 587–607. https://doi.org/10.1177/1350507609340808.

Cliff, Jennifer E., P. Devereaux Jennings, and Royston Greenwood. "New to the Game and Questioning the Rules: The Experiences and Beliefs of Founders Who Start Imitative versus Innovative Firms." *Journal of Business Venturing* 21, no. 5 (2006): 633–63. https://doi.org/10.1016/j.jbusvent.2005.02.010.

Coburn, Kathleen. *Samuel Taylor Coleridge – The Philosophical Lectures, Lecture XI.* London: The Pilot Press, 1949.

Cock, Christian de. "Jumpstarting the Future with Fredric Jameson: Reflections on Capitalism, Science Fiction and Utopia." *Journal of Organizational Change Management* 22, no. 4 (2009): 437–49. https://doi.org/10.1108/09534810910967198.

Cole, Courtney E. "Stories from the Lived and Living Fieldwork Process." *Qualitative Research in Organizations and Management: An International Journal* 8, no. 1 (2013): 50–69. https://doi.org/10.1108/17465641311327513.

Coleman, James S. "Social Capital in the Creation of Human Capital." *The American Journal of Socilogy* 94, no. Supplement (1988): S95–120.

Collins, Hilary, Hayley Glover, and Fran Jones Myers. "The Automation Game: Perceptions on the Impact of the Changes on Business School Tutors' Roles and Identity during the Introduction of Technological Student Retention Activities." In *2017 British Academy of Management Conference Proceedings*, 2017.

Collyer, Fran M. "Practices of Conformity and Resistance in the Marketisation of the Academy: Bourdieu, Professionalism and Academic Capitalism." *Critical Studies in Education* 56, no. 3 (2015): 315–31. https://doi.org/10.1080/17508487.2014.985690.

Conceição, Pedro, David V. Gibson, Manuel V. Heitor, and Giorgio Sirilli. "Beyond the Digital Economy: A Perspective on Innovation for the Learning Society." *Technological Forecasting and Social Change* 67, no. 2–3 (2001): 115–42. https://doi.org/10.1016/S0040-1625(01)00128-7.

Conceiçao, Pedro, Manuel V. Heitor, and Francisco Veloso. "Infrastructures, Incentives, and Institutions: Fostering Distributed Knowledge Bases for the Learning Society." *Technological Forecasting and Social Change* 70, no. 7 (2003): 583–617. https://doi.org/10.1016/S0040-1625(03)00046-5.

Cook, Laurence. "Coronavirus + the UK Entertainment Industr y — the Latest." Backstage, 2020. https://www.backstage.com/uk/magazine/article/coronavirus-the-uk-entertainment-industry-responds-70289/.

Cook, Scott D. N., and John Seely Brown. "Bridging Epistemologies: The Generative Dance between Organizational Knowledge and Organizational Knowing." *Organization Science* 10, no. 4 (1999): 381–400.

Cooke, Philip. "World Turned Upside down: Entrepreneurial Decline, Its Reluctant Myths and Troubling Realities." *Journal of Open Innovation: Technology, Market, and Complexity* 5, no. 2 (2019). https://doi.org/10.3390/joitmc5020022.

Cooper, Robert. "Primary and Secondary Thinking in Social Theory: The Case of Mass Society." *Journal of Classical Sociology* 3, no. 2 (2003): 145–72. https://doi.org/10.1177/1468795X030032003.

Cornelissen, Joep P. "Portrait of an Entrepreneur: Vincent van Gogh, Steve Jobs, and the Entrepreneurial Imagination." *Academy of Management Review* 38, no. 4 (2013): 700–709. https://doi.org/10.5465/amr.2013.0068.

Cornuel, Eric. "Challenges Facing Business Schools in the Future." *Journal of Management Development* 26, no. 1 (2007): 87–92. https://doi.org/10.1108/02621710710720130.

Courtney, Kathy. "Adapting Higher Education through Changes in Academic Work." *Higher Education Quarterly* 67, no. 1 (2013): 40–55. https://doi.org/10.1111/hequ.12002.

Cross, Michael. "Johnson Opens New Front in War on 'Lefty Lawyers.'" The Law Society Gazette, 2020. https://www.lawgazette.co.uk/news/johnson-opens-new-front-in-war-on-lefty-lawyers/5105891.article.

Crouch, Colin. "Models of Capitalism." *New Political Economy* 10, no. 4 (2005): 439–56. https://doi.org/10.1080/13563460500344336.

———. "The Paradoxes of Privatisation and Public Service Outsourcing." In *Rethinking Capitalism: Economics and Policy for Sustainable and Inclusive Growth*, edited by Michael Jacobs and Mariana Mazzucato, 156–71. Chichester, UK: John Wiley & Sons, 2014.

Cumming, Graeme S., and Stephan von Cramon-Taubadel. "Linking Economic Growth Pathways and Environmental Sustainability by Understanding Development as Alternate Social-Ecological Regimes." *Proceedings of the National Academy of Sciences of the United States of America* 115, no. 38 (2018): 9533–38. https://doi.org/10.1073/pnas.1807026115.

Cunliffe, Ann L. "Alterity: The Passion, Politics, and Ethics of Self and Scholarship." *Management Learning* 49, no. 1 (2018): 8–22. https://doi.org/10.1177/1350507617737454.

———. "Social Poetics as Management Inquiry: A Dialogical Approach." *Journal of Management Inquiry* 11, no. 2 (2002). https://doi.org/10.1177/10592602011002006.

D'Souza, Jeevan, and Michael Gurin. "The Universal Significance of Maslow's Concept of Self-Actualization." *Humanistic Psychologist* 44, no. 2 (2016): 210–14. https://doi.org/10.1037/hum0000027.

Dacin, M. Tina, Peter A. Dacin, and Paul Tracey. "Social Entrepreneurship: A Critique and Future Directions." *Organization Science* 22, no. 5 (2011): 1203–13. https://doi.org/10.1287/orsc.1100.0620.

Dahlbäck, Nils, Arne Jönsson, and Lars Ahrenberg. "Wizard of Oz Studies - Why and How." *Knowledge-Based Systems* 6, no. 4 (December 1993): 258–66. https://doi.org/10.1016/0950-7051(93)90017-N.

Damasio, Antonio R. *Descartes' Error*. London, UK: Random House, 2006.

Darity, William A., Patrick L. Mason, and James B. Stewart. "The Economics of Identity: The Origin and Persistence of Racial Identity Norms." *Journal of Economic Behavior and Organization* 60, no. 3 (2006): 283–305. https://doi.org/10.1016/j.jebo.2004.09.005.

Dator, Jim. "De-Colonizing The Future." *Journal of Futures Studies* 9, no. 3 (2005): 93–104.

Dau, Luis Alfonso. "Learning across Geographic Space: Pro-Market Reforms, Multinationalization Strategy, and Profitability." *Journal of International Business Studies* 44, no. 3 (2013): 235–62. https://doi.org/10.1057/jibs.2013.5.

Davidsson, Per. "Entrepreneurial Opportunities and the Entrepreneurship Nexus: A Re-Conceptualization." *Journal of Business Venturing* 30, no. 5 (2015): 674–95. https://doi.org/10.1016/j.jbusvent.2015.01.002.

Davis, Jack, and Kamlesh T. Mehta. "Reengineering a School of Business of the Future : A Mission/Vision Model for Higher Education in Transformational Times." *SAM Advanced Management Journal* 62, no. 2 (1997): 8.

Davis, John B. "Identity and Individual Economic Agents: A Narrative Approach." *Review of Social Economy* 67, no. 1 (2009): 71–94. https://doi.org/10.1080/00346760802431009.

Delanty, Gerard. "The Governance of Universities: What Is the Role of the University in the Knowledge Society?" *Canadian Journal of Sociology* 27, no. 2 (2002): 185–98. https://doi.org/10.2307/3341710.

Dennett, Daniel C. "Beliefs about Beliefs." *Behavioral and Brain Sciences* 1, no. 4 (1978): 568–70. https://doi.org/10.1017/S0140525X00076664.

———. "Conditions of Personhood." In *What Is a Person?*, edited by Michael F. Goodman, 145–67. Clifton, NJ: Humana Press, 1988.

Denning, Stephen. *The Age of Agile: How Smart Companies Are Transforming the Way Work Gets Done.* New York, NY: Amacon, 2018.

———. "Why Today's Business Schools Teach Yesterday's Expertise." *Forbes*, May 27, 2018.

Derbyshire, James, and George Wright. "Augmenting the Intuitive Logics Scenario Planning Method for a More Comprehensive Analysis of Causation." *International Journal of Forecasting* 33, no. 1 (2017): 254–66. https://doi.org/10.1016/j.ijforecast.2016.01.004.

Dewey, John. *Art as Experience.* New York, NY: Perigee (1934), 1980.

Diamond Jr, Arthur M. "Schumpeter's Creative Destruction: A Review of the Evidence." *Journal of Private Enterprise* 22, no. 1 (2006): 120–46.

Dick, Philip K. "Stability." In *Beyond Lies the Wub, Volume 1 of the Collected Stories of Philip K. Dick*, 1–11. London: Millennium, 1987, 1999.

———. *The Shifting Realities of Philip K. Dick: Selected Literary and Philosophical Writings.* Edited by L Sutin. New York, NY: Vintage Books, 1995.

Diethelm, Jerry. "Doughnut Economics: Seven Ways to Think Like a 21st Century Economist." *She Ji: The Journal of Design, Economics, and Innovation* 2, no. 4 (2016): 349–50. https://doi.org/10.1016/j.sheji.2017.05.002.

Dijkema, Gerard P.J., Paulo Ferrão, Paulien M. Herder, and Manuel Heitor. "Trends and Opportunities Framing Innovation for Sustainability in the Learning Society." *Technological Forecasting and Social Change* 73, no. 3 (2006): 215–27. https://doi.org/10.1016/j.techfore.2006.01.001.

Dörrenbächer, Christoph, and Jens Gammelgaard. "Critical and Mainstream International Business Research: Making Critical IB an Integral Part of a Societally Engaged International Business Discipline." *Critical Perspectives on International Business* 15, no. 2–3 (2019): 239–61. https://doi.org/10.1108/cpoib-02-2019-0012.

Dörrenbächer, Christoph, and Snejina Michailova. "Editorial." *Critical Perspectives on International Business* 15, no. 2–3 (2019): 110–18. https://doi.org/10.1108/cpoib-05-2019-103.

Dosi, Giovanni, Maria Enrica Virgillito, and Andrea Roventini. "Rebalancing Labour Power for an Innovation-Fuelled Sustainable Inclusive Growth." European Policy Brief. Pisa, 2018.

Douglass, Robin. "Morality and Sociability in Commercial Society: Smith, Rousseau-And Mandeville." *Review of Politics* 79, no. 4 (2017): 597–620. https://doi.org/10.1017/S0034670517000584.

Dow, Sheila C. "Smith's Philosophy and Economic Methodology." In *Elgar Companion to Adam Smith*, edited by J. T. Young, 100–111. Edward Elgar Publishing, 2009.

Dumitriu, Sam. "Educating Future Founders." London, UK, 2020.

Dunn, Phoebe, Lucinda Allen, Richard Humphries, and Hugh Alderwick. "Briefing: Adult Social Care and COVID-19 - Assessing the Policy Response in England so Far." The Health Foundation, 2020.

Dunne, Stephen. "Book Review: Thinking the Art of Management: Stepping into 'Heidegger's Shoes', David M. Atkinson. Hampshire: Palgrave, 2007. 272 Pp., £55.00, ISBN 139780230553743 (Hbk)." *Organization* 16, no. 6 (2009): 919–21. https://doi.org/10.1177/1350508409346264.

Duroy, Quentin. "North African Identity and Racial Discrimination in France: A Social Economic Analysis of Capability Deprivation." *Review of Social Economy* 69, no. 3 (2011): 307–32. https://doi.org/10.1080/00346764.2010.502834.

Dziuban, Charles, Charles R. Graham, Patsy D. Moskal, Anders Norberg, and Nicole Sicilia. "Blended Learning: The New Normal and Emerging Technologies." *International Journal of Educational Technology in Higher Education* 15, no. 1 (2018): 1–16. https://doi.org/10.1186/s41239-017-0087-5.

Earle, Bo. "Plato, Aristotle, and the Imitation of Reason." *Philosophy and Literature* 27, no. 2 (2003): 382–401. https://doi.org/10.1353/phl.2003.0044.

Eden, Lorraine. "Letter from the Editor-in-Chief." *Journal of International Business Studies* 39, no. 1 (2008): 1–7. https://doi.org/10.1057/palgrave.jibs.8400336.

Eden, Lorraine, Li Dai, and Dan Li. "International Business, International Management, and International Strategy: What's in a Name?" *International Studies of Management and Organization* 40, no. 4 (2010): 54–68. https://doi.org/10.2753/IMO0020-8825400405.

Edwards, Gareth, and Nicholas O'Regan. "Leading Through Art: An Interview With Vicki Heywood CBE, Chair, Royal Society of Arts." *Journal of Management Inquiry* 28, no. 1 (2019): 71–76. https://doi.org/10.1177/1056492617750491.

Egeland, Jonathan. "Imagination Cannot Justify Empirical Belief." *Episteme* 18, no. 4 (2021): 507–13. https://doi.org/10.1017/epi.2019.22.

Egri, Lajos. *The Art of Dramatic Writing: Its Basis in the Creative Interpretation of Human Motives.* 1st Touchs. New York, NY: Simon and Schuste, 1942, 2004.

Eisenhardt, Kathleen M. "Agency Theory: An Assessment and Review." *Academy of Management Review* 14, no. 1 (1989): 57–74. https://doi.org/10.5465/amr.1989.4279003.

Elliott, John E. "Marx and Schumpeter on Capitalism's Creative Destruction: A Comparative Restatement." *The Quarterly Journal of Economics* 95, no. 1 (1980): 45–68.

Elliott, Scott S. "'Witless in Your Own Cause': Divine Plots and Fractured Characters in the Life of Aesop and the Gospel of Mark." *Religion and Theology* 12, no. 3–4 (2005): 397–418. https://doi.org/10.1163/157430106776241187.

Ellis, Carolyn. "Fighting Back or Moving on an Autoethnographic Response to Critics." *International Review of Qualitative Research* 2, no. 3 (2009): 371.

Ellis, Carolyn, and Tony E. Adams. "The Purposes, Practices, and Principles of Autoethnographic Research." In *The Oxford Handbook of Qualitative Research*, edited by P. Leavy, 253–76. Oxford: University Press, 2014. https://doi.org/10.1093/oxfordhb/9780199811755.013.004.

Ellis, David. "Economic Freedom Mis-Sold: Neoliberalism and the Moral Economies of the PPI Scandal in the UK." In *Neoliberalism and the Moral Economy of Fraud*, edited by David Whyte and Jörg Wiegratz, 155–69, 2016.

Ellis, Vernon. “Can Global Business Be a Force for Good?” *Business Strategy Review* 12, no. 2 (2001): 15–20. https://doi.org/10.1111/1467-8616.00171.

Engelke, Henning, Stefanie Mauksch, Inga-Lena Darkow, and Heiko Von Der Gracht. “Heading Toward a More Social Future? Scenarios for Social Enterprises in Germany.” *Business & Society* 55, no. 1 (2016): 56–89. https://doi.org/10.1177/0007650314523096.

Envick, Brooke R. “Beyond Human and Social Capital: The Importance of Positive Psychological Capital for Entrepreneurial Success.” *Academy of Entrepreneurship* 10, no. 2 (2005): 41–52.

Eriksson, Clas. “Is There a Trade-off between Employment and Growth?” *Oxford Economic Papers* 49, no. 1 (1997): 77–88. https://doi.org/10.1093/oxfordjournals.oep.a028598.

Euromonitor International. “Global Economic Forecasts Q4 2019,” 2019.

Euromonitor Passport. “Understanding the Five Drivers Shaping Megatrends.” *Euromonitor International*, no. January (2019): 1–3.

European Commission. “2020 Strategic Foresight Report: Charting the Course Toowards a More Resilient Europe,” 2020. https://ec.europa.eu/info/sites/info/files/strategic_ foresight_report_2020_1.pdf.

———. “Commission Unveils Its First Strategic Foresight Report : Charting the Course towards a More Resilient Europe.” *European Commission - Press Release*. September 9, 2020.

Ewenstein, Boris, and Jennifer Whyte. “Beyond Words: Aesthetic Knowledge and Knowing in Organizations.” *Organization Studies* 28, no. 5 (2007): 689–708. https://doi.org/10.1177/0170840607078080.

Feenberg, Andrew. “Why Students of the Frankfurt School Will Have to Read Lukács.” In *The Palgrave Handbook of Critical Theory*, edited by Michael J. Thompson, 109–33. Palgrave Macmillan, 2017. https://doi.org/10.1057/978-1-137-55801-5_6.

Fehr, Drude von der. “Abduction as the Missing Link Between Aesthetics and Biology.” In *12th World Congress of Semiotics: New Semiotics. Between Tradition and Innovation*, 91–96. Sofia: The International Association for Semiotic Studies, 2014. https://doi.org/10.24308/iass-2014-013.

Fergnani, Alessandro, and Thomas J. Chermack. “The Resistance to Scientific Theory in Futures and Foresight, and What to Do about It.” *Futures & Foresight Science*, no. December (2020): 1–16. https://doi.org/10.1002/ffo2.61.

Fergnani, Alessandro, and Zhaoli Song. “The Six Scenario Archetypes Framework: A Systematic Investigation of Science Fiction Films Set in the Future.” *Futures* 124, no. September (2020): 102645. https://doi.org/10.1016/j.futures.2020.102645.

Field, Thalia. “Irrationality, Situations, and Novels of Inquiry.” The Review of Contemporary Fiction, 2013. link.gale.com/apps/doc/A424614989/ITOF?u=urjy&sid=ITOF&xid=cff72a31.

Filippi, Stefano, and Daniela Barattin. “Definition and Exploitation of Trends of Evolution about Interaction.” *Technological Forecasting and Social Change* 86 (2014): 216–36. https://doi.org/10.1016/j.techfore.2013.08.042.

Fine, Michelle. "Working the Hyphens: Reinventing Self and Other in Qualitative Research." *Handbook of Qualitative Research*, 1994. https://doi.org/10.1016/j.jconhyd.2010.08.009.

Fischer, Ronald, Maria Cristina Ferreira, Nathalie Van Meurs, Kubilay Gok, Ding Yu Jiang, Johnny R.J. Fontaine, Charles Harb, et al. "Does Organizational Formalization Facilitate Voice and Helping Organizational Citizenship Behaviors? It Depends on (National) Uncertainty Norms." *Journal of International Business Studies* 50, no. 1 (2019): 125–34. https://doi.org/10.1057/s41267-017-0132-6.

Fisher, Eran. "Contemporary Technology Discourse and the Legitimation of Capitalism." *European Journal of Social Theory* 13, no. 2 (2010): 229–52. https://doi.org/10.1177/1368431010362289.

Fisher, Mark. *Capitalist Realism: Is There No Alternative?* Alresford, Hants, UK: Zero Books, 2009.

Fitzsimmons, Stacey R. "Us, Them, and Others in Management Research." *Academy of Management Review*, no. 3 (n.d.). https://doi.org/10.5465/amr.2014.0041.

Flynn, Asher, and Jacqueline Hodgson. "Access to Justice and Legal Aid Cuts: A Mismatch of Concepts in the Contemporary Australian and British Legal Landscapes." In *Access to Justice & Legal Aid: Comparative Perspectives on Unmet Legal Need*, edited by Asher Flynn and Jacqueline Hodgson. Oxford and Portland, Oregon: Hart Publishing, 2017.

Forsman, Helena. "Innovation Capacity and Innovation Development in Small Enterprises. A Comparison between the Manufacturing and Service Sectors." *Research Policy* 40, no. 5 (2011): 739–50. https://doi.org/10.1016/j.respol.2011.02.003.

Foster, Peter. "Universities' Plea for £ 2bn Bailout Falls on Deaf Ears in Treasury," 2020, 8–10.

Fotaki, Marianna, and Ajnesh Prasad. "Questioning Neoliberal Capitalism and Economic Inequality in Business Schools." *Academy of Management Learning and Education* 14, no. 4 (2015): 556–75. https://doi.org/10.5465/amle.2014.0182.

Foucault, Michel. *Aesthetics, Method, and Epistemology*. Edited by James D Faubion. *Essential Works of Foucault, 1954-1984*. London: Penguin, 1998.

———. *Power/Knowledge: Selected Interviews and Other Writings 1972–1977*. New York: Pantheon, 1980.

Franck, Georg. "Mental Presence and the Temporal Present." In *Brain and Being: At the Boundary Between Science, Philosophy, Language and Arts*, edited by G.G. Globus, K.H. Pribram, and G. Vitiello, 47–68. Amsterdam: John Benjamins, 2004. https://doi.org/10.1075/aicr.58.05fra.

Frankel, Jeffrey. "Economic Shocks and International Politics." *Survival* 54, no. 3 (2012): 29–46. https://doi.org/10.1080/00396338.2012.690977.

Fraser, Nancy. "A Triple Movement? Parsing the Politics of Crisis after Polanyi." In *Beyond Neoliberalism? Social Analysis after 1989*, edited by Marian Burchardt and Gal Kirn, 29–42. Cham, Switzerland: Palgrave Macmillan, 2017. https://doi.org/10.1007/978-3-319-45590-7_1.

Freedland, Jonathan. "Don't Pity White, Middle-Aged Men. It's Ludicrous to Cast Them as Victims." The Guardian, 2018. https://www.theguardian.com/commentisfree/2018/jan/10/pity-white-middle-aged-men-may-cabinet-massacre.

Fresen, Jill W. "Embracing Distance Education in a Blended Learning Model: Challenges and Prospects." *Distance Education* 39, no. 2 (2018): 224–40. https://doi.org/10.1080/01587919.2018.1457949.

Freud, Sigmund. *The Essentials of Psycho-Analysis.* London, UK: Vintage, Random House, 2005.

Friedman, Milton. *Capitalism and Freedom.* 40th Aniv. The University of Chicago Press (1962), 2002.

———. "The Social Responsibility of Business Is to Increase Its Profits." September 13, 2020.

Fuchs, Christian. *Communication and Capitalism: A Critical Theory. Communication and Capitalism: A Critical Theory.* London, UK: University of Westminster Press, 2020. https://doi.org/10.16997/book45.

Fuller, Ted, and Krista Loogma. "Constructing Futures: A Social Constructionist Perspective on Foresight Methodology." *Futures* 41, no. 2 (2009): 71–79. https://doi.org/10.1016/j.futures.2008.07.039.

Fung, Brian. "Congress Grilled the CEOs of Amazon, Apple, Facebook and Google." *CNN Business*, 2020.

Garbuio, Massimo, Andy Dong, L. I.N. Nidthida, Ted Tschang, and Dan Lovallo. "Demystifying the Genius of Entrepreneurship: How Design Cognition Can Help Create the next Generation of Entrepreneurs." *Academy of Management Learning and Education* 17, no. 1 (2018): 41–61. https://doi.org/10.5465/amle.2016.0040.

Garcia-Lorenzo, Lucia, Paul Donnelly, Lucia Sell-Trujillo, and J. Miguel Imas. "Liminal Entrepreneuring: The Creative Practices of Nascent Necessity Entrepreneurs." *Organization Studies* 39, no. 2–3 (2018): 373–95. https://doi.org/10.1177/0170840617727778.

García-Olivares, Antonio, and Jordi Solé. "End of Growth and the Structural Instability of Capitalism-From Capitalism to a Symbiotic Economy." *Futures* 68, no. 2015 (2015): 31–43. https://doi.org/10.1016/j.futures.2014.09.004.

Garner, Benjamin R., Michael Gove, Cesar Ayala, and Ashraf Mady. "Exploring the Gap between Employers' Needs and Undergraduate Business Curricula: A Survey of Alumni Regarding Core Business Curricula." *Industry and Higher Education* 33, no. 6 (2019): 439–47. https://doi.org/10.1177/0950422219876498.

Garthwaite, Nina, Mick Hatter, Jon Jonn, Stewart Maxwell, Frank Benson, and Lynne Friedli. "A Commentary on Encountering Austerity; the Experiences of Four Men Living in a London Hostel." *Geoforum* 110, no. October 2018 (2020): 252–60. https://doi.org/10.1016/j.geoforum.2018.10.007.

Gartner, William B. "'Who Is an Entrepreneur?' Is the Wrong Question." *American Journal of Small Business* 12, no. 4 (1988): 11–32.

Gartner, William B., Eveline Stam, Neil Thompson, and Karen Verduyn. "Entrepreneurship as Practice: Grounding Contemporary Practice Theory into Entrepreneurship Studies." *Entrepreneurship and Regional Development* 28, no. 9–10 (2016): 813–16. https://doi.org/10.1080/08985626.2016.1251736.

Georgieva, Kristalina. "Facing a Darkening Economic Outlook: How the G20 Can Respond." IMF Blog, 2022. https://blogs.imf.org/2022/07/13/facing-a-darkening-economic-outlook-how-the-g20-can-respond/.

Gernsbacher, Morton Ann, and Melanie Yergeau. "Empirical Failures of the Claim That Autistic People Lack a Theory of Mind." *Arch. Sci Psychol. Sci Psychol.* 7, no. 1 (2019): 102=118. https://doi.org/10.1037/arc0000067.

Gessel, Micbael, Nancy Tystad Koupal, and Fred Erisman. "The Politics of Oz: A Symposium." *South Dakota History* 31, no. 2 (2001): 146–68.

Giannakakis, Vangelis. "Adorno, Badiou and the Politics of Breaking Out." *Theory and Event* 22, no. 1 (2019): 18–43.

Gibbons, Michael. "Mode 2 Society and the Emergence of Context-Sensitive Science." *Science and Public Policy* 27, no. 3 (2000): 159–63. https://doi.org/10.3152/147154300781782011.

Gilad, Benjamin, and Philip Levine. "A Behavioral Model of Entrepreneurial Supply." *Journal of Small Business Management* 24, no. February 1984 (1986): 45.

Gitlin, Todd. "The Black Lives Matter Protests Don't Evoke 1968. They're More like 1969." *The Washington Post.* June 12, 2020.

Gold, Jeff. "The Future of HRD: Scenarios of Possibility." *International Journal of Human Resource Development: Practice, Policy & Research* 2, no. 2 (2017): 71–82. https://doi.org/10.22324/ijhrdppr.2.117.

Goldin, Daniel. "Storylines." *Psychoanalysis, Self and Context* 14, no. 2 (2019): 161–77. https://doi.org/10.1080/24720038.2019.1582233.

Goldsby, Michael G., Donald F. Kuratko, Matthew R. Marvel, and Thomas Nelson. "Design-Centered Entrepreneurship: A Four Stage Iterative Process for Opportunity Development." *Journal of Small Business & Entrepreneurship* 29, no. 6 (2017): 477–90. https://doi.org/10.1080/08276331.2017.1377396.

Gordon, Theodore J., and Mariana Todorova. *Future Studies and Counterfactual Analysis: Seeds of the Future.* Ebook. Sringer, 2019. https://doi.org/10.1007/978-3-030-18437-7.

Gould, Stephen J. "The Emergence of Consumer Introspection Theory (CIT): Introduction to a JBR Special Issue." *Journal of Business Research* 65, no. 4 (2012): 453–60. https://doi.org/10.1016/j.jbusres.2011.02.010.

Graham, Gary. "Exploring Imaginative Futures Writing through the Fictional Prototype 'Crime-Sourcing.'" *Futures* 50 (2013): 94–100. https://doi.org/10.1016/j.futures.2013.04.002.

Graham, Gary, Anita Greenhill, and Vic Callaghan. "Exploring Business Visions Using Creative Fictional Prototypes." *Futures* 50 (2013): 1–4. https://doi.org/10.1016/j.futures.2013.04.001.

———. "Technological Forecasting and Social Change Special Section: Creative Prototyping." *Technological Forecasting and Social Change* 84 (2014): 1–4. https://doi.org/10.1016/j.techfore.2013.11.007.

Graham, Gary, and Rashid Mehmood. "The Strategic Prototype 'Crime-Sourcing' and the Science/Science Fiction behind It." *Technological*

Forecasting and Social Change 84 (2014): 86–92. https://doi.org/10.1016/j.techfore.2013.10.026.

Greene, Patricia Gene, and Terrence Edison Brown. "Resource Needs and the Dynamic Capitalism Typology." *Journal of Business Venturing* 12, no. 3 (1997): 161–73. https://doi.org/10.1016/S0883-9026(96)00060-2.

Gregory, Amanda. "The State We Are in: Insights from Autopoiesis and Complexity Theory." *Management Decision* 44, no. 7 (2006): 962–72. https://doi.org/10.1108/00251740610680613.

Grimmelikhuijsen, Stephan. "A Good Man but a Bad Wizard. about the Limits and Future of Transparency of Democratic Governments." *Information Polity* 17, no. 3–4 (2012): 293–302. https://doi.org/10.3233/IP-2012-000288.

Groves, Kevin S., Charles M. Vance, David Y. Choi, and John L. Mendez. "An Examination of the Nonlinear Thinking Style Profile Stereotype of Successful Entrepreneurs." *Journal of Enterprising Culture* 16, no. 2 (2008): 133–59. https://doi.org/10.1142/S0218495808000077.

Grundy, Tony. "Rethinking and Reinventing Michael Porter's Five Forces Model." *Strategic Change* 15, no. 5 (2006): 213–29. https://doi.org/10.1002/jsc.764.

Guercini, S., and B. Cova. "Unconventional Entrepreneurship." *Journal Of Business Research* 92 (2018): 385–91. https://doi.org/10.1016/j.jbusres.2018.06.021.

Gunderson, Ryan. "A Defense of the 'Grand Hotel Abyss': The Frankfurt School's Nonideal Theory." *Acta Sociologica (United Kingdom)* 58, no. 1 (2015): 25–38. https://doi.org/10.1177/0001699314559526.

Gupta, Nakul, and Sangeeta Shah Bharadwaj. "Agility in Business School Education through Richness and Reach: A Conceptual Model." *Education and Training* 55, no. 4 (2013): 370–84. https://doi.org/10.1108/00400911311326018.

Gutkind, L. "Roundtable: What Is Creative Nonfiction? Two Views - Why I Chose the Creative Nonfiction Way of Life." *Fourth Genre: Explorations in Nonfiction* 2, no. 1 (2000): 200–206. https://doi.org/10.1353/fge.2013.0378.

Gyamera, Gifty Oforiwaa, and Penny Jane Burke. "Neoliberalism and Curriculum in Higher Education: A Post-Colonial Analyses." *Teaching in Higher Education* 23, no. 4 (2018): 450–67. https://doi.org/10.1080/13562517.2017.1414782.

Hackley, Chris. "Auto-Ethnographic Consumer Research and Creative Non-Fiction: Exploring Connections and Contrasts from a Literary Perspective." *Qualitative Market Research* 10, no. 1 (2007): 98–108. https://doi.org/10.1108/13522750710720422.

Haggard, Stephan, and Robert R. Kaufman. "The Political Economy of Democratic Transitions." *Comparative Politics* 29, no. 3 (1997): 263–83. https://doi.org/10.2307/422121.

Hall, Peter A. "Varieties of Capitalism in Light of the Euro Crisis." *Journal of European Public Policy* 25, no. 1 (2018): 7–30. https://doi.org/10.1080/13501763.2017.1310278.

Hall, Peter A., and David Soskice. *Varieties of Capitalism.* Oxford: Oxford University Press, 2001.

———. “Varieties of Capitalism and Institutional Change: A Response to Three Critics.” *Comparative European Politics* 1, no. 2 (2003): 241–50. https://doi.org/10.1057/palgrave.cep.6110010.

Hall, Stuart. “The Problem of Ideology-Marxism without Guarantees.” *Journal of Communication Inquiry* 10, no. 2 (1986): 28–44. https://doi.org/10.1177/019685998601000203.

Hamilton, Barton H. “Does Entrepreneurship Pay? An Empirical Analysis of the Returns to Self-Employment.” *Journal of Political Economy* 108, no. 3 (2000): 604–31. https://doi.org/10.1086/262131.

Han, Jin, Yi Ruan, Yanmin Wang, and Haibo Zhou. “Toward a Complex Adaptive System: The Case of the Zhongguancun Entrepreneurship Ecosystem.” *Journal of Business Research*, no. November (2019): 0–1. https://doi.org/10.1016/j.jbusres.2019.11.077.

Hannibal, Martin, and Gary Knight. “Additive Manufacturing and the Global Factory: Disruptive Technologies and the Location of International Business.” *International Business Review* 27, no. 6 (2018): 1116–27. https://doi.org/10.1016/j.ibusrev.2018.04.003.

Hansen, Bradley A. “The Fable of the Allegory: The Wizard of Oz in Economics.” *Journal of Economic Education* 33, no. 3 (2002): 254–64. https://doi.org/10.1080/00220480209595190.

Hansen, Kenneth Reinecke. “News from the Future: A Corpus Linguistic Analysis of Future-Oriented, Unreal and Counterfactual News Discourse.” *Discourse and Communication* 10, no. 2 (2016): 115–36. https://doi.org/10.1177/1750481315611240.

Harley, Bill. “Confronting the Crisis of Confidence in Management Studies: Why Senior Scholars Need to Stop Setting a Bad Example.” *Academy of Management Learning & Education* 18, no. 2 (2019): 286–97.

Harris-Lovett, Sasha, Judit Lienert, and David Sedlak. “A Mixed-Methods Approach to Strategic Planning for Multi-Benefit Regional Water Infrastructure.” *Journal of Environmental Management* 233 (2019): 218–37.

Hartmann, Heinz. “Managers and Entrepreneurs: A Useful Distinction?” *Administrative Science Quarterly* 3, no. 4 (1959): 429–51. https://doi.org/10.2307/2390809.

Harvey, Karen. “Oeconomy and the Eighteenth-Century House: A Cultural History of Social Practice”. *Home Cultures* 11, no. 3 (2014): 375-389.

Harvey, David. “Neo-Liberalism as Creative Destruction.” *Geografiska Annaler, Series B: Human Geography* 88, no. 2 (2006): 145–58. https://doi.org/10.1111/j.0435-3684.2006.00211.x.

Hawkins, Christopher V., Sung Wook Kwon, and Jungah Bae. “Balance Between Local Economic Development and Environmental Sustainability: A Multi-Level Governance Perspective.” *International Journal of Public Administration* 39, no. 11 (2016): 803–11. https://doi.org/10.1080/01900692.2015.1035787.

Hay, Amanda, and Myra Hodgkinson. “More Success than Meets the Eye-a Challenge to Critiques of the MBA: Possibilities for Critical Management Education?” *Management Learning* 39, no. 1 (2008): 21–40. https://doi.org/10.1177/1350507607085170.

Hay, Colin. "Does Capitalism (Still) Come in Varieties?" *Review of International Political Economy* 27, no. 2 (2020): 302–19. https://doi.org/10.1080/09692290.2019.1633382.

Heck, Richard G. "Nonconceptual Content and the 'Space of Reasons.'" *Philosophical Review* 109, no. 4 (2000): 483–523. https://doi.org/10.1215/00318108-109-4-483.

Heidegger, Martin. *Being and Time.* First Engl. Oxford: Blackwell Publishing (1962), 2005.

Henderson, Rebecca. *Reimagining Capitalism In a World on Fire.* New York, NY: PublicAffiars, Hatchette, 2020.

Henrekson, Magnus, and Tino Sanandaji. "Schumpeterian Entrepreneurship in Europe Compared to Other Industrialized Regions." IFN Working Paper. Stockholm, 2017.

———. "Small Business Activity Does Not Measure Entrepreneurship." *Proceedings of the National Academy of Sciences* 111, no. 5 (2014): 1760–65. https://doi.org/10.1073/pnas.1307204111.

Hermann, Christoph. "Value and Knowledge: Insights from Marxist Value Theory for the Transformation of Work in the Digital Economy." *Rethinking Marxism* 21, no. 2 (2009): 275–85. https://doi.org/10.1080/08935690902743542.

Hernandez-de-Menendez, Marcela, Carlos Escobar Díaz, and Ruben Morales-Menendez. "Technologies for the Future of Learning: State of the Art." *International Journal on Interactive Design and Manufacturing,* no. November (2019). https://doi.org/10.1007/s12008-019-00640-0.

Hicks, Donna. *Leading with Dignity.* Yale University Press, 2018.

Hines, Andy, and Peter C. Bishop. "Framework Foresight: Exploring Futures the Houston Way." *Futures* 51 (2013): 31–49. https://doi.org/10.1016/j.futures.2013.05.002.

Hjorth, Daniel. "Absolutely Fabulous! Fabulation and Organisation-Creation in Processes of Becoming-Entrepreneur." *Society and Business Review* 8, no. 3 (2013): 205–24. https://doi.org/10.1108/sbr-02-2013-0020.

Hjorth, Daniel, and Robin Holt. "It's Entrepreneurship, Not Enterprise: Ai Weiwei as Entrepreneur." *Journal of Business Venturing Insights* 5 (2016): 50–54. https://doi.org/10.1016/j.jbvi.2016.03.001.

Hmieleski, Keith M., and Andrew C. Corbett. "The Contrasting Interaction Effects of Improvisational Behavior with Entrepreneurial Self-Efficacy on New Venture Performance and Entrepreneur Work Satisfaction." *Journal of Business Venturing* 23, no. 4 (2008): 482–96. https://doi.org/10.1016/j.jbusvent.2007.04.002.

Hodgson, Karen, Fiona Grimm, Emma Vestesson, Richard Brine, and Sarah Deeny. "Briefing : Adult Social Care and COVID-19 - Assessing the Impact on Social Care Users and Staff in England so Far." London: The Health Foundation, 2020.

Hoffmann, Christian Hugo, and André Dahlinger. "How Capitalism Abolishes Itself in the Digital Era in Favour of Robo-Economic Systems: Socio-Economic Implications of Decentralized Autonomous Self-Owned Businesses." *Foresight* 22, no. 1 (2019): 53–67. https://doi.org/10.1108/FS-03-2019-0014.

Hofstede, Geert. "Dimensionalizing Cultures: The Hofstede Model in Context." *Online Readings in Psychology and Culture* 2, no. 1 (2011): 1–17. https://doi.org/10.9707/2307-0919.1014.

Hofstetter, C. Richard. "Political Disengagement and the Death of Martin Luther King." *Public Opinion Quarterly* 33, no. 2 (1969): 174–79.

Hogg, Michael A., and Janice Adelman. "Uncertainty-Identity Theory: Extreme Groups, Radical Behavior, and Authoritarian Leadership." *Journal of Social Issues* 69, no. 3 (2013): 436–54. https://doi.org/10.1111/josi.12023.

Hogg, Michael A., Deborah J. Terry, and Katherine M. White. "A Tale of Two Theories: A Critical Comparison of Identity Theory with Social Identity Theory." *Social Psychology Quarterly*, 1995. https://doi.org/10.2307/2787127.

Holbrook, Morris B. "Customer Value and Autoethnography: Subjective Personal Introspection and the Meanings of a Photograph Collection." *Journal of Business Research* 58, no. 1 SPEC.ISS (2005): 45–61. https://doi.org/10.1016/S0148-2963(03)00079-1.

Holland, John H. *Emergence: From Chaos to Order*. Oxford: Oxford University Press, 1998.

Holling, Crawford S. "Resilience and Stability of Ecological Systems." *Annual Review of Ecology and Systematics* 4 (1973): 1–23.

Hook, Peter A. "Domain Maps: Purposes, History, Parallels with Cartography, and Applications." *Proceedings of the International Conference on Information Visualisation*, 2007, 442–46. https://doi.org/10.1109/IV.2007.42.

Hornaday, Robert. "Dropping the E-Words from Small Business Research: An Alternative Typology." *Journal of Small Business Management* 28, no. 4 (1990): 22–33.

Howcroft, Debra, and Phil Taylor. "'Plus ca Change, plus La Meme Chose?'-Researching and Theorising the 'new' New Technologies." *New Technology, Work and Employment* 29, no. 1 (2014): 1–8. https://doi.org/10.1111/ntwe.12026.

Hua, Jian, and Sanjay Bapna. "Who Can We Trust? The Economic Impact of Insider Threats." *Journal of Global Information Technology Management* 16, no. 4 (2013): 47–67. https://doi.org/10.1080/1097198x.2013.10845648.

Huan-Niemi, Ellen, Pasi Rikkonen, Jyrki Niemi, Olli Wuori, and Janne Niemi. "Combining Quantitative and Qualitative Research Methods to Foresee the Changes in the Finnish Agri-Food Sector." *Futures* 83 (2016): 88–99. https://doi.org/10.1016/j.futures.2016.03.007.

Hydle, Katja Maria. "Temporal and Spatial Dimensions of Strategizing." *Organization Studies* 36, no. 5 (2015): 643–63. https://doi.org/10.1177/0170840615571957.

Ingold, Tim. *The Perception of the Environment: Essays in Livelihood, Dwelling, and Skill. Technology and Culture*. E-Edition. Vol. 43. London, UK and New York, NY: Taylor & Francis (2000), 2002. https://doi.org/10.1353/tech.2002.0079.

Islam, Gazi. "Finding a Space for Story: Sensemaking, Stories and Epistemic Impasse." *Journal of Organizational Change Management* 26, no. 1 (2013): 29–48. https://doi.org/10.1108/09534811311307897.

İyigün, N. Öykü. "What Could Entrepreneurship Do for Sustainable Development? A Corporate Social Responsibility-Based Approach." *Procedia - Social and Behavioral Sciences* 195 (2015): 1226–31. https://doi.org/10.1016/j.sbspro.2015.06.253.

Jackson, Emma, and Tim Butler. "Revisiting 'Social Tectonics': The Middle Classes and Social Mix in Gentrifying Neighbourhoods." *Urban Studies* 52, no. 13 (2015): 2349–65. https://doi.org/10.1177/0042098014547370.

Jackson, Gregory, and Richard Deeg. "Comparing Capitalisms: Understanding Institutional Diversity and Its Implications for International Business." *Journal of International Business Studies* 39, no. 4 (2008): 540–61. https://doi.org/10.1057/palgrave.jibs.8400375.

Jackson, Michael C. "Critical Systems Thinking and Practice : What Has Been Done and What Needs Doing." *Systemist* 41, no. 1 (2021): 3–33.

———. *Critical Systems Thinking and the Management of Complexity : Responsible Leadership for a Complex World.* Ebook. Wiley, 2019.

Jacobs, Michael, and Mariana Mazzucato. "Rethinking Capitalism: An Introduction." In *Rethinking Capitalism: Economics and Policy for Sustainable and Inclusive Growth*, edited by Michael Jacobs and Mariana Mazzucato, 1–27. Chichester, UK: John Wiley & Sons, 2016.

Jari, Kaivo-Oja, and Theresa Lauraéus. "Analysis of 2017 Gartner' s Three Megatrends to Thrive the Disruptive Business, Technology Trends 2008 - 2016, Dynamic Capabilities of VUCA and Foresight Leadership Tools." *Advances in Technology Innovation* 4, no. 2 (2019): 105–15.

Jarrold, Christopher, D. W. Butler, E. M. Cottington, and F. Jimenez. "Linking Theory of Mind and Central Coherence Bias in Autism and in the General Population." *Developmental Psychology* 36, no. 1 (2000): 126–38. https://doi.org/10.1037/0012-1649.36.1.126.

Jeffries, Stuart. *Grand Hotel Abyss: The Lives of the Frankfurt School.* London, UK: Verso, 2017.

Johannisson, Bengt. "Between Arm's Length Research and Policy Practices: Interactive Approaches in Entrepreneurship Studies." In *13th Nordic Conference on Small Business Research.* Tromso, Norway, 2004.

———. "Disclosing Everyday Practices Constituting Social Entrepreneuring–a Case of Necessity Effectuation." *Entrepreneurship and Regional Development* 30, no. 3–4 (2018): 390–406. https://doi.org/10.1080/08985626.2017.1413770.

———. "Limits to and Prospects of Entrepreneurship Education in the Academic Context." *A Research Agenda for Entrepreneurship Education* 28 (2018): 139–63. https://doi.org/10.4337/9781786432919.00014.

Johansen, Bob, and James Euchner. "Navigating the VUCA World, An Interview with Bob Johansen." *Research Technology Management* 56, no. 1 (2013): 10–15. https://doi.org/10.5437/08956308X5601003.

Johnsen, Christian Garmann, and Bent Meier Sørensen. "Traversing the Fantasy of the Heroic Entrepreneur." *International Journal of Entrepreneurial Behaviour and Research* 23, no. 2 (2017): 228–44. https://doi.org/10.1108/IJEBR-01-2016-0032.

Johnson, Brian David. “Engineering Uncertainty: The Role of Uncertainty in the Design of Complex Technological and Business Systems.” *Futures* 50 (2013): 56–65. https://doi.org/10.1016/j.futures.2013.03.011.

Johnson, Jeffrey Kane. “The Colliding Reciprocal Dance Problem: A Mitigation Strategy with Application to Automotive Active Safety Systems∗.” *ArXiv*, 2019, 1417–22.

Joll, Nicholas. “Adorno’s Negative Dialectic: Theme, Point, and Methodological Status.” *International Journal of Philosophical Studies* 17, no. 2 (2009): 233–53. https://doi.org/10.1080/09672550902794413.

Jones, Campbell, and Andre Spicer. *Unmasking the Entrepreneur. Unmasking the Entrepreneur.* Edward Elgar Publishing Ltd., 2009. https://doi.org/10.4337/9781781952689.

Jones, Rupert. “The End of a Scandal: Banks near a Final Release from Their PPI Liabilities.” The Guardian, 2020. https://www.theguardian.com/money/2019/aug/23/ppi-end-of-a-scandal-banks-final-release-liabilities-deadline.

Jones, Steven. “Covid-19 Is Our Best Chance to Change Universities for Good.” *The Guardian*, March 31, 2020.

Jones, Steven, Katy Vigurs, and Diane Harris. “Discursive Framings of Market-Based Education Policy and Their Negotiation by Students: The Case of ‘Value for Money’ in English Universities.” *Oxford Review of Education* 00, no. 00 (2020): 1–18. https://doi.org/10.1080/03054985.2019.1708711.

Juille, Tom, and Dorian Jullien. “Narrativity and Identity in the Representation of the Economic Agent.” *Journal of Economic Methodology* 24, no. 3 (2017): 274–96. https://doi.org/10.1080/1350178X.2017.1286027.

Jünger, Ernst. *The Worker: Dominion and Form.* Edited by L. P. Hemming and (transl.) B Costea. Eng. Trans. Evanston, IL: Northwestern University Press (1932), 2017.

Kahneman, Daniel, Oliver Sibony, and Cass R. Sunstein. *Noise: A Flaw in Human Judgement.* London, UK: William Collins, 2021.

Kalika, Michel, Gordon Shenton, and Pierre Louis Dubois. “What Happens If a Business School Disappears? The Intellectual Foundations of BSIS.” *Journal of Management Development* 35, no. 7 (2016): 878–88. https://doi.org/10.1108/JMD-10-2014-0120.

Kallinikos, Jannis. “The Order of Technology: Complexity and Control in a Connected World.” *Information and Organization* 15, no. 3 SPEC. ISS. (2005): 185–202. https://doi.org/10.1016/j.infoandorg.2005.02.001.

Kauppinen, Antti, and Maria Daskalaki. “’Becoming Other’ : Entrepreneuring as Subversive Organising.” *Ephemera* 15, no. 3 (2015): 601–20.

Keane, John F., Gary Graham, and Bernard Burnes. “Literary Praxiphorical Analysis: Using Science Fiction and Fantasy to Shape Organizational Futures.” *Technological Forecasting and Social Change* 84 (2014): 54–65. https://doi.org/10.1016/j.techfore.2013.10.025.

Keegan, D. “The Future of Learning: From ELearning to MLearning.” Hagen: Inst. For Research into Distance Education, 2002.

Kerr, William R, Ramana Nanda, and Matthew Rhodes-Kropf. “Entrepreneurship as Experimentation.” *Journal of Economic Perspectives* 28, no. 3 (2014): 25–48. https://doi.org/10.1257/jep.28.3.25.

Keynes, John M. "The General Theory of Employment, Interest and Money." In *Volume VII of Collected Writings*. London, UK: Macmillan, 1936, 1973.

Kijek, Tomasz, and Arkadiusz Kijek. "Is Innovation the Key to Solving the Productivity Paradox?" *Journal of Innovation and Knowledge* 4, no. 4 (2019): 219–25. https://doi.org/10.1016/j.jik.2017.12.010.

Kilduff, Martin. "Performance and Interaction Routines in Multinational Corporation." *Journal of International Business Studies* 23, no. 1 (1992): 133–45. https://doi.org/10.1057/palgrave.jibs.8490262.

King, Martin Luther. "Showdown for Nonviolence." *Look Magazine (USA 1937-1971)*, April 1968.

King, Michael. "The 'Truth' about Autopoiesis." *Journal of Law and Society* 20, no. 2 (1993): 218. https://doi.org/10.2307/1410168.

Kinsley, Sam. "Futures in the Making: Practices to Anticipate 'Ubiquitous Computing.'" *Environment and Planning A* 44, no. 7 (2012): 1554–69. https://doi.org/10.1068/a45168.

Kirchhoff, Bruce. *Entrepreneurship and Dynamic Capitalism: The Economics of Business*. Westport, CT: Praeger, 1994.

Kirchhoff, Bruce A., Jonathan D. Linton, and Steven T. Walsh. "Neo-Marshellian Equilibrium versus Schumpeterian Creative Destruction: Its Impact on Business Research and Economic Policy." *Journal of Small Business Management* 51, no. 2 (2013): 159–66. https://doi.org/10.1111/jsbm.12018.

Kirchhoff, Bruce A. *Entrepreneurship and Dynamic Capitalism. The Economics of Business Firm Formation and Growth*. Vol. 75. Westport: Greenwood Publishing, 1994. https://doi.org/10.2460/ajvr.75.7.613.

Klein, Louis. "The Culturally Embedded Algedonics of Society: The Drivers and Controls of Integrating Culture." *Proceedings of 2015 IEEE World Conference on Complex Systems, WCCS 2015*, 2016. https://doi.org/10.1109/ICoCS.2015.7483273.

Klein, Sherwin. "The Head, the Heart, and Business Virtues." *Journal of Business Ethics* 39, no. 4 (2002): 347–59. https://doi.org/10.1023/A:1019762707218.

Kleinknecht, Alfred. "The (Negative) Impact of Supply-Side Labour Market Reforms on Productivity: An Overview of the Evidence1." *Cambridge Journal of Economics* 44, no. 2 (2020): 445–64. https://doi.org/10.1093/cje/bez068.

Knaus, Christopher. "Manufacturing Face Shields within Days: How Australian Industry Is Pivoting to Fight Coronavirus." The Guardian, 2020. https://www.theguardian.com/world/2020/apr/05/manufacturing-face-shields-mat-bowtell-3d-printing-australia-fight-coronavirus.

Knight, Barry. "Powering a Good Society." *Local Economy* 33, no. 6 (2018): 569–82. https://doi.org/10.1177/0269094218803001.

Knight, Frank H. "Profit and Entrepreneurial Functions." *The Journal of Economic History* 2, no. S1 (1942): 126–32. https://doi.org/10.1017/S0022050700083479.

———. *Risk, Uncertainty and Profit*. New York: Hart, Schaffner and Marx, 1921.

Koris, Riina, Anders Örtenblad, and Triinu Ojala. "From Maintaining the Status Quo to Promoting Free Thinking and Inquiry: Business Students' Perspective on the Purpose of Business School Teaching." *Management Learning* 48, no. 2 (2017): 174–86. https://doi.org/10.1177/1350507616668480.

Koskinen, Ilpo, and Gordon Hush. "Utopian, Molecular and Sociological Social Design." *International Journal of Design* 10, no. 1 (2016): 65–71.

Kotabe, Masaaki, and Munir Mandviwalla. "Information Technology and International Business: Theory and Strategic Development." *Journal of International Management* 11, no. 2 SPEC. ISS. (2005): 119–23. https://doi.org/10.1016/j.intman.2005.03.002.

Kranton, Rachel E. "Identity Economics 2016: Where Do Social Distinctions and Norms Come From?" *American Economic Review* 106, no. 5 (2016): 405–9. https://doi.org/10.1257/aer.p20161038.

Kristiansen, Stein. "Social Networks and Business Success the Role of Subcultures in an African Context." *American Journal of Economics and Sociology* 63, no. 5 (2004): 1149–71. https://doi.org/10.1111/j.1536-7150.2004.00339.x.

Kuratko, Donald F., and Michael H. Morris. "Examining the Future Trajectory of Entrepreneurship." *Journal of Small Business Management* 56, no. 1 (2018): 11–23. https://doi.org/10.1111/jsbm.12364.

Kuratko, Donald F., and Richard M. Hodgetts. *Entrepreneurship: Theory, Process, Practice.* Thomson/South-Western, 2004.

Lachmann, Ludwig M. *The Legacy of Max Weber.* Berkeley, CA: Glendessary, 1970.

Lamoureux, Marcel, and David M. Atkinson. "Email Correspondence: Insertions on Precarity (Capitalism)," 2021.

———. "Email Corrspondence: Chapter 2 and Some Thoughts," 2021.

Lancione, Michele, and Stewart R. Clegg. "The Lightness of Management Learning." *Management Learning* 46, no. 3 (2015): 280–98. https://doi.org/10.1177/1350507614526533.

Landgraf, Tim, Michael Oertel, Daniel Rhiel, and Raúl Rojas. "A Biomimetic Honeybee Robot for the Analysis of the Honeybee Dance Communication System." *IEEE/RSJ 2010 International Conference on Intelligent Robots and Systems, IROS 2010 - Conference Proceedings,* 2010, 3097–3102. https://doi.org/10.1109/IROS.2010.5650930.

Landström, Hans, and Gouya Harirchi. "The Social Structure of Entrepreneurship as a Scientific Field." *Research Policy* 47, no. 3 (2018): 650–62. https://doi.org/10.1016/j.respol.2018.01.013.

Landström, Hans, Gouya Harirchi, and Fredrik Åström. "Entrepreneurship: Exploring the Knowledge Base." *Research Policy* 41, no. 7 (2012): 1154–81. https://doi.org/10.1016/j.respol.2012.03.009.

Lauster, Michael, and Stephanie Hansen-Casteel. "On Some Fundamental Methodological Aspects in Foresight Processes." *European Journal of Futures Research* 6, no. 1 (2018): 1–8. https://doi.org/10.1186/s40309-018-0140-1.

Lawrence, Felicity, Rob Evans, David Pegg, Caelainn Barr, and Pamela Duncan. "How the Right's Radical Thinktanks Reshaped the Conservative Party." *The Guardian,* 2019, 1–12.

Lazonick, William. "Innovative Enterprise and the Theory of the Firm." In *Rethinking Capitalism: Economics and Policy for Sustainable and Inclusive*

Growth, edited by Michael Jacobs and Mariana Mazzucato, 77–97. Chichester, UK: John Wiley & Sons, 2016.

Lee, Clarissa Ai Ling. "Schrödinger's Notebook: Shifting Real." *Technological Forecasting and Social Change* 84 (2014): 143–54. https://doi.org/10.1016/j.techfore.2013.09.010.

Lefebvre, Henri. *Rhythmanalysis: Space, Time, and Everyday Life.* Edited by Stuart Elden and Gerald Moore. Transl. London, UK: Bloomsbury Academic (1992), 2013.

Lemley, Mark A., and Mark P. McKenna. "Unfair Disruption." *Boston University Law Review* 100 (2020): 71–131.

Lenway, Stefanie Ann, and Thomas P. Murtha. "The State as Strategist in International Business Research." *Journal of International Business Studies* 25, no. 3 (1994): 513–35. https://doi.org/10.1057/palgrave.jibs.8490210.

Leopold, Till Alexander, Vesselina Ratcheva, and Saadia Zahidi. "The Future of Jobs: Employment, Skills and Workforce Strategy for the Fourth Industrial Revolution." *Global Challenge Insight Report.* Geneva, 2016.

Lerner, Josh. "The Boulevard of Broken Dreams: Innovation Policy and Entrepreneurship." *Innovation Policy and the Economy* 13, no. 1 (2013): 61–82. https://doi.org/10.1086/668239.

Lever, Mark. "The Autism Employment Gap Too Much Information in the Workplace." *National Autistic Society*, 2016.

Lévinas, Emanuel. *Entre Nous.* Edited by Michael B. Smith and Barbara Harshav. Transl. London, UK and New York, NY: Continuum, 2006.

———. "Ethics and Infinity." *Cross Currents*, 1984, 191–204.

Levitt, Theodore. "The Globalization of Markets." *Harvard Business Review* 61, no. 3 (1983): 92–102.

Levy, Sidney J. "Olio and Intègraphy as Method and the Consumption of Death." *Consumption Markets and Culture* 18, no. 2 (2015): 133–54. https://doi.org/10.1080/10253866.2014.908287.

Levy, Sidney J., and Charles H. Kellstadt. "Intègraphy: A Multi-Method Approach to Situational Analysis." *Journal of Business Research* 65, no. 7 (2012): 1073–77. https://doi.org/10.1016/j.jbusres.2011.02.012.

Lewin, Kurt. *Frontiers in Group Dynamics: Concept, Method and Reality in Social Science; Social Equilibria and Social Change. Human Relations.* Vol. 1, 1947. https://doi.org/10.1177/001872674700100103.

Linton, Gabriel, and Markus Klinton. "University Entrepreneurship Education: A Design Thinking Approach to Learning." *Journal of Innovation and Entrepreneurship* 8, no. 1 (2019). https://doi.org/10.1186/s13731-018-0098-z.

Lipiec, Eva, Peter Ruggiero, Alexis Mills, Katherine A. Serafin, John Bolte, Patrick Corcoran, John Stevenson, Chad Zanocco, and Denise Lach. "Mapping out Climate Change: Assessing How Coastal Communities Adapt Using Alternative Future Scenarios." *Journal of Coastal Research* 34, no. 5 (2018): 1196–1208.

Livingston, Dennnis. "Science Fiction Models of Future World Order Systems." *International Organization* 25, no. 2 (1971): 254–70.

Loomes, Susan, Alison Owens, and Grace McCarthy. "Patterns of Recruitment of Academic Leaders to Australian Universities and Implications for the

Future of Higher Education." *Journal of Higher Education Policy and Management* 41, no. 2 (2019): 137–52. https://doi.org/10.1080/1360080X.2019.1565296.

Lott, Bret. "Roundtable: What Is Creative Nonfiction? Two Views - Toward a Definition of Creative Nonfiction." *Fourth Genre: Explorations in Nonfiction* 2, no. 1 (2000): 192–200. https://doi.org/10.1353/fge.2013.0378.

Lotz, Sebastian. "Engineering Fairness? Market Design as a Resource for Social Justice Research." *Social Justice Research* 28, no. 3 (2015): 391–99. https://doi.org/10.1007/s11211-015-0250-x.

Lucas, David S., Caleb S. Fuller, Ennio E. Piano, and Christopher J. Coyne. "Visions of Entrepreneurship Policy." *Journal of Entrepreneurship and Public Policy* 7, no. 4 (December 2018): 336–56. https://doi.org/10.1108/JEPP-D-18-00034.

Luhmann, Niklas. *Introduction to Systems Theory.* Edited by Dirk Baecker. Transl. Cambridge, UK: Polity Press (2002), 2013.

———. *Trust and Power.* Edited by Christian Morgner and Michael King. English. Cambridge, UK: Polity (1973), 2017.

Lüthy, Christina, and Chris Steyaert. "The Onto-Politics of Entrepreneurial Experimentation: Re-Reading Hans-Jörg Rheinberger's Understanding of 'Experimental Systems.'" *Entrepreneurship and Regional Development* 31, no. 7–8 (2019): 652–68. https://doi.org/10.1080/08985626.2019.1596360.

Luzzi, Alessandra, and Amir Sasson. "Entrepreneurial Skills or Reward for Success? Does Entrepreneurship Pay in Future Paid Employment?" In *75th Annual Meeting of the Academy of Management, AOM 2015*, 1425–30, 2015. https://doi.org/10.5465/AMBPP.2015.255.

Macfarlane, John. "Future Contingents and Relative Truth." *Philosophical Quarterly* 53, no. 212 (2003): 321–36. https://doi.org/10.1111/1467-9213.00315.

Machiavelli, Niccolo. *The Prince.* (1532). London: Penguin, 1981.

MacInnes, John. "Work-Life Balance in Europe: A Response to the Baby Bust or Reward for the Baby Boomers?" *European Societies* 8, no. 2 (2006): 223–49. https://doi.org/10.1080/14616690600644988.

MacIntyre, Alasdair. *After Virtue.* 2nd (1985). London: Duckworth, 2004.

MacLean, Nancy. *Democracy in Chains: The Deep History of the Radical Right's Stealth Plan for America.* London, UK: Scribe, 2017.

Maggio, Rodolfo. "The Anthropology of Storytelling and the Storytelling of Anthropology." *Journal of Comparative Research in Anthropology and Sociology* 5, no. 2 (2014): 89–106.

Maimone, Fabrizio, and Marta Sinclair. "Dancing in the Dark: Creativity, Knowledge Creation and (Emergent) Organizational Change." *Journal of Organizational Change Management* 27, no. 2 (2014): 344–61. https://doi.org/10.1108/JOCM-12-2012-0197.

Mandala, Susan. "Science Fiction and Fantasy: Language, Style, and the Critics." In *The Language in Science Fiction and Fantasy : The Question of Style*, 1–36. London: Continuum, 2010.

Mandeville, Bernard. *The Fable of the Bees.* Edited by Phillip Harth. London, UK: Penguin Classiscs (1724), 1989.

Mani, Venkatesh, Rajat Agrawal, and Vinay Sharma. "Impediments to Social Sustainability Adoption in the Supply Chain: An ISM and MICMAC Analysis in Indian Manufacturing Industries." *Global Journal of Flexible Systems Management* 17, no. 2 (2016): 135–56. https://doi.org/10.1007/s40171-015-0106-0.

Marchal, Jean. "The Construction of a New Theory of Profit." *The American Economic Review*, no. 4 (1951): 549–65.

Margolin, Victor, and Sylvia Margolin. "A 'Social Model' of Design: Issues of Practice and Research." *Design Issues* 18, no. 4 (2002): 24–30. https://doi.org/10.1162/074793602320827406.

Marks, Peter. "The Rich Haven't a Clue in 'Inspector.'" *Washington Post*. November 28, 2018.

Marshall, Aarian. "Uber Says Its UK Drivers Are 'Workers', but Not Employees." Wired, 2021. https://www.wired.com/story/uber-uk-drivers-workers-not-employees/.

Marshall, Catherine, and Gretchen B. Rossman. *Designing Qualitative Research*. London, UK: SAGE Publications, 1989.

Martin, Drew. "Uncovering Unconscious Memories and Myths for Understanding International Tourism Behavior." *Journal of Business Research* 63, no. 4 (2010): 372–83. https://doi.org/10.1016/j.jbusres.2009.04.020.

Marx, Karl. "'A Contribution to the Critique of Hegel's Philosophy of Right: Introduction,'" 1844. http://www.marxists.org/archive/marx/works/1843/critique-hpr/intro.htm.

———. *Capital*. Edited by Tom Griffith. Wordsworth. Ware, Hertfordshire: Wordsworth (1867/1884), 2013.

Maslow, Abraham H. *Motivation and Personality*. 3rd ed. New York, NY: Harper & Row, 1987.

Mason, Jennifer. *Qualitative Researching*. 2nd ed. London: Sage, 2002.

Mason, Paul. *Postcapitalism: A Guide to Our Future*. London, UK: Penguin Random House, 2016.

Massa, Silvia, and Stefania Testa. "Innovation and SMEs: Misaligned Perspectives and Goals among Entrepreneurs, Academics, and Policy Makers." *Technovation* 28, no. 7 (2008): 393–407. https://doi.org/10.1016/j.technovation.2008.01.002.

Mathias, Blake D., and David W. Williams. "Giving up the Hats? Entrepreneurs' Role Transitions and Venture Growth." *Journal of Business Venturing* 33, no. 3 (2018): 261–77. https://doi.org/10.1016/j.jbusvent.2017.12.007.

———. "The Impact of Role Identities on Entrepreneurs' Evaluation and Selection of Opportunities." *Journal of Management* 43, no. 3 (2017): 892–918. https://doi.org/10.1177/0149206314544747.

Mazzucato, Mariana. "The Covid-19 Crisis Is a Chance to Do Capitalism Differently." The Guardian, 2020. https://www.theguardian.com/commentisfree/2020/mar/18/the-covid-19-crisis-is-a-chance-to-do-capitalism-differently.

McCullagh, Paul. "Superhighway Patrolman." *Futures* 50, no. October 2012 (2013): 101–8. https://doi.org/10.1016/j.futures.2013.03.007.

McGaughey, Ewan. "Uber, the Taylor Review, Mutuality and the Duty Not to Misrepresent Employment Status." *Industrial Law Journal* 48, no. 2 (2019): 180–98. https://doi.org/10.1093/indlaw/dwy014.

McGregor, Rafe, and Miriam Sang-Ah Park. "Towards a Deconstructed Curriculum: Rethinking Higher Education in the Global North." *Teaching in Higher Education* 24, no. 3 (2019): 332–45.

McKee, Robert. *Story: Style, Structure, Substance, and the Principles of Screenwriting.* London: Methuen, 1999.

Mckeever, Edward, Alistair R. Anderson, and Sarah Jack. "Entrepreneurship and Mutuality: Social Capital in Processes and Practices." *Entrepreneurship & Regional Development* 26, no. 5–6 (2014): 453–77. https://doi.org/10.1080/08985626.2014.939536.

McKelvey, Maureen, and Olof Zaring. "Co-Delivery of Social Innovations: Exploring the University's Role in Academic Engagement with Society." *Industry and Innovation* 25, no. 6 (2018): 594–611. https://doi.org/10.1080/13662716.2017.1295364.

McKenzie, Brian, Steve D. Ugbah, and Norman Smothers. "'Who Is an Entrepreneur?' Is It Still the Wrong Question?" *Academy of Entrepreneurship Journal* 13, no. 1 (2007): 23–43.

McLean, Bethany, and Peter Elkind. *The Smartest Guys in the Room: The Amazing Rise and Scandalous Fall of Enron.* London and New York, NY: Penguin (2003), 2004.

McLuhan, Marshall. "The Medium Is the Message." In *Media and Cultutral Studies: Key Works,* edited by Meenakshi Gigi Durham and Doouglas M. Kellner, Revised., 107–16. Oxford: Blackwell Publishing, 2006.

McNary, Dave. "Entertainment Industry Seeks Legislative Relief From COVID-19 Impact." Variety, 2020. https://variety.com/2020/film/news/entertainment-industry-seeks-legislative-relief-covid-19-impact-1234693745.

McPherson, Michael S., and Lawrence S. Bacow. "Online Higher Education: Beyond the Hype Cycle." *Journal of Economic Perspectives* 29, no. 4 (2015): 135–54. https://doi.org/10.1257/jep.29.4.135.

Metcalfe, J. Stanley. "The Entrepreneur and the Style of Modern Economics." *Journal of Evolutionary Economics* 14, no. 2 (2004): 157–75. https://doi.org/10.1007/s00191-004-0210-3.

Mete, Barış. "Mimetic Tradition and the Critical Theory." *Selcuk Üniversitesi Sosyal Bilimler Enstitüsü Dergisi* 39, no. 39 (2018): 216–24.

Metzner-Szigeth, Andreas. "Contradictory Approaches? On Realism and Constructivism in the Social Sciences Research on Risk, Technology and the Environment." *Futures* 41, no. 3 (2009): 156–70. https://doi.org/10.1016/j.futures.2008.09.017.

Mićić, Pero. *The Five Futures Glasses.* London: Palgrave, 2010.

Miles, Ian. "Stranger than Fiction. How Important Is Science Fiction for Futures Studies?" *Futures* 25, no. 3 (1993): 315–21. https://doi.org/10.1016/0016-3287(93)90139-K.

Millar, Carla C.J.M., Olaf Groth, and John F. Mahon. "Management Innovation in a VUCA World: Challenges and Recommendations." *California Management Review* 61, no. 1 (2018): 5–14. https://doi.org/10.1177/0008125618805111.

Misra, Sasi, and E. Sendil Kumar. "Resourcefulness: A Proximal Conceptualisation of Entrepreneurial Behaviour." *The Journal of Entrepreneurship* 9, no. 2 (2000): 135–54. https://doi.org/10.1177/097135570000900201.

Mitchell, Timothy. *Carbon Democracy: Political Power in the Age of Oil.* London and New York, NY: Verso, 2011.

Modell, Harold, William Cliff, Joel Michael, Jenny McFarland, Mary Pat Wenderoth, and Ann Wright. "A Physiologist's View of Homeostasis." *Advances in Physiology Education* 39, no. 1 (2015): 259–66. https://doi.org/10.1152/advan.00107.2015.

Moeller, Hans Georg. "On Second-Order Observation and Genuine Pretending: Coming to Terms with Society." *Thesis Eleven* 143, no. 1 (2017): 28–43. https://doi.org/10.1177/0725513617740968.

Moeran, Brian. "Magical Capitalism." *Journal of Business Anthropology* 6, no. 2 (2017): 133. https://doi.org/10.22439/jba.v6i2.5409.

Molina-Azorin, José F., Donald D. Bergh, Kevin G. Corley, and David J. Ketchen. "Mixed Methods in the Organizational Sciences: Taking Stock and Moving Forward." *Organizational Research Methods* 20, no. 2 (2017): 179–92. https://doi.org/10.1177/1094428116687026.

Monat, Jamie, and Thomas Gannon. "Applying Systems Thinking to Engineering and Design." *Systems* 6, no. 3 (2018): 34. https://doi.org/10.3390/systems6030034.

Mooradian, Todd, Kurt Matzler, Borislav Uzelac, and Florian Bauer. "Perspiration and Inspiration: Grit and Innovativeness as Antecedents of Entrepreneurial Success." *Journal of Economic Psychology* 56 (2016): 232–43. https://doi.org/10.1016/j.joep.2016.08.001.

Moore, Geoffrey, A, and Regis Mckenna. *Crossing the Chasm.* Oxford: Capstone, 1999.

Moran, Dermot. *Introduction to Phenomenology.* London, UK: Routledge, 2000.

Morrish, Liz. "The Accident of Accessibility: How the Data of the TEF Creates Neoliberal Subjects." *Social Epistemology* 33, no. 4 (2019): 355–66. https://doi.org/10.1080/02691728.2019.1638991.

Moss, Rob. "Uber Drivers in Court over Ministers' Failure to Help Gig Workers." Personnel Today, 2020. https://www.personneltoday.com/hr/uber-drivers-adiatu-hm-treasury-coronavirus-cjrs-seiss/.

Muhr, Sara Louise, Christian De Cock, Magdalena Twardowska, and Christina Volkmann. "Constructing an Entrepreneurial Life: Liminality and Emotional Reflexivity in Identity Work." *Entrepreneurship and Regional Development* 31, no. 7–8 (2019): 567–82. https://doi.org/10.1080/08985626.2019.1596348.

Munjal, Surender, Pawan Budhwar, and Vijay Pereira. "A Perspective on Multinational Enterprise's National Identity Dilemma." *Social Identities* 24, no. 5 (2018): 548–63. https://doi.org/10.1080/13504630.2017.1386375.

Muñoz, Pablo, and Jonathan Kimmitt. "Entrepreneurship and the Rest: The Missing Debate." *Journal of Business Venturing Insights* 9 (2018): 100–106. https://doi.org/10.1016/j.jbvi.2018.03.003.

Murawski, John. "Critical Race Theory Is About to Face Its Day (s) in Court." *RealClear Investigations,* April 27, 2021.

Murphy, Peter. "Design Capitalism: Design, Economics and Innovation in the Auto-Industrial Age." *She Ji* 1, no. 2 (2015): 140–49. https://doi.org/10.1016/j.sheji.2015.11.003.

Nadkarni, Sucheta, Marc Gruber, Katy DeCelles, Brian Connelly, and Markus Baer. "New Ways of Seeing: Radical Theorizing." *Academy of Management Journal* 61, no. 2 (2018): 371–77. https://doi.org/10.5465/amj.2018.4002.

Nanda, Ramana, and Matthew Rhodes Kropf. "Financing Entrepreneurial Experimentation." *Innovation Policy and the Economy* 16, no. 1 (2016): 1–23. https://doi.org/10.1086/684983.

Narayan, Kirin. "Tools to Shape Texts: What Creative Nonfiction Can." *Anthropology and Humanism* 32, no. 2 (2007): 130–44. https://doi.org/10.1525/ahu.2007.32.2.130.Narayan.

Nash, Kate. "Neo-Liberalisation, Universities and the Values of Bureaucracy." *Sociological Review*, 2018. https://doi.org/10.1177/0038026118754780.

Nelder, Geoff. "Auditory Crescendo." *Futures* 50 (2013): 86–93. https://doi.org/10.1016/j.futures.2013.03.010.

Nietzsche, Friedrich W. "Beyond Good and Evil: Prelude to a Philosophy of the Future." In *Basic Writings of Nietzsche*, edited by Walter Kaufman, 179–435. New York, NY: Modern Library, Random House, 2000.

———. *Twilight of the Idols.* Edited by Duncan Large. Oxford: Oxford University Press, 1998.

Noorda, Sijbolt. "Future Business Schools." *Journal of Management Development* 30, no. 5 (2011): 519–25. https://doi.org/10.1108/02621711111133028.

Nussbaum, Martha C. *Not for Profit: Why Democracy Needs the Humanities.* Updated. Princeton University Press (2010), 2016.

O'Neil, Isobel, and Deniz Ucbasaran. "Balancing 'What Matters to Me' with 'What Matters to Them': Exploring the Legitimation Process of Environmental Entrepreneurs." *Journal of Business Venturing* 31, no. 2 (2016): 133–52. https://doi.org/10.1016/j.jbusvent.2015.12.001.

O'Neill, Kayte, Gurmak Singh, and John O'Donoghue. "Implementing ELearning Programmes for Higher Education: A Review of the Literature." *Journal of Information Technology Education: Research* 3 (2004): 313–23. https://doi.org/10.28945/304.

O'Regan, John P., and John Gray. "The Bureaucratic Distortion of Academic Work: A Transdisciplinary Analysis of the UK Research Excellence Framework in the Age of Neoliberalism." *Language and Intercultural Communication* 18, no. 5 (2018): 533–48. https://doi.org/10.1080/14708477.2018.1501847.

Ogrean, Claudia, and Mihaela Herciu. "The Complex, Yet Small World of Global Multinationals – Insights on Some Apparent Paradoxes." *Studies in Business and Economics* 8, no. 2 (2013): 90–101.

Omri, Anis. "Entrepreneurship, Sectoral Outputs and Environmental Improvement: International Evidence." *Technological Forecasting and Social Change* 128, no. August 2017 (2018): 46–55. https://doi.org/10.1016/j.techfore.2017.10.016.

Öner, M. Atilla, and Özlem Kunday. "Linking Technology Foresight and Entrepreneurship." *Technological Forecasting and Social Change* 102 (2016): 1. https://doi.org/10.1016/j.techfore.2015.11.021.

Orta, Andrew. "Imagining the Unmanageable: MBAs at the Limits of Neoliberalism." *Culture, Theory and Critique* 60, no. 1 (2019): 50–65. https://doi.org/10.1080/14735784.2018.1543604.

Österman, Marcus. "Varieties of Education and Inequality: How the Institutions of Education and Political Economy Condition Inequality." *Socio-Economic Review* 16, no. 1 (2018): 113–35. https://doi.org/10.1093/ser/mwx007.

Ouellet, Maxime, and Éric Martin. "University Transformations and the New Knowledge Production Regime in Informational Capitalism." *TripleC* 16, no. 1 (2018): 78–96. https://doi.org/10.31269/vol16iss1pp78-96.

Overall, Jeffrey, and Sean Wise. "The Antecedents of Entrepreneurial Success: A Mixed Methods Approach." *Journal of Enterprising Culture* 24, no. 03 (2016): 209–41. https://doi.org/10.1142/s0218495816500096.

Palumbo, Rocco, and Rosalba Manna. "The Need for Requisite Variety to Support Growth: An Organizational Life Cycle Perspective." *Journal of Strategy and Management* 11, no. 2 (2018): 241–56. https://doi.org/10.1108/JSMA-10-2016-0072.

Parker, Martin. *Shut Down the Business School. Shut Down the Business School.* University of Chicago Press, 2018. https://doi.org/10.2307/j.ctvqhtj8.

Partington, Richard. "Price of High Demand Food Bought Online in UK Rises Sharply." The Guardian, 2020. https://www.theguardian.com/world/2020/apr/16/price-of-high-demand-food-in-uk-rises-sharply.

Peach, Kathy, Aleks Berditchevskaia, Theo Bass, Geoff Mulgan, Kelly Duggan, Sonja Dahl, Brenton Caffin, et al. *The Collective Intelligence Playbook.* Edited by Kathy Peach, Aleks Berditchevskaia, and Theo Bass. V.001. NESTA, 2019.

Pearl, Judea. "Probabilities of Causation : Three Counterfactual 1 Introduction." *Synthese* 121, no. 1–2 (1999): 93–149.

Peng, Wenhui, and Yaling Zhou. "The Design and Research of Responsive Web Supporting Mobile Learning Devices." *Proceedings - 2015 International Symposium on Educational Technology, ISET 2015*, 2016, 163–67. https://doi.org/10.1109/ISET.2015.40.

Pepper, Stephen, C. "Emergence." *Journal of Philosophy* 23, no. 9 (1926): 241–45.

Permatasari, Indah, Dana I. Sensuse, and Harry B. Santoso. "Cultural Aspects Influencing the Application of E-Learning: A Literature Review." *Journal of Physics: Conference Series* 1235, no. 1 (2019). https://doi.org/10.1088/1742-6596/1235/1/012026.

Pesic, Peter. "Hearing the Irrational: Music and the Development of the Modern Concept of Number." *Isis* 101, no. 3 (2010): 501–30. https://doi.org/10.1086/655790.

Petriglieri, Gianpiero. "F**k Science!? An Invitation to Humanize Organization Theory." *Organization Theory* 1 (2020): 1–18. https://doi.org/10.1177/2631787719897663.

Peverelli, Peter J., and Jiwen Song. *Chinese Entrepreneurship: A Social Capital Approach. Chinese Entrepreneurship: A Social Capital Approach.* Vol. 9783642282. Heidelberg: Springer Science & Business Media, 2012. https://doi.org/10.1007/978-3-642-28206-5.

Pichler, J. Hanns. "In Quest of SME-Conducive Policy Formulation." *Entrepreneurial Business and Economics Review* 6, no. 1 (2018): 105–13. https://doi.org/10.15678/EBER.2018.060106.

Pimblott, Kerry. “Decolonising the University: The Origins and Meaning of a Movement.” *Political Quarterly* 91, no. 1 (2020): 210–16. https://doi.org/10.1111/1467-923X.12784.

Pissarides, Francesca. “Is Lack of Funds the Main Obstacle to Growth? Ebrd’s Experience with Small- and Medium-Sized Businesses in Central and Eastern Europe.” *Journal of Business Venturing* 14, no. 5 (1999): 519–39. https://doi.org/10.1016/S0883-9026(98)00027-5.

Plato. *The Symposium*. Edited by Christopher Gill. London, UK: Penguin, 1999.

Polanyi, Karl. *Economy and Society: Selected Writings*. Edited by Michele Cangiani and Claus Thomasberger. Cambridge, UK: Polity Press, 2018.

Polanyi, Michael, and Emile Tompa. “Rethinking Work-Health Models for the New Global Economy: A Qualitative Analysis of Emerging Dimensions of Work.” *Work* 23, no. 1 (2004): 3–18.

Ponte, Raquel, Daniele Ellwanger, and Lucy Niemeyer. “Social Design and Ethics in Peirce’s Philosophy.” In *12th World Congress of Semiotics: New Semiotics. Between Tradition and Innovation*, 237–41. Sofia: International Association for Semiotic Studies (IASS/AIS), 2014. https://doi.org/10.24308/iass-2014-018.

Popp, Andrew, and Robin Holt. “Entrepreneurship and Being: The Case of the Shaws.” *Entrepreneurship and Regional Development* 25, no. 1–2 (2013): 52–68. https://doi.org/10.1080/08985626.2012.746887.

Popper, Karl R. *Conjectures and Refutations*. 5th ed. London, UK and New York, NY: Routledge, 1989.

———. “What Is Dialectic?” *Mind* 49, no. 196 (1940): 403–26. https://doi.org/10.1093/mind/xlix.194.403.

Popper, Rafael. “Foresight Methodolgy.” In *The Handbook of Technology Foresight: Concepts and Practice*, edited by Luke Georghiou, Jennifer Cassingena Harper, Michael Keenan, Ian Miles, and Rafael Popper, 44–88. Edward Elgar Publishing Ltd., 2008.

Porter, Michael E., and Victor E. Millar. “How Information Gives You Competitive Advantage.” *International Journal of Cancer* 85, no. July (1985): 149–60. https://doi.org/10.1002/ijc.2910610124.

Pötzsch, Holger. “Critical Digital Literacy: Technology in Education beyond Issues of User Competence and Labour-Market Qualifications.” *TripleC* 17, no. 2 (2019): 221–40. https://doi.org/10.31269/triplec.v17i2.1093.

Prasad, Ajnesh, and Gabrielle Durepos. “From Margin to Center: Listening to Silenced Subjectivities in International Business.” *Critical Perspectives on International Business* 12, no. 3 (2016): 218–21. https://doi.org/10.1108/cpoib-10-2015-0048.

Priestley, John B. “An Inspector Calls.” In *An Inspector Calls and Other Plays*, 157–220. London, UK: Penguin Modern Classics (1947), 2000.

———. *The Arts Under Socialism*. London, UK: Turnstile Press, 1947.

Prud’homme, Dan, and Max von Zedtwitz. “Managing ‘Forced’ Technology Transfer in Emerging Markets: The Case of China.” *Journal of International Management* 25, no. 3 (2019): 100670. https://doi.org/10.1016/j.intman.2019.04.003.

Putney, LeAnn G., Judith L. Green, Carol N. Dixon, and Gregory J. Kelly. "Evolution of Qualitative Research Methodology: Looking Beyond Defense to Possibilities." *Reading Research Quarterly* 34, no. 3 (1999): 368–77. https://doi.org/10.1598/rrq.34.3.6.

Pyysiäinen, Jarkko, Alistair R. Anderson, Gerard McElwee, and Kari Vesala. "Developing the Entrepreneurial Skills of Farmers: Some Myths Explored." *International Journal of Entrepreneurial Behaviour and Research* 12, no. 1 (2006): 21–39. https://doi.org/10.1108/13552550610644463.

QAA. *Enterprise and Entrepreneurship Education: Guidance for UK Higher Education Providers.* Gloucester, UK: The Quality Assurance Agency for Higher Education, 2018.

Qian, Gang, Feng Guo, Todd Ingalls, Loren Olson, Jody James, and Thanassis Rikakis. "A Gesture-Driven Multimodal Interactive Dance System." *2004 IEEE International Conference on Multimedia and Expo (ICME)* 3 (2004): 1579–82. https://doi.org/10.1109/icme.2004.1394550.

Qian, Wei, and Roger L. Burritt. "The Development of Environmental Management Accounting: An Institutional View." In *Environmental Management Accounting for Cleaner Production*, edited by S. Schaltegger, M. Bennett, Roger. L. Burritt, and C. Jasch, 233–48. Dordrecht: Springer, 2008. https://doi.org/10.1007/978-1-4020-8913-8_12.

Ramsey, Caroline. "Reflective Practice or Poetic Mindfulness: A Role for Social Poetics in Constructing and Performing Futures." *Action Learning: Research and Practice* 15, no. 2 (2018): 90–101. https://doi.org/10.1080/14767333.2018.1464709.

Rathbone, Daniel. "The UK's next PM Should Build on R&D Spending Commitments." CaSE: Campaign for Science and Engineering-Comment, 2022. https://www.sciencecampaign.org.uk/news-media/case-comment/the-uk-s-next-pm-should-build-on-r-d-spending.html.

Rauch, Andreas, Johan Wiklund, G. T. Lumpkin, and Michael Frese. "Entrepreneurial Orientation and Business Performance: An Assessment of Past Research and Suggestions for the Future." *Entrepreneurship: Theory and Practice* 33, no. 3 (2009): 761–87.

Raven, Paul Graham. "The Future's Four Quarters: Proposing a Quadrant Methodology for Strategic Prototyping in Infrastructural Contexts." *Technological Forecasting and Social Change* 84 (2014): 115–30. https://doi.org/10.1016/j.techfore.2013.10.012.

Raworth, Kate. *Doughnut Economics: Seven Ways to Think Like a 21st-Century Economist.* London, UK: Penguin Random House, 2017.

———. "Why It's Time for Doughnut Economics." *IPPR Progressive Review* 24, no. 3 (2017): 217–22. https://doi.org/10.1111/newe.12058.

Rawski, Thomas G. "Human Resources and China's Long Economic Boom." *Asia Policy* 12, no. 1 (2011): 33–78. https://doi.org/10.1353/asp.2011.0028.

Rehn, Alf, Malin Brännback, Alan Carsrud, and Marcus Lindahl. "Challenging the Myths of Entrepreneurship?" *Entrepreneurship and Regional Development* 25, no. 7–8 (2013): 543–51. https://doi.org/10.1080/08985626.2013.818846.

Reich, Robert. "Reconsidered: The Team As Hero." *Harvard Business Review* 65, no. 3 (1987): 77–83.

Reijonen, Helen, and Raija Komppula. "Perception of Success and Its Effect on Small Firm Performance." *Journal of Small Business and Enterprise Development* 14, no. 4 (2007): 689–701. https://doi.org/10.1108/14626000710832776.

Rhisiart, Martin. "Exploring the Future for Arts and Culture Organisations through Scenarios and Vignettes." *Futures* 50 (2013): 1–10. https://doi.org/10.1016/j.futures.2013.03.008.

Rhisiart, Martin, and Dylan Jones-Evans. "The Impact of Foresight on Entrepreneurship: The Wales 2010 Case Study." *Technological Forecasting and Social Change* 102 (2016): 112–19. https://doi.org/10.1016/j.techfore.2015.03.010.

Rhisiart, Martin, Eckhard Störmer, and Cornelia Daheim. "From Foresight to Impact? The 2030 Future of Work Scenarios." *Technological Forecasting and Social Change* 124 (2017): 203–13. https://doi.org/10.1016/j.techfore.2016.11.020.

Rhoads, David M., Joanna Dewey, and Donald Michie. *Mark as Story: An Introduction to the Narrative of a Gospel.* 2nd ed. Minneapolis, MN: Fortress Press, 1999.

Rhodes, Chris. "Business Statistics." *Briefing Paper.* London, 2019. https://doi.org/10.2307/3607925.

Ricart, Joan Enric, Michael J. Enright, Pankaj Ghemawat, Stuart L. Hart, and Tarun Khanna. "New Frontiers in International Strategy." *Journal of International Business Studies* 35, no. 3 (2004): 175–200. https://doi.org/10.1057/palgrave.jibs.8400080.

Ricci, Ronald J. "Autoethnographic Verse: Nicky's Boy: A Life in Two Worlds." *The Qualitative Report* 8, no. 4 (2003): 591–96.

Rice, Carla, and Ingrid Mündel. "Story-Making as Methodology: Disrupting Dominant Stories through Multimedia Storytelling." *Canadian Review of Sociology* 55, no. 2 (2018): 211–31. https://doi.org/10.1111/cars.12190.

Rindova, Violina, Daved Barry, and David J. Ketchen. "Entrepreneuring as Emancipation." *Academy of Management Review* 34, no. 3 (2009): 477–91. https://doi.org/10.5465/amr.2009.40632647.

Ringer, Fritz K. "Education, Knowledge, and Vocation." In *Max Weber : An Intellectual Biography.* Chicago: University of Chicago Press, 2004.

Robert, Yola. "Here's Why You're Feeling Zoom Fatigue." Forbes Women, 2020. https://www.forbes.com/sites/yolarobert1/2020/04/30/heres-why-youre-feeling-zoom-fatigue/#191eb4432ac6.

Roberts, Deborah L., and Marina Candi. "Leveraging Social Network Sites in New Product Development: Opportunity or Hype?" *Journal of Product Innovation Management* 31, no. S1 (2014): 105–17. https://doi.org/10.1111/jpim.12195.

Roberts, James P., and Andrew Middleton. "Evolving Products: From Human Design to Self-Organisation via Science Fiction Prototyping." *Technological Forecasting and Social Change* 84 (2014): 15–28. https://doi.org/10.1016/j.techfore.2013.09.003.

Roberts, Joanne. "Luxury International Business: A Critical Review and Agenda for Research." *Critical Perspectives on International Business* 15, no. 2–3 (2019): 219–38. https://doi.org/10.1108/cpoib-02-2019-0018.

Robinson, Sarah, and Alexandra Bristow. "Riding Populist Storms: Brexit, Trumpism and beyond, Special Paper Series Editorial." *Organization*, 2020. https://doi.org/10.1177/1350508420910576.

Robinson, Sir Ken. "A Global Reset of Education." *Prospects*, no. 0123456789 (2020): 1–3. https://doi.org/10.1007/s11125-020-09493-y.

Robison, Lindon J., and Bryan K. Ritchie. *Relationship Economics: The Social Capital Paradigm and It's Application to Business, Politics and Other Transactions. Relationship Economics: The Social Capital Paradigm and It's Application to Business, Politics and Other Transactions.* Boca Raton, FL: CRC Press, 2016. https://doi.org/10.4324/9781315604701.

Rogers, Everett M. *Diffusion of Innovations, 3rd Ed.* New York, NY: The Free Press, 1983.

Rogers, Martha, and Allen Tough. "Facing the Future Is Not for Wimps." *Futures* 28, no. 5 (1996): 491–96. https://doi.org/10.1016/0016-3287(96)00021-3.

Rose, Nikolas, and Peter Miller. "Political Power beyond the State: Problematics of Government." *British Journal of Sociology* 43, no. 2 (1992): 173–205.

Roundy, Philip T., Mike Bradshaw, and Beverly K. Brockman. "The Emergence of Entrepreneurial Ecosystems: A Complex Adaptive Systems Approach." *Journal of Business Research* 86, no. February (2018): 1–10. https://doi.org/10.1016/j.jbusres.2018.01.032.

Runde, J. "Clarifying Frank Knight's Discussion of the Meaning of Risk and Uncertainty." *Cambridge Journal of Economics* 22, no. 5 (1998): 539–46. https://doi.org/10.1093/cje/22.5.539.

Sachs, Jeffrey, Joseph Stiglitz, Mariana Mazzucato, Clair Brown, Indivar Dutta-Gupta, Robert Reich, Gabriel Zucman, and others. "Letter from Economists: To Rebuild Our World, We Must End the Carbon Economy." The Guardian, 2020. https://www.theguardian.com/commentisfree/2020/aug/04/economists-letter-carbon-economy-climate-change-rebuild.

Saltman, Kenneth J. "Neoliberalism and Corporate School Reform: 'Failure' and 'Creative Destruction.'" *Review of Education, Pedagogy, and Cultural Studies* 36, no. 4 (2014): 249–59. https://doi.org/10.1080/10714413.2014.938564.

Sandberg, Birgitta, Leila Hurmerinta, and Peter Zettinig. "Highly Innovative and Extremely Entrepreneurial Individuals: What Are These Rare Birds Made Of?" *European Journal of Innovation Management* 16, no. 2 (2013): 227–42. https://doi.org/10.1108/14601061311324557.

Sandberg, Maria, Kristian Klockars, and Kristoffer Wilén. "Green Growth or Degrowth? Assessing the Normative Justifications for Environmental Sustainability and Economic Growth through Critical Social Theory." *Journal of Cleaner Production* 206 (2019): 133–41. https://doi.org/10.1016/j.jclepro.2018.09.175.

Sandel, Michael J. *The Tyranny of Merit.* Allen Lane, 2020.

Sanford, Carol. "A Theory and Practice System of 'Systems Thinking': With an Executive's Story of the Power of 'Developmental' and 'Evolutionary' Systems

Thinking. Why a New Typology of Systems Thinking?" In *International Conference on Systems Thinking in Management-ICSTM-ICSTM*, 2004.

Santos, Filipe M. "A Positive Theory of Social Entrepreneurship." *Journal of Business Ethics* 111, no. 3 (2006): 335–51. https://doi.org/10.1007/s.

Sarasvathy, Saras D. "The Questions We Ask and the Questions We Care about: Reformulating Some Problems in Entrepreneurship Research." *Journal of Business Venturing* 19, no. 5 (2004): 707–17. https://doi.org/10.1016/j.jbusvent.2003.09.006.

Sardar, Ziauddin. "The Namesake: Futures; Futures Studies; Futurology; Futuristic; Foresight-What's in a Name?" *Futures* 42, no. 3 (2010): 177–84. https://doi.org/10.1016/j.futures.2009.11.001.

Saritas, Ozcan, and Jack E. Smith. "The Big Picture - Trends, Drivers, Wild Cards, Discontinuities and Weak Signals." *Futures* 43, no. 3 (2011): 292–312. https://doi.org/10.1016/j.futures.2010.11.007.

Sarooghi, Hessam, Sanwar Sunny, Jeffrey Hornsby, and Stephanie Fernhaber. "Design Thinking and Entrepreneurship Education: Where Are We, and What Are the Possibilities?" *Journal of Small Business Management* 57, no. S1 (2019): 78–93. https://doi.org/10.1111/jsbm.12541.

Sarooghi, Hessamoddin, Dirk Libaers, and Andrew Burkemper. "Examining the Relationship between Creativity and Innovation: A Meta-Analysis of Organizational, Cultural, and Environmental Factors." *Journal of Business Venturing* 30, no. 5 (2015): 714–31. https://doi.org/10.1016/j.jbusvent.2014.12.003.

Sarpong, David, Eve Eyres, and Georgios Batsakis. "Narrating the Future: A Distentive Capability Approach to Strategic Foresight." *Technological Forecasting and Social Change* 140 (2019): 105–14. https://doi.org/10.1016/j.techfore.2018.06.034.

Sartre, Jean-Paul. *Being and Nothingness: An Essay on Phenomenological Ontology*. Edited by H. E. Barnes. Transl. London: Routledge Classics (1943), 2003.

Sayer, Andrew. "Moral Economy, Unearned Income, and Legalized Corruption." In *Neoliberalism and the Moral Economy of Fraud*, edited by David Whyte and Jörg Wiegratz, 44–56, 2016.

Schaltegger, Stefan, Markus Beckmann, and Kai Hockerts. "Collaborative Entrepreneurship for Sustainability. Creating Solutions in Light of the UN Sustainable Development Goals." *International Journal of Entrepreneurial Venturing* 10, no. 2 (2018): 131–52. https://doi.org/10.1504/IJEV.2018.092709.

Schaper, Michael. "The Essence of Ecopreneurship." *Greener Management International* 38 (2002): 26–30.

Scharmer, Claus Otto. "Presencing: Learning From the Future As It Emerges." In *Conference On Knowledge and Innovation*, Vol. 2000. Helsinki: Helsinki School of Economics, 2000.

Schick, Kate. "Speculative Dialectics." In *Gillian Rose: A Good Enough Justice*, 17–35. Edinburgh: Edinburgh University Press, 2012.

Schiller, Dan. "Digital Capitalism's Ascent to Crisis." In *Digital Depression : Information Technology and Economic Crisis*, 10–69. Chicago: University of Illinois Press, 2014.

Schneider, Marguerite, and Mark Somers. "Organizations as Complex Adaptive Systems: Implications of Complexity Theory for Leadership Research." *Leadership Quarterly* 17, no. 4 (2006): 351–65. https://doi.org/10.1016/j.leaqua.2006.04.006.

Schokkaert, Erik. "Review of Kate Raworth's Doughnut Economics. London: Random House, 2017, 373 Pp." *Erasmus Journal for Philosophy and Economics* 12, no. 1 (2019): 125–32. https://doi.org/10.23941/ejpe.v12i1.412.

Schouten, Fredreka. "These Democratic Billionaires Could Help Shape the 2020 Election." *CNN Politics*, June 1, 2019.

Schubert, Stefan F., and Stephen J. Turnovsky. "Growth and Unemployment: Short-Run and Long-Run Tradeoffs." *Journal of Economic Dynamics and Control* 91 (2018): 172–89. https://doi.org/10.1016/j.jedc.2017.11.003.

Schultz, Theodore W. "Investment in Human Capital." *The American Economic Review* 51, no. 1 (1961): 1–17.

Schumpeter, Joseph A. *Can Capitalism Survive?* Harper Per. New York, NY: Harper Collins (1942), 2009.

———. *Capitalism, Socialism, and Democracy.* Second. Floyd, Va: Wilder Publications (1946), 2018.

Schwab, K. *The Fourth Industrial Revolution.* New York: Crown Business, 2017.

Schwarz, Jan Oliver. "The 'Narrative Turn' in Developing Foresight: Assessing How Cultural Products Can Assist Organisations in Detecting Trends." *Technological Forecasting and Social Change* 90, no. PB (2015): 510–13. https://doi.org/10.1016/j.techfore.2014.02.024.

Schwarz, Jan Oliver, Rixa Kroehl, and Heiko A. von der Gracht. "Novels and Novelty in Trend Research - Using Novels to Perceive Weak Signals and Transfer Frames of Reference." *Technological Forecasting and Social Change* 84 (2014): 66–73. https://doi.org/10.1016/j.techfore.2013.09.007.

Schwarz, Jan Oliver, and Franz Liebl. "Cultural Products and Their Implications for Business Models: Why Science Fiction Needs Socio-Cultural Fiction." *Futures* 50 (2013): 66–73. https://doi.org/10.1016/j.futures.2013.03.006.

Segady, Thomas W. "The Utility of Weber's Ideal Type: Verstehen and the Theory of Critical Mass." *Sociological Spectrum* 34, no. 4 (2014): 354–61. https://doi.org/10.1080/02732173.2014.917249.

Segal, Gerry, Dan Borgia, and Jerry Schoenfeld. "The Motivation to Become an Entrepreneur." *International Journal of Entrepreneurial Behaviour and Research* 11, no. 1 (2005): 42–57. https://doi.org/10.1108/13552550510580834.

Selasky, Susan. "Food Prices Soar to Highest One-Month Increase since 1974; Price of Eggs up 16% in April." USA Today/ Detroit Free Press, 2020. https://eu.usatoday.com/story/money/2020/05/20/food-prices-soar-coronavirus-covid-19/5226969002/.

Seligman, Daniel, and Patty de Llosa. "God's Economics." *Fortune*, 1994.

Senge, Peter M., C. Otto. Scharmer, Joseph Jaworski, and Betty S. Flowers. *Presence: Exploring Profound Change in People, Organizations, and Society.* London: Nicholas Brealey Publishing, 2005.

Seo, Ju Hwan, Jeong Yean Yang, Jaewoo Kim, and Dong Soo Kwon. "Autonomous Humanoid Robot Dance Generation System Based on Real-Time Music Input." *Proceedings - IEEE International Workshop on Robot and*

Human Interactive Communication, 2013, 204–9. https://doi.org/10.1109/ROMAN.2013.6628446.

Shahrokhi, Manuchehr, Huifang Cheng, Krishnan Dandapani, Antonio Figueiredo, Ali M. Parhizgari, and Yochanan Shachmurove. "The Evolution and Future of the BRICS: Unbundling Politics from Economics." *Global Finance Journal* 32 (2017): 1–15. https://doi.org/10.1016/j.gfj.2017.03.002.

Shane, Scott, Edwin A. Locke, and Christopher J. Collins. "Entrepreneurial Motivation Objectives." *Entrepreneurial and Small Business Operations Commons*, 2003.

Shane, Scott, and S. Venkataraman. "The Promise of Entrepreneurship as a Field of Research." *Academy of Management Review* 25, no. 1 (2000): 217–26. https://doi.org/10.5465/AMR.2000.2791611.

Shapero, A. "Why Entrepreneurship? A Worldwide Perspective." *Journal of Small Business Management (Pre-1986)* 23, no. 4 (1985): 1.

Shattock, Michael. "Better Informing the Market? The Teaching Excellence Framework in British Higher Education." *International Higher Education* 92, no. Winter (2018): 21–22.

Shepherd, Dean A. "Party On! A Call for Entrepreneurship Research That Is More Interactive, Activity Based, Cognitively Hot, Compassionate, and Prosocial." *Journal of Business Venturing* 30, no. 4 (2015): 489–507. https://doi.org/10.1016/j.jbusvent.2015.02.001.

Short, John, Ederyn Williams, and Bruce Christie. *'The Social Psychology of Telecommunications.'* London: John Wiley & Sons Ltd, 1976.

Shotter, John, and Arlene M. Katz. "Articulating Practices: Methods and Experiences: Articulating a Practice from within the Practice Itself: Establishing Formative Dialogues by the Use of a 'Social Poetics.'" *Concepts and TransformationConcepts and Transformation International Journal of Action Research and Organizational Renewal* 1, no. 2–3 (1996): 213–37. https://doi.org/10.1075/cat.1.2-3.07sho.

Sia, P. Di. "Describing the Concept of Infinite among Art, Literature, Philosophy and Science: A Pedagogical-Didactic Overview." *The Journal of Education Culture and Society*, no. 1 (2014): 9–19. https://doi.org/10.15503/jecs20141-9-19.

Siddiqui, Kalim. "David Ricardo's Comparative Advantage and Developing Countries: Myth and Reality." *International Critical Thought* 8, no. 3 (2018): 426–52. https://doi.org/10.1080/21598282.2018.1506264.

Silvester, Andy. "Exclusive: Liz Truss : I'll Protect 'Crown Jewel' City of London as Prime Minister." *City AM.* August 31, 2022.

Singh, Gurmak, and Glenn Hardaker. "Barriers and Enablers to Adoption and Diffusion of ELearning : A Systematic Review of the Literature - a Need for an Integrative Approach." *Education and Training* 56, no. 2 (2014): 105–21. https://doi.org/10.1108/ET-11-2012-0123.

Skeates, Richard. "The Infinite City." *City* 2, no. 8 (1997): 6–20. https://doi.org/10.1080/13604819708713512.

Sklar, Julia. "'Zoom Fatigue' Is Taxing the Brain. Here's Why That Happens." National Geographic, 2020. https://www.nationalgeographic.co.uk/science-

and-technology/2020/04/zoom-fatigue-is-taxing-the-brain-heres-why-that-happens.

Sklaveniti, Chrysavgi, and Chris Steyaert. "Reflecting with Pierre Bourdieu: Towards a Reflexive Outlook for Practice-Based Studies of Entrepreneurship." *Entrepreneurship and Regional Development* 32, no. 3–4 (2020): 313–33. https://doi.org/10.1080/08985626.2019.1641976.

Skovgaard-Smith, Irene, and Flemming Poulfelt. "Imagining 'Non-Nationality': Cosmopolitanism as a Source of Identity and Belonging." *Human Relations* 71, no. 2 (2018): 129–54. https://doi.org/10.1177/0018726717714042.

Slater, Mel. "Presence and the Sixth Sense." *Presence: Teleoperators and Virtual Environments* 11, no. 4 (2002): 435–39. https://doi.org/10.1162/105474602760204327.

Slaughter, Richard A. "Farewell Alternative Futures?" *Futures,* 2020, 102496. https://doi.org/10.1016/j.futures.2019.102496.

———. "From Forecasting and Scenarios to Social Construction: Changing Methodological Paradigms in Futures Studies." *Foresight* 4, no. 3 (2002): 26–31. https://doi.org/10.1108/14636680210697731.

Smallbone, David. "Entrepreneurship Policy: Issues and Challenges." *Small Enterprise Research* 23, no. 3 (2016): 201–18. https://doi.org/10.1080/13215906.2016.1270227.

Smith, Adam. *The Theory of Moral Sentiments.* Edited by Ryan Patrick Hanley. 6th ed. London, UK: Penguin Classiscs (1759,1790), 2009.

———. *The Wealth of Nations: Books I-III.* Edited by Andrew Skinner. New 1982. London, UK: Penguin Classiscs (1776), 1970.

———. *The Wealth of Nations: Books IV-V.* Edited by Andrew Skinner. New 1982. London, UK: Penguin Classiscs (1776), 1999.

Smith, Peter A.C., and Carol Ann Sharicz. "The Bi-Modal Organization: Balancing Autopoiesis and Fluid Social Networks for Sustainability." *Learning Organization* 20, no. 2 (2013): 134–52. https://doi.org/10.1108/09696471311303773.

Snelson-Powell, Annie, Johanne Grosvold, and Andrew Millington. "Business School Legitimacy and the Challenge of Sustainability: A Fuzzy Set Analysis of Institutional Decoupling." *Academy of Management Learning and Education* 15, no. 4 (2016): 703–23. https://doi.org/10.5465/amle.2015.0307.

Snyder, David Pearce. "Extra-Preneurship: Reinventing Enterprise for the Information Age." *Futurist* 39, no. 4 (2005): 47–53.

Soin, Kim, and Tobias Scheytt. "Making the Case for Narrative Methods in Cross-Cultural Organizational Research." *Organizational Research Methods* 9, no. 1 (2006): 55–77. https://doi.org/10.1177/1094428105283297.

Solow, Robert M. "We'd Better Watch out, Review of SS Cohen and J. Zysman. Manufacturing Matters: The Myth of the Post-Industrial Economy." *New York Times Book Review* 12, no. 7 (1987): 36.

Sommers, Jeffrey, Rachel Hegland, and Patrick Delices. "American Public Policy and Full Employment: The Imperative of Martin Luther King's Political Economy in the 21st Century." *SAGE Open* 8, no. 3 (2018). https://doi.org/10.1177/2158244018802674.

Sonesson, Göran. "Phenomenology Meets Semiotics." *Metodo. International Studies in Phenomenology and Philosophy* 3.1, no. 1 (2015): 41–62. https://doi.org/10.19079/metodo.3.1.41.

Southern, Jen, Rebecca Ellis, Maria Angela Ferrario, Ruth McNally, Rod Dillon, Will Simm, and Jon Whittle. "Imaginative Labour and Relationships of Care: Co-Designing Prototypes with Vulnerable Communities." *Technological Forecasting and Social Change* 84 (2014): 131–42. https://doi.org/10.1016/j.techfore.2013.08.003.

Spangenberg, Joachim H., Ines Omann, and Friedrich Hinterberger. "Sustainable Growth Criteria Minimum Benchmarks and Scenarios for Employment and the Environment." *Ecological Economics* 42, no. 3 (2002): 429–43. https://doi.org/10.1016/S0921-8009(02)00125-8.

Spash, Clive L. "'The Economy' as If People Mattered: Revisiting Critiques of Economic Growth in a Time of Crisis." *Globalizations*, 2020, 1–18. https://doi.org/10.1080/14747731.2020.1761612.

Spencer, David A. "Fear and Hope in an Age of Mass Automation: Debating the Future of Work." *New Technology, Work and Employment* 33, no. 1 (2018): 1–12. https://doi.org/10.1111/ntwe.12105.

Srikantia, Jessica. "The Structural Violence of Globalization." *Critical Perspectives on International Business* 12, no. 3 (2016): 222–58. https://doi.org/10.1108/cpoib-09-2015-0040.

Stacey, Ralph D., Douglas Griffin, and Patricia Shaw. *Complexity and Management: Fad or Radical Challenge to Systems Thinking?* E-Book. Vol. 53. London, UK: Routledge, 2001.

Stahl, Bernd Carsten, Neil McBride, Kutoma Wakunuma, and Catherine Flick. "The Empathic Care Robot: A Prototype of Responsible Research and Innovation." *Technological Forecasting and Social Change* 84 (2014): 74–85. https://doi.org/10.1016/j.techfore.2013.08.001.

Standing, Guy. "Economic Insecurity and Global Casualisation: Threat or Promise?" *Social Indicators Research* 88, no. 1 (2008): 15–30. https://doi.org/10.1007/s11205-007-9202-7.

Stanfield, J. Ron. "Phenomena and Epiphenomena in Economics." *Journal of Economics Issues* 13, no. 4 (1979): 885–98.

Stankiewicz, Kevin. "Mark Cuban Says Coronavirus Will End up Improving Capitalism with Companies Putting Employees First." CNBC, 2020. https://www.cnbc.com/2020/04/08/mark-cuban-says-coronavirus-will-end-up-improving-capitalism-with-companies-putting-employees-first.html.

Starkey, Kenneth, Sue Tempest, and Silvia Cinque. "Management Education and the Theatre of the Absurd." *Management Learning* 50, no. 5 (2019): 591–606. https://doi.org/10.1177/1350507619875894.

Statler, Matt. "Developing Wisdom in a Business School? Critical Reflections on Pedagogical Practice." *Management Learning* 45, no. 4 (2014): 397–417. https://doi.org/10.1177/1350507614541198.

Stevenson, Angus, and Maurice Waite, eds. *Concise Oxford English Dictionary*. 12th ed. Oxford University Press, n.d.

Steyaert, Chris. "'Entrepreneuring' as a Conceptual Attractor? A Review of Process Theories in 20 Years of Entrepreneurship Studies." *Entrepreneurship and Regional Development* 19, no. 6 (2007): 453–77. https://doi.org/10.1080/08985620701671759.

———. "Entrepreneurship as in(Ter)Vention: Reconsidering the Conceptual Politics of Method in Entrepreneurship Studies." *Entrepreneurship and Regional Development* 23, no. 1 (2011): 77–88. https://doi.org/10.1080/08985626.2011.540416.

———. "Of Course That Is Not the Whole (Toy) Story: Entrepreneurship and the Cat's Cradle." *Journal of Business Venturing* 22, no. 5 (2007): 733–51. https://doi.org/10.1016/j.jbusvent.2006.10.004.

Stinchfield, Bryan T., Reed E. Nelson, and Matthew S. Wood. "Learning From Levi-Strauss' Legacy: Art, Craft, Engineering, Bricolage, and Brokerage in Entrepreneurship." *Entrepreneurship Theory and Practice* 37, no. 4 (2013): 889–921. https://doi.org/10.1111/j.1540-6520.2012.00523.x.

Stolman, Lara. "Entrepreneurship Is How Families Are Creating Meaningful Jobs for Their Children With Autism Spectrum Disorder." Entrepreneur.com, 2018. https://www.entrepreneur.com/article/321421.

Storey, D. J. *Understanding the Small Business Sector. London: International Thomson Business Press.* London: Routledge, 1994.

Streeck, Wolfgang. "E Pluribus Unum?1 Varieties and Commonalities of Capitalism." *The Sociology of Economic Life, Third Edition.* MPIfG Discussion Paper. Cologne, 2010.

———. *How Will Capitalism End?* London, UK: Verso, 2017.

Strömberg, Helena, Ingrid Pettersson, Jonas Andersson, Annie Rydström, Debargha Dey, Maria Klingegård, and Jodi Forlizzi. "Designing for Social Experiences with and within Autonomous Vehicles-Exploring Methodological Directions." *Design Science* 4, no. January (2018). https://doi.org/10.1017/dsj.2018.9.

Sun, Guoyu, Paisarn Muneesawang, Matthew Kyan, Haiyan Li, Ling Zhong, Nan Dong, Bruce Elder, and Ling Guan. "An Advanced Computational Intelligence System for Training of Ballet Dance in a Cave Virtual Reality Environment." *Proceedings - 2014 IEEE International Symposium on Multimedia, ISM 2014,* no. 1 (2015): 159–66.

Suvin, Darko. "On the Poetics of the Science Fiction Genre." *College English* 34, no. 3 (1972): 372–82.

Sylvan, David, and Stephen Majeski. "A Methodology for the Study of Historical Counterfactuals." *International Studies Quarterly* 42, no. 1 (1998): 79–108. https://doi.org/10.1111/0020-8833.00070.

Szentpéteri, Márton. "Changing the Rhythm of Design Capitalism and the Total Aestheticization of the World." *Hungarian Studies Yearbook 2019,* no. I (2019): 82–99. https://doi.org/10.2478/HSY-2019-0007.

Szostak, Michał, and Łukasz Sułkowski. "Manager as an Artist: Creative Endeavour in Crossing the Borders of Art and Organizational Discourse." *Creativity Studies* 13, no. 2 (2020): 351–68. https://doi.org/10.3846/cs.2020.11373.

Tarhini, Ali, Kate Hone, and Xiaohui Liu. "User Acceptance towards Web-Based Learning Systems: Investigating the Role of Social, Organizational and

Individual Factors in European Higher Education." *Procedia Computer Science* 17 (2013): 189–97. https://doi.org/10.1016/j.procs.2013.05.026.

Tavenner, Eugene. "Three as a Magic Number in Latin Literature." In *Transactions and Proceedings of the American Philological Association*, 47:117–43. The Johns Hopkins University Press, 1916.

Teske, Paul, and Mark Schneider. "The Bureaucratic Entrepreneur: The Case of City Managers." *Public Administration Review* 54, no. 4 (1994): 331–40.

Thatcher, Margaret. "No Such Thing as Society." Interview with Douglas Keay, Woman's Own (Sep 23), 1987. https://www.margaretthatcher.org/document/106689.

Thomas CBE, Richard. "The Impact of PPI Mis-Selling on the Financial Ombudsman Service." London, UK, 2016.

Thomas, Ken, and Tarini Parti. "Biden Calls Attack on Capitol an 'Insurrection.'" *The Wall Street Journal*. January 7, 2021.

Thompson, Neil A., Karen Verduijn, and William B. Gartner. "Entrepreneurship-as-Practice: Grounding Contemporary Theories of Practice into Entrepreneurship Studies." *Entrepreneurship and Regional Development* 32, no. 3–4 (2020): 247–56. https://doi.org/10.1080/08985626.2019.1641978.

Tie, Warwick John. "The Subject Supposed to Design." *CoDesign* 13, no. 1 (2017): 16–31. https://doi.org/10.1080/15710882.2015.1127388.

Tight, Malcolm. "Education, Education, Education! The Vision of Lifelong Learning in the Kennedy, Dearing and Fryer Reports." *Oxford Review of Education* 24, no. 4 (1998): 473–85. https://doi.org/10.1080/0305498980240404.

———. "The Neoliberal Turn in Higher Education." *Higher Education Quarterly* 73, no. 3 (2019): 273–84. https://doi.org/10.1111/hequ.12197.

Tiqqun. *The Cybernetic Hypothesis*. Edited by Robert Hurley. Transl. Semiotext(e) (2001), 2020.

Todorova, Mariana. "Counterfactual Construction of the Future." *World Futures Review* 7, no. 1 (2015): 30–38. https://doi.org/10.1177/1946756715587004.

Torre, José de la, and Richard W. Moxon. "Introduction to the Symposium E-Commerce and Global Business: The Impact of the Information and Communication Technology Revolution on the Conduct of International Business." *Journal of International Business Studies* 32, no. 4 (2001): 617–39. https://doi.org/10.1057/palgrave.jibs.8490988.

Trigg, Andrew B. "Deriving the Engel Curve: Pierre Bourdieu and the Social Critique of Maslow's Hierarchy of Needs." *Review of Social Economy* 62, no. 3 (2004): 393–406. https://doi.org/10.1080/0034676042000253987.

Trilling, Daniel. "Why Is the UK Government Suddenly Targeting 'Critical Race Theory'?" The Guardian, October 23, 2020. https://www.theguardian.com/commentisfree/2020/oct/23/uk-critical-race-theory-trump-conservatives-structural-inequality.

UN ESCWA. "Social Justice Matters: A View from the Economic and Social Commission for Western Asia." Pamphlet. Beirut, 2019.

United Nations. "World Food Prices Drop in March." United Nations Africa Renewal News, 2020. https://www.un.org/africarenewal/news/coronavirus/world-food-prices-drop-march-due-covid-19-and-oil.

Urueña, Sergio. "Understanding 'Plausibility': A Relational Approach to the Anticipatory Heuristics of Future Scenarios." *Futures* 111, no. August 2018 (2019): 15–25. https://doi.org/10.1016/j.futures.2019.05.002.

USAHEC. "Q. Who First Originated the Term VUCA (Volatility, Uncertainty, Complexity and Ambiguity)?" USAHEC Ask Us a Question. Accessed August 23, 2020. http://usawc.libanswers.com/faq/84869.

Valentinov, Vladislav. "From Equilibrium to Autopoiesis: A Luhmannian Reading of Veblenian Evolutionary Economics." *Economic Systems* 39, no. 1 (2015): 143–55. https://doi.org/10.1016/j.ecosys.2014.10.004.

Varoufakis, Yanis. *And the Weak Suffer What They Must?: Europe, Austerity, and the Threat to Global Stability.* London, UK: Vintage Books, 2017.

Veblen, Thorstein. "The Theory of Business Enterprise." In *The Complete Works of Thorstein Veblen*, Kindle edn., 270–506. e-artnow, 2016.

Vega Balbás, Rubén. "The Performative Nature of Dramatic Imagination." *Revista Brasileira de Estudos Da Presença* 10, no. 1 (2020): 1–26. https://doi.org/10.1590/2237-266092193.

Venkataraman, Sankaran. "The Distinctive Domain of Entrepreneurship Research." *Advances in Entrepreneurship, Firm Emergence and Growth* 3 (1997): 119–38.

Venkateswaran, Ramya Tarakad, and Abhoy K. Ojha. "Strategic Management Research on Emerging Economies: Cultural Imperialism in Universalizing Research Paradigms." *Critical Perspectives on International Business* 13, no. 3 (2017): 204–25. https://doi.org/10.1108/cpoib-05-2016-0012.

Venturini, Giada, Meiken Hansen, and Per D. Andersen. "Linking Narratives and Energy System Modelling in Transport Scenarios: A Participatory Perspective from Denmark." *Energy Research & Social Science* 52, no. 204–220 (2019).

Verbeke, Alain, Régis Coeurderoy, and Tanja Matt. "The Future of International Business Research on Corporate Globalization That Never Was…." *Journal of International Business Studies* 49, no. 9 (2018): 1101–12. https://doi.org/10.1057/s41267-018-0192-2.

Verduijn, Karen, Pascal Dey, Deirdre Tedmanson, and Caroline Essers. "Emancipation and/or Oppression? Conceptualizing Dimensions of Criticality in Entrepreneurship Studies." *International Journal of Entrepreneurial Behaviour and Research* 20, no. 2 (2014): 98–107. https://doi.org/10.1108/IJEBR-02-2014-0031.

Villo, Sofia, Minna Halme, and Tiina Ritvala. "Theorizing MNE-NGO Conflicts in State-Capitalist Contexts: Insights from the Greenpeace, Gazprom and the Russian State Dispute in the Arctic." *Journal of World Business* 55, no. 3 (2020). https://doi.org/10.1016/j.jwb.2019.101068.

Vine, Tom. "Brexit, Trumpism and Paradox: Epistemological Lessons for the Critical Consensus." *Organization*, 2019. https://doi.org/10.1177/1350508419855706.

Vliegenthart, Hans. "The Role of the University in Bridging the Communication Gap between Science and Technology and Society." In *International Symposium on Technology and Society*, 19–22. IEEE, 2000. https://doi.org/10.1109/istas.2000.915571.

Volchik, Vyacheslav, Anna Oganesyan, and Tadeusz Olejarz. "Higher Education as a Factor of Socio-Economic Performance and Development." *Journal of International Studies* 11, no. 4 (2018): 326–40. https://doi.org/10.14254/2071-8330.2018/11-4/23.

Volkmann, Christina, and Christian De Cock. "The Bauhaus and the Business School: Exploring Analogies, Resisting Imitation." *Management Learning* 38, no. 4 (2007): 389–403. https://doi.org/10.1177/1350507607080570.

Vroom, Victor H. *Work and Motivation*. New York, NY: Wiley, 1964.

Waehning, Nadine, Mike Hemmings, David M. Atkinson, Serge Koukpaki, David Weir, and Jeff Gold. "Social Justice in York, 2030 (Extended Summary)." York, UK, 2020.

Waldern, Barbara. "Impressing Heaven: Creative Non-Fiction as Reflective Practice in Foreign Language Teaching and Cross Cultural Study." *Universal Journal of Educational Research* 3, no. 7 (2015): 467–71. https://doi.org/10.13189/ujer.2015.030707.

Walker, Kenton B., and Ervin L. Black. "Reengineering the Undergraduate Business Core Curriculum: Aligning Business Schools with Business for Improved Performance." *Business Process Management Journal* 6, no. 3 (2000): 194–213. https://doi.org/10.1108/14637150010313366.

Wallace, Scott. "Brazil' s New Leader Promised to Exploit the Amazon — but Can He?" National Geographic, 2019. https://www.nationalgeographic.co.uk/2018/10/brazils-new-leader-promised-exploit-amazon-can-he.

Wallendorf, Melanie, and Merrie Brucks. "Introspection in Consumer Research: Implementation and Implications." *Journal of Consumer Research* 20, no. 3 (1993): 339. https://doi.org/10.1086/209354.

Wallmann, Elisabeth. "The Human-Animal Debate and the Enlightenment Body Politic: Emilie Du Châtelet's Reading of Mandeville's Fable of the Bees." *Early Modern French Studies* 42, no. 1 (2020): 86–103. https://doi.org/10.1080/20563035.2020.1775430.

Wang, Georgette, and Zhong Bo Liu. "What Collective? Collectivism and Relationalism from a Chinese Perspective." *Chinese Journal of Communication* 3, no. 1 (2010): 42–63. https://doi.org/10.1080/17544750903528799.

Wang, Yao. "What Are the Biggest Obstacles to Growth of SMEs in Developing Countries? – An Empirical Evidence from an Enterprise Survey." *Borsa Istanbul Review* 16, no. 3 (2016): 167–76. https://doi.org/10.1016/j.bir.2016.06.001.

Waring, Jack, Rebecca Price, and Carl Waring. "Business Empathy." *Conference Proceedings of the Academy for Design Innovation Management* 2, no. 1 (2019). https://doi.org/10.33114/adim.2019.01.200.

Warmington, Paul. "Critical Race Theory in England: Impact and Opposition." *Identities* 27, no. 1 (2020): 20–37. https://doi.org/10.1080/1070289X.2019.1587907.

Watanabe, Chihiro, Yuji Tou, and Pekka Neittaanmäki. "A New Paradox of the Digital Economy - Structural Sources of the Limitation of GDP Statistics." *Technology in Society* 55, no. June (2018): 9–23. https://doi.org/10.1016/j.techsoc.2018.05.004.

Waterworth, John A., and Eva L. Waterworth. "'The Meaning of Presence', Presence-Connect." *Presence-Connect* 3, no. 3 (January 2003): 3.

Watson, Tony J. "Entrepreneurship in Action: Bringing Together the Individual, Organizational and Institutional Dimensions of Entrepreneurial Action." *Entrepreneurship & Regional Development* 25, no. 5–6 (2013): 404–22. https://doi.org/10.1080/08985626.2012.754645.

Watt, Peter. "The Rise of the 'Dropout Entrepreneur': Dropping out, 'Self-Reliance' and the American Myth of Entrepreneurial Success." *Culture and Organization* 22, no. 1 (2016): 20–43. https://doi.org/10.1080/14759551.2015.1104682.

Weber, Max. "Science as a Vocation." In *Max Weber: Essays in Sociology*, edited by H.H Gerth and M. Wright. London: Routledge & Kegan Paul, 1948.

Webster, Frederick. "Entrepreneurs and Ventures: An Attempt at Classification and Clarification." *The Academy of Management Review* 2, no. 1 (1977): 54. https://doi.org/10.5465/amr.1977.4409165.

Weeks, John. *Capital and Exploitation*. Ebook. Princeton, NJ: Princeton University Press (1981), 2014.

Wegner, Douglas, Elisa Thomas, Eduardo Künzel Teixeira, and Alisson Eduardo Maehler. "University Entrepreneurial Push Strategy and Students' Entrepreneurial Intention." *International Journal of Entrepreneurial Behaviour and Research* 26, no. 2 (2019): 307–25. https://doi.org/10.1108/IJEBR-10-2018-0648.

Weick, Karl. E. *Sensemaking in Organizations (Vol. 3)*. Sage, 1995.

Weick, Karl E., Kathleen M. Sutcliffe, and David Obstfeld. "Organizing and the Process of Sensemaking." *Organization Science* 16, no. 4 (2005): 409–21. https://doi.org/10.1287/orsc.1050.0133.

Welsh, M. Ann, and Gordon E. Dehler. "Whither the MBA? Or the Withering of MBAs?" *Management Learning* 38, no. 4 (2007): 405–23. https://doi.org/10.1177/1350507607080572.

Welter, Friederike, Ted Baker, David B. Audretsch, and William B. Gartner. "Everyday Entrepreneurship—A Call for Entrepreneurship Research to Embrace Entrepreneurial Diversity." *Entrepreneurship: Theory and Practice* 41, no. 3 (2017): 311–21. https://doi.org/10.1111/etap.12258.

Whittle, Andrea, Frank Mueller, Alan Gilchrist, and Peter Lenney. "Sensemaking, Sense-Censoring and Strategic Inaction: The Discursive Enactment of Power and Politics in a Multinational Corporation." *Organization Studies* 37, no. 9 (2016): 1323–51. https://doi.org/10.1177/0170840616634127.

Wierzbinska, G. W. "The Future of Managerial Education." In *Economic and Social Development*, 48–54, 2018.

Wiklund, Johan, and Dean Shepherd. "Entrepreneurial Orientation and Small Business Performance: A Configurational Approach." *Journal of Business Venturing* 20, no. 1 (2005): 71–91. https://doi.org/10.1016/j.jbusvent.2004.01.001.

Wilde, Oscar. *The Soul of Man under Socialism & Selected Critical Prose*. Penguin, 2001.

Williams, Colin C., and Sara J. Nadin. "Beyond the Entrepreneur as a Heroic Figurehead of Capitalism: Re-Representing the Lived Practices of

Entrepreneurs." *Entrepreneurship and Regional Development* 25, no. 7–8 (2013): 552–68. https://doi.org/10.1080/08985626.2013.814715.

Willis, Katie. *Theories and Practices of Development.* Routledge, 2011.

Wilson, Edward O. *Origins of Creativity.* UK: Penguin Random House, 2017.

Wilson, Nick, and Lee Martin. "Entrepreneurial Opportunities for All?: Entrepreneurial Capability and the Capabilities Approach." *The International Journal of Entrepreneurship and Innovation* 16, no. 3 (2015): 159–69. https://doi.org/10.5367/ijei.2015.0189.

Winfield, Fiona, and Tabani Ndlovu. "'Future-Proof Your Degree': Embedding Sustainability and Employability at Nottingham Business School (NBS)." *International Journal of Sustainability in Higher Education* 20, no. 8 (2019): 1329–42. https://doi.org/10.1108/IJSHE-10-2018-0196.

Winslow, E.G. "Keynes and Freud: Psychoanalysis and Keynes's Account of the 'Animal Spirits' of Capitalism." *Social Research* 53, no. 4 (1986): 549–78.

Winston, Christine N. "An Existential-Humanistic-Positive Theory of Human Motivation." *Humanistic Psychologist* 44, no. 2 (2016): 142–63. https://doi.org/10.1037/hum0000028.

Winston, Christine N., Hemali Maher, and Veena Easvaradoss. "Needs and Values: An Exploration." *Humanistic Psychologist* 45, no. 3 (2017): 295–311. https://doi.org/10.1037/hum0000054.

Witt, Ulrich. "Capitalism as a Complex Adaptive System and Its Growth." *Journal of Open Innovation: Technology, Market, and Complexity* 3, no. 3 (2017). https://doi.org/10.1186/s40852-017-0065-0.

Wood, Andrew F., and Deanna L. Fassett. "Remote Control: Identity, Power, and Technology in the Communication Classroom." *Communication Education* 52, no. 3–4 (2003): 286–96. https://doi.org/10.1080/0363452032000156253.

World Commission on Environment and Development. "Our Common Future," 1987.

Xenakis, Ioannis, and Argyris Arnellos. "Aesthetics as an Emotional Activity That Facilitates Sense-Making: Towards an Enactive Approach to Aesthetic Experience." In *Aesthetics and the Embodied Mind: Beyond Art Theory and the Cartesian Mind-Body Dichotomy,* edited by Alfonsina Scarinzi, 245–59. Dordrecht: Springer, 2015. https://doi.org/10.1007/978-94-017-9379-7_15.

Yeou, Mohamed. "An Investigation of Students' Acceptance of Moodle in a Blended Learning Setting Using Technology Acceptance Model." *Journal of Educational Technology Systems* 44, no. 3 (2016): 300–318. https://doi.org/10.1177/0047239515618464.

YNYER LEP. "YNYER Local Industrial Strategy (Draft January 2020)." York, UK: York North Yorkshire East Riding Local Enterprise Partnership, 2020.

Zahorik, Pavel, and Rick L. Jenison. "'Presence as Being-in-the-World', Presence." *Presence* 7, no. 1 (1998): 78–89.

Zilbersheid, Uri. "The Utopia of Herbert Marcuse Part 1." *Critique* 36, no. 3 (2008): 403–19. https://doi.org/10.1080/03017600802434508.

Žižek, Slavoj. *Living in the End Times.* London: Verso, 2011.

———. *The Sublime Object of Ideology.* London and New York, NY: Verso, 2008.

Zornes, Deborah. "The Business of the University: Research, Its Place in the 'Business', and the Role of the University in Society," 2012. http://dspace.library.uvic.ca/bitstream/handle/1828/4249/Zornes_Deborah_PhD_2012.pdf.

Zuidervaart, Lambert. *Social Philosophy after Adorno*. Cambridge, UK: Cambridge University Press, 2007.

———. "Theodor W. Adorno." In *Stanford Encyclopedia of Philosophy*, Pdf versio., 1–32. Stanford University Press (2003), 2015.

Zwick, Detlev. "No Longer Violent Enough?: Creative Destruction, Innovation and the Ossification of Neoliberal Capitalism." *Journal of Marketing Management* 34, no. 11–12 (2018): 913–31. https://doi.org/10.1080/0267257X.2018.1536076.

Index

E

F

M

N

R

S

T

U

www.ingramcontent.com/pod-product-compliance
Ingram Content Group UK Ltd.
Pitfield, Milton Keynes, MK11 3LW, UK
UKHW021033041026
15470UKWH00017B/1835/J

9 781648 895951